Napoleon and the Operational Art of War

Photo: Courtesy of Florida State University

Napoleon and the Operational Art of War

Essays in Honor of Donald D. Horward

REVISED AND EXTENDED EDITION

Edited by

Michael V. Leggiere

BRILL

LEIDEN | BOSTON

Part of this book was originally published in History of Warfare 110 (2016).

Cover illustration: Bataille d'Austerlitz, 2 décembre 1805 (MV2765), Gérard François Pascal Simon, baron (1770-1837): Versailles, châteaux de Versailles et de Trianon. Photo © RMN-Grand Palais (Château de Versailles) / image RMN-GP.

The Library of Congress has cataloged the earlier edition as follows:

Names: Horward, Donald D., honouree. | Leggiere, Michael V., 1969- editor.
Title: Napoleon and the operational art of war : essays in honor of Donald D. Horward / edited by Michael V. Leggiere.
Description: Brill : Leiden, [2016] | Series: History of warfare, ISSN 1385-7827 ; volume 110 | Collection of essays in honor of Donald D. Horward. | Includes bibliographical references and index. | Description based on print version record and CIP data provided by publisher; resource not viewed.
Identifiers: LCCN 2015042278 (print) | LCCN 2015045344 (ebook) | ISBN 9789004270343 (hardback : alkaline paper) | ISBN 9789004310032 (e-book)
Subjects: LCSH: Napoleonic Wars, 1800-1815--Campaigns. | Napoleon I, Emperor of the French, 1769-1821--Military leadership. | France--History, Military--1789-1815.
Classification: LCC DC202.1 (print) | LCC DC202.1 .N27 2016 (ebook) | DDC 940.2/7--dc23
LC record available at http://lccn.loc.gov/2015042278

Typeface for the Latin, Greek, and Cyrillic scripts: "Brill". See and download: brill.com/brill-typeface.

ISBN 978-90-04-43441-7 (paperback, 2021)
ISBN 978-90-04-43840-8 (e-book, 2021)
ISBN 978-90-04-27034-3 (hardback, 2016)
ISBN 978-90-04-31003-2 (e-book, 2016)

Copyright 2021 by Koninklijke Brill NV, Leiden, The Netherlands.
Koninklijke Brill NV incorporates the imprints Brill, Brill Hes & De Graaf, Brill Nijhoff, Brill Rodopi, Brill Sense, Hotei Publishing, mentis Verlag, Verlag Ferdinand Schöningh and Wilhelm Fink Verlag.
All rights reserved. No part of this publication may be reproduced, translated, stored in a retrieval system, or transmitted in any form or by any means, electronic, mechanical, photocopying, recording or otherwise, without prior written permission from the publisher. Requests for re-use and/or translations must be addressed to Koninklijke Brill NV via brill.com or copyright.com.

This book is printed on acid-free paper and produced in a sustainable manner.

Contents

Foreword   VII
   Geoffrey Wawro
List of Maps   XI
Contributors   XIII
The Coalitions against France   XV
   John H. Gill

Introduction   1
   Michael V. Leggiere

1   The Prophet Guibert   8
      Jonathan Abel

2   The French Way of War   39
      Jordan R. Hayworth

3   The Campaign against Piedmont-Sardinia, April 1796   87
      Frederick C. Schneid

4   Napoleon's First Italian Campaign, 1796-1797   116
      Michael V. Leggiere and Phillip R. Cuccia

5   The Second Italian Campaign   194
      John F. Weinzierl

6   1805: Ulm and Austerlitz   221
      Mark T. Gerges

7   The Jena Campaign: Apogee and Perihelion   249
      Dennis Showalter

8   Napoleon's Operational Warfare During the First Polish Campaign, 1806–1807   275
      Alexander Mikaberidze and John H. Gill

9 An Ulcer Inflamed: Napoleon's Campaign in Spain, 1808   306
   Huw J. Davies

10 1809: The Most Brilliant and Skillful Maneuvers   342
    John H. Gill

11 The Limits of the Operational Art: Russia 1812   372
    Alexander Mikaberidze

12 Prometheus Chained, 1813–1815   423
    Michael V. Leggiere

13 Napoleon's War at Sea   493
    Kenneth G. Johnson

14 Britain's Royal Navy and the Defeat of Napoleon   542
    Kevin D. McCranie

Afterword   565
Robert M. Citino

Conclusion   583
John Severn

Index   591

Foreword

Geoffrey Wawro

It is a great pleasure to introduce the scholarship in this *Festschrift* dedicated to Donald D. Horward. From his own Fontainebleau in Tallahassee, Don raised a family of scholars who have left their mark on the dynamic field of the French Revolution and Napoleon. Like the emperor himself, Don identified key areas for further research, distributed the work to his marshals, and – unlike the emperor's marshals – Don's have never disappointed. This book contains incisive pieces by his students and admirers that probe into every corner of the Napoleonic world.

Fundamentally, Napoleon excelled by doing unexceptional things with exceptional speed, vigor, inspiration, and efficiency. His preferred stance in politics and war was the "central position" – stealing between two converging enemies, and holding off one while attacking the other. His famed *manoeuvre sur les derrières*, pinning an enemy's front while rolling him up from the flank, accounted for his greatest victories. The all-arms corps of 16,000 to 30,000 men, introduced and perfected between Marengo and Austerlitz, was the hook on which Napoleon hung this devastating new form of warfare. He could snare larger forces with a corps, and then wheel his other corps into their flanks and rear. He could parry one army with a corps – of oscillating strength – while annihilating the other with the bulk of his forces. At Waterloo, he famously (if unsuccessfully) sent Grouchy with a corps to drive Blücher away from Wellington.

Rick Schneid shows us Napoleon emerging from obscurity as the great captain in the 1790s. Bonaparte had an uncommon ability to wring maximum advantage from small troop numbers – just 40,000 mobile troops in that 1796 campaign against Piedmont. By 1805, Napoleon had institutionalized this dexterity, one *grognard* quipping to another during the envelopment of the Austrians at Ulm, that the "emperor makes war in a new way – with our legs." He wrung every advantage from speed and time, wrong-footing his foes. As Mark Gerges puts it in his chapter on Austerlitz, Napoleon dispersed his corps "like spread fingers," used them to locate his enemy, and then wrapped them around the enemy in a suffocating embrace. This kind of agility required expert use of roads, supplies, staff work, and combat power. Napoleon oversaw a pre-industrial war machine that had this expertise. He was, as Dennis Showalter reminds us, the very "father of operational war," as we know it.

And therein lay the problem. Napoleon was a father who directed but did not teach his sons. None of his marshals ever attained his level of ingenuity. And so, as most of the authors in this volume make clear, Napoleonic warfare was most effective when Napoleon himself commanded. This was no problem in the 1790s, when, as Rick Schneid shows, a relatively junior Bonaparte was put in charge of manageable theaters. He proved adept at manipulating his order of battle to achieve maximum impact, shifting brigades between divisions to almost magically attain numerical superiority in a series of battles. This operational and tactical genius – *coup d'oeil* – became harder to exercise as his power and responsibilities (and number of enemies) mounted.

As the empire grew, much work had to be subcontracted to the marshalate, especially given the emperor's reliance on detached *corps d'armée* after the Marengo campaign. Some of the marshals were generally accounted brilliant – Masséna, Davout, Soult, Lannes – some less so. Many of the marshals were the proverbial "good with a corps, bad with an army" type of general. Napoleon's "strong hand and short leash" system – evolved to inject the emperor's genius into ballooning French armies – threatened to collapse whenever a marshal escaped the leash, either willfully or due to isolation in a faraway theater of war.

Ney, particularly after he lost his staff chief Jomini, personified this undiscerning type – almost singlehandedly destroying the army at Waterloo in his last-ditch gasconade with the cavalry. Grouchy, another of that type, doomed that army to defeat by pursuing the rear of Blücher's army to Wavre, while its advanced guards smashed in Napoleon's withered flank at Waterloo. But long before Waterloo, the allies had already detected this vulnerability and resolved to exploit it via the Trachenberg–Reichenbach Plan of 1813. That plan, composed as a result of Allied (Russians, Prussians, and Swedes) negotiations with the Austrians in July, held that henceforth the Allies would give way before Napoleon-commanded troops – goading the emperor into fruitless pursuits – while swinging into action against the marshals on the emperor's flanks. This was the formula that culminated in the great victory of Leipzig.

Mike Leggiere makes us feel the full weight of Napoleon's emerging problems. Like a celebrity whose best career exploits were behind him, Napoleon now had to contend with ambitious new rivals who had taken the time to study his methods. Russia's desertion of the Continental System, Napoleon's failed 1812 invasion, the loss of 500,000 of 600,000 troops in Russia, and the defection of key French allies or tributaries, principally Prussia, were blows that all but doomed the French Empire. By the summer of 1813, Napoleon was confronted with the combined, *intelligent* strength of Europe's four other great powers. They came from all points of the compass – approaching the Rhine from the east, threading through the Pyrenees in the south, and threatening from the north and west with deployments in the Low Countries.

Dennis Showalter finds that, even under duress, Napoleon was uniquely gifted, able to intervene successfully at any level–policy, strategy, operations, or tactics – without degrading or destroying the whole. Showalter rightly points out that our own post-Vietnam insistence on establishing a hierarchy of importance – policy first, strategy second, then operations and tactics – blinds us to Napoleon's real genius. His talent and institutions wrung maximum advantage from all four levels of warfare and made them symbiotic and synergistic. Ferocious operations and tactical strokes could rescue an overreaching strategy or a tone-deaf policy.

Showalter sees the Austerlitz and Jena campaigns as outstanding examples of this virtuosity, Jena in particular. It was "a tactical victory that would fulfill his strategy and policy objectives." Contemporaries, like the stunned governor-general of India in 1808, Lord Minto, could only gape in wonderment: "What would have seemed impossible had become scarcely improbable, since we have seen one state after another in Europe, among them those we deemed most stable and secure, fall like a house of cards before the genius of one man."

But this versatility was also the seed of Napoleon's downfall. It tempted him to gamble, and to hazard wild strokes on the assumption that he would always find a way to make them work. As he said in 1809, "our past successes are a certain guarantee of the victory that awaits us." Of course they weren't. War, as Clausewitz said, is cards, not chess, and his adversaries were hiding their cards and preparing new gambits to stymie the emperor's increasingly familiar approach. His two greatest defeats–in Spain and Russia–were owed to this complacency. He became too confident in his intuition and master-strokes, and underestimated a rapidly evolving and improving enemy. "Napoleon's system," as Showalter puts it, "had outgrown Napoleon himself."

Rob Citino's chapter describes a Prussia that rebuilt from the debacle of Jena–Auerstedt: "The postcatastrophe period was the great era of Prussian reform." And the same went for the other armies. By Wagram in 1809 – "Napoleon's last victory" – all of Napoleon's adversaries were adopting French methods: all-arms divisions, more artillery, faster marches, French tactics, and even national guards like the Austrian and Prussian Landwehr.

Underestimation of the British may have been Napoleon's greatest blind spot. Huw Davies has Napoleon dismissing the British thusly in 1808, even as they embarked on the Peninsular Campaign: "the English are of little importance; they have never more than a quarter of the troops that they profess to have." And yet that overlooked Britain's key strength: seapower and money, the two things they would use to destroy Napoleon. As Kevin McCranie puts it:

"the Royal Navy was never far over the horizon." It picked off French ports and colonies all over the world and could decide great battles, like Trafalgar, or whittle away at Napoleon's alliances, like the one he constructed in the Baltic after Copenhagen, but which the British navy had essentially dismantled by 1811.

Seapower allowed the British to erode the Continental System, by smuggling to or even openly trading with countries that were technically forbidden to trade with Britain. Britain's other strength was strategic mobility, its use of naval power to open peripheral fronts such as Walcheren or Portugal, and use them to distract and bleed the Grande Armée. Kenneth Johnson has Napoleon lamenting this in 1809; the British were constantly "disturbing" his financial affairs by opening new fronts and forcing him to react. The English "continue to ruin me," he wrote then. Even the Walcheren Expedition, generally accounted a British fiasco, wounded the French Empire. "It has cost me 50,000,000," Napoleon fretted, money he would not recover as multiple threats – ferried by British subsidies – built and coalesced around him.

Alexander Mikaberidze's chapter on Russia in 1812 captures the strategic floundering of Napoleon. Cooler heads urged him merely to contain the Russian colossus, using the Turks, Poles, Swedes, and Germans as curbstones, but the emperor trusted in his ability to invade Russia, bring the tsar's army quickly to battle, and dictate devastating terms. He was under no illusions about the campaign, writing lyrically about the Polish mud and the bare Russian steppe, but he trusted his war luck. It ran out in 1812, Mikaberidze noting that "the very magnitude of the war" defeated Bonaparte: the "enormous forces, vast distances, [and] logistical challenges."

Of course a mind as great as Napoleon's should have predicted all of this. But Napoleon was a thruster, never content to sit or parley idly. He wanted to impose his will by force of arms. As Leggiere, who stands as Horward's Caulaincourt with this magnificent volume, affirms in the context of 1813: the Emperor Napoleon became the master of General Bonaparte. Sadly, that must be the brilliant but flawed emperor's epitaph. Ego always clashed with pragmatism in the mind of history's greatest commander.

Maps

3.1 The Italian theater, 1796   99
4.1 Theater of War, Northern Italy, 1796-1797   118
4.2 Piedmont Phase   121
4.3 Lombard Phase   133
4.4 Castiglione Offensive, Wurmser's advance, July 1796   141
4.5 Castiglione Offensive, Wurmser's advance, August 1796   142
4.6 Castiglione and Surrounding Area   148
4.7 Bassano and Arcole Offensives   163
4.8 Arcole and Surrounding Area   174
4.9 Rivoli Offensive   179
4.10 Austrian Phase   186
5.1 The Italian theater, 1800   198
5.2 The Marengo Campaign, 1800   205
6.1 Deployment of the Austrian Army, September 1805   229
6.2 Strategic envelopment of Austrian forces at Ulm   233
7.1 Theater of war, 1806   255
7.2 The twin battles of Jena-Auerstedt   268
8.1 Napoleon's forward corps deployment, early November 1806   278
8.2 The Grande Armée's corps deployments, mid-December 1806   282
8.3 The Grande Armée's corps deployments, late-December 1806   286
8.4 The Grande Armée's corps deployments, early January 1807   288
8.5 Russian Movements, early January 1807   291
8.6 The Grande Armée's positions, late January 1807   295
8.7 The Grande Armée's corps deployments, May 1807   297
9.1 Napoleon's advance to the Ebro   318
9.2 Moore's advance from Lisbon   326
9.3 Moore's flight to Coruña   333
10.1 The Danube Valley theater of war in 1809   343
10.2 The April 1809 Campaign in Bavaria   349
11.1 Napoleon's supply depots in 1812   379
11.2 Napoleon's invasion of Russia   399
11.3 Napoleon's retreat from Russia   411
12.1 Theater of war, spring 1813   430
12.2 Theater of war, fall 1813   441
12.3 Leipzig Campaign   446
12.4 Invasion of France 1813–1814   453
12.5 Theater of war, 1815   474

13.1 The Mediterranean Sea as a French lake   494
13.2 The Caribbean Sea   498
13.3 The Indian Ocean   500
13.4 French and British naval positions   504

Contributors

Jonathan Abel
Assistant Professor of Military History, US Army Command and General Staff College

Robert M. Citino
Executive Director of the Institute for the Study of War and Democracy and the Samuel Zemurray Stone Senior Historian, The National WWII Museum

Phillip R. Cuccia
United States Army War College

Huw J. Davies
Senior Lecturer in Defense Studies, King's College London

Mark T. Gerges
Associate Professor of Military History, US Army Command and General Staff College

John H. Gill
Associate Professor, Near East–South Asia Center, National Defense University

Jordan R. Hayworth
Assistant Professor of Military and Security Studies in the Department of Airpower, Air Command and Staff College

Kenneth G. Johnson
Associate Professor, US Air Command and Staff College

Michael V. Leggiere
Professor of History, University of North Texas

Kevin D. McCranie
Associate Professor of Strategy and Policy, US Naval War College

Alexander Mikaberidze
Professor of History, Ruth Herring Noel Endowed Chair for the Curatorship of the James Smith Noel Collection, Louisiana State University-Shreveport

Frederick C. Schneid
Professor of History, High Point University

John Severn
Professor of History (Emeritus), University of Alabama-Huntsville

Dennis Showalter
Professor of History (Emeritus), Colorado College

John F. Weinzierl
Associate Professor of History, University of Jamestown

Geoffrey Wawro
Professor of History, University of North Texas

The Coalitions against France

John H. Gill

The various alliances, formed to oppose Revolutionary and Napoleonic France are generally known as "coalitions" and often referred to as "the Allies" in this book. It is impossible to track all of the diplomatic shifts or to list all of the major engagements over this period of more than two decades, but the chart below provides a simplified outline to assist the reader. The "Peninsula War" in Iberia (1808–1814) and the Russian campaign (1812) are not generally included among the listings of "coalitions." Note that Napoleon also had coalitions and allies of his own; even if many of his partners were forced into alliance with France (as Prussia forced Saxony into an alliance in 1806) or were more vassals than true allies, the French emperor still had to contend with alliance politics of a sort.

	First Coalition	Second Coalition	Third Coalition	Fourth Coalition	Fifth Coalition	Sixth Coalition	Seventh Coalition
Active Period	1792–1797	1798–1802	1803–1805	1806–1807	1809	1813–1814	1815
Members	· Holy Roman Empire (incl. Austria)	· Holy Roman Empire (incl. Austria)	· Holy Roman Empire (incl. Austria)	· Prussia	· Austria	· Russia	· Great Britain
	· Great Britain	· Great Britain	· Great Britain	· Russia	· Great Britain	· Prussia	· Prussia
	· Prussia (to 1795)	· Russia (to 1799)	· Russia	· Great Britain	· Spain	· Austria	· Austria
	· Spain (to 1795)	· Portugal	· Naples/Sicily	· Saxony (to Dec 1806)	· Naples	· Great Britain	· Russia
	· Dutch Republic (to 1795)	· Tuscany	· Sweden	· Sweden	· Sicily	· Sweden	· Sweden
	· Portugal	· Ottoman Empire		· Sicily		· Spain	· Spain
	· Sardinia (to 1796)	· Naples				· Portugal	· Portugal
	· Naples	· Malta				· Sicily	· Sicily
	· French royalists	· French royalists				· Sardinia	· Sardinia
						· German states (from October 1813)	· German states
						· Netherlands (1814)	· Netherlands
						· Naples (1814)	· Tuscany
							· Switzerland
Key Neutrals	N/A	Prussia	Prussia	Austria	Prussia	N/A	N/A
Select Battles	General Bonaparte's First Italian Campaign	· Egypt	· Ulm	· Jena/Auerstedt	· Abensberg/ Eggmühl	· Lützen	· Waterloo
		· Marengo	· Trafalgar	· Eylau	· Aspern/Essling	· Bautzen	
		· Hohenlinden	· Austerlitz	· Friedland	· Wagram	· Leipzig	
						· Paris	

Introduction

Michael V. Leggiere

As a sophomore history major in the spring of 1989, I worked as a fitness instructor in the bowels of Florida State University's former student athletic complex, Tully Gym. One day, a colleague and fellow history major on the verge of graduating gave me some advice. He insisted that I take a class with a history professor by the name of Dr. Horward. I responded that I had seen the name "Howard" listed in the course catalogue and that his classes looked interesting. My colleague was quick to correct me: not Howard, but *Horward*. Sure enough, the following fall semester I took Dr. Horward's French Revolution course: a three-hour class every Monday night from 7:00 PM to 10:00 PM. Regardless of the football game that aired every Monday night and long before the DVR, Dr. Horward started each class at 7:00 PM sharp and almost always exceeded the 10:00 hour. I am certain that, like myself, not a soul in that classroom minded one bit, for taking a course with Dr. Horward was unlike anything I had experienced before or have since. I have now been teaching on the university level for twenty years and, despite my best efforts, I can never tell the story of Louis XVI's failed "Flight to Varennes" quite like Dr. Horward did that fall semester in 1989. Of course he kept us until 11:00 that night but no one complained as we hung on his every word. Like scores of students before and after, I was hooked.

By the fall semester of 1989, Donald D. Horward, a native of Pennsylvania, was already in his twenty-eighth year as a professor at FSU. Don had completed his undergraduate studies at Waynesburg College before pursuing an M.A. at Ohio University, where he defended his thesis, "Marshal Ney, Hero or Traitor: A Review of His Military Career," in August 1956. He then spent the next six years in a doctoral program at the University of Minnesota studying under Harold Deutsch, his *Doktorvater*, and John Wolf, the biographer of Louis XIV. Don's research focused on French operations during the Peninsular War. His dissertation, "The French Invasion of Portugal, 1810–1811" was based on extensive research in the French archives, including the papers of Marshal André Masséna, and broke new ground in the field of Peninsular War studies.

In 1961, while finalizing his dissertation, Don joined the faculty at Florida State University, where he remained for more than forty-four years. During his long and distinguished career, Don introduced some 16,000 students to the history of the French Revolution and Napoleon and developed a dynamic graduate studies program at FSU. He directed his first master's student in 1963, followed by the first PhD in Napoleonic history, Gordon Bond, in 1966. Thus began the process of establishing Florida State University as the leading American center for the study of the Revolutionary Era (1750–1850) in the western hemisphere. By the end of his career, Don had directed more than 100 doctoral dissertations and master's theses, making FSU one of the most prolific centers for the study of Napoleon in the world. Training several generations of Napoleonic historians represents Don's greatest contribution to the field of history. Dozens of his students remain active in academia, teaching at American institutions of higher learning and producing original research that breaks new ground in the field of the Napoleonic studies. Don put FSU on the map as the preeminent university in the nation for the study of the French Revolution and Napoleon.

Teaching was always Don's major commitment, and as a result he received seven university-wide awards from FSU, including the first Distinguished Teaching Award, established in 1990; three Excellence in Teaching awards (1988, 1994, and 1997); and the university's first Outstanding Graduate Faculty Mentor Award (2005). He held fifteen academic chairs at various American and European universities and institutions, including the Ben Weider Chair at FSU, the Chair of Military History at West Point, the Edwin P. Conquest Chair in Humanities at Virginia Military Institute, the Chair of Military Affairs at the Marine War College (renewed seven times), and the Chair of Military Studies at the School of Advanced War Fighting at Marine University. He has lectured on Napoleonic warfare at the US Naval War College, the US Army War College, the US Naval Academy, the US Air Force Academy, the US Marine Command and Staff College, the Naval Postgraduate School, the UK's Royal Military Academy at Sandhurst, the German General Staff College at Hamburg, the Czechoslovakia Military Academy, the Czech Military Academy at Brno, SHAPE Historical Society at Mons, NATO Headquarters at Brussels, and the Historical Service of the Portuguese Army at Lisbon. Don has lectured at universities throughout the United States, and the Smithsonian on several occasions, and has given presentations in Europe at universities such as Frederick Schiller University in Germany, Charles University and Masaryk University in the Czech Republic, Cambridge University and Southampton University in England, the University of Budapest in Hungary, and the Borodino/Mazajsk Center in Russia. In the fall of 2000, Don, as a contributor to the PBS four-hour documentary on Napoleon, attended the premiere showing of the film at the French Consulate General in New York City. He took part in a panel discussion of the film in New York, and in November of that year he lectured at West Point, the Naval Postgraduate School outside Washington, DC, and the Naval Academy at Annapolis.

Don played a decisive role in creating The French Revolution and Napoleonic Collection at the Special Collections Department of FSU's Strozier Library. On his arrival at FSU in 1961, the library possessed some 250 titles on the French Revolution and Napoleon. As a direct result of Don's efforts and hard work over four decades, which included twenty-eight trips to Europe doing research and searching for books, Strozier Library now houses a unique collection on the French Revolution and Napoleon that includes more than 22,000 items, some from renowned collections such as those of King Ernst August of Hanover and Achille Murat, King of Naples, and is one of the most extensive collections in the western hemisphere. The Collection contains numerous rare items and continues to attract students and scholars from across the United States and Europe.

In 1990, Don founded the Institute on Napoleon and the French Revolution (INFR) which was approved by the Board of Regents of the State University System of Florida that same year. In 1998, the INFR received a generous donation from Dr. Benjamin "Ben" Weider, OC CQ (1923–2008). Ben, the co-founder of the International Federation of Bodybuilding and Fitness (IFBB) along with brother Joe Weider, was a Canadian businessman from Montreal, well known in two areas: bodybuilding and Napoleonic history. His bequest to FSU allowed for the establishment of the first endowed chair devoted to Napoleonic studies; Don was designated as the first chair holder. In addition, several scholarships and research/travel fellowships were created for Institute students by the Weider Bequest and generous donations by the Institute's alumni and supporters. Among them are Baron Roger Jomini, a descendant of the famous 19th-century military theorist, who contributed funds for student scholarships; Dr. Proctor Jones, who provided substantial support for student grants to do research in Paris; and Dr. Skip Vichness and Dr. George Knight, graduates of the Napoleonic program at FSU, who established generous scholarships. These funds have also brought students from as far away as Hawaii and the Republic of Georgia to study the Napoleonic period at FSU and have helped send scores of students to European archives.

Much of the current research on Napoleon in the United States has been conducted by Don's former students. From the forty-eight PhD and fifty-two MA students that Don graduated in his forty-four years at FSU, more than forty-five books have been published and almost a thousand articles have been produced in scholarly journals. Six of their volumes have been awarded the International Book Prize of the International Napoleonic Society for the best book published in Napoleonic history in a particular year. Doctoral students who completed their research under Don's direction have taught at scores of universities and colleges from California to New York. Don was also instrumental in developing a close relationship with the US Military Academy at West Point, which regularly sent officers (seventeen in all), destined for the history faculty at West Point, to be trained in Napoleonic studies at the Institute. The officers who studied under Don have taught at the US Military Academy at West Point, where they imparted their knowledge of Napoleon's operational art to tens of thousands of cadets, the US Command and Staff College at Ft. Leavenworth, Kansas, the US Army Command College at the Von Braun Center in Huntsville, Alabama, the US Naval Post Graduate School at Monterey, California, the US Naval War College at Newport, Rhode Island, and the US Air Force Command and Staff College in Montgomery, Alabama. Others have occupied senior command positions in Italy, Afghanistan, Iraq, and South Korea as well as throughout the United States.

During a career that spanned four decades, Don made important contributions to the field of Napoleonic studies. He devoted his research primarily to the events of Napoleon's war in Portugal and Spain (1807–1814). Starting with *The Battle of Bussaco: Masséna vs. Wellington* (Tallahassee, FL, 1965), Don published three major works that offered detailed analysis of the French invasion of Portugal in 1810–1811. His subsequent books include *The French Campaign in Portugal* (Minneapolis, 1973); and *Napoleon and Iberia: The Twin Sieges of Ciudad Rodrigo and Almeida, 1810* (Tallahassee, FL, 1980; Spanish editions published in 1984 and 2006). In addition to these scholarly works, Don also published *The French Revolution and Napoleon Collection at Florida State University* (Tallahassee, FL, 1973) and *Napoleonic Military History: A Bibliography* (New York, 1986). He co-authored or contributed to twenty more books and has written more than fifty articles on the revolutionary and Napoleonic period that have appeared in scholarly journals published in France, Britain, the Republic of Georgia, Spain, Portugal, Sweden, the Czech Republic, and Italy, as well as the United States and Canada. In all, he has published and presented more than 220 book chapters, scholarly papers, and addresses on various Napoleonic topics at over 190 conferences in the United States, France, Britain, Portugal, Spain, Germany, Italy, Belgium, Germany, the Czech Republic, Hungary, Russia, and Iran.

Don is one of the original founders of the Consortium on Revolutionary Europe, established in 1972 to foster the study of Europe during the revolutionary period (1750–1850). The Consortium, which changed its designation to Consortium on the Revolutionary Era (1750–1850) to reflect its international nature, currently includes more than twenty universities and colleges and organizes an annual international conference that attracts hundreds of scholars from across the United States and Europe. Don served as editor-in-chief of the Consortium publications for over a decade. He also organized five international

Consortium Conferences at FSU including the Congress to Commemorate the Bicentennial of the French Revolution. This meeting, held in Tallahassee, was attended by the French ambassador and 250 participants from 8 countries; it was ranked by French scholars as being among the most significant of such conferences in the United States. He was a principal organizer of international conferences related to the Napoleonic period in France (Meaux), Spain (Ciudad Rodrigo), Portugal (Lisbon and Almeida), and England (Cambridge and Southampton), as well as in the United States.[1]

After forty-four years of distinguished service, Don retired in 2005. That year, he was asked what was it about Napoleon that so captivated him. "His footprint is gigantic," responded Don. "He changed warfare. The warfare we see today in Iraq is what Napoleon developed. Students at the US military academies still study Napoleon's military strategies." "In addition to his military exploits, Napoleon helped shape the modern world in myriad other ways," Don said. "He was a brilliant politician and administrator. The *Code Napoléon*, our modern educational system, transportation, social services – all of these were innovations established by Napoleon that have had a dramatic effect on the world we live in. This was not just a conqueror; this was a guy who understood life."[2]

For his work in the Napoleonic period, Don has been decorated by the French, American, and Portuguese governments, and recognized by the Czech Republic and Spain. He was elected to the Portuguese Academy of History in December 1991, and the following year he was decorated by the president of Portugal and named a Grand Officer of the Order of Infante Dom Henrique (Prince Henry the Navigator). In 2001, he was honored by the Napoleonic Alliance as the first John Elting Scholar "for his extraordinary contributions to the study of Napoleonic History." Although deeply honored by these awards, Don received his most distinguished awards from the French government, being named *Chevalier* (1984), *Officier* (1992), and *Commandeur* (2001) *de l'Ordres des Palmes Académique*, an order established by Napoleon in 1808 for contributions to historical studies and the sciences. In 2002, the French government recognized his contributions to the field of the Napoleonic studies by naming him *Chevalier* of the Légion d'Honneur, France's highest civilian honor, which was established by Napoleon in 1802. In a moving ceremony at the US Military Academy at West Point, General Jean-Philippe Douin, Grand Chancellor of the Legion of Honor, represented the French Republic and French president Jacques Chirac, in making the awards. Don later commented that "the Legion

---

1 See <http://www.napoleonicsociety.com/english/HorwardPalmesAcademiques.htm>.
2 See <http://www.napoleonicsociety.com/english/retraitehorward.htm>.

of Honor is the medal of Napoleon, the presidents of France, and battlefield heroes; but it is also the medal of Mme. Marie Curie, Louis Pasteur, Victor Hugo, George Sand, and Goethe." He continued, "For me, it is the most important medal in the world, and a direct link to Napoleon himself; for me it is the impossible dream that came true."[3]

Don, along with his twin sister, Barbara, was born in Pittsburgh in 1933 to Frank and Selina Horward. Born in 1897, Frank had migrated to the United States from Germany while Selina was born in Braddock, Pennsylvania, in 1899. Don had two older brothers, Frank and William. Don grew up in the wake of the Great Depression followed by the Second World War. Too young to serve, he fondly recalls collecting scrap metal for the war effort. A man who devoted his career to studying war, he abhors the human catastrophe that is war. Now in his eighties, Don and his stalwart chief of staff and wife, Annabel, split their time between Tallahassee, Florida, and their home on the shores of Lake Erie at Sandusky, Ohio, where Don enjoys caring for his junipers while Annabel's daylilies bloom in all their splendor: 670 for three consecutive days in July 2014. After fifty-eight trips across the Atlantic, Don took his first year off in decades in 2014.

All who have studied under Don or worked closely with him know that he was much more than a mentor and taskmaster. Don and Annabel often opened their home to his students, treating us and caring for us like we were their own children. The dinners, pool parties, Thanksgiving feasts, and late-night slide shows of Don navigating Devil's Bridge over the Schöllenen Gorge en route to the St. Gotthard Pass or inspecting Wellington's lines at Torres Vedras outside Lisbon will forever be part of Horwardian lore. In regard to our work, he drove us like a stern stepfather, but when it came to looking out for us both personally and professionally he was like a kind grandfather. He was a friend, a father figure, and a role model for us. He taught us how to teach and how to be scholars; he protected us yet pushed us out of the nest so that we had to take our first unsteady flight through the daunting halls of Europe's archives; he opened his international network to us so that we could develop professionally; he laughed with us and he cried with us; he was larger than life. He sacrificed his own research and scholarship to attend to read our dissertations and our theses. *Doktorvater* is truly an appropriate term describing Don, for he bequeathed a part of himself to each of us. We will forever be grateful for all that D.D.H. did for us and we will forever cherish the memory of our journey with him.

What follows is a tribute to Don's passion, Napoleon's operational art of war. Among the contributors, John Weinzierl, Mark Gerges, Alex Mikaberidze, Phil

---

3 See <http://www.napoleonicsociety.com/english/HorwardLegionHonor.htm>.

Cuccia, Kevin McCranie, Kenny Johnson, John Severn, and myself studied under Don at Florida State University. Geoff Wawro and Rob Citino – my dear colleagues at the University of North Texas – contributed out of respect and admiration for Don's many accomplishments. Don and the late Dennis Showalter both received their doctoral degrees from the University of Minnesota. Rick Schneid, Huw Davies, and Jack Gill – three of the foremost Napoleonic military historians working in the field today, have been long-time friends of Don, his students, and his program. Jon Abel and Jordan Hayworth are my doctoral students and are thus Don's academic grandchildren. Within the parameters of a festschrift, we have attempted to provide an operational history of Napoleon at war as well as an in-depth look at the war at sea. No attempt will be made to explain the Napoleonic Wars in a broader context nor was the writing team concerned with the issue of whether the wars were Napoleon's or whether they were caused by the numerous coalitions that he faced. Don himself would fall short of saying that the wars were completely Napoleon's fault but would be quick to point out that the emperor brought on many of his troubles and certainly made monumental mistakes and miscalculations. Space does not permit a detailed study of each of Napoleon's campaigns from start to finish yet scale is generously compensated with erudite analysis. For this second volume, we have added one chapter covering the entirety of Napoleon's First Italian Campaign (1796–1797) and one chapter covering the Polish campaign against the Russians in 1807. Comprehensive accounts of these two campaigns are necessary to see Bonaparte's genius at work in two very different situations. In Italy, his field forces rarely exceeded 50,000 men while in Prussian Poland he commanded well over 100,000. In both campaigns he faced challenges presented by difficult terrain and enemy armies that came close to matching his mobility.

We wish to thank Julian Deahl, Marcella Mulder, Kelly DeVries, John France, Michael Neiberg, Rick Schneid, and the staff at Brill for supporting this book and allowing us to write this tribute in Don's honor. We are also grateful to Alex Mikaberidze for making the maps. As editor, I would like to thank the authors for their wonderful contributions which far surpassed my expectations. Thanks to them, this book is truly a monument to a man who himself is monumental.

CHAPTER 1

The Prophet Guibert

Jonathan Abel

"Le *Dieu de la Guerre* est près de se révéler, car nous avons entendu son prophète."[1, 2] The "God of War" in this famous quote by historian Jean Lambert Alphonse Colin was of course Napoleon. Although this appellation rings of hyperbole, it also contains a truth that was recognized by the great captain's peers and especially his enemies. "Depend upon it, at the head of a French army there never was anything like him," recorded his famous adversary, Arthur Wellesley, the duke of Wellington. "I used to say of him that his presence on the field made the difference of 40,000 men."[3]

Napoleon cut his teeth commanding armies between 1796 and 1802 during the Wars of the French Revolution. After crowning himself emperor of the French, he smashed the combined powers of Europe between 1805 and 1807 and conquered or subdued much of the continent by 1810. In that time, Napoleon conducted several masterpiece battles that rivaled the great victories at Cannae, Agincourt, and Leuthen. He was undoubtedly the "God of War," developing his own way of war to defeat his enemies. Yet, for all his operational and strategic genius, Napoleon made very few drastic alterations to the French army. Instead, he inherited an army that had evolved from a long process of development stretching back through the Revolution to France's Old Regime, when the French were seeking to reform their army after its miserable performance in the Seven Years War. The period between 1763 and 1789 proved decisive for the evolution of a new French way of war. In particular, the *Règlement* of 1791, drafted in the early days of the Revolution and the standard manual of the French army until well after the fall of the empire, created an army that allowed Napoleon to develop the operational art of war.[4] Napoleon himself

---

1 The author wishes to thank Michael Leggiere, Alexander Mikaberidze, and Chad Tomaselli for their input and assistance on this project.
2 Jean Colin, *L'éducation militaire de Napoléon* (Paris, 1901), 107.
3 Philip Henry, Earl Stanhope, *Notes of Conversations with the Duke of Wellington, 1831–1851* (New York, 1888), 9.
4 Irenée Amelot de Lacroix, *Rules and Regulations for the Field Exercise and Maneuvers of the French Infantry issued August 1, 1791: and the Maneuvers Added Which Have Been Since Adopted by the Emperor Napoleon: Also, the Maneuvers of the Field Artillery with the Infantry* (Boston, 1810), Albert Latreille, *L'œuvre militaire de la révolution: l'armée et la nation à la fin de l'ancien régime: les derniers ministres de la guerre de la monarchie* (Paris, 1914), and Robert Quimby,

acknowledged this debt, noting that "we possess a masterpiece entitled *le Réglement sur les manœuvres de l'infanterie du 1er Août, 1791*. Any officer who would employ himself in forming a companion to this work, by collecting in a similar manner an account of whatever related to the plans and operations of an army in campaign, would be incontestably entitled to the gratitude of every military man."[5]

A thorough examination of this evolutionary process reveals one figure who stands out as Colin's "prophet of war": Jacques-Antoine-Hippolyte, comte de Guibert. In the last years of the Old Regime, Guibert developed a systematic doctrine for the French army that provided new organization and tactics which had evolved from the Old Regime practices of Frederician linear warfare. This in turn created the opportunity for operational-level warfare to develop in the decades after his death. Although Guibert died in 1790, his work proved instrumental in the development of the 1791 Regulations. While the Wars of the French Revolution provided the ideal laboratory for Guibert's doctrine, Napoleon's rise to power beginning in 1796 supplied the missing element to Guibert's system, the *homme de génie* who would carry it to even greater heights. Indeed, Napoleon's art and science of war evolved directly from the foundation provided by Guibert. This chapter will illustrate the development of Guibert's system and its singular importance to French military theory, the struggle to implement that doctrine during the Wars of the Revolution, and its culmination in the corps system of the Grande Armée of 1805–1807.

For centuries, feudal decentralization had resulted in an almost complete lack of doctrine within the French army. Each regiment conformed to the personal doctrine and beliefs of its commander and proprietor. Great captains such as Louis, prince de Condé; and Henri de La Tour d'Auvergne, vicomte de Turenne, held their own doctrinal principles independent of the larger army establishment. These operated only in the armies commanded by the individual and rarely outlasted their command. Systematic, army-wide doctrine simply could not develop within this structure.[6] During the 18th century, the French army underwent a long evolutionary process that began creating insti-

---

The Background of Napoleonic Warfare: The Theory of Military Tactics in Eighteenth-Century France (New York, 1957), provide the best surveys of this topic.

5 Quoted in Jean Sarrazin, *Confession of General Buonaparté to the abbé Maury* (London, 1811), 142. See also Auguste Frédéric Louis Viesse de Marmont, duc de Raguse, *The Spirit of Military Institutions,* trans. by Frank Schaller (Columbia, SC, 1864), 179; and Napoleon I, *Memoirs of the History of France During the Reign of Napoleon* (London, 1823), 3:327–328.

6 Jean Colin, *L'infanterie au XVIIIe siècle: la tactique* (Paris, 1907), 73–134; Brent Nosworthy, *The Anatomy of Victory: Battle Tactics, 1689–1763* (New York, 1990), 65–78, 199–222; R.R. Palmer, "Frederick the Great, Guibert, Bülow: From Dynastic to National War," in Peter Paret, ed., *Makers of Modern Strategy: From Machiavelli to the Nuclear Age* (Princeton, NJ, 1986), 91–122.

tutional doctrine for the first time, starting with the army of Louis XIV. During his reign, his secretaries of state for war greatly expanded the size of the army and worked to bring it more directly under the control of the ministry of war and its generals. As a result, the army began to conform more closely to a set of institutional norms. The replacement of the pike by the musket with fixed bayonet created an army with a uniform infantry for the first time in centuries. This was a critical step in the evolutionary process, as it allowed for infantry doctrine that encompassed the entire army rather than needing separate instructions for the shock and fire branches. Louis XIV's legacy was thus to produce a drive for further centralization and to initiate the process of developing doctrine in the early 18th century.[7]

In the decades that followed, the process of change was greatly accelerated by the rise of the Prussian army. In 1740, Frederick II launched an invasion of Silesia, beginning the first general European war in nearly three decades.[8] The effectiveness of the Prussian army greatly impressed French observers and theorists, who fervently praised Frederick and his methods. Nearly all argued that France had fallen behind Prussia as the continent's premier military power and suggested change. This produced a considerable increase in the number and volume of theoretical treatises written and published in France. A bevy of writers, many within the army itself, wrote and published works of theory in response. They argued that France's doctrine was at once both too formalistic and too lax.[9]

To some writers, Prussia's strict discipline had created an army that was far more centralized, doctrinally-minded, and articulated at the tactical and operational levels. This made it greatly superior to the French army. Proponents of this ideology argued that the Prussians fought in thin, linear formations and emphasized disciplined fire. The French writers named this system *l'ordre mince* and many declared it to be the superior doctrine extant in Europe. They concluded that only an adoption of rigid, Prussian-style discipline and formalism would lead France to future victory.[10] Other writers argued to the contrary, chief among them Jean-Charles, chevalier Folard. He found the French

---

7   Colin, *L'infanterie au XVIIIe siècle*, 2–71; Nosworthy, *Anatomy of Victory*, 34–75; and Quimby, *Background of Napoleonic Warfare*, 4–53.
8   See Reed Browning, *The War of the Austrian Succession* (New York, 2003).
9   Nosworthy, *Anatomy of Victory*, 183–198; Gunther Rothenberg, *The Art of Warfare in the Age of Napoleon* (Bloomington, IN, 1978), 11–30. See also Louis Drummond, comte de Melfort, *Tactique et manœuvres des Prussiens*, Service Historique de l'Armée de Terre (hereafter cited as SHAT), M¹ 1793, 11.
10 Nosworthy, *Anatomy of Victory*, 183–198, 243–260; Palmer, "Frederick the Great, Guibert, Bülow."

constitutionally incapable of such discipline. He instead proposed *l'ordre profond* as the basic doctrine of the French army. This system would make use of the French soldier's *élan* in dense, columnar formations using shock attacks. He concluded that this would better serve the naturally undisciplined French mentality rather than the stilted Prussian methodology.[11]

The period of the early 1750s launched a wave of reform, spurred in part by the increase in theoretical literature. Various secretaries of state for war under Louis XV pushed to introduce reforms, moving France toward an institutional army, one with a clearly enumerated and army-wide doctrine. The ministry of war annually promulgated a set of regulations from 1753 to 1755. Deployment on the firing line was established at three ranks, which would remain the standard for the remainder of the century. More importantly, for the first time in the army's history, the 1754 document established a standard cadenced step, decreeing a fixed march and battle step for the entire army rather than leaving to commanders the responsibility of determining the step used by their individual units. Cadenced step gradually became the basis for all maneuvers and deployments, bringing a uniformity that had not existed in prior periods. It was possible to promulgate doctrine for organization and maneuver to the entire army. A standard set of evolutions appeared in these regulations, imposing them across the army.[12]

These effects were felt at the level of grand tactics as well. Cadenced step provided the potential to divide regiments into smaller columns for march and deployment. Yet no official regulation suggested such a grand tactical system, and the opposite actually occurred in practice. The uniformity imposed by cadenced step along with the increasingly pro-Prussian voices within the military establishment led to increased formalism and attention to detail. This mired the army in pedantic conversations about the precise nature and substance of maneuvers and deployment. The standardization created by the regulations of the 1750s required maneuvers to be performed in closed rather than open columns.[13] Closed columns were necessary for officers to keep

---

11   Jean Charles, chevalier Folard, *Nouvelles découvertes sur la guerre, dans une dissertation sur Polybe, où l'on donne une idée plus étendue du commentaire entrepris sur cet auteur, et deux dissertations importantes detachées du corps de l'ouvrage* (Paris, 1726); *Histoire de Polybe* and *Traité de la colonne, la manière de la former et de combattre dans cet ordre*, 6 vols (Amsterdam, 1774). The latter works circulated for several decades before their formal publication in 1774. See Colin, *L'infanterie au XVIIIe siècle*, 27–40.

12   Colin, *L'infanterie au XVIIIe siècle*, 40–72; Quimby, *Background of Napoleonic Warfare*, 80–105.

13   Colin, *L'infanterie au XVIIIe siècle*, 3–72. Closed columns kept the units in the column, usually divisions, close to each other, no more than a few paces apart. This retained the dense nature of the column and allowed it to maneuver better as a unit. Open columns

control of their units as they maneuvered as a whole with the same step rather than individually, often in open columns, as in past practice. Battalions were placed in order within the column of march based on precedence or numerical order rather than to suit the needs of battle. The column of march, often comprising an entire army, then marched in a rigid pattern according to the now-established cadenced step.[14]

On reaching the battlefield, the march column deployed along a single axis. This was performed in the simplest fashion by marching the entire column to the desired front at a 90-degree angle and having each battalion perform a quarter-wheel at the leftmost or rightmost point of the parallel, then marching it along the front. The entire line would then quarter-wheel the opposite direction to face the enemy, having formed a line parallel to the opposing army.[15] Such a deployment could be performed from the right or left of the position, drawing the entire army across the enemy frontage to reach the desired place on the field. It could also be performed from the center on the square. To do this, the army would divide into two columns that would march parallel towards the desired front. On arriving, each unit with the column deployed on the square by quarter-wheels. This deployment was considered by contemporaries to be the most sophisticated and difficult, as it required a rapid series of geometrical calculations and maneuvers to be accomplished without lapsing into chaos.[16]

The combination of a traditional emphasis on precedence and the imposition of cadenced step inextricably linked march and battle order. French armies marching at the same step and using the same evolutions required a rigid system to keep them coherent and functional, limiting their options for maneuver to those that occurred in a linear formation rather than from the deployment column. Much emphasis was placed on perfecting these maneuvers during the middle of the century, particularly in training camps and in public demonstrations. Commanders became experts at beautifully geometric maneuvers that greatly impressed observers on the parade ground. Rival

---

increased the space between formations, allowing them more space to maneuver but virtually eliminating the ability of the entire column to move or deploy as a unit.

14   See ibid., and Quimby, *Background of Napoleonic Warfare*, 1–79.
15   Colin, *L'infanterie au XVIIIe siècle*, 40–72. See also Nosworthy, *Anatomy of Victory*, 261–280, and *With Musket, Cannon, and Sword*, 85–89.
16   Quimby, *Background of Napoleonic Warfare*, 80–105. Nosworthy, *With Musket, Cannon, and Sword*, 85–89, argues that the Prussians in the 1740s and 1750s "stumbled on" this method of deployment, which marked an incremental step in the transition away from the single axis of deployment.

theorists broke into schools around *l'ordre mince* and *l'ordre profond* and lobbed polemical arguments at each other in print and in person.[17]

Despite their rancorous nature, the mid-century reforms provided the foundation for an institutional army, rather than a decentralized one, by providing the germ of army-wide doctrine. In particular, cadenced step regularized march and maneuver. For the first time, the entire army trained and marched at the same speed. This allowed for battle drill, which increased the discipline and ability of the army. Despite this progress, the French army failed to become more fluid and articulated. Instead, the French created a rigid system that was far better suited to the parade ground than the battlefield. Universality of petty tactics led to stilted and processional maneuvers with little grounding in practicality.[18]

The reforms of the 1750s marked a significant advance in the development of French doctrine, but they were merely a foundation. Much work remained before the French army would have a true institutional doctrine. Few writers addressed combined arms, preferring instead to focus on the line infantry, thus allowing light infantry, cavalry, and artillery to languish. The polemical debate needed settling, either by army command selecting between *l'ordre mince* or *l'ordre profond*, or the development of a system that would aggregate the two. More importantly, the army still relied heavily on processional movements and deployment on the square at the petty tactical level, and march order still dictated battle order on the grand tactical level. To match Prussia, French doctrine would have to evolve beyond these impediments.

Guibert came of age during this time of great debate. His career was typical for a child of the lesser French nobility. Born in 1743 at Montauban, he entered the military in 1756 as an aide to his father, Charles-Benoît Guibert, himself an officer of long service in the French army. Both participated in the Seven Years War, where Guibert received his first taste of battle and decorations for valor. In the years after that conflict, he served as the second in command during the French pacification of Corsica, being stationed there from 1768 to 1772. By that year, he had made colonel, was acknowledged by the ministry of war for his service, and appeared to be destined for a provincial command.[19]

---

17   Quimby, *Background of Napoleonic Warfare*, 16–25. Jacques-François de Chastenet, marquis de Puységur, was perhaps most guilty of both processionalism and polemicism. See *Art de la guerre par principes et par règles*, 2 vols (Paris, 1749).
18   Colin, *L'infanterie au XVIIIe siècle*, 3–72, and Quimby, *Background of Napoleonic Warfare*, 16–25.
19   Charles-François Dumoriez, *The Life of General Dumouriez*, 3 vols (London, 1796), 1:132–137; Philip Dwyer, *Napoleon: The Path to Power* (New Haven, CT, 2007), 19–21; "Jacques-Antoine-Hippolyte, comte de Guibert," in *Biographie universelle ancienne et moderne*, ed.

In 1773, Guibert's career path sharply diverged from those of his peers. He had spent his leisure time in Corsica composing a treatise on military theory entitled the *Essai général de tactique*. Published in 1772, the *Essai* appeared in several editions and achieved widespread readership by the following year.[20] He received plaudits and attention from the salons, launching a literary career that would produce more works of theory, theatrical endeavors, and several treatises on politics.[21] He also served on the *Conseil de la Guerre*, a reform body and prototypical general staff, from 1775 to 1777 and again from 1787 to 1789.[22]

Guibert's work and career belonged to the reform movement within the French army detailed above, which itself reflected the Enlightenment push for the reforms of all levels of French society. The effort took on a different tone after 1763. France was humiliated in the Seven Years War by the Prussian army which was so admired by the French.[23] This demonstrated the superiority of Prussia's "military constitution," as contemporaries argued. Like the theoretical French political constitution, the French military constitution was a nebulous set of traditions and ideologies that often changed to suit time and necessity. After the crushing defeat in the Seven Years War, many, including Guibert, argued for an enumerated doctrine to clearly define the army's tactics, organization, and operations.[24]

Building on the work of the 1750s, many theorists and writers during the postwar period attempted to create this military constitution as a comprehensive doctrine, or an "art of war" in contemporary parlance. Most merely

---

by Louis-Gabriel Michaud, 45 vols (Paris, 1857), 28:87; Ethel Groffier, *Le stratège des lumières: le comte de Guibert (1743–1790)* (Paris, 2005), 28–30; Matti Lauerma, *Jacques-Antoine-Hippolyte de Guibert (1743–1790)* (Helsinki, 1989), 20–23; François-Emmanuel Toulongeon, "Notice historique de Jacques-Antoine-Hippolyte Guibert, écrite en 1790," in Jacques-Antoine-Hippolyte, comte de Guibert, *Journal d'un voyage en Allemagne* (Paris, 1803), 3–4.

20 Jacques-Antoine-Hippolyte, comte de Guibert, *Essai général de tactique*, 2 vols (Liège, 1773), is the definitive edition.

21 Dumouriez, *Life of General Dumouriez*, 1:186–189; and Groffier, *Le stratège des lumières*, 33–34.

22 SHAT, M¹ 1790–1794, contains most of the records of Guibert's work in the ministry of war. See also Latreille, *L'œuvre militaire de la révolution*, 54–134 and 236–288.

23 On 5 November 1757, Frederick II's Prussian army met a combined Franco-imperial force under Charles de Rohan, prince de Soubise, near the village of Roßbach. Despite having little over half the number of soldiers of the Allied army, Frederick won the battle. This devastated the French, who had long considered themselves to be the masters of land war in Europe. See Franz Szabo, *The Seven Years War in Europe, 1756–1763* (New York, 2008), 94–98; and Richard Waddington, *La guerre de sept ans: histoire diplomatique et militaire*, 5 vols (Paris, 1899–1914), 1:617–630.

24 Quimby, *Background of Napoleonic Warfare*, excellently details the development and course of these ideas.

generated lists of maxims and ideas that, while useful, did not accomplish their goal of producing doctrine.[25] This failure is the genesis of Napoleon's famous quote that "the works of [military theory] are only incomplete compilations and too voluminous to be read with any profit ... We have not yet a single work which can with justice be called the *Art of War*."[26]

Guibert's work would be different from his contemporaries, a fact that Napoleon failed to recognize in the statement quoted above. Unlike them, Guibert produced a complete doctrine for the tactical and operational levels that was both systematic and enumerated. He addressed far more than just the petty tactics and organization most of his contemporaries favored. Instead, he recognized the difference between parade-ground precision and functionality in battle. He addressed the question of operations, illustrating in detail how his reforms would produce an articulated and mobile army at both the tactical and operational levels. Guibert noted the need for excellent officers and commanders, *hommes de génie*, to lead an army. As such, he created a systematic doctrine that encompassed nearly the entire French army in all areas of its functionality, from the individual soldier through the highest command.

Guibert's first contribution to both his doctrine and to the French army came in 1769 as a partnership with his father.[27] In *L'instruction de 1769 pour les troupes légères*, an internal memorandum issued by Louis XV's chief minister, Étienne-François, duc de Choiseul, the Guiberts proposed their solution to the problem of processional and rigid maneuvers. Instead of deployment into line and then maneuvering, a deploying army should break into smaller closed columns of maneuver that would deploy either on the square, or preferably, on the oblique. This eliminated the need to deploy from a unitary or double column into line and then maneuver ponderously in that line imposed by the reforms of the 1750s.[28]

---

25 Folard, *Nouvelles découvertes sur la guerre*; François-Jean de Graindorge d'Orgeville, baron de Mesnil-Durand, *Projet d'un ordre français en tactique, ou la phalange coupée et doublée soutenue par le mélange des armes* (Paris, 1755); and Maurice de Saxe, *Mes rêveries* (Paris, 1895).

26 Sarrazin, *Confession of General Buonaparté to the abbé Maury*, 142.

27 Colin, *L'infanterie au XVIIIe siècle*, 73–134; Quimby, *Background of Napoleonic Warfare*, 90–105. See also Etienne-François, duc de Choiseul, "Comte que j'ai rendu au roi de mon administration depuis 1757 jusqu'à 16 mars 1770," in Choiseul, *Mémoires* (Paris, 1982), 218.

28 Colin, *L'infanterie au XVIIIe siècle*, and Quimby, *Background of Napoleonic Warfare*, elaborate this debate in great detail. See also Nosworthy, *Anatomy of Victory*, 183–198; Rothenberg, *Art of Warfare in the Age of Napoleon*, 11–30. Nosworthy, *With Musket, Cannon, and Sword*, 81–91, ascribes the origins of this reform to experiments conducted during the Seven Years War with "columns of waiting," where armies broke into smaller columns rather than the unitary linear formations of past practice to cope with battlefield terrain.

The 1769 memo marked Guibert's first foray into doctrine and would be a signal change in the French army. It proposed to dispense with much of the parade-ground formalism present in the army. Moreover, it laid the foundation and provided the detailed mechanism whereby units could deploy not as unitary bodies or by regiment but rather by being broken into smaller columns and deploying however necessary to suit the circumstance, be it on the square or on the oblique. Such deployment became standard from that point forward, and the smaller columns became known as *"colonnes de Guibert."* These Guibert Columns allowed French commanders to move away from stilted, processional movements toward more practical formations able to meet battlefield conditions.[29]

Consequently, Guibert's earliest work indicated the thrust of his doctrine. It dispensed with much of the traditional and processional past of France's "military constitution," offering instead to replace it with simple and pragmatic solutions. Much of Guibert's later treatises reflect this ideology. This becomes particularly apparent when examining his great works of theory. Guibert followed his 1772 *Essai général de tactique* with his second tome of military theory, the 1778 *Défense du système de guerre moderne*. This work was largely a response to criticism of his *Essai général de tactique* by rival factions within the army in the intervening years but contains much clarification of Guibert's thought. In sum, the *Essai* and the *Défense* provide the blueprint of Guibert's doctrine.[30]

Guibert's systemic doctrine originated with a call for an army "better constituted and more maneuverable ... easy to move and to conduct ... [with] simple, analogous, [and] flexible tactics."[31] The principles of his system were based on battlefield reality rather than the "pretension to precision and perfection on many points, meticulous and ridiculous."[32] Dispensing with much of the extant tactical manual, Guibert greatly simplified French tactics and operations. "The primitive, fundamental, and habitual order of infantry will be on three ranks of depth; the momentary and accidental order will be the column," maintained Guibert. "The natural and habitual order is the proper order of fire, that is to say *l'ordre mince*."[33] Armies deployed in three-deep lines, as required by the Regulations of 1754. This multiplied the volume of fire from an army

---

29 Quimby, *Background of Napoleonic Warfare*, 90–105.
30 Jacques-Antoine-Hippolyte, comte de Guibert, *Défense du système de la guerre moderne, ou réfutation complète du système de M[esnil] D[urand]*, in *Oeuvres militaires de Guibert*, vols 3–4 (Paris, 1803), and *Essai général de tactique*.
31 Guibert, *Essai général de tactique*, 1:xcvii–xcix.
32 Ibid., 1:25.
33 Ibid., 1:30–33.

deployed in such a formation.[34] They also deployed in smaller battalions than was common practice, as few as 400 men. Guibert's battalions marched at a faster rate of speed than was common, up to 100 steps per minute for march step, as compared to 75.[35] Taken together, this created an army of small, articulated units that would be more maneuverable and flexible than extant armies.

In his advocacy for *l'ordre mince* as primary doctrine, Guibert rejected the chief virtue of *l'ordre profond*. He argued that fire trumped shock in its ability to inflict mass damage to an enemy army in a variety of circumstances, not just the attack of the column. Unlike the theorists of that school, Guibert considered moral forces in his doctrine. He insisted that an army subjected to fire, particularly when deployed in close order, tended to panic. This reduced the ability of a column deployed in *l'ordre profond* from achieving its objective of rupturing the enemy line if under fire of any notable quantity.[36]

Despite his advocacy of *l'ordre mince*, Guibert acknowledged that "the circumstances, the nature of the terrain, the situation of the enemy can require that one go without fire and that one engages in shock action."[37] Thus, he identified several situations where a column would prove superior to a line, particularly during the assault on a "point." Crucially, unlike proponents of *l'ordre profond*, Guibert did not deploy columns in closed formation, but rather with intervals. This system, adapted from the 1769 *Instructions for Light Troops*, eliminated the need for processional movements, which were designed to prevent intervals from opening in the entire deployment column.[38]

Guibert's smaller battalions and quicker march speed were to be employed by the Guibert Columns of that document. When on the march or performing evolutions, the regiments broke into small columns rather than maintaining unitary order. March columns were united only by their direction and remained broken into battalion-sized columns within the larger march order. They deployed according to circumstance and practicality rather than precedence or march order. Rather than combining the attack in one or two columns, as *l'ordre profond* advocated, Guibert suggested the use of many small columns identical to his columns of maneuver. These columns would be separated by a short distance and screened by light cavalry. The columns would advance at normal step, gradually increasing pace as they neared the enemy's line. Officers maintained order and separation between the columns to

---

34 See Colin, *L'infanterie au XVIIIe siècle*, 55–72.
35 Guibert, *Essai général de tactique*, 1:29–37.
36 Ibid., 1:33–34, and Guibert, *Défense du système de guerre moderne*, 1:19–75.
37 Guibert, *Essai général de tactique*, 1:31.
38 Ibid., 1:131–160. See also Colin, *L'infanterie au XVIIIe siècle*, 113–134.

prevent bunching. If the attack succeeded, the light cavalry would pursue and harass the enemy to prevent a counterattack.[39]

Unlike many of his predecessors in military theory, Guibert held no rigid conception of the use of column or line. He allowed either to be used, even within the same plan of deployment. Although Guibert argued for the primacy of firepower in linear formations, he also provided the mechanics for combat in columns and squares, with fire or shock. He referred to the use of line and column in the same formation as *l'ordre mixte*. Guibert intended it as a general appellation, not the name for a specific formation. *L'ordre mixte* was neither a tactical formation nor a specific instruction for battle. Rather, it was a tactical system that stressed mobility, maneuverability, flexibility, and pragmatism. Guibert's *l'ordre mixte* provided commanders with the ability and option to fight in any formation to fit the tactical situation. This fulfilled the spirit of his system, which called for flexibility above all.[40]

These alterations in organization and petty tactics provided the foundation for the higher levels of war in Guibert's system. Much of his analysis concerned the operational level, which contemporaries referred to as "grand tactics." This illustrated his system in theoretical practice, further elucidating its principles.[41] Guibert's operations depended on restructuring the army. Quoting Maurice de Saxe, he argued that "all the secret of exercise, of war, is in the legs."[42] Operational mobility, like tactical speed, provide the foundation for success.[43]

The first step in achieving operational mobility was to divorce the march order from the battle order. As noted, contemporary armies were forced to maintain rigid order in the march column and into deployment in line. Guibert believed that the extant concept of keeping the infantry line perfectly intact while on the march or while deployed was nonsense. Instead, he called for "movements that are by battalion and never by regiment," essentially devolving march and battle order to the battalion level.[44] While the larger administrative units would provide an outline of the march and even its organization, Guibert expected the battalion to form in a Guibert Column and to maneuver around obstacles on its own authority. He allowed for a march or formation disrupted by terrain as long as the army as a whole maintained its cohesion.

---

39 Guibert, *Essai général de tactique*, 1:37–42, and Guibert, *Défense du système de guerre moderne*, 1:119–125 and 170–212.
40 Guibert, *Essai général de tactique*, 1:110–168.
41 Ibid., 2:1–149.
42 Ibid., 2:8.
43 Guibert, *Défense du système de guerre moderne*, 2:1–70. Much of the second volume of this work concerns the operational level of war.
44 Guibert, *Essai général de tactique*, 1:42.

Divorcing the march order from battle order freed the French army from almost all of its processional hindrances. It allowed battalion commanders to act autonomously within the larger plan, providing a much more supple and effective march and deployment. It also eliminated the unitary march column, allowing for a much greater operational mobility in an army no longer tied to a unitary march direction and formation.[45]

The second element of Guibert's operational system involved the adoption of a new form of organization at the operational level. "For a large mass to be moved with the most ease," Guibert maintained, "it must be divided ... into many parts; then each of the parts is susceptible to more movement and action; then one can, by these forces combined and multiplied, act on all the parts at a time; this is therefore an army." "[These] principles ... will be able to render march more rapid and easier, will separate the army into many bodies that reunite on a point, or to within range of a prepared point," he concluded.[46]

To this end, Guibert adopted the division system first experimented with by Victor-François, duc de Broglie, in the Seven Years War. Broglie's use of divisions provided a novel methodology and the inspiration for Guibert's adoption.[47] However, they failed to gain traction in the larger army at the time or immediately after. Broglie never created an enumerated doctrine surrounding the use of divisions in his many writings on the conflict. Thus, his system represented a personal doctrine unique to the commander rather than a systemic doctrine that could be institutionalized for the entire army's use.[48]

Unlike his contemporaries, Guibert created an army that included all three branches at the operational level. His divisions were combined-arms units composed of infantry, cavalry, and in some circumstances artillery.[49] The infantry, as the most numerous arm, remained the foundation and primary tool of Guibert's theoretical army and constitution. He noted that cavalry served several important roles in the support of infantry: scouting, raiding, screening,

---

45 Ibid., 1:48–70.
46 Ibid., 2:11, 24.
47 Ibid. Broglie created operational divisions for many of his campaigns during the Seven Years War on an ad hoc basis. He often divided his army into six such units and assigned them different march routes, uniting them before contact with the enemy for the battle. Guibert's father served on Broglie's staff, as did the young Guibert. See Colin, *L'infanterie au XVIIIe siècle*, 73–134; Quimby, *Background of Napoleonic Warfare*, 90–105. See also Victor-François, duc de Broglie, *Campagnes du maréchal duc de Broglie en Allemagne 1759–1761* (Frankfurt and Leipzig, 1761), and *Correspondance inédite* (Paris, 1903).
48 Guibert, *Essai général de tactique*, 2:26–30, and *Défense du système de guerre moderne*, 2:3–36, 59–70.
49 Guibert, *Essai général de tactique*, 2:8–36, and *Défense du système de guerre moderne*, 2:37–46.

pursuit, disrupting enemy lines of communication and supply, and shock attacks. Unlike many other authors of the period, Guibert refused to simply chain the cavalry to the infantry as a screening or protection force. He noted its utility as a supporting arm and its ability to function independently in certain circumstances.[50]

Artillery was "a utile and important accessory of the troops that compose armies... [because it] cannot fight alone and by [itself]," unlike cavalry and infantry.[51] To this end, Guibert proposed to increase its mobility via the Gribeauval system to allow it to better support the other arms. The much lighter and more maneuverable guns would allow Guibert's small batteries to maneuver quickly to the proper place on the battlefield, plugging gaps in the line or supporting attacks. The majority of guns could be left in the artillery park, quickly maneuvering to points of need rather than spreading across the entire battle line and slowing the entire army. These factors would combine to produce light, maneuverable, and flexible artillery units that could better support infantry.[52]

Guibert castigated Old Regime armies for becoming overly fond of light troops, employing as much as 20 per cent of an army's soldiers in the role. These light troops served as excellent skirmishers, he argued, embodying the principles of accurate and destructive fire central to his doctrine. However, they could perform only the function for which they were designed, namely skirmishing. They could not fight in line, thus greatly limiting their utility. To correct this problem, Guibert's system advocated flexibility of organization and use, principles that light troops directly countered as a single-use force. He allowed for the retention of limited light forces, particularly working with light cavalry. Their tasks included scouting, screening, and harassing the enemy.[53] To enhance the flexibility of his army, Guibert advocated the training of line troops as skirmishers. Rather than dedicate forces solely to skirmishing, this enabled his theoretical army to deploy in open or closed order to skirmish or fight a linear battle as circumstances dictated. Like his multi-use columns, Guibert's infantry would function as line or light as needed.[54]

Guibert's reduction in the number of artillery, cavalry, and light troops in favor of line infantry points to a key element of his doctrine: the concentration of force provided by a unitary army. The separation of an army into large detachments of line infantry, cavalry, light infantry, and artillery typical of

---

50 Guibert, *Essai général de tactique*, 1:169–172.
51 Ibid., 1:231–232.
52 Ibid., 1:253–272.
53 Ibid., 1:215–230.
54 Ibid., 1:70–90.

contemporary theory necessarily reduced the opportunity for concentration. Reducing the numbers of cavalry and light infantry in favor of line infantry and combining soldier's duties provided a highly skilled, unitary army. Such an army could use its superior maneuverability and flexibility to concentrate its force on the enemy's weak point and win the battle.[55]

Guibert's combined-arms division provided greater march security, discipline, and operational flexibility.[56] It also allowed divisions to disperse and use different march routes to arrive at the same destination.[57] Separate routes allowed divisions to move much more quickly than a unitary march. Dispersed divisions could fan out across the countryside until the enemy was encountered, whereupon they would converge on the proposed battlefield. This concentration supported the concept of local numerical superiority, as Guibert's mobile divisions would be able to concentrate much more easily than an Old Regime army similarly dispersed, which tended to remain fixed to a geographic *point d'appui* or "place" to form a cordon.[58] The tactical articulation of the battalion was mirrored in the operational articulation of the division. Guibert's divisions could maneuver as fluidly as his battalions, enabling an operational maneuver on the enemy's weak points, a kind of operational *ordre mixte*. This could be conducted by a division attached to the main body or one separate from it: Guibert's system provided for both usages.[59]

The operational innovation of Guibert's system came in the institutionalization of doctrine rather than any particular discovery of operations.[60] He maintained a unitary view of armies once the battlefield was reached,

---

55 Much of volume 2 of the *Essai général de tactique* elaborates Guibert's doctrine in this regard.
56 Ibid., 2:6–9.
57 Ibid., 2:8–38.
58 Ibid., 2:12–24. See Duffy, *The Military Experience in the Age of Reason* (New York, 1988), 151–188.
59 Guibert, *Essai général de tactique*, 2:39–60. Much of the above also occurs in Pierre-Joseph Bourcet, *Principes de la guerre de montagnes* (Paris, 1775), often considered to be the origin of French, and Napoleonic, operational warfare. The pamphlet circulated within the French army before its official date of publication, although no historian has discovered when exactly it received its authorship or, more importantly, its wide readership. Guibert's drafting of the *Essai général de tactique* was completed by 1770 or 1771, providing an intriguing historiographical debate with no apparent solution as to the origins of operational-level warfare.
60 This point has become one of great contention in historiography. Palmer argues that Guibert failed to grasp the implications of his theories. Telp insists on the contrary, that "Guibert was particularly important to the 'discovery' of the operational level of war." See Palmer, "Frederick the Great, Guibert, Bülow," 110, and Claus Telp, *The Evolution of Operational Art, 1747–1813: From Frederick the Great to Napoleon* (New York, 2005), 26.

imagining the divisions uniting in a single line and then performing maneuvers at the tactical level to overcome the enemy. He simply did not possess the Napoleonic genius for operational-level warfare, perhaps because he had never commanded troops at that level in combat.[61] Instead, the creation of his system established the framework that allowed future commanders to develop the operational art. In particular, his tactical and organizational reforms freed commanders from the processional strictures of past practice.

In addition to tactical and organizational reforms, Guibert dedicated much of his work to areas he considered vital for the success of his army. He strongly emphasized discipline and education, not in the mechanistic sense but rather in an elastic and practical model that would harness the French soldier's *élan* to the movements of the larger army.[62] Guibert counseled the staging of training camps as the "school of the officer," transforming them from mere military parades into valuable tools in the education and training of the officer corps.[63] He lamented the destruction that accompanied war, arguing for a nationalized and centrally controlled logistical department rather than the forage of contemporary practice.[64] Most of all, Guibert called for an army to be led by an *homme de génie*. This commander "rarely rested in action" and was able to "perceive many objects, embrace many combinations; and therefore by consequence, where the mediocre general does not see the position to defend or the possibility of acting, [*coup d'oeil*] presents to the imagination of the former [*l'homme de génie*] an advantageous movement."[65] When these reforms were combined with Guibert's tactics and organization, the army produced would once again surmount the Prussian as the most complete and effective in Europe.

Guibert's doctrine would remain purely theoretical until its implementation by the ministry of war, which would occur in stages between 1775 and 1791. His first foray into politics proved something of a trial run. He served as Recording Secretary to the Council of War under Claude-Louis, comte de Saint-Germain, the secretary of state for war from 1775 to 1777. Saint-Germain named Guibert as the primary inspiration for the reforms that would take place during his tenure.[66] Many of these consisted of cost-cutting measures, particularly by

---

61 Guibert, *Essai général de tactique*, 1:24–39, 90–94, and 2:13.
62 Ibid., 2:62–70.
63 Ibid., 1:1–9, 2:113–136, and Guibert, *Défense du système de guerre moderne*, 2, which discusses training camps and discipline in great detail.
64 Guibert, *Essai général de tactique*, 2:180–218.
65 Ibid., 2:2, 109, 139–161. See also Guibert, *Défense du système de guerre moderne*, 2:39–61.
66 *Observations relatives à la nouvelle constitution, Vices de l'ancienne constitution et avantages de la nouvelle constitution,* and *Project de travail relatif...*, SHAT, M¹ 1791, 13–15;

eliminating much of the bloated Maison du Roi and officer corps.[67] Guibert was largely stymied in the implementation of his tactical and organizational doctrine, as the majority of the Council preferred a mostly strict adherence to *l'ordre mince* as practiced in Prussia.[68] The experiment ended in 1777, as Saint-Germain fell out of favor at court and the entire ministry was dismissed.

Guibert's great chance finally arrived on the eve of the Revolution. Now an older and bitter man, Guibert applied great energy to the problems of reform as de facto chair of the *Conseil de la Guerre*. He implemented much of his doctrine in the provisional Regulations of 1788, calling for his tactical and organizational methods to become the doctrine of the French army. He also created an embryonic division system, dividing the kingdom into military districts with a division attached to each. This idea was a hybrid of the territorial system and an operational division system.[69] However, it remained the foundation for the implementation of a true division system in the near future. Guibert also envisioned the Council of War's becoming a General Staff, which also partially occurred during his tenure.[70] Together, these reforms would provide a better-

---

Lauerma, *Guibert*, 86–106; Claude-Louis, comte de Saint-Germain, *Mémoires* (Amsterdam, 1779), 31; and Joseph Alphonse de Véri, *Journal de l'abbé de Véri*, 2 vols (Paris, 1928–1930), 1:380. For Guibert's thoughts on these machinations, see Guibert to Lespinasse, 18 October 1775; Guibert to Lespinasse, 27 October 1775; and Guibert to Lespinasse, [March–April] 1776, in *The Love Letters of Mlle. de Lespinasse to and from the Comte de Guibert*, ed. by Armand Villeneuve-Guibert, trans. by E.H.F. Mills (London, 1929), 396–401, 419–424, and 507–508.

67 *Commentaires sur les mémoires de monsieur le comte de Saint-Germain* (Paris, 1780), 73. See also David D. Bien, "The Army in the French Enlightenment: Reform, Reaction and Revolution," *Past & Present* 85 (1979), 68–98; Rafe Blaufarb, *The French Army, 1750–1820: Careers, Talent, Merit* (New York, 2002), and "Noble Privilege and Absolutist State Building: French Military Administration after the Seven Years War," *French Historical Studies* 24 (2001), 223–246; and Julia Osman, "Patriotism as Power: The Old Regime Foundation for Napoleon's Army," *International Congress of Military History Conference Proceedings 2009* (2010).

68 Guibert to Lespinasse, [March 1776], [Winter 1776], and especially [Winter 1776], *Love Letters of Mlle. Julie de Lespinasse*, 505, 507, and 510–511. See also Colin, *L'infanterie au XVIIIe siècle*, 135–184; Quimby, *Background of Napoleonic Warfare*, 205–209.

69 A militia division system assigns the militia within a given territory to a territorial division, bringing them together for training, organization, and mobilization. A "true" division system functions in the field, as units are divided into combined-arms operational units capable of autonomous march and action. Guibert's system contained elements of both. He created territorial divisions for organizing the kingdom's militia but also envisioned them functioning as operational units in wartime.

70 *Rapport à faire au conseil de la guerre sur la formation de l'Armée*, SHAT, M¹ 1790, 25; *Armée – Infanterie*, and *Commandements dans les provinces*, SHAT, M¹ 1790, 26, 30. See also Latreille, *L'oeuvre militaire de la révolution*, 269–284.

controlled and -constituted army, rendering it more effective at the operational and tactical levels.

Guibert's doctrine was largely codified in the Provisional Regulations of 1788, the other work of the Council of War during that period.[71] However, political enemies conspired against him and saw to his removal in 1789 as the Revolution began. Guibert died the following year, never having had the opportunity to witness the implementation of his doctrine on the battlefield.[72] It would become the basic tactical manual of the French army, replacing those of prior use with Guibert's ideas. His legacy in print also succeeded him, inspiring many of the officers and theorists in the years of great conflict that would follow.

Nearly simultaneously with Guibert's death was the death of the Old Regime and its replacement by the various governments of Revolutionary France. The Revolution was a crucial period for both France and Guibert's ideas. His reforms would evolve during the wars of the Revolution as they were tested in battle and shaped for practical use. Like the previous government, those of the Revolutionary Era required an army with a governing doctrine. Rather than innovate, the army of the Revolution relied almost entirely on the Old Regime for its technical doctrine. As a result, Guibert's ideas would become the basis for French doctrine into the Napoleonic period.

In October of 1789, Guibert's *Conseil de la Guerre* was disbanded by France's first revolutionary government, the National Constituent Assembly, along with most of the old ministry of war. It was replaced by a new Military Committee, which included several of Guibert's collaborators, most notably Louis-François, baron Wimpffen-Bournebourg.[73] For the next two years, the Committee strove to recreate the army, much as the state was being recreated by the Assembly's other committees.[74] The result appeared in 1791. The Military Committee would be the governing body of the French army, a kind of General Staff

---

71 Much of the Council's work built on the Council of Saint-Germain in cutting costs, reducing the Maison du roi, and further centralizing and bureaucratizing the army. See ibid.

72 Louis-Joseph Amour, marquis de Bouillé, *Souvenirs et fragments pour servir aux mémoires de ma vie et de mon temps*, 3 vols (Paris, 1906–1911), 1:83–88; and André-François, comte Miot de Melito, *Mémoires*, 3 vols (Paris, 1858), 1:2–4.

73 "Louis-François, baron Wimpffen-Bornebourg," in *Biographie universelle ancienne et moderne*, 44:668.

74 Latreille, *L'œuvre militaire de la révolution*, 236–288, provides the clearest overview of this period. Many of the documents in SHAT, M¹ 1790, detail the work of the Council, especially *Mémoire servant à la fois d'intruction et résumé au plan général de réforme du département de la guerre*, *Plan général*, *Bureaux (Plan général)*, and *Idées particulières*, *Instruction du roi pour le conseil de la guerre*, *Résumé de la première division du travail du Conseil de la Guerre*, *Première séance – rapport pour Octobre 1787*, *Infanterie*, *Séance du 20*

chaired by Louis XVI as commander in chief and receiving its funding from the Assembly. Lacking permanent infantry regulations, it created a new set issued on 1 August 1791. This was essentially an update and formalization of the Provisional *Réglement* of 1788. It became the famous 1791 *Réglement* and would remain the official regulations until the 1830s, providing the Guibertian foundation of doctrine during that period.[75]

The Regulations adopted the Guibert Column for the document's method of deployment in closed column. These were designed after Guibert's recommendations.[76] Most notably, Guibert's hybrid of *l'ordre mince* and *l'ordre profond* became the standard deployment and tactics of the army. The 1791 Regulations allowed commanders to use both line and column in battle as they saw fit, including in the same formation and within smaller units. His hybrid became known as *l'ordre mixte*, after Guibert's term from his writings. It reflected not a particular tactical system, but rather the flexible and pragmatic nature of its inspiration.[77]

Like much of Guibert's theoretical doctrine, the Regulations were not intended as irrevocable and fixed dogmatic pronouncements. Rather, they were designed to be adapted to the battlefield as deemed necessary by commanders in the field. François Roguet illuminated this point in his valuable postwar analysis. He found that "the Regulations are perhaps only the grammar of tacticians, which then must be [tested] on the field and before the enemy; the enemy formations give them their regulations."[78] A facility with language requires an understanding of its grammar. As Roguet stated, the 1791 Regulations were the grammar of doctrine for all practitioners who followed. They could choose to accept or reject elements of the grammar, but the crucial learning process would have to be completed by the point at which a commander could justifiably make that choice, thus learning its basics. The language of the French army after 1791 was the Regulations of that year, and those regulations spoke a language with a grammar created by Guibert.

Novembre, and *Mémoire du Conseil de la Guerre à sa majesté sur les places des colonels-généraux et autres changes d'état-major*, SHAT, M¹ 1790, 4, 5, 6, 10, 14, 18, and 22–24.

75 Howard Brown, *War, Revolution, and the Bureaucratic State: Politics and Army Administration in France, 1791–1799* (New York, 1995), 19–23; Colin, *L'infanterie au XVIIIe siècle*, 260–278; and Steven T. Ross, *From Flintlock to Rifle: Infantry Tactics, 1740–1866* (London, 1995), 51–56.

76 Lacroix, *Rules and Regulations for the Field Exercise and Maneuvers of the French Infantry issued August 1, 1791*, 169–290.

77 Ibid.

78 François Roguet, "Etude sur l'ordre perpendiculaire," in Jean Maximilien Lamarque, ed., *Le spectateur militaire* (Paris, 1834), 18:523.

This notion, perhaps more so than any simple tactical or organizational innovation, illustrates Guibert's seminal influence on the French army after his death. Throughout his work, he railed against fixed regulations that did not function in practice and proposed solutions to correct those faults within the extant regulations, often in pedantic detail. Many technical reforms, like the Guibert Columns, were adopted into doctrine, but much of this detail was also simply ignored by future theorists and practitioners. Even if some of the specifics of his system, like the three-battalion regiment, were forgotten, its spirit of pragmatism and flexibility remained as the foundation of French doctrine going forward.

The Wars of the French Revolution provided the testing ground referenced by Roguet. Between 1792 and 1799, the French army gained much experience in battle. In particular, Guibert's tactical and organizational reforms revolutionized how war was fought. No longer would the army rely on difficult processional maneuvers in march or maneuver. Nor would it be chained to a rigid implementation of *l'ordre mince* or *l'ordre profond*, as many of Guibert's contemporaries had preached. Instead, it would develop a dynamic system of tactics and organization that produced a flexible and mobile army adaptable to any battlefield conditions.[79]

Exact usages of tactical formations and methods prove controversial in both contemporary debate and modern historiography. The theorists of the 18th century defined use of the line as *l'ordre mince* and the column as *l'ordre profond*.[80] Modern scholars have adopted this dichotomy, leading to much rancorous debate as to which system the French armies preferred. This debate is further exacerbated by the use of each formation. Contemporaries identified fire almost exclusively with *l'ordre mince* and shock with *l'ordre profond*, a distinction which has also entered modern historiography.[81] Paddy Griffith

---

79   See Jean-Paul Bertaud, *The Army of the French Revolution: From Citizen-Soldiers to Instrument of Power*, trans. by R.R. Palmer (Princeton, NJ, 1988). See also Nosworthy, *With Musket, Cannon, and Sword*, 83–102.

80   Folard, *Nouvelles découvertes sur la guerre*; Quimby, *Background of Napoleonic Warfare*, 7–105; and Mesnil-Durand, *Projet d'un ordre français*.

81   For example, see David Chandler, *The Campaigns of Napoleon: The Mind and Methods of History's Greatest Soldier* (New York, 1966), 188–190; John Elting, *Swords Around a Throne: Napoleon's Grande Armée* (New York, 1988), 207–226 and 536–538; Rory Muir, *Tactics and the Experience of Battle in the Age of Napoleon* (New Haven, CT, 1998), 68–71; and Rothenberg, *Art of Warfare in the Age of Napoleon*, 114–118. Quimby, *Background of Napoleonic Warfare*, 7–43, following Colin, argues to the contrary, that *l'ordre mixte* was never a formation and was never intended to be. Although Quimby found examples of mixed-order tactical formations dating back at least to the 1750s he concludes that no such official formation existed.

notably contends that the armies of Revolutionary France triumphed in large part because of tactics. He finds that, rather than a flexible doctrinal system, the armies of the period instead made use of a specific formation known as "*l'ordre mixte*." Griffith presents this in a diagram as a formation of one unit in column on the left of the formation, another unit in line facing the enemy, and a third unit in column on the right. Such a formation would ostensibly provide both fire and shock as well as protection of the flanks. This was superior to enemy tactics, allowing the French soldiers to win the majority of their battles.[82] This argument is carried into a number of other works, including attributing the formation to Guibert. While none of the cited works argues that the French won their battles exclusively through the use of this formation, many imply that it was a significant contributing factor in their success.[83]

These distinctions remained largely academic, even during the period. With the advent of Guibert's system, they were rendered entirely obsolete. He liberated the French army from its reliance on any single tactical system. The flexibility of his organization and tactics allowed an army to utilize any formation with fire or shock. Moreover, units could make use of several formations and methods within a single engagement.[84] Evidence from battles during the period bears out this argument. Few examples of the proposed *l'ordre mixte* exist. Rather, many chroniclers record the use of multiple tactics and formations.

The default tactical formation and method during the Revolutionary Wars appeared to be the line using fire. At the Battle of Neerwinden on 18 March 1793, the Armée du Nord began the battle by "divid[ing] into two columns [and] deploy[ing] in three lines ... fire engaged from one end to the other" to receive the initial Austrian attack, illustrating the classic deployment and use of a line.[85] Lines afforded the benefit of increasing the volume of fire and spreading the army across a larger portion of the battlefield, providing better control of the space. Most battles during the period involved some form of fighting in *l'ordre mince*.[86]

---

82 Griffith, *The Art of War of Revolutionary France 1789–1802* (Mechanicsburg, PA, 1998), 221–222. See also Michel Ney, *Marshal Ney's Military Studies*, in *Memoirs of Marshal Ney*, 2 vols (London, 1833), 2:291–384, for the possible origin of Griffith's argument.

83 Muir, *Tactics and the Experience of Battle in the Age of Napoleon*, 72–74; and Rothenberg, *Art of Warfare in the Age of Napoleon*, 117.

84 See John Lynn, *The Bayonets of the Republic: Motivation and Tactics in the Army of Revolutionary France, 1791–1794* (Urbana, IL, 1984).

85 Jacques Fricasse, *Journal de marche du sergent Fricasse de la 127e demi-brigade, 1792–1802* (Paris, 1882), 39.

86 See Louis-Joseph Bricard, *Journal du canonnier Bricard: 1792–1802* (Paris, 1894), 146–147, 220–221, 225–230; Auguste Colbert, *Le général Auguste Colbert (1793–1809): traditions, souvenirs, et documents touchant sa vie et son temps*, ed. by Marquis de Colbert-Chabanais

However, this did not preclude the use of either the column or *l'ordre profond* as necessary. In particular, the column became a vital element of tactical and grand tactical doctrine and organization during the period. Guibert Columns were the standard formation for deployment and maneuver. This eliminated the Old Regime practice of converting from march to battle order, a cumbersome process, as noted. The Revolution's nimble columns allowed their commanders to move and maneuver much more rapidly than their enemies, probing for a weak point and focusing on it once discovered.[87]

Attack columns became the most celebrated use of the column and the only direct implementation of *l'ordre profond* during the revolutionary period. They made the best use of French character and *élan*, as their proponents had long argued. For example, on 4 June 1796, General Michel Ney oversaw a prototypical attack on an entrenched Austrian position in the vicinity of Mainz. He divided his force into three columns, one led by the future marshal Nicolas Soult, and concentrated them against the weakest points in the Austrian defenses. Each column overran its assigned Austrian position, taking the field.[88] Similarly, John Money notes an attack in column by line infantry at Tavier on 1 December 1792.[89]

Other formations illustrate the flexibility given to the French army by Guibert's doctrine. Infantry squares appeared as a defensive formation, especially after 1794. Ney provides a model example of this deployment, speaking of the two battalions under his command near Amberg on 23 August 1796: "they … formed themselves into a square and continu[ed] their march. The Austrian cavalry made a charge upon them; they received it with calm firmness, and

---

(Paris, 1888), 2:15–18, 21, 335–337; Fricasse, *Journal de marche du sergent Fricasse*, 21–22, 32, 90, 114; Théodore Leclaire, *Mémoires et correspondance du général Leclaire, 1793* (London, 1904), 43–44; Louis François, baron Lejeune, *Memoirs of Baron Lejeune*, trans. by Arthur Bell (New York, 1897), 21; and Ney, *Memoirs of Marshal Ney*, 1:59–60 and 2:364.

87 Bricard, *Journal du canonnier Bricard*, 39–42, describes the use of maneuver columns to reach the battlefield and as a staging formation for the deployment into line at Neerwinden. See Griffith, *Art of War of Revolutionary France*, 207–234; and Ross, *From Flintlock to Rifle*, 51–87.

88 Ney, *Memoirs of Marshal Ney*, 1:110–112.

89 Jean-Roch Coignet, *The Narrative of Captain Coignet*, ed. Lorédan Larchey, trans. M. Carey (London, 1890), 131–134; J[ohn] Money, *The History of the Campaign of 1792, Between the Armies of France Under Generals Dumouriez, Valence, Etc. and the Allies Under the Duke of Brunswick* (London, 1794), 210. The latter example illustrates the use of disciplined attack columns in the early days of the Revolution, when many authors argue the French army was capable of little more than flinging disorganized hordes at their more professional enemies. See Chandler, *Campaigns of Napoleon*, 479–502; James Marshall-Cornwall, *Napoleon as Military Commander* (London, 1967), 146–166; Maximilian Yorck von Wartenburg, *Napoleon as a General*, 2 vols (London, 1902), 1:267–302.

having repulsed it, continued their movement."[90] French armies also dispersed into open order, or *en tirailleur*, in many engagements. They possessed dedicated light troops, particularly the *chasseurs à pied* and *chasseurs à cheval*, who engaged in much of the skirmishing. However, line infantry also dispersed into open order and skirmished on numerous instances during the period, fulfilling Guibert's doctrine as noted above.[91]

These examples illustrate the flexibility and utility of the tactical system designed by Guibert. Revolutionary armies fought not in predetermined order or according to a rigid and unitary system. Rather, they used line, column, shock, squares, or open order as demanded by the situation or the terrain. Fire could be delivered from lines, columns, squares, and open order. Shock could be effected with columns, lines, and occasionally open order. This was Guibert's true *l'ordre mixte*: not a tactical formation, but rather an entire tactical system. The false dichotomies introduced by contemporaries and continued in modern historiography in the "line vs. column" debate hold no traction on the actual practice of battle.[92] The armies of France developed a significant tactical flexibility in the crucible of the Revolutionary Wars, enabling them to fight in any formation using any methods as suited to the situation. Old Regime armies tended not to have this flexibility, marking it as the most significant change of Guibert's doctrine during the period.

Perhaps the most significant result of the increase in tactical flexibility was to provide the foundation for the development of operational-level warfare within the French system. The Guibert Column became the standard column of both march and maneuver, as noted. Instead of being chained to a larger battle plan, units marched and maneuvered freely into position for the battle. This enabled them to move much more quickly and fluidly. The liberation of march from battle order prescribed by Guibert eliminated almost every aspect of formalism and processionalism at the level of grand tactics.[93]

Commanders began to adapt Guibert's combined-arms divisions, as well. They created ad hoc units that functioned largely according to the prescriptions laid out by Guibert in 1788, which in large part were based on Broglie's

---

90 Ney, *Memoirs of Marshal Ney*, 1:186.
91 Muir, *Tactics and the Experience of Battle*, 51–67; and Nosworthy, *With Musket, Cannon, and Sword*, 245–262.
92 See James R. Arnold, "A Reappraisal of Column Versus Line in the Peninsular War," *Journal of Military History* 68 (2004), 535–552, for a recent example of this ongoing historiographical debate.
93 Colin, *L'education militaire de Napoleon*, 28–108; Nosworthy, *With Musket, Cannon, and Sword*, 85–93; Quimby, *Background of Napoleonic Warfare*, 300–344; and Telp, *Evolution of Operational Art*, 42–45.

experiments in the Seven Years War. For example, at the Battle of the Roer on 2 October 1794, General Jean-Baptiste Jourdan dispersed his forces by division to attack the Austrians on multiple fronts simultaneously, probing for a weak point. This method proved successful, and the Austrian army retreated from its position.[94] Nosworthy refers to these operational-level innovations as the "impulse system of grand tactics." Breaking up the unitary army of Old Regime practice enabled individual commanders to conduct their units autonomously within the larger battle plan. This allowed for operations on multiple axes rather than the single axis of the past. This in turn fed on the social reforms of the period, as officers promoted on merit rather than venality or title were much more autonomous, active, and capable of reacting to battlefield situations. He credits this impulse system with much of the French success during the period.[95]

Despite many victories, the French army largely failed to exploit the great advantages afforded it by Guibertian doctrine at the operational level. Like Guibert, most revolutionary commanders still thought in terms of a unitary army. It might disperse for march, but it would unite before the battle to form a single army in the face of the enemy. Few commanders grasped that the operational articulation of the army via the division could allow for dynamic operational warfare whereby divisions could unite during the battle at the point in time and space most beneficial to the victory. Fewer still had the necessary political and strategic control to affect such battles and campaigns.[96]

Only Napoleon Bonaparte fully realized the implications of the system created by Guibert and refined during the Revolutionary Wars. His command of the Army of Italy in 1796–1797 illustrated the potential of that system, particularly on the operational level. Despite being consistently undermanned, his army defeated both the Austrians and Sardinians and shifted the strategic balance of the War of the First Coalition. Napoleon effected this victory largely through superior operational-level warfare. He dispersed his units into prototypical divisions under his subordinate commanders. They moved with lightning speed and flexibility in large part because of their liberation from Old Regime tactics via Guibertian doctrine. Napoleon expertly directed them against his enemies, surprising them time and again as one division or two would erupt on their flanks or rear during critical battles and campaigns. The combination of Guibertian tactics and organization and Napoleon's

---

94 See Ramsay Weston Phipps, *The Armies of the First French Republic and the Rise of the Marshals of Napoleon I*, 5 vols (London, 1926–1939), 2:184–187.
95 Nosworthy, *With Musket, Cannon, and Sword*, 82–97.
96 Colin, *L'éducation militaire de Napoleon*, 47–64; Palmer, "Frederick the Great, Guibert, Bülow"; and Telp, *Evolution of Operational Art*, 35–58.

operational evolution swept them from the field and brought the conflict to an end.[97]

This campaign, and Napoleon's second in Italy in 1800, provided the prototype for the Napoleonic art of war. He would make no major alterations to its tactics or tactical organizations during the years of his great victories before 1810.[98] Instead, he used the system provided to him by Guibert and refined during the Revolution. From 1802 to 1805, France was at peace with every major power save Great Britain and fought no major conflicts, allowing Napoleon to implement his desired alterations to the army. Many of these took place on paper, as he reworked operational organization, logistics, and the command structure of the army between 1800 and 1802. He then put them into practice by ordering a great training camp to be held at Boulogne. From 1803 to 1805, Napoleon oversaw the remaking of the army, creating his Grande Armée.[99] Following that critical period, he would achieve his apotheosis as the "God of War."

The most significant change developed during the Napoleonic period was the creation of *corps d'armée*. These were an adaption of the division system of autonomous units. Napoleon entirely scrapped the notion of territorial divisions, preferring instead units that operated on the march and in battle. In their place he created *corps*, bodies consisting of at least two divisions of infantry with artillery, cavalry, and light infantry attached. They ranged in size from 10,000 to more than 40,000 men, especially later in the period. He numbered each corps, creating eight by 1805 and adding several later. Each corps was a permanent formation with a complete staff and headquarters. Each corps was also commanded by a senior general, many of whom were elevated to the marshalate in 1804.[100]

Napoleon intended his *corps d'armée* to be autonomous units capable of marching, maneuvering, fighting, and foraging without support for at least several hours, if not several days. Each corps contained all elements of an army, making them miniature armies. However, they were not intended to function alone. He created a grand staff system to oversee their operations as part of the

---

97   Colin, *L'éducation militaire de Napoleon*, 353–382; Rothenberg, *Art of Warfare in the Age of Napoleon*, 95–164; and especially Telp, *Evolution of Operational Art*, 35–144. See also Martin Boycott-Brown, *The Road to Rivoli: Napoleon's First Campaign* (London, 2001); and Guglielmo Ferrero, *The Gamble: Bonaparte in Italy 1796–1797*, trans. by Bertha Pritchard and Lily C. Freeman (London, 1961).
98   Ross, *From Flintlock to Rifle*, 88–125.
99   Scott Bowden, *Napoleon and Austerlitz* (Chicago, 1997), 11–142, provides an excellent and detailed summary of this period.
100 Chandler, *Campaigns of Napoleon*, 133–204; Elting, *Swords Around a Throne*, 55–66; and Rothenberg, *Art of Warfare in the Age of Napoleon*.

larger Grande Armée. Each corps would function within a larger operational battle plan, dispersing them across march routes for the campaign and bringing them together for the culminating battle.[101]

The prototype for this system has become known as the *bataillon carré*, or battalion square, after a jest of Napoleon's. This operational formation deployed four corps in a diamond formation, with one in the van, two on the flanks, and one in reserve. Each would be less than a day's march from its neighbor, and the army's headquarters would be in the center of the formation. This would enable Napoleon to disperse his army across the countryside, preventing it from clogging roads and exhausting supply along its route. It would move much more quickly and flexibly than other armies, particularly those of the Old Regime and even the Revolution from which it sprang.[102]

Perhaps most significantly, Napoleon represented the fulfillment of the *homme de génie* in Guibert's system. During the Revolution, commanders struggled with operational-level warfare. Few were able to use the army created by Guibert and refined on the tactical level at the higher levels of war. Fewer still could climb the treacherous ladder in Paris to command field armies without running afoul of intrigues and succumbing to sacking or the guillotine. Most importantly, France lacked a central command authority that could effectively dictate strategy and supply in both the government and the army.[103]

Napoleon's rise signaled the union of political and military power in the hands of a single man. Like the absolutist monarchs who preceded him, Napoleon emphasized order and effective functioning in both. He greatly increased the bureaucratization of both the government and the army, creating a number of bureaux and staffing them with specialists to ensure the functioning of his army. He also elevated to the ranks of brigade, division, and corps command within the Grande Armée a series of generals, fellow *hommes de génie*, who showed merit. This officer corps, forged in the fire of the Revolution, would be instrumental in leading it to victory. Like Napoleon, they were skilled and educated in both theory and practice. Most importantly, they had a coherent doctrine and political system to form the army that they lead. No prior era

---

101   Chandler, *Campaigns of Napoleon*, 133–204; Elting, *Swords Around a Throne*, 55–66; Rothenberg, *Art of Warfare in the Age of Napoleon;* and especially Telp, *Evolution of Operational Art*, 35–38.

102   Chandler, *Campaigns of Napoleon*, 161–190, provides an excellent description and diagram of this formation.

103   Lazare Carnot attempted to direct military operations and strategy throughout much of the revolutionary period, but chaos in Paris often prevented more than the most basic of direction, and the field commanders assumed much of the control over planning and operations. See Brown, *War, Revolution, and the Bureaucratic State*, 98–123.

had this union of positive factors, and it contributed to French success during the period.[104]

An army thus constituted required a centrally controlled and supplied logistical system, as Guibert had noted. The revolutionary governments never developed the centralized logistical system, in no small part because of the political chaos that often gripped Paris during the period. Armies became cut off from the center, especially as they ranged farther from France's traditional borders after 1795. They achieved a reputation as ravaging hordes, seizing whatever they chose and shipping it back to Paris or consuming it themselves.[105] Generals such as André Masséna developed reputations as particularly skilled looters, enriching themselves greatly to the detriment of the territories they occupied.[106] Napoleon famously chastised the state of the Army of Italy upon his arrival in 1796, finding it lacking in even the most basic supplies.[107]

As a result, the major innovation in logistics occurred during the Napoleonic period. After his seizure of power in 1799, Napoleon devoted much of his energy and time to solving the continuing issues. He created a supply bureau, the Intendance, in stages between 1800 and 1805. He staffed it with functionaries and junior officers skilled in requisitions and bookkeeping. Its goal was to oversee the logistics of the army, ideally with all supply and equipment flowing efficiently and in a disciplined way from the central government.[108] The chief overhaul he put into place was to nationalize the supply system, removing it from the hands of private contractors, at least in theory. Notoriously abusive and corrupt, contracting companies had spent generations skimming from government budgets and providing substandard service and equipment, profiteering from all conflicts the French army fought. He largely accomplished this goal, although contractors played a significant role in the functioning of the Intendance nonetheless.[109] In practice, the Intendance functioned more as an oversight body than a true supply bureau. The French army still requisitioned much of its supply from enemy territory. Instead of wasteful forage by individual soldiers, Intendance officers conducted orderly requisitions with at

---

104 Elting, *Swords Around a Throne*, 5–67; Rothenberg, *Art of Warfare in the Age of Napoleon*, 124–147; Telp, *Evolution of Operational Art*, 35–56.
105 Ibid.
106 James Marshall-Cornwall, "'Dear Child of Victory' – Masséna," in David G. Chandler, ed., *Napoleon's Marshals* (London, 2000), 270–295.
107 Despite melodramatic letters from soldiers and grandiose pronouncements from Napoleon, the Army of Italy retained adequate supply and wanted only for organization and regularization of its logistical systems, to which Louis-Alexandre Berthier quickly attended. See Boycott-Brown, *Road to Rivoli*, 123–161.
108 Elting, *Swords Around a Throne*, 555–563.
109 Ibid.

least some documentation. Corruption was perhaps inevitable, and much of the material that passed through the Intendance disappeared into the pockets of its officials. However, the system functioned far better than the preceding systems, as it freed soldiers from the threat of starvation and largely accomplished its work of feeding and supplying the Grande Armée in its great campaigns.[110]

With this system, Napoleon defeated the combined armies of Europe. His Grande Armée was more mobile and articulated at the operational level because of its Guibertian foundation and refinement during the Revolutionary Wars, allowing him to fight battles of annihilation against his enemies. Guibert's writings and career established him as the foremost military theorist of the late Old Regime. Unlike most of his contemporaries, he considered far more than tactical systems designed for the parade ground in his publications. He set aside processionalism in favor of flexible and pragmatic tactics and organization. Guibert provided the genesis of the division system, projecting his reforms to the operational level of war. Most importantly, he included these elements in the creation of a systematic doctrine that he desired to be implemented in France. That doctrine provided the foundation for a flexible, adaptable army. In his time on the *Conseil de la Guerre*, Guibert oversaw much of the implementation of that doctrine, particularly in the areas of organization and tactics, via the Regulations of 1788.

The Revolutionary Wars of 1792–1799 were a transitional period for both Guibert's doctrine and the French army. The *Réglement* of 1791 codified the provisional measures of 1788 for the new government, solidifying much of Guibert's ideology within the theoretical dictates of the army. The outbreak of war in 1792 forced a disunified and fractious France into the crucible of what would become more than two decades of near-constant warfare. Practice proved much different from theory, and the period of the Revolutionary Wars was one of upheaval and the search for true order. Much of the theoretical system was tested against practicality, and many of Guibert's ideas were borne out in this process. The armies of the Revolution sallied forth from France and fought nearly every power in Europe from 1792 to 1802. In that period, particularly the early years, Guibertian doctrine via the *Réglement* would be tested and refined in battle. Much of the success of these armies can be attributed to this doctrine. However, its implementation was not complete, as several key elements were lacking, particularly in the areas of command, organization, and logistics.

Only after 1799 did the system receive its culmination with the rise of Napoleon. Although he was loath to admit his debt to theory, much of Napoleon's

---

110   Ibid., 554–571.

success rested on Guibert's doctrine and reforms. Napoleon supplied the *homme de génie* to use Guibert's system to its fullest extent. Napoleon's art of war provided a near-perfect match with the science of Guibert's doctrine. In each of the areas examined, the transition from Guibert's system through the Revolution to Napoleon illustrates the efficacy of his system. In some, particularly tactics and organization, Guibert's doctrine furnished the theory that was realized during the revolutionary period. In others, such as operations and logistics, Napoleon's genius and sense of order added the final piece. In all, Guibertian ideas formed the basis or greatly informed the Grande Armée that scourged Europe during the years of its ascent.

Bibliography

Abel, Jonathan. "Jacques-Antoine-Hippolyte, comte de Guibert." *Oxford Bibliographies Online*, 2014 <http://www.oxfordbibliographies.com/view/document/obo-9780199791279/obo-9780199791279-0037.xml>.

Anderson, M.S. *War and Society in Europe of the Old Regime, 1617–1789*. New York, 1988.

Bachaumont, Louis Petit de. *Mémoires secrets pour servir à l'histoire de la République des Lettres en France*, 36 vols. London, 1788.

Bardin, Etienne-Alexandre. *Notice historique sur Guibert*. Paris, 1836.

Bertaud, Jean-Paul. *The Army of the French Revolution: From Citizen-Soldiers to Instrument of Power*, trans. by R.R. Palmer. Princeton, NJ, 1988.

Best, Geoffrey. *War and Society in Revolutionary Europe, 1770–1870*. New York, 1982.

Bien, David D. "The Army in the French Enlightenment: Reform, Reaction, and Revolution." *Past & Present* 85 (1979), 68–98.

Bien, David D. "Military Education in Eighteenth-Century France; Technical and Non-Technical Determinants." In Monte D. Wright and Lawrence J. Paszek, eds, *Science, Technology, and Warfare: Proceedings of the Third Military History Symposium, US Air Force Academy*, 8–9 May 1969 (1971), 51–59.

Bien, David D. and Nina Godneff. "Les offices, les corps et le credit d'état: l'utilisation des privilèges sous l'Ancien Régime." *Annales. Histoire, Sciences Sociales* 43e (1988), 397–404.

Bien, David D. and J. Rovet. "La réaction aristocratique avant 1789: l'exemple de l'armée." *Annales. Histoire, Sciences Sociales* 29e, 3 (1974), 505–534.

Bien, David D. and J. Rovet. "La réaction aristocratique avant 1798: L'exemple de l'armée." *Annales. Histoire, Sciences Sociales* 29e, 2 (1974), 23–48.

Bien, David D., et al. *Caste, Class, and Profession in Old Regime France: The French Army and the Ségur Reform of 1781*. St Andrews, UK, 2010.

Blanning, T.C.W. *The French Revolutionary Wars, 1787–1802*. New York, 1996.

Blaufarb, Rafe. *The French Army, 1750–1820: Careers, Talent, Merit.* New York, 2002.

Blaufarb, Rafe. "Noble Privilege and Absolutist State Building: French Military Administration After the Seven Years War." *French Historical Studies* 24 (2001), 223–246.

Bourcet, Pierre-Joseph. *Mémoires historiques sur la guerre que les français ont soutenue en Allemagne depuis 1757 jusqu'en 1762.* Paris, 1792.

Bourcet, Pierre-Joseph. *Mémoires militaires sur les frontières de la France, du Piémont, et la Savoie, depuis l'embouchure du Var jusqu'au Lac de Genève.* Paris: Chez Levrault, 1802.

Bourcet, Pierre-Joseph. *Principes de la guerre de montagnes.* Paris, 1888.

Brown, Howard. *War, Revolution, and the Bureaucratic State: Politics and Army Administration in France, 1791–1799.* New York, 1995.

Camon, Hubert. *Napoleon's System of War*, trans. by George Nafziger. West Chester, OH, 2001.

Camon, Hubert. *Quand et comment Napoléon a conçu son système de bataille.* Paris, 1935.

Camon, Hubert. *Quand et comment Napoléon a conçu son système de manœuvre.* Paris, 1931.

Childs, John. *Armies and Warfare in Europe, 1648–1789.* New York, 1982.

Choiseul, Etienne-François, duc de. *Mémoires.* Paris, 1982.

Colin, Jean. *L'éducation militaire de Napoléon.* Paris, 1901.

Colin, Jean. *L'infanterie au XVIIIe siècle : la tactique.* Paris, 1907.

Corvisier, André. *Armies and Societies in Europe, 1494–1789*, trans. by Abigail T. Siddall. Bloomington, IN, 1979.

Duffy, Christopher. *The Military Experience in the Age of Reason.* New York, 1988.

Dumouriez, Charles-François. *The Life of General Dumouriez*, 3 vols. London, 1796.

Elting, John. *Swords Around a Throne: Napoleon's Grande Armée.* New York, 1988.

Esdaile, Charles J. *Napoleon's Wars: An International History, 1803–1815.* New York, 2008.

Folard, Jean Charles, chevalier. *Nouvelles découvertes sur la guerre, dans une dissertation sur Polybe, où l'on donne une idée plus étendue du commentaire entrepris sur cet auteur, et deux dissertations importantes détaches du corps de l'ouvrage.* Paris, 1726.

Forestié, Emerand. *Biographie du Cte. de Guibert.* Montaubon, 1855.

Gates, David. *The Napoleonic Wars, 1803–1815.* New York, 1997.

Griffith, Paddy. *The Art of War of Revolutionary France 1789–1802.* Mechanicsburg, PA, 1998.

Groffier, Ethel. *Le stratège des lumières: le comte de Guibert (1743–1790).* Paris, 2005.

Guibert, Jacques-Antoine-Hippolyte, comte de. *Défense du système de guerre moderne, ou refutation complette du système de M. de M... D... Oeuvres militaires de Guibert,* vols 3–4. Paris, 1803.

Guibert, Jacques-Antoine-Hippolyte, comte de. *Eloge de maréchal de Catinat*. Edimbourg, 1775.

Guibert, Jacques-Antoine-Hippolyte, comte de. *Eloge du roi de Prusse*. London, 1787.

Guibert, Jacques-Antoine-Hippolyte, comte de. *Eloge historique de Michel de l'Hôpital, Chancelier de France*. 1777.

Guibert, Jacques-Antoine-Hippolyte, comte de. *Essai général de tactique*. Liège, 1773.

Guibert, Jacques-Antoine-Hippolyte, comte de. *Journal d'un voyage en Allemagne*. Paris, 1803.

Guibert ou le soldat philosophe, ed. by Jean-Paul Charnay. Paris, 1981.

Heuser, Beatrice. *The Evolution of Strategy: Thinking War from Antiquity to the Present*. New York, 2010.

Heuser, Beatrice. "Guibert: Prophet of Total War?" In Roger Chicking and Stig Forster, eds, *War in an Age of Revolution, 1775–1815*. New York, 2010.

Huntington, Samuel P. *The Soldier and the State: The Theory of Politics and Civil–Military Relations*. Cambridge, MA, 1957.

Lacroix, Irenée Amelot de. *Rules and Regulations for the Field Exercise and Maneuvers of the French Infantry issued August 1, 1791: and the Maneuvers added which have been since Adopted by the Emperor Napoleon: also, the Maneuvers of the Field Artillery with the Infantry*. Boston, 1810.

Latreille, Albert. *L'oeuvre militaire de la révolution. L'armée et la nation à la fin de l'ancien régime : les derniers ministres de la guerre de la monarchie*. Paris, 1914.

Lauerma, Matti. *Jacques-Antoine-Hippolyte de Guibert (1743–1790)*. Helsinki, 1989.

Lynn, John. *The Bayonets of the Republic: Motivation and Tactics in the Army of Revolutionary France, 1791–1794*. Urbana, IL, 1984.

Mas, Raymond. "L'éssai général de tactique (1770) de Guibert ou le rationalism des Lumières face à la guerre." In Paul Viallaneix and Jean Ehrard, eds, *La Bataille, l'armée, la gloire, 1745–1871: actes du colloque international de Clermont-Ferrand* I (1985), 119–134.

Muir, Rory. *Tactics and the Experience of Battle in the Age of Napoleon*. New Haven, CT, 1978.

Ney, Michel, duc d'Elchingen, prince de la Moskova. *Memoirs of Marshal Ney*, 2 vols. London, 1833.

Nosworthy, Brent. *The Anatomy of Victory: Battle Tactics 1689–1763*. New York, 1990.

Nosworthy, Brent. *With Musket, Cannon, and Sword*. New York, 1996.

Olsen, John Andreas and Martin van Creveld, eds, *The Evolution of Operational Art: From Napoleon to the Present*. New York, 2011.

Osman, Julia. "Ancient Warriors on Modern Soil: French Military Reform and American Military Images in Eighteenth-Century France." *French History* 22 (2008): 223–246.

Osman, Julia. "Patriotism as Power: The Old Regime Foundation for Napoleon's Army." *International Congress of Military History Conference Proceedings* 2009 (2010).

Palmer, R.R. "Frederick the Great, Guibert, Bülow: From Dynastic to National War." In Peter Paret, ed., *Makers of Modern Strategy: From Machiavelli to the Nuclear Age*, 91–119. Princeton, NJ, 1986.

Phipps, Ramsay Weston. *The Armies of the First French Republic and the Rise of the Marshals of Napoleon I*, 5 vols. London, 1926–1939.

Poirier, Lucien. *Les voix de la stratégie*. Paris, 1985.

Quimby, Robert. *The Background of Napoleonic Warfare: The Theory of Military Tactics in Eighteenth-Century France*. New York, 1957.

Ross, Steven T. *From Flintlock to Rifle: Infantry Tactics, 1740–1866*. London, 1979.

Rothenberg, Gunther F. *The Art of Warfare in the Age of Napoleon*. Bloomington, IN, 1978.

Scott, Samuel F. *From Yorktown to Valmy: The Transformation of the French Army in the Age of Revolution*. Niwot, CO, 1998.

Scott, Samuel F. *The Response of the Royal Army to the French Revolution: The Role and Development of the Line Army, 1787–1793*. Oxford, 1978.

Starkey, Armstrong. *War in the Age of Enlightenment, 1700–1789*. Westport, CT, 2003.

Telp, Claus. *The Evolution of Operational Art, 1740–1813: From Frederick the Great to Napoleon*. New York, 2005.

Toulongeon, François-Emmanuel. "Notice historique de Jacques-Antoine-Hipolite Guibert, écrit en 1790." In *Journal d'un voyage en Allemagne*, 1–85. Paris, 1803.

Van Creveld, Martin. *The Transformation of War*. New York, 1991.

Vivent, Jacques. "Un précurseur de la tactique moderne: le comte de Guibert." *Revue historique de l'armée; revue trimestrielle de l'état-major de l'armée, service historique.*

Wasson, James N. *Innovator or Imitator: Napoleon's Operational Concepts and the Legacies of Bourcet and Guibert*. Fort Leavenworth, KS, 1998.

Wilkinson, Spenser. *The French Army Before Napoleon: Lectures Delivered Before the University of Oxford in Michaelmas Term, 1914*. Oxford, 1915.

Wilkinson, Spenser. *The Rise of General Bonaparte*. Oxford, 1930.

CHAPTER 2

The French Way of War

Jordan R. Hayworth

According to historian Hew Strachan, "the techniques of Napoleonic warfare were all present before Bonaparte's first successful campaign in 1796."[1] Yet if Napoleon inherited a new way of war, it was not bequeathed to him in a perfect form by the *ancien régime*. Instead, a new French operational art emerged from the crucible of the French Revolutionary Wars. The emergence of the citizen soldier, organizational improvements, and superior numbers of troops provided the French with the confidence and ability to test more rigorous military practices devised by late *ancien régime* military reformers. In addition, French designs to transform the map of Western Europe required a new level of decisiveness in warfare.[2] Although the evolution of new operational approaches did not follow a linear model or necessarily revolutionize European warfare, the system that Napoleon inherited constituted an undeniably powerful force – one that he further improved as a general and used to conquer much of Europe after becoming the ruler of France.

Claus Telp argues that between 1740 and 1815 "a major change in the complexity of warfare occurred." Most important, Telp describes an evolution from a two-level model of warfare to a three-level model. While early modern warfare consisted of the strategic and tactical levels, the existence of an intermediate or operational level constitutes one key characteristic of modern warfare.[3] Modern military theorists possess clear definitions for strategy, operations, and tactics. Yet these terms remained in their infancy during the eighteenth and nineteenth centuries. For example, the French military theorist Guibert never utilized the term strategy, despite clearly discussing the use of war to achieve political objectives. Guibert divided war into "elementary tactics" and "grand tactics," the latter of which constituted modern operations and strategy.[4] Henry E.H. Lloyd coined the term "operation's line", which subsequent

---

1 Hew Strachan, *European Armies and the Conduct of War* (New York, 2004), 42.
2 Paul Schroeder, *The Transformation of European Politics* (New York, 1994), 115–116.
3 Telp, *Evolution of Operational Art*, 1–2.
4 Guibert did use the term *la stratégique*, yet historians remain divided on whether this conformed to modern strategy. See Palmer, "Frederick the Great, Guibert, Bülow: From Dynastic to National War," 107; Beatrice Heuser, *The Evolution of Strategy: Thinking War from Antiquity to the Present* (New York, 2010), 5.

theorists and practitioners such as Archduke Charles of Austria adopted as "lines of operation".⁵ Yet the use of the term operational warfare remains a 20th-century invention. Even after the Napoleonic Wars, theorists such as Antoine-Henri Jomini and Carl von Clausewitz continued to refer to the tactical and strategic levels of war without clearly defining an operational level. Nevertheless, both theorists discussed new developments in warfare resulting from changes in the late 18th century, especially an increased focus on understanding the overall conduct of military campaigns.⁶ The desire to thoroughly study and understand the level of war between the deployment of armies for strategic purposes and the commencement of battle required modern theorists to fully develop the terminology now understood as the operational level.⁷

Evolutionary and Revolutionary Changes in War

In terms of army organization, the French Revolution built on a system that emerged during the *ancien régime*. Progressive reforms initiated during and after the Seven Years War proved crucial in the evolution of the operational level of war. In part, these reforms aimed to overcome the limitations of Frederician operations by breaking the standard unitary army into several distinct parts or divisions. In the early 18th century, the term "division" meant any unit of the field army not directly commanded by the commander in chief. It could also function as a tactical unit similar to a modern platoon. The use of the term to describe a combined-arms unit commanded by a general of division appeared after mid-century.⁸ Between 1759 and 1761, the French marshal Victor-François de Broglie experimented with ad hoc divisions during marches. He found that these units allowed for greater speed and requisitioning on campaign than was possible with traditional unitary armies. While favoring dispersion on separate roads during the march, Broglie reunited the divisions when they reached the area of battle.⁹

---

5   Lee Eysturlid, *The Formative Influences, Theories, and Campaigns of the Archduke Carl of Austria* (Westport, CT, 2000), 53.

6   Geoffrey Wawro, *Warfare and Society in Europe, 1792–1914* (New York, 2000), 27–35.

7   For a discussion of these terms focused especially on the twentieth-century German and American armies, see Robert M. Citino, *Blitzkrieg to Desert Storm: The Evolution of Operational Warfare* (Lawrence, KS, 2004), 7–8.

8   Steven T. Ross, "The Development of the Combat Division in Eighteenth-Century French Armies," *French Historical Studies* 4, 1 (1965): 85; Quimby, *Background of Napoleonic Warfare*, 20, 157.

9   Colin, *L'éducation militaire de Napoléon*, 48–59.

At a most basic level, the organization and use of divisions and higher-level formations such as *corps d'armée* to achieve strategic objectives and promote tactical success on the battlefield constituted the operational art of war in this period. Not only did frustration with the Frederician system's failure to provide decisiveness lead to the emergence of the divisional system, but these reforms also corresponded with important changes in the European landscape. In particular, increased agricultural productivity led to the development of food surpluses while improvements in roads allowed for the enhanced mobility of larger armies.[10]

While Broglie tested ad hoc divisions, Guibert and Pierre-Joseph de Bourcet provided the theoretical underpinnings of an emerging divisional system, focusing especially on their operational use in campaigns. Guibert's 1772 *Essai générale de tactique* launched a comprehensive critique against *ancien régime* military orthodoxy. To increase marching speed for example, Guibert advised living off the land rather than maintaining burdensome lines of operation. Rather than committing forces to sieges and the pursuit of geographic objectives, he advocated a war of movement in order to envelop and destroy the enemy army.[11] In his 1775 essay *Principes de la guerre de montagnes*, Bourcet provided a model for the use of divisions as distinct units dispersing for the march and reuniting to deliver decisive battles. In addition, Bourcet emphasized the study of topography and cartography to achieve greater speed and maneuverability.[12]

In the 1770s and 1780s, the French formed administrative or territorial districts called divisions, which provided the framework for the creation of divisional army units during the French Revolutionary Wars. Although the 1788 reforms did not introduce permanent divisions that integrated infantry, light infantry, cavalry, and artillery, they created twenty-one divisional units that varied greatly in terms of composition.[13] Nevertheless, the nascent divisional system constituted an important example of the evolutionary nature of French military change during the late 18th century. Military innovations did

---

10 Strachan, *European Armies and the Conduct of War*, 40–41.
11 Guibert, *Essai générale de tactique*. See Beatrice Heuser, "Guibert: Prophet of Total War?," in Roger Chickering and Stig Förster, eds, *War in an Age of Revolution, 1775–1815* (New York, 2010), 49–68; Jonathan Abel, "Jacques-Antoine-Hippolyte, comte de Guibert: Father of the *Grande Armée*" (PhD diss., University of North Texas, 2014).
12 Pierre-Joseph de Bourcet, *Principes de la guerre de montagnes* (Paris, 1888); Armstrong Starkey, *War in the Age of Enlightenment, 1700–1789* (Westport, CT, 2003), 42–45.
13 Some of the divisions contained both infantry and cavalry units. Yet most contained either infantry or cavalry only. See Albert Latreille, *L'oeuvre militaire de la révolution: l'armée et la nation à la fin de l'ancien régime* (Paris, 1914), 263; Ross, "Development of the Combat Division," 85–86.

not emerge from a vacuum within the French Revolution; rather, the revolutionaries built on the reform movement initiated after the Seven Years War.[14]

Like the divisional system, the cult of the citizen soldier first appeared during the late *ancien régime* rather than the French Revolution.[15] Marshal Maurice de Saxe argued that the soldier could possess honor similar to his officer, a radical statement coming from a grandee of the mid-18th-century officer corps.[16] While the French army led the way in promoting a more humanitarian view of soldiering, other European armies tested these new ideas as well. For example, despite Russian officers' reputation for extreme brutality, official regulations instructed them to gain the trust and confidence of their men.[17] The archetypical patriot soldier could be trusted to fight for love of country and monarch. In addition, the Greco-Roman concept of the self-sacrificing citizen soldier received much discussion in late Enlightenment thought. Jean-Jacques Rousseau promulgated a veritable cult of the citizen soldier by depicting him as a virtuous superhuman capable of achieving great feats of heroism because of an indomitable willpower.[18]

Guibert expressed these positive views of the citizen soldier in his *Essai*, which combined technical military reform with the new military romanticism. In a seemingly prophetic passage, Guibert stated: "Only suppose the appearance in Europe of a people who should join to austere virtues and a citizen army a fixed plan of aggression … Such a people would subdue its neighbors and overthrow our feeble constitutions like the northern gale bends the reeds."[19] For curious European onlookers, the defeat of British regulars by American colonists during the War of American Independence appeared to provide concrete evidence that citizen soldiers possessed inherent superiority over regular

---

14 For examples of the evolutionary argument, see Jeremy Black, *European Warfare, 1660–1815* (New Haven, CT, 1994), 172; Ute Planert, "Innovation or Evolution? The French Wars in Military History," in Chickering and Förster, *War in an Age of Revolution*, 69–84.

15 This argument has been made most strongly in Julia Osman, *Citizen Soldiers and the Key to the Bastille* (New York, 2015); see also Bien, "Army in the French Enlightenment."

16 Maurice de Saxe, *Reveries, or, Memoirs Concerning the Art of War* (Edinburgh, 1759), 271–300; Geoffrey Best, *War and Society in Revolutionary Europe, 1770–1870* (New York, 1982), 53.

17 Christopher Duffy, *Russia's Military Way to the West: Origins and Nature of Russian Military Power, 1700–1800* (London, 1981), 132; Rothenberg, *Art of Warfare in the Age of Napoleon*, 196–197.

18 John Lynn, *Battle: A History of Combat and Culture* (New York, 2003), 185.

19 Quoted in Best, *Warfare and Society in Revolutionary Europe*, 58. Guibert recanted his support for the citizen soldier in his subsequent *Défense du système de guerre moderne*, which called for a professional army. Nonetheless, Guibert's support for a citizen army in the *Essai* probably made a greater public impact than his subsequent conservative turn. Many leaders of the Revolution viewed Guibert as too conservative. See Heuser, "Guibert," 62–63.

soldiers. In 1780, Joseph Servan's *Le soldat-citoyen* called for army reform involving a system of universal conscription, blurring the lines between soldier and citizen.[20]

French confidence in the absolute superiority of the citizen soldier dealt with an imaginary object rather than a material reality. Regardless, it proved significant for the evolution of operational warfare because it gave the French supreme confidence in the ability of their troops. Convinced of their superiority, the French demanded a more grueling pace of operations that required greater speed, maneuverability, and boldness. After 1789, the revolutionaries devoted much attention to the concept of the citizen soldier. Although sharply divided over issues of war and peace, leaders of the Revolution employed the rhetoric of the citizen soldier. Camille Desmoulins urged the royal army to support the New Regime: "You are no longer satellites of the despot, the jailors of your brothers. You are our friends, our fellows, citizens, and soldiers of the *patrie*."[21] Jacques-Pierre Brissot used the citizen soldier as a rhetorical device while promoting war in 1791 and 1792: "What soldiers of despotism can for any length of time withstand the soldiers of liberty!" Brissot offered the most cogent explanation for the citizen soldier's superiority relative to the *ancien régime* soldier: "The soldiers of tyrants are after pay; they have little fidelity, and desert on the first occasion. The soldier of liberty fears neither fatigue, danger, nor hunger – he runs, he flies at the cry of liberty, while despotism is scarcely taking a few tottering steps."[22] After the French declaration of war in April 1792, Revolutionary rhetoric not only venerated the virtues of the citizen soldier, but denigrated their opponents as "slave soldiers."

While promotion of the citizen soldier provided the French with the spirited confidence to support the technical innovations of the *ancien régime* reformers, the revolutionaries faced practical military concerns that demanded redress. Most significant, the French army suffered from declining manpower. In 1789, the royal line army consisted of approximately 180,000 troops.[23] The creation of the National Guard in July 1789 led to the gradual reduction in size of the royal army, as the better pay and more lax discipline of the National

---

20   Joseph Servan, *Le soldat-citoyen, ou vues patriotiques sur la manière la plus avantageuse de pourvoir à la défense du royaume* (Neufchatel, 1780). For a discussion of the reaction against a more egalitarian army, see Bien, "Army in the French Enlightenment," 96–98.
21   Quoted in Lynn, *Battle*, 187.
22   Jacques-Pierre Brissot, *Discours prononcé par M. Brissot à l'assemblée des Amis de la Constitution le 10 juillet, 1791, ou Tableau frappant de la situation actuelle des puissances de l'Europe* (Paris, 1791).
23   Samuel F. Scott, *The Response of the Royal Army to the French Revolution* (New York, 1978), 5; Rothenberg, *Art of Warfare in the Age of Napoleon*, 95.

Guard enticed line troops to desert. Moreover, the abolition of aristocratic privileges and Louis XVI's flight to Varennes led to the emigration of approximately 6,000 noble officers by the end of 1791.[24] Political disturbances in the army compelled the National Constituent Assembly to call for 100,000 volunteers in January 1791, yet the public response proved underwhelming: instead of the desired 162 volunteer battalions, they mustered only 60.[25] A second call for volunteers in 1792 and the formation of 20,000 *fédérés* somewhat alleviated the pressure on the French, but these troops continued to serve only as short-term volunteers. After the victories at Valmy and Jemappes in 1792, many of the volunteers simply went home, leaving a hardened core of troops from the royal army alongside the more committed volunteers.[26]

Although well suited for revolutionary ideology, the volunteer concept proved insufficient for the French war effort. In February 1793, France's third government of the Revolution, the National Convention, declared the nation to be in a permanent state of requisition and called for 300,000 troops based on *département* quotas. The *levée des 300,000* raised only 180,000 troops and incited a civil war in the Vendée, a brutal quagmire that sucked troops away from the major fronts. Finally, the *levée en masse* of 23 August 1793 produced an army based on long-term conscripts. The revolutionaries made military service in defense of *la patrie* an obligation of citizenship. By 1794, mobilization produced an army of approximately 750,000 troops, whom the government expected to serve until "every enemy has been driven from the territory of the Republic."[27] The *levée en masse* provided the French with a mass army capable of employing the new operational approach imagined by the *ancien régime* reformers and demanded by the revolutionary government.

The contradiction between the Revolution's egalitarian ethos and the structures of the military hierarchy demanded reconciliation. After the emigration of many noble officers, respect for authority declined in the royal army. Moreover, the National Guard and volunteer battalions initially authorized the election of officers, a system that did not promote obedience among the troops.[28] In its orthodox form, French veneration of the citizen soldier represented the

---

24 Timothy Tackett. *When the King Took Flight* (Cambridge, MA, 2003).
25 Samuel F. Scott, *From Yorktown to Valmy: The Transformation of the French Army in an Age of Revolution* (Niwot, CO, 1998), 159–160; Jean-Paul Bertaud, *The Army of the French Revolution: From Citizen-Soldiers to Instrument of Power*, trans. by R.R. Palmer (Princeton, NJ, 1988), 49–58.
26 Camille Rousset, *Les volontaires, 1791–1794* (Paris, 1870), 115.
27 *Archives parlementaires de 1787 à 1860: recueil complet des débats législatifs et politiques des chambres francaises* (Paris, 1907), 72:674.
28 Bertaud, *Army of the French Revolution*, 81–86; Alan Forrest, *Soldiers of the French Revolution* (Durham, NC, 1990), 48–50.

lack of discipline, training, and obedience as military virtues because they engendered a more spirited type of warrior, one who could easily defeat what the revolutionaries viewed as the suffering, mechanistic automatons of the *ancien régime*. After the commencement of war, the French government realized the truism of arguments made by military professionals such as Edmond Louis Alexis Dubois-Crancé: armies cannot function without discipline and training.[29] Consequently, the French returned to the discipline of the *ancien régime* to rehabilitate their war effort.

In fact, many politicians took an extreme turn in favor of draconian discipline. Brissot dramatically shifted his tone as early as June 1792: "What is the first means by which liberty can be made to triumph over the coalition of *slaves* armed against it? It is discipline. What is the second means? It is discipline. What is the third? It is discipline."[30] In 1793, Lazare Carnot instituted harsh punishments for nearly any infraction of the military code, especially the crimes of insubordination and pillage.[31] While promoters of the citizen soldier emphasized the spirit of the troops as essential, General Jean-Baptiste Jourdan referred to discipline rather than *élan* as "the force of armies."[32] By 1794, a fusion emerged within revolutionary rhetoric whereby the citizen soldier's purported superiority rested in his willful acceptance of discipline as a necessary requirement to achieve military success. The continuity of discipline being more purposeful and enlightened rather than arbitrarily brutal represents another aspect of evolutionary rather than revolutionary military change in this period.[33]

Armed with the a new confidence in their troops, superior numbers, and an improved disciplinary system, the armies of Revolutionary France proved highly effective in the new art of war devised by the late *ancien régime* reformers. The revolutionaries continued important reforms and instituted new military regulations. Most important, the *Règlement concernant l'exercice et les manoeuvres de l'infanterie du 1er août 1791* provided the basis of a formal tactical

---

29 Théodore Jung, *Dubois-Crancé (Edmond-Alexis-Louis): mousqeutaire, constituent, conventionnel, général de division, minister de la guerre* (Paris, 1884), 368–369.

30 Brissot, *Le Patriote françois: journal libre, impartial et national, par un société de citoyens, et dirigé par J.P. Brissot de Warville* (Paris, 1792), no. 1028.

31 John Lynn, *The Bayonets of the Republic: Motivation and Tactics in the Army of Revolutionary France, 1791–1794* (Boulder, CO, 1996), 114–115.

32 See Jourdan's memoir in SHAT, M¹ 608, 2.

33 Forrest, *Soldiers of the French Revolution*, 40–41; Lynn, *Bayonets of the Republic*, 104–107; Ian Germani, "Terror in the Army: Representatives on Mission and Military Discipline in the Armies of the French Revolution," *Journal of Military History* 75, 3 (2011), 733–768.

system to utilize during drill instructions.³⁴ While the 1791 regulations concentrated primarily on formal battlefield maneuvers and tactics, the *Règlement provisoire sur le service de l'infanterie au campagne du 5 avril 1792* explicitly called for a system of offensive attack followed by the rapid pursuit of the enemy.³⁵ In theory, this became the basis of the new operational art adopted by the armies of Revolutionary France.

In order to instill proper military skills among the volunteers and conscripts of 1792 and 1793, the French utilized the traditional institution of the training camp. Ideally, the raw troops would receive several months of training before being integrated into the field army. After 1793, the policy of amalgamation contributed to a better unified and professional army. According to this policy, the generals and "representatives on mission" of the National Convention would combine volunteer and conscript battalions with battalions of the line army to form demi-brigades.³⁶ In theory, the professionalism of the regulars would improve the abilities of the volunteers and conscripts while the *élan* and patriotism of the latter would spread to the former.³⁷

After the *amalgame*, the generals of Revolutionary France possessed the essential tools with which to forge a new operational art. Historians continue to dispute the evolutionary or revolutionary nature of the French system. Adopting either argument as a holistic paradigm inevitably overlooks important aspects of change and continuity depending on one's perspective and method of analysis.³⁸ The use of dichotomies provide a convenient but rather imperfect

---

34   *Règlement concernant l'exercice et les manoeuvres de l'infanterie du 1er août 1791* (Paris, 1791); Quimby, *Background of Napoleonic Warfare*, 107.

35   See Michael Bonura, "The '*Règlement provisoire sur le service de l'infanterie en campagne de 1792*': The Document That Provided the Armies of the French Revolution with the Intellectual Framework That Allowed It to Dominate Europe for Two Decades," in John Severn and Frederick C. Schneid, eds, *The Consortium on the Revolutionary Era: Selected Papers, 2008* (High Point, NC, 2009), 87, and *Under the Shadow of Napoleon: French Influence on the American Way of War from the War of 1812 to the Outbreak of WWII* (New York, 2012), 27–28.

36   "Representatives on mission" were deputies to the National Convention appointed to enforce government policy in either the provinces or the armies. While their duties focused on law enforcement and overseeing administrative matters, they often intervened in strategic and operational decisions. Demi-brigades emerged in August 1793 as a replacement for the *ancien régime* regimental system. The revolutionary government abolished the regiments because they associated them with the royal army. Napoleon restored the regimental system in 1803.

37   Jean Colin, *La tactique et la discipline dans les armées de la Révolution* (Paris, 1902); Forrest, *Soldiers of the French Revolution*, 50–54.

38   I have argued for an evolutionary model when examining French performance in battle. Yet this does not exclude the acceptance of revolutionary change in other areas, especially society, politics, and foreign policy. See Jordan R. Hayworth, "Evolution or

means of assessing the past. Typically, understanding historical reality requires a more willing admission of nuance.³⁹ In general, the French system represented the combination of an *ancien régime* intellectual framework with social and political structures transformed by the Revolution. More important, the forging of a new operational art required its implementation in practice after 1792. Understanding the evolution of the operational art in this period demands not only an analysis of the ideas and structures that brought it into being, but also an investigation of its emergence during the French Revolutionary Wars.

The new operational art of war that emerged in France after 1792 followed a trend developed by Frederick the Great: an increasing emphasis on the destruction of the enemy's army in battle. In the 18th century, battles typically happened for one of two reasons. First, both sides might agree to fight a pitched or set battle, either because both sides believed they could win or because one side viewed battle as the only means of overcoming inferior odds at the strategic level. Second, a battle could result after a chance encounter with enemy forces, a rare but not unknown occurrence. A third possibility existed in theory but not in practice: that of one side forcing the other to fight a battle against the other's will. Assuming that both sides act rationally, the third possibility occurs only in the event that one side possesses a clear superiority over the other, most often in speed, mobility, or overwhelming numbers.⁴⁰ At a macro-level, the French Revolutionary Wars constitute a transition period in which the French began to develop the superiority that allowed them to achieve the third possibility. However, this became possible only under Napoleon and remained a rare occurrence even at the French army's peak performance.

Regardless, an increased focus on battle resulted from these operational changes. Gunther Rothenberg calculates that 713 battles occurred in Europe between 1790 and 1820, while the Europeans fought a total of 2,659 battles between 1480 and 1790.⁴¹ Curiously, war did not necessarily become more brutal as a result of the increasing number of battles. Although revolutionary rhetoric called for the enemy's complete destruction in battles of annihilation, the French Revolutionary Wars revealed real limitations on the pursuit of absolute war in practice, especially in the essentially conventional campaigns fought

---

Revolution on the Battlefield? The Army of the Sambre and Meuse in 1794," *War in History* 21, 2 (2014), 170–192.

39 Jeremy Black discusses these theoretical problems in *Rethinking Military History* (New York, 2004).

40 Carl von Clausewitz, *On War*, ed. and trans. by Michael Howard and Peter Paret (Princeton, NJ, 1976), 225–227; Telp, *Evolution of Operational Art*, 13.

41 Rothenberg, *Art of Warfare in the Age of Napoleon*, 61.

between France and the other European powers.⁴² Only in cases of partisan warfare did the French engage in a form of conflict approaching "total war," yet even in these cases significant debate persists regarding the full extent of the brutality.⁴³

Although the French unquestionably pursued a new and more rigorous operational art of war, it remained imperfectly developed. While Napoleon attained consistent success against the forces of the *ancien régime* until the European powers reformed their armies on the French model, the other generals of Revolutionary France achieved a mixed record against armies that remained essentially *ancien régime* in organization and conduct. Thus, the changes adopted by the French did not necessarily gain an overwhelming dominance over the armies of the *ancien régime*. In the conventional campaigns against regular European armies, the French often lacked the discipline, organization, or logistical capacity to pursue the enemy after a battlefield victory. In contrast, the armies of their *ancien régime* opponents often did pursue the French, a situation that damaged the citizen army's sense of infallibility. While this chapter concentrates on the operational art of war, French victory in the War of the First Coalition cannot be explained by the military superiority of the citizen soldier but must be understood within a broader political, social, and diplomatic context, as well as within a framework that allows for contingency and human decision-making.

Conquest and Disaster: Charles-François Dumouriez

Although significant debate exists regarding his role in the French Revolution, the French foreign minister, Charles-François Dumouriez, functioned as the leading government figure at the beginning of war in April 1792. Dumouriez believed that an immediate French offensive into the Austrian Netherlands, which is now modern-day Belgium, would foster a people's uprising against Austrian rule and result in the creation of a Belgian republic.⁴⁴ Despite repeated warnings by Marshal Jean-Baptiste Donatien de Vimeur, comte de

---

42   Black, *European Warfare*, 168–172; Russell S. Weigley, *The Age of Battles: The Quest for Decisive Warfare from Breitenfeld to Waterloo* (Bloomington, IN, 1991), 280.

43   For the total war debate, see David Bell, *The First Total War: Napoleon's Europe and the Birth of Warfare as We Know It* (New York, 2007); Jean-Yves Guiomar, *L'invention de la guerre totale, XVIIIe–XXe siècle* (Paris, 2004); Michael Broers, "The Concept of 'Total War' in the Revolutionary–Napoleonic Period," *War in History* 15, 3 (2008), 247–268.

44   Patricia Chastain Howe, *Foreign Policy and the French Revolution: Charles-François Dumouriez, Pierre Lebrun, and the Belgian Plan, 1789–1793* (New York, 2008).

Rochambeau, concerning the Army of the North's unpreparedness, Dumouriez maintained that any delay would allow the Austrians and Prussians time to unite superior forces and disillusion the eager Belgian revolutionaries.[45] Moreover, the success promised by putting the theoretical concept of the citizen soldier into practice provided Dumouriez with sufficient confidence in the French army to dismiss the forewarnings of Rochambeau as the misinformed jeremiads of an old, worn-out soldier.[46]

Dumouriez viewed speed as essential in order to initiate an uprising in the Austrian Netherlands and to benefit from revolutionary enthusiasm. Prior to the declaration of war, the French ministry of war developed a number of strategic plans for the upcoming conflict. Given the prominence of French *émigrés* in the Rhineland, many leaders favored an immediate invasion of the Electorate of Trier and of the Palatinate, where Marshal Nicolas Luckner's Army of the Rhine would take the leading role. Commanding the Army of the Center, Gilbert du Motier, marquis de Lafayette, desired 50,000 reinforcements to facilitate a major offensive through Liège. Instead, Dumouriez remained committed to the liberation of Belgium and emphasized the operation against Brussels.[47] Although Rochambeau warned that his army lacked the strength to invade enemy territory, Dumouriez entrusted the Army of the North with the main offensive. While Lafayette advanced toward the Sambre River with only 12,000 men as a diversion, Luckner would remain on the defensive in Alsace. Dumouriez made the capture of Brussels Rochambeau's primary objective, yet Mons and Tournai stood as the immediate targets.

Whereas the French possessed approximately 94,700 combat-ready troops on the northern frontier in April 1792, the Austrians and Prussians commenced

---

45   A decree signed by King Louis XVI on 14 December 1791 created three French armies: the Army of the North, the Army of the Center, and the Army of the Rhine. At the beginning of the war, the Army of the North consisted of approximately 60,000 troops stationed between Dunkirk and Philippeville. General Gilbert du Motier, marquis de Lafayette, commanded the 25,000-man Army of the Center between Philippeville and the Lauter River. Marshal Nicolas Luckner defended Alsace with the 45,000-man Army of the Rhine. On 13 April 1792, the government appointed General Anne-Pierre de Montesquiou-Fézensac to command the 25,000-man Army of the Midi. See Claude Clerget, *Tableaux des armées françaises pendant les guerres de la révolution* (Paris, 1905), 5–13; Ramsay Weston Phipps, *The Armies of the First French Republic and the Rise of the Marshals of Napoleon I* (Oxford, 1931), 3:67–69.

46   See Charles-François Dumouriez, *La vie et les mémoires du général Dumouriez, avec des notes et des éclaircissemens historiques* (Paris, 1822), 2:230–232, but read along with Jean-Pierre Bois, *Dumouriez: héros et proscrit* (Paris, 2005), 205–209; see also Phipps, *Armies of the First French Republic*, 1:75–77.

47   Antoine-Henri Jomini, *Histoire critique et militaire des guerres de la Révolution* (Paris, 1819), 2:11–13.

negotiations at Potsdam for the details of their offensive. The need to organize an invasion force required several months. In the short term, the Austrians mustered only 30,000 men for the defense of the border between France and Belgium. Convinced of the strength of the 1756 Bourbon–Habsburg alliance, Joseph II of Austria had ordered the razing of the expensive barrier fortresses in the Austrian Netherlands in 1781. By 1792, the Austrians possessed first-class fortresses only at Namur and Luxembourg; as second-class fortresses, Mons and Tournai constituted the only practical obstacles on the road to Brussels. The weaknesses of the Austrian fortress system in this period make comparisons between the campaigns after 1792 and those of the earlier 18th century problematic. Although the Austrians soon reconstructed parts of older fortresses such as Ypres and Charleroi, they began the war from a position of inherent weakness based on the normal rules of 18th-century warfare. Moreover, the widespread confidence in peace that reigned in Brussels and Vienna meant that the Austrians did not prepare to sustain large-scale operations. Accordingly, they did not construct extensive magazines or depots but relied on supply lines that stretched to the Rhine.[48]

Despite the apparent strategic advantages and the promise of sparking revolutionary agitation in Belgium, Dumouriez's invasion revealed that the lack of training and discipline represented an existential threat to the French war effort. While political concerns compelled Dumouriez to utilize the elements of speed and decisiveness, the French army proved incapable of executing these operations effectively. Rochambeau formed the 54,000-man Army of the North into a field army of 34,000 with approximately 20,000 troops serving in the numerous garrisons stationed along the French border. Similarly, Lafayette reserved 24,000 troops at Dun and Tiercelet to cover the center from a force of *émigrés* that could advance through Trier and Luxembourg.[49] Not anticipating an Austrian offensive, the French could have concentrated a larger striking force by leaving the defense of these fortresses to National Guard battalions. Accordingly, the French did not utilize their full offensive power in the first campaign.

Rochambeau divided his army into three columns – 1,500 troops at Dunkirk, 4,000 at Lille, and 10,000 at Valenciennes – while Lafayette brought moved 12,000 men to Givet.[50] The offensive resulted in fiasco mainly because of ineffective discipline and organization. Rochambeau did not harness the power of

---

48 See Paul Foucart and Jules Finot, *La défense nationale dans le nord de 1792 à 1802* (Lille, 1890), 1:1–3, 6; Steven Ross, *Quest for Victory: French Military Strategy, 1792–1799* (New York, 1973), 25.
49 Jomini, *Histoire critique et militaire*, 2:13–14.
50 Lynn, *Bayonets of the Republic*, 4–6; Jomini, *Histoire critique et militaire*, 2:14–15.

the combined-arms division but instead remained committed to the traditional brigade system. Infantry, artillery, and cavalry served in distinct units and under different commanders. Instead of forming divisions, the French relied on the system of ad hoc columns consisting of two-regiment brigades common in *ancien régime* warfare. Although the column at Dunkirk advanced quickly toward Furnes, Rochambeau's two additional and larger columns met with disaster before reaching Tournai and Mons. Halfway between Lille and Tournai, General Théobald Dillon's column of 4,000 troops encountered an Austrian patrol and panicked. Harassed by Austrian cavalry and artillery, the frightened infantry fled and reached the safety of French territory. There, after claiming that they had been betrayed, the soldiers executed the unfortunate Dillon. General Armand-Louis Biron's larger force of 10,000 men advanced from Valenciennes toward Mons and also panicked after encountering an Austrian cavalry picket. Fortunately for Biron, he escaped with his life. These reverses revealed serious disciplinary problems among both the line and volunteer battalions. Moreover, the French faced severe deficits in both artillery and cavalry. On encountering enemy cavalry and artillery, the French infantry panicked and received little support from their own specialized forces. The brigade system did not allow for the central direction of the specialized services within each column, severely weakening the army's flexibility.[51]

Despite the reverses, taking the offensive remained the default mindset among the French. Rather than personally direct an operation he did not support, Rochambeau resigned in early May. Dumouriez subsequently blamed the defeats on a Jacobin plot. He portrayed Rochambeau's resignation as an act of honor by a revered warrior.[52] Luckner transferred from the inactive Army of the Rhine to take command of the Army of the North. On 19 May, Lafayette and Luckner organized a second invasion of Belgium. Unlike the first, Luckner proposed striking Courtrai, sixteen miles northeast of Tournai, while Lafayette advanced toward Mons. Considering the vulnerability of the Austrian lines of operation that led to the Rhine, a major strike toward Liège appears more likely to have produced significant results than an attack in maritime Flanders, where the Austrians possessed greater troop strength. The French emphasis on battle appears the only viable explanation for this decision, yet it allowed the more professional Austrian troops to fight battles on ground chosen by their

---

51   Matti Lauerma, *L'artillerie de campagne française pendant les guerres de la Révolution* (Helsinki, 1956), 153–155; Édouard Desbrière and Maurice Sautai, *La cavalerie pendant la Révolution: du 14 juillet au 26 juin 1794* (Paris, 1907), 103–116; Bois, *Dumouriez*, 2:208–209; Phipps, *Armies of the First French Republic*, 1:77–78.

52   See Dumouriez, *La vie et les mémoires*, 2:239.

commanders instead of forcing them to fight battles to defend their lines of operation.

On 9 June, Luckner led 28,000 men in four columns toward Courtrai, which they captured after a minor combat on the 18th. While a small Austrian detachment contained Lafayette's advance, the Austrians dispersed more than 20,000 troops around Courtrai. Instead of using his central position to attack these weak and dispersed forces with his 28,000 men, Luckner felt surrounded and ordered the retreat after a brief engagement on 19 June. By month's end, both Luckner and Lafayette had returned their armies to France.[53] On 11 July, the Legislative Assembly declared *la patrie en danger* and called for a new batch of volunteers.[54]

Ignoring the military situation, Luckner and Lafayette engaged in political conspiracy. Desiring to be closer to Paris in order to possibly execute a *coup d'état*, Lafayette convinced Luckner to switch commands. However, fearing that Luckner's troops would not rally to him, Lafayette decided to actually shift the positions of their respective armies. Conducted in the presence of enemy forces, the *chassé-croisé* remains one of the more bewildering events of the French Revolutionary Wars and shows that political concerns dominated the French in the first year of the war: not until the officer corps was refurbished and professionalized in 1793 and 1794 would a truly new operational art of war develop.[55]

French passivity allowed the Austrian and Prussians to gain the initiative. In May, the two powers agreed to joint operations against France, which they both hoped would result in significant territorial aggrandizement. Prussia sought territory in Germany and Poland while Austria revived the Belgian–Bavarian exchange plan.[56] The Prussians decided to contribute 42,000 troops to the campaign while the Austrians planned to muster approximately 70,000 men. Combined with *émigré* forces, the Allies possessed at most 122,000 troops

---

53   Jomini, *Histoire critique et militaire*, 2:18–24.
54   For the declaration of the *patrie en danger*, see *Archives parlementaires*, 46:323–367; Blanning, *French Revolutionary Wars*, 73; Arthur Chuquet, *La première invasion prussienne (11 août–2 septembre 1792)* (Paris, 1886), 33–38.
55   Lynn, *Bayonets of the Republic*, 6; Phipps, *Armies of the First French Republic*, 1:90–93.
56   Austria gained control of Belgium after the end of the War of the Spanish Succession in 1714. According to Robert Howard Lord, the idea of exchanging Belgium for Bavaria "haunted the minds of Austrian statesman for almost a century": *The Second Partition of Poland: A Study in Diplomatic History* (Cambridge, MA, 1915), 262. The possession of Belgium required the Austrians to commit resources to defend territory far from the Habsburg heartland. In contrast, the possession of Bavaria would strengthen Austria's defensive borders in southern Germany.

for operations against France.[57] Yet these numbers did not reflect the true military strength of the Coalition. The Prussian commander, Charles William Ferdinand, duke of Brunswick-Wolfenbüttel, led the main Allied invasion force: 42,000 Prussians, 30,000 Austrians, 5,500 Hessians, and 4,500 émigrés. The emerging crisis in Poland caused by Russia's invasion proved more significant to both Austria and Prussia in 1792 than the war against France. Accordingly, the vast majority of their military forces remained in their home territories, prepared to intervene in Eastern affairs if necessary.[58]

Brunswick's command in 1792 epitomized the orthodox art of war that had developed during the 18th century. Unlike the French, the Allies did not view speed as essential and remained committed to a typically slower pace of operations. Moreover, both the Prussians and Austrians relied on long lines of operation that extended across the Rhine to sustain their advance. Rather than attack French armies, Brunswick directed his force toward Longwy and Verdun, indicating a preference for sieges and geographic objectives over battle.[59] Yet the slowness of Brunswick's advance proved disastrous for one of the key Allied objectives: restoring the French monarchy to full authority. After declaring his intention to destroy Paris should any harm befall the royal family, Brunswick delayed operations for several weeks, which ultimately doomed Louis XVI.[60] On 10 August with the Allied advance stalled, an armed mob stormed the Tuileries Palace, massacred the king's Swiss Guard, and suspended the monarchy.[61] After failing to rally the Army of the North to march on Paris and restore Louis XVI, Lafayette fled to the Austrians.[62]

Two weeks after the fall of the Tuileries, Brunswick commenced his operation in earnest by capturing Longwy. On 29 August, the Prussians surrounded the fortress of Verdun, where poor supply and insufficient manpower

---

57   Jomini, *Histoire critique et militaire*, 2:25–28; Bois, *Dumouriez*, 207–208; Rothenberg, *Napoleon's Great Adversaries*, 44–45.
58   Schroeder, *Transformation of European Politics*, 103–110; Chuquet, *La première invasion prussienne*, 90–105; Blanning, *French Revolutionary Wars*, 37–41, emphasizes the point that war began in Europe as a result of the crisis of 1787.
59   See the memoir of Louis Alexandre Andrault, comte de Langeron, in Léonce Pingaud, *L'invasion austro-prussienne (1792–1794)* (Paris, 1895); Austro-Hungarian Monarchy, *Krieg gegen die Französische Revolution, 1792–1797*, 2 vols (Vienna, 1902), 2:89–107; Chuquet, *La première invasion prussienne*, especially chs. 4–6.
60   For the infamous "Brunswick Manifesto," see J.H. Robinson, ed., *Readings in European History* (Boston, 1906), 2:443–445.
61   David P. Jordan, *The King's Trial: Louis XVI vs. the French Revolution* (Berkeley, CA, 2004), 1–10; Michel Vovelle, *La chute de la monarchie, 1787–1792* (Paris, 1999), 288–289.
62   See Lafayette to William Short, Nivelle, 26 August 1792, in Étienne Charavay, *Le Général Lafayette, 1757–1834: notice biographique* (Paris, 1898), 582.

undermined the superior fortress's defensibility. After the commander of Verdun committed suicide, the garrison surrendered to the Allies on 2 September, news of which led to a general hysteria in Paris that culminated in the September Massacres.[63] The French Executive Council advocated the government's abandonment of Paris in order to rehabilitate the military situation. A member of the Legislative Assembly, Georges Jacques Danton, rejected this plan and called for an unflinching war effort.[64] On 20 September 1792, the National Convention met for the first time, inaugurating the First French Republic two days later. Thus, the Allied strategy of pursuing geographic objectives instead of crushing the French armies served only to radicalize revolutionary politics and preserve French military power.

Yet the French likewise did not initially abandon geographic objectives to seek the destruction of the Allied army. As noted, the offensives in April, May, and June required the French to conquer specific geographic positions rather than destroy the enemy's army. After Lafayette's treason, Dumouriez took command of the Army of the North.[65] A variety of considerations convinced Dumouriez to ignore Brunswick's army, even after the fall of Longwy. At Sedan, his war council agreed to invade Belgium instead of marching east to attack Brunswick. The French minister of war, the aforementioned Joseph Servan, rejected Dumouriez's plan and suggested that he march to the Argonne Forest to defend the Meuse River. Dumouriez refused and prepared to march north, leaving Verdun practically undefended.[66] Only after Verdun's fall did Dumouriez temporarily concern himself with Brunswick's army.

The famous French victory at the 20 September Battle of Valmy did not result from an aggressive operational approach on Dumouriez's part. In fact, the French failure to concentrate their forces gave Brunswick an advantage. While Dumouriez's field army consisted of only 23,000 troops at Sedan, the French placed 25,000 troops to defend the frontier in Flanders and 45,000 men to guard Alsace. Another 25,000 troops stood at Metz, from where they could assist Dumouriez. After gaining Longwy and Verdun, Brunswick decided to advance through Champagne and perhaps force the perceived French rabble

---

63 The best detailed account of these operations remains Chuquet, *La première invasion prussienne*, esp. chs. 4–8; see also Heinrich von Sybel, *History of the French Revolution*, trans. by Walter C. Perry (London, 1867), 2:112–129; Blanning, *French Revolutionary Wars*, 74.

64 See Danton's speech of 2 September 1792 in *Archives parlementaires*, 49:209. For background, see David Lawday, *The Giant of the French Revolution: Danton, A Life* (New York, 2009), 130–135.

65 Dumouriez, *La vie et les mémoires*, 2:358–361, 373–377.

66 Ibid., 2:380–386; Howe, *Foreign Policy and the French Revolution*, 93–100; Bois, *Dumouriez*, 218–220.

to give battle. Dumouriez attempted to guard the Meuse but could not stop the Allied breakthrough at La Croix au Bois on 12 September. Rather than marching directly against the enemy force, he retreated thirty miles west of Verdun to Sainte-Menehould, where he appealed for support from the new commander of the Army of the Center, General François Kellermann. Kellermann complied, marching with approximately 36,000 troops and 58 cannon to assist Dumouriez. The two commanders united on 19 September, with Dumouriez at Sainte-Menehould and Kellermann occupying a position on the French left flank at the small hamlet of Valmy.[67] The French allowed Brunswick to position his army between them and Paris. Rather than immediately target the French capital, Brunswick decided to attack the French armies to secure his extensive lines of operation before continuing the advance.[68]

According to the rules of *ancien régime* warfare, a commander could not ignore an enemy army camped on his lines of operation. Thus, Brunswick decided to attack the French in positions of their choosing and which they prepared to defend.[69] Kellermann's artillery harassed Brunswick's troops as they advanced through heavy fog on 20 September. The Prussian cannon responded and kept the French infantry from charging. However, French artillery repulsed two Prussian infantry assaults and Brunswick canceled plans for a third. In reality, Valmy proved more of an artillery duel than a battle; both sides suffered minimal loss.[70] Rather than pursue the Prussians, Dumouriez agreed to negotiate with Frederick William II of Prussia, who hoped to prevent a French attack while Brunswick's forces retreated to the safety of the Rhine. Although an important victory, Valmy proved indecisive because both sides remained perfectly capable of continuing the war. Moreover, the entire campaign demonstrates that the French did not clearly comprehend the new way of war idealized by Guibert and Bourcet. The focus on geographic objectives rather than the enemy army, alongside ineffective organization and training, limited the implementation of the operational art proposed by the reformers.

Nonetheless, the French remained committed to the offensive spirit of the new operational approach. Accordingly, the offensive resumed shortly after Valmy. General Adam Philippe Custine advanced the 17,000-man Army of the Rhine into the Rhineland at the end of September mainly to attain resources. Within weeks, Allied resistance on the Rhine virtually collapsed. The Austrians

---

67 Bois, *Dumouriez*, 218–219.
68 The best overall work on Valmy is Jean-Paul Bertaud, *Valmy: la démocratie en armes* (Paris, 1970). On the fighting at Valmy, the most judicious source is Bois, *Dumouriez*, 220–231.
69 Phipps, *Armies of the First French Republic*, 1:126–129.
70 Casualty estimates are 300 troops for the French and fewer than 200 for the Prussians: Ross, *Quest for Victory*, 33; Bois, *Dumouriez*, 231.

and Prussians withdrew to the right bank while the Rhenish princes fled their lands. Rhineland radicals welcomed the French as long-awaited liberators while the majority of the population, as in Belgium, responded with apathy or fear. By the end of October, Custine occupied Mainz, Worms, and Frankfurt-am-Main.[71] Concomitantly, forces from the Army of the Midi under General Anne-Pierre, marquis de Montesquiou-Fézensac, invaded Nice and Savoy.[72] Given Dumouriez's leadership, these operations constituted diversions compared to the main offensive: Dumouriez's long-awaited invasion of Belgium. Dumouriez formed an operational force of 40,000 troops and advanced toward Mons, which the Austrians defended with approximately 14,000 men. On 6 November, he attacked the Austrians outside Mons and won the Battle of Jemappes. Demonstrating little tactical finesse, the French victory resulted from overwhelming numerical superiority.[73] Although a better-organized and -trained French army might have delivered a battle of annihilation, the Austrians conducted an effective fighting withdrawal east of the Meuse.[74] Instead of pursuing the Austrians, Dumouriez took the opportunity to capture Brussels, which fell to the French by mid-November.

Buoyed by military success, the French National Convention passed the Liberty and Fraternity decree in November, which claimed that France would support foreign liberation movements. However, in December the Convention declared that foreign peoples must pay for their own liberation and outlined a coherent occupation policy in Belgium, the Rhineland, and Savoy. By early 1793, the policy of liberation had switched to a policy of *réunions*, whereby foreign territories were directly annexed to France.[75] This aggressive foreign policy, along with the execution of Louis XVI in January 1793, the territorial expansion of France, and the overthrow of established diplomatic agreements led to the expansion of the First Coalition against France. By the beginning of the campaign season of 1793, France fielded approximately 270,000 troops

---

71   See Sydney Seymour Biro, *The German Policy of Revolutionary France: A Study in French Diplomacy During the War of the First Coalition, 1792–1797* (Cambridge, MA, 1957), 1:93–111; Phipps, *Armies of the First French Republic*, 2:29–43.
72   Phipps, *Armies of the First French Republic*, 3:67–70.
73   See Chuquet, *Jemappes et la conquête de la Belgique (1792–1793)* (Paris, 1890); Bois, *Dumouriez*, 253–278; Lynn, *Bayonets of the Republic*, 9.
74   Austro-Hungarian Monarchy. *Krieg gegen die Französische Revolution*, 2:223–258.
75   For the decrees, see *Archives parlementaires*, 53: 472–474, 55: 72–73; Schroeder, *Transformation of European Politics*, 12–13; Blanning, *The French Revolution in Germany: Occupation and Resistance in the Rhineland, 1792–1802* (New York, 1983), 64–65.

against 330,000 Austrian, Prussian, British, Dutch, Spanish, Hanoverian, and Sardinian troops.[76]

After taking Belgium, Dumouriez remained committed to the offensive and invaded the Netherlands with a small portion of the Army of the North, the remainder of which performed occupation duties in Belgium and besieged the fortress of Maastricht. Encountering little resistance from the unprepared and largely isolated Dutch, Dumouriez captured the fortress city of Breda in early March. Nevertheless, the Austrians under Prince Frederick Josias of Saxe-Coburg-Saalfeld demonstrated their own offensive zeal to recover their Belgian provinces and attacked the French around Maastricht. In two days of fighting, the Austrians forced the French to retreat west of the Meuse River and inflicted more than 6,000 casualties. Coburg did not divert his attention from the French army but continued to pursue. Dumouriez terminated his offensive into the Netherlands to reunite the Army of the North.[77] Demonstrating the fallacy behind the argument that the French won every time they possessed superior numbers, 39,000 Austrians defeated 45,000 French troops at the 18 March Battle of Neerwinden.[78] After retreating to Louvain and Brussels, Dumouriez became convinced that he could not defend Belgium and so attempted to rally the army against Paris. As part of a secret agreement with the Austrians, Dumouriez retreated from Belgium and arrested the French commissioners sent by the National Convention to monitor his behavior. After the troops refused to support his coup, Dumouriez defected to the Austrians.

Dumouriez's treason confirmed the suspicions of French politicians over the loyalty and reliability of *ancien régime* military commanders.[79] Although political designs committed Dumouriez to offensive operations, he never demonstrated supreme talents in the new operational art of war as envisioned by

---

76 Ross, *Quest for Victory*, 45, reaches these figures based on archival sources; see also Blanning, *French Revolutionary Wars*, 95, for similar approximations. Blanning notes that the Allies did not come close to mobilizing their maximum strength. See also Bois, *Dumouriez*, 278–286, 293–294.

77 For Dumouriez's account of the campaign, see the conversation between Dumouriez and the future Austrian ambassador to Great Britain, Count Louis Starhemberg, in Alfred Ritter von Vivenot and Heinrich Ritter von Zeissberg, eds, *Quellen zur Geschichte der deutschen Kaiserpolitik Österreichs während der Französischen Revolutionskriege, 1790–1801* (Vienna, 1882), 3:4–9; see also Alfred von Witzleben, *Prinz Friedrich Josias von Coburg-Saalfeld, Herzog zu Sachsen* (Berlin, 1859), 2:113–144; Sybel, *History of the French Revolution*, 2:426–447.

78 The official French and Austrian reports on Neerwinden are printed in Dumouriez, *La vie et les mémoires*, 4:266–276; the best account is now Bois, *Dumouriez*, 307–312.

79 R.R. Palmer, *Twelve Who Ruled: The Year of Terror in the French Revolution* (Princeton, NJ, 1941), 24–25.

the late *ancien régime* reformers. His defeat proved disastrous for France and culminated in a more rigorous conduct of the war out of necessity. Yet his loss paved the way for a new class of generals and a new French leader who better comprehended the new operational art.

Lazare Carnot and the Emergence of the Operational Art

While the situation in Belgium collapsed, France's other armies likewise suffered reverses. In the Alps, the Army of Italy failed to repulse a Piedmont-Sardinian invasion of France. Two French armies in the Pyrenees retreated from a larger Spanish force that besieged Perpignan and approached Bayonne. Thus, by July 1793, the French war effort had reverted to a defensive on all fronts.[80] Following an Allied council of war at Antwerp in April, Coburg invaded France from Belgium and besieged Valenciennes on 30 May after driving the French from the Camp of Famars.[81] Meanwhile, after taking Frankfurt-am-Main in December 1792, Brunswick besieged Mainz in April 1793. Rather than attack Brunswick's superior force, Custine retreated to Landau with approximately 40,000 men. Throughout spring and summer, the French launched several relief efforts to save the 20,000-man garrison at Mainz. Regardless, the garrison surrendered on 22 July, allowing Brunswick to resume his offensive.[82]

The military crisis that faced France as well as continued domestic unrest led to the implementation of the Reign of Terror in the summer of 1793. Under Maximilien Robespierre, the Committee of Public Safety assumed chief executive power and management of the nation's diplomatic and military efforts.[83] In August, it proposed the *levée en masse* to the National Convention, providing the bulk of the manpower for France's mass army. Moreover, the Committee of Public Safety oversaw a national requisition and the organization of all resources for the war effort. Learning from the examples of Lafayette and Dumouriez, it maintained strict oversight and correspondence with the Convention's representatives on mission attached to the field armies, allowing the Committee to ensure effective control over the generals.[84]

---

80 Ross, *Quest for Victory*, 47–55.
81 Coburg to Francis II, Boussu, 12 April 1793, in Vivenot and Zeissberg, *Quellen zur Geschichte*, 3:11.
82 See Arthur Chuquet, *Wissembourg (1793)* (Paris, 1893), 42–62.
83 Peter McPhee, *Robespierre: A Revolutionary Life* (New Haven, CT, 2013), 158–159.
84 Palmer, *Twelve Who Ruled*, ch. 2; David Andress, *The Terror: The Merciless War for Freedom in Revolutionary France* (New York, 2005), 318–319, 325–326; Marie-Cécile Thoral, *From*

Most important, committee member Lazare Carnot became the leading figure of the French war effort in July 1793. Carnot demanded strenuous efforts from the Republic's military commanders. The Committee of Public Safety arrested and ultimately executed Custine after he failed to act decisively to relieve the besieged fortress of Condé. General Jean Nicolas Houchard met the same fate after failing to pursue the Anglo-Dutch army under Prince Frederick, duke of York and Albany, at the 6–8 September Battle of Hondschoote.[85] By the end of 1793, the revolutionary government had raised a new cadre of republican officers and generals drawn mainly from the middle class. As demonstrated below, these new commanders generally lacked strategic genius yet possessed sufficient determination to implement the new operational measures demanded by the Committee of Public Safety.

The new French way of war emerged most fully under Carnot's direction in the fall of 1793 and the spring of 1794. During this period, the French built a powerful mass army based on conscription, which brought their strength to 750,000 men under arms by August 1794. Organizational reforms allowed the generals to harness the power of this army. Demi-brigades appeared in 1793 and generals started dividing their armies into combined-arms divisions. By 1794, the divisional system became fully realized in the French army.[86] Carnot understood the significance of these changes and made them effective through a broad program of central control of the war effort involving matters of planning, mobilization, training, supply, and strategy.[87] Most important, Carnot and the other committee members rejected the concept of negotiation with the Allies and demanded the Coalition's annihilation. Only decisive battles could achieve a quick victory for the salvation of the Republic. Carnot understood that, in order to achieve these types of victories, the French revolutionary armies had to force the Allies to fight battles against their will and in situations that promised the French decisive victory. Operational art combined with the concentration of superior numbers of troops in areas deemed strategically vital provided the only means of annihilating the enemy.[88] In addition, Carnot realized that operational art required effective organization and command and control alongside the offensive spirit. An increasingly sophisticated General Staff allowed the divisional system to function smoothly. Provided

---

Valmy to Waterloo: France at War, 1792–1815, trans. by Godfrey Rogers (New York, 2011), 94–95.
85 Blanning, *French Revolutionary Wars*, 125–127.
86 Ross, "Development of the Combat Division," 89.
87 See Jean Dhombres and Nicole Dhombres, *Lazare Carnot* (Paris, 1997), 354–366; Marcel Reinhard, *La Grande Carnot* (Paris, 1952), 2:102–118.
88 Telp, *Evolution of the Operational Art*, 36–37.

with information and maps by the Topographical Bureau, the commanders and chiefs of staff of the French armies proved highly capable at the operational level.[89]

General Jean-Baptiste Jourdan assumed command of the Army of the North in September 1793. Jourdan's plan utilized Bourcet's concept of dispersed divisions for the approach and concentration for battle. After gathering supplies at Paris, Carnot joined Jourdan's headquarters at Guise to assist the new commander's efforts. Ironically, Jourdan and Carnot committed to a broad attack on 15 October that reflected little operational or tactical finesse. Nevertheless, the French executed an impressive maneuver that allowed them to concentrate superior strength against the Austrian left at Wattignies on the 16th.[90] Although the French victory at Wattignies repulsed an Allied invasion effort, it did not represent an annihilation battle as envisioned by Carnot. In early November, he urged Jourdan to attack Coburg in Belgium north of the Sambre River. Jourdan refused after claiming that the army lacked proper supplies and equipment. In January, the Committee recalled Jourdan to Paris and, according to some accounts, nearly executed him for insubordination.[91]

Following Wattignies, Carnot feared that an Austro-Prussian offensive through Alsace would disrupt the ability to exploit the success of Wattignies. Accordingly, he sent reinforcements to the Army of the Moselle and the Army of the Rhine commanded by Generals Lazare Hoche and Jean-Charles Pichegru respectively. Imbued with the spirit of the offensive, Hoche quickly pursued Brunswick toward Kaiserslautern with dispersed divisions, which he united on 28 November for an attempted envelopment of the Prussian position. For three days, Hoche repeatedly assailed Brunswick's force but finally retreated on 30 November after his losses became too significant. Insufficient topographical knowledge and poor coordination ruined Hoche's attack, and the Prussians scored a significant tactical victory.[92] Following the defeat at Kaiserslautern, the Committee ordered Hoche to march through the Vosges Mountains to help Pichegru drive the Austrians from Wissembourg. By 26 December, the two

---

89   Carnot to Representatives on Mission, Paris, 3 September 1793, in Étienne Charavay, ed., *Correspondance générale de Carnot* (Paris, 1897), 3:78–79; Howard Brown, *War, Revolution, and the Bureaucratic State: Politics and Army Administration in France, 1791–1799* (New York, 1995), 149.
90   SHAT, M¹ 608, 2: Victor Dupuis, *La campagne de 1793 à l'armée du Nord et des Ardennes*, 2 vols (Paris, 1906); Witzleben, *Coburg*, 311–332.
91   Phipps, *Armies of the First French Republic*, 2:269–273.
92   See Arthur Chuquet, *Hoche et la lutte pour l'Alsace* (Paris, 1893), 61–91; Michael V. Leggiere, *Blücher: Scourge of Napoleon* (Norman, OK, 2014), 41–45; Phipps, *Armies of the First French Republic*, 2:85–90.

armies had forced the enemy to retire north, even after Brunswick's Prussians had attempted to reinforce the Austrians at Wissembourg.[93]

Along with French success against Allied offensives in Savoy and the Pyrenees, the victories at Wattignies and Wissembourg brought an end to the major Allied offensive following Dumouriez's treason. Moreover, the French successfully defeated the Federalist Revolt at Lyons, recaptured Toulon from the British and counterrevolutionaries, and defeated the Royal and Catholic Army in the Vendée. In addition, crippling divisions emerged within the Coalition. The second partition of Poland by Russia and Prussia in 1793 contributed greatly to the deterioration of relations. Learning of Austrian plans for a third partition, King Frederick William II refused to provide troops to defend the Austrian Netherlands in the approaching campaign.[94]

In the context of this Allied discord, Carnot determined to seek a decisive victory that would potentially end the war in the 1794 campaign. Recognizing the principle of economy of force, Carnot decided to concentrate French strength in the decisive theater: Belgium. French spies in Brussels kept the Committee of Public Safety informed of Allied troop movements in the Low Countries.[95] In his general instructions of 2 February 1794, Carnot outlined a coherent operational plan for achieving a "battle of annihilation," which he defined as a victory that would impede the Allied ability to continue the war after the end of the year.[96] Although he specified a few key geographic positions that the French armies should occupy, Carnot indicated his intention to force the Allies to relieve these positions, forcing them to give battle under unfavorable circumstances. Thus, Carnot sought to utilize siege warfare rather than operational maneuver to facilitate a battle of annihilation. Nevertheless, he urged the generals to engage in battles whenever possible. Most important, he demanded that they act offensively and pursue the enemy to convert tactical success into strategic victory.

The 1794 Belgium campaign represents the pinnacle of the new French way of war before the advent of Bonaparte. Strategically, Carnot developed a plan to envelop Allied forces in Belgium by launching two attacks: one in Flanders and the other further east toward the Sambre and Meuse region. Pichegru received command of the Army of the North, the force that would make the

---

93   Chuquet, *Wissembourg*, 181–200.
94   See Schroeder, *Transformation of European Politics*, 135–137; Ross, *Quest for Victory*, 71–73; Lord, *Second Partition of Poland*.
95   These reports can be found in SHAT, B¹ 169. French intelligence operations during the Revolutionary Wars have received little attention.
96   "General System of Military Operations in the Approaching Campaign," 2 February 1794, in Charavay, *Correspondance générale de Carnot*, 4:279–283.

main assault through Flanders. Jourdan returned to command the Army of the Moselle, which Carnot had initially kept in reserve at Arlon ready to advance to Belgium or fight in Alsace or Trier if the Prussians launched an offensive. Regardless, Carnot's instructions clearly explained that the French should campaign rigorously to achieve a battle of annihilation.[97]

In the first phase of the spring campaign, an Allied offensive through Flanders upset Carnot's plan and forced Pichegru to respond to Coburg's aggressive movements. Following the principles of *ancien régime* warfare, Coburg aimed to capture Landrécies, Le Cateau, and Cambrai before marching on Paris. Like the French, Coburg would accept battle to repulse enemy relief efforts: at the tactical level, the Allies remained convinced of their parity – if not their absolute superiority – with the French. On 21 and 26 April, Coburg defeated the French and captured Landrécies on the 30th. Yet Pichegru did not send considerable forces against Coburg at this stage; instead, he avoided the enemy army and invaded Flanders.[98]

By the end of April, each side threatened the other's lines of operation. While Pichegru could tolerate this situation, Coburg could not. Accordingly, Coburg postponed his offensive and redirected his army against Pichegru in Flanders to defend his rear. Unfortunately for the French, they lacked the tactical strength to fully destroy the Allied army. On 17 May, Coburg drove the French from Tourcoing in a frontal assault that utilized shock columns. The French escaped with few casualties and counterattacked on the morning of the 18th by attempting an envelopment with 60,000 troops. Unable to resist the French advance, Coburg retreated to Tournai with heavy casualties. Four days later, on 22 May, Pichegru attacked Coburg at Tournai in an attempt to both capture the city and destroy the main Allied army. Traditional defensive tactics won the day for the Austrians, and Pichegru suffered approximately 6,000 casualties.[99] The fact that Coburg managed to repulse Pichegru's attack at Tournai four days after the 18 May Battle of Tourcoing refutes the notion that the latter battle constituted a French decisive victory. Instead, Tourcoing proved to be the first of many tactical victories in the 1794 campaign that the French failed to convert into annihilation battles.

The decision to send Jourdan's Army of the Moselle to the Sambre and Meuse Rivers to support the operations of the right wing of the Army of the North and two divisions of the Army of the Ardennes constituted the key

---

97 Carnot to Jourdan, Paris, 27 May 1794, ibid., 4:383–384; also SHAT, M^1 608, 2.
98 See Witzleben, *Coburg*, 107–136; Phipps, *Armies of the First French Republic*, 1:285–290.
99 Ross, *Quest for Victory*, 77–78; Lynn, *Bayonets of the Republic*, 15–16; Witzleben, *Coburg*, 139–148.

factor in the success of the Belgium campaign. This proved possible simply because the French possessed numbers capable of firmly defending multiple fronts while concentrating overwhelming strength in the decisive theater. In late April, the Committee instructed Jourdan to advance to Charleroi, Namur, and Liège with 42,000 troops divided into four divisions. Although the Committee provided Jourdan specific geographic objectives to gain, they insisted that he seek any opportunity to destroy the Allied army through battle. Moreover, Carnot insisted on absolute speed.[100] Contrary to conventional understanding, the French did not abandon lines of supply and magazines in order to quicken their pace of march by living off the land. From May to June, Jourdan's Moselle Army advanced quickly but methodically to the Sambre and Meuse region, benefiting from a line of operation developing along the Meuse. In addition, the representatives on mission conducted orderly requisitions and imposed contributions on local towns and villages while executing nearly every soldier accused of pillaging. In fact, the generals and representatives on mission outlawed pillage because they associated it with lack of discipline and feared it would turn civilian populations against them.[101]

On 5 June 1794, Jourdan reached his destination and received command of all forces in the region: approximately 90,000 battle-hardened troops. Jourdan's force became known as the Army of the Sambre and Meuse.[102] Carnot's plan for a strategic envelopment of the Allies in Belgium forced Coburg to make a decision: should he defend Flanders while sacrificing his lines of operation to the Rhine or move east to protect his left flank on the Sambre and Meuse?[103] On 16 June, an Allied force commanded by the William Frederick, crown prince of Orange, drove Jourdan's army south of the Sambre and reinforced the besieged garrison at Charleroi in the Battle of First Fleurus. This victory convinced the Allies that they could defeat the new army forming on their strategic left flank and salvage the situation in Belgium.[104] Accordingly, Coburg moved east intending to save Charleroi and decisively defeat Jourdan's

---

100 Committee of Public Safety (CPS) to Jourdan, Paris, 6 May 1794, in SHAT, M¹ 608, 2, no. 40; Jourdan to CPS, 16 May 1794, in SHAT, M¹ 608, 3, no. 43; CPS to Jourdan, Paris, 27 May 1794, SHAT, M¹ 608, 2, no. 55.

101 On punishments for pillaging, see SHAT, B ¹ 311; on logistics, see Peter Wetzler, *War and Subsistence: The Sambre and Meuse Army in 1794* (New York, 1985), and Alan Forrest, "The Logistics of Revolutionary War in France," in Chickering and Förster, *War in an Age of Revolution*, 177–196.

102 Order of the CPS, Paris, 8 June 1794, SHAT, M¹ 608, 2, no, 64. The army did not officially become the Army of the Sambre and Meuse until 29 June.

103 Ross, *Quest for Victory*, 78–79.

104 Victor Dupuis, *Les opérations militaires sur la Sambre en 1794: bataille de Fleurus* (Paris, 1907), 261–290.

army. On 18 June, Jourdan crossed the Sambre again and reestablished the positions his army had lost on the 16th. Following Carnot's directives as established in February, Jourdan awaited Coburg's attack, forming his troops in defensive positions bolstered by field works and entrenchments.[105]

On 26 June, Coburg attacked across a front of more than thirty miles to commence the Battle of Second Fleurus. Although Jourdan's army nearly broke on multiple occasions, the French held and benefited tremendously from the fact that the Charleroi garrison had surrendered the previous evening. Coburg learned of Charleroi's fall in the afternoon of the 26th and decided to retreat, a decision that infuriated the Austrian commanders and many of the troops. Believing that Coburg had sacrificed a chance for victory, Austrian morale did not recover in 1794. Although a battle of annihilation required a vigorous pursuit, Jourdan could not give chase after Second Fleurus because of the exhaustion of his troops. While the Austrians retreated in perfect order, the grueling battle required the French to take two days of rest before they could advance.[106]

Although Second Fleurus proved less decisive than traditionally thought, the French followed the victory with an impressive campaign. After capturing Ypres, Pichegru's Army of the North advanced to Ghent on the road to Brussels, meeting little resistance from the duke of York and the crown prince of Orange. Meanwhile, Jourdan's army launched a more significant operation against Coburg. Crucially, Jourdan's 75,000-man field army could not advance in a unitary form even with the organizational improvements afforded by the divisional system.[107] Therefore, Jourdan maintained a system of wing commands that he had first developed for the battles at Fleurus. General Jean-Baptiste Kléber commanded the left wing, Jourdan led the center, and General François-Séverin Marceau directed the right wing. At Second Fleurus, the wing-command system allowed Jourdan to maintain effective command and control over a massive front. In the subsequent campaign, it enabled his army to consistently outmarch and outmaneuver the main Allied army, clearly demonstrating the advantages of the new French organization and operational art. By the end of the 1794 campaign, the French were referring to these formations as *corps d'armée* in their battle reports. Although they lacked the sophisticated staff systems and uniformity of Napoleon's corps system, the wing commands functioned in a similar manner. Each wing constituted several divisions of

---

105 SHAT, M¹ 608, 2 Witzleben, *Coburg*, 3:280–299.
106 Witzleben, *Coburg*, 299–324, prints Coburg's report on Second Fleurus.
107 Situation report, 3 July 1794, in SHAT, B¹ 254.

infantry, a cavalry attachment, and an artillery unit. Jourdan retained control over the center and a central cavalry reserve.[108]

The Thermidorean Republic and the Directory: Transition and Degeneration

Although they failed to annihilate the Allied armies in battle, the French conquered Belgium and the Rhineland while invading the Netherlands by the end of 1794. The accomplishment of these objectives resulted from Allied weakness and French strategic and operational superiority.[109] Jourdan understood the possibilities of the new French operational art. In early September, he devised an impressive plan that utilized many of the principles developed by the *ancien régime* reformers. Continuing the system of wing commands, Jourdan decided to deceive the Austrians, who remained dispersed in a cordon along the Meuse and the Ourthe Rivers. Jourdan tasked Kléber with executing a diversionary attack at Maastricht to compel the Austrians to reinforce their right flank while the French army's center and right wing prepared for the main attack at Sprimont on the Ourthe. Jourdan hoped to unravel the Austrian left flank in a *manoeuvre sur les derrières*.[110] On 17 September 1794, Kléber launched the diversionary attack and the Austrian commander, François Sébastien de Croix, count von Clerfayt, reinforced his right flank in anticipation of the main French attack. Following Jourdan's plan, General Barthélemy Louis Joseph Schérer led the left wing against Sprimont the next day. Austrian forces could not stop the French attack and soon retreated after losing the key passages across the Ourthe. Made possible by the wing-command system, the French maneuver effectively outperformed the Austrians at the operational level, completing the French conquest of Belgium.[111]

Still, the Battle of the Ourthe did not achieve the complete destruction of the Austrian army. Clerfayt's army retreated in good order to Aachen. Again the French could not aggressively pursue the Austrians because of exhaustion and disorganization after the battle. In fact, Jourdan allowed Clerfayt two weeks in

---

108 On the formation of wing commands, see SHAT, M¹ 608, 2, and Louis Jouan, *La campagne de 1794–1795 dans les Pays-Bas* (Paris, 1915), chs. 3 and 4.
109 Carnot to Jourdan, 2 July 1794, SHAT, B¹ 35; Jourdan to CPS, 20 August 1794, SHAT, M¹ 608, 2, no. 105.
110 SHAT, M¹ 608, 2.
111 The best work remains Louis Thiry, *Après Fleurus: la bataille de Sprimont (18 septembre 1794)* (Brussels, 1936).

which to retreat to a new defensive position on the Roer River.[112] Moreover, Austrian troops remained stationed at Maastricht. Carnot repeatedly urged Jourdan to ignore the Maastricht garrison and pursue the enemy army. As he stated, after destroying the Austrian army, the French could capture fortresses with ease. Accordingly, Jourdan left a small covering force at Maastricht and concentrated his strength for the campaign's climactic battle.[113] On 2 October, the French attacked the Austrians across a fifty-mile front on the Roer. Instead of utilizing deception and surprise as he had at the Ourthe, Jourdan organized a direct frontal attack. As a result, the French assault achieved less success than it should have against a demoralized army. Nevertheless, the wing-command system allowed Kléber and Schérer to direct separate assaults while Jourdan led the army's center. Because Jourdan delegated authority to his wing commanders within an overall operational plan, the army acted with unity of purpose despite the extended front. It is at this point that the French started referring to these wing commands as *corps d'armée*.

Although Jourdan expected to continue the battle on the 3rd, the French awoke to find that the Austrian army had retreated. By the 6th, Clerfayt's army had reached the right bank of the Rhine at Koblenz. While the new operational art allowed the Sambre and Meuse Army to conquer the left bank of the Rhine by the end of the year, it did not achieve the battle of annihilation desired by Carnot. Regardless, its victories mark the peak of French military effectiveness before Bonaparte's victories in 1796.[114]

Following the 1794 campaign, the French war effort underwent a transitional phase closely related to political changes in France and Europe. The Thermidorean Reaction ended the Reign of Terror and instituted constitutional reforms that introduced the fourth of France's revolutionary governments, the Directory, in October 1795.[115] The third partition of Poland in 1795 eroded European interest in the war against France. Content with territorial aggrandizement in the east and tired of war, Prussia made peace with France at Basel. Spain left the war in the summer of 1795, bringing an end to operations in the Pyrenees. Nonetheless, ongoing economic and financial problems made the French unable to negotiate peace with Britain and Austria. Instead, the French continued the war to plunder supplies from neighboring states. French armies pursued offensive operations to wage war on enemy territory, thereby allowing

---

112   See the Austrian reports in Alfred Ritter von Vivenot, *Thugut, Clerfayt, und Wurmser* (Vienna, 1869).
113   CPS to Jourdan, 23 September 1794, SHAT, M^1 608, 2, no. 115.
114   Ibid.; see also Schérer's report in SHAT, B^1 40.
115   Denis Woronoff, *La république bourgeoise de Thermidor à Brumaire, 1794–1799* (Paris, 1972).

war to feed war instead of placing the costs of the war effort on the French state.[116]

The financial and economic weaknesses of the French state made this policy necessary in order to maintain the supply of the Republic's armies, which now stood on the frontiers away from the metropole and beyond normal supply networks. In addition, the winter of 1794–1795 proved incredibly cold and greatly weakened the armies. Desertion and disease increased tremendously so that, by 1795, the 750,000-man army of the previous fall stood at only 480,000 troops. Such a drastic rate of attrition in a period of relatively little combat reveals the army's genuinely horrible material condition. Indeed, in many ways this period witnessed the degeneration of the famed army of the Year II.[117]

Despite the economic returns from foreign requisitions, the logistical deterioration took a significant toll on the armies operating along the Rhine. Constant campaigning by large armies in this region significantly disrupted normal patterns of agriculture and reduced the food supply. In this circumstance, the French system of living off the land became highly problematic.[118] Continuing his command of the Army of the Sambre and Meuse, Jourdan battled the supply situation through 1795. Rather than an isolated lack of certain items, Jourdan faced a systemic crisis. For example, it took the general approximately three months simply to gather enough wood to construct bridges to allow the French to cross the Rhine. At the opening of the campaign, he warned the government that his army alone lacked 35,000 draft horses necessary to conduct operations on the right bank.[119] Accordingly, during the 1795 campaign the French marched not with the intention of attacking the enemy army but because starvation drove the soldiers to constantly search for food. In fact, Jourdan refrained from seeking battle against the Austrians because he feared his army would collapse. After Clerfayt crossed the Main River and threatened to outflank Jourdan's left at Frankfurt, the general ordered a retreat to save his army. By the end of 1795, the Sambre and Meuse Army had withdrawn to the

---

116 Schroeder, *Transformation of European Politics*, 150–151.
117 H. Bordeau, *Les armées du Rhin au début du Directoire* (Paris, 1909); see also Bertaud, *Army of the French Revolution*, 272–291.
118 See SHAT, M¹ 608, 3; although secondary sources do not adequately address the extent of the logistical crisis in this period, see Ross, *Quest for Victory*, 90–91, for general observations.
119 In addition to SHAT, M¹ 608, 3, see Jean Adam Pflieger, "Survey of the State of the Cavalry of the Republic," in *Carnet de la Sabretache: revue militaire retrospective* (Paris, 1900), 8:6–12.

left bank of the Rhine and the Austrians were preparing an offensive to possibly recover the Low Countries.[120]

In 1796, the French armies on the Rhine developed a more flexible supply system that combined requisitions from enemy territory with a system of supply contractors coordinated by the Directory. Although these measures fell short of perfect and suffered from corruption, they allowed the French to conduct a full-scale offensive deep within enemy territory.[121] In fact, Carnot expected the offensives in Germany to provided decisive results in the war. Although French strategy provided the Austrians under Archduke Charles with the advantage of interior lines, Carnot confidently maintained that the speed of the two French armies would allow them to deliver a decisive battle. According to the plan, Jourdan's Army of the Sambre and Meuse would advance along the Main River while the Rhine and Moselle Army under General Jean Victor Marie Moreau marched toward the Danube. After defeating Charles in detail, the two forces would unite for an advance against Vienna, thereby forcing the Austrians to accept French peace terms.[122]

In late May 1796, Jourdan led approximately 80,000 troops across the Rhine at Düsseldorf and advanced south toward the Lahn River, which the French reached on 6 June. Accordingly, Charles left a garrison at Mainz and advanced west toward the Lahn with numbers superior to Jourdan's. In early June, Moreau claimed that he could not cross the Rhine because of the Austrian presence on the right bank of the Rhine. On the 24th, Moreau crossed the Rhine at Strasbourg to take advantage of Charles's march north to confront Jourdan.[123] Rather than seek battle with Charles, Jourdan repeated his actions of the previous year's campaign and retreated to the left bank of the Rhine. Meanwhile, Moreau advanced toward Rastatt and fought Charles on 5 July. After a series of clashes that favored the French, Charles withdrew eastward. On 16 July, the Sambre and Meuse Army captured Frankfurt-am-Main.[124]

With both French armies east of the Rhine and within striking distance of Charles, the moment for the climax of Carnot's plan seemed opportune. Ultimately, Carnot's strategy failed for two reasons. First, Jourdan and Moreau

---

120 Jourdan even possessed orders from the CPS authorizing him to avoid battle. See CPS to Jourdan, Paris, 12 September 1794, SHAT, M¹ 608, 3, nos. 55, 63, 64.
121 Bertaud, *Army of the French Revolution*, 286–291.
122 See Executive Directory to Jourdan, Paris, 29 March 1796, in SHAT, B¹ 70; Executive Directory to Moreau, Paris, 10 April 1796, in SHAT, M¹ 608, 4, no. 1. The copies of these orders reprinted in Jean-Baptiste Jourdan, *Mémoires pour servir à l'histoire de la campagne de 1796* (Paris, 1818), 215–232, cannot be relied on for accuracy.
123 Phipps, *Armies of the First French Republic*, 2:288.
124 SHAT, M¹ 608, 3; Archduke Charles, *Principes de la stratégie, développés par la relation de la campagne de 1796 en Allemagne*, 3 vols (Paris, 1818).

proved incapable of operating with the skill and energy demanded by Carnot. Moreover, instead of uniting their armies to pursue a decisive battle against Charles, the two French armies operated outside supporting distance. Second, the archduke performed a perfectly executed fighting withdrawal that brought him closer to his base of operations while simultaneously stretching the French lines of operation too far from the Rhine.

While Moreau invaded Bavaria and captured Ulm in August, Jourdan advanced along the Main to Bamberg, Nuremberg, and Amberg. The slowness of the French advance, their focus on geographic positions, and the lack of coordination between their armies allowed Charles to defeat both armies in detail. On 24 August, Charles attacked Jourdan's right flank at Amberg while General Wilhelm von Wartensleben pinned his front. After an indecisive combat, Jourdan retreated because he feared the Austrian threat to his rear and did not expect support from Moreau. Receiving orders from the Directory to remain on the right bank of the Rhine, Jourdan concentrated his army at Würzburg. On 3 September, Charles attacked with superior numbers and forced the French to withdraw to the Lahn. Moreau remained passive and the Austrians pursued the Sambre and Meuse Army aggressively. Jourdan withdrew to the left bank of the Rhine on the 20th and resigned his command in disgust. Due to low morale and poor supply, the Sambre and Meuse Army remained inactive for the rest of the year. Predictably, Charles turned against Moreau and easily drove him from the Black Forest region in a brilliant campaign. By the end of October, Moreau's army had joined the Sambre and Meuse Army on the left bank of the Rhine. Although both of these armies possessed the advantages of the French military system, they proved unable to replicate the successes of 1793–1794 and demonstrated the incomplete development of the new operational art in practice.[125]

The Napoleonic Operational Art in Italy

While the armies in Germany suffered defeats against Charles, another French army, the Army of Italy, achieved victories that demonstrated the full potential of the new operational art.[126] Led by General Bonaparte, the small and poorly supplied Army of Italy knocked Piedmont-Sardinia out of the war and took

---

125 For other reliable assessments of this understudied campaign, see Ross, *Quest for Victory*, 94–97; Blanning, *French Revolutionary Wars*, 149, 156–158; Rothenberg, *Napoleon's Great Adversaries*, 55–63; Eysturlid, *Archduke Carl*, 69–84.

126 On the Army of Italy, see Gilles Candela, *L'Armée d'Italie: des missionnaires armés à la naissance de la guerre napoléonienne* (Paris, 2011).

most of northern Italy from the Austrians within a few months of the start of campaigning. Although both sides viewed Germany as the main theater at the beginning of the year, both sent reinforcements to Italy after Bonaparte's successes. Thus, Bonaparte's supreme operational skill completely overturned the strategic calculations in the war.[127]

Strategically, Bonaparte possessed few advantages against the superior forces of Piedmont-Sardinia and Austria. Although the French victory at Loano in November 1795 gained control of the Alpine passes, Bonaparte's army remained pinned along the Ligurian coast. Moreover, his forces received even fewer supplies than the armies in Germany. Bonaparte's negotiation of a loan from Genoa and careful preparations in March 1796 somewhat improved the situation but the charismatic leader told his men that they would have to feed and clothe themselves through victory.[128] In this respect, he enjoyed an advantage over the commanders in Germany. While Jourdan and Moreau operated in a region depleted by years of campaigning and requisitioning, Bonaparte stood on the doorstep of the lush plains and wealthy towns and cities of Lombardy. If his army could crush the immediate barrier of Austro-Sardinian armies to his north, it could enter this paradise.[129]

Throughout the First Italian Campaign, Bonaparte utilized the new operational art to great effect. Like the French commanders in 1794, he organized the divisions into higher formations similar to the more fully refined corps system that appeared later. These formations allowed Bonaparte's army to march divided and achieve mass at the decisive point of attack on a number of occasions throughout the campaign. In April, General Masséna commanded 17,000 troops, General Charles Pierre François Augereau led 11,500, and General Jean-Mathieu-Philibert Sérurier directed 9,500. Another force under General Amédée Emmanuel François Laharpe functioned as a reserve but primarily supported Masséna.[130] Utilizing speed, maneuver, and central position, Bonaparte drove a wedge between the 52,000 Piedmontese and Austrians defending Piedmont and Lombardy. After Masséna and Laharpe forced the Austrians from Montenotte and Dego, Bonaparte concentrated the army against the Piedmont-Sardinians at Ceva, ultimately defeating them on 21 April at

---

127   Schroeder, *Transformation of European Politics*, 161–164.
128   See Boycott-Brown, *Road to Rivoli*, ch. 7.
129   See Napoléon Bonaparte, *Correspondance générale, publiée par la Fondation Napoléon* (hereafter cited as CG), Nos. 453 and 455, 1:317–318, 320; Dwyer, *Napoleon*, 200–201; Candela, *L'Armée d'Italie*, 260–274.
130   Candela, *L'Armée d'Italie*, 234–235, gives Bonaparte 43,000 effectives without breaking the total down for each division; Chandler, *Campaigns of Napoleon*, 62, gives the more typical figure of 37,000–38,000.

Mondovi. Five days later, he forced the Piedmontese to sign the Armistice of Cherasco, thus removing Piedmont-Sardinia from the First Coalition. Throughout this decisive campaign, Bonaparte used divisions to achieve operational superiority. Moreover, speed and maneuver proved essential factors in his ability to defeat larger armies and to achieve the Directory's strategic goals.[131]

After forcing Piedmont-Sardinia to surrender, Bonaparte pursued the Austrians into Lombardy. In the Lombard phase, Bonaparte utilized the new operational art to great effect and added the elements of deception and surprise. Violating the neutrality of the Duchy of Parma, he ordered Masséna to cross the Po River at Piacenza. In the same way that Jourdan's invasion of Belgium endangered Coburg's lines of operation in 1794, Bonaparte's decision to cross at Piacenza threatened to strategically envelop the Austrian army under the native Belgian General Jean-Pierre de Beaulieu.[132] Rumors swept through the Austrian army that Bonaparte possessed more than 100,000 troops: the result of his insistence on speed, maneuver, and concentration at the decisive point of attack. Consequently, the Austrians evacuated Lombardy. Bonaparte's commitment to battle explains his decision to postpone the capture of Milan in favor of pursuing the Austrian army at Lodi. Although he defeated the Austrian rearguard rather than Beaulieu's army, the 10 May Battle of Lodi provided much inspiration for the Napoleonic legend; more importantly, it demonstrates the further development of the operational art.[133]

After Lodi, Bonaparte entered Milan and spent several weeks reorganizing and resupplying his army. Shortly afterward, the French prepared to pursue the Austrians into Venetia. Beaulieu hoped that the Quadrilateral Fortresses would allow him to defend Venetia from Bonaparte. The fortresses of Mantua, Peschiera, Legnago, and Verona defended all the road junctions and river crossings in the region. Beaulieu placed a strong Austrian garrison in Mantua and initially retreated further east into Venetia. Even Bonaparte could not ignore the strong fortress of Mantua on the Mincio River. Accordingly, on 15 July he ordered Sérurier to mask and then fully invest the fortress. Yet instead of pursuing Beaulieu, Bonaparte executed the Directory's orders to plunder central and southern Italy.[134]

---

131 The most detailed account of the Piedmont phase of the First Italian Campaign remains Félix Bouvier, *Bonaparte en Italie, 1796* (Paris, 1899).
132 CG, No. 582, 1:389.
133 Ibid., No. 589, 1:393; Boycott-Brown, *Road to Rivoli*, 320–327; on the significance of Lodi to Napoleonic propaganda, see Dwyer, *Napoleon*, 211–218.
134 See especially Phillip R. Cuccia, *Napoleon in Italy: The Sieges of Mantua, 1796–1799* (Norman, OK, 2014); see also CG, Nos. 802 and 806, 1:516, 518; Dwyer, *Napoleon*, 334–338; Boycott-Brown, *Road to Rivoli*, 328–405.

By the end of July, the Austrians had regrouped and attempted to drive the French from Venetia. Field Marshal Dagobert Sigismund von Wurmser received the task of liberating Beaulieu's forces at Mantua. Attempting to envelop Bonaparte by marching south on both sides of Lake Garda, Wurmser's operational plan inhibited his army's effective coordination and communication.[135] Although Bonaparte dispersed his army across a front of nearly seventy-five miles to await the Austrians, he prepared to concentrate against them as soon as he discovered where they would attack. After the Austrian offensive commenced on 28 July, he grouped four divisions in the triangle formed by Lonato, Castiglione, and Solferino. As he had done in Piedmont, Bonaparte utilized the central position to defeat a divided opponent in detail. Victories against the two sections of the Austrian army at Lonato and Castiglione on 3 and 5 August demonstrated his mastery of the central position. Unlike Jourdan's passive defense of Charleroi at First and Second Fleurus, Bonaparte used Mantua to goad the Austrians to attack but responded with an active offensive operation against them.

Moreover, Bonaparte allowed his exhausted troops little rest and pursued the Austrians through the Brenner Pass. Masséna's division reached Trento on 5 September as scheduled. Wurmser marched southeast down the Brenta River valley to escape Bonaparte and to strategically outflank the French in eastern Venetia. The French commander maintained the pressure by boldly ordering Masséna and Augereau to chase the Austrians down the Brenta. On 8 September, the French caught and defeated Wurmser's Austrians at Bassano. Wurmser found himself enveloped and marched to the safety of Mantua, which he entered on the 13th.[136]

To be sure, the grueling pace of Napoleonic operations took a toll on the French. The Army of Italy had 14,000 sick and 4,000 wounded in hospital by September 1796. Nearly 10,000 troops did not participate in the campaign but remained at Mantua. Many of these troops, including Sérurier, contracted malaria, which spread rapidly in the river and swamps around the fortress. Only the divisions of Masséna and Augereau remained fit for mobile operations.[137] A lesser commander than Bonaparte would have acted with extreme caution in these circumstances. Yet Bonaparte responded with boldness and daring when the Hungarian field marshal, József Alvinczi de Borkerek, assembled another Austrian relief effort in November. Alvinczi planned to march west from

---

135 Rothenberg, *Napoleon's Great Adversaries*, 60; Chandler, *Campaigns of Napoleon*, 90–95.
136 CG, Nos. 815–816, 836, 838, 855–856, and 906, 1:524–525, 534–539, 546–547, 578–581; Boycott-Brown, *Road to Rivoli*, 345–360, 406–438; Chandler, *Campaigns of Napoleon*, 98–99.
137 Chandler, *Campaigns of Napoleon*, 100.

eastern Venetia with 29,000 troops while a smaller force outflanked Bonaparte from the Brenner Pass. Instead of concentrating to defend Mantua, Bonaparte ordered General Claude-Henri Belgrand de Vaubois's division to guard the Brenner Pass while Masséna and Augereau repulsed Alvinczi. Although he suffered his first defeat at the 12 November Battle of Caldiero, Bonaparte quickly recovered and ordered Masséna and Augereau to outflank Alvinczi's left flank by using the Adige River as a screen. Demonstrating the ultimate combination of daring, speed, and deception, Bonaparte's victory at the 15–17 November Battle of Arcola ended Alvinczi's second effort to relieve Mantua. Most important, the Austrians missed their best opportunity to defeat Bonaparte and possibly reverse the French gains in northern Italy.[138]

In January 1797, Bonaparte repulsed Alvinczi's third relief operation in another brilliant campaign. At this point, the Army of Italy contained approximately 35,000 troops in the field army while 8,500 men besieged 24,000 Austrians at Mantua.[139] As in previous phases of the campaign, Bonaparte initially dispersed his army in order to gain flexibility at the operational level. Alvinczi decided to command the attack down the Brenner Pass while General Giovanni Marchese di Provera assailed the French right flank from eastern Venetia. Bonaparte tasked General Barthélemy Catherine Joubert with defending Rivoli in the Brenner Pass while Augereau, Masséna, and General Louis Emmanuel Rey contained Provera. After realizing that Alvinczi's main attack was coming from the Brenner, Bonaparte reacted by sending Masséna, Augereau, Rey, and General Claude Victor-Perrin to support Joubert.

The maneuver at Rivoli constitutes the most impressive example of concentration at the decisive point during the First Italian Campaign. In addition to repulsing Alvinczi, Bonaparte sought to destroy Provera's Austrian relief force. Consequently, when Provera advanced toward Mantua, Bonaparte ordered Masséna's victorious troops to march from the field of Rivoli to assail him. Sérurier stopped Provera at La Favorita and Masséna attacked the Austrian right flank on 16 January 1797. Masséna's rapid march proved decisive because Wurmser attempted to break out of Mantua to assist Provera. After covering fifteen miles from Verona to Rivoli on the night of 13–14 January, Masséna advanced his division at 5:00 AM on the 15th for a thirty-mile march to La Favorita. Without Masséna's timely arrival on the 16th, Sérurier might have

---

138 CG, Nos. 1050, 1059, and 1060, 1:661, 664–667; Boycott-Brown, *Road to Rivoli*, 438–480.
139 The army reached this strength after the arrival of approximately 14,250 troops from Germany. See Boycott-Brown, *Road to Rivoli*, 488, 494.

been defeated and a large Austrian force would have threatened the rear of Bonaparte's army.[140]

Following Rivoli, the Austrians sent Archduke Charles to defend Austria proper from Bonaparte. Admittedly in an unenviable situation, Charles proved no match for his French counterpart. Bonaparte rapidly crossed the Alpine passes into Austria in early March. Although a long-time critic of the cordon defense, Charles failed to concentrate his forces against the French, allowing Masséna to defeat the Austrians piecemeal with the French advance guard. By 7 April, Charles recognized defeat and sought an armistice with the French, essentially bringing the War of the First Coalition to an end.[141]

The First Italian Campaign provides a textbook example of the new French operational art. Napoleon utilized the principles of war that he first encountered as a student, especially the ideas of Bourcet and Guibert. The Piedmont phase demonstrated Napoleon's mastery of the central position, speed, maneuver, mass, and economy of force. In the Lombard phase, Bonaparte added deception and surprise to his arsenal. Throughout the campaign in Venetia, he used a flexible operational approach to defend Mantua and destroy the Austrian army. More than any other revolutionary commander, Bonaparte internalized the ideas of the *ancien régime* military theorists so that the application of their concepts became nearly second-nature. Furthermore, he recognized the strengths of the military system that had emerged after the French Revolution. Understanding the French army's potential for speed and maneuver, Bonaparte utilized flanking attacks to force his opponents to give battle or retreat. Napoleon's success in war did not ultimately result from luck or from an innate ability to scramble, although he possessed a large quantity of both. Rather, he succeeded by committing to the new operational approach, sustained by the confidence he possessed in his own abilities and those of his troops.

Conclusion: Jean Victor Moreau in 1800

Although the French enjoyed an improved military system because of the post-Seven Years War reforms and the French Revolution's social and political changes, success and failure in war rested largely on the shoulders of those who commanded France's armies. None proved more adept in this new

---

140 Bonaparte called Masséna *"l'enfant chéri de la victoire"* for his accomplishments at Rivoli and La Favorita.
141 CG, Nos. 1287–1290, 1294, 1:785–787, 790; Rothenberg, *Napoleon's Great Adversaries*, 60–63.

system, especially at the operational level, than Bonaparte. Although he struggled a great deal during the invasion of Egypt of 1798–1799, he returned to form during the Second Italian Campaign of 1800.

Certainly, Bonaparte benefited from effective subordinates and the mistakes and misjudgements of his enemies throughout most of his career. Yet a comparison of his performance with those of his French contemporaries reveals the difference between his genius and their effectiveness. French generals such as Jourdan, Pichegru, Hoche, and Moreau could effectively employ the new operational art in the right circumstances; but only Bonaparte demonstrated its true mastery, even against unfavorable odds. The performance of Moreau during the campaign of 1800 demonstrates this final point quite clearly.

In 1800, Moreau probably commanded the best-organized and -supplied army ever fielded by a general of revolutionary France: the 108,000-man Army of the Rhine.[142] Although the winter of 1799–1800 and the neglect of the Directory brought suffering to the army, Bonaparte quickly repaired the situation after becoming First Consul and virtual dictator of France. By 31 January 1800, Moreau received as much as 6,200,000 francs to rehabilitate the army.[143] He faced the 96,000-man Austrian army of the Hungarian field marshal Krajovai és Topolyai, báró Kray Pál (better known as Paul Baron Kray von Krajova und Topola), on the right bank of the Rhine. The French possession of Switzerland provided Moreau with a strategic advantage over previous commanders in the various Rhine campaigns of the Revolutionary Wars. Yet he failed to exploit the opportunity provided by an incredibly strong army and strategic position. While the Austrians planned to take the initiative in the campaign by breaking through the French line at Belfort, Moreau spread his 108,000 troops in a cordon along the Rhine and slowly prepared for operations.[144]

In March, Bonaparte proposed that Moreau take the offensive on the Rhine as part of his strategy for the destruction of the Austrian army. The First Consul even directed him to organize his army into four corps. Bonaparte believed that Moreau could utilize these corps according to the principles of the French

---

142   The French army increased in size as a result of the Jourdan Law of 1798, which institutionalized annual conscription. See James R. Arnold, *Marengo and Hohenlinden: Napoleon's Rise to Power* (Barnsley, UK, 2004), 199–200. Frédéric Hulot in *Le général Moreau* (Paris, 2001), 60–61, depicts the army as poorly equipped but does not consider its strength relative to other French armies of the period. See also Ernest Picard, *Hohenlinden* (Paris, 1909).

143   CG, Nos. 4874 and 4915, 3:40–41, 60–61. According to Arnold, "Moreau's Army of the Rhine was in excellent condition. It had received first call on men, equipment, and munitions." See Arnold, *Marengo and Hohenlinden*, 199.

144   Arnold, *Marengo and Hohenlinden*, 200.

operational art.[145] In February, he sent his aide de camp, Colonel Géraud-Christophe-Michel Duroc, to Moreau's headquarters at Basel to ascertain the army's situation. Bonaparte utilized Duroc and the minister of war, Louis-Alexandre Berthier, to convey his strategic and operational plans to Moreau.[146] Accordingly, he advised Moreau to execute a *manoeuvre sur les derrières* against the Austrians by crossing the Rhine at Schaffhausen and advancing from Constance through the Black Forest. Bonaparte hoped that Kray would accept battle in order to defend his lines of operation, providing Moreau the opportunity to deliver a battle of annihilation against the main Austrian army. After achieving this decisive victory, Moreau could then advance on Vienna nearly unimpeded.[147]

Thus, Bonaparte's instructions to Moreau envisioned a decisive spring campaign resulting from an aggressive operation against the Austrians on the Rhine. Clearly, Bonaparte understood the new operational art and expected other French commanders to execute it effectively. However, Moreau failed to live up to the First Consul's expectations. Stressing his inability to secure passages over the Rhine, Moreau resisted Bonaparte's plan. Moreover, Moreau remained committed to maintaining supply lines and expressed his unwillingness to live off the land. Instead of executing a decisive strike through the Black Forest, Moreau desired to make a feint against Kray's right flank while performing a complicated maneuver on the left bank of the Rhine that would allow him to cross at Basel. Moreau even threatened to resign if Napoleon rejected his plan.[148]

For a variety of reasons, Bonaparte accepted Moreau's less aggressive plan and shifted his own focus to the Italian theater. Historians often cite a claim attributed to Bonaparte by Jomini: "I was not yet sufficiently firm in my position to come to an open rupture with a man who had numerous partisans in the army, and who only wanted the energy to attempt to put himself in my place. It was necessary to negotiate with him as a separate power, as indeed, at that time, he really was. I therefore left him the command of the finest army which France had seen for a long time, and allowed him to move upon the Danube at his pleasure."[149] Although Bonaparte's victory at the 14 June 1800 Battle of Marengo turned the war in France's favor, Moreau's unwillingness to

---

145 CG, Nos. 5032 and 5033, 3:113–114.
146 Ibid., No. 4991, 3:94.
147 In March, Bonaparte relied on General Jean-Joseph-Paul-Augustin Dessolles to communicate these views to Moreau. See ibid., no. 5110; 3:148, and Jomini, *Life of Napoleon*, trans. by H.W. Halleck (New York, 1864), 1:315.
148 Arnold, *Marengo and Hohenlinden*, 201.
149 Quoted in Jomini, *Life of Napoleon*, 1:315–316.

execute Napoleon's original campaign plan reduced French chances for achieving a decisive victory in the spring and summer of 1800. While he often addressed Moreau with pleasantries, Bonaparte did not remain silent concerning his opinion of the general's conduct between March and May. As he wrote to the new minister of war, Lazare Carnot, on 24 April: "Reiterate the order to General Moreau to attack the enemy. Make him feel that his delays compromise the security of the Republic." On the same day, he informed Moreau that "all delays will be extremely disastrous for us."[150] These statements attest to Bonaparte's frustration with Moreau's flawed operational approach.

During the first phase of the 1800 campaign in Germany, Moreau gained a few tactical victories against Kray's forces but never concentrated overwhelming mass at the decisive point of attack. Coincidentally, Moreau actually crossed the Rhine one day after Bonaparte wrote his letter of 24 April to express his frustrations with his slowness. On the 25th, Moreau commenced a diversion toward the Black Forest while the bulk of the Rhine Army maneuvered on the left bank around Basel. Instead of concentrating against Kray's extreme left flank at Constance, Moreau advanced from Basel to Schaffhausen with approximately 85,000 troops. Kray attempted to defend his supply base at Stockach with 12,000 men. Moreau only brought 20,000 troops to attack Stockach, which he captured on 3 May. The larger body of troops fought at Engen on the same day, which resulted in a draw in which both sides suffered approximately 7,000 casualties. On 5 May, Moreau pursued Kray to Möskirch and achieved an indecisive tactical victory despite outnumbering Kray's 40,000 Austrians with 50,000 French. Kray sought shelter for his army at Ulm, which Moreau refused to attack. Instead, the French marched around the Austrian lines of operation, attempting to entice Kray to give battle.[151] Curiously, Bonaparte praised Moreau for his victories at Stockach and Möskirch despite their lack of decisiveness.[152] Yet he continued to urge Moreau to act with greater boldness: "The success of the campaign depends on the speed with which you operate ... If you execute a swift movement, decisively, and with all determination, Italy and the peace will be ours."[153] In this instance, the First Consul demonstrated a desire to see his subordinates succeed. Moreau's failure to gain a decisive victory over Kray proved consequential: the Austrian army remained an effective force even after the armistice that ensued in July, forcing the

---

150   *CG*, Nos. 5195, 5197, 3:187–188.
151   These operations remain essentially unstudied. A brief account is provided in Arnold, *Marengo and Hohenlinden*, 201–203.
152   *CG*, No. 5245, 3:216.
153   Ibid., No. 5301, 3:240.

French to fight a subsequent campaign to conclude the War of the Second Coalition.[154]

Thus, the first half of the campaign of 1800 demonstrates the different operational approaches utilized by Bonaparte and Moreau. Nonetheless, Moreau deserves much credit for ultimately ending the war with Austria. In fact, Bonaparte allowed Moreau to continue command of the Army of the Rhine. The First Consul expected to end the war the following spring.[155] Moreau's victory at the 3 December Battle of Hohenlinden ranks as one of the most decisive of the French Revolutionary Wars. Yet the victory did not result from Moreau's utilization of the new operational art. In fact, the 100,000-man Austrian army under Archduke John took the initiative after the expiration of the Franco-Austrian armistice on 22 November. John outflanked Moreau's army in Bavaria and on 1 December defeated General Paul Grenier's division at Ampfing while taking heavy casualties.[156] Like Jourdan at Second Fleurus, Moreau defeated John at Hohenlinden with an initial defensive posture that he turned into an attack after the Austrian columns became disconnected while marching through a thickly wooded area. Although he utilized little operational art, Moreau demonstrated excellent flexibility at the tactical level. The Austrian army practically disintegrated after the battle from low morale and high casualties.

Despite his impressive victory, Moreau did not immediately pursue. In fact, he waited one week before authorizing any major advance against John's scattered forces while pursuing geographic objectives such as Salzburg. According to James R. Arnold, "[Moreau] showed himself to be a general more comfortable with the prior strategic era than with the new style of war the First Consul was perfecting."[157] However, after 8 December, the vulnerability of the Austrian army became so apparent that Moreau finally ordered a general pursuit, although he remained anxious concerning the Austrian fortresses along his lines of operation. Regardless, within fifteen days the Army of the Rhine marched 186 miles and camped 50 miles from Vienna. As in 1797, Archduke Charles received the task of defending the capital. The archduke considered his task hopeless and requested an armistice, which Moreau happily signed.[158]

---

154   A.B. Rodger, *The War of the Second Coalition, 1798 to 1801: A Strategic Commentary* (New York, 1964), 231–234.
155   Philip Dwyer, *Citizen Emperor: Napoleon in Power* (New Haven, CT, 2014), 63–65.
156   See Picard, *Hohenlinden*, and Arnold, *Marengo and Hohenlinden*, 217–221.
157   Arnold, *Marengo and Hohenlinden*, 256.
158   Much debate exists over Moreau's conduct after Hohenlinden. Dwyer, *Citizen Emperor*, 64, criticizes Moreau's march toward Vienna as "a leisurely pace by anyone's standards." Arnold, *Marengo and Hohenlinden*, 256, explains that Moreau's pursuit did not com-

Moreau's victory at Hohenlinden ended the War of the Second Coalition and ranks him as one of Revolutionary France's most effective generals. Nonetheless, his refusal to execute Bonaparte's far bolder plan in the spring campaign reveals a major difference between the two commanders in terms of the operational art. Moreau performed effectively in excellent circumstances whereas Bonaparte's First Italian Campaign demonstrated his capacity to achieve decisive victory against long odds. While both command styles proved capable of winning wars, Bonaparte's method clearly held greater potential.

In his 1772 *Essai générale de tactique*, Guibert suggested the need for a great man to emerge in order to make the new system of war function to perfection. Although Bonaparte suffered from numerous personal flaws, he possessed the talent and determination necessary to master the new operational art of the late 18th century. The operational art evolved in several stages between 1763 and 1800, reaching its peak under Bonaparte. Political beliefs and ambition committed Dumouriez to offensive operations. He never fully understood the new operational art. Carnot recognized the possibilities of the new approach but did not hold a position that allowed him to personally implement his designs. Instead, he urged a new class of determined generals to annihilate the enemy army through rigorous campaigns and maneuver. Bonaparte understood the new operational art even better than Carnot. Most important, he occupied a position that allowed him to master it in practice. Bonaparte's frustrated relationship with Moreau partly reflected the divergence in their respective military talents and their understanding of war. Throughout his career, the former showed his mastery of the late 18th-century operational art, even when his strategic and tactical skills failed him. If Bonaparte inherited a new way of war from the 18th century, it required his genius and skill to make it the dominant force in Europe.

Bibliography

Alder, Ken. *Engineering the Revolution: Arms and Enlightenment in France, 1763–1815.* Princeton, NJ, 2010.

Andress, David. *The Terror: The Merciless War for Freedom in Revolutionary France.* New York, 2005.

---

mence until 8 December. However, Moreau marched rapidly when he decided to pursue. According to Arnold, "He exhibited commendable flexibility by changing plans to take advantage of unexpected opportunity."

Anon. *Règlement concernant l'exercice et les manoeuvres de l'infanterie du 1er août 1791.* Paris, 1791.

Arnold, James R. *Marengo and Hohenlinden: Napoleon's Rise to Power.* Barnsley, UK, 2004.

Austro-Hungarian Monarchy. *Krieg gegen die Französische Revolution, 1792–1797*, 2 vols. Vienna, 1902.

Bell, David. *The First Total War: Napoleon's Europe and the Birth of Warfare as We Know It.* New York, 2007.

Bertaud, Jean-Paul. *The Army of the French Revolution: From Citizen-Soldiers to Instrument of Power*, trans. by R.R. Palmer. Princeton, NJ, 1988.

Bertaud, Jean-Paul. *Valmy: la démocratie en armes.* Paris, 1970.

Bertaud, Jean-Paul and Daniel Roche. *Atlas de la Révolution française: l'armée et la guerre.* Paris, 1989.

Best, Geoffrey. *War and Society in Revolutionary Europe, 1770–1870.* New York, 1982.

Bien, David. "The Army in the French Enlightenment: Reform, Reaction and Revolution." *Past & Present* 85 (1979), 68–98.

Biro, Sydney Seymour. *The German Policy of Revolutionary France: A Study in French Diplomacy during the War of the First Coalition, 1792–1797*, 2 vols. Cambridge, MA, 1957.

Black, Jeremy. *British Foreign Policy in an Age of Revolutions, 1783–1793.* New York, 1994.

Black, Jeremy. *European Warfare, 1660–1815.* New Haven, CT, 1994.

Black, Jeremy. *Rethinking Military History.* New York, 2004.

Blanning, T.C.W. *The French Revolution in Germany: Occupation and Resistance in the Rhineland, 1792–1802.* New York, 1983.

Blanning, T.C.W. *The French Revolutionary Wars, 1787–1802.* New York, 1996.

Blanning, T.C.W. *The Origins of the French Revolutionary Wars.* New York, 1986.

Blaufarb, Rafe. *The French Army, 1750–1820: Careers, Talent, Merit.* London, 2002.

Bois, Jean-Pierre. *Dumouriez: héros et proscrit.* Paris, 2005.

Bonura, Michael. "The '*Règlement provisoire sur le service de l'infanterie en campagne de 1792*': The Document that Provided the Armies of the French Revolution with the Intellectual Framework that allowed it to Dominate Europe for Two Decades." In John Severn and Frederick C. Schneid, eds, *Selected Papers of the Consortium on Revolutionary Europe, 2008.* High Point, NC, 2009.

Bonura, Michael. *Under the Shadow of Napoleon: French Influence on the American Way of War from the War of 1812 to the Outbreak of WWII.* New York, 2012.

Bordeau, H. *Les armées du Rhin au début du Directoire.* Paris, 1909.

Bourcet, Pierre-Joseph de. *Principes de la guerre de montagnes.* Paris, 1888.

Bouvier, Félix. *Bonaparte en Italie, 1796.* Paris, 1899.

Boycott-Brown, Martin. *The Road to Rivoli: Napoleon's First Campaign.* London, 2001.

Brissot, Jacques Pierre. *Discours prononcé par M. Brissot à l'assemblée des Amis de la Constitution le 10 juillet, 1791, ou Tableau frappant de la situation actuelle des puissances de l'Europe*. Paris, 1791.

Brissot, Jacques Pierre. *Le Patriote françois: journal libre, impartial et national, par un société de citoyens, et dirigé par J.P. Brissot de Warville*. Paris, 1792.

Broers, Michael. "The Concept of 'Total War' in the Revolutionary–Napoleonic Period." *War in History* 15, 3 (2008), 247–268.

Brown, Howard. "Politics, Professionalism, and the Fate of Army Generals After Thermidor." *French Historical Studies* 19, 1 (1995), 133–152.

Brown, Howard. *War, Revolution, and the Bureaucratic State: Politics and Army Administration in France, 1791–1799*. New York, 1995.

Candela, Gilles. *L'Armée d'Italie: des missionnaires armés à la naissance de la guerre napoléonienne*. Paris, 2011.

Cardoza, Thomas. *Intrepid Women: Cantinières and Vivandières of the French Army*. Bloomington, IN, 2010.

Chandler, David G. *The Campaigns of Napoleon: The Mind and Method of History's Greatest Soldier*. New York, 1966.

Charavay, Étienne. *Le général Lafayette, 1757–1834: notice biographique*. Paris, 1898.

Charles, Archduke. *Principes de la stratégie, développés par la relation de la campagne de 1796 en Allemagne*, 3 vols. Paris, 1818.

Chickering, Roger and Stig Förster, eds. *War in an Age of Revolution, 1775–1815*. New York, 2010.

Chuquet, Arthur. *Hoche et la lutte pour l'Alsace*. Paris, 1893.

Chuquet, Arthur. *Jemappes et la conquête de la Belgique (1792–1793)*. Paris, 1890.

Chuquet, Arthur. *La première invasion Prussienne (11 août–2 septembre 1792)*. Paris, 1886.

Chuquet, Arthur. *Wissembourg (1793)*. Paris, 1893.

Citino, Robert M. *Blitzkrieg to Desert Storm: The Evolution of Operational Warfare*. Lawrence, KS, 2004.

Clarke, Joseph. "'Valour Knows Neither Age Nor Sex': The *Recueil des Actions Héroïques* and the Representation of Courage in Revolutionary France." *War in History* 20, 1 (2013), 50–75.

Clausewitz, Carl von. *On War*. Ed. and trans. by Michael Howard and Peter Paret. Princeton, NJ, 1976.

Clerget, Claude. *Tableaux des armées françaises pendant les guerres de la révolution*. Paris, 1905.

Cole, Juan. *Napoleon's Egypt: Invading the Middle East*. New York, 2007.

Colin, Jean. *L'éducation militaire de Napoléon*. Paris, 1901.

Colin, Jean. *La tactique et la discipline dans les armées de la Révolution*. Paris, 1902.

Cuccia, Philip R. *Napoleon in Italy: The Sieges of Mantua, 1796–1799*. Norman, OK, 2014.

Desbrière, Édouard and Maurice Sautai. *La cavalerie pendant la Révolution: du 14 juillet au 26 juin 1794*. Paris, 1907.
Dhombres, Jean and Nicole Dhombres. *Lazare Carnot*. Paris, 1997.
D'Huart, Suzanne. *Brissot: la Gironde au pouvoir*. Paris, 1999.
Duffy, Christopher. *Eagles over the Alps: Suvorov in Italy and Switzerland, 1799*. New York, 1999.
Duffy, Christopher. *Russia's Military Way to the West: Origins and Nature of Russian Military Power, 1700–1800*. London, 1981.
Dupuis, Victor. *La campagne de 1793 à l'armée du Nord et des Ardennes*, 2 vols. Paris, 1906.
Dupuis, Victor. *Les opérations militaires sur la Sambre en 1794: Bataille de Fleurus*. Paris, 1905.
Dwyer, Philip. *Citizen Emperor: Napoleon in Power*. New Haven, CT, 2014.
Dwyer, Philip. *Napoleon: The Path to Power*. New Haven, CT, 2007.
Eloise, Ellery. *Brissot de Warville: A Study in the History of the French Revolution*. New York, 1915.
Eysturlid, Lee. *The Formative Influences, Theories, and Campaigns of the Archduke Carl of Austria*. Westport, CT, 2000.
Forrest, Alan. *Conscripts and Deserters: The Army and French Society during the Revolution and Empire*. New York, 1989.
Forrest, Alan. *The Legacy of the French Revolutionary Wars: The Nation-in-Arms in French Republican Memory*. New York, 2009.
Forrest, Alan. "The Logistics of Revolutionary War in France." In Roger Chickering and Stig Förster, eds, *War in an Age of Revolution, 1775–1815*. New York, 2010.
Forrest, Alan. *Napoleon's Men: The Soldiers of the Revolution and Empire*. London, 2002.
Forrest, Alan. *Soldiers of the French Revolution*. Durham, NC, 1990.
Foucart, Paul and Jules Finot. *La défense nationale dans le nord de 1792 à 1802*. 2 vols. Lille, 1890.
Germani, Ian. "Military Justice Under the Directory: The Armies of Italy and of the Sambre and Meuse." *French History* 23, 1 (2009), 47–68.
Germani, Ian. "Reports from the Front: The Representation of Military Events in the Parisian Press, 1792–1793." In *Selected Papers of the Consortium on Revolutionary Europe, 1994*, 44–57. Tallahassee, FL, 1994.
Germani, Ian. "Terror in the Army: Representatives on Mission and Military Discipline in the Armies of the French Revolution." *Journal of Military History* 75, 3 (2011), 733–768.
Griffith, Paddy. *The Art of War of Revolutionary France, 1789–1802*. London, 1998.
Guibert, Jacques-Antoine-Hippolyte. *Essai générale de tactique*. Liège, 1773.
Guiomar, Jean-Yves. *L'invention de la guerre totale, XVIIIe–XXe siècle*. Paris, 2004.

Hayworth, Jordan R. "Evolution or Revolution on the Battlefield? The Army of the Sambre and Meuse in 1794." *War in History* 21, 2 (2014), 170–192.

Heuser, Beatrice. *The Evolution of Strategy: Thinking War from Antiquity to the Present.* New York, 2010.

Heuser, Beatrice. "Guibert: Prophet of Total War?" In Roger Chickering and Stig Förster, eds, *War in an Age of Revolution, 1775–1815.* New York, 2010.

Hippler, Thomas. *Citizens, Soldiers and National Armies: Military Service in France and Germany, 1789–1830.* London, 2008.

Howe, Patricia Chastain. "Charles-François Dumouriez and the Revolutionizing of French Foreign Affairs in 1792." *French Historical Studies* (1986), 367–390.

Howe, Patricia Chastain. *Foreign Policy and the French Revolution: Charles-François Dumouriez, Pierre Lebrun, and the Belgian Plan, 1789–1793.* New York, 2008.

Hulot, Frédéric. *Le général Moreau.* Paris, 2001.

Hulot, Frédéric. *Le maréchal Jourdan.* Paris, 2010.

Hyatt, A.M.J. "The Origins of Napoleonic Warfare: A Survey of Interpretations." *Military Affairs* (1966), 177–185.

Jomini, Antoine-Henri. *Histoire critique et militaire des guerres de la Révolution*, 15 vols. Paris, 1820–1824.

Jomini, Antoine-Henri. *Life of Napoleon*, trans. by H.W. Halleck. New York, 1864.

Jordan, David P. *The King's Trial: Louis XVI vs. the French Revolution.* Berkeley, CA, 2004.

Jouan, Louis. *La campagne de 1794–1795 dans les Pays-Bas.* Paris, 1915.

Jourdan, Jean-Baptiste. *Mémoires pour servir à l'histoire de la campagne de 1796.* Paris, 1818.

Jourdan, Jean-Baptiste. *Opérations de l'armée du Danube.* Paris, 1799.

Jung, Théodore. *Dubois-Crancé (Edmond-Alexis-Louis): mousqeutaire, constituent, conventionnel, général de division, ministre de la guerre.* Paris, 1884.

Knox, Macgregor. "Mass Politics and Nationalism as Military Revolution: The French Revolution and After." In Macgregor Knox and Williamson Murray, eds, *The Dynamics of Military Revolution, 1300–2050,* 57–73. New York, 2001.

Latreille, Albert. *L'oeuvre militaire de la révolution: l'armée et la nation à la fin de l'ancien régime.* Paris, 1914.

Lauerma, Matti. *L'artillerie de campagne française pendant les guerres de la Révolution.* Helsinki, 1956.

Lawday, David. *The Giant of the French Revolution: Danton, A Life.* New York, 2009.

Leggiere, Michael V. *Blücher: Scourge of Napoleon.* Norman, OK, 2014.

Lord, Robert Howard. *The Second Partition of Poland: A Study in Diplomatic History.* Cambridge, MA, 1915.

Lynn, John. *Battle: A History of Combat and Culture.* New York, 2003.

Lynn, John. *The Bayonets of the Republic: Motivation and Tactics in the Army of Revolutionary France, 1791–1794.* Boulder, CO, 1996.

Lynn, John. "En avant! The Origins of the Revolutionary Attack." In John Lynn, ed., *Tools of War: Instruments, Ideas and Institutions of Warfare, 1445–1871*. Urbana, IL, 1990.

Lynn, John. "French Opinion and the Military Resurrection of the Pike, 1792–1794." *Military Affairs* 41, 1 (1977), 1–7.

Lynn, John. "Toward and Army of Honor: The Moral Evolution of the French Army, 1789–1815." *French Historical Studies* 16, 1 (1989): 152–173.

McPhee, Peter. *Robespierre: A Revolutionary Life*. New Haven, CT, 2013.

Moran, D. and A. Waldron, eds. *The People in Arms: Military Myth and National Mobilization Since the French Revolution*. New York, 2003.

Mori, Jennifer. *William Pitt and the French Revolution, 1785–1795*. London, 1997.

Osman, Julia. *Citizen Soldiers and the Key to the Bastille*. New York, 2015.

Ozouf, Mona. "War and Terror in French Revolutionary Discourse." *Journal of Modern History* 56 (1984), 579–597.

Palmer, R.R. *The Age of the Democratic Revolution: A Political History of Europe and America, 1760–1800*, 2 vols. Princeton, NJ, 1959–1964.

Palmer, R.R. "Frederick the Great, Guibert, Bülow: From Dynastic to National War." In Peter Paret, ed., *Makers of Modern Strategy: From Machiavelli to the Nuclear Age*. Princeton, NJ, 1986.

Palmer, R.R. ed. *Makers of Modern Strategy: From Machiavelli to the Nuclear Age*. Princeton, NJ, 1986.

Palmer, R.R. *Twelve Who Ruled: The Year of Terror in the French Revolution*. Princeton, NJ, 1941.

Phipps, Ramsey Weston. *The Armies of the First French Republic and the Rise of the Marshals of Napoleon I*, 5 vols. London, 1929–1934.

Picard, Ernest. *Hohenlinden*. Paris, 1909.

Pingaud, Léonce. *L'invasion Austro-Prussienne (1792–1794)*. Paris, 1895.

Planert, Ute. "Innovation or Evolution? The French Wars in Military History." In Roger Chickering and Stig Förster, eds, *War in an Age of Revolution, 1775–1815*. New York, 2010.

Quimby, Robert S. *The Background of Napoleonic Warfare: The Theory of Military Tactics in Eighteenth-Century France*. New York, 1957.

Reinhard, Marcel. *La Grande Carnot*, 2 vols. Paris, 1952.

Rodger, A.B. *The War of the Second Coalition, 1798 to 1801: A Strategic Commentary*. New York, 1964.

Roider, Karl. *Baron Thugut and Austria's Response to the French Revolution*. Princeton, NJ, 1987.

Ross, Steven T. "The Development of the Combat Division in Eighteenth-Century French Armies." *French Historical Studies* 4, 1 (1965).

Ross, Steven T. *Quest for Victory: French Military Strategy, 1792–1799*. New York, 1973.

Rothenberg, Gunther E. *The Art of Warfare in the Age of Napoleon*. Bloomington, IN: Indiana University Press, 1978.

Rousset, Camille. *Les volontaires, 1791–1794*. Paris, 1870.

Saxe, Maurice de. *Reveries, or, Memoirs Concerning the Art of War*. Edinburgh, 1759.

Schroeder, Paul. *The Transformation of European Politics*. New York, 1994.

Scott, Samuel F. *From Yorktown to Valmy: The Transformation of the French Army in the Age of Revolution*. Niwot, CO, 1998.

Scott, Samuel F. *The Response of the Royal Army to the French Revolution: The Role and Development of the Line Army, 1787–1793*. New York, 1978.

Sécher, Reynald. *A French Genocide: La Vendée*, trans. by George Holoch. Notre Dame, IN, 2003.

Servan, Joseph. *Le soldat-citoyen, ou vues patriotiques sur la manière la plus avantageuse de pourvoir à la défense du royaume*. Neufchatel, 1780.

Soboul, Albert. *Les soldats de l'an II*. Paris, 1959.

Starkey, Armstrong. *War in the Age of Enlightenment, 1700–1789*. Westport, CT, 2003.

Strachan, Hew. *European Armies and the Conduct of War*. New York, 2004.

Strathern, Paul. *Napoleon in Egypt*. New York, 2007.

Sybel, Heinrich von. *History of the French Revolution*, 4 vols, trans. by Walter C. Perry. London, 1867.

Tackett, Timothy. *The Coming of the Terror in the French Revolution*. Cambridge, MA, 2015.

Tackett, Timothy. *When the King Took Flight*. Cambridge, MA, 2003.

Telp, Claus. *The Evolution of Operational Art, 1740–1813: From Frederick the Great to Napoleon*. New York, 2005.

Thiry, Louis. *Après Fleurus: la Bataille de Sprimont (18 septembre 1794)*. Brussels, 1936.

Thoral, Marie-Cécile. *From Valmy to Waterloo: France at War, 1792–1815*, trans. by Godfrey Rogers. New York, 2011.

Vivenot, Alfred Ritter von. *Thugut, Clerfayt, und Wurmser*. Vienna, 1869.

Vivenot, Alfred Ritter von and Heinrich Ritter von Zeissberg. *Quellen zur Geschichte des deutschen Kaiserpolitik Oesterreichs während der Französischen Revolutionskriege, 1790–1801*. Vienna, 1882.

Vovelle, Michelle. *The Fall of the French Monarchy, 1787–1792*, trans. by Susan Burke. New York, 1984.

Wawro, Geoffrey. *Warfare and Society in Europe, 1792–1914*. New York, 2000.

Weigley, Russell S. *The Age of Battles: The Quest for Decisive Warfare from Breitenfeld to Waterloo*. Bloomington, IN, 1991.

Wetzler, Peter. *War and Subsistence: The Sambre and Meuse Army in 1794*. New York, 1985.

Witzleben, Alfred von. *Prinz Friedrich Josias von Coburg-Saalfeld, Herzog zu Sachsen*, 2 vols. Berlin, 1859.

Woloch, Isser. *The French Veteran: From the Revolution to the Restoration*. Chapel Hill, NC, 1979.

Woronoff, Denis. *The Thermidorean Regime and the Directory, 1794–1799*, trans. by Julian Jackson. New York, 1984.

CHAPTER 3

The Campaign against Piedmont-Sardinia, April 1796

Frederick C. Schneid

The most astounding aspect of Napoleon's campaign in 1796 was not the speed and decisiveness of his operations, but their scope and depth. To be sure, "scope and depth" refer to the parameters initially placed on the young general and, second, the distances covered in his operations over a course of eight weeks. The orders Lazare Carnot issued to Napoleon in anticipation of the forthcoming campaign were well defined in their short- and long-term objectives. They clearly established operational goals within the larger strategic plan: first the defeat of Piedmont-Sardinia and then the advance south of the Po River. In extent and detail, Carnot's orders to Bonaparte indicate a serious expectation that a decisive campaign could be waged in the Italian theater of war in 1796. The question that arises, however, is why was the Directory so confident that the next campaign in Italy would be decisive?

France's military situation in Italy did not engender bravado, and all previous military directives for that theater between 1793 and 1795 had been limited in scope. Forces that had previously served in Spain provided valuable reinforcements for all French armies, although only a very small percentage went to Italy. Thus, the expectation that a decisive stroke would be delivered in Italy in 1796 derived from the erosion of the First Coalition, the changing diplomatic climate, and the prospect that Piedmont-Sardinia could be forced from the war. This confidence stemmed from the awareness of the severely strained relationship between Turin and Vienna. Carnot therefore designed operations and Napoleon conducted them to achieve victory as quickly as possible.

On the same day that the Directory accepted General Schérer's letter of resignation as commander of the Army of Italy, they dispatched instructions to his replacement, General Napoleon Bonaparte.[1] These orders reflected the

---

1 A. Debidour, *Recueil des actes du Directoire Exécutif, Procès-verbaux, arrêtés, Instruction, Lettres et actes divers, Instructions pour le général en chef de l'Armée d'Italie*, 2 vols (Paris, 1911), 1:718–719. The *Instructions pour le général en chef de l'Armée d'Italie* appear in edited form in Léonce Krebs and Henri Moris, *Les campagnes dans les Alpes pendant la Révolution*, vol. 2, *1794, 1795, 1796* (Paris, 1895), the classic comprehensive work on the war in Italy, but are reprinted in full in *Recueil des actes du Directoire Exécutif*. The version in *Campagnes dans les Alpes* includes

Directory's clear understanding of the broader context of Piedmontese politics. The French understood that they had forced the war on Piedmont by their 1792 invasion, which in turn prompted the House of Savoy to join a coalition consisting of Austria, Prussia, Britain, Spain, Naples, and the Holy Roman Empire. They also recognized that, despite this wartime necessity, the relationship between Piedmont and Austria was strained. This, however, was not a new situation for Piedmont, but an essential part of its historic role as a buffer between Austria and France. Consequently, by 1796, the French government believed that, if Piedmont could be politically and militarily separated from its recent dependency on Austria, King Victor Amadeus III would be willing to withdraw from the Coalition.

Carnot provided unambiguous instructions on how to cleave Victor Amadeus from his Habsburg alliance. Piedmont-Sardinia could be compensated, he explained, with the Milanese (Austrian Lombardy). Previous French governments before and during the current war made similar proposals.[2] Furthermore, the Directory would offer Victor Amadeus an offensive–defensive alliance against Austria. Carnot intended for Napoleon to "chase" the Austrians from Italy, which would enable Piedmont to safely annex Lombardy.[3] On this final point, Carnot made it clear that the Directory would not accept the simple neutrality of Piedmont, but would demand an active alliance against Austria. In this regard, the Directory had already achieved success when Spain signed the Peace of Basel on 22 July 1795. According to its stipulations, Spain not only withdrew from the First Coalition, but entertained negotiations to establish a military alliance with France. The broader context of Directoral foreign policy therefore called not only for the defeat of Coalition powers, but also the turning of their former enemies against the two main powers they understood as existential threats: Britain and Austria.

Military planning should reflect the strategic and foreign policy goals of a state, and this was the case in Italy. To achieve their ends, the French deployed two armies: the Army of the Alps and the Army of Italy on the Piedmontese frontier. The latter was subordinate to the former, and was smaller in manpower. The Army of Italy provided a supporting role in the Italian theater from 1793 to 1795. Thereafter, its commanders and their respective orders reflected a growing independence of action from the Army of the Alps. This changing relationship reflected limited strategic opportunities until 1795 when the

---

only the military operations, not the first part of the *Instructions*, which provide the diplomatic and strategic context of the operations. See Appendices I and II to this chapter.
2   The first similar offer was made in the Treaty of 1697 between Louis XIV and Victor Amadeus II.
3   Debidour, *Instructions pour le général en chef de l'Armée d'Italie*, 1:719.

Genoese Republic reluctantly permitted the French access to their territory. The operational objectives for the Army of Italy in the years preceding Bonaparte's campaign were merely incremental in scope.

In 1793, the operations focused on pressing the Alpine passes and seizing control of the Piedmontese forts guarding them. The attainment of these objectives would permit the French to conduct a campaign into Piedmont the following year. Nevertheless, the limited extent of the 1793 operations was a function of the need for expanded operations in Germany, the Austrian Netherlands, and Spain. Furthermore, the outbreak of civil war in the form of the Federalist Revolt at Lyons, Toulon, and Marseille drew troops away from the Italian theater at that time.[4]

Strategy in the Italian theater in 1794 was governed by two sets of war plans, one issued in January, and the other after the Thermidorean Reaction in July. Both sets of orders remained narrow in objective, but reflected a changing geopolitical reality in Italy. The January *Instructions* considered opportunities by both the armies of the Alps and Italy. Although a successful seizure of Piedmontese fortifications northwest of the city was possible, it would only place the French army before the fortifications of Susa, west of Turin. Thus, only after a successful siege of Susa could the French advance on the Piedmontese capital. An approach from the north via the Little and Great Saint Bernard Passes would enable the French army to move directly on Turin, but the French war ministry concluded that an offensive by the Army of Italy along the Riviera offered better prospects.[5] An advance into neutral Genoa combined with the capture of Oneglia would provide the French army in the Alpes Maritime – the Army of Italy – the opportunity to strike north via the Col de Tende and down the Tanaro River. By controlling these passes in the Ligurian Alps, the French could move against the fortress of Coni, which defended the southwestern approaches to Turin. Furthermore, Carnot believed that "the taking of Oneglia would also provide us with the advantage that the Republic of Genoa would probably decide in our favor."[6]

---

4 François Christophe de Kellermann, commanding the Army of the Alps, and Gaspard Jean-Baptiste de Brunet, commanding the Army of Italy, conducted a defensive campaign for much of the year due to the extraordinary demands of the civil war. Operational orders were therefore quite limited, and very little direction was provided by Paris. See Virgilio Ilari, Piero Crociani, and Ciro Paoletti, *La guerra delle Alpi (1792–1796)* (Rome, 2000), chs. IV and V.

5 Krebs and Moris, *Campagnes dans les Alpes*, 1, *Pièces justificatives* 216, "Extrait du système générales operations militaries de la campagne prochaine par Carnot, le 11 pluv., an II de la Rép."

6 Ibid.; Charavay, *Correspondance générale de Carnot*, 4:281, "Système general des opérations militaires de la campagne prochaine," 2 February 1794.

Following the capture of Oneglia in the spring of 1794, Carnot issued new orders in June for the advance on Coni, Demont, and Ceva. The latter was the easternmost fortress guarding the southern approaches to Turin. The presence of the Army of Italy along the Ligurian coast permitted a broader offensive against Piedmont. As the artillery commander, Napoleon was present with the army at this time. The Army of Italy was able to conduct a second campaign late in the year, advancing along the Savona–Carcare–Dego line, which was the same line of advance Napoleon would utilize in 1796.[7] The campaign failed as a consequence of a Piedmontese counteroffensive in the Bormida valley.

In 1795, Schérer's operations focused again on the Savona–Carcare–Dego axis. The *Instructions* of 1795 remained focused on the defeat of Piedmont by seizing the fortress of Ceva. The last line of the *Instructions* mentioned, almost as an afterthought, that if Piedmont were defeated the campaign would progress into Lombardy.[8] No further elaboration was given for this brief comment. Schérer's army enjoyed a great familiarity with the few roads, trails, mule tracks, and paths that bisected the mountains dividing Genoa and Piedmont. Yet an Austrian counteroffensive and a severe lack of supply undermined the French campaign and threw Schérer back. Only a hard-won victory at Loano in November saved the French position on the Ligurian coast.

A month following these events, Schérer presented the Directory with a rather cautious and unimpressive plan for 1796. He argued that the Army of Italy required more troops. His current strength of merely 19,000 men was insufficient for combat operations. The remainder of his forces guarded the various mountain passes. He proffered that, with an army of 60,000, he could move against the Piedmontese and Austrians respectively at Ceva and Cairo. A victory would then force the Allies to withdraw on Mondovi and Alessandria, thereby awarding the French control of much of the right bank of the Po.[9] Here in Schérer's plans we first see a significant discussion of the potential for operations, but *only* if the army received substantial reinforcements, and *only* after

---

7 Krebs and Moris, *Campagnes dans les Alpes*, 1, *Pièces justificatives*, 286, "Copie de l'arrêté du comité de Salut public de la Convention national, du 15 messidor, l'an II de la Republique Française, une et indivisible." For the orders issued at the end of August, see *Les représentants du peuple prés l'armée d'Italie, 26 August 1794*, 1, *Piéces justificatives*, 295–296; and a month later on 24 September 1794, *Les représentants du peuple prés l'armée d'Italie aux représentants du people composant le comité de Salut public de la Convention nationale*, 1, *Piéces justificatives*, 298–299.

8 Napoleon I, *Correspondance de Napoleon I* (hereafter referred to as CN) (Paris, 1858), No. 52, *Instruction militaire pour le général en chef de l'armée d'Italie*, 1:71–75.

9 Schérer's Plan can be found in *Mémoire au Directoire Exécutif*, 3 February 1796, in Krebs and Moris, *Campagnes dans les Alpes*, 1, *Pièces justificatives*, 358–364.

Ceva was taken. As is well known, this was not to be, and Schérer resigned from command, making room for Bonaparte.

All of this provides the context for 1796, but in French planning alone; there is little that offers insight to the question of why Carnot and Napoleon believed they could achieve a decisive blow in Italy. Events at the court of Turin, however, provide significant evidence. After war was forced on Piedmont in 1792, Victor Amadeus sought Austrian assistance to defend the Alpine gates. Baron Johann Amadeus Franz de Paula Thugut, the Austrian chancellor, had little inclination to extend Vienna's military commitments, particularly as the main theaters had been the Austrian Netherlands and the Rhine. After several months of negotiations, Thugut agreed to a military alliance, but with the clear stipulation that Austro-Piedmontese forces would serve under a Habsburg commander. Although Victor Amadeus remained commander in chief of the Piedmontese army, a Habsburg commander would direct the field army.[10] *Feldmarschall-Leutnant* Josef Nikolaus de Vins initially received command of the Austro-Piedmontese army, but in 1793 was replaced by Baron Michaelangelo Alessandro Colli, who remained in that position through 1796.[11] By 1794, Coalition forces in Piedmont included the Austro-Piedmontese army under Colli, an Austrian auxiliary corps – actually no more than a brigade – under General Provera, and the Austrian army based in Lombardy.[12] The operations of the Austrian and Austro-Piedmontese armies from 1794 to 1796 were coordinated between the courts of Vienna and Turin in a rather vague sense, but specifically directed by two Habsburg generals.

The dynamic of this uneasy military alliance revealed a palpable Piedmontese lack of trust based on historical memory. Throughout the War of the First Coalition, Victor Amadeus reflected upon past wars when Piedmont had found itself caught between French ambitions and Austrian intransigence. Although the last significant event had occurred during the War of Austrian Succession (1740–1748), references to the Wars of Louis XIV seemed more applicable to the current situation. During the Nine Years War (1689–1698) and the War of the Spanish Succession (1701–1714), Piedmont had had to balance the real and perceived intentions of Austria and France. More than once the kingdom considered changing sides, and in fact eventually did.[13] History appeared

---

10   Ilari et. al., *La guerra delle Alpi*, 43. The agreement was made on 21 December 1792.
11   Ibid.
12   Ibid.
13   Joseph-Henri Costa de Beauregard, *Mémoires historiques sur la maison royale de Savoie* (Turin, 1816), 3:369. See Ciro Paoletti, *Dal ducato all'unità: tre secoli e mezzo di storia militare piemontese* (Rome, 2011), chs. XXII and XXIII, for the intricacies of Piedmontese foreign policy during these wars.

to be repeating itself when, in the wake of the 1795 Peace of Basel, the Grand Duchy of Tuscany and the Republic of Venice entered into negotiations with France. Victor Amadeus worried that both the Kingdom of Naples and Austria were also secretly negotiating with the French. If true, this would leave Piedmont isolated.[14]

The Peace of Basel completely altered the nature and direction of the War of the First Coalition. As noted, Spain took advantage of the peace, by signing on to the treaty ending their conflict with France. Indeed, the Spanish pledged diplomatic assistance in mediating between France and the states of Italy. In particular, the Spanish Bourbons offered to employ their dynastic ties with the Neapolitan Bourbons and Duke Ferdinand of Parma. They also had a great deal of influence with the papacy. Although the French did not take full advantage of Madrid's diplomatic clout until 1796, the end of the war with Spain provided France with troops that were redeployed to the German and Italian fronts, and diplomatic support from a state that had enormous influence in the Italian peninsula.[15]

By the end of 1795, Victor Amadeus was contending with two court factions: one supported the continuation of the conflict against Revolutionary France, and the other advocated peace. The changing face of the First Coalition created opportunity for Piedmont to actively negotiate with France. Negotiations were not so simple, as Piedmont's alliance with Austria meant that withdrawing from the Coalition would be more complicated than simply ending the war with France. The Directory was clearly amenable to reasonable settlements, when compared to its predecessor, the Committee of Public Safety. Although French and Piedmontese agents conducted secret negotiations for years prior, the current talks were inaugurated by the French. During the summer of 1795, the Spanish – as per their treaty requirements – offered to mediate between France and Piedmont. Victor Amadeus initially refused, but decided to return to the table in late autumn 1795.

Prior to the French victory at Loano, Victor Amadeus sent the French ambassador at Genoa, Jean-Baptiste Dorothée Villars, a set of demands that served as the foundation of a Franco-Piedmontese treaty. This diplomatic initiative came at a time when the Coalition had thrown the Army of Italy back onto the Riviera, and was rolling it up along the coast. The favorable situation permitted Victor Amadeus to negotiate. Yet the subsequent defeat of the Austrians at

---

14 Domenico Carutti, *Le corte di Savoia durante le rivoluzione e l'impero francese* (Turin, 1888), 1:289–293.

15 Spain signed on to the Peace of Basel, 22 July 1795. The treaty and its articles can be found in full in M. de Clerq, *Recueil des traités de la France*, 10 vols (Paris, 1880), 1:245–249.

Loano on 23 November and their precipitous retreat eliminated any Piedmontese leverage but by no means their desire to seek terms.[16]

Victor Amadeus's four conditions were quite important, because they represented the baseline for a settlement. These terms indicated the general parameters of a lasting peace:

1. That the king wants a final peace, and not one changing sides that would prolong and aggravate the horrors of the war.
2. That His Majesty wants a peace that is favorable and at the same time assured.
3. That His Majesty rejects with indignation the proposals that are made to him and that would wound his honor and his interests.
4. He is, however, always disposed to discuss terms which are fair and equitable.[17]

The king viewed Prussian neutrality as the model and greatly desired similar guarantees. Joseph-François-Jerôme Perret d'Hauteville, the foreign minister of Piedmont, appointed Count Charles-François Thaon de Revel to conduct the negotiations with the French. Heated talks followed between the respective agents over the next several months. Victor Amadeus's specific demands included the return of French-occupied Nice and Savoy, a suspension of arms, and the neutrality of Piedmont based on the Prussian model, meaning no permission of transit for French troops to reach Lombardy.[18]

The French response, which arrived on 17 December 1795, countered that an armistice was possible only if the French had permission to transit through Piedmont to Lombardy; that the neutrality of Piedmont would be respected; that the process would follow the Prussian model in regard to the separation of forces, to prevent issues when the French marched on Lombardy; and, lastly, that Nice and Savoy would be left in the temporary possession of France. Certainly, the first and fourth points were unacceptable, and a counteroffer was sent. Negotiations continued through January 1796.[19]

Victor Amadeus was frustrated with Austrian performance in the wake of Loano. Not only had the Coalition offensive failed, but the French had also

---

16   Carutti, *Le corte di Savoia*, 307–308. French and Piedmontese agents regularly exchanged diplomatic notes through the course of 1795. The difference with the November note, however, is that the Piedmontese initiated it.
17   Ignace Thaon de Revel, *Mémoires sur la guerre des Alpes et les évenéments en Piémont pendant la Révolution française* (Turin, 1871), 317.
18   Carutti, *Le corte di Savoia*, 307–308.
19   Ibid., 308.

managed to reclaim their former positions and push their forward posts into the Apennine passes. Indeed, he believed that the Austrian commanders, particularly Vins, were incompetent. By January, the king was angered by hollow Austrian promises of reinforcements. Victor Amadeus informed Francis II of his negotiations with the French, but vowed that, if these talks failed, he would take personal command of the Allied armies in order to instill greater energy and direction. His ire stemmed from news of an armistice on the Rhine, and he feared that this might be a precursor to Austrian negotiations with France.[20] He further demanded that the Austrians commit themselves seriously to the defense of Piedmont and not simply to protecting the route to Lombardy. Without a greater Austrian commitment, he stressed, the Piedmontese could not trust the Austrians. Thaon de Revel remarked, "They [the Viennese court] always spoke of battalions *en marche* from Germany to Italy, but nothing ever arrived."[21]

For their part, Francis and Thugut feared Piedmont would withdraw from the Coalition as had Prussia and Spain. The campaign on the Rhine ended in 1795 with an Austrian-sponsored truce, and Thugut did not trust the Prussians after they moved large forces into Poland. With troops to spare for Italy, Francis ordered a paltry five battalions as a pledge of continued support for his only substantive ally on the European continent.[22] Victor Amadeus's concerns about the performance of Habsburg generals led to the shuffling in Austrian command, and the eventual appointment of the seventy-year-old

---

20   Ludovic Sciot, *Le Directoire* (Paris, 1895), 1:620; Heinrich von Sybel, *Geschichte der Revolutionszeit von 1789 bis 1800* (Düsseldorf, 1870), 4:147, cites a letter from Thugut to Count Ludwig von Cobenzl, 20 January 1796, in which Thugut discusses a letter received from Victor Amadeus relating to the armistice and the king's threats. Sciot referred to Sybel on this issue, but mistranslated the passage. Sciot stated that Victor Amadeus informed Thugut that Piedmont had signed an armistice with France and was in the process of negotiations. In fact, Sybel says that Victor Amadeus informed the Austrians that he was seeking peace because of the Austrian armistice.

21   The issue of war with Austria if Piedmont accepted Lombardy was raised as early as 1795, prior to the events of Loano. See Carlo Botta, *Storia d'Italia dal 1789 al 1814* (n.d., 1824), 1, Book V, 326; quote in Thaon de Revel, *Mémoires sur la guerre*, 321. Botta, like Revel, was a contemporary to events. He too stressed the difficult situation of the court of Turin.

22   Alfred von Vivenot, *Thugut, Clerfayt und Wurmser*, Francis to Wallis, 19 January 1796, 417. Sciot states that Thugut could not send more men because of concerns on the Rhine and in Poland: Sciot, *Directoire*, 620–621, n. 1. By January 1796, Austria and Britain were the two remaining European powers in the Coalition. Catherine the Great was on the verge of committing Russia. In Italy, only Piedmont and Naples fought for the Coalition, and few Neapolitan troops had made their way to the north Italian front. In Germany, only great pressure from Austria kept the South German princes in the Coalition.

Feldzeugmeister Beaulieu in March 1796.[23] Nevertheless, the Piedmontese continued their negotiations with France.

By the middle of January, the French had increased their demands. In addition to those points presented in December, they wanted the king to unite his army with those of France or grant passage to the French. Piedmont also would open the cities of Susa, Alessandria, and Tortona along the route to Lombardy and furnish supplies for the French army.[24] The king, however, had little reason to believe that the French would be in a position to offer Lombardy as compensation for Nice and Savoy. Moreover, the request for a suspension of arms accompanied by French troops in transit through Piedmont to Lombardy would neither guarantee the integrity of the kingdom, nor be seen favorably by the Austrians. Victor Amadeus wanted an honorable peace that eventually would include a separate peace, the neutralization of the Italian theater, and an eventual end to the general conflict.[25]

French representatives tried to threaten the king with imminent revolution if he did not conclude a peace.[26] This threat effectively ended negotiations as Victor Amadeus would not brook such disrespect and intimidation. In any event, the loss of Nice and Savoy remained a sticking point, and the French offer to exchange those territories for Lombardy was a nonstarter. First, it would win the eternal enmity of Austria and, second, Victor Amadeus was all too aware of the history of empty French promises regarding Habsburg Lombardy, dating back to the Wars of Louis XIV.

The Piedmontese ambassador at Vienna demanded promises from the Austrians that imperial forces would not merely guard the road to Lombardy, but do a better job defending Piedmont from French invasion. Francis replied in the affirmative, and backed his words with the appointment of Beaulieu and the dispatch of reinforcements. In the face of impossible French demands, these actions sufficed to keep Piedmont in the Coalition. Therefore, it can be surmised that the French government was keenly aware of both that Victor Amadeus was interested in concluding the war and that its own demand for

---

23 Joseph-Henri Costa de Beauregard, *Un homme d'Autrefois: souvenirs recueillis par son Arrière-Petit Fils* (Paris, 1877), 297, 301. The author's grandfather was a prominent member of the Piedmontese court and later participated in the negotiations at Cherasco. According to his grandfather, Vins was the cause of the military disasters more than the French.
24 Thaon de Revel, *Mémoires sur la guerre*, 315, and Carutti, *Le corte di Savoia*, 310–311. Carutti states that the French wanted to occupy Susa, Tortona, and Alessandria as well.
25 Thaon de Revel, *Mémoires sur la guerre*, 315–316; cf. Botta, *Storia d'Italia*, Book V, 329, and Book VI, 3–11. Carutti, *Le corte di Savoia*, 309, explicitly states that Victor Amadeus sought a peace analogous to that of Ryswick in 1697, which saved Piedmont from the vice-like grip of Austria and France during the Nine Years War (1688–1697).
26 Thaon de Revel, *Mémoires sur la guerre*, 317–319.

Piedmont to do more than simply end its conflict with France remained an insurmountable obstacle. Regardless, the Directory believed that military victory in Piedmont would realistically lead to a conclusion of the war with that kingdom, thereby opening northern Italy and the road to Lombardy.

Carnot's vision for the French army, which was introduced in 1794, came to fruition in 1796. It is within the context of the general situation of the war, and the diplomatic negotiations with Piedmont, that the *Instructions* of 1796 were developed and issued. The strategic and operational parameters of Napoleon's campaign were clearly relayed by the Directory. Bonaparte understood the diplomatic climate, and certainly believed that he could crack the barrier posed by the Apennines. During the course of the campaign Napoleon fulfilled his orders, although not necessarily following them to the exact letter. This is not a significant issue, as he ultimately achieved the most important goal of cleaving Piedmont from Austria. The subsequent phase of operations took him to the Adige River, where he spent the next six months on the defensive until Mantua fell. Nevertheless, the conduct of the campaign through the month of April created an impetus that had yet to be seen in this theater of war. Napoleon's operational art can be seen in the speed and flexibility of his command.

To that end, the Army of Italy fielded fewer than 40,000 men for the campaign, deducting troops in garrison, guarding supplies, or en route to the theater. It is important to note, however, that the army comprised four active divisions and two coastal divisions as well as two blocking divisions that guarded the Alpine passes.[27] Both Kellermann and Schérer believed that all of the passes required substantial forces to secure them against Coalition forces. This severely reduced the troops available for operations. They had a legitimate fear. In June 1795, the Austro-Piedmontese army launched an offensive to drive the French from the Riviera. Piedmontese forces under Colli marched down the Tanaro valley while the Austrians advanced toward Savona and Voltri. Allied operations on the Tanaro continued through June and into July. Their advance threatened to cut off the Army of Italy from France. Kellermann withdrew the army from the Riviera to prevent this.[28] Subsequently, Schérer determined to insure that this would not happen again by strengthening the divisions holding the passes.[29]

---

27 Illari, et al., *La guerra della Alpi*, 200.
28 Krebs and Moris, *Campagnes dans Alpes*, 2:316, 322–323; Illari, et al., *La guerra della Alpi*, 204–207.
29 Schérer's concern for guarding the passes is clear in his war plan sent to the Directory, *Mémoire au Directoire Exécutif*, 3 February 1796, in Krebs and Moris, *Campagnes dans Alpes*, 2, *Pièces justificatives*, 358–364.

Schérer had reason to be cautious. His army received supplies, pay, and reinforcements only after those on the Rhine. He had little confidence that his army would be in any condition to pursue offensive operations. As noted, the closing of the Spanish front the previous year enabled the Directory to shift forces to the remaining theaters of war. While General Augereau's division arrived from Spain to increase the strength of the Army of Italy by 7,000 men, it certainly did not provide the numbers to launch a pivotal campaign.[30] Moreover, the insufficient size of the Army of Italy did not allow Carnot to believe a decisive action could be achieved in Piedmont.

Although the size of the contending forces indicated that the events of 1796 in Italy would not differ from previous years, the diplomatic climate had changed. In particular, Thugut worried about the resolve of the Italian princes in the face of a determined French offensive, noting on 6 September 1795 that "the king of Sardinia is in our constellation but one cannot doubt that he remains in the Coalition only out of fear of our army, greatly disposed to join the enemy as soon as the occasion offers considerable advantages." On 10 March 1796, Thugut wrote that Piedmontese fears concerning a French invasion were overdone; nevertheless, Beaulieu "should give them [reason for] greater confidence, in order to prevent their defection."[31] Thus, the Austrian chancellor had little concern for a French offensive, but believed that Victor Amadeus's disaffection with the Coalition could have significant repercussions.

Napoleon received command of the Army of Italy in the same month that Thugut tried to allay Piedmontese concerns. Although appointed on 2 March 1796, General Bonaparte did not reach Nice until the 26th. Until that time, Schérer remained general in chief. Schérer had his own ideas concerning future operations and precipitously directed the brigade commanded by the native Corsican Jean-Baptiste Cervoni to Voltri, as a precursor to a larger movement of divisions in that direction. After Napoleon arrived, he countermanded the grander orders, but left Cervoni in position.[32] General Masséna likewise pushed his advanced posts to Cadibona and Monte Legino, several miles south

---

30 Ramsay Weston Phipps, *The Armies of the First French Republic*, 3:261.
31 Karl Roider, *Baron Thugut and Austria's Response to the French Revolution* (Princeton, NJ, 1987), 201–202, quotes Thugut to Cobenzl on 6 September 1795 concerning the "King of Sardinia," but in December wrote to Vice Chancellor Franz Gundacker von Colloredo-Mansfeld that the French victory at Loano could be stemmed by "redoubling our zeal and efforts." cf. Alfred Vivenot, ed., *Quellen zur Geschichte der Deutschen Kaiserpolitik Österreichs während der Französischen Revolutionskriege* (Vienna, 1809), 5:350. See Thugut to Colloredo, 10 March 1796, in Alfred Vivenot, ed., *Vertrauliche Briefe des Freiherrn von Thugut* (Vienna, 1872), 1:287.
32 CG, No. 428, Napoleon to Masséna, 28 March 1796, 1:305; Ilari, et al., *La guerra della Alpi*, 262. Antoine Christophe Salicetti, the *representative en mission* with the Army of Italy,

of Montenotte. Therefore, Napoleon inherited the position of the Army of Italy, and Schérer's actions precipitated an Allied response before his successor was prepared to inaugurate his campaign.[33]

To push the French from the Riviera, Beaulieu and Colli intended for the Piedmontese to hold the Apennine passes, while the Austrian army advanced with its left toward Voltri and Genoa, and the right to Cadibona and then Savona.[34] The "swinging door" of such an Allied operation was similar to but more conservative than the one conducted in 1795 prior to Loano. The belief that the French would respond in 1796 as they had the previous year was reasonable, and the appointment of a new French general, let alone an unknown such as Bonaparte who possessed no practical experience directing an army, increased Allied confidence. Beaulieu ordered his troops from their winter quarters at the end of March and began their concentration and subsequent advance during the first week of April. Despite agreeing to a general plan of combined operations, Beaulieu did not keep Colli apprised of Austrian movements. Although the two generals met at Acqui to establish a relationship, little if any communication flowed between them.

Napoleon did not hold a council of war or inform his subordinates of his plan of operations. He spent much of the two weeks prior to the campaign improving the logistics, feeding and clothing his troops, and gathering intelligence on the enemy's whereabouts.[35] He intended to see Masséna at Garessio around 8 April, but that meeting never occurred. It is possible that he met with General Sérurier, whose division stood between Ormea and Garessio, but only saw Augereau at Finale on 9 April.[36] It appears that Napoleon informed his division commanders separately about his intentions. He wrote to Masséna on 4 April to keep watch from his advanced posts, concerned that the Austrians might push down the valley to Cadibona and the coast; otherwise no orders were issued to commence operations until 11 April.[37] The "Ordres du jour" for 1,

---

encouraged the movement to Genoa to extort greater funds from its Senate. In addition, the Genoese were secretly negotiating with the Austrians.

33 Illari, et al., *La guerra della Alpi*, 259.
34 Ibid., 259; J.B. Schels, "I. Die Gefechte in den Apenninen, bei Voltri, Montenotte, Millesimo, Cossaria, und Dego im April 1796," *Streffleurs Österreicher Militarzeitschrift* 5 (1822), 159–161; these pages include full citation of Beaulieu's plans for the opening campaign.
35 Boycott-Brown, *Road to Rivoli*: see chs. 7 and 8.
36 Ibid., 187. The author argues that news of the Austrian advance against Voltri and Monte Legino prevented Masséna's journey. Phipps, *Armies of the First French Republic*, 3:15, claims that Napoleon met with Augereau on 9 April en route to Savona.
37 CG, No. 457, Napoleon to Masséna, 4 April 1796, 1:321; Nos. 475, 476, 477, Napoleon to Augereau, Laharpe, and Masséna respectively, 11 April 1796, 1:330–331.

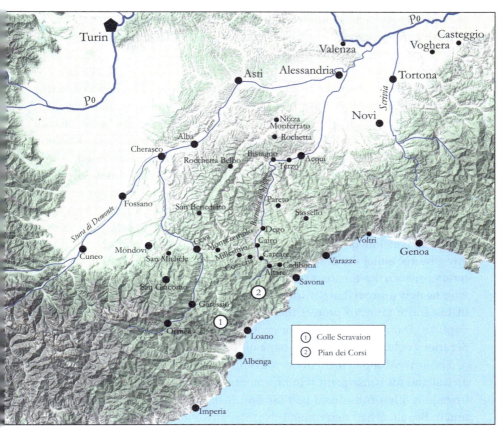

MAP 3.1   The Italian theater, 1796

3, and 5 April relate to preparations for campaign and logistics, but state nothing that relates to a plan of campaign.[38]

The poor condition of the French army is well known, yet it had no impact on Napoleon's plans other than his steps to secure transport, supplies, and funds from the Genoese. Conscious that the Austrians and Piedmontese were already moving, he intended to set his divisions in motion as soon as possible.[39] Napoleon's familiarity with the theater and his work in the Topographical

---

38 CN, No. 114, Ordre du jour, 1:120; No. 115, Ordre du jour, 1:121; No. 120, Ordre du jour, 1:124. The archival correspondence between Napoleon's headquarters and the respective division commanders prior to 9 April affirm the view given in the published correspondence.

39 CG, No. 450, Napoleon to Faipoult, 1 April 1796, 1:316; Napoleon told Guillaume-Charles Faipoult, the French representative at Genoa, that spies had informed him that Allied

Bureau in 1795 provided him with the opportunity to create a plan in the midst of a campaign. This reality would be clearly seen in the reactions of the French, Austrian, and Piedmontese generals over the next month.

Napoleon's operations during 11–26 April are uniformly characterized as employing the strategy of the "central position." This term is used to describe how Napoleon imposed his army between the Piedmontese and Austrians, keeping them apart, holding one while attacking the other. It became the hallmark strategy he employed throughout his various campaigns. Napoleon certainly never used this term, nor does it really matter. He intended to concentrate three of his four divisions in the Bormida valley from Savona to Carcare. This axis of advance had been effectively used in 1794, when newly promoted *General de brigade* Bonaparte experienced his first field battle at Dego. This route was again used in early 1795 with initial success. Now, in 1796, Napoleon concluded that the Piedmontese concentration at Ceva meant that any advance along the Bormida could be threatened by a Piedmontese counteroffensive on the Tanaro. As the Piedmontese had advanced on the Tanaro in 1795, he now insured that Sérurier's division had sufficient strength, one-fourth of his entire army, to protect the valley. Indeed, he detached General Jean-Baptiste Dominique Rusca's brigade from Augereau's division to cover Sérurier's right flank on the east bank of the Tanaro.[40]

The forward deployment of Cervoni's brigade in the week prior to Napoleon's arrival and his subsequent reinforcement of the position at Voltri by a demi-brigade is often considered bait for Beaulieu. This, however, is assuming too much. Beaulieu had determined to strike at Genoa prior to Napoleon's dispatch of reinforcements, and it seems highly presumptive that a single brigade at Genoa would be sufficient to lure the Austrians. The movement of Austrian forces toward Genoa occurred well before Napoleon's general orders to advance and was in response to the Austro-Piedmontese desire to protect Genoa against French occupation.[41] Indeed, Schérer had sent the brigade forward, and

---

troops were moving; ibid., No. 451, Napoleon to Masséna, 1 April 1796, 1:317, and No. 455, Napoleon to Berthier, 4 April 1796, 1:320, on obtaining supplies and transport from the locals; No. 453, Napoleon to Súcy, 1 April 1796, 1:317–318, on obtaining similar from Nice and Marseille.

40 SHAT, B3 352 *Armée d'Italie Situations avril–mai 1796*, "Tableau general de l'Armée d'Italie," 4 April 1796, indicates that Sérurier's division numbered 5,855 present under arms on 4 April. To guarantee Sérurier's strength, Napoleon approved the reinforcement of Rusca's brigade and its temporary detachment to Sérurier's command. Augereau's order to Rusca indicated Napoleon's affirmation is found in SHAT B3 20 *Armée des Alpes et d'Italie Correspondence 16 mars–15 avril 1796*, Augereau to Rusca, 7 April 1796.

41 A French agent in Genoa, François Cacault, reported that Beaulieu intended to move against French troops at Voltri: Cacault to French foreign minister, 2 April 1796; the French

Napoleon merely let the order stand. The Allied offensive worked to Napoleon's advantage. Beaulieu expected that his offensive toward Voltri and Genoa would draw Napoleon east along the Riviera, permitting *Feldmarschall-Leutnant* Eugène-Guillaume Argenteau's division to eventually advance on Savona. The fact that Napoleon ignored the Austrian success at Voltri is a reflection of his *sangfroid*; French defeat provided the Austrians no advantage and drew them further away from his objective.

Thus, the campaign began in earnest with Napoleon pursuing his operational directives in the face of an Austro-Piedmontese offensive. Beaulieu, however, began his movement before his forces were properly arrayed. Neither of his two divisions had concentrated and their battalions remained strung out along the roads. The advance against Voltri was premature. *Feldmarschall-Leutnant* Karl Philipp Sebottendorf van der Rose's division needed another several days to be in position to reach Genoa and push down the Ligurian coast. Argenteau's division equally required several days to concentrate and, although its purpose was to defend the route from Savona to Cairo, it lacked sufficient strength for the task.

It is abundantly clear that Napoleon did not intend to inaugurate his campaign prior to 11 April, when he became aware of the Austrian offensive. He was still assessing the state of his army and, other than the forward deployment of posts on Monte Legino, in the Savona valley, and west at Garessio, his divisions were not in position.[42] The Austrian offensive, therefore, preempted Napoleon's plans by several days. Nonetheless, it did not deter Napoleon from moving ahead with his operations. He ordered Masséna, General Laharpe, and Augereau to make their way north by the primary and secondary routes toward Carcare–Cairo–Dego. Augereau's division – only two brigades, as Rusca's was deployed to the west, protecting the gap between Augereau and Sérurier – advanced along the mountain paths "by the shortest route" to first Mallare and then Cairo.[43] Masséna, leading General Jean-François-Xavier de Menard's brigade, advanced upon Carcare–Cairo, with Laharpe on his right marching toward Montenotte.[44] This latter movement is significant because, as in 1794,

---

plenipotentiary at Genoa, Faipoult, informed Napoleon of Beaulieu's intention to move toward Genoa: SHAT B3 20, Faipoult to Napoleon, 3 April 1796; Illari, et al., *La guerra della Alpi*, 262–263.

42 Napoleon spent much of 8–10 April dealing with political and economic matters related to Genoa and the raising of funds for his army. See *CG*, no. 471, Napoleon to the Directory, 8 April 1796, 1:328; No. 473, Napoleon to Cacault, 10 April 1796, 1:329; No. 474, Napoleon to Faipoult, 10 April 1796, 1:329–330.

43 *CN*, No. 131, Napoleon to Augereau, 11 April 1796, 1:130.

44 Ibid., No. 133, Napoleon to Masséna, 11 April 1796, and No. 134, Napoleon to Masséna, 11 April 1796, 1:131.

Austrian forces at Montenotte threatened the French advance up the Savona–Cairo road. Napoleon's intent to press the Austrians along the flanks of the Savona–Carcare–Cairo road indicate an understanding of past failures and future threats. On 11 April, Napoleon ordered Masséna to "seek to engage the enemy between Carcare, Altare, and Montenotte."[45] In a letter to Sérurier that same day, he confirmed that Augereau's movement on Cairo was intended to turn Austrian positions between Carcare and Montenotte.[46]

The Austrian attack at Voltri followed by the assault on Monte Legino signaled the opening of the campaign. Yet the Allies believed that the French had not yet concentrated their forces. Beaulieu imagined that these movements would have similar results as the 1795 fall offensive, which had driven the French beyond Oneglia. Cervoni's resistance at Voltri and his subsequent withdrawal fully supported the Austrian commander's notion. What he did not expect was the ability of French troops at Monte Legino to repel Argenteau's assault and then respond rapidly with a counteroffensive in front and flank on 11–12 April at Montenotte.[47] Nevertheless, Argenteau withdrew upon his battalions, strung out behind, which permitted him to gather strength in the wake of the attack. In addition, Beaulieu believed that Provera's brigade at Cosseria and Colli's army would threaten the French advance.[48] His thoughts on this matter were reasonable, but Beaulieu remained completely unaware of the number of French troops Napoleon had moved into the area between Cosseria and Montenotte.

When on 11 and 12 April Argenteau and Masséna's troops engaged at Monte Legino and Montenotte, more than half of Beaulieu's forces were too distant to assist. Napoleon, however, had two-thirds of his army in the vicinity. Certainly, the close proximity of the area of operations permitted Napoleon to manipulate his divisions and brigades with relative ease. The divisions of Augereau, Laharpe, and Masséna were initially thirteen or fourteen miles apart on 9 April, but within days were merely six or seven miles distant along two parallel routes connected laterally by trails and small roads. This region was well known by all parties. Both the Austro-Piedmontese and French armies had fought in this same area for the previous two years. Perhaps a large part of Napoleon's success at this time resulted from his enemy's believing that French operations would follow a predictable pattern, as in the past. Schérer was a capable yet cautious commander, and Kellermann was methodical. Napoleon had a

---

45 Ibid., No. 133, Napoleon to Masséna, 11 April 1796, 1:131.
46 Ibid., No. 136, Napoleon to Sérurier, 11 April 1796, 1:133.
47 Schels, "Die Gefechte in den Apenninen," 179–184.
48 Ibid., 186–187.

completely different leadership style and energy. Beaulieu's and Colli's estimations of French actions or reactions were therefore based on false assumptions.

Napoleon's ability to direct his divisions during this initial phase of the campaign was facilitated by his own energy, and the small, manageable size of his forces. The higher organizational structure of the army followed the standard French pattern, but the brigade composition and its allocations during the campaign differed somewhat from common practice. During the course of the first phase of the campaign Napoleon manipulated brigades, shifting them as needed from one division to another with great fluidity. Although brigades were clearly assigned to parent divisions, the modest size of the Army of Italy permitted Napoleon this greater flexibility.[49] Indeed, necessity often drove his orders to detach brigades and move them as needed, either attaching them temporarily to another division, or using them independently for specific operations. This was particularly critical during the first days of operations, the initial assault at Montenotte, and again at Cosseria–Millesimo, Dego, Ceva, and Mondovi. The ability to shift forces at will and with relative ease permitted Napoleon to increase the weight of numbers and outflank Austrian positions

---

49 The French armies of the Revolution were organized into infantry divisions, which were further subdivided into brigades and then regiments. A division comprised two or more brigades and a brigade was composed of two or more regiments. Napoleon standardized the army after 1800, establishing permanent brigades and divisions for the respective armies, and introducing *corps d'armée* of two or more divisions instead of the ad hoc formation occasionally employed during the French Revolutionary Wars. Those familiar with the Napoleonic Wars understand the corps and divisional system as having these formations, and their respective regiments as permanent fixtures in the table of organization. Thus, a regiment assigned to a brigade of a particular division in a specific corps is fixed for one or two campaigns. Furthermore, a Napoleonic corps was a combined-arms unit, possessing artillery and cavalry components. During the French Revolutionary Wars, however, the organization remained fluid. In 1796, the Army of Italy contained divisions and brigades, yet Napoleon continually shifted brigades among divisions as the situation dictated. Indeed, the standardization of regimental strength did not occur until after 1796. This meant that regiments varied in number of men and, subsequently, the brigades and divisions did too. Cavalry, which remained independent and too few in numbers, was therefore organized into separate brigades and later divisions. Artillery too was insufficient and played little role in the early stages of the campaign. While batteries could be assigned to divisions, they too were shifted as needed. Regimental strengths also varied at the start of the 1796 campaign. The second amalgam was still in process; therefore not all regiments were at full strength. Some regiments had a mere 1,400 men, while others stood at 2,000–3,000. The number of men "present under arms" just prior to the opening of the campaign was as follows: 1st division had 11,075 men and 2nd division 5,428, while 3rd had 7,908 men and 4th had more than 5,855: SHAT, B3 352, *Tableau general de l'Armée d'Italie*, 4 April 1796.

at Montenotte and then Dego. Colli's Austro-Piedmontese forces at Cosseria were able to delay Augereau's offensive due to this shifting of French brigades, yet the intent of Napoleon's operations was to defeat Argenteau's Austrians and push them east and away from Colli. Thus, holding the Piedmontese and throwing the weight of forces against the Austrians was well in line with Napoleon's orders.

Sérurier's division was distant from the main area of operations, but his purpose was to keep Colli's attention. At the time of Montenotte on 12 April 1796, only Provera's Austro-Piedmontese brigade formed the link between Argenteau and Colli. The latter held most of his forces around Ceva, covering the Tanaro valley. Supported by Rusca's brigade to the east, Sérurier's advance from Garessio down the valley restricted Colli's options. He wrote to Beaulieu on 13 April that "the enemy is in strength in the Tanaro valley."[50] Even so, Colli remained unaware of the Austrian offensive several days earlier, and was clueless about the French offensive toward Montenotte and Cairo. Only a few battalions were pushed east toward Millesimo and Cosseria on the night of 12 April, shortly before Augereau's division attacked.

The day after the victory at Montenotte, Napoleon shifted brigades once again. Brigades commanded by Generals Joubert and Elzéar-Auguste Cousin de Dommartin, from Masséna's division, did not participate at Montenotte, but were marching concomitant with Augereau's division. Napoleon directed them to Cosseria, seeking to shift the weight of forces against Provera. Menard's brigade, which participated in the turning movement at Montenotte on the second day, shifted west to support this operation. Masséna gathered his other brigades, including those of Laharpe's division, and directed them to Cairo and thence Dego.[51] The chart illustrates the result of Napoleon's shifting of brigades to achieve numerical superiority on the battlefields of Piedmont between 11 and 16 April.

Stiff Piedmontese resistance at Millesimo–Cosseria to the west caused Napoleon some concern, as the Austrians regrouped and advanced on Dego in the east. Napoleon, however, benefited from the piecemeal Austrian advance and the fact that Beaulieu's battalions remained strung out. Therefore, Argenteau's troop strength would prove insufficient to counter the impending

---

50   Schels, "Die Gefechte in den Apenninen," 187, quoting Colli to Beaulieu, 13 April 1796; Augereau kept Sérurier informed of his movements, writing the general that his division was moving upon Cairo and that Sérurier should further reinforce Rusca, SHAT, B3 20; : Augereau to Sérurier, 11 April 1796, and Augereau to Rusca, 11 April 1796.

51   Original found, SHAT B3 20 Napoleon to Laharpe, 12 April 1796; published in CN, No. 137, Napoleon to Laharpe, 12 April 1796, 1:134: "Augereau, Dommartin, and Joubert ... will move tomorrow on Montezemolo [Millesimo–Cosseria], in order to fight the Piedmontese."

TABLE 3.1   Opening battles of 1796

Date	Engagement	French	Austrians and Piedmontese
11 April	Montenotte	16,500	4,000
12 April	Millesimo	11,000	2,100
13 April	Cosseria	4,000	1,200
14 April	Dego	13,000	5,400
15 April	Dego	16,000	4,000

French advance on Dego. The result was a failed attack on the second day, when it became clear to the Austrians that the French were in strength. While it is true that Napoleon reinforced his position at Dego, he also rushed Rusca's brigade toward the fighting at Millesimo–Cosseria to free additional troops that could be used to reinforce Masséna. The fighting at Millesimo–Cosseria raged for three days, with the initial engagement occurring on the night of 12 April at Millesimo, followed by combat at Cosseria and Montezomolo on 13 and 14 April. Montezemolo was some miles to the west of Millessimo–Cosseria, and east of Ceva. Napoleon determined to outmaneuver Colli, by swinging forces around Millesimo–Cosseria through a *manoeuvre sur les derrières*. Formidable resistance came from Provera's brigade, which gradually received reinforcements from Colli. Determined and often successful Piedmontese opposition frustrated Napoleon. Nonetheless, the manipulation of his brigades and divisions meant that any tactical setbacks would be offset by operational maneuver.[52]

In all, the small theater of operations and the short distances between key points permitted a rapid redeployment of French brigades to threatened areas. Furthermore, the success in breaking through the Apennines permitted Napoleon to operate over roads that ran laterally along the north Italian plain, rather than over mountain paths as in previous campaigns.[53] He separated the Piedmontese from the Austrians by pushing Provera's brigade to Cosseria while advancing on Dego. As Sérurier's and Rusca's movement down the Tanaro valley pinned Colli at Ceva, the Piedmontese commander could send only minimal reinforcements. Indeed, Napoleon's orders to Rusca on 13 April called

---

52   Schels, "Die Gefechte in den Appeninen," 186–199; cf. Ilari, et al., *La guerra della Alpi*, 271–276, who provides a detailed discussion of Provera's resistance and French failures in ejecting the Piedmontese and Austrian battalions from their respective positions. Provera essentially conducted an effective rearguard action, slowing the French advance.
53   Hubert Camon, *La guerre napoléonienne: précis des campagnes* (Paris, 1911), 14–15.

for an attack on Montezemolo. Clearly, Napoleon intended to sever Provera from Colli, and prevent the latter from reinforcing the former.[54]

That same day, 13 April, Napoleon ordered Sérurier to "make your plans to insert one of your columns into the town of Ceva at the moment that I master Montezemolo."[55] Thus, while Napoleon overwhelmed Piedmontese resistance east of Ceva, Sérurier would keep Colli's eyes fixed to the south, preventing him from moving his forces to support Provera. By 15 April, Colli held the line of the Tanaro, with his defenses centered on the entrenched camp at Ceva. He faced Sérurier coming from the Apennines, Rusca to his east, and an undetermined number of Bonaparte's forces coming up from Montezemolo.[56] With Colli pinned at Ceva and the Austrians retreating after Dego, Napoleon achieved the operational separation of forces.

Masséna's advance after Dego gave the impression of a French offensive toward Acqui and also kept the Austrians further removed from the Piedmontese. The separation of the Coalition armies initially severed communication between them. This lengthened the time of lateral communication due to the French presence between Cairo and Dego. Thus, Beaulieu and Colli could communicate only by a circuitous route. Consequently, the Piedmontese remained unaware of Beaulieu's actions and the condition of his army as late as 17 April. Joseph-Henri Costa de Beauregard, a Piedmontese officer at Turin, remarked, "I fear that the imperial army has experienced some new and quite considerable disaster, judging by the letter of the 15th from General Beaulieu, in which he said that the remnants of Comte d'Argenteau['s force] and all of those concentrated and sent to support [the position at] Dego arrived in disorder at Terci, without any information on the events which precipitated this retreat."[57] This palpable anxiety permeated the royal court.

Beaulieu and Colli may have been without communication for several days, but the Austrian commander wrote to Victor Amadeus on 18 April. Wanting to bolster the king's resolve, Beaulieu assured him that he had sixteen battalions concentrated at Acqui and implied that he intended to move.[58] Despite this reassurance, he did not move, but remained in position on 19 April. At that time, Colli achieved relative success holding Ceva and the west bank of the Tanaro by repulsing attacks by Sérurier and Rusca. The Tanaro line, anchored

---

54   CN, No. 146, Napoleon to Rusca, 13 April 1796, 1:139.
55   Ibid., 1: no. 143, Napoleon to Sérurier, 13 April 1796, 137.
56   Ilari, et al., *La guerra della Alpi*, 288.
57   Costa de Beauregard to d'Hauteville, 17 April 1796, in Thaon de Revel, *Mémoires sur la guerre en Alpes*, 337–338.
58   Beaulieu to Victor Amadeus, 18 April 1796, ibid., 338–339.

at Ceva, was defended by more than 12,000 Piedmontese.[59] Napoleon faced the real possibility that his army's momentum would falter against this imposing barrier. His orders from Paris called for the taking of Ceva, and the early discussions between Napoleon and Carnot included the possibility of besieging its entrenched camp. Nevertheless, the thought did not appeal to Napoleon at this time and, instead of throwing his troops against this obstacle, he used his numerical superiority to outmaneuver Colli and force him from the security of Ceva.

Between 17 and 19 April, Napoleon directed Augereau and Sérurier's divisions to maneuver along the Tanaro to the north and northwest of Ceva. By 19 April, their divisions were beyond Ceva, and in position to force a passage at Castellino, threatening the rear of the Piedmontese position down river. Napoleon followed this achievement and directed Sérurier against the Piedmontese positions at San Michele. He intended to break through to the north and, with the recent arrival of *Général de division* Henri Christian Michel de Stengel's cavalry, cut Colli's communication with Mondovi and perhaps trap him in Ceva. Colli saw the snare and immediately abandoned the fortified camp for the security of Mondovi.[60]

Although anticipating Napoleon's trap, Colli had not heard from his Austrian counterpart, and remained unaware of his circumstances. On 18 April he wrote to Beaulieu, who replied the following day that he had forces available and agreed with Colli's decision to withdraw. Beaulieu further encouraged Colli to concentrate his army between Modovi and Mulassano (Murazzano), indicating that he would march to his aid.[61] As heartening as this may have been, Beaulieu's forces were still only partially concentrated. Regardless, Napoleon did not give Colli any respite.

Sérurier's orders were clear, but Piedmontese resistance at San Michele – a vital crossing on the Corsaglia River en route to Mondovi – delayed the advance. Several French attempts to force the passage failed. This delay threatened to again stall French momentum, but the continual flow of troops permitted Napoleon to increase pressure. He reinforced Sérurier with Dommartin's brigade, and coordinated an attack on the Piedmontese position with Augereau. The latter was directed northwest of the Tanaro–Corsaglia line, with the intent to attack across the river and flank the Piedmontese positions. On 20 April, the

---

59 Ilari, et al., *La guerra della Alpi*, 287–291.
60 *CN*, Nos. 183, 188, 189, Napoleon to Sérurier, 17, 19 April 1796, 1:160–161; No. 190, Napoleon to Augereau, Dommartin, and Masséna 19 April, 1:163; Costa de Beauregard, *Mémoires historiques*, 384.
61 Beaulieu to Colli, 19 April 1796, in Thaon de Revel, *Mémoires sur la guerre en Alpes*, 339–340.

divisions moved, but Colli feared that his successes the previous day would be undone by French assaults to the front and flank of the Corsaglia line. To avoid any perceived disaster, he ordered a withdrawal to Mondovi.[62]

The Battle of Mondovi (21 April 1796) was a rearguard action fought by the Piedmontese against a determined French advance guard composed largely of cavalry. Although a cursory examination of the French offensive and the Piedmontese withdrawal from Ceva to San Michele to Mondovi would indicate Colli's intention to fall back upon his fortified positions and reinforce his command, it equally illustrates the increasing separation between the Piedmontese army and Turin. Napoleon understood the advantages of this development and so forced Colli out of his positions by maneuver. These actions from 17 to 21 April are in fact, the first operational use of the *manoeuvre sur les derrières*. Although nothing as dramatic as the one to come in May, it was equally effective. After the victory against the Piedmontese rearguard east of Mondovi, Napoleon intended to separate Colli from the capital.

Beaulieu's intransigence in the days after Dego permitted Napoleon to leave Laharpe to observe the Austrians while Masséna moved with the rest of his troops (General Jean-Baptiste Meynier's division) to support operations against the Piedmontese. On 22 April, Napoleon intended another maneuver to isolate Colli from Turin. Masséna was ordered north of the Tanaro to Carrú, while the rest of the French army kept Colli in check.[63] The Piedmontese general, however, understood the implications of his situation. Mondovi was a strongly fortified position, but irrelevant if Napoleon could march directly on the capital. Therefore, Colli decided to avoid the trap, abandon Mondovi, and rapidly march north toward Cherasco.[64]

At the moment the Piedmontese army avoided the French net, Kellermann launched his Army of the Alps in an offensive. Indeed, Napoleon, seeing the Piedmontese withdraw upon Mondovi, and potentially Cuneo, had earlier ordered his divisions in the Stura valley to advance on Cuneo. The broad French offensives in the Alps, combined with Napoleon's movement on Mondovi, created a crisis at Turin.

After the French separated the Piedmontese from the Austrians, discord in Turin followed. On 21 April, the king called a special council meeting that included the Austrian and British ambassadors to discuss a situation that had significantly deteriorated. Beaulieu indicated that reinforcements from

---

62 SHAT, B3 21, Berthier to Augereau, 20 April 1796, states that Dommartin was under the orders of Sérurier; *CN*, No. 194, Napoleon to Sérurier, 20 April 1796, 1:165; Ilari, et al., *La guerra della Alpi*, 293–297.
63 *CN*, No. 209, Napoleon to Masséna, 22 April 1796, 1:173.
64 Ilari, et al., *La guerra della Alpi*, 304.

Lombardy were en route, but moving slowly. According to Thaon de Revel, the king was loath to treat with the French, despite the failure of the Austrians to comply with their part of the alliance.[65] Victor Amadeus vacillated for twenty-four hours over his next course of action. Finally, he decided to make peace on 22 April, but suspended the diplomatic mission after receiving word that Beaulieu was moving. Shortly thereafter, the king decided that he had nothing to lose by restarting negotiations with the French.[66] Rather than indecision, this reflected his hope that the situation would change for the better.

Any chance for success rested with the Austrians marching on Turin. This chance, however, proved illusory as Beaulieu procrastinated. He wrote on 23 April that he was marching west, but did not know the specific situation facing Colli. He complained that his colleague had not written in three days.[67] Without word or evidence of Austrian support, Colli withdrew from Mondovi and the Tanaro to Cherasco, south of the capital. On 25 April, the king learned that Beaulieu had halted his movement after only a few miles, and the military situation around Cherasco was critical. The cabinet debate that followed centered on Turin's ability to hold out until the Austrians arrived. Again, Piedmontese historical memory recalled the events of 1706, when the French had besieged the city, and it was narrowly saved by the timely arrival of Austrian forces under Prince Eugene of Savoy. Nevertheless, the king worried about the damage to his city, and the potential for revolution among the population. Furthermore, the Habsburgs had no Prince Eugene available to save the day. This conclusion led to the fateful ceasefire signed by Colli and Napoleon on 26 April 1796. It ended a three-week campaign and an unwanted war with France.

War plans are not drawn up in a vacuum, but reflect grand strategic realities. The most significant factor in shaping the objectives and operations appears to be the diplomatic climate, and the real possibility of concluding a peace with Piedmont, either through successful negotiations or the arm-bending of an aggressive military campaign. The strain on the Austro-Piedmontese alliance provided the French with the realistic belief that they could achieve a decision in Italy in 1796. Napoleon executed those orders and succeeded in forcing Victor Amadeus to surrender. All players in the campaign looked to contemporary events and interpreted them within the context of historic memory. For years the court at Turin debated the merits of continuing the war versus the

---

65 Ibid., 343.
66 Ibid., 345. Botta, *Storia d'Italia*, Book VI: 45–49, says that Colli's and Beaulieu's actions were interpreted as betrayal. Cf. Costa de Beauregard, *Mémoires historiques*, 3:383, who makes it clear that the Piedmontese court believed Colli's precipitous retreat and Beaulieu's lethargy reeked of foul play.
67 Thaon de Revel, *Mémoires sur la guerre*, 345.

territorial cost of an agreement with France. They desperately wanted out of the Coalition, but the king's wariness and hatred of the revolutionaries weighed the scales against peace. The Piedmontese continually advocated an aggressive strategy, and begged Austria first in 1793 to commit more men to a counteroffensive across the Alps in order to recapture Savoy and Nice and perhaps link with the counterrevolutionaries in Lyons, Toulon, and Marseille. The Austrians rejected any notion of moving the Italian theater beyond the Alpine frontier. For them, it was a matter of grand strategy and resources. The preservation of Habsburg power on the Rhine and in the Austrian Netherlands remained paramount to their strategic and dynastic goals. All of this meant that whatever forces and manpower were delegated to the Italian theater would be secondary to other military efforts. This hamstrung Piedmontese options and limited any Coalition offensive to the operational scale such as the counteroffensives along the Riviera in 1794, 1795, and planned in 1796.

Napoleon's operational art in April 1796 reflected the fundamental principle that the enemy must be given no rest and no opportunity to reorganize. Although the small size and limitation of resources had hampered previous commanders, Napoleon saw an opportunity to make a name for himself. Indeed, he was not as sanguine as his predecessor but, having previously served with the Army of Italy, knew that its officers and soldiers were professionals and experienced. In all cases, Napoleon relied upon his men to conduct themselves with *activité*, to prevent the momentum of his offensive from stalling. Any history of the Napoleonic Wars will refer to the two strategic principles exhibited in April 1796 as the "central position" and in May, "*manoeuvre sur les derrières*." To the former, Napoleon's insinuation of his divisions between the Austrians and Piedmontese was a matter of his orders from Paris, the position of enemy forces as they dictated, and the fact that the Savona–Carcare–Dego road was the only axis not protected by Piedmontese fortifications. French operations in 1794 and 1795 focused on breaking into the Piedmontese plain along this route. In fact, the Austro-Piedmontese strategy counted on Napoleon doing the same in 1796, but did not take into account the personality and determination of the new young commander.

In regard to the *manoeuvre sur les derrières*, Napoleon consistently employed it throughout the first three weeks of the campaign to threaten Colli's communications, first with Ceva, then Mondovi, and finally Turin. By manipulating his brigades, Napoleon rolled around Austrian positions at Montenotte, outmaneuvered them again at Dego, forced the Piedmontese to withdraw at Millesimo–Cosseria with a maneuver at Montezemolo, and compelled Colli to abandon Ceva and fall back upon Mondovi. In this last encounter, Napoleon threatened to cut the Piedmontese from their capital, leaving Colli no option but retreat toward Turin. The Piedmontese army performed admirably, and Colli's intentions to rely upon fortified camps and fortresses were sound. These plans, however, did not consider an aggressive French offensive that emphasized engagement and maneuver. In many ways, it combined the best elements of traditional 18th-century warfare with a commitment to battle. Napoleon did not, however, have the luxury of manpower and could not dedicate his army to sieges. Carnot's instructions did not require Napoleon to conduct his campaign in this manner, but merely stated that Ceva must be taken.[68] Napoleon was free to determine the best means to achieve this objective. In any event, the instructions are clear that Ceva was not an end, but a means to an end, which was the march on Turin, and the conclusion of the war with Piedmont. Napoleon achieved this through operational maneuver when battle failed to eject the enemy from their positions in a timely fashion. What is clear throughout the April campaign is that Napoleon's operational art fulfilled the strategic vision of the Directory, as manifest in Carnot's orders of February 1796.

Bibliography

Botta, Carlo. *Storia d'Italia dal 1789 al 1814*, 8 vols. Rome, 1824.

Boycott-Brown, Martin. *The Road to Rivoli: Napoleon's First Campaign*. London, 2002.

Carutti, Domenico. *Le corte di Savoia durante le rivoluzione e l'impero francese*, 8 vols. Turin, 1888.

Charavay, Étienne, ed. *Correspondance générale de Carnot*. Paris, 1907.

Clerq, M. de. *Recueil des traités de la France*, 10 vols. Paris, 1880.

Costa de Beauregard, Joseph-Henri. *Un homme d'Autrefois: souvenirs recueillis par son Arrière-Petit Fils*. Paris, 1877.

Costa de Beauregard, Joseph-Henri. *Mémoires historiques sur la maison royale de Savoie*. Turin, 1816.

Debidour, A. *Recueil des actes du Directoire Exécutif, Procès-verbaux, arrêtés, Instruction, Lettres et actes divers, Instructions pour le général en chef de l'Armée d'Italie*, 2 vols. Paris, 1911.

France, Château de Vincennes, Service Historique de la Defense: B3 20 Armée des Alpes et Italie, Correspondance 16 Mars – 16 Avril 1796

Ilari, Virgilio, Piero Crociani, and Ciro Paoletti. *La guerra delle Alpi (1792–1796)*. Rome, 2000.

Krebs, Léonce and Henri Moris. *Les campagnes dans les Alpes pendant la Révolution*, vol. 2, *1794, 1795, 1796*. Paris, 1895.

---

68   Krebs and Moris, *Campagnes dans les Alpes*, 2, *Piéces justificatives*, 375–378.

Napoleon I, *Correspondance de Napoléon I*, 32 vols. Paris, 1858–1862.
Napoleon I, *Correspondance générale, publiée par la Fondation Napoléon*, 12 vols. Paris, 2004.
Paoletti, Ciro. *Dal ducato all'unità: tre secoli e mezzo di storia militare piemontese*, 2 vols. Rome, 2011.
Phipps, Ramsay Weston. *The Armies of the First French Republic and the Rise of the Marshals of Napoleon I*, 5 vols. London, 1929–1934.
Revel, Ignace Thaon de. *Mémoires sur la guerre des Alpes et les évenéments en Piémont pendant la Révolution Française*. Turin, 1871.
Roider, Karl. *Baron Thugut and Austria's Response to the French Revolution*. Princeton, NJ, 1987.
Schels, J.B. "I. Die Gefechte in den Apenninen, bei Voltri, Montenotte, Millesimo, Cossaria, und Dego im April 1796." *Streffleurs Österreicher Militarzeitschrift* 5 (1822), 123–217.
Sciot, Ludovic. *Le Directoire*. Paris, 1895.
Sybel, Heinrich von. *Geschichte der Revolutionszeit von 1789 bis 1800*. Düsseldorf, 1870.
Vivenot, Alfred, ed. *Quellen zur Geschichte der Deutschen Kaiserpolitik Oesterreichs während der Französischen Revolutionskriege*. Vienna, 1809.
Vivenot, Alfred, ed. *Vertrauliche Briefe des Freiherrn von Thugut*. Vienna, 1872.
Vivenot, Alfred, *Thugut, Clerfayt und Wurmser*. Vienna, 1869.

Appendix 1: Unexpurgated orders for the Army of Italy

Instructions pour le général en chef de l'Armée d'Italie[69]

The French Republic has two main enemies to fight in Italy, the Piedmontese and the Austrians: the latter, though less numerous [in Italy], are formidable, both in their hatred for France, resources which are infinitely greater, and, by their close relationship with our natural enemies, the English, and especially by their imperial possessions which they hold in Italy, allowing them to pressure the court of Turin, which is obligated to submit to their demands and even their whims. The result of this state of things is that the more immediate interest of the French government should be directing its main efforts against the Austrian army and their possessions in Italy.

Indeed, it is easy to feel that any military movement against the Piedmontese and their territory is somehow of no concern to the Austrians, who, as we saw in the previous campaign, seem to care very little about the disasters of their allies, who in times

---

69 Debidour, *Recueil des actes du Directoire exécutif, Instructions pour le général en chef de l'Armée d'Italie*, 718–719.

of danger – far from seeking to protect them effectively – break away to only cover the country that belongs to them, and provides an abundance of resources they need …

When you consider the real interests of the court of Turin is mainly related to ours, and there is no doubt about the desire of this court to see the determined Austrians fully expelled from Italy and Milan … Why, if the interests of Piedmont are to join the French and drive the Germans out of Italy, does the court of Turin not hasten to join its arms to those of the Republic, to move as quickly as possible for this purpose, profitably and gloriously?

The answer to this question should help shed light on our political position vis-à-vis Italy, as well as the best way forward in order to defeat our enemies, especially Austrian satellites. Placed between countries, the latter and the French Republic, Piedmont is forced to play a role in the current war, and if she would remain in a state of neutrality, she would have suffered all the evils of war without power, enjoy a precious prerogative for a moderately strong state with respect to its neighbors, that is to say, the respect that they can join forces with those of one of the warring parties, and the danger of defection on their part to move toward its enemy, ensuring that they will experience the least possible harassment, from the power with which it is combined. Without absolutely rejecting the idea that the King of Sardinia has been driven by family considerations into the coalition against France, it is true to say that our position at the beginning of the present war, and the need in which we found it necessary to take Savoy and the one-time County of Nice … forced the court of Turin to embrace the our enemies and oppose our effort, but since our success of Frimaire hope of compensation to take the Austrian possessions in Italy would probably change is the court of Turin …

… the Executive Directory sets its sights on a system of offensive war, directed primarily against the Austrian forces in Italy and, so combined, it has given the French army in Italy the opportunity to attain, by the defeat of the Piedmontese at the beginning of military operations … to bring the court of Turin in a forced alliance with France, and finally a way to expedite the conclusion of an advantageous peace for us, the total rout the Austrians in Italy. The first military operations are confined within this limited sphere and require little elaboration.

The Directory shall limit their statements, leaving the execution of details to the commander in chief, whom they trust. They will be submitted to the Executive Directory, as time and circumstances permit, and in extraordinary cases where the opinion becomes absolutely necessary to determine military movements of major importance and that would not be provided.

Appendix II: The second part of the document above, and the extract often quoted when discussing Napoleon's orders

Archives de la Guerre					2 March 1796

CERTIFIED DOCUMENT [EXTRACT]
OF INSTRUCTIONS FOR THE GENERAL IN CHIEF OF THE ARMY OF ITALY

You will find that your command has all the means, which are in our power to cross the Po against the enemy and carry our great effort in the direction of the Milanese [Lombardy].

This essential operation will not have an impact without the French army taking Ceva. The Directory leaves to the General in Chief the liberty to begin the operations by attacking the enemy at this point, and in a manner by which he can obtain a complete victory, which will force them [the Piedmontese] to retire on Turin. The Directory authorizes the pursuit and new attacks, including a bombardment of this capital if circumstances render it necessary.

After you have mastered Ceva and having brought the left wing of the Army of Italy closer from Coni ... the General in Chief will be able, as much as possible, to see to the needs of the army in terms of resources, which will be drawn from Piedmont. He will thereafter direct his forces toward the Milanese and principally against the Austrians. He will throw the enemy across the Po; will occupy the various places to cross the river; and will seek to capture the places of Asti and Valence [Valenza].

The General in Chief will not, at this time, lose sight of the Austrians, which is of principal importance, in order to take proper measures to press the advance, if possible, on the right and toward Tortona ...

The General in Chief will not make this critical movement of troops to our right, until after taking Ceva, achieving a clear victory over Piedmont. We will improve the situation by imposing ourselves on the Genoese Republic and will send a French agent to that government to maintain negotiations ...

The more wealthy their government, the more they must attend to furnishing our troops with money, which will guarantee them our loyalty and favorable circumstances in this war ...

The entrance of the Republican army in Piedmont is considered only a preliminary and will place us in a position to attack Austrian forces to our great advantage. They will not have the means possible to advance without proper supplies in this situation without the defeat of Piedmont.

The following movements of the right of the French army will be made toward Alessandria and Tortona. It will become indispensible to subsequent operations that we have in our possession Gavi, which the Genoese by their good graces will give us during the war, and this will be done by the appearance of forces threatening this town if they do not consent. The Directory is convinced that the General in Chief will be prudent in executing these measures and consider the circumstances and our political relationship with the Genoese Republic ...

By moving the principal Republican forces of the Army of Italy on the right ... we will gain several important advantages: we force the Piedmontese, already defeated, to join our side. We intimidate all of Italy, and we will dissolve the coalition of small powers which are in support of the Austrian cause.

The march, which the Directory has indicated to the General in Chief, is considered primary ... This is the first upon which all the secondary movements will follow and placed in proper succession: it goes without saying that the conduct of all these operations should be entirely favorable ...

Signed: Le Tourneur, president

By the Executive Directory, for the secretary general,

Signed: Carnot[70]

---

[70] Carnot's orders reprinted can be found in Krebs and Moris, *Campagnes dans les Alpes*, 2, *Piéces justificatives*, 375–378.

CHAPTER 4

Napoleon's First Italian Campaign, 1796–1797

Michael V. Leggiere and Phillip R. Cuccia

Napoleon fundamentally changed warfare during his campaigns in northern Italy in 1796–1797. He did so not by introducing a completely new facet of warfare. Instead, he combined several aspects of competing theories of conducting war, which allowed him to lead his ragged army to astounding victories and end the War of the First Coalition on a front that both sides initially regarded as secondary. During this campaign, Napoleon established the principles of war that are still studied by today's professional military establishments: objective, offensive, mass, economy of force, maneuver, unity of command, security, surprise, and simplicity. He also implemented the strategy of the single point, the *manœuvre sur la position centrale*, the *manœuvre sur les derrières*, and the concept of victory through a decisive battle of annihilation and the destruction of the opposing force. The causes of Napoleon's tactical victories, his operational success, and ultimately his strategic triumph over Piedmont and Austria can be attributed to his aggressive implementation of the changes in the character of war produced by the French Revolution: living off the land of conquered territories[1] instead of relying on lengthy supply chains; task-organizing his commands for the next battle based on his understanding of the enemy's forces; making the most of speed on the march, which in turn was facilitated by a reduced reliance on magazines; and capitalizing on the new formations of column attacks made possible by mass conscript armies. The immutable nature of war that Napoleon grasped included the building and maintaining of a high level of morale in his army; appreciating and exploiting the value of time; being able to "see" the battlefield and anticipate the enemy's next move; and his relentless aggressiveness, calmness under pressure, and indefatigable energy. For these reasons, we will take a closer look at the events already discussed in the previous chapter as well as the remainder of the campaign.

---

1 For example, on 9 May 1796, Napoleon forced Duke Ferdinand of Parma to provide the French army with 1,000,000 kilograms (2,204,623 pounds) of wheat and 500,000 kilograms (1,102,311 pounds) of oats as well as 2,000 oxen. See François-René-Jean de Pommereul, *Campagne du général Buonaparte en Italie, pendant les années IVe et Ve de la République Française* (Paris, 1797), 1:24.

In late March 1796, Bonaparte's talent and determination inspired new life and hope in a French army that had struggled for four years in a prolonged war of attrition against Piedmontese (Sardinian) and Austrian troops in northwest Italy. The fighting on the Italian front began after France annexed the Piedmontese provinces of Savoy and Nice in late 1792 and sent the Army of Italy to claim the territory. From 1792 through early 1796, the French fought at the base of the Ligurian Alps[2] between Nice and Genoa but never achieved a decisive victory. The days of fighting indecisive battles in northern Italy ended after Bonaparte took command of the Army of Italy. To assist the reader, we divide the First Italian Campaign into four phases: Piedmont, Lombard, Venetian, and Austrian.[3] The Venetian Phase is further broken down into four offensives: Castiglione, Bassano,[4] Arcole, and Rivoli.

The strategic situation in 1796 found the main French and Austrian armies concentrated in the Rhine theater: French armies commanded by Generals Moreau (79,500 men) and Jourdan (78,000) faced Austrian forces led by Archduke Charles (94,000 men) and General Dagobert Sigismund von Wurmser (83,000 men). In addition, the Austrians posted an army of observation (80,000 men) in Bohemia to monitor their former allies, the Prussians. A small French army of 18,000 men under Kellermann held the alpine passes between France and Italy, while a second small army of 15,000 under Hoche guarded the French coastline along the English Channel. Carnot remained convinced that the Italian theater served only to distract Austrian attention and resources.

On the day that Napoleon received command of the Army of Italy, 2 March 1796, Carnot issued him instructions, based on plans that Bonaparte himself had drafted while assigned to the Topographical Bureau the previous year. These simple orders called for Napoleon to: (1) take the entrenched Piedmontese camp at Ceva and force King Victor Amadeus to quit the war; (2) resupply the Army of Italy at Piedmont's expense; (3) drive the Austrians beyond the Po River Valley; and (4) capture Milan, the capital of Lombardy.

---

2 The Ligurian Alps in northwestern Italy form the southwestern extremity of the Alps, separated from the Apennines by the Colle di Cadibona and from the Maritime Alps by the Col de Tende; they form the border between Piedmont in the north and Liguria in the south.

3 Regarding maps, space does not allow us to provide a map for each section and subsection of the chapter. However, Maps 4.1, 4.2, and 4.3 are the general geographic maps to be consulted for the Piedmont, Lombard, and Venetian Phases.

4 Here we follow Clausewitz in using Bassano to describe the "series of actions from Bassano to the walls of Mantua that are collectively known as the First Battle of Bassano." See Carl von Clausewitz, *Hinterlassenes Werk: der Feldzug von 1796 in Italien* (Berlin, 1858), 142.

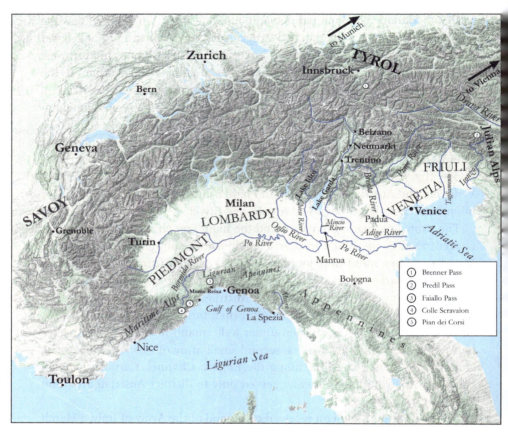

MAP 4.1   Theater of War, Northern Italy, 1796–1797

1   **Piedmont Phase**

Beaulieu widely dispersed his 37,000 Austrian troops and 148 guns in the mountains northeast of the French Army of Italy to protect Lombardy.[5] His advance guard of 11,500 under Argenteau stood closest to the French. He positioned 10,000 men under the Croatian colonel Josip Filip Vukasović and Colonel Sebottendorf between his main supply base at Alessandria and Argenteau's troops. To the southwest, Provera's 2,000 men near Millesimo served as a tenuous link with the Piedmontese army under Colli. An Austrian

---

5   J.B. Schels, "Die Gefechte in den Apenninen, bei Voltri, Montenotte, Millesimo, Cossaria und Dego im April 1796," *Streffleurs Österreicher Militärzeitschrift* Bd 5 (1822):157.

officer on loan to Sardinia, Colli extended his 25,000 Piedmontese troops along a thirty-mile front on the line of Cuneo (Coni)–Mondovi–Ceva–Millesimo. Beaulieu intended to launch an offensive designed to drive the French from the Italian Riviera[6] and (1) secure the city and port of Genoa, (2) gain possession of the passes through the Maritime Alps,[7] and (3) secure communication with the British fleet off the Ligurian coast.[8]

As for the Army of Italy, Masséna's command, which consisted of divisions led by Laharpe and Meynier, formed the army's right flank and advance guard. From Meynier's division, Cervoni's brigade (3,500 men) stood on the extreme right at Voltri in an isolated and exposed position. Augereau's division formed the army's center with Sérurier's division providing the left wing. Accompanied by General Jean Joseph Pijon's brigade from Laharpe's division, Napoleon transferred his headquarters from Nice to Savona on 9 April so that his line of communications now extended more than 100 miles. Planning a *manœuvre sur la position centrale* to place his forces between the two enemy armies, Bonaparte identified the Dego–Cairo–Carcare region as his objective, with particular emphasis on Carcare and its valuable crossroads, which the Piedmontese and Austrians utilized for communication.[9] According to Napoleon's plan, Masséna and Augereau would march north to Carcare while Sérurier and Cervoni provided diversions on the extreme flanks. After seizing central position, he planned to mask the Austrians near Dego and strike the Piedmontese first, as they stood closer to his line of communications than did the Austrians. Napoleon determined to commence his offensive on 15 April. Carl von Clausewitz provides an extensive explanation of his agreement with Bonaparte's decision to attack the Piedmontese first rather than the Austrians:

> As long as the two armies operated close together in the same theater of operations under unified command, the Austrians were undoubtedly the part of the enemy force that contained the center of gravity. This would have remained the case for the whole campaign, even if they had been

---

6 The Italian Riviera, or Ligurian Riviera, is the narrow coastal strip that lies between the Ligurian Sea and the mountain chain formed by the Maritime Alps and the Apennines. It includes nearly all the coastline of Liguria; historically the "Riviera" extends along the French coast as far as Marseille.
7 The Maritime Alps are a mountain range in the southwestern part of the Alps that form the border between southeastern France and the Italian regions of Piedmont and Liguria. They are the southernmost part of the Alps.
8 G.A. von Erdmannsdorff, *Der Feldzug von 1796 in Italien* (Magdeburg, 1847), 43–44.
9 Clausewitz explains that where Napoleon intended to commence his offensive "is the junction of the Apennines with the Alps and is a saddle in the mountains, from which the Alps rise more steeply to the west and the Apennines to the east": Clausewitz, *Der Feldzug von 1796*, 17.

driven out of Italy entirely, if the Piedmontese could have been completely isolated. But ... with the separation of the Austrians from the Piedmontese, it would cease to apply; the Piedmontese would effectively become independent and, by virtue of their positions, would become more important than the Austrians. ... if he [Napoleon] did succeed in driving the Austrians back beyond the Po, he could not leave 10,000 of his 40,000 men facing Colli and cross the Po with 30,000, drive the Austrians out of the province of Milan, then cross the Mincio, besiege Mantua, and move up the Adige – not while leaving 30,000–40,000 Piedmontese to his rear with a mass of fortified positions that were closed against him, standing like a gatekeeper on his exceptionally poor line of communications. ... We believe the question of where to direct the main force must be answered in this manner, insofar as it helps us determine the location of the enemy's *Schwerpunkte* [center of gravity]. But the enemy's center of gravity is not decided in isolation; there is a second consideration, concerning the immediate successes that are offered. As a rule, of course, these will be greatest if the main force is used continuously in a single direction, but this is not of exclusive importance; rather, chance circumstances may mean that one can expect much greater rewards from victory in the subordinate direction. This particular immediate advantage may outweigh the more distant general one. ... Thus, in our opinion, we believe Bonaparte's view was completely justified.[10]

Yet the seventy-one-year-old Beaulieu surprised Bonaparte by launching his own offensive on Sunday, 10 April, in an attempt to destroy Cervoni's brigade at Voltri. According to his plan, Beaulieu himself would converge on Cervoni's 5,000 men with 8,000 soldiers, while in the center Argenteau advanced from Sassello to Savona to separate the French right from the rest of Bonaparte's army. Beaulieu provided Colli and Provera with a general outline of his plan as well as an invitation to participate in the offensive, but offered no specific instructions on how they should proceed to achieve a common purpose; Colli ultimately remained idle at Ceva.[11]

On 10 April, Beaulieu attacked the French at Voltri. Outnumbered, Cervoni conducted a masterful withdrawal west that night to unite with Laharpe, who held Savona with Pijon's brigade. As for Argenteau, instead of attacking Savona on 10 April, he spent the day concentrating his forces and reconnoitering his

---

10   Ibid., 15–17.
11   Ibid., 6; Schels. "Die Gefechte in den Apenninen," 173; Erdmannsdorff, *Der Feldzug von 1796*, 45.

NAPOLEON'S FIRST ITALIAN CAMPAIGN, 1796–1797 121

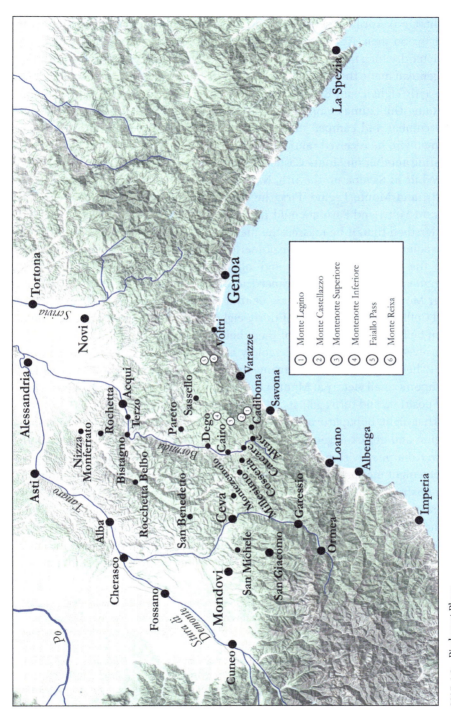

MAP 4.2 Piedmont Phase

front. On 11 April, he could delay no longer and commenced his march with only 3,000 men. A few miles north of Savona, Argenteau ran into Laharpe's vanguard, which held a strong redoubt on Monte Legino.[12] With his 3,000 men, Argenteau made three unsuccessful assaults on the redoubt and its defenders: the 17th Light Demi-Brigade and 32nd Line, both commanded by General Antoine-Guillaume Rampon. Having no artillery on hand, Argenteau broke off the combat and camped under arms near Montenotte Superiore. During a rainy night, he received reinforcements, placing one battalion on his left and posting another on Monte Castellazzo to protect his right and rear.[13]

While at Savona on the 11th, Napoleon learned of the Austrian attacks at Voltri and Monte Legino. First, he recognized that the columns advancing toward Voltri and Savona could not support each other directly. Second, he understood that, if he massed the majority of his forces against one of these two columns, he would achieve numerical superiority over it. Therefore, utilizing the principles of mass and offensive, Napoleon resolved to attack Argenteau's column as it advanced toward Savona. By defeating Argenteau near Montenotte, he would gain central position between Beaulieu at Voltri and Colli at Ceva, a distance of thirty-eight miles of difficult terrain. He would then be free to attack either of them before the other could provide support. His revised plan centered on rapidly utilizing interior lines to concentrate overwhelming force against Argenteau. In short, Bonaparte resolved to exploit Rampon's small victory at Monte Legino to crush Argenteau, firmly secure central position, and turn against the Piedmontese.

That night, Bonaparte ordered Laharpe to move his division north to Monte Legino and attack Argenteau at dawn on 12 April. With three brigades (one from Laharpe's division and two from Meynier's division), Masséna would conduct a night march northeast toward the Carcare – Montenotte region to turn the Austrian right and strike Argenteau's rear. To both complete the envelopment and shield Masséna's rear, Augereau received orders to advance from Loano on the coast to the central position between the Austrians and Piedmontese at Cairo. Bonaparte instructed Masséna and Augereau to block any attempt by the Piedmontese to march east to support Argenteau. Finally,

---

12 Fifteen miles northwest of Argenteau's position, General Matija Rukavina Bojnogradski held Dego with five companies from Provera's brigade to maintain communication with Beaulieu. He reached Castellazzo, just west of Montenotte Superiore, with two battalions in time to support Argenteau on the 11th.

13 CN, No. 148, Napoleon to the Directory, 1:161–162; Clausewitz, *Der Feldzug von 1796*, 20–21; Gabriel Fabry, *Campagne de l'armée d'Italie, 1796–1797* (Paris, 1914), 4:237–241; Schels, "Die Gefechte in den Apenninen," 174–178; Erdmannsdorff, *Der Feldzug von 1796*, 50–51; Martin Boycott-Brown, *The Road To Rivoli: Napoleon's First Campaign* (London, 2001), 197–215.

he tasked Sérurier with keeping Colli occupied by advancing north from Ormea toward Ceva.[14] In this manner, Napoleon planned to concentrate some 25,000 men against Argenteau and near the junction of two allied armies. Tactically, this would be "a combined attack in full force on the right wing of the Austrian column advancing via Montenotte, and strategically, a piercing of the enemy's center."[15]

Overnight, Laharpe moved his two brigades and artillery to Monte Legino. Early on the extremely foggy morning of 12 April, his guns opened fire on the unsuspecting Austrians. Between 8:00 and 9:00 a.m., the sun finally broke through the fog, revealing to the Austrians almost 4,000 French soldiers and numerous guns on Monte Legino. Moreover, locals warned Argenteau of a French force approaching his right. Laharpe launched an energetic attack to fix the Austrians and provide time for Masséna to complete his envelopment. With his five battalions, Argenteau commenced a slow retreat *en échelon* toward Montenotte Superiore. Laharpe pursued and managed to pin the Austrians, thus facilitating the Battle of Montenotte.

Masséna led Meynier's division around Argenteau's right, nearly enveloping the Austrians, who retreated to Montenotte Inferiore. The Austrians barely managed to evacuate Montenotte Inferiore before Masséna and Laharpe converged on the village. The engagement saw 16,500 French troops engage 4,000 Austrians, and ended with the Austrians losing 1,800 men and 12 guns to some 880 French casualties.[16] Napoleon now held central position between the two enemy armies, forming a wedge between them that would prevent their junction. This marked the first occasion that Bonaparte, an artillery officer, handled infantry in the field and fought a pitched battle. The brilliant result cannot be attributed to innate genius or luck, but to Napoleon's use of the tactical lessons he had learned from Bourcet and Guibert. He applied them with clear perception, quick decision, and rapidity of action.

Allowing his troops no rest, Napoleon sought to exploit the victory by continuing operations that same day – despite the forced night march through a spring thunderstorm that Masséna's troops had endured. Thus, still on 12 April,

---

14   CN, No. 136, Napoleon to Sérurier, 11 April 1796, 1:150–151; No. 135, Napoleon to Laharpe, 11 April 1796, 1:149–150; Nos 133–134, Napoleon to Masséna, 11 April 1796, 1:148–149; Nos 130–131, Napoleon to Augereau, 11 April 1796, 1:146–147; Fabry, *Campagne de l'armée d'Italie*, 4:241–242; G.J. Fiebeger, *The Campaigns of Napoleon Bonaparte of 1796–1797* (West Point, NY, 1911), 6–7.

15   Hans Ludwig David Maximilian Yorck von Wartenburg, *Napoleon as a General*, 2 vols (London, 1897–1898), 1:30.

16   CN, No. 148, Napoleon to the Directory, 14 April 1796, 1:162–163; Fabry, *Campagne de l'armée d'Italie*, 4:242–245; Erdmannsdorff, *Der Feldzug von 1796*, 50–54; Schels, "Die Gefechte in den Apenninen," 183–186; Boycott-Brown, *Rivoli*, 223–230.

Masséna led Meynier's division north toward Dego to pursue the Austrians while Laharpe marched west from Montenotte to Cairo. Augereau had reached San Giacomo and was heading east on the road to Cairo when he received orders to march west toward Millesimo. Sérurier continued marching northeast from Ormea toward Colli's entrenched position at Ceva. During the course of 12 April, Bonaparte remained at Altare on the Savona–Carcare road, but that night he established his headquarters at Cairo. A few miles south of Carcare, he positioned his reserve of six battalions and the 1st Cavalry Division so that he could use it to rapidly reinforce either wing of the army.[17]

For Wednesday, 13 April, Napoleon wanted to concentrate 25,000 men against the Piedmontese. He ordered Meynier and Laharpe to follow Augereau toward the Piedmontese positions at Millesimo and Ceva; Sérurier's division would continue its northeast march. He decided to have Masséna occupy Dego with Meynier's 21st Demi-Brigade.[18] This maneuver would serve two purposes: first, Masséna would be able to block any Austrian attempt to reach the Piedmontese, as control of Dego would enable the French to close the only road that would allow the two Allied armies to link with each other. Second, Dego remained strategically important because of its proximity to Napoleon's line of communications, which ran northeast along the coast on the Nice–Savona road before turning northwest at Savona and running through Cadibona and Carcare to Cairo. The position of Dego on the right bank of the Bormida di Spigno[19] consisted of a chain of five to six hills that formed sheer bluffs overlooking the river valley. Earthworks crowned each hill, with the highest hill that dominated the region – Monte Magliani – containing a large redoubt; altogether eighteen guns defended the fortifications.[20]

Thus, on the morning of 13 April, Augereau advanced west with 11,000 men and 23 guns toward Millesimo. With an Austro-Piedmontese force of some 2,100 men, Provera held a ridge at Cosseria, east of Millesimo. Forming three large columns, Augereau attacked and defeated Provera, who with 600 soldiers took refuge in the ruins of the old Cosseria castle situated on a high hill. His

---

17 CN, No. 138, Napoleon to Masséna, 12 April 1796, 1:152–153; No. 137, Napoleon to Laharpe, 11 April 1796, 1:151–152; Clausewitz, *Der Feldzug von 1796*, 22.

18 CN, Nos 142–145, Napoleon to Meynier, Sérurier, Masséna, and Laharpe, respectively, 13 April 1796, 1:155–158.

19 The headwaters of the Bormida di Spigno are located above Pian dei Corsi at 1,000 meters (3,300 ft) above sea level in a transitional zone between the Alpine and Apennine mountain ranges. It joins with the Bormida (or Bormida di Millesimo) north of Rivoli near Bistagno. The Bormida di Millesimo rises in Liguria and flows through Piedmont. After converging with the Bormida di Spigno near Bistagno, it joins the Tanaro, of which it is the major tributary, northeast of Alessandria.

20 Fabry, *Campagne de l'armée d'Italie*, 4:247–248; Boycott-Brown, *Rivoli*, 243–245.

main body withdrew through Millesimo to Montezemolo and united with Colli's detachment. Bonaparte arrived to oversee Augereau's launching of several unsuccessful assaults that cost the French 700 casualties to 96 Austrians and Piedmontese. During these attacks, Colli did nothing, out of fear of being attacked by Sérurier's division as it approached along the Tanaro. Napoleon then received news from Masséna that "6,000" Austrians held the entrenchments at Dego. Leaving Augereau to invest Cosseria, he returned to Cairo, concerned by the threat to his right flank posed by the Austrian force at Dego.[21]

As for Beaulieu, instead of marching on Savona and proceeding in unison with Colli, he decided to retreat from Voltri on 12 April. He weakened his force by dispatching Vukasović with three battalions northwest to the Faiallo Pass near Monte Reixa in the Ligurian Apennines[22] to obtain news of Bonaparte's movements. Hearing the sound of the guns from Montenotte, Vukasović marched west toward Sassello. He arrived there on 13 April and found four of Argenteau's battalions that had not participated in the Battle of Montenotte. As for Beaulieu himself, he withdrew on 12 April with the aim of reaching Acqui, where he arrived on 13 April. Before learning of Argenteau's defeat, the Austrian commander issued orders for Colli and Provera to harass the enemy and drive back his posts.[23]

After the Battle of Montenotte, Argenteau had escaped ten miles north to Pareto on 12 April with barely 700 men under arms.[24] That afternoon, he received an urgent request for support from General Matija Rukavina Bojnogradski, who had returned to Dego after the Battle of Montenotte: his posts were under heavy pressure from the French. Arriving at Dego, Argenteau found two Piedmontese battalions, two Austrian companies, and a wounded Rukavina. After being battered at Montenotte, Argenteau had no desire to engage the French again and had already decided to continue his retreat to Acqui and thus returned to Pareto. In fact, at 8:00 on the morning of 13 April,

---

21   In his report to the Directory, Napoleon cites the number of "6,000" Austrians: CN, No. 165, Napoleon to the Directory, 15 April 1796, 1:170–172; Clausewitz, *Der Feldzug von 1796*, 25–27; Fabry, *Campagne de l'armée d'Italie*, 4:248–249; Schels, "Die Gefechte in den Apenninen," 188–196; Erdmannsdorff, *Der Feldzug von 1796*, 56–58; Yorck von Wartenburg, *Napoleon as a General*, 1:31; Boycott-Brown, *Rivoli*, 234–239.

22   The Ligurian Apennines border the Ligurian Sea in the Gulf of Genoa, from Savona below the upper Bormida River Valley to La Spezia below the upper Magra River Valley. The range follows the Gulf of Genoa, separating it from the upper Po River Valley.

23   Clausewitz, *Der Feldzug von 1796*, 23; Schels, "Die Gefechte in den Apenninen," 186; Erdmannsdorff, *Der Feldzug von 1796*, 54, 61.

24   "Incomprehensibly," notes Clausewitz, in *Der Feldzug von 1796*, 22–23, "Argenteau did not lead his remnants toward the four battalions at Sassello, not toward the three and one-half battalions at Dego, but right between the two along the road to Acqui as far as Pareto."

he wrote to Beaulieu to inform him that he could do little to hold Dego with 1,800 men and 18 guns. Beaulieu responded that same day with orders for him to do his utmost to hold Dego for two days and cover the road to Acqui. If Argenteau could keep the road to Acqui open, Beaulieu would arrive at Dego with his main body.[25]

After reaching Cairo on the afternoon of 13 April, Napoleon conducted a leader's reconnaissance at Dego. Concerned that the Austrian force there represented the lead elements of Beaulieu's main body, he decided to delay Masséna's assault until Provera surrendered Cosseria, which would make Laharpe and Augereau available to support Masséna if the circumstances required. Yet Provera's small Austro-Piedmontese force held throughout 13 April, costing Napoleon almost one full day, which meant that if Beaulieu intended to attack Masséna, he now stood even closer to Dego. Knowing that time was short, Napoleon gave Augereau the economy of force mission of masking Cosseria while Meynier led his brigade back to Cairo. Massing his forces that day, Napoleon also ensured that Laharpe's division and the cavalry moved from Cairo to Dego.[26]

In the end, the Austrians failed to take advantage of the brave sacrifice made at Cosseria by Provera's men, who capitulated to Augereau early on the morning of the 14th due to a lack of food, water, and ammunition.[27] As soon as Napoleon received news of the surrender by way of a large signal fire, he launched an attack with Masséna, Laharpe, and Meynier that enveloped Argenteau's position at Dego. In this Second Battle of Dego,[28] during which some 13,000 French faced 5,400 Austrians, the Allies lost 3,000 casualties as well as 18 guns, compared to 1,500 French killed and wounded. The survivors fled twenty-five miles north along the western bank of the Bormida River to Terzo near Acqui.[29]

After the Second Battle of Dego, Laharpe received orders to turn west and cooperate with Augereau on the following day, 15 April, against the

---

25 Ibid., 27–28; Schels, "Die Gefechte in den Apenninen," 200–203; Fabry, *Campagne de l'armée d'Italie*, 4:245–246; Erdmannsdorff, *Der Feldzug von 1796*, 54, 58–61; Boycott-Brown, *Rivoli*, 241–243.
26 *CN*, Nos 151–156, Napoleon to Masséna, Laharpe, Augereau, Joubert, and Meynard, 14 April 1796, 1:164–167.
27 Schels, "Die Gefechte in den Apenninen," 198.
28 The First Battle of Dego, during which the French commanded by Masséna defeated a small Austro-Sardinian force, took place on 21 September 1794.
29 *CN*, No. 165, Napoleon to the Directory, 15 April 1796, 1:172–173; Schels, "Die Gefechte in den Apenninen," 203–206; Erdmannsdorff, *Der Feldzug von 1796*, 54, 60–61; Boycott-Brown, *Rivoli*, 243–248. According to Erdmannsdorff, 2,160 Piedmontese and 3,260 Austrians, altogether 5,420 men, fought at Dego.

Piedmontese.[30] Masséna again occupied Dego with one of Meynier's brigades; its starving men immediately started looting Dego and did not observe the approach of Vukasović's battalions. Owing to the drunk and disordered state of the French troops, the Austrians smashed through them and retook Dego around 11:00 a.m. At this time, Masséna, who had passed the night at Cairo, met his troops at Rocchetta as they staggered south from Dego. There, he managed to reorganize some 3,000–4,000 men and lead them back to Dego.

At Carcare, Bonaparte received the news of this unexpected turn of events. Concerned that Beaulieu had finally arrived with his main force, he immediately ordered Laharpe and Meynier to lead their exhausted men yet again to Dego. Securing the five-road intersection at Dego became his new immediate objective, as it would allow him to maintain central position and further separate Beaulieu from Colli. Around 2:00, Laharpe's division arrived so that Vukasović's 2,800 Austrians faced more than 13,000 French. Despite the disparity in numbers, the Austrians offered a ferocious fight, costing the French 933 casualties. It took all afternoon before exhaustion, the shortage of ammunition, and the realization that no friendly units would arrive to support him finally convinced Vukasović to order a retreat. However, before he could withdraw, a general assault by the French destroyed the cohesion of his units. In the aftermath, the French either cut down or captured all seven of his battalions. Fewer than 1,000 of his men managed to escape. News of these events convinced Beaulieu to abandon his plans to drive the French from the Italian Riviera. Now, he would reorganize the remains of his shattered army north of the Bormida around Acqui.[31]

On 16 April, Napoleon spent the entire day at Dego with Masséna and Meynier's division awaiting Beaulieu's arrival. Laharpe marched northeast to Sassello, sending patrols in all directions in search of the Austrians, but he returned to Dego late on 16 April after finding no signs of them. Strategically, Napoleon faced a choice. He could advance northeast and seek to finish the Austrians, or he could resume his plan and turn against the Piedmontese. In keeping with his general plan of operations, he decided on the latter, on moving against Colli.[32] Consequently, Bonaparte ordered Masséna to lead Meynier's

---

30   CN, Nos 158–161, Napoleon to Joubert, Augereau, Dommartin, and Sugny, 14 April 1796, 1:167–169.

31   CN, No. 174, Napoleon to the Directory, 16 April 1796, 1:178–179; Erdmannsdorff, *Der Feldzug von 1796*, 62–63; Yorck von Wartenburg, *Napoleon as a General*, 1:32; Boycott-Brown, *Rivoli*, 249–253.

32   Clausewitz, in *Der Feldzug von 1796*, 37, is critical of Napoleon's decision to turn against Colli instead of driving Beaulieu across the Po, which would have forced Colli to abandon his positions out of fear of being cut off from Turin: "Bonaparte was motivated to turn

troops west to a position at San Benedetto. There, he would be able to support Laharpe at Dego should Beaulieu suddenly appear, just as Vukasović had on the previous day. More importantly, from San Benedetto, Masséna could support Augereau against the Piedmontese. Bonaparte rode west late on 16 April, transferring his headquarters to Millesimo.[33]

Meanwhile, after Provera surrendered at Cosseria, Colli realized that Beaulieu's forces would not be able to support him in the near future. Thus, on 15 April, he led his main body west to Ceva with the idea of utilizing its entrenched camp to hold the French until the Austrians recovered. That same day, his rearguard of 6,000 men commanded by General Giuseppe Felice di Vital took a position at Montezemolo. However, Sérurier's advance north along the west bank of the Tanaro River threatened to cut him off from Ceva. Not only did Sérurier's approach threaten to strand Vital east of Ceva, but it also jeopardized Colli's line of retreat to Turin. Consequently, the Piedmontese conducted another general retreat west on 16 April: Colli led the main body across the Corsaglia River while Vital and the rearguard withdrew to Ceva.

Early on 16 April, Augereau's 8,000 men cleared Montezemolo in pursuit of Vital. Reaching Ceva at noon, Augereau spent the next four hours launching futile, uncoordinated attacks on Vital's fortified positions. After sustaining 600 casualties, Augereau ordered his men to make camp and wait for Sérurier to arrive. Although the Piedmontese fought a successful rearguard action, concern over Sérurier's approach prompted Colli to order Vital to leave one battalion in Ceva's citadel and withdraw the rest of his troops west of the Corsaglia during the night of 16/17 April. This proved to be a wise precaution as Sérurier's men camped within sight of Ceva that night. On 17 April, Augereau and Sérurier formed their troops across the Corsaglia from Colli's first line of

---

    toward Colli by the danger the latter posed to his flank. ... We do not wish to dwell on this any longer, but nobody can persuade us that, in the few days the French army would have needed to drive Beaulieu across the Po, Colli would have been in a position to do any serious damage against their flank. Thus, in this case, we find it impossible to recognize Bonaparte's reasoning as correct." Here, Clausewitz is wrong. Beaulieu managed to assemble his army at Acqui. Had Napoleon pursued him on 16 April with Masséna, Laharpe, and Augereau, he would have had to leave Sérurier at Carcare to mask Colli. This would have meant that rather than achieving mass for a battle with Beaulieu, Napoleon's forces would have been equal to or even fewer than the Austrian army. Had he concentrated his entire force against Beaulieu at Acqui, Napoleon would have exposed his line of communications to Colli. According to Jean Collin, the French army had enough ammunition for only one battle with Beaulieu and would have had to be resupplied, which the Piedmontese could have prevented in this scenario. See also Carl von Clausewitz, *La campagne de 1796 en Italie*, trans. Jean Collin (Paris, 1899), 49.

33   CN, Nos 170 and 173, Napoleon to Laharpe and Masséna, 15 April 1796, 1:176–178; Clausewitz, *La campagne de 1796 en Italie*, trans. Collin, 51.

8,000 men and 15 guns posted around Bicocca di San Giacomo and San Michele. The following day, the Piedmontese commander, General Jean-Gaspard Dichat de Toisinge, utilized his well-placed artillery to repulse a combined attack by Augereau and Sérurier.[34]

On 19 April, applying the principles of simplicity and security, Bonaparte rerouted the army's line of communications from the Nice–Imperia–Albenga–Savona–Cadibona–Carcare route to along the Nice–Imperia–Ormea–Ceva road, thus shortening it considerably and avoiding the exposed stretch through the Cadibona Pass. This new line rendered Dego less important strategically, as an Austrian force there could no longer threaten the French army's line of communications. Consequently, Napoleon instructed Laharpe to post one brigade in the Dego–Cairo region and send his other brigade to San Benedetto, which allowed Masséna to move south from there to Ceva to support Sérurier and Augereau as they massed to engage the Piedmontese at the new French objective: San Michele.[35]

Also on 19 April, Napoleon attempted a double envelopment maneuver against the Piedmontese position at San Michele with Sérurier and Augereau. In the ensuing Battle of San Michele, the flooding Corsaglia and stiff enemy resistance stymied the French operation. In light of this setback, Bonaparte halted operations for twenty-four hours while Augereau and Sérurier rested their men, Masséna moved his division into the line, and Laharpe marched to Ceva, leaving only one brigade as a rearguard at Cairo. Correctly reading the situation, Colli ordered a retreat west from the Corsaglia to Mondovi on the night of 20 April to prevent the French from surrounding him at San Michele. Before dawn on 21 April, the French poured across the Corsaglia and smashed through the Piedmontese rearguard, thus commencing the Battle of Mondovi, which pitted 17,500 French against 13,000 Piedmontese. As the speed of the French attack prevented Colli from preparing the defense of Mondovi, he ordered the retreat to continue. At 6:00 p.m., Bonaparte reached Mondovi; the battle cost him another 600 killed and wounded to 1,600 Mondovi casualties.[36]

---

34 CN, Nos 174 and 203, Napoleon to the Directory, 16 and 22 April 1796, 1:179, 195–196; Nos 183–185, Napoleon to Sérurier, 17 April 1796, 1:185–186; Erdmannsdorff, *Der Feldzug von 1796*, 63–64; Boycott-Brown, *Rivoli*, 262–265.

35 CN, No. 189, Napoleon to Sérurier, 19 April 1796, 1:187–188; No. 190, Napoleon to Augereau, Dommartin, and Masséna, 19 April 1796, 1:188; Erdmannsdorff, *Der Feldzug von 1796*, 64.

36 CN, No. 193, Napoleon to Masséna, 20 April 1796; No. 203, Napoleon to the Directory, 22 April 1796, 1:190, 196–197; Erdmannsdorff, *Der Feldzug von 1796*, 64–67; Gunther E. Rothenberg, *The Art of Warfare in the Age of Napoleon* (Bloomington, IN, 1980), 248; Boycott-Brown, *Rivoli*, 265–272; Yorck von Wartenburg, *Napoleon as a General*, 1:34–35.

Napoleon rested the army where its divisions stood on 22 April partly in an effort to curb the rampant looting and partly because he expected Colli to counterattack. After being assured that the Piedmontese were retreating north to Turin, on the 23rd he ordered the pursuit to begin. That same day, Colli requested an armistice. With only 10,000 troops barring the road to Turin and Beaulieu doing little to support them, the Piedmontese wanted to end the unpopular war. Nevertheless, Napoleon continued the advance on Turin; negotiations did not begin until late on 27 April, after Masséna took Cherasco, thirty-five miles south of Turin. Bonaparte offered lenient terms that the Piedmontese accepted at 2:00 a.m. on the following day, 28 April. The Armistice of Cherasco effectively removed Piedmont-Sardinia from the War of the First Coalition and awarded the French the fortresses of Ceva, Cuneo, Tortona, and, temporarily, Alessandria. The acquisition of Cuneo proved vital, as it linked directly with Nice and provided additional security for Napoleon's line of communications, which could now completely avoid the Ligurian coast and the ever-present British fleet. Moreover, the Piedmontese not only declared complete neutrality and granted the French free passage through the kingdom, but they also pledged to guard Napoleon's new line of communications that ran east-northeast along the Cuneo–Ceva–Acqui–Tortona route.[37] Bonaparte also added a clause to the armistice, stating that the French army could cross the Po River at the Piedmontese town of Valenza as soon as it began the pursuit of Beaulieu. Here we see the brilliant mind of the young general at work. Knowing that news of this clause would reach the Austrians, he was already setting the conditions to deceive Beaulieu using the principle of surprise in the next phase of the campaign.[38]

Clausewitz and Yorck von Wartenburg adequately summarize the strategic and operational lessons of the Piedmont Phase. According to Clausewitz:

> This overall success rested mainly on the very successful French strategic combinations, which set up all the individual decisions so advantageously that they could not fail. Consequently, one may say that here, strategy[39]

---

37   Fiebeger, *The Campaigns of Napoleon*, 10.
38   Clausewitz, *Der Feldzug von 1796*, 51.
39   It is important to note that Clausewitz sometimes uses the term "strategy" for what is today called the "operational art." Clausewitz's definition of strategy is close to a mixture of "strategy" and "operations" in their modern definitions. Clausewitz rarely uses the term "strategic combinations" and the definition is hard to nail down. It could be the concept of planning the operations for the situation in front of you; the plan to attain strategic points (key terrain, cities, road networks/intersections, harbors, etc.) or it could be the combination of key principles of war: identifying how much force is needed and where to deliver battle, thus mass, economy of force, and maneuver.

was very strongly dominant to a degree rarely seen elsewhere and, indeed, this factor was decisive almost on its own. ... Bonaparte followed very simple plans, and where great decisions are concerned, such plans are *eo ipso* always the best. We must especially applaud the great energy, the hunger for victory, with which he progressed from one operation to the next.[40]

According to Yorck von Wartenburg:

In this opening of the campaign, we immediately recognize the characteristic stamp of Napoleon's whole generalship: a clear perception of what masses can effect. ... The execution of this principle was the secret of Napoleon's strategy; but, in addition, it is always necessary to be able to distinguish readily the point at which the concentrated attack should be delivered and to possess the strength of mind to disregard all secondary matters, however important they may seem to be, in order to bring your whole force to bear at the decisive point. It is above all this clearness and logical pursuit of strategical [and operational] plans that we admire in Napoleon, and which make the study of him as a general profitable.[41]

11   Lombard Phase

With his rear thus secured, Napoleon prepared to resume the pursuit of Beaulieu. Bonaparte reorganized his army, demanding a higher level of discipline throughout after the officers failed to control the excesses of widescale looting. To curb the problem, he mercilessly requisitioned the Piedmontese for food and clothing to augment the supplies he had captured at Mondovi. After

---

40   Ibid., 31–32.
41   Yorck von Wartenburg, *Napoleon as a General*, 1:38–39. The grandson of Prussian field marshal Hans David Ludwig, Count Yorck von Wartenburg, of the Napoleonic era, Hans Ludwig David Maximilian Yorck von Wartenburg (1850–1900) was a Prussian officer, military attaché, and historian. After serving in the Franco-Prussian War, he attended the Kriegsakademie in Berlin. Upon graduation, he assumed duties on the German General Staff. During this time, he wrote *Napoleon as a General*, which was translated into English ten years later. The two volumes and accompanying atlas served as the standard textbook for the Napoleonic Wars at the U.S. Military Academy at West Point for almost two-thirds of the twentieth century. For a while, Yorck was considered the heir apparent to Alfred von Schlieffen, Chief of the German General Staff, until Yorck's untimely death while serving with the German Expeditionary Force during the Boxer Rebellion in 1900 in China, where he was accidentally killed by carbon monoxide.

posting 5,000 men in the Piedmontese fortresses, Napoleon commenced the Lombard Phase with a field army of 40,000 troops thanks to the arrival of reinforcements. Full of confidence in his offensive plan, he boasted to the Directory on 24 April that in one month's time, he would "be able to seize the whole of Austrian Lombardy up to Mantua and drive Beaulieu from Italy." Four days later, on 28 April, Bonaparte revealed his plans "to be in the mountains of the Tyrol, to meet the Army of the Rhine, and in conjunction with it carry the war into Bavaria." He then assured Carnot that, "with reinforcements, Italy is ours, as I can then march on Naples and Mantua simultaneously."[42]

After Piedmont surrendered, Beaulieu withdrew north from Acqui with some 26,000 men. After vain attempts to secure Tortona and Alessandria south of the Po, he continued to retreat, crossing the Po at Valenza on 2 May and moving his headquarters to Valeggio on the eastern bank of the Agogna. He spread the divisions of Vukasović, Sebottendorf, and General Anton Lipthay de Kisfalud in a cordon along the northern bank of the Po from west to east between its junctions with the Sesia and the Ticino. Believing Bonaparte would cross the Po at Valenza, he positioned 20,000 men along a line of twenty miles.[43]

Having baited Beaulieu into thinking that he would directly follow the Austrians across the Po at Valenza, Napoleon planned to cross east of Valenza and effect a *manœuvre sur les derrières*. Not only would this maneuver surprise the enemy, but it would also place his army on the flank and rear of the Austrians and turn their positions on the Agogna, the Terdoppio, the Ticino, and the Lambro, thus cutting Beaulieu's line of communications. "Thus the French commander planned his crossing according to the simplest and most sweeping strategic principles, and there is certainly no doubt that these were on his mind."[44] Starting on 28 April, Napoleon steadily moved the army toward the Po, spreading false intelligence that he intended to cross at Valenza. He formed a special, handpicked advance guard division consisting of six infantry battalions (3,000 bayonets in total), 1,500 cavalry, and 6 guns under the command of General Claude Dallemagne to execute the crossing. Shortly after 12:00 a.m. on 6 May, Napoleon selected Piacenza as the crossing point. "This river [the Po] is very large," he explains to the Directory, "and difficult to cross. My intention is to cross as close to Milan as possible to avoid any further obstacles before I reach that capital. Today, I march on Piacenza; Pavia will be turned

---

42 CG, Nos 523 and 541, Napoleon to the Directory, 24 and 28 April 1796, 1:358, 368; No. 545, Napoleon to Carnot, 29 April 1796, 1:370.

43 CG, No. 583, Napoleon to the Directory, 9 May 1796, 1:389; Erdmannsdorff, *Der Feldzug von 1796*, 84.

44 Clausewitz, *Der Feldzug von 1796*, 52.

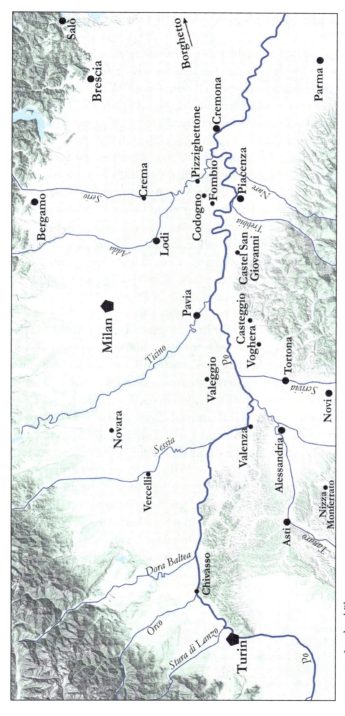

MAP 4.3 Lombard Phase

and, if the enemy determines to defend that town, I will be between him and his depots."[45]

Napoleon applied the principle of simplicity with his plan. With Sérurier's division remaining at Valenza, Dallemagne's division commenced the thirty-mile march east from Casteggio to Piacenza on 6 May with the rest of the army in tow. For security, cavalry screened the southern bank of the Po, itself forming a curtain that concealed French movements. After marching twenty miles, Dallemagne's men camped at Castel San Giovanni that night. Remaining south of Valenza at Tortona to continue the ruse until the last moment, Napoleon finally joined Dallemagne at Castel San Giovanni in time to commence the march to Piacenza at 4:00 a.m. on 7 May. Arriving at Piacenza five hours later, the French seized a ferry. Led by the intrepid Colonel Jean Lannes, they quickly crossed the river. After scattering an Austrian cavalry post of 150 troopers, the infantry established a bridgehead, and the engineers constructed a pontoon bridge. By 2:00 p.m., all of Dallemagne's men had reached the opposite bank, and Laharpe's division started to cross. French patrols soon made contact with Beaulieu's outposts only five miles north of Piacenza. From Fombio, Lipthay's 4,000 infantry and 1,000 cavalry quickly drove the French back to the northern bank of the Po but failed to take the bridgehead, which meant Laharpe's men continued to cross; Lipthay retired to Fombio that evening. After receiving Lipthay's report, Beaulieu directed Vukasović to move from Valeggio to Fombio to support Lipthay. Alertly, Beaulieu also ordered the entire Austrian army to retreat east in the direction of the Adda River.[46]

On the morning of 8 May, Laharpe's division supported Dallemagne's infantry as it assaulted the village of Fombio and forced Lipthay to retreat northeast to Codogno. Allowing the Austrians no respite, the French drove them from Codogno and another five miles east to the Adda, where Lipthay's men escaped to the safety of the east bank via the bridge at Pizzighettone. As Lipthay retreated across the Adda, the rest of the Austrian army was likewise streaking eastward. At 10:00 p.m., General Anton Schübirz von Chobinin's detachment of 1,000 infantry and 500 cavalry collided with Laharpe's 51st Demi-Brigade at Codogno. In the confusion, friendly fire claimed Laharpe's life before Schübirz withdrew around dawn on 9 May.[47]

---

45 CG, Nos 539 and 573, Napoleon to the Directory, 27 April and 6 May 1796, 1:367, 384; Yorck von Wartenburg, *Napoleon as a General*, 1:42.
46 Erdmannsdorff, *Der Feldzug von 1796*, 86–87.
47 CG, No. 583, Napoleon to the Directory, 9 May 1796, 1:389–390; Erdmannsdorff, *Der Feldzug von 1796*, 87–83; Boycott-Brown, *Rivoli*, 299–304; Yorck von Wartenburg, *Napoleon as a General*, 1:46–47.

Beaulieu intended to launch a general offensive to drive the French across the Po and even issued the pertinent orders on the evening of 8 April. However, unable to concentrate his scattered forces, he issued new orders just after 12:00 a.m. on 9 May for the army to withdraw across the Adda at Lodi. With 7,000 men, Sebottendorf received the task of covering Beaulieu, who planned to retreat another seventy miles east to the Mincio River. After crossing that river, the Austrian commander planned to use Lake Garda to the north and the fortress of Mantua to the south to shield his army from Napoleon's flanking movements. For the moment, he turned southeast at Lodi and followed the Adda through Pizzighettone toward Cremona.[48]

Napoleon responded by directing his army, which completed its crossing of the Po on 9 May, to Lodi. Around 9:00 a.m. on 10 May, Dallemagne's vanguard made contact with Sebottendorf's rearguard under Vukasović. After a brief engagement, the Austrians continued their march to Lodi, pursued by Dallemagne. Near Lodi, an Austrian covering force took in Vukasović's tired soldiers and moved across the 250-yard-long bridge, leaving one battalion to hold the weakly fortified western part of the town and take in stragglers. As soon as the French arrived, this battalion also withdrew across the Adda. Deeming it inadvisable to retreat in daylight, Sebottendorf planned to defend the bridge and eastern bank with twelve battalions, four cavalry squadrons, and fourteen guns. In the face of these numbers, Dallemagne decided to await the arrival of reinforcements before attempting to cross the bridge, but French artillery foiled Austrian attempts to destroy the structure.[49]

In brief, Napoleon reached Lodi at 11:30 a.m. and placed several cannon on the west bank. After a lengthy artillery duel with the Austrians, he sent his cavalry to ford the Adda upstream and formed an assault column consisting of the 2nd Battalion of Carabiniers followed by four grenadier battalions. At 7:00 p.m., carabiniers stormed out of Lodi's eastern gate and onto the bridge. As the French approached the halfway point across the bridge, the Austrians opened fire. The French wavered and halted, but Masséna, Cervoni, Dallemagne, Lannes, and Bonaparte's chief of staff, Alexandre Berthier, rushed to the head of the column and led their men forward. Exhausted, hungry, demoralized, and concerned about French cavalry cutting their line of retreat, the Austrians

---

48 J.B. Schels, "Die Kriegsereignisse in Italien vom 15 April bis 16 Mai 1796 mit dem Gefechte bei Lodi," *Österreichische Militärische Zeitschrift* Bd 4 (1825), 57; Erdmannsdorff, *Der Feldzug von 1796*, 88–89.

49 Erdmannsdorff, *Der Feldzug von 1796*, 90–91. Sebottendorf had not attempted to destroy the bridge earlier due to his task of taking in stragglers and detachments that had yet to reach the Adda. He did not believe that the French would make a serious attack on the bridge and so believed that his measures would suffice to defend it.

broke after the carabiniers resumed their advance across the bridge. The Austrians soon regained their composure and conducted an orderly retreat but not after losing 5,200 men, 12 guns, 2 howitzers, and 30 caissons compared to 1,000 French casualties.

The unforgettable storming of the bridge at Lodi had a tremendous psychological effect on both the Austrians and the French and, most of all, on Napoleon himself. "This performance," notes Yorck von Wartenburg, "which he himself described as the boldest of the campaign, inspired him with unwavering confidence in his lucky star. Even at Saint Helena he said: 'Vendémiaire, and even Montenotte, had not yet led me to consider myself a being apart. Not until after Lodi did I feel that I was destined in to play a foremost part on our political stage: that first kindled the spark of boundless ambition in me.'"[50]

Intending to pursue Beaulieu and deliver another blow, Napoleon kept the army concentrated around Lodi on 11 May. Forward detachments spread south toward Cremona and northwest toward Milan. After receiving reports indicating that Beaulieu had retreated southeast to Pizzighettone, Napoleon directed the army there early on the morning of 12 May along both banks of the Adda. Pizzighettone's small garrison surrendered on 13 May, but Beaulieu had already cleared Cremona and crossed the Oglio River *en route* to Mantua. A strong detachment of French cavalry pursued the Austrians as far as Cremona while Dallemagne's advance guard and Augereau's division followed. Convinced that even his swift-moving troops could not overtake Beaulieu, Napoleon decided to complete the conquest of Lombardy. Posting Dallemagne's advance guard and Laharpe's division along the Adda, he directed Augereau to Pavia and Masséna to Milan while Sérurier's division held Piacenza.[51]

Napoleon entered Milan on 15 May, a mere seventeen days after the Armistice of Cherasco and forty-six after he assumed command of the Army of Italy. His occupation of Milan marks the end of the Lombard Phase. Although short, this phase again showcased some of the principles of war necessary for the operational art to succeed: objective, offensive, maneuver, security, surprise, and simplicity. Compliance with these essential requisites assured the success of Napoleon's operational *manœuvre sur les derrières*. He has received some criticism for "needlessly" waging the battle of Lodi. In his defense, he believed that Beaulieu would defend the river crossing with his entire force and justified his

---

50 CG, No. 589, Napoleon to the Directory, 11 May 1796, 1:393–394; Yorck von Wartenburg, *Napoleon as a General*, 1:47–48; Boycott-Brown, *Rivoli*, 310–315; Erdmannsdorff, *Der Feldzug von 1795*, 91–93; Fiebeger, *The Campaigns of Napoleon*, 13–14.

51 CG, No. 588, Napoleon to Carnot, 11 May 1796, 1:392; CN, Nos 417 and 418, Napoleon to Faypoult, and 'Extrait de l'Ordre du Jour," 13 May 1796, 1:332–333; Yorck von Wartenburg, *Napoleon as a General*, 1:49; Fiebeger, *The Campaigns of Napoleon*, 14.

actions by claiming that the battle "won all of Lombardy for the Republic."[52] Clausewitz also supports the result:

> The storming of the bridge at Lodi is an operation that, on the one hand, deviates so far from all conventional practice and, on the other, seems to have so little reason that we must ask ourselves whether it was justified. If it had been repulsed with a bloody nose, then it certainly would have been condemned as an utter blunder. But its very success warns us not to agree so readily; it indicates that there is food for thought here. But it is all the more important not to neglect this point, for here we find, virtually isolated, an element of war and especially of strategy to which we attach the greatest value throughout our thinking: we mean the moral effect of victory, as it exerts its influence on both sides in opposite directions. ... If one now states that there was no strategic reason for storming the bridge at Lodi, that Bonaparte could have had the bridge for free the next day, then one is only thinking of the spatial dimensions of strategy. But is moral weight not also an object of strategy? He who doubts this does not understand war in its entirety, in its living being.[53]

III Venetian Phase

While at Milan, Napoleon did not lose focus on the military situation. He already knew the Austrians intended to reinforce Mantua. He also had to contend with the imminent peril of Austrian reinforcements arriving north of his position from Germany via the Tyrol. Moreover, he remained concerned about the French armies in Germany. On 20 May, he wrote to the French minister in Switzerland, François-Marie Barthélemy, begging for details about the movements of the French Army of the Rhine and the Austrian forces in Bavaria and Swabia. Napoleon specifically asked Barthélemy: "Can the [Holy Roman] Emperor weaken his Rhine army to reinforce the one in Italy? What troops could he still send to the Tyrol?" He directed Barthélemy to dispatch spies to ascertain the size of the forces that Vienna could redirect to Italy.[54] Bonaparte's aggressive quest for operational intelligence proved extremely beneficial later in the campaign.

---

52 CG, No. 588, Napoleon to Carnot, 11 May 1796, 1:392.
53 Clausewitz, *Der Feldzug von 1796*, 73, 75.
54 CN, No. 468, Napoleon to Barthélemy, 20 May 1796, 1:375.

Meanwhile, Beaulieu did not stop retreating until he reached Roverbella, just north of Mantua, where he established his headquarters. During the retreat, he committed troops only to Milan and Pizzighettone, gathering the remainder of his army at Mantua to prepare for the imminent French offensive.[55] Upon arrival, he posted twenty-three battalions and three squadrons – some 8,000 of his 20,000 troops – in the fortress, increasing the garrison to 12,800 men.[56] Beaulieu decided that the entire line of the Mincio River from Mantua to Lake Garda needed to be guarded and so formed a cordon along the nineteen-mile stretch of the Mincio between Peschiera and Mantua.[57] He confided to Colonel Thomas Graham, the British liaison officer attached to his headquarters, that "on the one hand, he had to provide for the defense of Mantua, the key of Italy, and on the other, to keep open his communications, with ... the Tyrol being the only way by which his reinforcements could come or his retreat be made."[58]

On 19 May, Napoleon issued orders for the army to cross the Adda. He commenced operations with the aim of duping Beaulieu into thinking that he intended to march north along the western shore of Lake Garda to the Tyrol. On 24 May, he turned his 25,000-man army northeast to cross the Oglio River and proceed through Brescia to the Chiese.[59] Early on the morning of 28 May, the vanguard, now commanded by General Charles-Edouard Kilmaine, crossed the Chiese and advanced as far as Lonato, sending one demi-brigade north to Salò on the western shore of Lake Garda.[60] Satisfied that his march northeast would confuse the Austrians, Napoleon quickly pivoted southeast, concentrated the army for mass, and utilized the *stratégie de pénétration* to force the crossing of the Mincio at Borghetto on 30 May.

During the course of the fighting, Kilmaine's infantry drove the Austrian defenders east through Valeggio and then six miles north to Castelnuovo.

---

55 CG, No. 598, Napoleon to the Directory, 14 May 1796, 1:399.
56 This figure includes *extrabrachen*, the Austrian term for artillery, engineer, and other combat support troops: J.B. Schels, "Die Verteidigung von Mantua im Juni und Juli 1796," *Österreichische Militärische Zeitschrift* Bd 1 (1830), 87; Graham to Grenville, 19 May 1796, as quoted in John Holland Rose, "The Despatches of Colonel Thomas Graham on the Italian Campaign of 1796–1797," *English Historical Review* 14/53 (January 1899), 112.
57 Schels, "Die Verteidigung von Mantua," 87. Beaulieu posted 3,900 men at Peschiera; 4,500 between Salionze and Oliosi; 2,600 between Campagnola and Pozzolo, and 3,100 in and around Valeggio. Mantua's garrison numbered 10,300 after Beaulieu committed more of its battalions to field service.
58 Graham to Grenville, 22 May 1796, as quoted in Rose, "The Despatches of Colonel Thomas Graham," 113.
59 CG, No. 639, Napoleon to the Directory, 1 June 1796, 1:421.
60 Yorck von Wartenburg, *Napoleon as a General*, 1:57.

Napoleon pursued, expecting Beaulieu to make a stand in that area, but his quarry escaped: Beaulieu retreated north along the eastern shore of Lake Garda to Rivoli and eventually from there to Rovereto in the Tyrol.[61] "As he [Napoleon] had done on the Po," concludes Yorck von Wartenburg, "he turned rapidly to the point chosen for his passage [of the Mincio] and crossed before the scattered Austrians had time to oppose him in sufficient force. It was natural, considering the concentration of Napoleon's forces and the distribution of Beaulieu's, that the former should break the latter's line merely by marching on Valeggio. He thus furnished a good illustration of the principle that the art of strategy consists in assembling the largest possible force at the most important points of any line of operations."[62]

Castiglione

At Vienna, Francis II grew increasingly alarmed by the bad news that he had been receiving since the end of April. Bonaparte's success in Piedmont and Lombardy now forced him to focus much more attention on this secondary theater of operations. Thus, on the same day that the French pushed across the bridge at Lodi, 10 May, eleven infantry battalions and eight cavalry squadrons commenced the march from Austria to northern Italy. Moreover, on 30 May, the Austrians transferred 25,000 men from their Army of the Upper Rhine to the Italian theater. Although Beaulieu desperately awaited the arrival of these reinforcements, he did not know that the officer commanding these troops was his replacement.[63] After news of Beaulieu's defeats in Lombardy reached Francis, he decided to transfer Field Marshal Wurmser from the Lower Rhine theater to Lombardy. "According to the present situation in Italy," Francis explained to Wurmser in a letter dated 29 May, "this theater of war [Italy] is the most important to me. Further enemy progress will result in the devastation of my interior German provinces, while success there promises the most important results with the retaking of the rich provinces I have just lost. The French must be prevented from entering the Tyrol, and prevented from marching

---

61   CG, No. 653, Napoleon to the Directory, 4 June 1796, 1:429.
62   Yorck von Wartenburg, *Napoleon as a General*, 1:55–56.
63   Beaulieu actually left the army on 21 June, handing over command to the Transylvanian-born general of Saxon descent, Michael Friedrich Benedikt von Melas, who had arrived in theater from the Rhine in May. See Carl von Decker, *Der Feldzug in Italien* (Berlin, 1825), 103–104; Clausewitz, *Der Feldzug von 1796*, 102; Erdmannsdorff, *Der Feldzug von 1796*, 178–179.

through and looting Italy or laying siege to the fortress of Mantua, which is to be supplied with everything necessary for a long and vigorous defense."[64]

The seventy-two-year-old Wurmser arrived at Trento in mid-July eager to challenge the young upstart, who was born four years after he had attained the rank of general. After posting 10,000 men as garrison forces in the Tyrol, Wurmser moved south through Trento with his main body. He planned to attack the French in four main columns. The Croatian general Petar Vid Gvozdanović would lead the 18,000 men and 56 guns of Wurmser's right wing south along the western shore of Lake Garda through Gavardo and Salò to reach Brescia and the rear of the French army by 30 July. In the center, Melas would direct the center column of 14,000 men and 58 guns south between Lake Garda and the right bank of the Adige to the Monte Baldo ridgeline; Wurmser wanted this column at Rivoli by 30 July. The ethnic Serb general Pavle Davidović would command the left-wing column of 10,000 men and 60 guns and march south along the left bank of the Adige through Ala to Dolcè. At Dolcè, Davidović would throw a pontoon bridge across the Adige so that his main body could unite with Melas's column. With both columns under Wurmser's direct supervision, they would proceed to Mantua. Finally, a much lighter and faster flank column, consisting of one brigade each of infantry and cavalry (5,000 men and 18 guns total) under the Magyar Johann Mészáros von Szoboszló, would march south-southwest through the Brenta River Valley to Vicenza to mislead the French and force Napoleon to divert forces to guard his flank. Should the French not take the bait, Mészáros would secure Verona and Legnago as soon as the French departed those posts to react to the advance of the main Austrian column.[65]

After Beaulieu's retreat north into the Adige River Valley, Napoleon ordered Masséna to guard the southern approaches of the Tyrol between Lake Garda

---

64   Francis II to Wurmser, 29 May 1796, in Vivenot, *Thugut, Clerfayt und Wurmser*, 447–448; Viktor Hortig, *Bonaparte vor Mantua: Ende Juli 1796* (Rostock, 1903), 25. Clausewitz, in *Der Feldzug von 1796*, 119–120, explains the importance of Mantua to the Austrians: "In July [1796], Mantua was in danger of falling to siege; that would have meant the loss of a great fortress and its 14,000-man garrison, which together were capable of pinning down the French army in Italy, thus preventing a strong, suuccessful offensive through the mountains against the Austrian states. This is the importance of the fortress to the Austrians as defenders; but the other half of its importance concerned the Austrians as attackers. If the French ever conquered Mantua, there would be little chance of [the Austrians] retaking Lombardy through a successful blow, because everything would first depend on the conquest of Mantua. ... Indisputably, the Austrian cabinet thought that, if the relief of Mantua succeeded, the reconquest of the province of Milan [Lombardy] must follow."

65   Decker, *Der Feldzug in Italien*, 104, 106–107; Erdmannsdorff, *Der Feldzug von 1796*, 185–187. Altogether, Wurmser's field army totaled 41,171 infantry, 5,766 cavalry, and 192 guns.

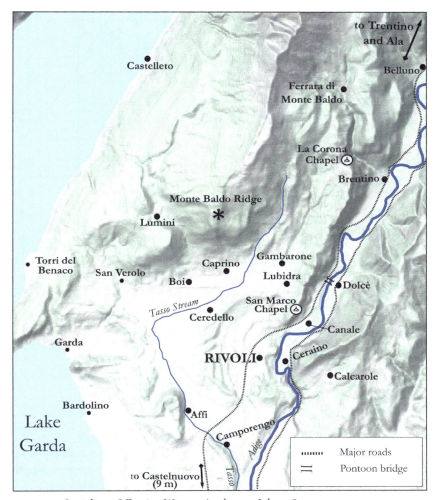

MAP 4.4   Castiglione Offensive, Wurmser's advance, July 1796

and the Adige and to cover the besieging forces of Mantua with his 15,000 men.[66] Bonaparte placed a garrison in the fortress of Verona[67] and tasked

---

66   Clausewitz explains that "Bonaparte was relying on a stout resistance in the Adige Valley to buy him enough time to use the rest of his troops the way he wanted, an absolute defense of the valley was not his intention, or at least not an important element of his plan": Clausewitz, *Der Feldzug von 1796*, 104.

67   Jomini identifies Verona as "an excellent pivot of operations for all of Napoleon's enterprises around Mantua for eight months" in 1796. According to Jomini, "points of support on the strategic front are called pivots of operations ... a material point of both strategical and tactical importance, [which] serves as a point of support and endures

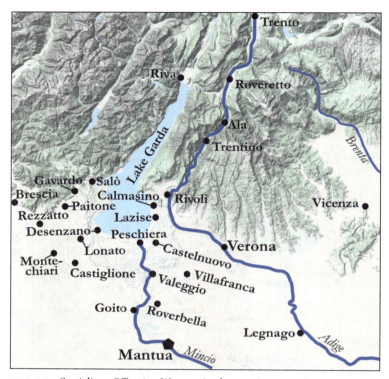

MAP 4.5   Castiglione Offensive, Wurmser's advance, August 1796

Augereau with securing the Adige around Legnago. Laharpe's replacement, General Pierre Franconin Sauret, assumed command of his 4,500-man division as it guarded Bonaparte's main line of communications running through Brescia to Milan. Only three infantry companies held Brescia. This apparent lack of concern over his line of communications likely indicates Napoleon's belief that major Austrian forces could not operate in the mountains west of Lake Garda. With 12,000 men, Sérurier received the task of besieging Mantua and its huge garrison of 11,000 men protected by 316 guns.[68] Altogether,

---

throughout a campaign": Henri de Jomini, *The Art of War*, trans. G.H. Mendell U.S. Army and W.P. Craighill U.S. Army (Westport, CT, 1971), 98.

68   Both Bonaparte and the Directory wanted Mantua in French hands before continuing any further operations. The Austrian commander of Mantua, Joseph Canto d'Yrles, remained determined to put up a stout resistance. On the afternoon of 23 July, he received a message from Wurmser stating that his army would relieve Mantua no later than 2 August. Further messages arrived from Wurmser, repeating the promise of relief. See Phillip R. Cuccia, *Napoleon in Italy: The Sieges of Mantua, 1796–1799* (Norman, OK, 2014), 33–42, 44, 48.

Wurmser enjoyed a considerable numerical superiority over Napoleon's field army: 47,000 Austrians to 35,000 French. Adding the Austrian garrison besieged in Mantua and the French besieging force to these numbers increases the total to 58,000 Austrians and 45,000 French.[69]

Wurmser could not have asked for a better start to his offensive on 29 July. West of Lake Garda, Gvozdanović's brigades caught Sauret by surprise and drove his troops from Salò and Gavardo. After losing 500 men and 2 guns, Sauret ordered a retreat to Desenzano.[70] Gvozdanović himself raced toward Brescia with the brigades commanded by Prince Heinrich XV of Reuß and General Johann Rudolf von Sporck. East of Lake Garda, the Austrians drove through Masséna's advance guard at Brentino and then made straight for Rivoli, nine miles south of Brentino. At Dolcè, Davidović's engineers hastily assembled a pontoon bridge. His main body crossed to the western bank of the Adige and likewise marched to Rivoli. Faced by the Austrian onslaught, Masséna ordered a retreat to Camporengo, three miles south of Rivoli, after losing 1,200 casualties in addition to 1,600 men and 9 guns captured by the Austrians.[71]

At Montichiari on the afternoon of 29 July, Napoleon received news of the Austrian movements and Masséna's retreat. Initially, he appeared shocked and gravely concerned about his line of communications from Verona through Brescia to Milan. To keep open a line of retreat for his army, he established a secondary line of communications to the Po along the Cremona–Pizzighettone–Milan road by clearing its rear of all baggage and sick.[72] "I am obliged to take serious precautions for the retreat," he confides to Sérurier.[73] Yet for Masséna, fighting on the front line, he provides philosophical encouragement: "the fate of arms is daily, my dear general; we will regain, tomorrow or the day after, what you have lost today." Bonaparte's measures indicate that he believed that the Austrians would limit their offensive to the area between the eastern shore of Lake Garda and the banks of the Adige. To support Masséna, he ordered the 4,772 men of General Joseph Despinoy's division along with Kilmaine's cavalry

---

69 CG, Nos 641 and 656, Napoleon to the Directory, 1 and 7 June 1796, 1:424, 431; Erdmannsdorff, *Der Feldzug von 1796*, 187.

70 CG, No. 836, Napoleon to the Directory, 6 August 1796, 1:534.

71 Erdmannsdorff, *Der Feldzug von 1796*, 188–191. On 29 July, Mészáros led his column from Vicenza to Montebello.

72 "The events at La Corona [Brentino] require that the heavy baggage and the treasury proceed to Milan by the roads of Cremona and Pizzighettone. The circumstances are quite critical. Evacuate all of the sick from Cremona, Piacenza, and Milan, and, in general, all of the property belonging to the Republic": CG, No. 818, Napoleon to Gaultier, 29 July 1796, 1:525–526.

73 CG, No. 821, Napoleon to Sérurier, 29 July 1796, 1:527.

of 1,535 troopers to Castelnuovo, twelve miles south of Rivoli. Augereau received instructions to abandon the Adige and withdraw west from Legnago to Villafranca and Roverbella, from where his troops could turn north to Castelnuovo. Napoleon informed Masséna that he planned to be at Castelnuovo by 1:00 a.m. on 30 July.[74]

Wurmser spent the day of 30 July preparing multiple columns to reach Peschiera at the mouth of the Mincio and to drive Masséna beyond Castelnuovo. The advance did not commence until the afternoon, and the Austrians encountered the French sooner rather than later; the two combined to prevent Wurmser from achieving his goals on 30 July. Just south of Rivoli, Davidović's vanguard under Sebottendorf encountered the majority of Masséna's division assembled on the hills by Camporengo. Masséna repulsed the Austrians twice, but the arrival of Davidović's main body prompted him to withdraw eight miles south to Castelnuovo after losing 4 guns and 250 prisoners. Rather than pursue, Davidović's column passed the night at Camporengo. Melas's main body halted and remained at Calmasino, seven miles north of Castelnuovo, for unknown reasons. Due to the late start and the tough French resistance, Sebottendorf only reached the hills of Lazise, six miles north of Peschiera. On a more positive note for the Austrians, Mészáros occupied Verona and Legnago as soon as the French departed.[75]

That same morning, 30 July, the vanguard of Gvozdanović's right wing, led by Colonel Johann von Klenau, surprised the French garrison at Brescia. The Austrians gained the town by *coup de main*, capturing 700 effectives plus 2,000 wounded and sick recovering in the hospital.[76] Among the prisoners were the future marshals Jean Lannes and Joachim Murat, who were quickly exchanged. By taking Brescia, the Austrians managed to crush Napoleon's left flank and cut his line of communications to Milan on the second day of their offensive. That afternoon, Gvozdanović reached Brescia. Around midnight, he continued the march toward Montichiari, fourteen miles southeast of Brescia. From Salò, the Hungarian general Péter Károly Ott von Bátorkézi led one of Gvozdanović's brigades twelve miles south toward Lonato in an attempt to envelop Bonaparte's left. However, Ott's brigade, exhausted from hard marching and a shortage of

---

74 CG, No. 816, Napoleon to Augereau, 29 July 1796, 1:525; No. 820, Napoleon to Masséna, 29 July 1796, 1:526.
75 Erdmannsdorff, *Der Feldzug von 1796*, 191–193; Decker, *Der Feldzug in Italien*, 107–108, 110–111; Clausewitz, *Der Feldzug von 1796*, 106, 109.
76 The Austrians lost only three killed and eleven wounded. Among the prisoners were two generals, four colonels, and twenty other officers. The Austrians also captured 2 guns, 500 muskets, and considerable supplies. See CG, No. 836, Napoleon to the Directory, 6 August 1796, 1:534; Erdmannsdorff, *Der Feldzug von 1796*, 193–194.

provisions, reached only Ponte San Marco, where the Brescia–Verona highway crossed the Chiese River just west of Lonato. The failure to reach Lonato on 30 July would prove costly. Despite this shortfall on 30 July, Gvozdanović planned to occupy Lonato and Montichiari the following day, 31 July.[77]

Before transferring his headquarters to Castelnuovo on the night of 29–30 July, Napoleon learned that Austrian columns advancing down the western shore of Lake Garda had reached Salò. Thanks to his central position, which allowed information to reach him quickly, he gained an overview of the situation and, with it, an appreciation for the tremendous danger that threatened his army. "Here is the perilous situation of the army," he explains to Augereau. "The enemy has pierced our line at three points; he is master of the important positions of La Corona[78] and Rivoli; Masséna and Joubert have been forced to concede to larger forces; Sauret has abandoned Salò and is retreating to Desenzano; the enemy had seized Brescia and the bridge at San Marco. You see that our communications between Milan and Verona are now cut."[79] Too late, he recognized that Wurmser intended to use the Austrian right wing to take Brescia and thus sever the Army of Italy's line of communications to Milan and ultimately France itself. Napoleon concluded that Wurmser then intended to crush the French army by converging on it from the west (from Brescia) and from the east (from the Adige). At this early stage of the Austrian offensive, his options remained limited, as Gvozdanović had already enveloped the French left and would soon threaten the army's rear.[80]

With Gvozdanović at Brescia, Bonaparte decided to exploit the advantages of his central position. Using his interior lines, he planned to mass the army against Gvozdanović and reopen his primary line of communications through Brescia to Milan. Napoleon did not have to execute a *manœuvre sur la position centrale*, as the Austrian advance south along both sides of Lake Garda combined with his own dispositions to give him central position by default. Moreover, with the lake between them, Wurmser and Gvozdanović operated on exterior lines making maneuver, mass, simplicity, and offensive more difficult to attain. With 42,000 men, Bonaparte commanded sufficient manpower

---

77 Erdmannsdorff, *Der Feldzug von 1796*, 194–195.
78 Shortened in military dispatches to La Corona, the full name of the chapel is the Santuario Madonna della Corona (Sanctuary of the Lady of the Crown). Built right into a vertical cliff face of Monte Baldo, the chapel appears to be suspended in mid-air.
79 CG, No. 822, Napoleon to Augereau, 30 July 1796, 1:527.
80 Clausewitz is quick to declare that "it is highly unlikely that Bonaparte, who never lost his head easily, would have lost it over an event whose development he had anticipated for several weeks and for which he was entirely prepared": Clausewitz, *Der Feldzug von 1796*, 108; CG, No. 836, Napoleon to the Directory, 6 August 1796, 1:534–535.

to mask Wurmser long enough to use his interior lines to concentrate overwhelming numbers against Gvozdanović. As Clausewitz notes: "When one is united, in the best case, there is everything to hope for and, in the worst, there is nothing to fear."[81] In an even bolder move, instead of allocating considerable forces to hold the Mincio against Wurmser, Napoleon decided to open the road to Mantua and raise the siege to see if the Austrian would make for the fortress rather than support Gvozdanović.[82]

From Castelnuovo, Napoleon instructed Masséna to withdraw west from Castelnuovo to Peschiera on the west bank of the Mincio. There, he would abandon the east bank of the Mincio and move the bulk of his division eight miles west to Desenzano, leaving 1,500 men at Valeggio to guard its bridge over the Mincio. Napoleon also ordered Masséna to send reinforcements to Augereau in the form of one demi-brigade.[83] Masséna's division reached Peschiera on the evening of 30 July and crossed the Mincio.[84] After transferring his headquarters to Desenzano, Bonaparte summoned Despinoy's division to march twelve miles west from Castelnuovo to Desenzano to unite with Sauret early on 31 July. From there, they would advance eleven miles north to Salò that same day, attack the Austrians at daybreak, and then drive west toward Brescia; Dallemagne received a firm directive to take Lonato.[85] As for Sérurier, Napoleon instructed him to raise the siege of Mantua. His troops that stood east of the Mincio would unite with Augereau's division, while those posted on the west bank of the Mincio would assemble at Marcaria to guard its bridge over the Oglio and secure the new line of communications of Cremona–Pizzighettone–Milan. After uniting with the reinforcements provided by Masséna and Sérurier, Augereau, whose division assembled at Roverbella on the evening of 30 July, would march to Montichiari via Goito. Napoleon intended to withdraw the entire army west of the Mincio both to evade Wurmser and to mass his forces against Gvozdanović; the Mincio would provide a temporary obstacle to Wurmser. "Given how matters stood on 29 July," judges Clausewitz, "Bonaparte's defense was indisputably one of the most beautiful examples in the history of warfare."[86]

---

81 Clausewitz, *Der Feldzug von 1796*, 18.
82 Erdmannsdorff, *Der Feldzug von 1796*, 195.
83 CG, No. 824, Napoleon to Masséna, 30 July 1796, 1:528.
84 CG, No. 836, Napoleon to the Directory, 6 August 1796, 1:535.
85 CG, No. 825, Napoleon to Sauret and Despinoy, 30 July 1796, 1:528.
86 CG, Nos 827 and 829, Napoleon to Sérurier, 30 and 31 July 1796, 1:529, 531; No. 828, Napoleon to Masséna, 31 July 1796, 1:530; Clausewitz, *Der Feldzug von 1796*, 106–108, 130; Erdmannsdorff, *Der Feldzug von 1796*, 195–196.

As noted, Gvozdanović planned to occupy Lonato and Montichiari on 31 July. Thus, the First Battle of Lonato on 31 July occurred as a collision of Gvozdanović's forces moving east-southeast and Bonaparte's army moving west-northwest. Ott's brigade marched seven miles east from Ponte San Marco to Lonato, where he engaged Despinoy and Masséna. During four hours of hard combat directed by Napoleon himself, the French drove Ott's outnumbered soldiers from Lonato and through Ponte San Marco. North of Lonato, Sauret marched from Desenzano to Salò and defeated the Slovenian general Joseph Ocskay von Ocskó's brigade but suffered a wound that forced him to turn over command to General Jean Joseph Guieu. With Despinoy detained at Lonato, Guieu did not feel that his troops sufficed to march on Brescia and so evacuated Salò and returned to Desenzano.

During the fighting on 31 July, Gvozdanović moved his two vanguards and the brigades commanded by Reuß and Sporck fourteen miles southeast from Brescia to Montichiari, itself five miles south of Ponte San Marco and less than six miles southwest of Lonato. Arriving at Montichiari at 9:00 a.m., Gvozdanović spent most of the day there planning his next operation rather than marching to the sound of the guns. How different from Napoleon's command style! Around 9:00 p.m. that night, Gvozdanović received news of Ocskay's defeat and subsequent retreat three miles north from Salò to Vobarno. Ocskay's report emphasized the brigade commander's doubt that he could secure Gvozdanović's line of retreat to the Tyrol: the Austrians did not know that Guieu had evacuated Salò and returned to Desenzano. Concerned about his own line of retreat through Salò and with the French massing at Lonato, Gvozdanović decided to suspend his offensive until he could retake Salò and secure his communications. At 10:00 p.m. on the night of 31 July, he ordered Reuß and Sporck to retreat from Montichiari through Ponte San Marco toward Gavardo. Klenau remained at Montichiari with a small rearguard while Ott and Ocskay followed Gvozdanović toward Gavardo on the morning of 1 August. Gvozdanović planned to remain at Gavardo until he gained a clear picture of French intentions or until he received word from Wurmser, who thus far had remained silent.[87]

Elsewhere on 31 July, Wurmser continued his movements between the eastern shore of Lake Garda and the west bank of the Adige. Sebottendorf arrived at Peschiera and the Mincio but did not cross the river; Melas and Davidović reached Castelnuovo. From the hills of Castelnuovo that afternoon, Wurmser could see all the way to Ponte San Marco. In the distance, he observed Gvozdanović's columns in combat with the French. He also could discern the

---

87   Erdmannsdorff, *Der Feldzug von 1796*, 199.

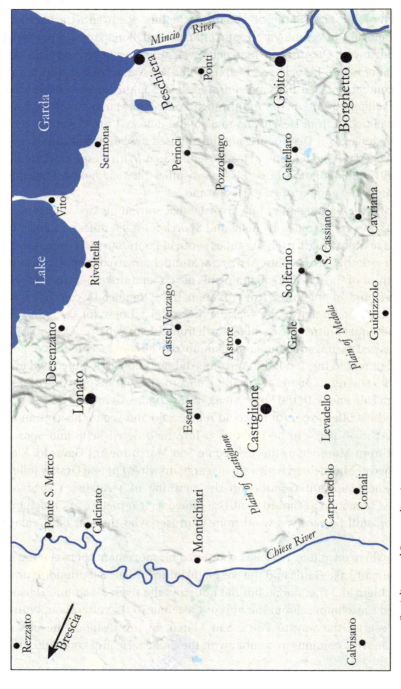

MAP 4.6 Castiglione and Surrounding Area

numerous French reinforcements moving toward Gvozdanović's position. That view convinced Wurmser to continue another six miles south with Melas and Davidović to Valeggio, cross the Mincio there, and move west in an attempt to link with Gvozdanović. Aware of a French force under Augereau seven miles south of Valeggio at Roverbella, Wurmser decided to post three brigades east of Valeggio at Villafranca to observe the French. With his remaining troops, he commenced the march from Castelnuovo south to Valeggio at 4:00 p.m. on 31 July but concern about the French force at Roverbella froze his operations throughout 1 August.[88]

As noted, Augereau had reached Roverbella on the evening of 30 July to cover Sérurier's troops as they raised the siege of Mantua.[89] Napoleon then led Augereau's 12,000-man column northwest on a thirty-mile march starting on the evening of 31 July from Goito through Montichiari toward Brescia. As Augereau's rearguard, Napoleon posted one brigade of 1,800 men under General Antoine La Valette at Castiglione, with orders to hold the position at all costs. On Bonaparte's right, Despinoy and Masséna marched early on 1 August on a parallel road from Lonato through Ponte San Marco toward Brescia. Bonaparte reached Brescia with Augereau's vanguard at 11:00 a.m., concluding a maneuver that Clausewitz describes as "eccentric and wonderful"; the divisions of Masséna and Despinoy arrived later in the day.[90] Napoleon instructed Sauret, who had taken back command of his division, to make another attempt on Salò on 1 August. Due to confusion over his orders, Sauret camped his division west of Lonato. Napoleon had reached his limits with Sauret; he ordered him to surrender command of the division to Guieu.[91] Regardless, by taking Brescia, Bonaparte restored his primary line of communications with Milan.

As for Wurmser, on the morning of 1 August, he masked Peschiera and concentrated his main body at Valeggio, but would not cross the Mincio until he received clarification about the situation at Roverbella. Thus, Lipthay led the

---

88 CG, No. 836, Napoleon to the Directory, 6 August 1796, 1:535; Erdmannsdorff, *Der Feldzug von 1796*, 196–198; Decker, *Der Feldzug in Italien*, 111–112; Clausewitz, *Der Feldzug von 1796*, 109–110.

89 According to an Austrian report, between 19 and 31 July, the French fired 4,000 mortar bombs, 2,000 exploding shells, and 6,000 hotshot at the fortress; the number of roundshot fired is not known. At 10:00 the following night, Sérurier bade the city farewell with hotshot and explosive shells before moving westward behind the Oglio. After raising the siege, Sérurier left behind a siege train consisting of 100 guns, 12 mortars, and 9,000 cannonballs. See Schels, "Die Verteidigung von Mantua," 149, 152.

90 Clausewitz, *Der Feldzug von 1796*, 110.

91 CG, No. 831, Napoleon to Sauret, 1 August 1796, 1:532; No. 836, Napoleon to the Directory, 6 August 1796, 1:535; Erdmannsdorff, *Der Feldzug von 1796*, 200.

army's vanguard south to Roverbella, found it evacuated by the French, and pursued the enemy west to Goito. There, his cavalry crossed the Mincio thanks to the locals who had already repaired the bridge after the French had damaged the structure. Lipthay's lead elements pursued La Valette all the way to Castiglione.[92]

During the course of 1 August, Wurmser received a report from Mantua that completely changed the situation. According to the Austrian commandant, Canto d'Yrles, his patrols "noticed an extraordinary silence in the enemy lines around the fortress this morning." Reports then arrived that the French had abandoned all of the trenches and siege works around Mantua. Not only did the French disappear, but they left behind all of their artillery and ammunition. On all of the roads leading west, the Austrians found discarded muskets and baggage: the signs of a precipitous flight. By the time Canto wrote this report, his patrols had already captured one French colonel, ten other officers, and more than one hundred prisoners. Nine miles southwest of Mantua, at Borgoforte, the Austrians located the French army's entire artillery park of almost 100 cannon, 12 huge mortars, 80,000–90,000 bombs and balls, 40,000 hundredweight in lead, a multitude of small firearms, bayonets, and sabers, four boats fully loaded with ammunition, two powder magazines, and a large quantity of lumber and spades.[93]

In a letter written from Valeggio on 2 August, Wurmser informed Francis that the French had raised the siege of Mantua thanks to the "force of maneuvering and converging on General Bonaparte." Colonel Graham seconded this opinion in his report to London: "These well concerted and rapid movements determined General Buonaparte to an immediate retreat across the Po and the Mincio."[94] Wurmser believed that, by occupying Brescia, Gvozdanović had prompted the French to mass at that location, thus providing Wurmser with an excellent opportunity to strike the rear of the enemy army. Thus, he planned to lead his entire army across the Mincio at Goito and proceed in great haste to Brescia. To catch the retreating French, Wurmser ordered Mészáros to cross the Po. "I love Milan too much," wrote the Austrian commander, "to leave the army for even a short time, and we must not give the enemy time to continue to damage Lombardy; for this reason I cannot go to Mantua myself." Expecting to drive the French completely out of Lombardy, Wurmser sent General Franz von Lauer to Mantua to determine if the fortress contained enough cannon to

---

92   Erdmannsdorff, *Der Feldzug von 1796*, 201.
93   Canto d'Yrles to Wurmser, 1 August 1796, in Vivenot, *Thugut, Clerfayt und Wurmser*, 475–476; Schels, "Die Verteidigung von Mantua," 151–152.
94   Graham to Grenville, No. 18, 1 August 1796, in "The Despatches of Colonel Thomas Graham," 119.

support the future sieges of Tortona and Alessandria or if the artillery train currently in the Rhine theater should be transferred to Italy.[95]

From Valeggio, Wurmser informed Canto d'Yrles that Bonaparte intended to move his entire army against Brescia and the Austrian right wing. To prevent this, and with the threat to his rear eliminated by the French abandonment of their position at Roverbella, Wurmser decided that all of his forces, including the three brigades at Villafranca, would cross the Mincio at Goito. Mészáros received orders to advance to the Po by forced marches. Wurmser also instructed Canto d'Yrles to send the Croatian generals, Vukasović and Rukavina, with seven infantry battalions and three-quarters of one cavalry squadron of the Mantua garrison by way of Goito to join the main army. Canto d'Yrles protested, claiming that the French siege corps, which remained thirteen miles west of Mantua near Marcaria, still posed a viable threat to the fortress. Eventually, on the following day, 3 May, Canto d'Yrles sent Vukasović with four battalions and four companies: fewer than 2,000 men.

Consequently, the main body of the Austrian army commenced the ten-mile march south from Valeggio to Goito at 3:00 a.m. on 2 August. Ahead of it, Lipthay led the vanguard across the Mincio at Goito, marched northwest in excessive heat to Castiglione, and ejected Valette's rearguard from the town, taking 600 prisoners.[96] Wurmser's main body reached Goito but did not cross the Mincio.[97] Clausewitz sheds light on the reasons why Wurmser did not rush across the river:

> Wurmser probably thought the French army was in full retreat. He found the siege [of Mantua] apparently abandoned in the greatest haste and confusion, the whole siege park and all its associated equipment left behind, and General Sérurier withdrawing. It was like finding a room with everything left just as it was when its occupants suddenly fled. The Austrians were overcome with joy and amazement. Wurmser believed this was the result of his superior numbers, his enveloping attack, and his successful actions ...; thus he believed he had obtained a complete victory and achieved his goal. Thus, on 2 August, he rested at Mantua, just letting

---

95   Wurmser to Francis II, 2 August 1796, in Vivenot, *Thugut, Clerfayt und Wurmser*, 474–475; Hortig, *Bonaparte vor Mantua*, 120; Antoine de Jomini, *Histoire critique et militaire des Guerres de la Révolution*, 15 vols (Paris, 1821), 8:256–257; Decker, *Der Feldzug in Italien*, 113, 115; Clausewitz, *Der Feldzug von 1796*, 110–112.
96   Graham to Grenville, Nos 19 and 20, 2 and 4 August 1796, in "The Despatches of Colonel Thomas Graham," 119.
97   Erdmannsdorff, *Der Feldzug von 1796*, 201–202; Decker, *Der Feldzug in Italien*, 113; Hortig, *Bonaparte vor Mantua*, 116.

General Lipthay advance from Goito to Castiglione in continued pursuit of the defeated enemy.[98]

While Wurmser believed he had achieved a great strategic victory, Gvozdanović regrouped three of his four brigades around Gavardo on 2 August while Ocskay's brigade occupied Salò to reopen the line of communications to Riva. Around noon, Gvozdanović received a letter from Wurmser, dated 1 August, stating that he would cross the Mincio on 2 August and drive against the rear of the French army. To support Wurmser's operation, Gvozdanović ordered three of his brigades to conduct a search-and-destroy mission between Lonato and Desenzano on 3 August. With Ocskay forming the left, Reuß the center, and Ott the right, the Austrians would advance south and attack any French columns they encountered; Sporck's brigade and Klenau's vanguard would remain in reserve at Gavardo.[99]

Aside from restoring his primary line of communications by retaking Brescia, Napoleon probably hoped to find Gvozdanović's main body there, so he could attack it and cut its line of communications across the Chiese River. Although Gvozdanović proved to be more elusive, Bonaparte gained a better understanding of the overall situation. As a result, he ordered Augereau and Kilmaine to march back to Montichiari at dawn on 2 August to shield the rear of the army while he concentrated it to attack Gvozdanović on the following day. To do so, Bonaparte instructed Dallemagne to lead his brigade from Rezzato to pin Gvozdanović's main body at Gavardo while Despinoy led the majority of his division from Brescia to Gavardo to turn his right. From Lonato, Guieu would lead his division back to Salò to turn Gvozdanović's left. To support the operation, Masséna received orders to concentrate at Ponte San Marco and then march to Lonato. After defeating Gvozdanović, Napoleon planned to rush the majority of his forces to the Mincio to engage Wurmser.[100]

On the evening of 2 August, reports arrived to inform Bonaparte that Wurmser was closer than he thought, with the Austrian vanguard having driven La Valette's rearguard from Castiglione. Although Napoleon had advised La Valette to hold the town at all costs, the vastly outnumbered French retreated

---

98 Clausewitz, *Der Feldzug von 1796*, 110–111. Clausewitz concludes by stating: "It was not until the evening of 2 August that he learned that Gvozdanović had been attacked on all sides and thrown back with considerable loss." However, in his brief of 2 August from Goito, Graham states that "no report had yet been received from General Gvozdanović": Graham to Grenville, No. 19, 2 August 1796, in "The Despatches of Colonel Thomas Graham," 119.
99 Erdmannsdorff, *Der Feldzug von 1796*, 203–204.
100 Clausewitz, *Der Feldzug von 1796*, 112–113; *CG*, No. 836, Napoleon to the Directory, 6 August 1796, 1:535.

six miles northwest to Montichiari pursued by Lipthay. Augereau managed to stem the panic caused by La Valette's flight and to push Lipthay back to Castiglione, where the Austrians remained.[101] Wurmser's movements placed Napoleon in a predicament: Lipthay's march threatened to cut his line of retreat to Pizzighettone while an advance by Gvozdanović would again threaten to sever his line of communications with Milan. Bonaparte again considered a general retreat, this time west of the Adda. Quickly regaining his *sangfroid*, he ordered Augereau to Castiglione, halfway between Brescia and Goito, to contain Wurmser should he advance. This would gain space to maneuver between the two Austrian forces and secure his line of communications with Milan. Napoleon proceeded with his decision to have Despinoy, from Brescia, Dallemagne, from Rezzato, and Guieu, from Lonato – altogether some 6,000 men – push Gvozdanović's forces north beyond Salò and Gavardo. Bonaparte planned to remain in central position at Lonato with Masséna's division and proceed according to circumstances. "I shall seize the first occasion to deliver battle to the enemy," he declared; "it will decide the fate of Italy. Beaten, I will retire to the Adda; victorious, I will not stop at the marshes of Mantua."[102] The resulting encounters between the French and Austrian columns initiated the Second Battle of Lonato on 3 August 1796.[103]

The combatants started their marches long before sunrise. On the French left, Despinoy's division did little. After making contact with Gvozdanović's forward posts, Despinoy's vanguard panicked, broke, and carried the rest of the division back to Brescia. On the French right, Guieu took a little-known path that the locals revealed to him, leading north from Lonato across the hills between Lake Garda and the Chiese River to Salò. After finding Salò clear of Austrian forces, Guieu marched west toward Gavardo with his vanguard, taking Gvozdanović's artillery park in the process and turning the guns against Austrian headquarters. With his camp and headquarters in complete confusion, Gvozdanović personally led a counterattack with three of Sporck's battalions that drove the French back to Salò. In the meantime, Guieu's main body as well as four battalions from Masséna's division had reached Salò. With the French massing at Salò, Gvozdanović halted on the hills west of the town.

In the French center, Dallemagne started the eight-mile march northeast from Rezzato toward Gavardo. At Paitone, the French passed around Ott's right

---

101 *CG*, No. 836, Napoleon to the Directory, 6 August 1796, 1:535. A furious Napoleon demoted La Valette in front of his troops the following day; he was later court-martialed and cashiered.
102 *CG*, No. 833, Napoleon to Salicetti, 2 August 1796, 1:533.
103 Erdmannsdorff, *Der Feldzug von 1796*, 205; Clausewitz, *Der Feldzug von 1796*, 112–113; Elijah Adlow, *Napoleon in Italy 1796–1797* (Boston, MA, 1948), 100–101.

without being detected and quickly crossed the remaining three miles to reach Gavardo. Dallemagne arrived at Gavardo after Guieu's attack and Gvozdanović's counterattack and pursuit to Salò. The French drove the remaining Austrians from Gavardo, but Sporck managed to reorganize his troops and retake Gavardo. Dallemagne led his troops back to Rezzato. On Gvozdanović's left, Ocskay reached Desenzano and then continued three miles southwest to Lonato, scattering Masséna's pickets near Ponte San Marco. At Lonato, he defeated Masséna's vanguard, the 4th Light Demi-Brigade, capturing its commander, General Pijon, in the process. Ocskay occupied Lonato, where he awaited Reuß and Ott. For reasons unknown, Ott did not move beyond Paitone, but Reuß, with Gvozdanović's center column, continued toward Lonato. In the meantime, Napoleon assembled Masséna's entire division of some 10,000 men at Ponte San Marco. From there, he led it to Lonato, arriving around noon and attacking Ocskay's 5,000 Austrians. To block Ocskay's retreat, Bonaparte directed his adjutant, Colonel Jean-Andoche Junot, who now commanded Pijon's 4th Light Demi-Brigade, to take a side road to Desenzano with that brigade, along with the Guides Squadron and the 15th Dragoon Regiment.

Overwhelmed at Lonato, the Austrians fell back toward Desenzano, pursued by Masséna. As the Austrians approached the hills just west of Desenzano, they found Junot's force blocking the road. The arrival of Masséna's troops forced Ocskay to surrender along with the majority of his troops. As they stacked their arms, the Austrians heard the fighting resume: Reuß's column of 1,800 men had reached the outskirts of Desenzano and overwhelmed Junot's force. Reuß held Desenzano for one hour until Napoleon himself arrived at the head of Masséna's troops. Reuß withdrew north, hoping to reach Salò with his column. After locals informed him that the French held Salò, Reuß turned northwest via Gavardo before arriving at Gvozdanović's headquarters outside Salò.

Gvozdanović remained on the hills facing Salò, intending to retake the position the next day, 4 August. For this purpose, he attempted to assemble the majority of his troops. Due to the exhaustion of their troops and the shortage of victuals and ammunition, Ott and Sporck advised against attacking the French at Salò. The two generals suggested falling back twenty miles to reassemble the army, but Gvozdanović remained committed to taking Salò, after which he would resume his plan to march southeast to facilitate Wurmser's operation on the Mincio. This resolution broke after Reuß arrived at midnight and brought news of the destruction of Ocskay's brigade.

Although Gvozdanović suffered considerable losses with respect to Ocskay's column, his three other brigades (Sporck, Ott, and Reuß) clearly defeated Despinoy, Dallemagne, and Guieu at Gavardo. However, instead of focusing on the success at Gavardo, Gvozdanović obsessed over Ocskay's defeat at Lonato and the losses suffered there. Having heard nothing from Wurmser since the letter he received on 2 August, Gvozdanović concluded that the Austrian commander-in-chief had failed to cross the Mincio. Reports that Napoleon himself had commanded the troops that defeated Ocskay served to support this assumption. According to his estimates, Gvozdanović believed that his brigades had faced at least three-quarters of the Army of Italy during the Second Battle of Lonato on 3 August 1796.

Assuming that Napoleon had little concern about Wurmser attacking his rear, Gvozdanović expected the French commander to launch another general attack against him on 4 August. With fewer than 10,000 effectives, weakened by the shortages of provisions and munitions, Gvozdanović decided that he could not withstand an attack by Napoleon's entire army. He ordered the retreat north to Riva to begin immediately. He planned to round the northern tip of Lake Garda and then march down its eastern shore to unite with Wurmser in one week. In his haste to retire on 4 August, Gvozdanović reopened Napoleon's line of communications with Milan and removed any further chances of the two Austrian forces uniting. Critically, his decision to retreat allowed Napoleon to concentrate more than 25,000 men against Wurmser's 20,000.[104]

Elsewhere on 3 August, at daybreak, Wurmser's army finally crossed the Mincio and took the road that ran northwest to Brescia through Guidizzolo, Castiglione, and Montichiari. Lipthay planned to continue from Castiglione to Montichiari to support Gvozdanović, but Augereau attacked with 11,000 men before the Austrians commenced their march. Outnumbered three to one, Lipthay eventually withdrew four miles southeast to Solferino. Moving toward the sound of the guns from the direction of Goito, General Anton Schübirz's brigade counterattacked Augereau, halting the French advance and securing the village of Solferino.

Although Lipthay was unable to support Gvozdanović, the former's defense of Castiglione allowed Wurmser to cross the Mincio unmolested and concentrate his forces in battle order on the hills of Solferino by the afternoon of 3 August. At this point in the campaign, Wurmser squandered an opportunity. With almost 20,000 men at his disposal, Wurmser enjoyed a considerable numerical advantage over Augereau and should have attacked. Unfortunately

---

104   CG, No. 836, Napoleon to the Directory, 6 August 1796, 1:535–536; Erdmannsdorff, *Der Feldzug von 1796*, 203–210; Decker, *Der Feldzug in Italien*, 115; Clausewitz, *Der Feldzug von 1796*, 113–115; Adlow, *Napoleon in Italy*, 101–102; Boycott-Brown, *Rivoli*, 393–395. In the fighting on 3 August, the Austrians lost more than 3,000 killed, wounded, and captured, along with 20 guns; French losses numbered at least 2,000.

for the Austrians, the crossing of the Mincio and march to Solferino satisfied Wurmser's objectives for that day.

With Wurmser remaining idle, Augereau launched repeated probing attacks on the Austrian position until late in the night that kept the Austrian camp in a state of unease. Wurmser's losses on 3 August amounted to 1,000 men. That night, Wurmser wrote to Gvozdanović, who he believed had assembled his brigades at Brescia, informing him that he had reached Castiglione. Moreover, Wurmser claimed that his troops needed a day of rest on 4 August and would not attack the French army but he expected to be assaulted at Castiglione. Should this occur, he wanted Gvozdanović to launch a general attack against all French forces on his front. He instructed Gvozdanović to place greater weight in numbers on his left wing while Wurmser would do the same on his right so that the two Austrian forces could break through the French position at Desenzano and unite. Little did Wurmser know that Gvozdanović would be retreating north on 4 August.[105]

Napoleon himself arrived at Castiglione on the evening of 3 August. Dissatisfied with the operation against Gvozdanović, he issued orders for Despinoy, Guieu, and Louis-Vincent-Joseph de Saint-Hilaire, who had replaced the sick Dallemagne, to again attack the Austrians at Gavardo on the following morning, with Masséna's division in support. In compliance with these orders, the French columns marched west from Salò on the road to Gavardo at 5:00 on the morning of 4 August, engaging Gvozdanović's rearguard, commanded by Sporck. One hour later, Sporck ordered the retreat to commence.[106]

Although Wurmser managed to concentrate his army at Solferino on 3 August, he continued to waste precious time on 4 August by resting his troops and making secondary arrangements that yielded little benefit during the following day's battle. In short, he ordered Mészáros to unite with him and shield the army's left. Unfortunately for the Austrians, Mészáros reached Mantua with his 5,021 men only on 5 August and could not arrive in time for the battle. Moreover, to increase the strength of his right, Wurmser summoned the brigade blockading Peschiera – Colonel Franz Weidenfeld's three battalions and one squadron – to march *west* and unite with the main army. He then ordered Vukasović's brigade, which had already reached Solferino, to march *east* and assume the blockade of Peschiera. Consequently, neither Vukasović's troops nor Weidenfeld's participated in the Battle of Castiglione. Sometime during

---

105   Erdmannsdorff, *Der Feldzug von 1796*, 210–213, 216; Decker, *Der Feldzug in Italien*, 115–116; Clausewitz, *Der Feldzug von 1796*, 113.
106   CG, No. 836, Napoleon to the Directory, 6 August 1796, 1:536–537; Erdmannsdorff, *Der Feldzug von 1796*, 216–218.

the night of 4–5 August, Wurmser received news of Gvozdanović's "defeat" on 3 August. This made a union between the two Austrian forces appear impossible. Wurmser realized that he could not withdraw in the face of the enemy, especially with his back to the Mincio. He had no choice but to prepare for battle on 5 August.[107]

Satisfied that Gvozdanović no longer posed a threat, Napoleon decided to attack and attempt to destroy Wurmser on 5 August. He ordered Despinoy to advance with haste from Brescia to Castiglione. Sérurier's illness caused him to turn command of his division over to General Pascal Antoine Fiorella, who would conduct a *manœuvre sur les derrières* by marching seventeen miles north from Marcaria through Guidizzolo to Castiglione, enveloping Wurmser's left and attacking the rear of his army. Meanwhile, Masséna's troops marched from Lonato and Desenzano to take a position west of Solferino on Augereau's left. From Salò, Guieu's division would monitor Gvozdanović's retreat.[108]

Analyzing the actions of each commander on 4 August reveals stark differences. Wurmser was not efficient in concentrating his forces to ensure a numerical superiority at the decisive point. He also failed to coordinate with Gvozdanović effectively.[109] Conversely, Napoleon concentrated his forces and selected Fiorella's line of advance to ensure that the enemy was not simply beaten, but annihilated.

The two armies faced each other the following morning, with the Austrian right and the French left anchored on the hills south of Solferino. The Austrian line of 19 battalions, 4 companies, and 10 cavalry squadrons, totaling some 20,000 men, extended from Solferino to Monte Medalano. On the French left, Masséna's division of about 10,000 men deployed on one line west of Solferino; Augereau's division of 9,000 troops deployed in two lines on the right, southwest of Solferino. Despinoy was *en route* from Brescia with 7,500 men. Kilmaine's Reserve Cavalry, 1,200 men, deployed *en echelon* to the right of Augereau on the Brescia–Castiglione–Mantua road. As noted, Napoleon ordered Fiorella on 4 August to march that night for Guidizzolo, where his force of 5,000 men would serve as the principal maneuver element for the attack and bring the total French army present on the field to about 32,000 combatants. Napoleon awaited Fiorella's arrival throughout the morning of 5 August as the two sides skirmished.

---

107 Erdmannsdorff, *Der Feldzug von 1796*, 201, 212, 219.
108 Ibid.; Clausewitz, *Der Feldzug von 1796*, 114–115; Decker, *Der Feldzug in Italien*, 116; Boycott-Brown, *Rivoli*, 395–398; Fiebeger, *The Campaigns of Napoleon*, 27–28.
109 With his right threatened by Guieu at Salò, Gvozdanović commenced the retreat to Riva on 4 August: Clausewitz, *Der Feldzug von 1796*, 115–116.

After marching all night, Fiorella's troops reached Guidizzolo and continued to Cavriana. There, they surprised the unsuspecting Austrians and overran Wurmser's command post. Meanwhile, after learning that Fiorella's lead elements had reached Cavriana on the Austrian left rear, Napoleon launched a general attack. Vastly outnumbered at the critical point on the battlefield, Wurmser's troops retreated to Borghetto, leaving the field to the French. Wurmser initially attempted to defend along the Mincio on 8 August, but Napoleon sent Augereau across the river at Valeggio and Masséna at Peschiera, which turned the Austrian right. That evening, Wurmser ordered a general retreat to the Tyrol.[110]

Following Castiglione, Wurmser began the task of extracting his army. He arrived at the gates of Verona on the night of 7 August, hotly pursued by the French, and continued his retreat north that same night. Meszaros's cavalry covered the retreating Austrian columns, but he directed his four infantry battalions to Mantua. By nightfall, these troops entered Mantua, increasing the garrison to 16,423, of which 12,224 were fit for service. In front of the advancing French, the Austrian columns withdrew along the same roads on which they had advanced less than two weeks earlier. Mészáros retired as far as Bassano; Wurmser established his headquarters north of Trento on 19 August. In hindsight, Wurmser's failings are easy to point out. However, we must remember that, throughout his offensive, he felt that the relief of Mantua was his main objective.[111]

Napoleon ordered Fiorella to blockade Mantua on 8 August with Sérurier's division; lacking heavy artillery, the French could not resume the siege. As for the rest of the army, Sauret advanced north along the Lake Idro road, west of Lake Garda, while east of the lake Masséna reached Rivoli on 10 August and Augereau moved into Verona. The rapid Austrian retreat afforded the French time to refit their divisions and exchange prisoners of war. Napoleon also adjusted his army's command structure based on leader performance. Unhappy with Despinoy, he dispatched him to a fortress command in Piedmont, placing his soldiers under Sauret. He then replaced Sauret with General Claude Henri Vaubois. Bonaparte also replaced Fiorella with General Jean Joseph Sahuguet to command Sérurier's division. By the end of August,

---

110 CG, No. 836, Napoleon to the Directory, 6 August 1796, 1:537; Erdmannsdorff, *Der Feldzug von 1796*, 219–223; Decker, *Der Feldzug in Italien*, 119–121; Bernhard Voykowitsch, *Castiglione 1796: Napoleon Repulses Wurmser's First Attack* (Vienna, 1998), 73–76; Adlow, *Napoleon in Italy*, 106–108.

111 CG, Nos 838 and 855, Napoleon to the Directory, 6 and 14 August 1796, 1:538, 546; Clausewitz, *Der Feldzug von 1796*, 116–118; Hortig, *Bonaparte vor Mantua*, 177; Pommereul, *Campagne du général Buonaparte*, 1:123.

Sahuguet had blockaded Mantua with 8,000 men; Augereau held Verona with 9,000; Masséna stood at Rivoli with 13,000; and Vaubois remained west of Lake Garda with 11,000. The French gained a series of minor victories pursuing the Austrians north to Rivoli and east to Verona and beyond.[112]

For the French, nine days of campaigning from the start of Wurmser's advance to his retreat resulted in Austrian losses of 17,000 men including 391 officers. The major cost for Napoleon was the interruption of the siege of Mantua and the loss of his entire siege train.[113] As he was not strong enough to continue siege operations and simultaneously fight the relieving Austrian army, Napoleon's decision to abandon his siege train and concentrate all of his forces against the enemy force on his left was not simply the best and simplest plan according to Clausewitz, but it was the only logical plan.[114] Although his immediate objective was the capitulation of Mantua, his primary task was to hold the line on the Mincio with the purpose of protecting Lombardy.[115] His decision to retreat behind the Mincio and mass all of his forces in a central position (*manœuvre sur la position centrale*) at the base of Lake Garda between Gvozdanović and Wurmser's columns so that he could operate against one at a time, even while his line of communications was threatened, demonstrates Bonaparte's resolve and ability to "see the battlefield." Although Wurmser possessed the larger army, the Austrian failed to get even half of his army to the battlefield, while Napoleon managed to mass a larger force at the point of attack, where numbers mattered most. His use of the besieging forces from

---

112 CN, No. 854, Napoleon to Fiorella, 8 August 1796, 1:663; No. 866, Napoleon to Sahuguet, 10 August 1796, 1:671; CG, No. 855, Napoleon to the Directory, 14 August 1796, 1:546; Decker, *Der Feldzug in Italien*, 122–123; Clausewitz, *Der Feldzug von 1796*, 118–119; Yorck von Wartenburg, *Napoleon as a General*, 1:73; Pommereul, *Campagne du général Buonaparte*, 1:123.

113 Decker, *Der Feldzug in Italien*, 121. In itself, this constituted a victory for Wurmser. "The siege of Mantua was lifted," explains Clausewitz in *Der Feldzug von 1796*, 120–121, "so the fortress was out of danger; thus the first part of the objective was achieved, but the second part [the reconquest of Lombardy] failed. The first part is obviously the primary objective.... Thus, while the Austrians had lost the offensive value of Mantua for the time being, it retained its defensive significance, which was now the main issue given the current state of affairs."

114 Clausewitz, *Der Feldzug von 1796*, 130.

115 Yorck von Wartenburg, *Napoleon as a General*, 1:67–69, 71; CN, Nos 847–849, Bonaparte to Fiorella, Pelletier, and Augereau, respectively, 6 August 1796, 1:658–659. According to Yorck von Wartenburg, "Here we disagree with Clausewitz, who attributes equal value to Bonaparte's tasks of holding the line of the Mincio and covering the siege of Mantua." In light of Napoleon's failure to maintain the siege, Clausewitz argues that Wurmser "achieved his central aim" and that "Bonaparte's method was new, fast-paced, of great decisiveness, and unprecedented activity; one could call it brilliant; but it was not correct and could not achieve the task set before him": Clausewitz, *Der Feldzug von 1796*, 124.

Mantua to provide the *manœuvre sur les derrières* against Wurmser clearly demonstrates Napoleon's use of the principles of war with respect to simplicity, mass, maneuver, and surprise.

Bassano

By diverting 30,000 troops from their army along the Rhine for Wurmser's first expedition to relieve Mantua, the Austrians reduced the strength of their forces in the German theater to such an extent that the French were able to cross the Rhine and resume offensive operations. Jourdan moved his Army of the Sambre and Meuse across that river north of the Main while Moreau crossed at Strasbourg with his Army of the Rhine and Moselle. By 20 August, Jourdan's forces were closing on the Imperial Free City of Nuremberg on Bavaria's northern border while Moreau's approached the Imperial Free City of Ulm on Bavaria's western border. The Directory instructed Moreau to move another 130 miles south-southeast to Innsbruck. There, he would be in position to threaten Wurmser's line of communication with Vienna, which would enable Bonaparte to remain on the offensive. In fact, the Directors believed that Moreau's advance would cause Wurmser to evacuate the Tyrol and rejoin Archduke Charles north of the Alps. Napoleon received a copy of this plan along with orders to launch an offensive in the Tyrol and to leave the garrison of Mantua "to die of sickness."[116]

The Austrians also prepared their next move on a strategic chessboard that spanned from Germany to Italy. General Franz von Lauer, Wurmser's new chief of staff, recommended dividing the army into two corps[117] of approximately 20,000 men each. Davidović would command one of the two and remain in the Lower Tyrol to defend the upper Adige Valley east of Lake Garda and attract Napoleon's attention. Wurmser would take the second corps, consisting of divisions commanded by Gvozdanović and Sebottendorf, through the Valsugana (Sugana Valley) and the Brenta Valley to Bassano. There, Wurmser would unite with Mészáros's 7,000-man division and proceed to the crossing over the Adige at Legnago with the same objective: relieving Mantua. Each corps could independently advance with caution; if Napoleon attacked one, the other would relieve Mantua and threaten the French line of

---

116   Antonin Debidour, ed., *Recueil des Actes du Directoire Exécutif: procès-verbaux, arrêtés, instructions, lettres et actes divers*, 3 vols (Paris, 1913), 3:332–334, 336–337; J.B. Schels, "Die zweite Einschließung Mantuas im August 1796 und gleichzeitige Ereignisse bei dem k. k. Heere unter dem FM. Grafen Wurmser in Tirol und Vorarlberg," *Österreichische Militärische Zeitschrift* Bd 4 (1831), 277.

117   In this sense, "corps" means a body of troops and not the combined arms "mini-armies" that Napoleon would develop later in his career.

communication. On 1 September 1796, Wurmser's corps began its movement to unite with Mészáros's division at Bassano. The threat posed by Moreau's army approaching from the north caused Davidović to send 7,000 men to Neumarkt, twenty miles north of Trento. His main body of 8,000 soldiers, located near Rovereto, had outposts to the south at Ala and a reserve of 5,000 men to the north at Trento.[118]

On 31 August, Napoleon informed the Directory and Moreau that on 2 September he would commence the advance on Trento and arrive there on 4 or 5 September. He planned to advance north in three columns: Vaubois up the west side of Lake Garda, and Masséna and Augereau to the east.[119] On 2 September, Masséna crossed the Adige and marched north along its eastern bank. He arrived at Ala on 3 September, forcing Davidović's outposts to fall back to Rovereto. That same day, Vaubois rounded the northern shore of Lake Garda. On 4 September, he united with Masséna and engaged Davidović at the Battle of Rovereto, capturing the town of Rovereto at a cost of 750 killed and wounded, and sending the Austrians staggering north after they sustained 3,000 casualties. Meanwhile, Wurmser continued his advance along the Brenta despite receiving word of Davidović's debacle. In response, he simply ordered Davidović to hold Trento. Regardless, Davidović failed to contain Masséna, who entered Trento unopposed at 8:00 a.m. on 5 September after the Austrians withdrew five miles north to Lavis. Vaubois's division reached Trento at noon on 5 September while Augereau's men continued their march north toward Trento. From Trento, Napoleon led Vaubois's division and one brigade from Masséna's division to Lavis in pursuit of Davidović, who continued his retreat another ten miles north from Lavis. Satisfied with his progress in that sector, Napoleon left Vaubois at Lavis to mask Davidović and returned to Trento.[120]

During the course of 5 September, Napoleon attempted to obtain a complete picture of the situation. He learned that Davidović's troops at Lavis did not represent the Austrian main force. Instead, Wurmser apparently had led his main force east and into the Brenta Valley to escape Masséna's onslaught. Thus, Bonaparte incorrectly concluded that Wurmser's movement constituted a retreat rather than an advance to relieve Mantua. Instead of retreating south

---

118   Decker, *Der Feldzug in Italien*, 131–132; Wurmser to Francis II, 1 September 1796, as quoted in Vivenot, *Thugut. Clerfayt und Wurmser*, No. 198, 486–489; Schels, "Die zweite Einschließung Mantuas im August 1796," 280.

119   See CG, No. 891, Napoleon to Berthier, 1 September 1796, 1:566–567.

120   CG, No. 886, Napoleon to Moreau, 31 August 1796, 1:563; No. 894, Napoleon to the Directory, 6 September 1796, 1:569–570; Decker, *Der Feldzug in Italien*, 133–135. According to Napoleon's report to the Directory, the Austrians lost 6,000–7,000 prisoners, 25 guns, 50 caissons and 7 flags to only 200 French killed and wounded.

along the eastern shore of Lake Garda, he decided to pursue Wurmser east and through the Brenta Valley with Augereau and Masséna on 6 September while Vaubois masked Davidović.[121]

Davidović's defeat at Rovereto prompted Wurmser to accelerate his march as Napoleon had succeeded in cutting him off from Trento and the Tyrol. The Austrian commander realized that he had to concentrate his corps at Bassano as quickly as possible in order to establish a new line of communications that ran northeast through the Friuli. On the other hand, it appears that he did not believe Napoleon would pursue him. Instead, Wurmser believed that Napoleon would march on Innsbruck to unite with Jourdan and Moreau coming from the Rhine. Mészáros, whose division formed Wurmser's vanguard, reached the suburbs of Vicenza on 6 September and proceeded to Montebello as Wurmser's main body reached Bassano, twenty miles northeast of Vicenza.[122]

Advancing on 6 September, Augereau's troops marched hard to reach Primolano, seventeen miles north of Bassano, on the morning of 7 September. There, the 5th Light Demi-Brigade and 4th Demi-Brigade practically destroyed Wurmser's rearguard of three Croatian battalions.[123] Augereau continued his advance that same day, leading the army to Cismon, where Napoleon established his headquarters. Wurmser's disbelief about Napoleon's appearance behind him could not have been slight, as he expected Bonaparte to be marching on Innsbruck. With the French commander so close, Wurmser decided to make a stand at Bassano. He posted his rearguard under the Croatian general Adam Bajalić von Bajaházy at Solagna on the eastern bank of the Brenta, five miles north of Bassano. Outside Bassano, Sebottendorf's division deployed on the western bank of the Brenta and Gvozdanović's on the eastern bank; Mészáros's division, which had attacked the French garrison at Verona on 7 September, remained too far away to support Wurmser.

---

121   Regarding Davidović, Jomini determines: "If Davidović on the Lavis had driven Vaubois from Trento, he might have embarrassed Napoleon; but this Austrian general, previously beaten at Rovereto, and ignorant of what the French army was doing for several days, and thinking it was all upon him, would scarcely have thought of resuming the offensive before Napoleon beaten at Bassano would have been on his retreat. Indeed, if Davidović had advanced as far as Rovereto, driving Vaubois before him, he would there have been surrounded by two French armies, who would have inflicted upon him the fate of Vandamme at Kulm." For the Kulm reference, see chapter 11. See Jomini, *Art of War*, 131; *CG*, Nos 894–895, Napoleon to the Directory, 6 September 1796, 1:570–572; *CN*, No. 971, Napoleon to Vaubois, 6 September 1796, 1:751–752; Decker, *Der Feldzug in Italien*, 136, 138; Yorck von Wartenburg, *Napoleon as a General*, 1:75–76; Adlow, *Napoleon in Italy*, 128.
122   Decker, *Der Feldzug in Italien*, 137.
123   *CG*, No. 897, Napoleon to the Directory, 7 September 1796, 1:573.

NAPOLEON'S FIRST ITALIAN CAMPAIGN, 1796–1797   163

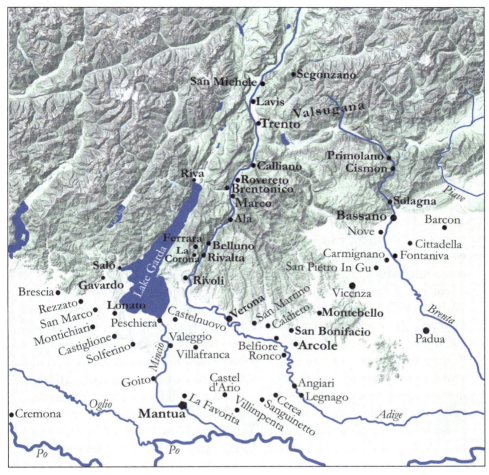

MAP 4.7   Bassano and Arcole Offensives

At 2:00 a.m. on 8 September, Napoleon continued the advance from Cismon down the Brenta Valley toward Bassano with some 20,000 French troops. Five hours later, Augereau's division routed Bajalić's rearguard. Augereau and Masséna then proceeded down the eastern and western banks of the Brenta, respectively, and engaged the Austrians. On both sides of the Brenta, the French coordinated their attacks better than the Austrians, whose artillery park returned from its post at Cittadella just in time to clog all of the roads in Bassano. Augereau's troops stormed Bassano while Masséna's soldiers gained the bridge over the Brenta. Forced to abandon the town, Wurmser narrowly escaped but personally led the wreck of two grenadier battalions to Montebello, halfway between Vicenza and Verona, where he united with Mészáros's division. Sebottendorf's weary survivors reached Vicenza but the French cut off Gvozdanović, who retreated eastward to the Friuli. Wurmser's losses in the Battle of Bassano amounted to 600 killed and wounded, 3,000 captured along with 35 guns, a bridge train, and 200 caissons, compared to 400 casualties on the French side.[124]

"In six days," Napoleon triumphantly reported to the Directory, "we have fought two battles and four engagements. We have taken 16,000 prisoners, among whom are many generals; the rest [of the enemy] have been killed, wounded, or scattered. In six days, always fighting in inexpugnable gorges, we have marched forty-five leagues [112 miles], taken seventy cannon with their caissons and horses, a part of their grand park, and considerable magazines spread along the route."[125] Although exaggerated, Napoleon's letter demonstrates the incredible speed of his army's pursuit through the Brenta Valley, his command of the principle of offensive, and the culminating effect of his victory at the Battle of Bassano.

Following Bassano, Napoleon wanted to complete the destruction of Wurmser's army, which still numbered 10,000 infantry and 4,000 cavalry. Yet, following the battle, the Austrians scattered in so many directions that he could not discern the actual road that Wurmser had taken. Therefore, Bonaparte took steps to counter any possible Austrian movement. To prevent Wurmser from retreating to the Piave River in the east, he sent Augereau thirty miles south of Bassano to Padua. To stop the Austrians from advancing west on Verona or Mantua, Bonaparte instructed Masséna to pursue the enemy force under Sebottendorf that had retreated to Vicenza. With Augereau and Masséna thus closing off the Brenta, Wurmser had little choice but to continue west to Mantua.[126]

On 9 September Wurmser crossed the Adige at Legnago and continued his march to Mantua. Also reaching the Adige, Masséna's vanguard crossed the river twelve miles north of Legnago at Ronco. Napoleon directed Masséna southwest to intercept Wurmser's advance at Sanguinetto on the Legnago–Mantua road. To press Wurmser from the rear, Augereau received orders to march southwest from Padua toward Legnago. Napoleon's plan to cut off Wurmser started to unravel on 11 September after Masséna's guide led him to

---

124   *CG*, Nos 898, 899, and 906, Napoleon to the Directory, 9, 10, and 16 September 1796, 1:574–575, 578; Pommereul, *Campagne du général Buonaparte*, 1:139–141; Decker, *Der Feldzug in Italien*, 138–139; Boycott-Brown, *Rivoli*, 431.
125   *CG*, No. 898, Napoleon to the Directory, 9 September 1796, 1:574.
126   *CG*, No. 906, Napoleon to the Directory, 16 September 1796, 1:578; Decker, *Der Feldzug in Italien*, 140; Adlow, *Napoleon in Italy*, 132.

Cerea, twenty-five miles east of Mantua, rather Sanguinetto. Likewise on the Legnago–Mantua road, Cerea marked the mid-point between Legnago and Sanguinetto. By marching to Cerea rather than Sanguinetto, Masséna lost the element of surprise due to Cerea's closer proximity to Legnago, where Austrian patrols spotted the French movement.

Leading Wurmser's vanguard, Ott reached Cerea before the French but failed to hold the town against Masséna's vanguard. After Cerea changed hands several times, Wurmser's main body started to arrive. The fresh Hungarian troops of the Alvinczi Infantry Regiment drove the French back along the road toward Ronco, capturing 736 men and 7 cannon. During the combat at Cerea, Napoleon rode up to the village just as the Hungarians completed their rout of the French. He quickly fled the field with his troops just minutes before Wurmser himself arrived.[127]

In the aftermath of the Austrian victory at Cerea, Sahuguet evacuated his investing lines at Mantua, moved his troops north along the western bank of the Mincio, crossed the river at Goito, and proceeded to Castel d'Ario east of Mantua on the Legnago–Mantua road. There, he and Kilmaine prepared to attack Wurmser.[128] The Austrian continued his march on 11 September, reaching Sanguinetto, where he learned that Sahuguet would attempt to stop him near Castel d'Ario. A local offered to lead Wurmser's troops along a route supposedly unguarded by the French. Thus guided, Wurmser and his troops commenced the march at midnight on 12 September. Marching through the night, the Austrians turned off the Legnago–Mantua road before reaching Castel d'Ario, headed south, and then turned west once again at Villimpenta. Despite hard marching all day, Masséna could not catch up with Wurmser, who reached Mantua's San Giorgio suburb on the morning of 13 September.[129]

Meanwhile, on 12 September, Augereau's division reached Legnago and invested the town. Augereau fell sick and turned over his command to General Louis-André Bon, who accepted the surrender of Legnago's garrison on 13 September. With Legnago in French hands, Napoleon could concentrate on

---

127 CG, No. 906, Napoleon to the Directory, 16 September 1796, 1:578–579; Decker, *Der Feldzug in Italien*, 140–141; Boycott-Brown, *Rivoli*, 433–434; Fiebeger, *Campaigns of Napoleon*, 34.
128 On 10 September, Bonaparte had ordered Sahuguet to unite all of his forces at Goito: CN, No. 984, Napoleon to Sahuguet, 10 September 1796, 1:761.
129 CG, No. 906, Napoleon to the Directory, 16 September 1796, 1:579; Napoleon Bonaparte, *Memoirs of the History of France during the Reign of Napoleon, Dictated by the Emperor at Saint Helena to the Generals Who Shared His Captivity, and Published from the Original Manuscripts Corrected by Himself* (hereafter cited as *Memoirs at Saint Helena*) (London, 1823), 3:270–271; Decker, *Der Feldzug in Italien*, 140–142; Fiebeger, *Campaigns of Napoleon*, 35; Boycott-Brown, *Rivoli*, 434.

blockading Mantua and trapping Wurmser. Consequently, Bon led Augereau's division west toward the fortress.[130]

Reinforced by Mantua's garrison, Wurmser deployed 25,000 men on the field between the San Giorgio suburb and La Favorita, with 5,000 inside the fortress to defend the city walls. He developed a forward position east of San Giorgio with an advance post at the village of Due Castelli. Unfortunately for the Austrians, on 14 September Masséna's vanguard advanced from Castel d'Ario, surprised the Austrians at Due Castelli, and quickly took the position. Ott and Klenau counterattacked from San Giorgio, forcing the French to abandon their artillery. Both sides committed reinforcements, but the first day of the Battle of San Giorgio ended in a draw.[131]

This gave Bonaparte the opportunity to again display his ability to turn a seemingly lost situation into a clear victory. Never accepting defeat, or in this case a stalemate, he planned a well-organized attack for the following day, 15 September, against the 18,000 Austrians in the area between San Giorgio and La Favorita.[132] The Battle of San Giorgio resumed on 15 September with Sahuguet driving back the Austrian left under Ott to the La Favorita palace, while Bon led Augereau's division up the east bank of the Mincio to hit the Austrian right at San Giorgio. Although Wurmser successfully countered Bon's troops at San Giorgio, the Austrian commander believed that he was facing both Augereau and Masséna. Realizing he needed more manpower, Wurmser summoned battalions from his center. After Sahuguet launched a fresh attack on La Favorita, Wurmser directed another 6,000 men from his center to reinforce his left. Thus reinforced, Ott managed to repulse Sahuguet's attacks throughout the day, but Bonaparte had won the chess match by prompting Wurmser to strip his center. Napoleon launched Masséna's columns from a concealed position that hit the Austrian center at the precise moment that it was most vulnerable.

---

130 At Legnago, the French took 22 cannon and 1,673 prisoners, and freed the 500 French prisoners whom the Austrians had captured during the combat at Cerea. See *CG*, No. 906, Napoleon to the Directory, 16 September 1796, 1:579; Bonaparte, *Memoirs at Saint Helena*, 3:271–272; Decker, *Der Feldzug in Italien*, 142.

131 *CG*, No. 906, Napoleon to the Directory, 16 September 1796, 1:580; André Masséna, *Mémoires de Masséna*, ed. by Jean Baptiste Frédéric Koch, 8 vols (Paris, 1848), 2:194; Bonaparte, *Memoirs at Saint Helena*, 3:271–272; Édouard Gachot, *Histoire militaire de Masséna: le première campagne d'Italie* (Paris, 1901), 180–182; Fiebeger, *Campaigns of Napoleon*, 36.

132 The 25,000 men in the above represents the total number of Austrians outside Mantua, including those south of San Giorgio on the east bank of the Mincio, the advanced post at Due Castelli, and any soldiers west of La Favorita in the Sant'Antonio area. The 18,000 represent the soldiers between San Giorgio and La Favorita.

After crushing Wurmser's center, Masséna's division wheeled south and attacked the flank of the Austrians defending San Giorgio and then occupied that suburb. The troops on the Austrian right, which was southeast of San Giorgio, heard the increasing sound of artillery and musketry behind them to the north. Despairing, they gave way to Bon's steady attacks. The Austrians at San Giorgio managed to reach Mantua while those in the center and on the left flank retired to the protection of the citadel. The Austrians lost some 2,500 casualties, 2,000 prisoners, and 25 guns compared to 1,500 killed and wounded and 9 guns lost by the French. That night, the French bivouacked at the captured San Giorgio suburb and celebrated their success. Once again, Napoleon orchestrated a textbook battle at San Giorgio, capitalizing on his use of maneuver, surprise, mass, and offensive.[133]

Now trapped in the fortress that he had marched to relieve, Wurmser had 29,676 men at his disposal, yet combat effectives numbered only 18,000 men, as the other 12,000 were sick or wounded. Napoleon bottled Wurmser in the island fortress after what Clausewitz terms a "complete strategic defeat," and the Army of Italy again had a brief respite from the fighting.[134] Kilmaine remained around Mantua with his two divisions under Sahuguet and Dallemagne, each consisting of approximately 4,500 troops. Vaubois took 8,000 troops into the Tyrol to observe the valley of the Adige and cover Trento. Masséna with 5,500 men and Augereau with 5,400 first marched to Verona and then to positions along the Brenta.[135]

The extraordinary decision Napoleon made on 5 September to pursue Wurmser from Trento through the Brenta Valley to Bassano provides an excellent example of his use of maneuver. "Bonaparte's conduct against the second Austrian offensive," judges Clausewitz, "is beyond all praise. He chose the most decisive course of action because he was certain of his objective, and he

---

133 Future marshals Lannes, Murat, and Victor sustained wounds in the battle. Napoleon estimated that 5,000 of Wurmser's troops joined the Mantua garrison. See *CG*, No. 906, Napoleon to the Directory, 16 September 1796, 1:579–580; *CN*, No. 998, Bonaparte to Sahuguet, 14 September 1796, 1:770; Bonaparte, *Memoirs at Saint Helena*, 3:272–273; Masséna, *Mémoires de Masséna*, 2:196–198; Gachot, *Histoire militaire de Masséna*, 183–186.
134 Clausewitz, *Der Feldzug von 1796*, 154.
135 *CG*, No. 907, Napoleon to Kilmaine, 16 September 1796, 1:581; No. 958, Napoleon to the Directory, 1 October 1796, 1:608; "Früh Rapport," 17 September 1796, Festung Mantua, Karton 1121, May through September 1796, Österreichisches Staatsarchiv, Kriegsarchiv (ÖstA KA); Bonaparte, *Memoirs at Saint Helena*, 3:273; J.B. Schels, "Die Begebenheiten in und um Mantua von 16 September 1796 bis 4 Februar 1797; nebst der Schlacht von Rivoli," *Österreichische Militärische Zeitschrift* Bd 2 (1832), 163.

executed it with a force and ferocious pace that had no equal."[136] According to Jomini:

> There were but three courses open to him, – to remain in the narrow valley of the Adige at great risk, to retreat by Verona to meet Wurmser, or the last, – which was sublime, but rash, – to follow him into the valley of the Brenta, which was encircled by rugged mountains whose two passages might be held by the Austrians. Napoleon was not the man to hesitate between three such alternatives. He left Vaubois on the Lavis to cover Trento, and marched with the remainder of his forces on Bassano. The brilliant results of this bold step are well known. The route from Trento to Bassano was not the line of operations of the army, but a strategic line of maneuver.... However, it was an operation of only three or four days' duration, at the end of which Napoleon would either beat or be beaten at Bassano: in the first case, he would open direct communication with Verona and his line of operations; in the second, he could regain in great haste Trento, where, reinforced by Vaubois, he could fall back either upon Verona or Peschiera. The difficulties of the country, which made this march audacious in one respect, were favorable in another; for even if Wurmser had been victorious at Bassano he could not have interfered with the return to Trento, as there was no road to enable him to anticipate Napoleon.[137]

Arcole

In November 1796, the Austrians sent a new army to Italy to relieve Mantua. To command it, they selected the sixty-one-year-old Hungarian József Alvinczi de Borberek. Lieutenant-Colonel Franz von Weyrother, his chief of staff, based the upcoming operations on two corps: the "Tyrol corps" under Davidović (18,500 men) and the "Friuli corps" under Gvozdanović (28,700 men). Weyrother divided Gvozdanović's Friuli corps into two wings: Gvozdanović would lead the right wing across the Piave to Bassano on the Brenta while Provera led the left wing to Fontaniva on the same river nine miles south of Bassano. The Austrian plan called for Davidović to march south along the eastern bank of the Adige. After retaking Trento and Rovereto, he would seek to unite with Alvinczi, who would be with Gvozdanović's corps, near Verona. After defeating Napoleon at Verona, Alvinczi wanted to push the French west of the Mincio; a column of mostly militia led by General Johann Ludwig von

---

136 Clausewitz, *Der Feldzug von 1796*, 155.
137 Jomini, *Art of War*, 131.

Loudon would march from the Tyrol south along the western shore of Lake Garda toward Brescia to hit the rear of the French army. The plan called for Wurmser's troops to sortie from Mantua and cooperate with Alvinczi's field army. A simple plan in concept, it proved difficult to execute with a newly created army operating on two separate lines of operation. Regardless, given their numerical superiority, Austrian confidence in the plan remained high.[138]

Austrian movements did not escape Napoleon. However, Bonaparte severely underestimated Davidović's strength. Having received reinforcements, Davidović's 18,000 men decisively outnumbered Vaubois's 8,000. Regardless, Vaubois attacked the Austrians at San Michele and Segonzano on 2 November in accordance with Napoleon's orders but had to fall back to Lavis that same evening. On 4 November, Davidović's superior numbers forced Vaubois to evacuate Trento. Therefore, Napoleon directed Joubert, who was very familiar with the Adige Valley, to reinforce Vaubois with two battalions and assist him with organizing a retrograde movement that would delay Davidović for as long as possible.[139]

On 2 November, Alvinczi's corps crossed the Piave, reaching Barcon, halfway between the Piave and Bassano, the following day. His right wing under Gvozdanović then departed for Bassano while the left wing, under Provera, marched to Fontaniva. Masséna evacuated Bassano and withdrew west to Vicenza early on 4 November, allowing Alvinczi to occupy Bassano that same day. Napoleon sent Augereau east to Montebello, nine miles southwest of Vicenza, and followed him in person from Verona. Provera reached Fontaniva with the left wing, erected a pontoon bridge over the Brenta, and sent Lipthay's brigade across. On 5 November, Masséna's division marched east to Montebello as Augereau's division, accompanied by Napoleon, reached Vicenza. From this position, Bonaparte could attack north-northwest along the road to Bassano or northwest along the road toward Fontaniva. With Davidović occupying Trento and Gvozdanović at Bassano, Napoleon recognized that the Austrians could use the Brenta Valley as an interior line of communications to unite their two

---

138   Decker, *Der Feldzug in Italien*, 155; Roider, *Baron Thugut*, 226; Friedrich M. Kircheisen, *Napoleons Feldzug in Italien und Österreich 1796–1797* (Munich, 1913), 225, 228. Gvozdanović's brigade commanders were Prince Friedrich Franz Xaver von Hohenzollern-Hechingen (vanguard), Philipp Pittoni von Dannenfeld, Gerhard von Roselmini, Anton Lipthay de Kisfalud, Anton Schubirz von Chobinin, and Adolf Brabeck.

139   CN, No. 1144, Napoleon to Masséna, 2 November 1796, 2:114; No. 1168, Napoleon to Joubert, 5 November 1796, 2:129; CG, No. 1043, Napoleon to Baraguey D'Hilliers, 3 November 1796, 1:656; No. 1059, Napoleon to the Directory, 13 November 1796, 1:665; Boycott-Brown, *Rivoli*, 447–450; Yorck von Wartenburg, *Napoleon as a General*, 1:81–82.

corps. Therefore, he decided to attack the Austrians at Bassano with the goal of pushing them east and out of the Brenta Valley.[140]

On the morning of 6 November, Napoleon sent Augereau toward Bassano and Masséna to Fontaniva, ten miles south of Bassano, to cross the Brenta with the intention of driving Alvinczi across the Piave. After doing so, Bonaparte intended to mask Alvinczi and conduct a *manœuvre sur les derrières* through the Valsugana to reach Trento and thus be behind Davidović's army. However, Alvinczi likewise advanced. Most of his troops had crossed the Brenta at Bassano and Fontaniva before the French arrived. Thus, the two forces collided on the west bank of the Brenta in the Second Battle of Bassano. Four miles southwest of Bassano near Nove, Augereau engaged Prince Friedrich von Hohenzollern-Hechingen's brigade in a back-and-forth struggle during which Nove changed hands several times. Seven miles south of this action, Masséna's troops ran into Lipthay's brigade at Carmignano. Lipthay withdrew across the Brenta and disassembled the pontoon bridge, but Masséna's troops attacked his position on the east bank ten times.[141] The French and Austrians fought until nightfall, when Napoleon ordered a withdrawal to Verona after failing to force the passage of the Brenta. In response, Alvinczi pushed his left to San Pietro in Gu, forty miles east of Verona, and his right to Vicenza.[142]

In the Adige Valley, Davidović defeated Vaubois at the Battle of Calliano on 6 and 7 November. In response, Joubert started a thirty-five-mile retreat south to La Corona, losing 3,000 killed and wounded in the process. After receiving news from Vaubois about the French retreat, Napoleon decided to abandon the offensive against Alvinczi to prevent Davidović from reaching Verona. Thus, he ordered Augereau and Masséna to countermarch and reach Verona by 8 November. On that day, Vaubois's 8,000 men reestablished a position along an eight-mile line that stretched south from La Corona to Rivoli. Davidović pushed his 16,000 men to Rivalta, two miles northeast of Vaubois's post at La Corona. Also on 8 November, Alvinczi reached Vicenza, placing the Austrian

---

140 Napoleon wanted to cross the Brenta that same night, 5 November, and eagerly pressed his subordinates to move up his pontoon train: *CN*, No. 1144, Napoleon to Masséna, 2 November 1796, 2:114; *CG*, No. 1045, Napoleon to Berthier, 4 November 1796, 1:658; No. 1049, Napoleon to Augereau, 5 November 1796, 1:660; No. 1050, Napoleon to Berthier, 5 November 1796, 1:661; No. 1059, Napoleon to the Directory, 13 November 1796, 1:665; Decker, *Der Feldzug in Italien*, 156–157; Yorck von Wartenburg, *Napoleon as a General*, 1:81–82; Kircheisen, *Napoleons Feldzug in Italien*, 228–229; Adlow, *Napoleon in Italy*, 152.

141 No mention is made in the sources of the French building a bridge over the Brenta so they likely found a ford.

142 In his report to the Directory, Napoleon claims that "the advantage was ours ... the field of battle remained ours; we took from them 518 prisoners": *CG*, No. 1059, Napoleon to the Directory, 13 November 1796, 1:665; Decker, *Der Feldzug in Italien*, 158.

commander only thirty miles from Napoleon's headquarters at Verona and fifty miles from Davidović's at Rivalta. Only one road connected Vicenza and Rivalta, and it passed through Verona, where Napoleon was assembling the 21,000 men of Masséna and Augereau's divisions and a reserve in his central position.[143]

Napoleon believed that Davidović would take full advantage of the situation and push further south to threaten the rear of the French main body at Verona. Therefore, he resolved to focus on Davidović. After receiving positive information on the strength of Joubert's position, Napoleon decided to await further developments on 9 and 10 November. At this point, he was still wrestling with the possibility of having to pull all of his forces west of the Mincio and so wanted to await Alvinczi's next move to determine where he (Napoleon) should direct his main effort and where he should conduct a holding action using economy of force.

On 9 November, Alvinczi's columns continued their advance toward Verona but Davidović, disturbed by rumors that Vaubois had received reinforcements, remained idle.[144] On the following day, Alvinczi's two columns united on the Vicenza–Verona road while Hohenzollern-Hechingen led the vanguard to San Martino, five miles east of Verona. During the afternoon of 11 November, as the Austrian vanguard approached Verona, Napoleon launched an attack with Augereau's division that forced Hohenzollern-Hechingen to retreat. The Austrians retraced their steps some ten miles east to Caldiero, where Hohenzollern-Hechingen decided to make a stand the next day. In the ensuing Battle of Caldiero on the morning of 12 November, Augereau attacked the Austrian position at Caldiero, and Masséna turned the Austrian right by marching to two miles north of Caldiero. However, a snowstorm blinded the French as the brigades of Provera and Anton Schubirz reached the battlefield. In the ensuing Austrian counterattack, the French lost 2 guns and nearly 1,000 men. Late in the afternoon, Alvinczi ordered a general advance that compelled Masséna and Augereau to conduct a disorderly retreat to Verona as night fell. According to Bonaparte's estimate, 12,000 French soldiers fought 22,000 Austrians.

On the following day, 13 November, Alvinczi advanced cautiously toward Verona, reaching San Martino on 14 November while his cavalry patrolled to the outskirts of Verona itself. At this stage of the campaign, Alvinczi

---

143   CG, No. 1059, Napoleon to the Directory, 13 November 1796, 1:665; Decker, *Der Feldzug in Italien*, 157–158; Boycott-Brown, *Rivoli*, 450–452; Yorck von Wartenburg, *Napoleon as a General*, 1:82–83.
144   Decker, *Der Feldzug in Italien*, 158.

squandered his best opportunity. Instead of attacking the French at Verona sometime between 13 and 15 November, he delayed. Before taking action, the Hungarian commander decided to await Davidović's success in the Adige Valley, news of Loudon's march down the western shore of Lake Garda toward Brescia, and the arrival of General Anton Ferdinand Mittrowsky von Mittrowitz und Nemyšl's brigade from the Brenta Valley.[145]

Meanwhile, in the Adige Valley, Davidović resumed his offensive, slowly pushing Vaubois south. This in turn caused Napoleon's overall situation to become extremely perilous. Although he could have retreated west across the Mincio or linked with his besieging force at Mantua, either alternative would have allowed the two Austrian forces to unite.[146] It is here, at this most dangerous time, that we see Napoleon's genius for the operational art on full display. In this perplexing and disadvantageous situation, he relied on his own skill and determination. In essence, he created opportunities rather than merely waiting for them to arise. In later years, he spoke of his star, the good fortune that followed him like a shadow. If a star did indeed shed its light on Napoleon and luck favored him, it was due to his energy, fortitude, and ability to create the circumstances that allowed him to achieve positive outcomes in the most dangerous and hopeless situations. It should be noted that a commander must never ignore the fact that failures and mistakes occur in operations; campaigns and battles are either won or lost. Most generals in Napoleon's situation would have retreated to save their army, but the young French general seized the initiative and created opportunities for victory. Thus, he determined to go completely around Alvinczi, capture his supply train and reserve artillery, and conduct a *manœuvre sur les derrières* to attack the Austrians from the east.[147]

On 14 November, Napoleon left General François Macquard with a small force of 1,500 at Verona and moved his army sixteen miles southeast along the

---

145 CG, No. 1059, Napoleon to the Directory, 13 November 1796, 1:665; Decker, *Der Feldzug in Italien*, 158–159; Boycott-Brown, *Rivoli*, 456.

146 CG, No. 1059, Napoleon to the Directory, 13 November 1796, 1:665–666. Napoleon warned the Directors about the predicament of his army. He informed them that he had withdrawn his exhausted and barefoot troops in the face of mounting Austrian pressure. He estimated that his field force of only 18,000 men (Masséna's 6,000, Augereau's 5,000, and Vaubois's 7,000) faced some 50,000 Austrians. According to his intelligence, Loudon was advancing on Brescia with an Austrian column while another column had reached the southern Tyrol, 115 miles north of Verona. Bonaparte also warned that, if he did not receive reinforcements, his army would be compelled to retreat behind the Adda.

147 CG, No. 1062, Napoleon to the Directory, 19 November 1796, 1:668; CN, No. 1171, Napoleon to Vaubois, 8 November 1796, 2:131; Decker, *Der Feldzug in Italien*, 159–161; Yorck von Wartenburg, *Napoleon as a General*, 1:83–84, 87–88; Reginald George Burton, *Napoleon's Campaigns in Italy 1796–1797 and 1800* (London, 1912), 74–75.

west bank of the Adige to Ronco, keeping himself between Alvinczi and Mantua. Using economy of force, Napoleon intended Vaubois to fix Davidović in the Adige Valley and Macquard's small force at Verona to prevent Alvinczi from linking with Davidović. With the majority of his army, Bonaparte himself would prevent a juncture between Alvinczi and Wurmser at Mantua. By maintaining his interior lines between the three Austrian forces of Davidović, Alvinczi, and Wurmser, Napoleon knew that he could exploit his central position to support Vaubois should Davidović force him to retreat to Verona. Likewise, if Vaubois held his ground at Rivoli and Alvinczi attacked Verona, Napoleon could equally relieve the pressure on Macquard's 1,500 troops by attacking Alvinczi in the flank from his position at Ronco. Napoleon observed that Ronco, itself a good defensive position, had several roads from which he could attack the Austrians. After bridging the Adige at Ronco, he planned to attack Alvinczi's left flank at Arcole and thus threaten the Austrian rear at Caldiero and line of operations on the Vicenza–Verona road.[148] Between Ronco and Arcole flowed the deep Alpone, a tributary of the Adige. The small village of Arcole stood some 150 yards east of the Alpone and just north of the confluence of the two rivers; a wooden bridge spanned the Alpone along the road to Arcole. The roads that Napoleon intended to utilize for the attack ran along dikes that traversed the marshy terrain between the two rivers.

Napoleon's movement on the night of 14 November to Ronco placed his concentrated force on the left flank of Alvinczi's troops as planned. On the opposite side of the Adige, one dike provided an eight-mile path northwest through Belfiore to Caldiero while a second dike provided a two-mile path northeast to the bridge over the Alpone at Arcole. Early on 15 November, the French started crossing the newly constructed bridge over the Adige at Ronco. Masséna's division commenced the operation, marching north on the dike toward Belfiore; Augereau's division then crossed and took the path east to Arcole.

Alvinczi had placed large forces at both Belfiore and Arcole to protect his left flank so that both French divisions encountered stiff resistance. Although Masséna took Belfiore, he could not push north of that village; Augereau reached the Alpone bridge at Arcole but could not cross. Mittrowsky's infantry and artillery made Augereau's men suffer every step they advanced. Generals Lannes, Verdier, Bon, and Verne sustained wounds while storming the bridge. To motivate his men, Napoleon personally led a charge across the bridge but fell into the marsh. By nightfall, Mittrowsky remained master of Arcole and its bridge while Provera contained Masséna at Belfiore. Nevertheless, Alvinczi sensed the danger these operations posed to his army. As a result, he decided

---

148   CG, No. 1062, Napoleon to the Directory, 19 November 1796, 1:668.

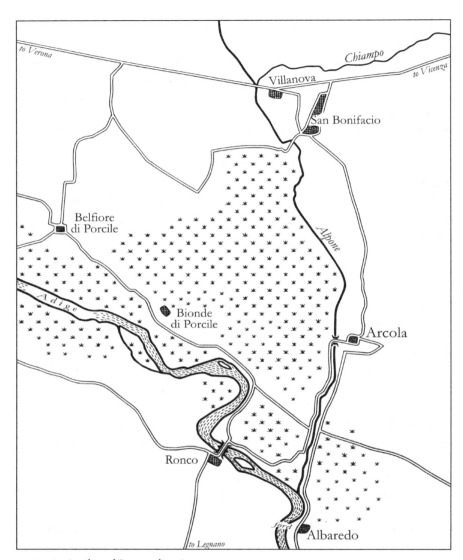

MAP 4.8   Arcole and Surrounding Area

to leave a rearguard of four battalions under Hohenzollern-Hechingen east of Verona and have the army retrace its steps east from Caldiero to Villanuova; he sent his supply trains even further east from Villanuova to Montebello. Thus, he removed his pressure on the French at Verona and considerably reduced his chances of uniting with Davidović. For his part, Napoleon ordered Masséna and Augereau to withdraw their divisions across the pontoon bridge at Ronco, posting a strong rearguard on the east bank of the Adige. Regardless, Bonaparte's operation had caused Alvinczi to retreat, abandon his plan to cross the Adige, and engage in battle near Arcole at a place and time of his adversary's choosing.[149]

That night, Bonaparte learned that Davidović had again remained idle during the course of 15 November. In light of this news, he ordered Vaubois to send 1,000 reinforcements to Verona and directed 3,000 men from the blockade of Mantua to Verona to reinforce his central position, thus allowing him to resume his offensive in the morning. Consequently, on 16 November, Masséna and Augereau again led their divisions along the dikes against Belfiore and Arcole respectively. Provera counterattacked Masséna from Belfiore with six battalions while Mittrowsky assaulted Augereau from Arcole with a portion of his sixteen battalion-sized units. Aside from Masséna taking 1,600 prisoners and 7 guns at Belfiore, neither side gained an advantage. Bonaparte again decided to withdraw to Ronco. Not only did the Austrians again stop him but also, to the north, Davidović drove Vaubois from La Corona to Rivoli on 16 November.[150]

Napoleon attributed his decision to return to Ronco to Vaubois's setback and need of support. He also decided to flank Arcole by bridging the Alpone south of Arcole and just north of its confluence with the Adige. On the morning of 17 November, Bonaparte received incorrect news that Vaubois had held La Corona against Davidović. Sensing that Vaubois did not require immediate support, he decided to send Masséna and Augereau across the Adige for a third time. Masséna took the same path northwest toward Belfiore, but Augereau marched south to cross the Alpone over the newly built bridge south of Arcole. Regardless, the results remained the same. The Austrians stopped Masséna and initially pushed him back to Ronco while Augereau's attack failed to wrest Arcole from Mittrowsky's troops. Erroneous reports of the French withdrawing to Mantua encouraged the Austrians to take the offensive at Arcole and cross the Alpone, but the French opened a murderous flanking fire on them. In addition, Masséna's troops retreating south from Belfiore turned the flank of the Austrian attack. Counterattacking from three sides, the French either killed or captured most of the attacking enemy force. These Austrian losses, along with Augereau's appearance on the east bank of the Alpone, convinced Alvinczi to

---

149   CG, No. 1062, Napoleon to the Directory, 19 November 1796, 1:668; Decker, *Der Feldzug in Italien*, 161–165; Boycott-Brown, *Rivoli*, 467; Adlow, *Napoleon in Italy*, 155–157; Burton, *Napoleon's Campaigns in Italy*, 76–78.
150   CG, No. 1062, Napoleon to the Directory, 19 November 1796, 1:669; Decker, *Der Feldzug in Italien*, 165–166; Yorck von Wartenburg, *Napoleon as a General*, 1:90; Adlow, *Napoleon in Italy*, 158; Burton, *Napoleon's Campaigns in Italy*, 79.

order a retreat around 3:00 p.m. Thus, the Battle of Arcole ended with Alvinczi withdrawing his forces toward Montebello. Clausewitz deems that "better leadership during the individual engagements, braver troops, more determined persistence, [and] more audacious daring" enabled Bonaparte to emerge as the victor.[151]

In the Adige Valley that same day, Davidović attacked Vaubois at Rivoli, capturing one-third of his division along with two of his three brigade commanders. With his remaining force, Vaubois retreated to Castelnuovo, thirteen miles south of Rivoli and thirteen miles due west of Verona. Davidović halted the pursuit halfway between Rivoli and Castelnuovo to await orders from Alvinczi. The next day, 18 November, Davidović remained idle, still awaiting directives from Alvinczi. Meanwhile, Masséna and Augereau moved their divisions north along both banks of the Alpone to Villanuova, causing the remaining Austrian forces to withdraw from the area. The two French divisions then marched west to Verona while French cavalry pursued Alvinczi east toward Montebello. After receiving word of Vaubois's retreat to Castelnuovo, Bonaparte ordered Masséna to Villafranca, where he could support Vaubois's shattered division. Napoleon himself accompanied Augereau's division to Verona, where the 3,000 troops from the blockade of Mantua arrived. With Augereau remaining at Verona, Masséna marched ten miles southwest to Villafranca, arriving on 20 November.[152]

Learning of Alvinczi's defeat and withdrawal, Davidović prepared to commence his own retrograde movement north toward the Tyrol on the afternoon of 19 November. On 20 November, Alvinczi received news of Davidović's 17 November victory over Vaubois; such was the state of communication between the respective Austrian headquarters that it took three days for Alvinczi to learn of these developments. Consequently, he decided to resume his march west to Verona the following day.

---

151   Clausewitz, *Der Feldzug von 1796*, 196; Decker, *Der Feldzug in Italien*, 166–167; Yorck von Wartenburg, *Napoleon as a General*, 1:90; Adlow, *Napoleon in Italy*, 159–160; Burton, *Napoleon's Campaigns in Italy*, 79.
152   Villafranca stood ten miles southwest of Verona and eight miles southeast of Castelnuovo. By directing Masséna there, Napoleon was resecuring central position between Davidović and Alvinczi as well as securing the army's rear against a major sortie from Mantua. Believing that Alvinczi's army was near, Wurmser finally sortied from Mantua on 23 November with 4 columns totalling 7,917 men including 2,005 cavalry. The Austrians attacked the French positions, which Napoleon had considerably weakened by detaching 3,000 men to Verona, but Wurmser's failure to concentrate his forces resulted in another French victory. See *CG*, Nos 1062 and 1077, Napoleon to the Directory, 19 and 24 November 1796, 1:669, 677; Cuccia, *Napoleon in Italy*, 85–87; Fiebeger, *Campaigns of Napoleon*, 46–47.

On 21 November, Masséna marched north to Rivoli as Augereau likewise moved north along the east bank of the Adige toward Davidović's line of communications. The approaching French columns prompted Davidović to accelerate his retreat, but not before Masséna attacked his rearguard at Rivoli and Augereau's vanguard struck his flank at Peri, nine miles north of Rivoli. Convinced that his troops could not continue the campaign, Davidović decided to withdraw further north to Rovereto. On 22 November, he informed Alvinczi, who had again marched west on the Vicenza–Verona road to Caldiero, of his plans. In response, Alvinczi likewise decided to withdraw to the Brenta; he had no desire to face Napoleon without the possibility of linking with Davidović's corps.[153] Alvinczi's three-week campaign to relieve Mantua had failed. He would try again.

While in exile at St. Helena, Napoleon wrote much concerning battles between equally matched and equally exhausted opponents. He commented that the smallest reserve force could settle the matter by providing a moral spark. Throughout the Arcole offensive, Alvinczi failed to provide that spark, while Napoleon's superior operational ability provided it in every crucial situation.[154] Applying the principles of objective, maneuver, surprise, mass, and simplicity at Arcole and that of economy of force at La Corona and Verona, Napoleon achieved a complete victory at Arcole on 17 November. Once again, Napoleon defeated a collectively larger enemy by concentrating his available units at the decisive point on the battlefield through a bold but calculated use of economy of force, which allowed him to achieve a local numerical superiority. In addition, utilizing the strategy of central position afforded him the flexibility he needed to support his economy of force troops if necessary while maintaining a firm control of his entire battlefront between three separate Austrian forces. In the end, Napoleon was able to defeat a combined Austrian force of 55,000 men with only 34,000 soldiers, counting garrison and besieging forces alike. His operations in this campaign demonstrate the value of offensive tactics at the tactical level of war by a numerically inferior force while conducting an operational defensive.

Rivoli

Implementing orders from Vienna and understanding Wurmser's beleaguered situation at Mantua, Alvinczi again started planning for a rapid relief of the fortress. Following the failure of his first campaign to relieve Mantua, he

---

153 CG, No. 1077, Napoleon to the Directory, 24 November 1796, 1:677; Decker, *Der Feldzug in Italien*, 170–174; Fiebeger, *Campaigns of Napoleon*, 47.
154 Yorck von Wartenburg, *Napoleon as a General*, 1:90.

concentrated the bulk of his army, some 28,000 men, at Rovereto, leaving Bajalić with 5,000 at Bassano and Provera with 9,000 at Padua. Weyrother decided to divide the Rovereto corps into six brigade columns for an advance on Verona. According to his plan, Franz Joseph de Lusignan would lead the first column (4,556 men) south along the eastern shore of Lake Garda. Columns under Lipthay (5,065 men) and General Sámuel Köblös de Nagy-Varád (4,138) would march to the left (east) of Lusignan, utilizing a mountain road through La Corona. Gvozdanović received command of two columns (Ocskay with 2,692 men and Reuß with 6,986) that would proceed south along the western bank of the Adige while Vukasović would lead the sixth column (2,795 men) south along the river's eastern bank to a point south of Rivoli where he would bridge the Adige. To deceive the French, Provera received orders to march southwest on 7 January, seize Legnago by 9 January, and relieve Mantua. Alvinczi tasked Bajalić with commencing his march likewise on 7 January, taking Verona by 12 January, and preventing the French garrison there from attacking either Austrian flank. Through the demonstrations made by Provera and Bajalić, Alvinczi hoped to paralyze at least half of Napoleon's forces so that they could not stop the columns of the Rovereto corps.[155]

Alvinczi's plan hinged on securing the plateau of Rivoli so that his columns could unite there. Rivoli itself was not situated on the main road from Trento to Verona. The mountainous terrain between Lake Garda and the Adige made vehicular and mounted traffic impractical, which forced the artillery and cavalry to follow the roads on either bank of the Adige to reach Rivoli. On the Adige's western bank, the road skirts the river as far as Canale, where the river meets the base of the southernmost part of the Monte Magnone Ridge. At this junction, a one-mile long defile follows a steep ascent to the village of Osteria situated on the border of the Rivoli plateau just south of the San Marco Chapel. The entire Rivoli plateau is higher in elevation than the Adige River. Stretching two miles in radius with the center at Rivoli, the plateau itself resembles a semicircle contained by the Monte Magnone Ridge, the Trambasore Heights, and the Tasso Stream. The Trambasore Heights run perpendicular to the Monte Magnone Ridge and thus the Adige; the Tasso encloses the entire battlefield. It was vital for the Austrians to secure both the Trambasore Heights and the Monte Magnone Ridge with the three eastern columns (Lusignan, Lipthay, and Köblös) to open the Osteria Defile and enable the artillery moving south on either side of the Adige to unite with them.

---

155 Decker, *Der Feldzug in Italien*, 181–184, 186; Boycott-Brown, *Rivoli*, 492–494; Adlow, *Napoleon in Italy*, 175; Fiebeger, *Campaigns of Napoleon*, 51; Yorck von Wartenburg, *Napoleon as a General*, 1:94; Burton, *Napoleon's Campaigns in Italy*, 83–84.

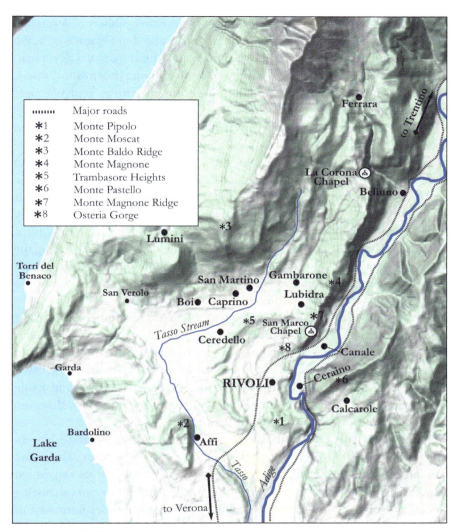

MAP 4.9 Rivoli Offensive

During the pause in operations, Napoleon reestablished the siege of Mantua, and reorganized and resupplied his army. He also relieved inefficient officers from operational command positions, exchanging them for officers newly promoted based on their skills, talent, and bravery. For example, he replaced Vaubois with Joubert, who took command of the former's reinforced division of 10,300 men that stood at Rivoli. On the southern end of the French line, Augereau had more than 8,300 men guarding the Adige from Ronco to Legnago.

From Verona, Masséna's 8,500 men could support either Joubert or Augereau. As a reserve, General Claude Victor commanded one demi-brigade of 2,000 infantry at Villafranca. West of the Mincio, General Antoine Gabriel Rey spread 4,000 reinforcements from the Army of the Vendée among Desenzano, Brescia, Peschiera, Lonato, and Salò. With about 10,200 men, Sérurier kept Wurmser bottled inside Mantua.[156]

In late December, Napoleon received an intercepted dispatch that detailed Alvinczi's plan to relieve Mantua. Believing that neither Provera nor Bajalić possessed sufficient numbers to force a passage of the Adige, he decided to concentrate the army against Alvinczi's columns moving down the Adige; once again, he already possessed central position when the enemy commenced his operation. Already familiar with the topography, he knew that only infantry columns and small mobile guns could cross the mountain passes in winter. Thus, Napoleon concluded that Alvinczi's heavy field guns would be using the roads on either bank of the Adige to reach Rivoli. Therefore, he planned to have Joubert's division hold the Osteria Defile on the western bank of the Adige. Victory would be certain if Joubert blocked that defile.[157]

On 7 January, Provera departed Padua, leading the Austrian left southwest toward Legnago while Bajalić marched west from Bassano as planned. By 11 January, Provera had reached the Adige near Angiari, two miles north of Legnago. He ordered a bridge built across the Adige on 12 January and crossed the river the following day. Meanwhile, Bajalić cleared Vicenza and made steady progress, coming within three miles of Verona on 12 January. However, on that day, Masséna drove him all the way back to Caldiero.

To the north, Alvinczi's columns experienced unexpected difficulties marching south toward Rivoli. Departing Brentonico on 10 January, Lusignan's column struggled to make progress along the thirty miles of snow-covered road through the western slopes of the Monte Baldo Ridge. After an exhausting three-day march, his troops finally reached Lumini, eight miles northwest of Rivoli, on the evening of 12 January. East of Lusignan, Lipthay and Köblös started their march south on 11 January along the eastern feet of the Monte Baldo Ridge. At 9:00 a.m. on 12 January, they encountered Joubert's forward

---

156   Decker calculates the Army of Italy to have comprised 39,720 infantry in 83 battalions and 2,990 cavalry in 16 regiments: Decker, *Der Feldzug in Italien*, 179; CG, No. 1077, Napleon to the Directory, 24 November 1796, 1:677; No. 1154, Napoleon to Joubert, 13 December 1796, 1:717–718; CN, Nos 1295, 1304–1305, Napoleon to Berthier, 20 and 21 December 1796, 2:229–231, 240–247; Anon., *Guerres des Français en Italie depuis 1794 jusqu'à 1814 avec 26 cartes et plans des principales batailles*, 2 vols (Paris, 1859), 239–240.

157   CG, Nos 1101 and 1210, Napoleon to the Directory, 6 and 28 December 1796, 1:690, 747–748; Cuccia, *Napoleon in Italy*, 90, 99.

post at Ferrara, three miles north of La Corona. The two Austrian generals disagreed on whether to halt and wait for the French to retreat as soon as they learned of Lusignan's flank march, or to attack Ferrara. In the end, Köblös assaulted and took Ferrara but the French counterattacked with such ferocity that the Austrians withdrew, hoping that Lusignan's maneuver would force the French to retreat.

As for Joubert, reports of Lusignan's force marching south to turn his left flank reached his headquarters at 4:00 a.m. on 12 January. He responded by ordering his troops to concentrate on 13 January at Caprino, three miles northwest of Rivoli and six miles southwest of La Corona. This meant that the troops who had bravely fought at Ferrara abandoned their positions just as the Austrians had hoped. Lipthay and Köblös followed on 13 January to Caprino while Lusignan started his nine-mile march south from Lumini to Affi, itself three miles southwest of Rivoli and thus in the rear of Joubert's position. A French detachment managed to slow his march and convince the Austrian colonel to wait for Lipthay and Köblös to make further progress. At this time, Alvinczi, who accompanied Gvozdanović's columns along the Adige, became worried that his center (Lipthay and Köblös) did not contain sufficient strength. To remedy this, he dispatched Ocskay's brigade from Belluno on the right bank of the Adige to link with Lipthay and Köblös. In turn, Ocskay experienced delays finding a path west from the Adige Valley, which prompted Alvinczi to postpone a general attack on 13 January.

As for Joubert, he felt that he did not have sufficient forces to withstand the Austrian offensive and started to withdraw further south to Castelnuovo on 14 January. While on the march, he received Napoleon's order to hold the plateau of Rivoli at all costs. In fact, he learned of General Bonaparte's imminent arrival at Rivoli with considerable reinforcements. The reports Napoleon had received from Joubert indicated that his initial thought had been correct: the Austrian columns approaching Rivoli represented the enemy's main effort. Thus, Bonaparte issued orders for Victor, Masséna, and Rey to march to Rivoli. Leaving nothing to chance, he also reinforced Sérurier at Mantua in case Provera forced the passage of the Adige.[158]

The columns commanded by Lipthay, Köblös, and Ocskay passed the bitterly cold night of 13–14 January camped on the snow-covered southern slopes of Monte Baldo. On the morning of Saturday, 14 January, their advance units

---

158 Masséna left a small garrison at Verona and a detachment to mask Bajalić, who was already withdrawing toward Vicenza: CG, No. 1285, Napoleon to Clarke, 12 January 1797, 1:784; No. 1287, Napoleon to Murat, 13 January 1797, 1:785; Nos 1288 and 1289, Napoleon to Joubert, 13 and 15 January 1797, 1:786; No. 1294, Napoleon to the Directory, 17 January 1797, 1:790; Decker, *Der Feldzug in Italien*, 183–184, 189–190.

occupied the Trambasore Heights as Lipthay prepared to lead his main body through Caprino. On Lipthay's left, Köblös and Ocskay marched toward the San Marco Chapel on the Monte Magnone Ridge. With Reuß's column, Gvozdanović marched south along the western bank of the Adige while Vukasović's column steadily progressed on the east side of the river toward Canale. Alvinczi ordered Lusignan to press his march from Lumini through Affi to the Monte Pipolo height south of Rivoli. Although Alvinczi's attack disposition was sound, it came twenty-four hours too late.

Napoleon reached Joubert's position around 2:00 a.m. on 14 January. After visiting the outposts and reconnoitering the Austrian positions from a distance, he ordered a general advance at 7:00 a.m. to drive back the forward Austrian positions and secure the Trambasore Heights, which would buy time for his reinforcements to arrive. At the start of the Battle of Rivoli, the Austrians outnumbered the French 17,000 men to 10,000, but Alvinczi lacked artillery. Joubert arrived at San Marco in time to prevent Ocskay's brigade from occupying the chapel. Despite this, Lipthay's brigade broke the 29th and 85th Demi-Brigades on Joubert's left, which folded and started to fall back. The panic spread to the French center, which faced Köblös. Just as Joubert's center started to break around 10:00 a.m., Masséna arrived on the left with the lead elements of his 32nd Demi-Brigade to drive Lipthay's column back to the Trambasore. To their credit, the determined Austrians regained their footing and slowly pushed the French back and toward the Osteria Defile. As the Austrians advanced, the risk of their juncture with Gvozdanović's column became apparent to the French. While Ocskay drove the French from San Marco, Gvozdanović moved Reuß's column south, but the long, steep-sided ridge of the Monte Magnone prevented him from linking with Ocskay. At Canale, Reuß turned west and awaited a favorable opportunity to ascend the defile to the Rivoli plateau. On the eastern bank of the Adige, Vukasović advanced to Ceraino, opposite Osteria, and trained his cannon on the French guarding the defile as Gvozdanović prepared Reuß's column to advance. Meanwhile, on Alvinczi's extreme right, Lusignan's column steadily worked around Bonaparte's left to sever his line of retreat. Around 11:00 a.m., Lusignan's brigade finally reached Affi and Monte Moscat after its long flank march. There, Lusignan's troops turned east, making for Monte Pipolo and the rear of the French position. Although the Austrians now surrounded Napoleon, the steady arrival of fresh troops allowed him to halt Lusignan's progress with Masséna's 18th Demi-Brigade and reopen the army's line of communications.

Yet, on Napoleon's right, Vukasović's artillery cleared the French from Osteria, thus opening the Canale Defile for Gvozdanović with Reuß's column. As noted, Napoleon had already determined that victory would be certain if

Joubert could hold the Osteria Defile. With most of Masséna's troops already committed, and Rey and Victor still en route, Bonaparte had no choice but to redirect some of the troops supporting Joubert to Osteria. An Austrian dragoon squadron followed by an infantry battalion emerged from the defile but a French combined-arms attack drove them back. As more Austrians emerged from the defile, the 18th Light Demi-Brigade, commanded by Napoleon's future brother-in-law, Charles Leclerc, engaged the column frontally, while Joubert's troops enfiladed them from San Marco. Realizing that his column could not break out of the defile, Gvozdanović withdrew out of range of the fifteen-gun French battery that was pouring canister into the Austrians at pointblank range. On the opposite side of the battlefield, Rey and Victor directed their arriving troops against Lusignan, whose column finally succumbed to superior French numbers after being assailed in the flank and rear.

Although Lipthay, Köblös, and Ocskay pushed the French down the Trambasore Heights and onto the Rivoli plateau, the broken ground had so disorganized the units that they could not coordinate an effective junction with Gvozdanović. A counterattack by French cavalry caused Ocskay's troops to turn back, spreading panic among the other Austrian brigades and prompting a disorderly retreat to the positions they had occupied in the morning north of the Tasso between Caprino and San Martino with detachments holding the Monte Magnone Ridge and the San Marco Chapel. The Battle of Rivoli ended in a French victory, which earned Clausewitz's admiration for Napoleon's combination of the "offensive defense" with an excellent position.[159]

Late on 14 January, Napoleon learned that Provera had crossed the Adige. In response, he ordered Joubert and Rey to pursue Alvinczi come morning. Despite the exhaustion of their troops, Masséna and Victor received instructions to depart the following morning to assist Sérurier at Mantua. As soon as Joubert no longer needed Rey, he too would march to Mantua. Joubert resumed the Battle of Rivoli early on 15 January, launching a frontal assault on the Austrians and retaking San Marco on the Austrian left. Another French column turned the Austrian right, prompting Alvinczi to order a general retreat north toward La Corona. Thus ended the battle, with the Austrians losing some 4,000 killed and wounded, along with 8,000 men and 40 guns captured. Bonaparte's losses were not slight: 3,200 killed and wounded and 1,000 captured in a battle that pitted 28,000 Austrians against 23,000 French.[160]

---

159 Clausewitz, *Der Feldzug von 1796*, 245.
160 *CN*, Nos 1371 and 1381, Napoleon to Masséna, 12 and 13 January 1797, 2:300–301, 308–309; *CG*, Nos 1294 and 1300, Napoleon to the Directory, 17 and 18 January 1797, 1:790, 793–795; Jomini, *Histoire critique*, 11:266, 288; Decker, *Der Feldzug in Italien*, 190–195; Adlow,

During the night of 15–16 January, Napoleon rode to the Sant'Antonio suburb of Mantua. He felt confident that he could stop Provera at San Giorgio and predicted where Wurmser would attempt to sortie from Mantua. For his part, Provera informed Wurmser of his arrival and planned to attack La Favorita and Sant'Antonio on the morning of 16 January. Around 5:00 a.m., Provera commenced his advance. At the same time, Wurmser made a sortie with 5,000 men toward La Favorita to link with Provera's troops. The lead elements of Sérurier's column engaged the troops coming from Mantua. After failing either to take La Favorita or link with Provera's relieving forces, the sortie assaulted and entered Sant'Antonio, but Victor repulsed the attack. This forced Wurmser to retreat into the fortress, leaving behind 400 men as prisoners. Approaching La Favorita, Provera suffered a three-pronged attack: Masséna pressed the attack on his right, General Sextius-Alexandre Miollis from San Giorgio attacked his left, and Lannes attacked his rear. Now inside the fortress, Wurmser could not support Provera, who surrendered to Sérurier 6,000 infantry, 700 cavalry, and 20 guns. Napoleon informed the Directory that the Battle of La Favorita had yielded a total of 7,000 prisoners as well as the entire Austrian army's baggage train and a large convoy of corn and cattle destined for Mantua. Thus ended Alvinczi's second and the Austrians' fourth and final attempt to relieve the besieged fortress of Mantua.[161]

Once again, ill-coordinated Austrian operations provided Napoleon with the precious time he needed to defeat in detail the separate Austrian columns. Once again, Napoleon's use of economy of force, in this case at Mantua and Legnago, permitted him to concentrate forces at the decisive point: Rivoli. As with his previous campaign against Alvinczi, he utilized the strategy of central position and applied the principles of mass, maneuver, simplicity, and offensive to achieve the decisive victory at Rivoli and then another at La Favorita. The overall effect of Alvinczi's second attempt to relieve Mantua cost the Austrians 25,000 men, including 5,000 killed. "This success," notes Clausewitz, "achieved with a smaller army and with the insignificant loss of a few thousand men, is one of the most glorious that military history can offer, and one can say that Bonaparte surpassed even himself."[162] With five successive armies defeated

---

Napoleon in Italy, 174–180; Fiebeger, *Campaigns of Napoleon*, 52–55; *Guerres des Français en Italie*, 241; Rothenberg, *The Art of Warfare in the Age of Napoleon*, 248.

161 Scorza, "Memorie sul Blocco ed Assedio di Mantova," 184–185; *CN*, No. 1394, Napoleon to the Directory, 17 January 1797, 2:319–320; *CG*, No. 1300, Napoleon to the Directory, 18 January 1797, 1:793–796; Pommereul, *Campagne du général Buonaparte*, 1:233, 248–249; Jomini, *Histoire critique*, 11:289–293; Decker, *Der Feldzug in Italien*, 195–200; Yorck von Wartenburg, *Napoleon as a General*, 1:98–99.

162 Clausewitz, *Der Feldzug von 1796*, 239.

by Napoleon, Austrian morale reached its nadir. Bonaparte correctly predicted that the Austrians would not make another attempt to relieve Mantua and that the fortress would soon fall. Wurmser, whose troops at Mantua resorted to eating their own horses, eventually had no alternative but to surrender the fortress with its garrison of 16,000 men to Sérurier on 2 February.[163]

IV Austrian Phase

The Battle of Rivoli and the fall of Mantua produced similar effects in Paris and Vienna, with both sides feeling compelled to reinforce their respective armies in Italy. In the middle of February, Kaiser Francis sent the army's most successful commander, his brother, Archduke Charles, to take command and restore the situation in northern Italy. By 10 March, Charles had posted 10,000 men under Hohenzollern-Hechingen along the Piave as an advance guard; 17,000 men under his direct control along the western bank of the Tagliamento River in a fifteen-mile stretch between Spilimbergo and San Vito; and 14,000 under Loudon in the Tyrol supported by an additional 10,000 Tyrolese volunteers. Lusignan's brigade stood in the region of Feltre to maintain communication between Charles and Loudon. After seeing the condition of his troops, Charles decided that his best course of action would be to defend the Austrian frontier until he could reorganize and reinforce the army. The twenty-six-year-old archduke organized the troops on the Tagliamento into six brigades with four consisting of some 4,000 men each. He positioned the two remaining smaller brigades to protect his line of communications: one in the gorge of the Tagliamento, south of Pontebba, and one in the gorge of the Isonzo River, south of Tarvisio. Charles believed that these would be reinforced by the replacements en route from Vienna before the French could strike.[164]

As for Napoleon, his operational success caused the Directory to change strategy and declare that northern Italy would now constitute the war's primary theater. In November 1796, the Directors decided to increase the Army of Italy to 80,000 men. They started by sending twelve regiments totaling 18,000 men under General Jean-Baptiste Bernadotte and General Antoine Guillaume Delmas to Italy. These troops reached the Adige as Bonaparte commenced his offensive. According to Napoleon's intelligence, his army of some 60,000 men

---

163 *CG*, Nos 1294 and 1300, Napoleon to the Directory, 17 and 18 January 1797, 1:790, 793–796; Cuccia, *Napoleon in Italy*, 103–104, 122–125; Fiebeger, *Campaigns of Napoleon*, 63; Adlow, *Napoleon in Italy*, 186–187.
164 Decker, *Der Feldzug in Italien*, 214, 216; Yorck von Wartenburg, *Napoleon as a General*, 1:103; Fiebeger, *Campaigns of Napoleon*, 64–65.

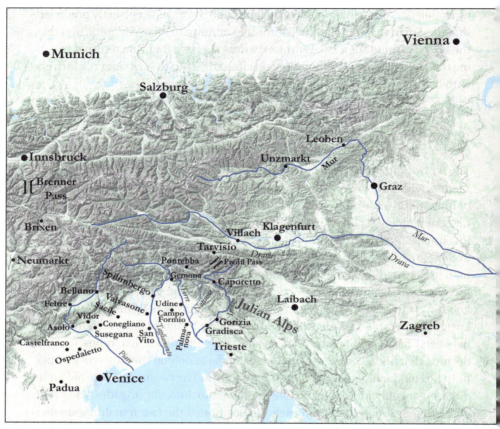

MAP 4.10 Austrian Phase

outnumbered the scattered Austrian forces in the Friuli and the Tyrol by approximately 10,000 men. However, he assumed that the Austrians would receive considerable reinforcements. Thus, every day that passed offered Charles the opportunity to increase his troop strength and concentrate his forces. For these reasons, Napoleon felt he could not wait for his own reinforcements to arrive. To take advantage of his present numerical superiority and the disorganized state of Austrian forces, he had to commence the offensive as soon as possible. By 10 March 1797, Bernadotte's 10,000 men stood at Padua, with Sérurier's 9,000 at Asolo, Masséna's 11,000 at Bassano, and 10,000 under Guieu, commanding in place of Augereau, who was on leave, at Castelfranco. Napoleon's left wing consisted of 21,000 men under Joubert at Trento. Bonaparte planned to have Joubert operate against the Austrian forces in the

Tyrol while he led the 40,000 troops of his right wing on a general offensive through the Friuli toward Vienna.[165]

Napoleon targeted the Predil Pass at Tarvisio, 125 miles northeast of Bassano, as his immediate objective since it provided the shortest route through the defiles of the Julian Alps to Vienna. He expected to encounter Charles and an Austrian army of at least 30,000 men in the Friuli. As his first step, he would execute a *manœuvre sur la position centrale* to place his main army between Loudon in the Tyrol and Charles in the Friuli. Then, he would isolate the archduke by having Masséna turn the Austrian right by marching through Feltre to Belluno to prevent Charles from linking with the troops in the Tyrol.

This plan entailed a considerable degree of risk. Knowing he would have to cross the Piave and the Tagliamento to reach Tarvisio, Bonaparte realized that he would expose his flanks and rear to an enemy force approaching from the Adige and Brenta Valleys. To prevent attacks on his lines of operation, Bonaparte decided to advance on all three routes guarded by the Austrians. Joubert would confront Loudon in the Tyrol while Masséna advanced up the Piave Valley to defeat Lusignan and secure the road to Tarvisio. Napoleon himself would lead the remainder of his army (32,000 men) against Archduke Charles on the Tagliamento. Should Joubert be overwhelmed, an Austrian force could drive down the Adige, reach Verona, and sever Napoleon's line of communications. Moreover, the distance between Joubert and Napoleon would increase as the latter moved further northeast. Regardless, Bonaparte would retain the advantage of interior lines. Should a large Austrian force emerge from the Tyrol, Joubert would conduct a fighting withdrawal for ten days south to Verona while Napoleon used his interior lines to march up the Brenta to Trento and fall on the rear of the Austrians pursuing Joubert. If no threat developed, Joubert would rendezvous with Bonaparte in the Drava River Valley.[166]

Operations started on 10 March with Masséna marching east from Bassano. Three days later, he attacked Lusignan at Belluno, capturing him along with 800 prisoners. Masséna then crossed the Piave and commenced a fifty-mile march east toward Spilimbergo on the Tagliamento with the intent of marching upriver to Gemona to turn the Austrian right and drive them from the feet of the Julian Alps. Meanwhile, on 12 March, Sérurier crossed the Piave at Vidor and proceeded east to Castello San Salvatore near Susegana. Eighteen miles south of Vidor, Guieu crossed the Piave at Ospedaletto and marched northeast

---

165   Decker, *Der Feldzug in Italien*, 215–216; Fiebeger, *Campaigns of Napoleon*, 64; Adlow, *Napoleon in Italy*, 199; Yorck von Wartenburg, *Napoleon as a General*, 1:103.
166   CG, No.1452, Napoleon to Joubert, 15 March 1797, 1:874.

to Conegliano, moving ahead of Sérurier's division, which formed the reserve. South of Guieu, Bernadotte led his division northeast from Padua. The following day, 13 March, Guieu engaged Hohenzollern-Hechingen twelve miles northeast of Conegliano at Sacile; the Austrians withdrew toward Valvasone on the western bank of the Tagliamento.

As Austrian forces fell back along their entire front, it became clear to Napoleon that Charles was not going to risk losing his field army in open battle. Nevertheless, the French general hoped to catch the Austrians at Valvasone on the Tagliamento and force Charles to accept battle. For this purpose, Bonaparte united the three divisions of his main body, those of Guieu, Sérurier, and Bernadotte, to attack the Austrians at Valvasone on 16 March. The Austrian rearguard formed on both sides of the river to stop the French from crossing, but the archduke had already started withdrawing his main body. During the ensuing Battle of Valvasone, Napoleon forced the passage of the Tagliamento, mainly because the Alpine snows had yet to melt and raise the level of the river, meaning that the French did not need a bridge to cross. Charles retreated east through Palmanova, thus opening the road to Tarvisio. To defend the Predil Pass, he detached 4,000 men and 26 cannon under Bajalić to march north along the Isonzo and link with the brigades commanded by Ocskay and Köblös, likewise en route to Tarvisio.[167]

Full of confidence, Napoleon wrote to the Directors on 17 March to urge them to order the French armies on the Rhine to conduct a general offensive across southern Germany and into Austria.[168] Before moving northeast toward Tarvisio, Napoleon wanted to push the archduke further east and away from the French line of communications. Charles obliged by continuing his retreat east, crossing the Isonzo at Gradisca on 18 March with Gvozdanović and the rest of the army. The French continued their general advance, pursuing the Austrians across the Torre River at Palmanova on 19 March. Accompanied by Napoleon, Bernadotte's division crossed first followed by Sérurier, but Guieu turned north to follow the Natisone River, a tributary of the Torre, to Caporetto (Kobarid). After reaching Gorizia just west of the Isonzo, Napoleon also moved north with Sérurier's division in pursuit of Bajalić. Bernadotte continued to follow the Austrians northeast toward Laibach (Ljubljana). Charles ordered General Johann Rudolf von Sporck to mask Bernadotte with 5,000 men while he led Gvozdanović's column through Laibach to Villach in the valley of the

---

167   CG, No. 1455, Napoleon to the Directory, 17 March 1797, 1:877; Nos 1451–1453, Napoleon to Joubert, 11 and 15 March 1797, 1:874–875; Decker, *Der Feldzug in Italien*, 216–219.

168   CG, No. 1454, Napoleon to the Directory, 17 March 1797, 1:876.

Drava.[169] Bernadotte reached Laibach on 25 March and remained there until 2 April.[170]

Meanwhile, Bajalić displayed little energy after finding his column blocked by Masséna, whose vanguard drove Ocskay from Tarvisio on 21 March. Marching southwest from Villach, General Charles-Philippe Vinchant de Gontroeul attacked Masséna from the opposite direction later that same day, clearing the French from Tarvisio. On the next day, Masséna launched a fierce counterattack, driving Vinchant's troops north through Tarvisio and forcing them to withdraw toward Villach. With Masséna in firm control of Tarvisio, Bajalić and Köblös found themselves on the wrong side of the Predil Pass and cut off from Villach. Meanwhile, Guieu's division arrived at the head of Napoleon's army to sandwich the Austrians between himself and Masséna. With few options, Bajalić and Köblös surrendered 4,000 men, 25 guns, and 500 supply wagons on 23 March.[171]

After gaining Tarvisio, Napoleon granted the army a few days of rest before entering Austria proper on 26 March. Although Charles planned to reassemble his army at Klagenfurt, the Austrians had lost heart. Masséna and Guieu advanced on Villach but the Austrians evacuated the town and retreated to Sankt Veit before the French arrived. Having reached the Drava Valley, Napoleon dispatched a detachment from Villach to follow the river to Joubert's position. Joubert had commenced his operation in the Tyrol as soon as he learned that Napoleon had crossed the Tagliamento. Fifteen miles north of Trento, he defeated General Wilhelm Lothar Maria von Kerpen's 12,000 Austrians on 20 March at the Battle of Salorno. Marching another fifty miles northeast, Joubert reached Brixen on 26 March to ensure than an Austrian force could not advance from Innsbruck along the Brenner Pass and attack

---

169   Some seventy miles northeast of Laibach, Villach stood on the Austrian side of the Predil Pass. The archduke's decision to try to reach Villach via Laibach–Krainburg (Kranj)–Kronau (Kranjska Gora) before the French arrived makes little sense. He should have turned his entire army north and followed the Isonzo to Tarvisio.

170   CG, No. 1457, Napoleon to Berthier, 17 March 1797, 1:879; CN, No. 1600, Napoleon to the Directory, 20 March 1797, 2:518–520; Préau, *Victoires*, 8:87–89; Decker, *Der Feldzug in Italien*, 219–221; Adlow, *Napoleon in Italy*, 207–208; Yorck von Wartenburg, *Napoleon as a General*, 1:110.

171   CG, Nos 1466, 1471, and 1476, Napoleon to the Directory, 22, 24, and 25 March 1797, 1:883, 886, 889–890; Préau, *Victoires*, 8:91–92; Pommereul, *Campagne du général Buonaparte*, 1:332; Decker, *Der Feldzug in Italien*, 221–222; Kircheisen, *Napoleons Feldzug in Italien*, 295–296; Adlow, *Napoleon in Italy*, 202–206.

Napoleon's rear at Klagenfurt.[172] He remained at Brixen, some 135 miles east of Villach, and awaited further orders.[173]

On 29 March, Napoleon's troops reached Klagenfurt, pushing on to Sankt Veit on 30 March. There, he learned that the French armies on the Rhine had not moved east to participate in an invasion of Austria. Moreover, the extension of his line of communications alarmed him: he was 200 miles from his base at Verona. With his lines of communication not completely secure, he realized that the archduke could rally a much larger force than his own. Continuing to advance on Vienna would be foolhardy, and withdrawing into Italy would be equally dangerous, as it would destroy the morale of his troops. He decided to send a letter to Charles on 31 March suggesting an armistice; he received a positive response. During the ensuing negotiations, Napoleon continued to push his army deeper into Austria. On 7 April, his main body reached Leoben, less than 100 miles from Vienna, after engaging the Austrians at Neumarkt on 1 April and Unzmarkt on 3 April. At Leoben, the Austrians presented a flag of truce, and work began on the preliminaries for the armistice that the belligerents signed on 18 April to end hostilities and arrange a conference to finalize the peace. Napoleon deliberated and finalized the peace treaty at Campo Formio on 17 October 1797.[174]

Napoleon's First Italian Campaign of 1796–1797 was one of the most fast-paced strategic and operational masterpieces in military history. Bonaparte's application of the principles of war proved devastating to his Piedmontese and Austrian foes, who applied the tenets of limited war based on lines of communication established along a series of magazines and fortresses. Napoleon demonstrated his operational expertise by his *manœuvre sur la position centrale* in the Arcole and Rivoli campaigns, and his *manœuvre sur les derrières* at Castiglione against Wurmser and at Arcole against Alvinczi's supply trains. In addition, Napoleon's use of the principles of objective, offensive, mass, economy of force, unity of command, security, surprise, and simplicity throughout his First Italian Campaign clearly demonstrated a change in the character of war. According to Jomini:

---

172   CG, No. 1486, Napoleon to the Directory, 1 April 1797, 1:895–896; Préau, *Victoires*, 8:94–95; Marcel Reinhard, *Avec Bonaparte en Italie d'après les lettres inédites de son aide de camp Joseph Sulkowski* (Paris, 1946), 276; Adlow, *Napoleon in Italy*, 208–209.

173   Joubert eventually defeated the Austrians at Innsbruck on 28 March 1797. See CG, No. 1489, Napoleon to the Directory, 5 April 1797, 1:898; Decker, *Der Feldzug in Italien*, 223–226.

174   CG, No. 1484, Napoleon to Charles, 31 March 1797, 1:894; No. 1490, Napoleon to the Directory, 5 April 1797, 1:898–899; Decker, *Der Feldzug in Italien*, 223, 228–231; Adlow, *Napoleon in Italy*, 211–213.

To detect at a glance the relative advantages presented by the different zones of operations, to concentrate the mass of the forces upon that one which gave the best promise of success, to be indefatigable in ascertaining the approximate position of the enemy, to fall with the rapidity of lightning upon his center if his front was too much extended, or upon that flank by which he could more readily seize his communications, to outflank him, to cut his line, to pursue him to the last, to disperse and destroy his forces, – such was the system followed by Napoleon in his first campaigns. These campaigns proved this system to be one of the very best.[175]

During the First Italian Campaign, Napoleon demonstrated that he had mastered these aspects of the science and art of war at the young age of twenty-six. The character of war was forever changed.

Bibliography

Adlow, Elijah. *Napoleon in Italy 1796–1797*. Boston, MA, 1948.

Anon. *Guerres des Français en Italie depuis 1794 jusqu'à 1814 avec 26 cartes et plans des principales batailles*. 2 vols. Paris, 1859.

Boycott-Brown, Martin. *The Road to Rivoli: Napoleon's First Campaign*. London, 2001.

Burton, Reginald George. *Napoleon's Campaigns in Italy 1796–1797 and 1800*. London, 1912.

Clausewitz, Carl von. *Hinterlassenes Werk: der Feldzug von 1796 in Italien*. Berlin, 1858.

Clausewitz, Carl von. *La campagne de 1796 en Italie*, trans. Jean Collin. Paris, 1899.

Cuccia, Phillip R. *Napoleon in Italy: The Sieges of Mantua, 1796–1799*. Norman, OK, 2014.

Debidour, Antonin, ed. *Recueil des Actes du Directoire Exécutif: procès-verbaux, arrêtés, instructions, lettres et actes divers*, 3 vols. Paris, 1913.

Decker, Carl von. *Der Feldzug in Italien*. Berlin, 1825.

Erdmannsdorff, G.A. von. *Der Feldzug von 1796 in Italien*. Magdeburg, 1847.

Fabry, Gabriel. *Campagne de l'armée d'Italie, 1796–1797*. Paris,1914.

Fiebeger, Gustav Joseph. *The Campaigns of Napoleon Bonaparte of 1796–1797*. West Point, NY, 1911.

"Früh Rapport." Festung Mantua, Karton 1121 May through September 1796, Österreichisches Staatsarchiv, Kriegsarchiv (ÖstA). Mantua, 17 September 1796

Gachot, Édouard. *Histoire militaire de Masséna: le première campagne d'Italie (1795 à 1798)*. Paris, 1901.

---

175 Jomini, *Art of War*, 90.

Hortig, Viktor. *Bonaparte vor Mantua: Ende Juli 1796.* Rostock, 1903.
Jomini, Antoine Henri de. *The Art of War,* trans. G.H. Mendell U.S. Army and W.P. Craighill U.S. Army. Westport, CT, 1971.
Jomini, Antoine Henri de. *Histoire critique et militaire des Guerres de la Révolution.* 15 vols. Paris, 1821.
Kircheisen, Friedrich M. *Napoleons Feldzug in Italien und Österreich 1796–1797.* Munich, 1913.
Masséna, André. *Mémoires de Masséna,* ed. by Jean Baptiste Frédéric Koch, 8 vols (Paris, 1848).
Napoleon I. *Correspondance de Napoléon I,* 32 vols. Paris, 1858–1862.
Napoleon I. *Correspondance general, publiée par la Fondation Napoléon,* 12 vols. Paris, 2004.
Napoleon I. [as Napoleon Bonaparte]. *Memoirs of the History of France during the Reign of Napoleon, Dictated by the Emperor at Saint Helena to the Generals Who Shared His Captivity, and Published from the Original Manuscripts Corrected by Himself.* London, 1823.
Phipps, Ramsay Weston. *The Armies of the First French Republic,* 5 vols. Oxford, 1931.
Pommereul, François-René-Jean de. *Campagne du général Buonaparte en Italie, pendant les années IVe et Ve de la République Française.* Paris, 1797.
Préau, Charles-Théodore Beauvais de. *Victoires, conquêtes, désastres, revers et guerres civiles des Français, de 1792 à 1815,* 29 vols. Paris, 1817–1825.
Reinhard, Marcel. *Avec Bonaparte en Italie d'après les lettres inédites de son aide de camp Joseph Sulkowski.* Paris, 1946.
Roider, Karl. *Baron Thugut and Austria's Response to the French Revolution.* Princeton, NJ, 1987.
Rose, John Holland. "The Despatches of Colonel Thomas Graham on the Italian Campaign of 1796–1797." *English Historical Review* 14/53 (January 1899), 111–124.
Rothenberg, Gunther E. *The Art of Warfare in the Age of Napoleon.* Bloomington, IN, 1980.
Schels, J.B. "Die Begebenheiten in und um Mantua von 16 September 1796 bis 4 Februar 1797; nebst der Schlacht von Rivoli." *Österreichische Militärische Zeitschrift* Bd 2 (1832), 3–61, 161–193, 254–277.
Schels, J.B. "Die Gefechte in den Apenninen, bei Voltri, Montenotte, Millesimo, Cossaria, und Dego im April 1796." *Streffleurs Österreicher Militarzeitschrift* Bd 5 (1822), 123–217.
Schels, J.B. "Die Kriegsereignisse in Italien vom 15 April bis 16 Mai 1796 mit dem Gefechte bei Lodi." *Österreichische Militärische Zeitschrift* Bd 4 (1825), 57–97, 267–268.
Schels, J.B. "Die Verteidigung von Mantua im Juni und Juli 1796." *Österreichische Militärische Zeitschrift* Bd 1 (1830), 83–100, 115–152.

Schels, J.B. "Die zweite Einschließung Mantuas im August 1796 und gleichzeitige Ereignisse bei dem k. k. Heere unter dem FM. Grafen Wurmser in Tirol und Vorarlberg." *Österreichische Militärische Zeitschrift* Bd 4 (1831), 251–295.

Scorza, Baldassare. "Memorie sul Blocca ed Assedio di Mantova," Manuscript in Dott. Archille Bertarelli Collection, Vol. 50 at the Museo del Risorgimento, Milan, n.d. [1796?].

Vivenot, Alfred, ed. *Quellen zur Geschichte der Deutschen Kaiserpolitik Oesterreichs während der Französischen Revolutionskriege.* Vienna, 1809.

Vivenot, Alfred, ed. *Thugut, Clerfayt und Wurmser.* Vienna, 1869.

Vivenot, Alfred, ed. *Vertrauliche Briefe des Freiherrn von Thugut.* Vienna, 1872.

Voykowitsch, Bernhard. *Castiglione 1796: Napoleon Repulses Wurmser's First Attack.* Vienna, 1998.

Yorck von Wartenburg, Hans Ludwig David Maximilian. *Napoleon as a General*, 2 vols. London, 1897–1898.

CHAPTER 5

The Second Italian Campaign

John F. Weinzierl

The Campaign of 1800 provides penetrating insight into the early career of Napoleon Bonaparte. Little doubt exists that in this second Italian campaign Napoleon proved himself to be a general of exceptional talent, able to overcome challenges by way of sheer will and a superb *coup d'oeil*. For the first time he faced the complexities of both commanding an army and serving as head of state. In 1800, Napoleon would not only control the operational and tactical aspects of war-making, but would also direct all strategic considerations as well. Still evolving as a commander, Napoleon demonstrated a sophisticated understanding of war at every level, in particular, the operational level of war. Although his *corps d'armée* were still in their infancy, he managed to execute a dramatic *manoeuvre sur les derrières* to set the stage for the climactic Battle of Marengo. Such a bold operational scheme would become the hallmark of Napoleonic warfare. In 1800, it was the execution of his plan, particularly when transitioning from the operational to the tactical level, which caused the young First Consul problems. Napoleon's experience in this campaign would prove instrumental in his development as a commander, and the lessons he learned would clearly inform his planning and execution in 1805 and beyond.

Napoleon emerged from the Coup of Brumaire as First Consul and leader of France but the Republic was far from stable and remained embroiled in the War of the Second Coalition. Bonaparte appealed to both Britain and Austria for peace as war-weariness in France had mounted and the condition of its armed forces left much to be desired. Both British prime minister William Pitt the Younger and Austrian foreign minister Baron Thugut rejected his peace overtures, prompting the First Consul to raise funds and gather troops to assemble the 55,000-strong Army of the Reserve at Dijon under the command of General Berthier.[1] With this newly created striking force, Napoleon hoped to decisively defeat the Coalition and bring both victory and peace to France, thereby consolidating his own political position as First Consul.

---

1   Napoleon to Berthier (minister of war), 25 January 1800, in Captain de Cugnac, *Campagne de L'Armée de Réserve en 1800* (Paris, 1900), I, 22–24. Many of the troops of the Reserve Army came from the conflict in the Vendée, which had recently been brought to an end. Funds for the upcoming war were secured via loans from the Netherlands and some of the German free cities.

Initially, the War of the Second Coalition was disastrous for the French, who had been driven back to the Rhine River and out of Italy. Specifically in Italy, a combined Austro-Russian force led by *General der Kavallerie* Michael Friedrich Benedikt von Melas and Generalissimo Aleksandr Vasiliyevich Suvorov had overwhelmed French forces in mid-1799, forcing them back into Switzerland. Near defeat and under threat of invasion, the French Republic sent forth Masséna and, in a brilliant campaign, he defeated the Austro-Russian army at Zurich on 25–26 September 1799. This victory not only saved France and the Revolution, but it also preserved the salient of Switzerland from which future French armies could invade Germany or Italy through the use of interior lines.[2] Soon, Allied bickering caused Russia to withdraw from the Coalition, thereby setting up a dramatic duel between France and Austria. The Aulic Council's and Thugut's strategy was to keep *Feldzeugmeister* and his Austrian force of more than 100,000 men in a defensive position behind the Rhine, and order Melas to take the offensive in Italy where he commanded 100,000 men in Piedmont (including 20,000 garrisoned across northern Italy). It was hoped that Melas could again defeat the French in Italy, just as he had in 1799.[3]

For the upcoming campaign, Napoleon made organizational changes. Chief among them and a crucial innovation in operational warfare was the general adoption of the *corps d'armée* system.[4] This system had been experimented with since the aftermath of the Seven Years War and found sustenance on the ideas of Guibert, Bourcet, and others who envisioned a more mobile and flexible system of war less dependent on logistical supply.[5] The First Consul called for each corps to contain elements of all arms including cavalry, artillery, a couple of divisions of infantry, and a small staff. The result was a military formation that resembled a small army and was capable of independent maneuver. A corps had the ability to engage an enemy of larger size until reinforcements arrived and concentration of the army was achieved. In the hands of a military genius of the caliber of Napoleon, it became an operational tool the rest of Europe would soon fear. With it the French army was able to increase its speed, range, and flexibility of operations and, as Martin van Creveld states, "for the first time in history, it became possible to compel an enemy to give battle, even if there were no borders or natural obstacles against which he

---

2   Donald Horward et al., *Warfare in the Western World* (Lexington, MA, 1996), 1:209.
3   Named commander in chief of the Austrian Army of Italy in April 1799, Melas, under Suvorov's overall command, defeated the French at Cassano (27 April 1799), on the Trebbia River (17–20 June 1799), and at Novi (15 August 1799). After the Russians withdrew from Italy, Kray was the victor at Savigliano (18 September 1799) and Genola (4 November 1799).
4   Napoleon to Berthier, 25 January 1800, in Cugnac, *Réserve*, 1:22–24.
5   For further discussion of this topic, see Quimby, *Background of Napoleonic Warfare*.

could be forced."[6] Although the French *corps d'armée* system was formally introduced in 1800, it was far from its institutionalized form of 1805. Napoleon had only two corps in 1800 and these were reconfigured several times, with divisions being detached and used as needed. Eventually, Napoleon's innovation of the corps system would become synonymous with his method of operational warfare.

The capture of Vienna and the destruction of both Austrian armies under Kray and Melas was Bonaparte's ultimate objective in 1800. Napoleon's first plan envisioned Germany as the main theater of war. He aimed to split the armies of Melas and Kray by launching a spring offensive with a French force consisting of both the Army of the Rhine and the newly formed Army of the Reserve. This combined French force was to make a concentrated thrust over the Rhine at Schaffhausen to turn Kray's left flank and defeat him, pushing him back toward Ulm and opening the road to Vienna. At this point, the Army of the Reserve would advance southward over the Alps and into Italy to fall on Melas from behind and thereby achieve decisive victories on both fronts.[7] Such a plan has that distinctive Napoleonic feel to it and resembles the operational design of 1805. There can be little doubt that Germany was the primary and potentially decisive theater. If Kray was defeated and Vienna exposed, Melas would be completely out of position and could have done nothing to halt the French advance on the Austrian capital. In considering the opposite outcome, if the French were defeated by Kray, the results would have been catastrophic and opened France to invasion.[8]

Napoleon understood the primacy of the German theater, but the implementation of such a grand design is never easy and Clausewitzian friction works against all the best-laid plans. General Moreau, the commander of the Army of the Rhine, from the start had reservations about Napoleon's audacious plan. He objected to it, delayed against it, and even threatened to resign his command over it. Much of this had to do with his overall cautious nature as well as his personal rivalry with the newly established First Consul. Napoleon tried to placate him by way of flattering communications, but to no avail.[9]

---

6   Martin van Creveld, "Napoleon and the Dawn of Operational Warfare," in John Andreas Olsen and Martin van Creveld, eds, *The Evolution of Operational Art: from Napoleon to the Present* (Oxford, 2011), 30.

7   Antoine H. Jomini, *Life of Napoleon* (Kansas City, MO, 1897), 1:241.

8   For more discussion on this topic, see Chandler, *Campaigns of Napoleon*, and Yorck von Wartenburg, *Napoleon as a General*, vol. 1.

9   Napoleon to Moreau, 16 March 1800, in John E. Howard, ed., *Letters and Documents of Napoleon I* (New York, 1961), 1:386. Napoleon wrote: "no one takes a greater interest than I in your personal glory and happiness ... Today I am a kind of puppet who has lost liberty and happiness. Grandeur is fine but in memory and imagination. I envy your happy lot: at

Bonaparte did not relieve him of command for insubordination, simply because the young First Consul realized he did not yet have the political clout to take down a general of Moreau's standing no matter what the reason. Moreau had powerful allies in both the army and in Paris: Bonaparte had to be careful in his dealings with him. Interestingly, and perhaps not surprisingly, Moreau later would be implicated in a plot against Napoleon and exiled in 1804. But for the present, a frustrated Napoleon simply ended his attempts to work directly with the recalcitrant general, stating: "Moreau is not capable of appreciating and executing the plan that I have conceived. Let him do as he pleases, provided he throws Marshal Kray upon Ulm."[10]

By way of tremendous intellectual energy and agility, Napoleon created a new plan toward the end of March that made Italy the primary theater of war and relegated General Moreau to a secondary role. Accordingly, Moreau would open the campaign between 10 and 20 April by crossing the Rhine and turning the Black Forest to sever Kray's communication with Melas. Moreau would then then drive Kray into Bavaria so he "would be unable to reconquer the ground they [the Austrians] have lost in less than ten or twelve days."[11] Napoleon was not asking Moreau for the decisive victory his first plan had sought, only a window of time just short of two weeks. An important component of this new plan was that Moreau was to leave a reserve corps of 25,000 experienced veterans under General Claude Jacques Lecourbe in Switzerland. Its mission was to first support the right flank of the Army of the Rhine as it advanced against Kray. Then, after Moreau's offensive had made headway and was secure, Lecourbe and his corps would march south through the Saint Gothard Pass and join the Army of the Reserve. At the same time that Lecourbe advanced south, the Reserve would initiate its advance into Italy by several Alpine passes further to the west. The junction of these two forces would take place in Lombardy, with Lecourbe's corps providing vital reinforcements for the Army of the Reserve as it began to move into position behind Melas in Piedmont. The final component of this plan was that, at precisely the same time as French forces entered Italy, the beleaguered Army of Italy, now commanded by the

---

the head of brave men you are going to do splendid things. I would gladly exchange my consular purple for the epaulettes of a colonel under your command. I much hope that circumstances will allow me to come and shake your hand. But, in any case, my confidence in you is complete, in all respects."

10 Louis Adolphe Thiers, *History of the Consulate and the Empire of France under Napoleon* (Philadelphia, 1893), 1:146. Thiers states that these words came from a heated conversation between Moreau's chief of staff, General Jean-Joseph Dessolles, and the First Consul. Thiers "received this account from the lips of General Dessolles himself."

11 Berthier to Moreau, 25 March 1800, in Cugnac, *Réserve*, 1:110–111.

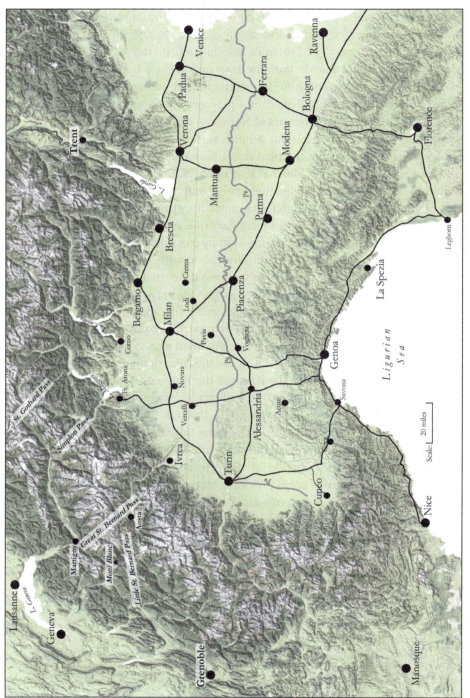

MAP 5.1   The Italian theater, 1800

talented Masséna but pressed against the Mediterranean Sea in the vicinity of Genoa, would capture the attention of Melas's much larger Austrian force. It was crucial for Masséna to stay on the defensive and utilize the mountain terrain in efforts to negate the influence of the Austrian cavalry and artillery. If Masséna could survive and keep Melas's attention long enough, the trap could be set.[12]

Such a bold march over the Alps and invasion of Italy would certainly seize the initiative and force Melas to defend Piedmont. The weakness of this plan, as hinted above, was that, unlike the first plan, it lacked the potential to bring the War of the Second Coalition to a decisive end. Even if the destruction of Melas was achieved, it was unlikely that Austria would sue for peace while Kray remained in the field and defended the road to Vienna. Although Bonaparte's second plan demonstrates tremendous flexibility and improvisation in response to Moreau's intransigence, it would most likely prolong the war. Nevertheless, this second plan gave Bonaparte the ability to strike and, by use of the Swiss salient, potentially fall on at least one of the Austrian armies with great consequence.

Since late January 1800, the Army of the Reserve had been assembling in the vicinity of Dijon to mislead any Allied spies as to its true destination. Berthier received command of this force until the First Consul could leave Paris and command it himself. As First Consul, Napoleon was understandably hesitant to depart for Italy and relinquish immediate control over the fledgling revolutionary government he had helped establish. There was no way to be certain the Consulate would survive his absence, especially should he be defeated, and the fact that Paris had already seen four revolutionary regimes come and go in the past decade did little to inspire Napoleon's confidence. Berthier was a trusted and loyal subordinate who would do exactly as Bonaparte indicated, and his attention to detail as chief of staff was unmatched; however, his talents as a commander in chief left something to be desired. He always needed encouragement and complained often. Understandably, Berthier was dismayed that, as late as April, the Reserve still numbered fewer than 30,000 men; moreover, this army was in woeful need of everything. In particular, he complained to Bonaparte about the lack of transport, stating that, while expecting to receive news of Moreau opening the campaign, he would find it difficult to begin the advance given the absence of a single means of transport either for the army or the supply services.[13]

---

12   Carnot to Masséna, 9 April 1800, ibid., 1:112–115.
13   Berthier to Napoleon, 23 April 1800, ibid., 1:159–161.

It was at this time, in mid-April, that Napoleon learned the dramatic news that Melas had taken the offensive against Masséna more than two weeks before and had driven him back into Genoa and was now besieging that city.[14] Bonaparte realized at once that the fate of the campaign now hinged on Masséna's ability to survive the Austrian onslaught with a numerically inferior and undersupplied army. How long could Masséna hold out in Genoa? This question weighed heavily on Bonaparte's mind. A premature collapse of Genoa could potentially compromise the entire campaign by freeing Melas to advance north, wait for the Army of the Reserve to emerge from the Alps, and defeat it in detail. Moreover, if Masséna surrendered, Genoa could provide Melas and the Austrians with a stronghold from which they could establish direct support from the British fleet. In addition, Genoa could serve as a base from which they could launch an invasion of France.

Bonaparte's response to this news was to accelerate the movement of the Army of the Reserve. He wanted it to reach Geneva and begin crossing the Alps as soon as possible. Initially, Napoleon had considered using the Saint Gothard or Simplon Passes. As time became of the essence, he increasingly felt that the more westward and closer Great Saint Bernard Pass should be utilized by the army's main body. Although other passes were to be used as feints (Little Saint Bernard, Simplon, and Mont Cenis), the Great Saint Bernard Pass offered the significant logistical advantage of utilizing Lake Geneva for water transport of supplies. Bonaparte especially liked that the advance from Villeneuve to Aosta would take only four days and that this route assured a secure line of operations back to Paris. The Great Saint Bernard also offered the advantage of opening onto the Po valley at Ivrea, where the army could maneuver in a more covered territory that was purportedly held by relatively few Austrian troops.[15]

To complicate matters even more, Moreau had yet to open the campaign. Napoleon repeated the order, telling Moreau that his delay was essentially "compromising the safety of the Republic."[16] Moreau's attack was needed before the Reserve could begin its march across the Alps; otherwise the Reserve's left wing, perhaps even its rear, would be exposed to Kray. Moreau finally attacked Kray on 25 April with excellent results, and soon Kray was in full retreat toward Ulm, driven from the vital areas of Switzerland. After his

---

14   Ibid. Berthier received a letter from Nice dated 14 April, stating that Masséna had been attacked. It would not be known for another week that Masséna was confined within Genoa; regardless, Napoleon realized that this was a very real possibility.
15   Napoleon to Berthier, 27 April 1800, ibid., 1:216–217. See also *Napoleon's Memoirs Dictated by the Emperor at Saint Helena*, ed. by Somerset de Chair (London, 1986), 453–454.
16   Napoleon to Carnot, 24 April 1800, in Cugnac, *Réserve*, 1:92–93. Napoleon actually told Carnot to relate the message.

initial success, Moreau became reluctant to release Lecourbe and his veterans; soon he could provide only General Bon-Adrien Jeannot de Moncey and half the numbers he had promised.[17]

As Napoleon readied to leave Paris and join the Reserve Army at Geneva, he received confirmation that Masséna was indeed besieged in Genoa and had supplies to hold out for one month (until the end of May).[18] Napoleon hoped Melas would remain focused on Genoa to give the Reserve time to cross the Alps. Rumors and reports from Vienna revealed that the enemy was not expecting the Reserve Army to cross the Alps in force and believed only a small force would be sent to relieve Masséna. Moreover, intelligence indicated that the Austrians, Melas in particular, had little respect for the Reserve Army, assuming it was not fit to march and consisted only of ignorant recruits. Melas's underestimation of the Reserve was a serious mistake that Napoleon, provided Masséna could hold out long enough, wanted the Austrian commander to regret.[19]

The massive operation of moving 40,000 troops over the Alps began on 15 May. The Army of the Reserve's advance guard was commanded by General Jean Lannes and numbered some 8,000 men of the divisions of Generals François Watrin, Joseph Antoine Marie Michel Mainoni, and the cavalry of Jean-Baptiste Rivaud. The rest of the army was formed into two corps: General Philibert-Guillaume Duhesme commanding one that consisted of divisions led by Generals Louis-Henri Loison and Jean Boudet; and General Claude Victor commanding the other, composed of the divisions of Generals Jean-Jacques-Antoine Chambarlhac and Joseph Chabran (who was to march by way of the Little Saint Bernard and join with the main army at Aosta). General Joachim Murat commanded all cavalry and General Auguste Frédéric Louis Viesse de Marmont all forty-eight guns of the artillery. The Consular Guard would bring up the rear of the army.[20] Deep snow, steep gradients, and the constant threat of avalanche made the going difficult. The greatest challenge was getting the artillery over the 8,000-foot-high pass. Berthier reported that the army's sledges on rollers were useless and that locals instructed them to hollow out a tree trunk, then place the artillery piece in it and, with sixty men,

---

17   Napoleon to Berthier, 4 May 1800, ibid., 1:274–277. Moreau continued to disappoint Napoleon. The First Consul told Berthier to "let General Moreau know by messenger the situation with the Army of Italy, make him feel that a few brigades more will amount to nothing for him, but that a few brigades less would compromise the Army of the Reserve."
18   Berthier to Napoleon, 3 May 1800, ibid., 1:249–250.
19   Napoleon to Berthier, 2 May 1800, ibid., 1:258–262.
20   Berthier to Dupont, 10 May 1800, ibid., 1:315–318.

drag it to the top.[21] The troops rested briefly at the Hospice of Saint Bernard, then began the descent into the Po valley. The advance guard under Lannes made good progress, reached Aosta, and pushed eighteen miles east to Châtillon, where a small force of Austrians was repulsed.

However, fourteen miles south-southeast of Châtillon, the advance guard was forced to halt on 19 May before a small fort perched atop a towering crag that dominated the whole narrow valley: this was Fort Bard. The geographic position of the small fortress alone made it almost impervious to harm. Beyond its location, the structure itself had no apparent defensive weaknesses and no salient angles, and it bristled with guns; there could be no doubt that such a stronghold would be difficult if not impossible to take. On 20 May, General Pierre Antoine Dupont summoned the commander of the fort and asked for its surrender "to avoid a useless spilling of blood," but the determined Captain Josef Otto Stockard von Bernkopf responded that he would never surrender Bard.[22] Evidence indicates that Napoleon had received flawed intelligence regarding Bard that underestimated the strength of the fort and thus the effort needed to take it.[23] As a result, Napoleon now found this "insignificant" mountain stronghold blocking the advance of his army and jeopardizing the future of the campaign, or at least delaying it significantly. The First Consul knew that as of 13 May Melas stood at the Var River and calculated that the Austrians could not concentrate before the 25th. If Bard detained the Army of the Reserve beyond 25 May, the French initiative could be lost to Melas who could feasibly be waiting fourteen miles to the south at Ivrea for the French to debouch from the valley.

Berthier reported that "Fort Bard is a greater obstacle than we had foreseen, since it is impossible to pass the artillery until we are masters of it. As for the infantry and cavalry, they can turn the fort by taking a mule path which runs [east across Mont Albaredo]."[24] The fort was shelled and assaulted but with no success. Napoleon wanted pressure to be kept on the fort, but also gave orders to begin work widening the "mule path" to facilitate circumventing the stronghold. Lannes and the advance guard had already used the path and continued on to Ivrea, but now General Armand Samuel de Marescot, commander of the

---

21 Berthier to Napoleon, 16 May 1800, ibid., 1:399–400.
22 Dupont to Stockard von Bernkopf, 20 May 1800, ibid., 1:444.
23 Mainoni to Berthier, 6 May 1800, ibid., 1:288–290. Mainoni, a divisional commander and part of Lannes's advance guard, underestimated the formidable nature of Bard even though he had been born in Switzerland and was well acquainted with the Aosta valley.
24 Berthier to Napoleon, 20 May 1800, ibid., 1:440–441. Berthier mentions a worst-case scenario resulting from Bard, which would be to achieve a junction with General Louis Marie Turreau operating in the region of Mount Cenis.

engineers, with the help of 1,500 sappers and soldiers, began to widen the path by filling holes, lowering the grade of some parts, and leveling out others. Such tireless work succeeded in creating a navigable road for all but the artillery: the Army of the Reserve was moving again.[25]

Berthier cleared the village of Bard and completely isolated the fort. Again he asked for its surrender, but again Stockard von Bernkopf refused and stood defiant. Napoleon became increasingly concerned that Lannes, who was advancing on Ivrea, would be vulnerable without artillery support.[26] Thus, Marmont received the task of somehow moving the artillery past Bard. In desperation he turned to stealth and one evening during a thunderstorm was able to drag several pieces of artillery passed Bard before the garrison noticed and began firing on the exposed men. In total, the French managed to pass only six of their guns in this manner.[27] Bonaparte was frustrated by Bard; he had underestimated the little fort and he knew it, but the delay thus far had not compromised the campaign. The First Consul gave charge of the siege operations to Chabran's division (recently arrived by way of the Little Saint Bernard Pass) and then advanced with the rest of the army into Piedmont.[28] Bard would finally fall to Chabran in early June, having held up the passage of the majority of the Reserve Army's artillery for more than a week.[29]

The crossing of the Alps, even with the difficulties presented by Fort Bard, had been successful and security had been maintained. Napoleon informed his brother Joseph that "the worst obstacles have been overcome ... we have come down like a thunderbolt; the enemy was not expecting us."[30] There were no indications that Melas intended to contest the Reserve Army's entrance

---

25 Marescot to Berthier, 23 May 1800, in US Army Service Schools, *Source Book of the Marengo Campaign in 1800*, ed. by Conrad Lanza (Fort Leavenworth, KS, 1922), 41. Marescot wrote to Berthier: "It is unfortunate that the strength of Bard, a strength dependent on its position and but slightly on itself, was unknown."
26 Watrin to Lannes, 22 May 1800, in Cugnac, *Réserve*, 1:470–471. Lannes and the advance guard would successfully take Ivrea on 22 May without any artillery support. Watrin claims that 6,000 Austrians were forced out, but this estimate seems high. A survey of secondary sources indicates 2,500 to 3,000 Austrians; 6,000 Austrians could have held Ivrea and perhaps indicated Melas's intention of seriously defending the Great Saint Bernard Pass.
27 Berthier to Napoleon, 21 May 1800, ibid., 1:455–457; and Berthier to First Consul, 22 May 1800, ibid., 1:464.
28 Napoleon to Berthier, 22 May 1800, ibid., 1:469–470.
29 For a more detailed discussion of the Army of the Reserve's crossing of the Alps, see Chandler, *Campaigns of Napoleon*, 274–281; Yorck von Wartenburg, *Napoleon as a General*, 1:170–180; and Herbert H. Sargent, *The Campaign of Marengo* (Chicago, 1901), 140–150.
30 Napoleon to Joseph, 24 May 1800, in Howard, *Letters and Documents of Napoleon*, 1:433.

into the Po valley. Bonaparte, it seemed, was free to maneuver and the campaign was open to him.

Now came the central operational question of the campaign: should Napoleon advance on Genoa, Turin, or Milan? The plan was always to fall on the rear of Melas's army and relieve Masséna, but precisely how that was to be done remained unconfirmed. Masséna's situation was becoming critical. Forced to eat rations of horsemeat and improvised "bread" made with linseed, starch and cocoa, the Army of Italy was held together increasingly by only the will of Masséna. The surrender of Genoa was not far off.

A move on Turin would achieve a junction with Turreau's division advancing by way of the Mont Cenis Pass (Susa), but it was the sector where the Austrians most expected Bonaparte to appear.[31] The advantage would go to Melas and his potential ability to concentrate a larger force than the French. Even if Bonaparte could defeat his Austrian counterpart, there would still be a large Austrian force to be dealt with before Genoa. Yorck von Wartenburg asserts that Turin was the "ordinary" general's choice because one would defeat Melas and relieve Genoa only to meet the enemy again behind the Po.[32] If all went well, the Turin choice might have made Bonaparte master of Piedmont, but it would not have been a decisive victory that would have brought an immediate end to the campaign. Bonaparte, when reevaluating the campaign while on Saint Helena, felt that a move on Turin "was contrary to the principles of war since Melas had considerable forces with him; the French army would have run the risk of fighting without having a certain retreat, because Fort Bard had not yet been secured."[33]

The choice of advancing on Genoa would bring immediate succor to the beleaguered Army of Italy and Masséna. Bonaparte asserts that a direct advance on Genoa, with Melas in force at Turin, would have carelessly exposed the French line of communication.[34] Another argument, callous to the suffering of Masséna and his troops, was that even if Genoa fell it was not a permanent loss to France because once Melas was defeated Genoa would again be returned to French hands. Unfortunately for Masséna and his men, the immediate relief of Genoa paled in comparison to pursuing a means to more decisively defeat Melas.

---

31 Turreau commanded the left wing of the Army of Italy until it was detached to the Army of the Reserve in April 1800. See Georges Six, *Dictionnaire biographique des généraux et amiraux Français de la Révolution et de l'Empire (1792–1814)* (Paris, 1934), 2:517.
32 Yorck von Wartenburg, *Napoleon as a General*, 1:181–182.
33 *Napoleon's Memoirs*, 458.
34 Ibid.

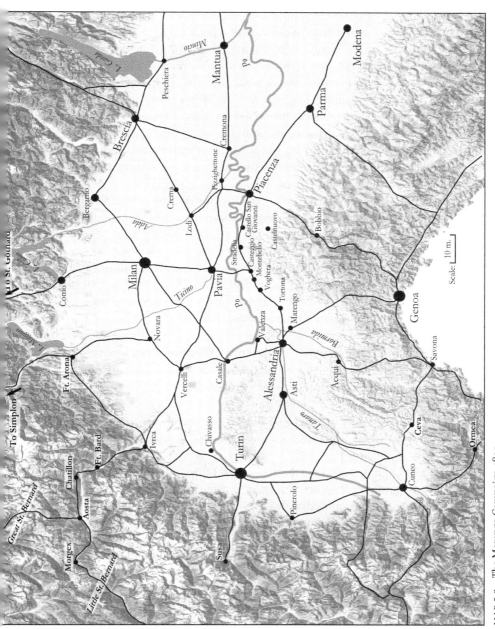

MAP 5.2 The Marengo Campaign, 1800

The third option, to march on Milan, "presented every advantage."[35] The taking of Milan would allow the French army to secure all that the main Austrian depot had to offer: supplies, munitions of war, hospitals, etc. Unlike a march on Turin, such a move would be unexpected and would facilitate junctions with the other French contingents advancing from the Simplon and Gothard Passes. An advance to Milan would also allow the French to transfer their lines of communication to the east, achieving more security than Aosta offered. Most significantly, the advance on Milan offered the possibility of maneuvering over the Po and cutting Melas's lines of retreat and communication. Such an audacious maneuver would not only test Austrian morale, but would also (it was hoped) force a quick Austrian withdrawal, perhaps even lift the siege of Genoa, and make Melas risk his army in a climactic battle.

Critics have blamed Bonaparte for not having placed the relief of Genoa above all other considerations. Despite the advantages of the Milan option, some believe that Masséna was wrongly abandoned. James Marshall-Cornwall, in fact, argues that Napoleon could have relieved Genoa before Melas could have arrived but "chose the third alternative, sacrificed Masséna and won the campaign, although only with the assistance of a certain amount of luck."[36] Defenders of the Milan choice, specifically David Chandler, state that this attitude is not really justifiable because Napoleon's main objective was the destruction of Melas's field army, not saving a friend.[37]

The situation of the approaching French army, to say the least, must have been confusing for the Austrian commander. Melas received reports of French activity in all the alpine passes from Mont Cenis to Saint Gothard and found it difficult to determine where the main French thrust would come. In Melas's defense, it would only be logical to believe that it was Turreau's division acting as the advance guard, pushing General Johann Konrad Valentin von Kaim back at Susa. Mont Cenis was the most direct line an invading force from France could take and it was practical for artillery as well. Turreau had artillery from the outset; Lannes, as long as Fort Bard held firm, could only dream of such support. Regardless, after news arrived of thousands of French soldiers filing past Fort Bard, Melas immediately left Nice with 10,000 men and joined Kaim, who had retreated from Susa, and General András Hadik Futaki (recently driven from the Aosta valley by Lannes) at Turin. With the majority of the Austrian forces still before Genoa, Melas united 18,000 men at Turin and fully anticipated that Bonaparte would cross the Po and attack him there.[38]

---

35 Ibid.
36 James Marshall-Cornwall, *Napoleon as Military Commander* (London, 1967), 105.
37 Chandler, *Campaigns of Napoleon*, 299.
38 Sargent, *Campaign of Marengo*, 148–149.

Meanwhile, 30,000 men of the Reserve Army concentrated thirty-two miles north-northeast of Turin at Ivrea; thus far, only eight guns had arrived. As Napoleon prepared for the 75-mile march east to Milan, he sent Lannes and the advance guard twenty miles due south toward Chivasso both to engage Hadik Futaki and to threaten Turin in an effort to misdirect the Austrians. Bonaparte knew that, as long as Lannes threatened Turin, the Reserve Army's march to Milan would be covered. Lannes aggressively attacked Hadik Futaki, which only reinforced Melas's idea that the French were moving on Turin.[39] Lannes would remain as a decoy before Chivasso until 31 May – a total of three days.

The Reserve Army advanced rapidly eastward on Milan by way of Vercelli and Novara. Murat and the cavalry acted as the advance guard and drove the Austrian division of General Josip Filip Vukasović across the Ticino River and from the vicinity of Milan. The Reserve Army continued to perform with a conspicuous lack of many things, in particular artillery, but at this juncture Bonaparte complained bitterly to Minister of War Carnot about the lack of engineers and sappers, not to mention transport and bridging equipment.[40] Such a lack of specialists and equipment would only hamper the army's impending passage of the Po, and Napoleon knew that soon all would depend on a successful crossing.

On 2 June, Napoleon entered Milan with the vanguard, claiming that the Milanese had not only enthusiastically received the French, but were also astonished to see Bonaparte because it had been reported that he had drowned in the Red Sea and it was actually his brother who commanded the French army(!).[41] Once situated in Milan, Bonaparte ordered Duhesme east to drive Vukasović's division across the Adda River in an effort to protect the Reserve Army's area of operations. In addition, Bonaparte immediately transferred and secured his lines of operation through the Simplon and Gothard Passes to the north.[42] Although he never needed it at the height of his glory, Napoleon always took care to identify a safe path of retreat and was as meticulous about

---

39   *Extrait du journal de la campagne de l'Armée de Réserve par l'adjudant commandant Brossier*, 28 May 1800, in Cugnac, *Réserve*, 2:14–16.
40   Napoleon to Carnot, 29 May 1800, ibid., 2:44–45. Bonaparte mentions a lack of *ouvriers d'artillerie* who would be related to engineers, but more specifically armory/artillery repair.
41   In regards to Bonaparte's entry into Milan, see *Napoleon's Memoirs*, 460, and *Bulletin de l'Armée de Réserve*, 29 May 1800, in Cugnac, *Réserve*, 2:41–42. The only bulletin that refers to Italians thinking Napoleon perished in the Red Sea was issued from Vercelli on 29 May. His *Memoirs* recall this "Vercelli scene" in Milan and add the detail about his unnamed brother commanding the army.
42   Napoleon to Berthier, 4 June 1800, in Cugnac, *Réserve*, 2:106–107.

securing his own communications as he was ruthless about attacking his enemy's.

While awaiting the arrival of Moncey's corps, which was still a few days march north of Milan after having exited the Saint Gothard Pass, Napoleon began planning the next phase of campaign in which he hoped to sever Austrian communications. Once reinforced by Moncey, Napoleon planned to advance south over the Po and concentrate in the vicinity of the important communications link provided by the Stradella Pass. With the French controlling Austrian communications and the Po valley from Milan to Stradella, Napoleon was convinced that Melas would be forced to fight. If bridgeheads could be established over the Po, the trap could be closed on Melas.

On 4 June, Napoleon dispatched Murat and Lannes as a dual vanguard to secure the crossings of the Po. Lannes advanced seventy miles due east from Chivasso toward Pavia, where he forced a crossing just south of Belgiojoso in the face of Austrian resistance. On 6 June, Lannes reported from Stradella that, after some intense fighting, he had been able to complete the bridge and have the rest of his troops cross to the right bank.[43] Murat appeared before Piacenza with his cavalry on 4 June. After sporadic fighting and a desperate search for boats, he last crossed the Po and seized the feebly held city on the 7th. The Po was flooding and the rising waters made it difficult to bridge, but on the 8th the First Consul was in possession of his second crossing over the river and the concentration on Stradella could proceed.[44]

The greatest prize yielded by Piacenza was a packet of Melas' latest dispatches to Vienna. It was from these documents that Napoleon learned that Genoa had fallen on 4 June and Masséna had formally surrendered to General Károly Péter Ott von Bátorkézi on 5 June. The Army of Italy was not taken prisoner, but allowed to join General Louis-Gabriel Suchet behind the Var River where it could recommence hostilities.[45] Yet Masséna's men, looking like skeletons from their ordeal, were unable to resume the offensive and impact the campaign in a meaningful way. Masséna's defense of Genoa became legendary and only enhanced his reputation as a military commander. However, much later on Saint Helena, Napoleon considered Genoa's fall premature and "less excusable because he [Masséna] knew of the arrival of my Army upon the Po."[46] The loss of Genoa was an important, but not an unforeseen blow to the First Consul's plan. The immediate result was to release General Ott von Bátorkézi

---

43   Berthier to Lannes, 4 June 1800, ibid., 2:112–113; see also Lannes to Berthier, 6 June 1800, ibid., 2:178–179.
44   Lauriston to Napoleon, 7 June 1800, ibid., 2:198–199.
45   Napoleon to Berthier, 8 June 1800, ibid., 2:227–231.
46   *Napoleon's Memoirs*, 462.

and thousands of Austrians to march northward on Alessandria to oppose the Army of the Reserve. In addition, now that Genoa was under Austrian control, the city could be used as a refuge and center of operations supported by the British navy.[47] If the latter scenario became a reality, Bonaparte's plan of a decisive battle could potentially vanish only to be replaced by a grueling siege. Waiting to counter Melas's breakthrough attempt was a luxury the French did not have at this point. Instead, Napoleon recognized that he would have to go on the offensive immediately and hunt down Melas before the Austrian commander could even consider falling back on Genoa.

Although surprised by the French move to first Milan and then the Po, Melas still seemed to underestimate the threat it represented. Still in Turin with Generals Kaim and Hadik Futaki, Melas ordered a general concentration at Alessandria on 31 May.[48] However, General Franz Anton von Elsnitz, badly mauled by Suchet while marching northward from Nice, was delayed while Ott von Bátorkézi was tied to Genoa until its capitulation.[49] In response, Melas remained at Turin and did nothing, preferring to wait until the formal surrender of Genoa was concluded before finally advancing to Alessandria on 6 June. Melas's obsession with Genoa hindered the Austrian ability to concentrate effectively and to contest the French presence on the Po; at the same time, such a delay provided Napoleon with valuable time to finish concentrating his own army on the right bank at Stradella.

Bonaparte initially feared the worst, but after further considering the captured correspondence, he became more confident and believed Melas could not unite his forces at Alessandria before 12 or 13 June. Napoleon estimated incorrectly that the Austrian forces, once concentrated, would number no more than 22,000 men (Elsnitz's 7,000, Ott von Bátorkézi's 9,000, and Hadik Futaki's 6,000). In response, Napoleon decided to have Lannes's corps continue to serve as the advance guard and resume the offensive rather than defend Stradella. On 8 June from Milan, Napoleon directed Berthier to have Lannes, supported by Victor's corps, advance from Stradella sixteen miles east-southeast to Voghera, crushing everything in his path.[50]

Berthier hastened the army's crossing of the Po. The Army of the Reserve proceeded toward the few completed bridges on the Po, but continuous rain

---

47	Chandler, *Campaigns of Napoleon*, 285–286.
48	Vincent S. Esposito and John R. Elting, *A Military History and Atlas of the Napoleonic Wars* (New York, 1965), 38.
49	Napoleon to Berthier, 8 June 1800, in Cugnac, *Réserve*, 2:227–231.
50	Ibid. Bonaparte issued several orders to Lannes that reflected his uncertainty over whether the general should defend Stradella or resume the offensive; he eventually committed to the latter.

made the river rise swiftly, and for several days it was a struggle to maintain the bridges. Repeated repairs slowed the passage of the army down to a crawl, allowing only portions to cross at a time. Berthier had to inform Napoleon that the crossing was not yet completed and only one of Victor's divisions (Chambarlhac's) was able to cross in time to support the advance guard.[51] Nonetheless, Berthier conveyed the First Consul's orders to Lannes who, with Victor's support, advanced toward Voghera on the morning of 9 June.[52]

Meanwhile, General Ott von Bátorkézi marched from Genoa upstream the Scrivia River to reach Voghera on 8 June, some four days earlier than Bonaparte had anticipated him. He would have made it sooner but was slowed by the flooding Scrivia. Ott had received orders to retake Piacenza and reopen the road to Mantua. Such a directive betrays the fact that the Austrians still had no clear idea of how large the Army of the Reserve was or the progress it had made. Although Lannes and Ott did not know it, they were now on a collision course.[53]

Ott's 18,000 men occupied a position on the heights in and around the village of Casteggio. After reconnaissance confirmed this, Lannes immediately attacked the larger Austrian force with his 5,000 men on 9 June but was repulsed by blistering artillery fire. As Napoleon had intended, Victor now hurried Chambarlhac's division forward to reinforce Lannes's entire line. After some intense combat, the French successfully turned the Austrian flank, crushing Ott's forces, and chasing them through Montebello. Lacking sufficient cavalry, the French could not pursue effectively, thus rendering the most significant combat of the campaign so far, the Battle of Montebello, inconclusive. Ott von Bátorkézi lost 4,000 men and hardly expected the French to be in such strength; confused and shaken, he fell back on Alessandria.[54] Realizing that he now held the initiative, Napoleon assumed that the Austrians had completed their concentration at Alessandria. What the First Consul did not know was that Melas would remained fixed to Alessandria for the next five days without making any significant movement.

---

51 Berthier to First Consul, 8 June 1800, ibid., 2:236–237; Claude-Perrin Victor, duc de Bellune, *Extraits de mémoires inedits de feu Claude Victor Perrin, duc de Bellune* (Paris, 1846), 148; Bulletin of the Reserve Army, 9 June 1800, in Howard, *Letters and Documents of Napoleon*, 1:460–461. Before the eventual five bridges across the Po were completed, it was necessary to impress the local peasantry into service. See Levasseur to Dupont, 11 June 1800, in Cugnac, *Réserve*, 2:303–304.
52 Berthier to Lannes, 8 June 1800, ibid., 2:237–238.
53 Quoted from *Österreichische Militarische Zeitschrift*, ibid., 2:264–269.
54 Victor, *Extraits de mémoires inedits de feu Claude Victor Perrin*, 151–155.

Napoleon arrived at Stradella to join the army in person, investigating as far as Casteggio to survey where Lannes and Victor had defeated Ott. He oversaw the completion of the bridges over the Po and the concentration of his forces. By the end of the 11th, Napoleon had 30,000 troops concentrated and ready for action on the right bank, while the entire Army of the Reserve (including detachments and troops in rear areas) numbered 55,000. It was at this time that General Louis Charles Antoine Desaix joined the Army of the Reserve, arriving directly from Toulon where he had been in quarantine after returning from Egypt. Napoleon immediately gave this talented general command of two divisions led by Jean Boudet and Jean-Charles Monnier.[55] Desaix was to play a crucial role in the approaching climax of the campaign. Also at this time, the balance of the artillery (forty guns) finally arrived from Bard.

Napoleon did not want to allow Melas to break contact; however, despite the First Consul's best intentions, that is exactly what happened. All energy was now focused on learning the whereabouts and intentions of the enemy army. Victor's advance guard commander, General Gaspard Amédée Gardanne, reported from Voghera that the Austrians did not seem to be preparing for an attack, simply because they had retreated in such disorder the previous evening (9 June). Many locals confirmed this. Some patrols had not yet returned, but thus far only vague information confirmed the claim that the Austrian position was somewhere "below [south of] Tortona."[56] Gardanne voiced his anger for not receiving more cavalry to execute his responsibilities: "[I have not] a single cavalryman to serve as an orderly ... you must realize that the advance guard cannot get along without a body of cavalry to hasten its operations!"[57] Without proper reconnaissance, or even the right tools to complete the task, it is not surprising that Napoleon lost contact with Melas. The French had failed to obtain any reliable information concerning the Austrians since the Battle of Montebello, more than four days previously. A frantic Berthier dispatched patrols here and there, demanding reports, even sending a "French officer who spoke Italian" to secure any possible news from locals on the left bank of the Po opposite Voghera.[58]

Confident that Melas was still in the vicinity of Alessandria, Napoleon sought contact with the Austrians on 13 June. He ordered the corps of Victor (Chambarlhac and Gardanne) and Lannes (Watrin) to advance westward from Voghera across the Scrivia with orders to attack and overthrow any enemy

---

55 Berthier to Dupont, 11 June 1800, in Cugnac, *Réserve*, 2:306–307; *Napoleon's Memoirs*, 462. Desaix and Napoleon had exchanged letters weeks earlier, and his arrival was expected.
56 Gardanne to Dupont, 11 June 1800, in Cugnac, *Réserve*, 2 :298–299.
57 Ibid., 299.
58 Berthier to Dupont, 12 June 1800, ibid., 2:328–329.

forces they encountered.⁵⁹ Murat lent one brigade of cavalry to each and Desaix followed as a reserve. As they neared San Giuliano three hours later, they had yet to make contact with the Austrians. Napoleon realized the plain of Marengo offered the Austrians an excellent chance to exploit their numerically superior cavalry; Melas's decision to relinquish such an opportunity only helped to convince the First Consul that the Austrian commander had decided to avoid combat.⁶⁰ Napoleon projected that Melas would pursue one of two courses: shift northward on Valenza in efforts to turn the French right and sever the Army of the Reserve's communications, or retire south on Genoa to make a stand with the support of the British fleet. Accordingly, Napoleon commanded Jean François Cornu de Lapoype's division to guard against a potential Austrian thrust to the north and for Desaix with Boudet's division to advance south and observe the road from Alessandria to Novi.⁶¹

It would seem Napoleon was more interested in blocking Melas's escape than defeating him in battle. To detach Desaix and Lapoype at this point, as he transitioned from the operational to the tactical, was imprudent and dangerous. As Yorck von Wartenburg states, "Napoleon sinned here against one of those great principles which can rarely be violated with impunity."⁶² Although Napoleon had lost contact with the Austrians, everything seemed to indicate that a climactic battle was only days away yet, instead of concentrating, the First Consul became consumed with blocking all avenues of retreat. The concentration of his army, that activity that Napoleon would elevate to the level of art, was performed inadequately prior to Marengo. Beyond detaching Desaix and Lapoype, Moncey remained at Milan, and Duhesme was still near Piacenza; all should have left behind minimal garrisons and started concentrating for battle days earlier.

As night fell, Victor found the Austrian rearguard at the small village of Marengo. After a brief combat, a bayonet charge sent the Austrians retreating across the Bormida River toward Alessandria in complete disorder.⁶³ Reports

---

59 Napoleon to Lannes, 13 June 1800, in Howard, *Letters and Documents of Napoleon*, 1, 463. See also Cugnac, *Réserve*, 2:338–339. Captain de Cugnac, the editor of the General Staff Publication at the turn of the 20th century, was probably most familiar with the sources of the campaign. He points out that very few if any official correspondence exists from 12, 13, and 14 June; he believes that the missing items were removed to protect the reputation of Napoleon and to rewrite the history of Marengo.
60 Berthier's campaign account from 1803, cited in Cugnac, *Réserve*, 2:339.
61 *Napoleon's Memoirs*, 464.
62 Yorck von Wartenburg, *Napoleon as a General*, 1:189.
63 Report on the Battle of Marengo, by *Lieutenant-général* Joachim Quiot, then aide de camp of General Victor, SHAT, Mémoires reconnaissances: Armée des Alpes et d'Italie, MR 463. See also Victor, *Extraits de mémoires inedits de feu Claude Victor Perrin*, 163.

incorrectly indicated that the Austrians had destroyed the bridges over the Bormida and only a small garrison held Alessandria.[64] All of this of course only confirmed in Napoleon's mind that Melas had no intention of fighting. As Napoleon retired for the night to Torre di Garafoli eight miles to the rear, anxious to read the latest reports, the last thing he considered was Melas bursting out of Alessandria in an all-out attack. Napoleon based his actions on the intelligence he had received, but at some point he needed to confirm the vital information concerning the absence of the bridges over the Bormida.

By this time, Melas realized the danger of his position. He defended his predicament by characterizing Napoleon's offensive as "so impetuous and so rapid that the division of Marshal Vukasović ... found itself unable to oppose ... [it] at any point."[65] After Napoleon had taken Milan and was in the midst of crossing the Po, Melas sent Ott von Bátorkézi to attack, but this attempt became for the Austrians "the unfavorable and bitter combat" of Montebello.[66] In other words, Melas had done very little to contest the Army of the Reserve's impressive maneuver that spanned well over 100 miles. The resistance the French had met since emerging from the Great Saint Bernard Pass had been remarkably light until Montebello. Melas simply did not take the Army of the Reserve seriously until it was too late. He explained in an almost casual manner: "Because of this change in situation [the French crossing of the Po at Piacenza], I decided to assemble all available troops on the right bank of the Po, near Alessandria."[67]

By the 11th, Melas had finally gathered all his troops at Alessandria. A tremendous influence upon his decision to launch a breakout attack from Alessandria was that he felt increasingly that Suchet and Masséna commanding what he believed to be 20,000 men were moving toward Acqui.[68] Although this was not the case, Melas decided "to attack the enemy with the object of opening the road [from Piacenza to Mantua] ... along the right bank of the Po."[69] Melas was confident in the Austrian superiority in artillery and cavalry, and in the "courage with which the whole army was animated."[70] The attack was planned for the morning of the 14th.

---

64 Auguste F. Marmont, *Mémoires du maréchal Marmont duc de Raguse de 1792 à 1841* (Paris, 1857), II, 127–128; and *Napoleon's Memoirs*, 465. Marmont, in regard to the French failure to confirm the status of the bridges over the Bormida, is content to place the blame entirely on General Gardanne.
65 Report of General Melas to Archduke Charles, 19 June 1800, in Cugnac, *Réserve*, 2:437.
66 Ibid., 438.
67 Ibid.
68 Ibid.
69 Ibid., 439.
70 Ibid.

At 8:00 AM, the Austrians burst forth from Alessandria and began surging over the two bridges that the French did not know existed. Nearly 30,000 troops supported by 100 cannon deployed in 3 columns and advanced on Marengo. Seeing this onslaught, Victor positioned his forces behind a small creek that appeared on the plain as a ravine and presented a considerable tactical obstacle for cavalry and artillery.[71] He sent word to the First Consul that the whole Austrian army was advancing from Alessandria with the intention of giving battle. Napoleon initially thought it was a feint and that Melas was making a distraction to cover his withdrawal; when he finally understood the reality of the situation, he immediately recalled Desaix.

Numbering only 8,000 men with 7 guns, Victor's corps presented a front to the enemy that extended from Marengo to the marshes of the Bormida. The Austrians battered his line three separate times. After being attrited by one-third, Victor's corps began to waver. Lannes's corps arrived just as the Austrians began to envelop Victor's right.[72] The Consular Guard, about 800 infantry, reinforced the line at this time and brought much-needed ammunition.[73] The third Austrian attack, even though repulsed, weighed heavily on the French line. With attacks well developed on the French flanks, Melas came forward with the fourth assault against the French center supported by artillery, which poured grapeshot into the French ranks. The corps of Victor and Lannes began to give way and were soon in full retreat.[74]

By this time, about 2:00 PM, the First Consul arrived and directed troops to prevent Ott von Bátorkézi from collapsing the French right and severing communications.[75] Napoleon tried to rally the retreating troops by giving them reassurances and praise; in response the soldiers shouted "save the Republic" and "save the Consul," but continued to withdraw.[76] With only about 20,000 men available, Napoleon had concentrated less than half of the total number of the troops that composed the Reserve Army. The First Consul was in a desperate situation. Would Desaix return in time?

For whatever reason, the Austrians at this point hesitated and failed to aggressively pursue the retreating French. If they had, the day no doubt would

---

71   Ibid.; see also Jean Gaspar Cugnac, *La campagne de Marengo* (Paris, 1904), 222.
72   Report on the Battle of Marengo, Joachim Quiot, SHAT, MR 463.
73   Jean-Rouche Coignet. *The Note-books of Captain Coignet: Soldier of the Empire 1799–1816* (London, 1989), 76. Coignet states that the arrival of the Consular Guard, and the desperately needed ammunition they brought, allowed the French to retreat in order and not collapse.
74   Lannes to Berthier, 15 June 1800, and Victor to Berthier, 16 June 1800, in Cugnac, *Réserve*, 2:383–386 and 389–391.
75   Report on the Battle of Marengo, Joachim Quiot, SHAT, MR 463.
76   Victor, *Extraits de mémoires inedits de feu Claude Victor Perrin*, 177.

have been won. After being slightly wounded and having two horses shot out from under him, Melas handed over command to his chief of staff, General Anton von Zach. Presumably it was this change of command and Melas's misplaced confidence that caused the inexplicable lull in the action. Zach would renew the attack, but only after Austrian hesitation allowed the French to break contact and gave Napoleon valuable time to restore order and seize the initiative.[77]

It was at this time that Desaix arrived with Boudet's division following. These reinforcements would prove instrumental in the crucial second phase of this battle. Desaix had advanced southward toward Novi, but had encountered high waters on the Scrivia which slowed his progress. Desaix may have indeed marched to the sound of the guns, but evidence indicates that he also received dispatches from Napoleon recalling him. Boudet states that he was only one mile "from Rivalta when an aide of the First Consul arrived in haste to bring me orders to march on San Giuliano and from there on to Marengo where the armies had been fighting since daybreak."[78]

Desaix brought up Boudet's relatively fresh division of 5,000 around 5:00 PM, and, after a short council of war, placed them on each side of the road from San Giuliano leading to Marengo.[79] What remained of Victor's and Lannes's corps was placed to the right of Boudet's position. As the Austrian column now under Zach's command approached, General Marmont's eighteen-gun battery opened up with loads of canister.[80] Immediately after the fusillade, an ammunition wagon exploded, momentarily stunning the Austrians. At this time, General Kellermann seized the moment and brought his heavy cavalry brigade down on the Austrian left and then the entire French line advanced at the charge.[81] General Desaix fell dead almost immediately, struck by a ball in the heart, never to speak of the day's events. At this point, the "victory" of Melas fell apart and the Austrians retreated in disorder over the Bormida. By 10:00 PM the Battle of Marengo was over, and Napoleon had managed to snatch victory

---

77   Melas to Archduke Charles, 19 June 1800, in Cugnac, *Réserve*, 2:441–442. Melas is very careful not to explicitly state that he had turned command over to Zach; however, he is mentioned as leading an attack in hopes of restoring order in the ranks. Melas mentions nothing about a delay in following up the French retreat, and he attributes the Austrian loss to Bonaparte bringing up his reserves (more than one division) at the last moment.

78   *Report of Boudet*, cited ibid., 2:393–395.

79   Ibid.

80   Marmont, *Mémoires du maréchal Marmont*, II, 131–135.

81   *Report of Boudet*, cited in Cugnac, *Réserve*, 2:401. See also François C. Kellermann, *Histoire de la campagne de 1800* (Paris, 1854), 182.

from the jaws of defeat. The combatants had fought for thirteen hours with the Austrians suffering 9,500 casualties and the French 5,800.[82]

Instead of continuing the battle, Melas chose to come to terms and sign the Convention of Alessandria the next day. While the First Consul strengthened his political position as a result of Marengo, he certainly did not achieve the decisive military victory he wanted. Far from being annihilated, more than half of Melas's army survived and was able to fight another day. Although Napoleon inflicted a serious setback on the Austrians at Marengo, it would be other French victories later in the year, most notably Moreau's triumph near the small Bavarian village of Hohenlinden in December, that finally brought Vienna to the peace table and caused the collapse of the Second Coalition.

The Campaign of 1800 challenged the First Consul and has generated both criticism and praise. Along with the Hundred Days and Waterloo, it is probably the most controversial of Napoleon's campaigns. Although faults of execution can be identified, the overall strategic and operational concepts utilized by Napoleon were sound: in particular, that relentless drive to operationally outflank, master enemy lines of communication, and then give battle, all of which would be the scenario he utilized repeatedly on the battlefields of Europe. His brilliant use of the salient of Switzerland to invade Italy allowed him to seize the initiative, maintain security, and facilitate his maneuver on the Po.

In this campaign, Napoleon demonstrated his natural ability to react to the unfolding situation and to respond instinctively to events. Napoleon stated:

> My great and most distinctive talent is to see everything in a clear light; even my eloquence is of the kind that sees the core of each question from all its facets at once – like the perpendicular, which is shorter than the diagonal. The great art of winning a battle consists in changing one's lines of operation in the middle of the action. This idea is entirely my own and altogether new. It's what made me win at Marengo.[83]

His decisions such as the one to use the Great Saint Bernard Pass, to overcome the delay of Fort Bard, to use misdirection at Chivasso, and to employ the dramatic *manoeuvre sur les derrières* to cut Melas's communications were all, to some degree, spontaneous and reflective of his *coup d'oeil.* So often commanders slavishly follow the set plan, afraid or incapable of deviating from it (like Melas's exclusive focus on Genoa). Bonaparte excelled in responding in real time, constantly recalculating the probable outcomes in his formidable mind

---

82   Kellermann, *Histoire de la campagne de 1800*, 194.
83   Christopher Herold, ed., *The Mind of Napoleon* (New York, 1955), 222.

to place the enemy at a disadvantage. There was simply no substitute for his genius, and this would only become more apparent in future campaigns.

As stated above, the Campaign of 1800 did not end with the destruction of Melas's army as Napoleon had intended. He must accept blame for this fact, but it is important to remember that the First Consul tried to implement another more audacious plan, which called for combined operations with Moreau's Army of the Rhine. This plan had excellent potential to defeat both Austrian armies decisively but, because of Moreau's refusal to collaborate, Napoleon was forced to develop the alternative plan which focused on the Italian theater exclusively. Napoleon's interactions with Moreau in 1800 provide a unique view of the future emperor having to work with an insubordinate commander and being able to do little about it: a situation he would never face again. Although Moreau enjoyed success against Kray Krajovai és Topolyai in 1800, Moreau's performance frustrated the First Consul. Not only did Moreau refuse to cooperate, but he was dilatory in initiating his offensive against Kray to open the campaign, and later refused to supply Lecourbe's corps of veterans as agreed upon and instead sent Moncey with fewer men. Such insubordination could have compromised the campaign – for many generals it would have – but Napoleon maintained his focus and tenaciously overcame these challenges.

There are valid criticisms to be made of Napoleon's actions immediately leading up to Marengo. The ineffectiveness of French intelligence is striking. To actually lose contact with Melas demonstrates a complete collapse in the ability to gather information. Just prior to Marengo, Napoleon did not know the location, size, or intent of the enemy. The overall shortage of cavalry certainly impacted the French ability to gather intelligence; however, Napoleon could have made more productive use of the Reserve's five brigades of cavalry. The lamenting of General Gardanne while trying to locate Melas without sufficient cavalry is evidence of this shortcoming. Also, instead of detaching entire divisions such as Desaix (Boudet) and Lapoype to seek Melas, a couple of cavalry brigades could have been as effective in reconnoitering and allowed the First Consul to concentrate greater numbers at the point of attack.

Napoleon's most serious miscalculation was his conclusion that Melas would not engage in combat. This assumption was based on faulty intelligence, but Napoleon was so convinced of this that he became reckless and detached troops in the face of imminent battle. Such imprudence risked disaster on the battlefield. It was so uncharacteristic of Napoleon not to consider all possibilities and outcomes and is indicative of his underestimating his opponent. In many ways Melas was an accommodating or obliging enemy, but his morning attack caught every person in the French army by surprise and was something Napoleon would never forget.

It is safe to conclude that Napoleon, the master of war himself, learned a great deal from his experience in 1800. This is evidenced by the fact that he would never again make the same mistakes. In future campaigns, most importantly, he would never again fail to place importance on the concentration of his army (with the possible exception of Waterloo). Another valuable lesson was never to engage without adequate reserves, both infantry and artillery. After Marengo, Napoleon improved reconnaissance methods; in particular, he made better use of light cavalry. It is not an exaggeration to say that the Campaign of 1800 was foundational in Bonaparte's development as a commander. Already a respected, innovative commander in his own right, Napoleon came face to face with defeat at Marengo but it did not break him; instead fate and Desaix's intervention gave him a second chance. Such a brush with defeat, with his and France's future on the line, had to be an intense learning experience.

Finally, often the political significance of the Campaign of 1800 and the culminating Battle of Marengo gets lost within the military analysis. Never in Napoleon's career were the political stakes as high as they were in 1800. Not only did he need to defeat the Austrians, but he needed victory to confirm what he had started with the Coup of Brumaire. Had Napoleon been forced from the field at Marengo, he may well have been able to retreat over the Po to fight again, but politically it would have been his death, and instead of being First Consul he would have faced potential political obscurity. Paris was still the scene of political intrigue where ambitious and jealous Jacobins roamed free. The victory at Marengo, François Furet states,

> had been the true coronation of his power and his regime. This was a coronation which no longer came by divine right, since it was the result of the most one-sided contract that a nation had ever made with its leader, who was forced into a commitment never to be vanquished. It is in this sense that, between Marengo and Waterloo, between the arrival of Desaix and the absence of Grouchy, between fortune and misfortune, there is a difference which is both minute and tremendous: the regime was itself dependent on it. In June 1800, therefore it was founded.[84]

Napoleon was aware of this commitment, this cult of victory, and the importance of Marengo. As a result, he immediately rewrote the official accounts of

---

84   François Furet, *Revolutionary France 1770–1800* (Oxford, 1992), 218.

the battle and continued to remove or revise documents in efforts to cleanse the historical record of any indecision or panic, and to make it appear as if the outcome was never in doubt.[85] In this way the future emperor nurtured and constructed the origins of his imperial power and ended the revolutionary upheaval that began in 1789.

Bibliography

Adye, John. *Napoleon of the Snows*. London, 1931.

Bertaud, Jean-Paul. *The Army of the French Revolution: From Citizen-Soldiers to Instrument of Power*, trans. by R.R. Palmer. Princeton, NJ, 1988.

Chandler, David G. *The Campaigns of Napoleon: The Mind and Method of History's Greatest Soldier*. New York, 1966.

Cugnac, Gaspar Jean. *Campagne de l'armée de reserve en 1800*, 2 vols. Paris, 1900.

Cugnac, Gaspar Jean. *La campagne de Marengo*. Paris, 1904.

Doughty, Robert and Ira Gruber. *Warfare in the Western World*, 2 vols. Lexington, MA, 1996.

Esposito, Vincent and John Elting. *A Military History and Atlas of the Napoleonic Wars*. New York, 1968.

Furet, Francois. *Revolutionary France 1770–1800*. Oxford, 1995.

Herold, J. Christopher, ed. *The Mind of Napoleon*. New York, 1955.

Howard, John E., ed. and trans. *Letters and Documents of Napoleon I*. New York, 1961.

Jomini, Antoine H. *Life of Napoleon*, 3 vols. Kansas City, MO, 1897.

Kellermann, François Christophe. *Histoire de la campagne de 1800*. Paris, 1854.

Lachouque, Henry and Anne S.K. Brown. *Anatomy of Glory*. Providence, RI, 1962.

Marmont, August F. *Mémoires du maréchal Marmont duc de Raguse de 1792 à 1841*, 9 vols. Paris, 1857.

Marshall-Cornwall, James. *Napoleon as Military Commander*. London, 1967.

Napoleon I. *Napoleon's Memoirs: Dictated by the Emperor at Saint Helena*. Ed. by Somerset de Chair. London, 1986.

Olsen, John Andreas and Martin van Creveld. *The Evolution of Operational Art: From Napoleon to the Present*. Oxford, 2011.

Quimby, Robert S. *The Background of Napoleonic Warfare: The Theory of Military Tactics in Eighteenth-Century France*. New York, 1957.

Rodger, Alexander B. *The War of the Second Coalition, 1798–1801: A Strategic Commentary*. Oxford, 1964.

Sargent, Herbert Howland. *The Campaign of Marengo*. Chicago, 1897.

---

85   Napoleon had Berthier rewrite the official accounts of Marengo in 1803 and again in 1805.

Thiers, Louis Adolphe. *History of the Consulate and the Empire of France under Napoleon*, 12 vols. Philadelphia, 1893.

US Army Service Schools. *Source Book of the Marengo Campaign in 1800*. Fort Leavenworth, KS, 1922.

Victor, Claude-Perrin, duc de Bellune. *Extraits de mémoires inedits de feu Claude Victor Perrin, duc de Bellune*. Paris, 1847.

Wilkinson, Spenser. *The French Army Before Napoleon: Lectures Delivered Before the University of Oxford in Michaelmas Term, 1914*. Oxford, 1915.

Yorck von Wartenburg, Maximilian, graf. *Napoleon as a General*, 2 vols. London, 1902.

CHAPTER 6

1805: Ulm and Austerlitz

Mark T. Gerges

> And at the moment of writing this, the boredom which is consuming me in cantonments (at Schönbrunn) and four months of marching about, months of fatigue and wretchedness, have proved to me that nothing is more hideous, more miserable, than war. And yet our sufferings in the Guard are not to be compared with those of the line.[1]

∴

The 1805 Ulm–Austerlitz campaign ranks among the greatest of Napoleon's victories. The newly organized, highly trained, and superbly led Grande Armée destroyed two *ancien régime* armies and shook the European political order in a period of less than three months. It was the display of a new system of warfare, created during the French Revolution and then perfected and systematized at the training camps around Boulogne. The differences between the *ancien régime* militaries and the new French system would be decisive.

The Treaty of Amiens of 25 March 1802 proved to be nothing more than a trial peace between the French and British governments. Waves of British tourists descended on the continent, able to visit for the first time in a decade. The changes in the balance of power in Europe still needed to be resolved, and the failure to continue further negotiations on outstanding issues such as trade deepened the mistrust over the course of the following year. Great Britain refused to evacuate Malta as stipulated in the treaty, furthering the suspicion between the two countries. To compel British compliance, Napoleon created an army under *Général de division* Adolphe Édouard Casimir Joseph Mortier at Nijmegen to threaten the Electorate of Hanover, a hereditary territory of the British crown. With Mortier's "Army of Hanover" threatening the electorate, the British Parliament declared an embargo of France on 16 May 1803. Two days later, a British warship fired on and seized a French vessel. With the peace effectively broken, Napoleon ordered the arrest of British citizens found in

---

[1] Jean-Baptiste Barrès, *A Memoir of a French Napoleonic Officer* (London, 1988), 55.

France. On 23 May, Mortier's army marched into Hanover. The war that would last for over a decade had begun.[2]

Initially, the war remained a strictly Anglo-French conflict but over the next two years European opposition toward First Consul Napoleon Bonaparte grew into active participation against France. The apprehension of Louis Antoine de Bourbon, duc d'Enghien, by French forces from his home in Baden and subsequent execution at Paris in March 1804 caused immediate repercussions across Europe. In general, the French violation of Badenese territory suggested that Napoleon would disregard other states' sovereignty with impunity.[3] Specifically, the act drew the ire of Tsar Alexander I of Russia, whose father-in-law, Elector Charles Frederick, ruled Baden. Two months later, a new French constitution made Napoleon hereditary "emperor," a title that implied he would seek to resurrect Charlemagne's empire in Germany and Italy. His reorganization of Italy and creation of the Kingdom of Italy in June 1805 appeared to confirm this fear. Russia, already angry with what it viewed as a lack of French respect, broke off diplomatic relations with France.

The military changes that had taken place in Revolutionary France during the previous decade had made little impact on the Russian army, which consisted of serfs conscripted for 25-year enlistments. Consequently, service in the tsar's armies was virtually a death sentence as families had little hope of seeing their loved ones again. When Tsar Alexander opted for war in 1805, almost one-quarter of his army was from the 1805 conscription class, meaning these soldiers had received little training.[4] The doctrine of the great Russian general Aleksandr Vasiliyevich Suvorov, stressing the bayonet over firepower with strict discipline to drive home the attack, continued to hold sway with followers such as Field Marshal Mikhail Illarionovich Kutuzov, who had commanded the field army during the 1805 campaign. The army had received extensive combat experience against the Turks in the latter half of 18th century, when the warfare tended to be without quarter. Russian soldiers had a well-earned international reputation for being brave, solid under fire, and well disciplined while the officers were generally considered poorly educated, and the lack of a General Staff with administrative abilities meant that the army suffered from poor planning.[5]

---

2   Robert Goetz, *Austerlitz 1805: Napoleon and the Destruction of the Third Coalition* (London, 2005), 23–24; Steven Englund, *Napoleon: A Political Life* (New York, 2004), 222–223.
3   Frederick Kagan, *The End of the Old Order* (Cambridge, MA, 2006), 91.
4   Scott Bowden, *Napoleon and Austerlitz: An Unprecedentedly Detailed Combat Study of Napoleon's Epic Ulm–Austerlitz* (Chicago, 1997), 96–97.
5   Bowden, *Napoleon and Austerlitz*, 115–116.

Turning to Austria, Habsburg hostility to France was deeply rooted but Vienna maintained strict neutrality because the Austrians could do little given their army's poor condition. Increasing tensions with Russia over Saint Petersburg's expanding influence in the German states and the Mediterranean reduced the likelihood of an Austro-Russian partnership.[6] In fact, Austria had declined a Russian offer in early 1804 for a defensive alliance that promised the support of 100,000 Russians in case of a Franco-Austrian war.[7] Not only did the Habsburgs distrust the Russians, but Austria's focus was on reversing its loss of influence and territory in both Germany and northern Italy. Harsh peace treaties with France in 1797 and 1801 had undercut the Habsburg position in both areas. Austrian fears of additional loss of prestige resurfaced in February 1803 when the Imperial Recess confirmed all French gains made along the left bank of the Rhine during the Wars of the French Revolution.[8]

Militarily, the Austrians had few options, as their armies had been devastated in the campaigns in Germany and Italy that had led to Austria's defeats in the Wars of the First and Second Coalitions. In the aftermath of these defeats, the state faced enormous debt as revenues declined due to the loss of territory in the two peace treaties.[9] The army's problems were difficult to remedy, with the military budget reduced by more than half since 1801, which resulted in a drastic reduction of troop strength. The army's most serious shortages were in men and horses. After Austria and Russia reconciled their differences to conclude a military alliance in November 1804, Vienna pledged to field 275,000 men in a war against Napoleon.[10] However, by January 1805, the Austrian army consisted of 186,446 infantry, 37,095 cavalry, and 11,224 artillerymen, approximately 40,000 men short of 275,000. Overall, the Austrians needed an additional 97,152 men to meet their full wartime organization, and the artillery batteries lacked horses.[11]

By April 1805, Archduke Charles of Austria, in charge of army reform, saw his influence wane with his brother, Emperor Francis I.[12] His report on the

---

6   Frederick Schneid, "The Grand Strategy of the Habsburg Monarchy During the War of the Third Coalition," in *Selected Papers of the Consortium on Revolutionary Europe, 2007* (High Point, NC, 2007), 317.
7   Goetz, *Austerlitz 1805*, 25.
8   John H. Gill, *1809: Thunder on the Danube – Napoleon's Defeat of the Habsburgs*, 3 vols (London, 2008–2010), 1:2.
9   Schneid, "Grand Strategy of the Habsburg Monarchy," 313.
10   Gunther E. Rothenberg, *Napoleon's Great Adversaries: The Archduke Charles and the Austrian Army, 1792–1814* (Bloomington, IN, 1982), 80.
11   Schneid, "Grand Strategy of the Habsburg Monarchy," 316–317.
12   The Habsburg emperor, Francis, was Holy Roman Emperor Francis II, a title that would disappear with the disbanding of the Holy Roman Empire in 1806. He declared himself

army's lack of readiness was poorly received by the more aggressive members of the Aulic Council. Francis, listening to his more belligerent advisors, recreated the Hofkriegsrat, the Court Council of War, to limit Charles's power. An optimistic report by *Feldmarschall-Leutnant* Karl Mack von Lieberich regarding Habsburg readiness was better received and, when war finally came in September 1805, Mack was appointed quartermaster-general of the army – not because of his capabilities but because, as one historian termed it, "he was expedient." His appointment and access to Francis further limited Charles's influence.[13]

Along with this power struggle atop the Habsburg command structure, the Austrian army was in the midst of transition when the campaign began. With Archduke Charles out of favor, Mack directed the reforms, but it was too late to make significant organizational changes without disrupting the army's mobilization. Officially adopted in April 1805, the reforms came too late for full implementation. More than symbolic changes, the reforms that were implemented affected basic army organization. Cavalry regiments grew to eight squadrons and fought in two ranks instead of three, while infantry regiments added a fourth battalion. Changes in logistics were also pushed through in September just as the army prepared to invade Bavaria, a French ally. This caused the army to be disorganized, poorly formed, and only partially trained in the new regulations just as it went to war with an army that had spent the past two years training.[14]

The plans of the Third Coalition provided a general operational focus, not a concrete operational framework. On paper, the coalition that faced France appeared formidable, with armies and detachments operating from the North Sea coast to the heel of Italy. On paper, the Habsburgs would provide 125,000 men, Russia 140,000, Sweden, Denmark, and Saxony each 16,000 men, Hesse and Brunswick together 16,000, and Mecklenburg-Strelitz 3,000 men, totaling 332,000 men, not including contingents provided by Great Britain and the Kingdom of the Two Sicilies.[15] Each participant was united in a broad strategic goal – to defeat France – but not operationally with mutually supporting objectives. Austria's main concern was to reassert its influence in southern Germany and northern Italy. Therefore, the largest Habsburg army, 94,000-strong, would deploy against the Kingdom of Italy under Archduke Charles with the goal of reconquering Milan and reestablishing of the House of Savoy in Piedmont.

Austrian Emperor Francis I in December 1804; because this paper is examining his role as Habsburg emperor, it will use the title Francis I throughout.

13 Schneid, "Grand Strategy of the Habsburg Monarchy," 318.
14 Rothenberg, *Napoleon's Great Adversaries*, 86–87.
15 Alfred Krauss, *Beilagen zu 1805 der Feldzug von Ulm* (Vienna, 1912), 4.

After accomplishing these objectives, Charles would cross the Alps and operate along the Rhine, in the flank of the expected French advance.[16] A joint Austro-Russian army would march to the southern German states to threaten France directly. Archduke Ferdinand Karl Joseph of Austria-Este, the 24-year-old brother-in-law of Francis I, would command the Austrian contingent of this force, but the true commander would be Mack. Maintaining contact between these two forces would be a 34,000-man Austrian army operating in the Tyrol and Voralberg. Other Coalition plans included Anglo-Russian landings in Naples to threaten the French rear, while an Anglo-Russian force recaptured Hanover with the assistance of a small Swedish contingent.[17] The goal was to reestablish the European status quo prior to 1792. However, the plans were fraught with assumptions that proved to be unfounded. The first was Mack's optimistic belief that Napoleon's forces would take sixty-nine days to move from their camps along the English Channel to southern Germany while the Russian army would take only sixty-four to reach the theater of war. The second fatal assumption was that the combined Austro-Russian army (100,000 men) would be a match for Napoleon's Grande Armée.[18]

The French army of 1805 ranks as one of the greatest armies in history. Its origins can be found in 1803 when, with the resumption of war with Great Britain in June 1803, Napoleon established the Armée des Côtes de l'Océan (Army of the Ocean Coasts), more commonly known as the Armée de l'Angleterre (Army of England), in six camps along the English Channel.[19] Although all camps from Brest to Utrecht are generally referred to as being part of the camp at Boulogne, the site of the main French camp, the various formations of the Armée des Côtes de l'Océan initially were identified by each camp's name. Later, corps numbers replaced these names as unit designations. Nearly half of the army had combat experience but training remained thorough and demanding so that, by 1805, these corps were incredibly well drilled and disciplined.[20] One regiment's riding school conducted classes from 4:00 AM to 10:00 PM to train recruits, some of whom had never ridden a horse. At Brest, cavalry in Marshal Augereau's corps learned additional tasks such as firing artillery.[21]

---

16 Schneid, "Grand Strategy of the Habsburg Monarchy," 319.
17 Schneid, "Grand Strategy of the Habsburg Monarchy," 313–314, 319.
18 Rothenberg, *Napoleon's Great Adversaries*, 83–84.
19 Following the Peace of Lunéville that ended the War of the Second Coalition in February 1801, Napoleon had reduced the French army and administrative overhead to a peace footing to save money.
20 Elting, *Swords Around a Throne*, 59–60.
21 B.T. Jones, ed., *Napoleon's Army: The Military Memoirs of Charles Parquin* (London, 1988), 11–12, 17.

For two years, France's only opponent was Great Britain, and Napoleon's plan to invade Britain was no idle threat. Yet he postponed the proposed invasion several times, which resulted in the army remaining in a high state of readiness for an invasion that could commence with little notice.[22] While 93,000 men were physically located along the Channel coast, 35-ton barges capable of carrying 151,940 men were ready by July 1805.[23] The additional 60,000 men were within a few days march of the embarkation points. If the combined French, Dutch, and Spanish fleets could wrest control of the Channel, this would give enough time for those outlying units to march to their ports of departure. To speed their movement, Napoleon spent 20,000,000 francs improving the roads between Paris and his naval bases at Brest, Cherbourg, and Boulogne. Ironically, he spent nothing on improving the roads he would actually use to reach the South German states and Austrian lands.[24]

Even after Sweden and Russia joined with Great Britain to form the Third Coalition, the opposing sides could not get at each other, so Napoleon continued his invasion plans. After Austria joined the Coalition on 9 August 1805, this changed the strategic situation by placing enemy armies within striking distance of France. As the first step in defending against this threat, Napoleon formally created the Grande Armée on 26 August.[25] Much like the Army of the Reserve in 1800, the Grande Armée could operate in any theater without tipping off its destination.[26] Against the Third Coalition, Napoleon fielded 177,000 soldiers in the Grande Armée, 30,000 in the new Armée des Côtes at the Boulogne camp along the English Channel, 40,000 in northern Italy, and 20,000 in Naples.[27]

The Habsburg army destined to operate in the South German states suffered from a number of issues, mostly from the unsettled command relationships. As this army would form part of the combined Austro-Russian army, Francis I resolved to exercise personal command over it. Until that time, his brother-in-law, Ferdinand, served as the commander. Yet, as noted, Francis appointed

---

22 Kagan, *End of the Old Order*, 58.
23 Paul Thiébault, *The Memoirs of Baron Thiébault*, trans. by Arthur John Butler (London, 1896), 2:123–134.
24 Richard Glover, *Britain at Bay: Defence Against Bonaparte, 1803–1814* (London, 1973), 14.
25 CN, No. 9137, 11:141–145.
26 The naval aspects of the war of the Third Coalition are significant for the Napoleonic era but do not fall within this discussion of the campaign. The French navy's inability to wrest control of the Channel in 1805 was less important than the Habsburg Empire's joining the coalition in August. Russia and France had no access to each other as long as Austria and Prussia remained neutral, so Austria joining the coalition was the key element that changed the campaign's dynamic, not naval actions.
27 Bowden, *Napoleon and Austerlitz*, 167; Chandler, *Campaigns of Napoleon*, 384–385.

Mack quartermaster-general of this army. With two senior commanders both reporting directly to the emperor, a crisis was bound to occur. Problems began in mid-September with arguments over where to deploy the Austrian army. Ferdinand received instructions from Francis to defer to Mack's judgement, thus making Mack the de facto commander, which only worsened the relationship between him and Ferdinand and created a hostile atmosphere that permeated the army. By the end of the campaign, Mack and Ferdinand were barely on speaking terms, communicating only in writing. Regardless of the instructions Mack received, he tended to ignore Ferdinand's commands and act independently.[28]

The Russian contingent of this army marched as each element was mobilized. The lead group was 38,000 men under Kutuzov; farther east was another 40,000 under the native Estonian German Friedrich Wilhelm von Buxhöwden, and 20,000 under Levin August Gottlieb Theophil von Benningsen. When combined with Ferdinand's army, the overall command of the Austro-Russian force would pass to Emperor Francis for a drive into France through the Black Forest.[29]

Postponing their mobilization as long as possible, the Austrians finally started at a measured pace in July; when Vienna ordered full wartime mobilization on 27 August, Napoleon's troops were already marching to the Rhine.[30] Austrian forces first entered Bavarian territory on 2 September; on 5 September, Austrian diplomats traveled to Munich to present an ultimatum to the Bavarian elector, Maximilian IV Joseph. The Habsburgs demanded free transit for Austrian forces and, as Bavaria was a member of the Holy Roman Empire, for the 22,000-man Bavarian army to operate with the Austro-Russian army.[31] Although weeks ahead of Russian reinforcements, the Austrian advance reasserted Habsburg influence and compelled the South German states, all members of the Holy Roman Empire, to support their emperor.[32] In Italy, Austrian forces had mobilized much earlier, mainly in response to Napoleon's review of his Army of Italy in April–May 1805.

After analyzing Napoleon's previous victories, Mack concluded that a portion of Napoleon's success was the rate at which his forces marched. "The enemy has conducted all his campaigns without transport columns and his

---

28 Kagan, *End of the Old Order*, 420–421.
29 Owen Connelly, *Blundering to Glory: Napoleon's Military Campaigns* (New York, 2006), 78; Chandler, *Campaigns of Napoleon*, 382–383.
30 Kagan, *End of the Old Order*, 297.
31 Schneid, "Grand Strategy of the Habsburg Monarchy," 318; Bowden, *Napoleon and Austerlitz*, 168.
32 Schneid, "Grand Strategy of the Habsburg Monarchy," 320.

infantry officers marched on foot," declared Mack. Consequently, he issued orders during the mobilization to reduce tents and supply wagons, and to allow soldiers to forage. The foraging system, with payments in the new Austrian paper currency, added more confusion when the Bavarians refused the script and soldiers used the opportunity of foraging to desert.[33]

The Grande Armée broke camp along the English Channel on 27 August and moved along multiple routes toward the Rhine. Napoleon's first concern was to get to the Rhine, concentrate the army, and then decide on the next step of the campaign. To deceive the enemy, Napoleon himself did not leave Paris until the third week of September, by which time Marshal Joachim Murat's cavalry had reported the Austrian advance into southern Germany and position behind the Iller River but had no information on the Russian armies, which remained far to the east. Additional reports on 25 and 26 September shed further light on the Austrians. Between 18 and 30 September, Mack won the argument with Ferdinand over the forward deployment of the army and so pushed west. An Austrian advance guard patrolled into the defiles of the Black Forest while the main army advanced to the Iller, making a front eighty kilometers wide with the northern end anchored on the cities of Ulm and Grünzburg. The army stood south of the Danube, on the right bank, facing west. A detached corps under *Feldmarschall-Leutnant* Michael von Kienmayer secured the lines of communication and guarded against the Bavarian army, which withdrew toward Würzburg.[34] The thought that the Grande Armée was preparing to descend not from the west, but from northeast of the Austrian positions, was never considered.[35]

The Danube River makes a gentle arc across southern Germany, flowing west to east. Starting in the west behind the Swabian Jura Mountains, it passes through the city of Ulm, where it is fed by the Iller. The Danube continues rising through Donauwörth until it hits its maximum arc at Regensburg where it begins to run southward into Austrian territory through Passau and Linz in the east. Near the center of this arc, sixty miles south of Regensburg, is Munich. To the west, behind the Juras, stood the fortifications of Ulm, which in part protected a bridgehead leading to the north bank of the Danube. During the French Revolutionary Wars, this strong position held out against superior French forces. Except for Ulm's position near the very western end of this arc, the city seemed a natural point to await Russian reinforcements. Mack thought his north secure because the French would not risk Prussia's intervention by

---

33 Rothenberg, *Napoleon's Great Adversaries*, 88.
34 Krauss, *Beilagen zu 1805 der Feldzug von Ulm*, map 11.
35 Bowden, *Napoleon and Austerlitz*, 174–176.

1805: ULM AND AUSTERLITZ

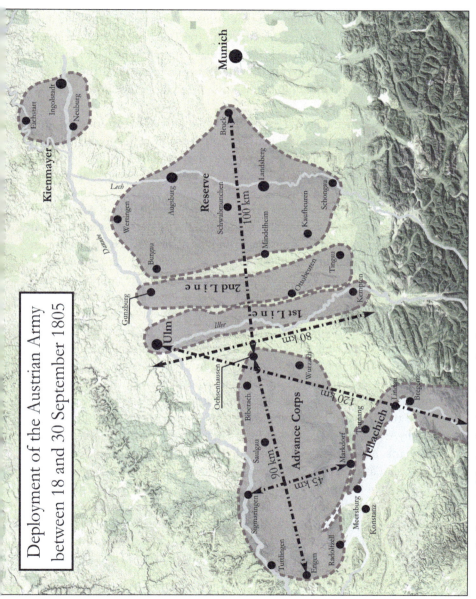

MAP 6.1 Deployment of the Austrian Army, September 1805

marching through its territory of Ansbach. At the Iller River, the Austrians planned to wait for the Russians before beginning active operations. However, the estimate that the Russians would arrive in sixty-four days proved optimistic. Delays in the mobilization meant that Kutuzov departed ten days late and, even then, a portion of his force remained on the Turkish border. Poor roads slowed the march, until the Russians crossed the Moravian border into Habsburg lands and the Austrians provided wagons to improve their march rate. Poorly provisioned, the Russians drew their supplies from Austrian depots.[36]

The Grande Armée's march from the Channel coast experienced fine weather in early September. As the army massed around Strasbourg, the men received fifty cartridges each, rations for four days, and their campaign utensils.[37] Only Marshal Jean-Baptiste Bernadotte's I Corps, the occupation force of Hanover, and *Général de division* Marmont's II Corps near Amsterdam remained separated from the French forces that assembled at Strasbourg. Napoleon tasked Bernadotte with protecting the Bavarian troops that had fled the Austrian invasion and took post near Würzburg. The French disposition in early September revealed their main effort to be near Strasbourg, due west of Mack's army. As the army began to cross the Rhine River, the remaining corps shifted north, almost evenly dispersed along a 259-kilometer front from Strasbourg in the south to Mainz in the north, suddenly altering the main weight of the French forces much further north.[38]

Napoleon believed that Mack would have four options available to him. If he realized that the French were approaching from the north, retention of the bridges over the Danube would prove paramount to prevent the French from severing his lines of communication with Vienna. In this option, as long as Mack held the bridges, the Danube would act as a barrier that would prevent the Grande Armée on the left bank from engaging the Austrian forces on the opposite bank. After the Russians arrived, those same bridges would allow the Austro-Russian army to cross the river and attack the Grande Armée. Mack's second option, in Napoleon's judgement, would be to retire eastward through Augsburg and Munich toward Austrian territory until he met the approaching Russian forces. Napoleon thought that the rapid French pace would enable him to inflict serious losses on the retreating Austrians. The third, and in Napoleon's opinion least likely, scenario was for Mack to stand and fight on the

---

36 Rothenberg, *Napoleon's Great Adversaries*, 89.
37 Barrès, *Memoir of a French Napoleonic Officer*, 57.
38 Krauss, *Beilagen zu 1805 der Feldzug von Ulm*, map 14; Bowden, *Napoleon and Austerlitz*, 176.

Danube. One final option – the one that Napoleon could do little to prevent – pictured Mack retiring south into the Tyrol and combining with Habsburg field marshal Archduke John's force.[39]

Crossing the Rhine in the final days of September, the Grande Armée headed east, aiming for the area between Ulm and Donauwörth. The pace was harsh. Troops marched from dawn to dusk, halting only for the night. Operating in friendly German territory, French quartermasters coordinated with local magistrates to ensure that, as units reached their destinations for the night, the town's inhabitants would be waiting in the square to quarter and feed the soldiers.[40] The fine weather of early September turned to rain later in the month, slowing the army's movement. Instead of the thirty kilometers a day averaged while crossing France, the men managed nineteen to twenty in the poor weather.[41] In comparison, Kutuzov's Russians averaged ten kilometers a day as they reached the frontier of Austrian territory and Kutuzov noted that his "soldiers [had] already endured much fatigue and they [were] suffering badly."[42]

As late as 3 October, Mack still believed that Napoleon's army would approach him from the west through the Black Forest. Only after Murat's cavalry withdrew into the forest did Austrian patrols report that no infantry stood behind the French troopers, and Mack determined that Napoleon must be approaching from the north.[43] This realization led to more dissent in the Austrian command. Ferdinand wanted the army to fall back but Mack simply ignored these orders; Francis later upheld his decision, which further undermined the nominal commander.[44] Although Mack favored attacking the French piecemeal as they crossed the Danube, his subordinate commanders, alarmed by the threat of losing their lines of communication back to Vienna, favored an immediate withdrawal. Mack feared that the poor weather, heavy rains, and lower temperatures would hamper the army's retreat and instead wanted to utilize the strong position at Ulm to resist the French advance and await Russian reinforcements.

Napoleon's *Proclamation of the Emperor to the Army* on 29 September 1805 explained to the soldiers why they were fighting and what they could expect in the upcoming campaign. Beginning with a list of the Austrian transgressions, including treaty violations and invading a French ally, Napoleon urged his

---

39 Bowden, *Napoleon and Austerlitz*, 176.
40 Barrès, *Memoir of a French Napoleonic Officer*, 58–59.
41 George Eberle, "March Performances of Napoleonic Armies," US Army Command and General Staff School student paper (Fort Leavenworth, KS, 1934), 8.
42 Quoted in Bowden, *Napoleon and Austerlitz*, 172.
43 Ibid., 176.
44 Rothenberg, *Napoleon's Great Adversaries*, 90.

soldiers to be prepared for fatigue, forced marches, and privations. He urged them not tp rest until their imperial eagles were planted on the territory of the enemy.[45] On 2 October, French and Austrian outposts clashed west of Ulm. Three days later Mack learned that the French had indeed violated the Prussian territory of Ansbach and were heading toward Donauwörth. He further concentrated his army near Ulm, pulling it northward and ordering a corps under *Feldmarschall-Leutnant* Fanjo Jelačić Bužimski to march from the Tyrol to support his army.[46] The next day, Mack issued orders for reconnaissance columns to determine the French location. To the north, a brigade-sized force under General Konstantin Ghilian Karl d'Aspré von Hoobreuk protected the bridgehead at Günzberg. A column of 5,000 infantry with 400 cavalry under *Feldmarschall-Leutnant* Franz Xaver von Auffenberg marched north toward Donauwörth in response to reports of the presence of French troops. After a forced night march, the Austrians arrived near Wertingen on 8 October.

Mack based his assessment of the situation on the retention of Ulm. In a letter to Kutuzov dated 8 October, he expressed his thought that the Austrian army had achieved a significant advantage by holding the Iller River line, though he admitted that Napoleon could seize Donauwörth and cross the Danube, thus hampering the union of the Austrians and Russians. He urged Kutuzov to push west, claiming that the Austrian army controlled the area from Ulm to Augsburg. He assured the Russian commander that, as long as the Austrians held the bridgeheads over the Danube, the situation was acceptable. Mack speculated that the Austro-Russian army, totaling 70,000 men when combined, would defeat Napoleon if he crossed the Danube and advanced toward the Lech. He closed with a statement that his army was in the best spirit and conditions, and hoped the Russians were the same.[47]

The next few days were disastrous for the Austrians. On 8 October, Murat's cavalry, supported by lead elements of Lannes's V Corps, crushed Auffenberg at Wertingen; the survivors retreated east and away from Mack. The next day, Marshal Ney's VI Corps fought D'Aspré von Hoobreuk's detachment that held the bridgehead at Günzberg and crossed to the southern bank of the Danube. Realizing the danger of his position at Ulm, Mack sent a force to Haslach-Jungingen on the Danube's north bank to observe the roads that ran north. There, on 11 October, 25,000 Austrians ran into *Général de division* Dupont's isolated 1st Division of VI Corps, nearly destroying it, but inexplicably the

---

45 J. David Markham, *Imperial Glory: The Bulletins of Napoleon's Grande Armée, 1805–1814* (London, 2003), 9–10.
46 Rothenberg, *Napoleon's Great Adversaries*, 91.
47 Ferdinand to Kutuzov, 8 October 1805, in Krauss, *Beilagen zu 1805 der Feldzug von Ulm*, 3–4.

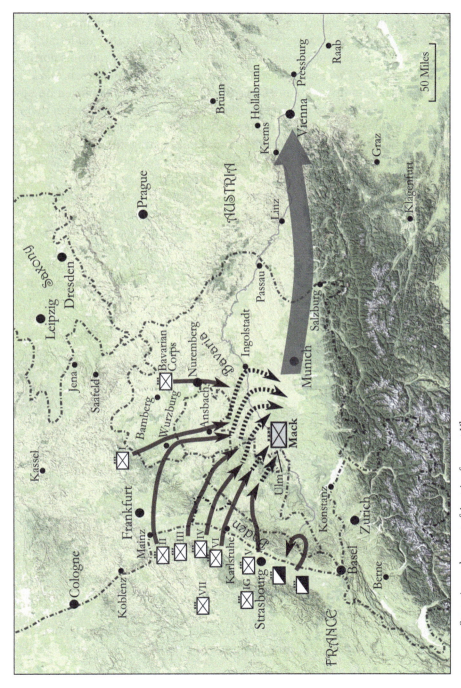

MAP 6.2 Strategic envelopment of Austrian forces at Ulm

Austrians returned to Ulm that night. Mack decided to attempt another break out to the north but the string of Austrian defeats affected army morale, and the poor relationship between the senior commanders further undermined the army's confidence. Regardless, on 13 October, he sent two columns north. Commanded by *Feldmarschall-Leutnant* Johann Sigismund von Riesch, Mack's right wing column of 25,000 men engaged French forces at Elchingen on 14 October, while *Feldmarschall-Leutnant* Franz von Werneck's 9,000-man division on the left slowly moved northeast. At Elchingen, Riesch's column fought against the men of Ney's VI Corps in brutal street-fighting but ultimately lost the town's bridge to the French. Ney practically destroyed Riesch's force, which lost 4,000 killed or wounded and 3,000 captured of the 15,000 engaged in the battle. Werneck attempted to march to Elchingen but Dupont's division blocked the road, forcing the former to retreat northwest and away from Ulm. Murat's cavalry and Dupont's infantry pursued Werneck's rearguard, overwhelming the Austrians at Neresheim; Werneck himself surrendered the next day. Not wanting to become French prisoners, Ferdinand and several other Austrian generals fled north and away from Napoleon's forces escorted by twelve squadrons of cavalry.[48]

Positioned between Mack and the Russians, the French had nearly completed the encirclement of the Austrian position by the time Ney won the struggle at Elchingen. While I and III Corps, commanded by Bernadotte and Marshal Louis-Nicolas Davout respectively, moved east to Munich to protect the left flank, the rest of the Grande Armée wheeled west toward Ulm. On 13 October, Marshal Soult's IV Corps defeated an Austrian force south of Ulm at Memmingen, cutting off the escape route to the Tyrol. Only Jelačić's column, hastily called from the Tyrol to reinforce Mack at Ulm, was able to flee south. On 15 October, Ney's troops stormed the Michelsberg fortifications along the ridge that overlooked Ulm, which allowed French artillery to hit Austrian positions in the town itself. When the French bombardment commenced the next day, Napoleon sent an officer to demand an Austrian surrender.

Although Mack clearly knew the end was near, he refused to surrender to the first emissary. Yet when Napoleon granted Mack an eight-day grace period for relief to arrive, the Austrian commander accepted on 17 October. Thus, if no Russian force large enough to raise the siege reached Ulm by 25 October, Mack would surrender. However, even in this last face-saving gesture Mack was frustrated. The weather, which had been cold with rain and snow, turned worse. On the night of 18 October a torrential thunderstorm caused the Danube to flood. Its rising waters carried away unburied Austrian dead, causing discipline

---

48   Bowden, *Napoleon and Austerlitz*, 236–240.

to collapse. French observers crudely commented that Vienna would certainly learn of the defeat when the Austrian dead floated by the capital.[49] Consequently, a demoralized Mack capitulated on 20 October with 23,000 men under his direct command. Including various detachments that likewise surrendered, the Austrians lost 60,000 men, 192 guns, and 90 standards in the Ulm campaign.[50] It was a devastating loss.

To confront the main Austrian army under Archduke Charles, Napoleon posted 40,000 men in northern Italy commanded by Marshal Masséna. He instructed Masséna to "wear down the enemy so he cannot support Vienna," an ambitious task considering that Charles outnumbered him 92,000 men to 40,000.[51] Fortunately for Masséna, Charles received poor intelligence about French troop strengths. As late as 20 September, the Austrian commander believed that he faced 102,000 French infantry and 6,000 cavalry; consequently, his actions were cautious.[52] A mid-September armistice bought the French time while fixing the largest Austrian army in place and preventing it from reinforcing the other theaters. With the Grande Armée across the Rhine and heading for the Danube, Masséna informed Charles that he planned to resume hostilities on 15 October.[53] Despite the expiration of the armistice, Masséna did not advance toward the Adige River for another three days; Charles slowly withdrew to Caldiero.[54] After news of Mack's surrender reached Charles on 24 October, the archduke prepared to withdraw his army from Italy. Before this could be accomplished, Masséna launched the first of four attacks at Caldiero on 29 October. Although this was familiar ground for Masséna, who had fought two battles there earlier in his career, the French could not break through. Seemingly halted by superior Austrian numbers, the French launched their last attack on 2 November, but Charles had already retreated with the main body of the Austrian army.[55]

With the disaster on the Danube front, Francis issued his brother new orders. The first concerned the dire need to prevent Masséna's forces from linking with Napoleon's army; the second involved protecting Hungary; and the final alerted Charles to prepare to march to Vienna's aid.[56] Napoleon's

---

49 Barrès, *Memoir of a French Napoleonic Officer*, 66.
50 Bowden, *Napoleon and Austerlitz*, 245.
51 Berthier to Masséna, 17 September 1805, in Frédéric Koch, *Mémoires de Masséna* (Paris, 1850), 5:361–364.
52 Donald D. Horward, "Austerlitz and Masséna's Army of Italy," in *Selected Papers of the Consortium on Revolutionary Europe, 2006* (High Point, NC), 206.
53 Ibid., 207–208.
54 Kagan, *End of the Old Order*, 520–521.
55 Horward, "Austerlitz and Masséna's Army of Italy," 209.
56 Ibid.

complete dominance of Habsburg thinking is evident in these contradictory and passive orders. None of these instructions sought to wrest the initiative from Napoleon but instead only to further protect Austrian interests, and all depended on French actions. The fears of a Hungarian uprising played an important role, as did preventing the capture of Vienna. Charles's operations changed little after he received these instructions. By 23 November, the Habsburg army still remained in Italy but a French army half the size of it continued to determine the pace of the Austrian retreat.

Despite rumors that an army consisting of 25,000 Russians, 10,000 British, and 40,000 Neapolitans had advanced into his rear areas, Masséna aggressively pressed Charles. Communication with Napoleon remained difficult, but Masséna finally received an order dated 8 November to press Charles because the Grande Armée had reached the outskirts of Vienna. By late November, Charles was isolated, 350 miles from the main Allied army in Moravia. Despite replacements that brought his army back up to 85,000 men, he now confronted Masséna's army as well as VI and II Corps that were converging on him from Vienna. Charles marched northeast toward Kormend and then Oldenburg, where he remained passively waiting for an armistice after learning of the French victory at Austerlitz.[57]

Returning to Mack's surrender at Ulm on 20 October, the removal of this Austrian army from the campaign presented Napoleon with a new situation. The French army had responded brilliantly thus far in the campaign; even the soldiers realized the significance of this innovative style of campaigning. "The emperor makes war in a new way – with our legs," as one soldier put it, relying on the speed and initiative of subordinate commanders to recognize opportunities and respond.[58] The rain and snow of October should have paralyzed the movement of a conventional force, but the Grande Armée was still able to make impressive marches. Despite the rains that caused the Danube to flood with what Napoleon termed "a violence unequalled in one hundred years," the Grande Armée still average twelve miles a day.[59] Thus far in the campaign, when the Austrians had gained a momentary advantage, such as finding Dupont's isolated division at Haslach, the size of the area covered by the Grande Armée, combined with the speed of maneuver, had caused Mack to

---

57 Ibid., 212.
58 J.F.C. Fuller, *The Conduct of War, 1789–1961* (New Brunswick, NJ, 1961), 50.
59 The daily march speed of an 1805 French infantry division was a point of comparison for students in the 1930s trying to increase the march rate of American infantry divisions. The French division moved longer distances and was able to maintain that rate over a longer period than the comparable American division. See Eberle, "March Performances of Napoleonic Armies," 8.

temporize and hesitate, unable to act due to the fragmentary nature of his information.

Napoleon still faced an impressive array of forces. If surprise and speed allowed him to gain the advantage in the first weeks of the campaign, these factors became less relevant as the campaign continued. Archduke John was still operating in the Tyrol, hindering communication between Napoleon and Masséna. Without rapid communication, Napoleon had no way of learning whether Masséna still held Archduke Charles's large army in place or whether that army was already marching on Vienna. Rumors of Allied landings in Italy and the North Sea added to the threats facing the French emperor. Bernadotte's violation of Prussian territory posed one final challenge. Although known for vacillating, the Prussian government could still join the Coalition in response. Backed by a fresh army of 200,000 men, Prussia, serving either as an active belligerent or as an armed mediator, threatened to undo all French gains and could not be lightly dismissed. As for the Russians, Napoleon assumed that Kutuzov had halted in anticipation of retreating on his line of communication, picking up various detachments until his force was large enough to confront the French.

Napoleon's greatest strength, the one skill that stood out, was his ability to see through the myriad of distractions to find the most important element and focus all his energies on that point. Defeating Austria would overturn any losses in Italy so, instead of dissipating his strength to meet the peripheral threat there, Napoleon decided to leave Masséna on his own. Likewise, the 30,000 men left at Boulogne would have to confront the possibility of British and Swedish landings along the Channel coast. Even the Prussian occupation of Hanover after Bernadotte's departure was an item for the future – after the surrender of Austria.

The immediate challenge was to destroy those isolated elements of the Austrian army that had escaped Ulm before they could seek safety. Already Napoleon had surrendered much of the initiative gained by not pushing east between 15 and 20 October.[60] Some fault Napoleon for losing the focus and aggressiveness that had brought success to this point. They argue that, after he had destroyed Mack, Napoleon simply expected the Austrians to surrender. Yet this analysis fails to address the weather conditions in October. French infantry had already been marching for two months before the snows and rains of October made the conditions "detestable."[61] By the time the great wheel began,

---

60 Kagan, *End of the Old Order*, 442–444.
61 Barrès of the Imperial Guard was an apt observer of the weather conditions and the challenges they brought for the soldiers, who often bivouacked in the open: *Memoir of a French Napoleonic Officer*, 60.

additional snow slowed the movement. Heavy rains, mixed with snow, turned the roads to mud; during one battle, soldiers complained of standing in mud up to their knees.[62] The emperor himself was reported not to have taken off his boots in a week. In the aftermath of Ulm, the need to sort corps routes and repair the army's logistics took time.[63]

Napoleon's poor intelligence about the location of the Russian army played a role in the ensuing delays. At the time of Mack's surrender, Kutuzov arrived at Braunau am Inn on the Bavarian border with 27,000 Russians. At first, Kutuzov waited and soon learned of the rumors of the Austrians being trapped at Ulm. The Russians then united with Kienmayer's exhausted corps and other minor Austrian detachments, increasing the combined strength to 38,000 men. Kutuzov's willingness to hold his position at Braunau am Inn changed when Mack arrived on 25 October, bringing definitive news of the Austrian disaster.[64] As a result, Kutuzov slowly withdrew east toward Buxhöwden's force.

According to the terms of Mack's surrender, Ney's corps remained at Ulm until 25 October. By that time, the Grande Armée was ready for the next phase of the campaign. The small Austrian detachments and the advancing Russians were the next target. To protect the army's southern flank, I, II, and the newly arrived VII Corps observed the roads coming from the Tyrol and northern Italy. Ney's VI Corps advanced to Innsbruck, blocking the Brenner Pass while VII Corps trapped Jelačić's corps in the Vorarlberg. The corps that remained under Napoleon's direct command advanced in two columns, but the limited road network in Austria forced multiple corps to share the same route, which increased column length and decreased march speed. Delaying the pursuit for five days meant that only the most advanced French elements could establish contact with the Russian rearguard.

The situation remained unclear, with no firm intelligence on the operations of the Austrian and Russian forces. Napoleon wrote to his brother that he thought he was facing 60,000 Austrians withdrawn from Italy and 100,000 Russians. He ordered Murat to gain more intelligence on enemy movements.[65] Finally, on 31 October, the Grande Armée made contact with the Russian rearguard. Kutuzov's army had stood for two days between Enns and Steyr before Davout's III Corps turned this position, prompting the Austro-Russian force to

---

62   Ibid., 64–66.
63   Napoleon spent considerable time and energy in ordering Augsburg converted into a fortified base for future operations: Kagan, *End of the Old Order*, 443.
64   Kagan, *End of the Old Order*, 445.
65   *CN*, No. 9431, 11:369.

again withdraw.[66] Poor logistics hampered the French pursuit, with additional effort being needed just to feed the troops because of Austria's poor roads.

The dilemma facing the Allies was the need for Kutuzov to maintain his position in the face of growing French pressure so that other forces could join his nucleus. As soon as an army large enough coalesced, it would turn and fight Napoleon. Forced out of the Enns–Steyr position that protected Vienna, Kutuzov retreated to Amstetten, Saint Polten, and then north to Krems an der Donau, crossing to the north bank of the Danube on 9 November. Murat's pursuit, hampered by poor roads, faltered. The Russian army moved north, but to the east stood the Habsburg capital. Left to his own devices, Murat decided to continue on to Vienna. Instead of vigorously pursuing the Russians, Murat sent a single brigade north while his main body moved toward the political prize.[67] When Napoleon learned of this diversion, he was furious at the opportunity lost.[68] Crossing the Danube without pressure, Kutuzov burned the bridges behind him.

The pursuit of Kutuzov continued along the southern bank of the Danube, and only the new provisional VIII Corps under Marshal Mortier, formed of three divisions taken from other corps, operated on the northern bank, where the terrain was much more restricted. With the bridges destroyed, this single corps remained isolated and on the same side of the river as the Austro-Russian forces. This error came to haunt the French on 11 November at Dürrenstein when Kutuzov trapped Mortier's lead division under *Général de division* Honoré Théodore Maxime Gazan de la Peyrière. Gazan fought desperately for the entire day, and only the arrival of Dupont's division late in the battle saved French honor. As a corps, Mortier's was *hors de combat* and relegated to secondary missions.

This French check was short-lived. Through a bold ruse two days later, Murat's cavalry and Lannes's V Corps captured Vienna's Tabor Bridge intact, reopening French communication with the north bank. Soon, Murat's Reserve Cavalry, Lannes's V Corps, and Soult's IV Corps marched north into Moravia in pursuit of Kutuzov. By 12 November, Kutuzov had abandoned the position at Krems an der Donau and withdrew along the Vienna–Olmütz (Olomouc) road to receive additional reinforcements. With V and IV Corps and the Reserve Cavalry operating along the Vienna–Olmütz road on the right, Bernadotte's I

---

66   Kagan, *End of the Old Order*, 458.
67   Napoleon expressed his dissatisfaction with Murat: "My cousin, I cannot approve of your manner of marching" (*CN*, No. 9470, 11:392–393).
68   Kagan does a good job analyzing the orders and situation of this period. Murat, without direct orders, made a mistake, but it was a mistake that Napoleon had had multiple opportunities to correct prior to its execution: Kagan, *End of the Old Order*, 463–469.

Corps crossed the Danube at Krems an der Donau and with Mortier's VIII Corps formed the left column, which received the task of advancing directly on the Russians to fix Kutuzov before he could unite with Buxhöwden's advancing army. Thus, Napoleon attempted another *manoeuvre sur les derrières*, a turning movement, to destroy the bulk of the Russian army by maintaining pressure with his left column while turning the enemy position with his right. However, Murat missed the opportunity by falling for the trick he himself had used earlier to cross the Tabor Bridge in Vienna. Without seeking confirmation, he believed a Russian emissary who reported that an armistice had been signed. While Murat halted his advance, the Russians continued their retreat for eighteen unmolested hours. On 16 November at Schöngrabern, the French vanguard once again fell on the Russian rear commanded by General Prince Pyotr Ivanovich Bagration. Despite his troops outnumbering the Russians almost three to one, Murat's recent scolding by the emperor resulted in a hasty and unwise deployment; the haphazardly handled battle allowed the Russian rearguard to escape – as did Kutuzov's army, which had been using the time bought by the rearguard to withdraw to better ground.[69] The Austro-Russian forces escaped Napoleon's trap, retiring to Brünn (Brno) and then toward Olmütz.

By the third week of November, the French situation was poor. After winning a stunning victory at Ulm, the pursuit yielded only the capture of isolated Austrian forces in late October and November. The advanced elements of the Russian army had conducted a skillful withdrawal along the length of Austria, beating back the French and in some instances inflicting serious losses, particularly at Dürrenstein. Falling back along its line of communication, bolstered by fresh reinforcements, and still undefeated, the Russian army was a formidable foe. On the other hand, Napoleon's army was at the end of what today would be called its logistical tether, with supplies being transported from as far away as France. The troops, although their morale remained high, had dwindled to 53,000 effectives. As they had been on the road since late August, the pace and exhaustion showed. The weather made them "half dead of cold" and the poor conditions left the men near exhaustion with the rapid marching, poor weather, and limited rations.[70] Moravia was less productive in terms of farming, which made prolonged foraging impossible. Hovering in the 20s (Fahrenheit) during the day, temperatures dipped into the teens at night. Ominously, Prussia continued to mobilize its army, threatening to add 200,000 fresh troops to the Coalition while additional Austrian troops, including those

---

69 Ibid., 492.
70 Men such as Barrès who kept detailed journals often left large gaps in their writings as the conditions deteriorated.

of Archduke Charles coming from Italy, could be expected to soon play a role. Napoleon understood he must end this campaign or see what had begun so favorably be wasted in another campaign season.

The Austrians and Russians, 82,000 strong, were near Olmütz.[71] Of this number, the Austrian contingent was a mere token force of 16,000 men, which forced Emperor Francis to play a secondary role to Tsar Alexander, whose still undefeated Russian forces were anxious for a fight with the French.[72] On 14 November, Napoleon began establishing the conditions for a set battle. Near Gratz in the south, Marmont's II Corps remained on the defensive, facing the passive Charles. Bernadotte was to the north, observing the route from Prague, while III and VIII Corps were at Vienna, eight miles south of Napoleon's position. Ney's VI Corps supported by Bavarian troops operated in the Tyrol while Augereau's VII Corps held Ulm. Various French and Bavarian detachments protected the depots along the Grande Armée's line of communication back to France. Napoleon had only four corps and the Reserve Cavalry – half of his army – with him in Moravia. On 21 November, he summoned IV and V Corps and the Reserve Cavalry to Brünn. With only 53,000 men, the emperor planned to advance against the Russian position on the Pratzen Heights and around the town of Austerlitz (Slavkov u Brna).[73]

The ground Napoleon chose was significant for his plan. Central Moravia consisted of gently rolling farmland with few dominant features. Sixteen kilometers to the north, the Moravian mountains restricted movement. A major road ran east–west between Brünn and Olmütz. South of the road, a gentle plateau known as the Pratzen Heights extended from north to south, ending above the village of Tellnitz (Tellnice). The Pratzen Heights rose only 200–250 feet above the surrounding farmland. Looking at the Pratzen from the east, the ground rose rapidly, providing an excellent position for defense. However, from the west, the plateau rose gently over two to three kilometers and offered no impediment to movement. As Napoleon examined this ground, he recognized the terrain's value, telling his staff to study the area carefully because it would be the site of a great battle.[74]

Expecting the Austro-Russian army to seek revenge for Ulm, he sent his aide, *Général de division* Anne-Jean Savary, to discuss an armistice. Prince Mikhail Petrovich Dolgorukov, a young, hot-headed member of Tsar Alexander's entourage, came to the French lines to deliver a list of demands, some of which

---

71 Kagan, *End of the Old Order*, 552.
72 Rothenberg, *Napoleon's Great Adversaries*, 101.
73 Chandler, *Campaigns of Napoleon*, 410.
74 Ibid.

were insulting – including a message addressed not to the emperor, but to the head of the French government. Napoleon ignored the slights. Dolgorukov reported to the tsar that the French troops looked demoralized and weak.[75] The bulk of the French army stood north along the Olmütz road, with only a single division extending the line southward. French troops improvised fortifications on the Santon and Zuran Hills, the only two pieces of defensible terrain, and both near the Olmütz road. On 29 November, Napoleon pulled Murat's cavalry and Soult's IV Corps off the Pratzen, abandoning the best defensible position in the area. The Allies knew the ground well, having conducted training in the area in 1804; Napoleon expected that, with 83,000 Austrian and Russian troops, his opponents would be unable to resist the opportunity to destroy the weaker French army.[76]

The next day, the Austro-Russian army occupied the vacant Pratzen Heights. The Austrian chief of staff, General Franz von Weyrother, developed a plan that would cut off the French from Vienna, trap them against the Moravian highlands, and destroy Napoleon's army. In his plan, Weyrother required the Austro-Russian army to divide into seven elements, each timed to hit the French at various critical moments in the battle.[77] Two small detachments would fix the French into position; one would attack along the Olmütz–Brünn highway and the other would hold the center of the position along the Prazten Heights. The main body, 59,300-strong, arranged in four columns, would form on the Pratzen, attack the weakly held southern sector of the battlefield between Tellnitz and Sokolnitz (Sokolnice), cut the road to Vienna, and then swing north to drive the French into the mountains.

Weyrother's complex plan depended on moving columns from the Pratzen through a small opening between the villages of Tellnitz to Sokolnitz before shifting north. Complicating the plan further was the need to translate it from German to Russian and make copies in time to execute it on 2 December. It was not until 1:00 AM on 2 December that the commanders assembled for the orders briefing. In Leo Tolstoy's novel *War and Peace*, he captures the atmosphere of the briefing well. Packed into a small dining room in a simple farmhouse dimly lit by candles, the Austrian chief of staff droned on in German, not understood by the Russian commanders. Weyrother presented the order "like a college teacher reading a lesson to young scholars."[78] Sitting in the front row was the nominal army commander, Kutuzov, who slept through

---

75 30th Bulletin of the Grande Armée, 3 December 1805, in Markham, *Imperial Glory*, 51.
76 Chandler, *Campaigns of Napoleon*, 410; Kagan, *End of the Old Order*, 572.
77 Connelly, *Blundering to Glory*, 86.
78 Adolphe Thiers, *Histoire du Consulat et de l'Empire* (Paris, 1845), 5:159.

the orders brief. His influence with the Russian tsar had been limited because of his loudly expressed desire to await the arrival of additional troops before giving battle; he had little say in developing the plan.[79] General Louis Alexandre Andrault de Langeron, a French *émigré* in Russian service, reported that most senior commanders stood in silence, and that only General Dmitry Sergeyevich Dokhturov examined the map. Only when the briefing ended in the early morning hours were the orders issued to the troops; most did not reach the units before the time scheduled for movement to begin. Moving columns cut through stationary ones still waiting for orders, creating confusion before the first shot was even fired.

The scene in the French camp was vastly different, and Napoleon's understanding of time, space, and his enemy's attitudes was key. The Austro-Russian plan to destroy the French army was exactly the one that Napoleon wanted them to adopt. On 28 November, he ordered Davout's III Corps, eighty miles to the south at Vienna, and Bernadotte's I Corps to march to Brünn; by 1 December Bernadotte's corps had arrived but Davout was still marching.[80] The army rested along the shallow Goldbach (Říčka) Stream. Oriented along the Olmütz road to the north, Lannes's V Corps and Murat's Reserve Cavalry defended the Santon Hill. The center contained Bernadotte's I Corps, the Imperial Guard, and Soult's IV Corps, hidden from Allied view by fog and campfire smoke that hung along the Goldbach. Napoleon spent 1 December visiting troops, sleeping from 8:00 AM to 12:00 PM and then riding south to investigate a skirmish that has developed in the early morning hours. The soldiers, seeing their emperor in the early morning hours, cheered "*Vive l'empereur*" and lit straw torches; his aides ordered the troops to quieten down lest they alert the enemy sentries to his presence. Napoleon spent the early morning hours of 2 December in the Imperial Guard's camp, on a bale of hay with his feet on a drum, keeping warm by a fire.

After a cold night thick with fog, the French sounded the call to arms before daylight.[81] The Austrian advance toward Sokolnitz began at 7:00 AM.[82] As the pressure against the French right or southern flank mounted, Napoleon refused to reinforce it with any troops from the center of his line. The right threatened to break several times, but at each moment of crisis reinforcements from Davout's hard-marching corps arrived to stabilize the fighting. The units of III Corps covered the eighty miles from Vienna in fifty hours, and often entered

---

79   Leo Tolstoy, *War and Peace*, trans. by Ann Dunnigan (London, 1968), 595–601.
80   Berthier to Davout, 28 November 1805, *Operations of the 3rd Corps*, trans. by Scott Bowden (Boalsburg, PA, 2006), 5. Davout received the order at 4:00 PM on 29 November.
81   Barrès, *Memoir of a French Napoleonic Officer*, 75.
82   Chandler, *Campaigns of Napoleon*, 425.

the desperate fighting straight from the march.[83] Weyrother's plan did not consider the Goldbach Stream and villages a significant obstacle, but the stone buildings made excellent defensive positions for the French troops.

By 8:00 AM on 2 December, 12,000 French were holding back 35,000–40,000 Allied troops. One hour later, additional Allied troops moved down the Pratzen Heights to support the assault on Sokolnitz and attempt to seal the Austro-Russian victory.[84] Yet the Austro-Russian attacks were poorly coordinated and hampered by the fog and French reinforcements. From Napoleon's headquarters on the Zuran Hill, he observed the Russian columns begin to descend the Pratzen as he expected. As the Allied ranks pressed into a narrow, dense mass between Sokolnitz and Tellnitz, the French line slowly bowed backward. The Pratzen appeared nearly empty as the second and third columns cleared the heights to add their weight to the attack in the south.[85] Tsar Alexander and Emperor Francis arrived on the Pratzen at 9:00 and, seeing the fourth column idle the tsar asked Kutuzov why it was not in motion. Kutuzov's answer that they were not yet ready led to the tsar's famous retort that "we are not on Empress' Field where the parade does not begin until all of the regiments are up," and ordered the fourth column forward – and off the Pratzen Heights.[86]

Napoleon waited for Marshal Soult, whose troops would execute the main attack, to move up his IV Corps. The fog and smoke in the valley continued to hide the mass of French troops. From the Zuran Hill, Napoleon watched as Austrian and Russian forces moved south until the Pratzen was nearly bare. Turning to Soult, he asked how long it would take his troops to reach the crest; Soult replied "less than twenty minutes, Sire." "Then we'll wait a further quarter of an hour," was Napoleon's answer.[87] The last Allied combat units finally cleared the plateau so that just a few knots of headquarters personnel, watching the deployment, marked where the Allied army had stood.

Napoleon issued the order and two divisions advanced from the fog. At that moment, the cloud cover parted and the sun shone through – the sun of Austerlitz was a favorable omen that many of the French participants later would comment on.[88] The Russian tsar and his staff on the Pratzen suddenly heard the French bands come alive; a few moments later to their amazement

---

83   Davout to Berthier, 3 December 1805, in *Operations of the 3rd Corps*, 14.
84   Chandler, *Campaigns of Napoleon*, 425.
85   The Pratzen was not as empty as it appeared because the fourth column, delayed due to the confused orders, still remained on the heights. See Christopher Duffy, *Austerlitz: 1805* (London, 1977), 106.
86   Quoted in Kagan, *End of the Old Order*, 591.
87   Quoted in Chandler, *Campaigns of Napoleon*, 425.
88   Duffy, *Austerlitz: 1805*, 102.

the lead French units appeared out of the fog.[89] Near Prace, the first contact occurred as the fourth column, marching southwest and hidden from view, was hit in the flank by Soult's advancing troops.[90] Although struck in the flank, this fourth column managed to deploy but was soon overwhelmed. Kutuzov ordered the only troops available – the Russian Imperial Guard, east of the heights – to attack, and he recalled units to return to the Pratzen.[91] Heavy fighting both to the north between Lannes and Bagration and in the center on the Pratzen itself led to the crisis between 9:30 and 11:00 AM. Despite desperate fighting by the fourth column and the recalled elements of the third and second columns, the greater French numbers and superior position were too much. Fierce fighting between the Russian Imperial Guard supported by Russian cavalry and the French cavalry and Bernadotte's I Corps in the vineyards that dotted the northern sector of the Pratzen turned the battle there in favor of the French. By 2:00 PM, with the commitment of I Corps to the Pratzen, the Allied center shattered.[92] After clearing the center of the heights, the French wheeled south, and artillery fired into the flanks and rear of Allied troops below. The second and third Allied columns, caught between fighting on the Pratzen and Sokolnitz, ceased to exist as organized forces. Some fled across the frozen fishponds to the south. The story of thousands of Russians and Austrians sinking to their death is a myth; although the ice did break, the shallow ponds contained few dead the next spring.[93] Instead, the ponds created bottlenecks that destroyed unit cohesion and therefore increased panic in the Austro-Russian army. By dusk, around 4:00 PM, the battle was effectively over. In the north, the outnumbered French counterattacked the Russians along the Olmütz road; French cavalry pursued broken Allied units, furthering the panic and destruction. Tsar Alexander, heartbroken over the loss, rode away in tears and left Austrian territory. The Allied army lost heavily – 12,000 captured and 19,545 dead and wounded.[94] Fifty stands of regimental colors and 180 cannons were captured compared to French losses of 8,000 men dead and wounded.[95] Napoleon spent the night in the Austerlitz castle where he wrote Josephine one of the greatest letters of understatement: "I defeated the

---

89 Chandler, *Campaigns of Napoleon*, 425.
90 Kagan, *End of the Old Order*, 595.
91 Duffy, *Austerlitz: 1805*, 135.
92 Chandler, *Campaigns of Napoleon*, 431.
93 Duffy, *Austerlitz: 1805*, 148–149; Markham, *Imperial Glory*, 54.
94 Kagan, *End of the Old Order*, 621.
95 Chandler, *Campaigns of Napoleon*, 432.

Russian and Austrian army commanded by the two emperors. I am a little tired ..."96

Speaking to his soldiers the next day, Napoleon said *"Soldats! Je suis content de vous"* ("Soldiers! I am pleased with you").97 The victory effectively destroyed the Third Coalition. In London, William Pitt, after hearing the news of the victory declared, "Gentlemen, roll up that map of Europe. We will not need it the next ten years."98 Austria signed a peace within the month, losing one-sixth of its territory including lands in Italy, the Balkans, and Germany. Bavaria became a kingdom as a reward for its support of France. The Holy Roman Empire virtually ceased to exist, and the next year Napoleon formally abolished the thousand-year *Reich* and created the Confederation of the Rhine that looked to France for leadership. Napoleon showered his soldiers with rewards – each man who had fought at Austerlitz received 200 francs; widows of the fallen received large pensions and their children, officially adopted by the state, received a free education and could add "Napoleon" as a baptismal name.99

When evaluating Napoleon's campaigns, the 1805 Ulm–Austerlitz campaign is considered Napoleon's masterpiece. The maneuver showed the capabilities of the French system, and its contrast with the Austrian and Russian armies of the *ancien régime* was drastic. Yet the results of cataclysmic battle on 2 December were not preordained or necessarily unavoidable. Austrian military reforms, which started too late and were too limited in scope, were hindered due to the time needed to recover from the losses suffered during the War of the Second Coalition. Organizing an army during mobilization and deployment is a risk; organizing an army as it deploys against an enemy who for the past two years had perfected his military system is foolhardy. The Russian forces, particularly those under Kutuzov, acquitted themselves well in battle with French forces during the withdrawal from Braunau am Inn to Olmütz, maintaining unit integrity and inflicting losses on their French pursuers. Yet it was still an *ancien régime* army that moved at one-third the rate of the French and ultimately did not have the resilience that the corps system provided for the French. While Austrian and Russian troops fought well at Austerlitz, the Allies lacked operational-level leadership which resulted in poor coordination that hampered operations.

---

96   Napoleon to Josephine, 3 December 1805, in Claude Manceron, *Austerlitz: The Story of a Battle* (New York, 1966), 55.
97   Quoted in Markham, *Imperial Glory*, 55.
98   Quoted in James Richard Joy, *Ten Englishmen of the Nineteenth Century* (New York, 1902), 3.
99   Markham, *Imperial Glory*, 61–62; Chandler, *Campaigns of Napoleon*, 439.

Napoleon's performance should also be examined. Far from being a perfectly planned and executed campaign, much of it saw confused and poorly understood situations. Napoleon seemed overconfident after the Austrian surrender at Ulm, expecting that defeat to demoralize the Habsburg emperor and lead to peace. His lack of an aggressive pursuit immediately following Ulm may have been impossible to overcome due to the weather and physical condition of the French army but it allowed the Russian army to escape, remedied only by the brilliant battle at Austerlitz. The true success of this campaign was the flexibility of the French corps system that allowed Napoleon to disperse his corps, like spread fingers, to seek his opponent and then bring them rapidly together in a mass to strike. This flexibility allowed mistakes made in corps disposition to be overcome through aggressive marching and seeking battle.

Bibliography

Barrès, Jean-Baptiste. *A Memoir of a French Napoleonic Officer.* London, 1988.
Bowden, Scott. *Napoleon and Austerlitz: An Unprecedentedly Detailed Combat Study of Napoleon's Epic Ulm–Austerlitz.* Chicago, 1997.
Bowden, Scott. trans. *Operations of the 3rd Corps.* Boalsburg, PA, 2006.
Burton, Reginald. *From Boulogne to Austerlitz: Napoleon's Campaign of 1805.* London, 1912.
Castle, Ian. *Austerlitz: Napoleon and the Eagles of Europe.* Barnsley, UK, 2005.
Chandler, David G. *Napoleon's Marshals.* London, 1987.
Connelly, Owen. *Blundering to Glory: Napoleon's Military Campaigns.* New York, 2006.
Duffy, Christopher. *Austerlitz: 1805.* London, 1977.
Englund, Steven. *Napoleon: A Political Life.* New York, 2004.
Esdaile, Charles. *Napoleon's Wars: An International History, 1803–1815.* New York, 2007.
Fuller, J.F.C. *The Conduct of War, 1789–1961.* New Brunswick, NJ, 1961.
Goetz, Robert. *Austerlitz 1805: Napoleon and the Destruction of the Third Coalition.* London: Greenhill Books, 2005.
Grab, Alexander. *Napoleon and the Transformation of Europe.* Basingstoke, 2003.
Horward, Donald D. "Austerlitz and Masséna's Army of Italy." In *Selected Papers of the Consortium on Revolutionary Europe, 2006.* High Point, NC, 2007.
Jones, B.T., ed. *Napoleon's Army: The Military Memoirs of Charles Parquin.* London, 1988.
Kagan, Frederick. *The End of the Old Order.* Cambridge, MA, 2006.
Lachouque, Henry. *The Anatomy of Glory: Napoleon and His Guard*, trans. by Anne S.K. Brown. Providence, RI, 1961.
Lefebvre, Georges. *Napoleon: From 18 Brumaire to Tilsit 1799–1807*, trans. by Henry F. Stockhold. New York, 1969.

Manceron, Claude. *Austerlitz: The Story of a Battle*, trans. by George Unwin. New York, 1966.

Maude, F.N. *The Ulm Campaign, 1805*. London, 1912.

Rothenberg, Gunther E. *Napoleon's Great Adversaries: The Archduke Charles and the Austrian Army, 1792–1814*. Bloomington, IN, 1982.

Schneid, Frederick C. "The Grand Strategy of the Habsburg Monarchy during the War of the Third Coalition." In *Selected Papers of the Consortium on Revolutionary Europe, 2007*. High Point, NC, 2007.

Schneid, Frederick C. *Napoleon's Conquest of Europe: The War of the Third Coalition*. Westport, CT, 2005.

Schneid, Frederick C. *Napoleon's Italian Campaigns: 1805–1815*. Westport, CT, 2002.

Schroeder, Paul. *The Transformation of European Politics, 1763–1848*. Oxford, 1994.

Thiébault, Paul. *The Memoirs of Baron Thiébault*, trans. by Arthur John Butler. London, 1896.

Thiers, Adolphe. *History of the Consulate and Empire of France*, trans. by D. Forbes Campbell. London, 1856.

Woolf, Stuart. *Napoleon's Integration of Europe*. New York and London, 1991.

CHAPTER 7

The Jena Campaign: Apogee and Perihelion

Dennis Showalter

Napoleon Bonaparte is increasingly credited with being if not the father, then certainly the facilitator of operational war as it is generally understood. Martin van Creveld suggests three relevant factors. Information could not move much faster than soldiers could. Limitations in communications – including maps – inhibited both planning and command. The relatively small size of armies restricted the scope of campaigns. And, until the emergence of Napoleon, no commander had possessed the inspiration and the energy to provide the dynamic application of the Revolutionary Era's simultaneous improvement in long-distance communications and its enabling of mass armies.[1]

A fourth, no less significant element may be profitably added to van Creveld's trio: authority. War is made at four levels. Policy determines its fundamentals. In turn strategy focuses, operations implements, tactics executes. The post-Vietnam insistence on a hierarchy is, however, a red herring. The true relationship among the levels is symbiotic. Defects or overemphasis anywhere can gridlock and collapse the system. Napoleon was the first modern ruler to possess, through a combination of institutional structure and personal ability, effective control of all four.[2] And in that context Napoleon was the first executive consistently able to "run the table": making his plays and sinking his shots not only one after the other, but on all four levels simultaneously.

Paradoxically, Napoleon was also the last head of state able to perform that feat. As early as the mid-19th century, war-making had grown too complex to be directly controlled by a single individual – though that has not deterred repeated attempts. A strong case can be made that by 1812 at least, and arguably earlier, Napoleon's system had outgrown Napoleon himself.[3] At its peak, however, the imperium was the terror and the wonder of Europe and the world. And, while acknowledging the claims of the Austerlitz campaign, Napoleon's overthrow of Prussia and his breaking of the Fourth Coalition in 1806–1807 offer an even better illustration of the synergy of war-making's four levels that

---

1 Van Creveld, "Napoleon and the Dawn of Operational Warfare."
2 See particularly Philip Dwyer's magisterial *Citizen Emperor*.
3 On this point, see Robert M, Epstein, "Patterns of Change and Continuity in Nineteenth-Century Warfare," *Journal of Military History*, 56 (1992), 375–388.

was the matrix of Napoleon's operational art. It was an apogee, taking war to the furthest distance from its existing matrices. And it was a perihelion, coming nearest to the maximum possible for a person and a system in a specific context.

I   The Fourth Coalition

The Jena campaign might be considered a perihelion as well for bringing Napoleon closest to realizing his always unfocused ambitions. Austria's prostration and Russia's withdrawal after the catastrophe of Austerlitz seemed to confirm the French army's limitless capacity to fulfill its commander's pretensions. At a stroke Napoleon abolished the Holy Roman Empire, replacing it by a French-oriented Confederation of the Rhine, and by making the middle-sized states of Baden, Württemberg, and Bavaria an offer they could not refuse: territorial gains and sovereign status under French protection. Simultaneously he turned to – and on – Prussia.[4]

That state's strategy for more than a decade had been to avoid war with France, using its highly regarded army as a deterrent and a makeweight. Prussia had dodged the column of the Third Coalition despite heavy pressure from France and Austria. Its recompense had been a suggestion from Paris that continued neutrality might be rewarded with possession of the Electorate of Hanover, a source of tension since occupied by French troops in 1803. In the event, Prussia did enter Hanover without resistance – only weeks before Austerlitz and the resulting paradigm shift.[5] The Holy Roman Empire's imminent dissolution also created a North German political vacuum Prussia was unable to stabilize. Napoleon had no immediate reasons to be anything but overbearing. A series of one-sided negotiations bound Prussia to supply resources for Napoleon's ongoing war with Russia, to close its ports to British ships and goods, to surrender territories in its east and south. The final straw came in the summer of 1806, when Napoleon offered to restore Hanover's sovereignty in return for a British alliance. Prussia began mobilization in August. When King Frederick William III sent Napoleon a letter expressing, even at such a late date, hope for reconciliation based on mutual respect, Napoleon dismissed the document as a tissue of insults and declared that within a month

---

4   See Kagan, *End of the Old Order*; and the contributions to Alan Forrest and Peter H. Wilson, eds, *The Bee and the Eagle: Napoleonic France and the End of the Holy Roman Empire* (New York, 2009).

5   Philip Dwyer, "The Politics of Prussian Neutrality, 1795–1805," *German History* 12 (1984), 351–373.

Prussia's situation would be very different. The tone and the words alike left no room for misinterpretation.[6]

In the context of policy, the contrast between the rivals could hardly have been greater. Napoleon's France was by this time a society structured by war: a political culture of obedience, sustained by an administration whose comprehensiveness and effectiveness surpassed anything seen in Europe since imperial Rome's heyday. Censorship was the order of the day. Judicial independence and collective organization were alike conspicuous by their absence. Nor was this a superimposed authoritarian/absolutist order. Compulsion was complemented by assent. Public opinion and public discussion were widely held responsible both for the collapse of the *ancien régime* and the excesses of its successors. Careers were widely open to talent – and to opportunism – and to venality. The burdens of empire were still bearable, not least because of their unequal distribution in a society where *égalité* had been reduced to an abstraction.[7]

Prussian policymaking, on the other hand, was driven hither and yon by combinations of high political, foreign political, and personal factors that still challenge analysis. The number of participants was small. The king was deft at avoiding decision by playing them against each other. That the outcome amounted to gridlock mattered relatively little to this game of the throne – until Napoleon's pretensions to hegemony in Central Europe became undeniable. Even then the decision for war did not create a coherent policy. Increasingly acrimonious debates over what to do, when, and how were further complicated by international considerations. A new coalition, the Fourth, built around Britain and Russia, was forming against France. One of its underlying postulates was that this time Prussia would participate. By October 1806 there seemed no doubt on the point – except for Prussia's limited credibility. Negotiations had remained tentative throughout the summer. Now it seemed incumbent on Prussia either to tackle France alone – an obvious nonstarter – or to show goodwill (and burn its bridges) by engaging Napoleon immediately.[8]

The only item of importance on which a consensus developed was the Saxony question. The end of the Holy Roman Empire opened the possibility of

---

6   Christopher Clark, *Iron Kingdom: The Rise and the Downfall of Prussia, 1600–1947* (Cambridge, 2006), 301–305, is brief and balanced.
7   A good introduction is Howard Brown, "From Organic Society to Security State," *Journal of Modern History* 69 (1997), 661–696. Marie-Cecile Thoral, *From Valmy to Waterloo. France at War, 1789–1815*, trans. by.Godfrey Rogers (New York, 2011), and Louis Bergeron, *France Under Napoleon*, trans. by R.R. Palmer (Princeton, NJ, 1981), are more developed.
8   Best in any language on this complex subject is Brendan Simms, *The Impact of Napoleon: Prussian High Politics and the Creation of the Executive* (Cambridge, 1997).

a North German counterpart to the Confederation of the Rhine, dominated by Prussia but with Saxony elevating its status to a kingdom. That was the offer made to Elector Frederick Augustus III on July 25. It was met by temporizing. Left to its own devices, the Saxon government would certainly have preferred neutrality, and probably a French connection. Given the Electorate's position on Prussia's exposed southwestern frontier, however, these were not options in Berlin. The strong – even the relatively strong – do what they can; the weak bear what they must. The Saxon army, 22,000 strong, joined the 150,000 Prussians moving toward the prospective theater of war.[9]

11   Strategy, Policy and Operations

At that point policy segued into strategy. From Prussia's perspective, there remained just enough time in the campaigning season to bloody France's nose – a feat that did not seem clearly beyond its army's powers. That would secure Saxony's cooperation, however unenthusiastic. Of greater importance, it would buy a winter for Russian bayonets and British guineas to bring their powers to bear across Europe. In pursuit of these objectives no fewer than five distinct plans emerged. These ranged from waiting on the Russians while fighting delaying actions, to meeting the French head on, mass against mass.[10] All were preliminary moves without a long-term objective. Specific implementation remained a subject of discussion as the generals, and the king, left Berlin for Erfurt in Thuringia – Prussian territory but only since 1802.

Napoleon for his part expected Prussia to continue temporizing. In public contexts, not until 5 September did he recall reservists and mobilize conscripts. Not until informed that Prussia would use armed force to defend Saxony's right to remain outside the Confederation of the Rhine did the emperor formally warn Frederick William to cease and desist. By then it scarcely mattered. Since late August, Napoleon had been studying his maps and planning to take the field once more with the Grande Armée. The policy aim was to prevent invasion, not only of France but of its freshly minted German allies and clients: the empire might not mean peace, but it needed to offer security. The strategic intention was to preempt and defeat any Prussian offensive before Russia

9   Karlheinz Blaschke, "Von Jena 1806 nach Wien 1815. Sachsen zwischen Preussen und Napoleon," in Gerd Fresser and Reinhard Jonscher, eds, *Umbruch im Schatten Napoleons. Die Schlachten von Jena und Auerstaedt und ihre Folgen* (Jena, 1998), 144–145.
10 Olaf Jessen, "Ohne Jena kein Verdun. Vom Nutzen einer neuen Operationsgeschichte: Feldzug und Schlacht 1806," in M. Tullner, ed., *1806: Jena, Auerstedt, und die Kapitulation von Magdeburg. Schande oder Chance?* (Halle, 2007), 19–23, 33–34.

could intervene. The means to those ends was tactical: a decisive battle: another Austerlitz that would remove Prussia from the playing field, intimidate Russia into negotiating peace – and arguably encourage Britain to accept the imperium's continental hegemony. In analytic terms, Napoleon sought a tactical victory that would fulfill his strategy and policy objectives. The crucial enabler, as we shall see, would be operational art.[11]

Napoleon had reached his decisions at the policy and strategy levels autonomously. In operational contexts he began by ordering Marshal Berthier, who served both as minister of war and chief of staff, to bring the Grande Armée up to strength from the depots in France.[12] In the aftermath of Austerlitz it had been moved into South Germany to underwrite Napoleon's political restructuring. But since Napoleon was marketing himself as an ally and patron, the individual corps had been so distributed as to make minimum demands on the German governments feeding them. Nine months of inactivity had also, inevitably, loosened discipline – particularly since with the completion of Germany's reconstruction the army was preparing to return to France. Furloughs and demobilization were livelier subjects of camp discussion than a potential new campaign.

That changed rapidly. On 5 September 1806, Napoleon instructed Berthier to prepare a report on the army's condition and begin reconnoitering the region's road network. On the 10th, he gave Berthier preliminary orders to concentrate three corps at Würzburg immediately on learning of Prussian troop movements into Saxony. Napoleon began issuing initial directives to his corps commanders and preparing his field headquarters for movement. On the 15th,

---

[11] Chandler, *Campaigns of Napoleon*, 452–506, remains the modern standard in English. Most of the detailed studies were more or less inspired by the first centennial. F.N. Maude, *The Jena Campaign* (New York, 1909), is still useful at the tactical level. F.L Petre, *Napoleon's Conquest of Prussia: 1806* (London, 1907), has a broader perspective. On the French side, Paul Jean Foucart, ed., *Campagne de Prusse, 1806: d'aprés les archives de la guerre*, 2 vols (Paris, 1887), is an early, still useful, documentary source. Henri Bonnal, *La manoevre de Iena* (Paris, 1904), prefigures Chandler. Pascal Bressonnet's massive 1909 work, the best of its kind, has been translated by Scott Bowden as *Napoleon's Apogee* and published by the Military History Press in 2009 (hereafter cited as Bressonnet, *Apogee*). The far larger body of German-language work is dominated by scapegoating and apologetics. Best for who, what, when, and where is Oscar von Lettow-Vorbeck, *Der Krieg von 1806–1907*, vol. I, *Jena und Auerstedt*, 2nd edn. (Berlin, 1896). And for those new to the subject or who are impatient, the best choice is David G. Chandler, *Jena 1806: Napoleon Destroys Prussia* (London, 1993), a hundred-page distillation of a career's worth of scholarship. Gerd Fesser, *Die Doppelschlacht bei Jena und Auerstedt* (Jena, 2006), is a similarly sized centennial volume. These works form the basis of the chapter's narrative element, and are specifically referenced only when necessary.

[12] *CN*, No. 10743, 13:148–149.

he learned that Prussian troops had entered Saxony. The same day he began issuing instructions for the mobilization – 120 separate orders in 48 hours. Some of these sent the Imperial Guard to Mainz in wagon convoys, ensuring their arrival as travel-worn but not march-exhausted – the first troop movement of that kind on that scale, and the last until the development of railroads.[13] On the 21st, informed by Berthier that the Prussians were moving southwest across the Elbe, the emperor left Paris for the emerging theater of war.

Initially, Napoleon had also considered two straightforward approaches: a direct advance into Prussia through Hanover and an offensive from Mainz into Saxony – the Cold War's Fulda Gap option in reverse. Both, however, required significant French redeployment. Both posed the risk of merely pushing the Prussians back toward their Russian allies. A drive northeast toward Berlin took advantage of existing French positioning. It offered, as well, the kind of objective that might tempt the Prussians into doing something more or less logical, more or less predictable, in contrast to their initial movements that Napoleon had found "quite extraordinary."[14]

South Germany was a new theater of operations, and information on its topography was correspondingly scanty. The Thuringian Forest alone invited consideration as a serious obstacle to major troop movements. It barred the way into Saxony and into Prussia, and cartography was not exactly a major concern of its subsistence economy. Berthier, however, had been instructed to send engineers to reconnoiter the roads leading to Berlin, while the Grande Armée's light cavalry was expert in scouting, screening, and – usually – reporting. On 30 September, Napoleon outlined his intentions to his brother, Louis, the king of Holland. He proposed to concentrate his entire force on the right, leaving the region from Bamberg to the Rhine River uncovered for the sake of having 200,000 men available for the decisive battle he expected to force. Should the enemy attempt a serious initiative against the theoretically exposed French left, Napoleon would simply "throw him into the Rhine."[15]

This rather simplified presentation might well have been intended simultaneously to impress and reassure the emperor's unmartial sibling. The "General

---

13   The men dismounted outside some villages, marched through them, then reboarded their vehicles – thus simultaneously resting the horses and demonstrating that the Guard had not gone soft: Chandler, *Campaigns of Napoleon*, 462.

14   The early stages of Napoleon's operational plan are most clearly summarized in English by David G. Chandler, "Napoleon, Operational Art, and the Jena Campaign," in *Historical Perspectives of the Operational Art*, ed. Michael D. Krause and R. Cody Philips (Washington, DC, 2007), 39–44. Telp, *Evolution of Operational Art*, 59–97, is an excellent contextualized study of the entire Jena campaign from an operational perspective.

15   CN, No. 10920, 13:292–296.

THE JENA CAMPAIGN: APOGEE AND PERIHELION

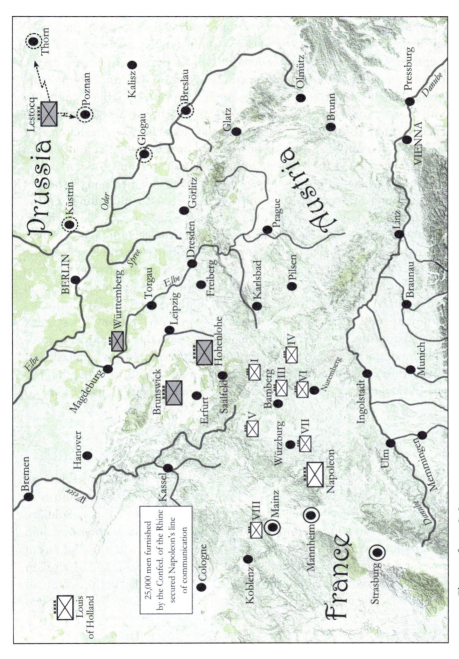

MAP 7.1 Theater of war, 1806

Dispositions for the Assembly of the Grand Army" were another matter. Six corps and the Imperial Guard were available. The VII, VI, and I were ordered to concentrate at Frankfurt, Nuremberg, and Ansbach, respectively, and to be ready to march by 2 October. The III Corps would join Napoleon and the Guard at Bamberg; V Corps would center on Würzburg; IV Corps, furthest east on the Inn River, would be at Amberg by the 4th. The Army of Italy under Napoleon's stepson, Eugène de Beauharnais, was to restrain any Austrian ambitions. Another 25,000 men, mostly from depots and garrisons, would secure the French northern coast against British raids and descents. And a freshly created VIII Corps, this one made up of first-line regiments, would support Louis against unexpected Prussian initiatives in northeast Germany.

Taken as a whole these directives clearly indicate the operational aspect of the Jena campaign. Securing other threatened areas with minimum force, the emperor concentrated a massive main army in the decisive theater – concentrated it without gridlocking. By this time, his knowledge of the road network sufficed to enable his final orders for the advance. On the left, the 40,000-strong V and VII Corps would march toward Saalfeld. On the right, IV and VI Corps followed by a Bavarian contingent, totaling more than 50,000 men, would move through Hof. Napoleon would march with the center: I and III Corps, the Guard, and most of the Reserve Cavalry – some of the army's best men. Napoleon informed one of his subordinates that, with this superiority of force in that limited a space, he was determined to leave nothing to chance.[16] But maneuvering a "battalion square" of 200,000 men in 7 corps along dubious roads and trails on a 40-mile front of advance would require skill and luck.

III   The Grande Armée

Napoleon enjoyed both – especially if luck is understood as the residue of design. At Bamberg he announced to his assembling army: They want us to evacuate Germany even though they are brandishing their arms ... Soldiers, there is not one of you who wants to return to France by any other way than that of honor. We must only return through the arches of triumph."[17] If any of the audience wondered whether that "we" meant the emperor had a mouse in his pocket, the records are silent. The army that Napoleon led in the autumn of 1806 was arguably at the peak of its effectiveness. It had been trained for two

---

16   Ibid., No. 10941, 13:309–310.
17   Quoted in F.G. Hourtoulle, *Jena–Auerstedt: The Triumph of the Eagle*, trans. by A.F. Mackay (Paris, 2006), 8.

years while preparing for the abortive invasion of England, tempered during the Ulm–Austerlitz campaign, and then given eight months to rest and refit. About a fourth of the rank and file had worn uniform since sometime during the Revolutionary Wars. Another fourth were veterans of more recent fighting in South Germany and upper Italy. The remaining half were conscripts, mostly drafted between 1800 and 1803. That provided a near-optimal mixture of not yet exhausted veterans and still willing, even enthusiastic, replacements. The regiments had not yet been attenuated by casualties. Their morale was a potent mix of revolutionary memories and imperial loyalties. Only in the troops led by William T. Sherman in the final eighteen months of the American Civil War does this hard veteran force find a match during the Age of Mass War in terms of numbers synchronized with quality.[18]

The Grande Armée was no less well served by its command structure. It was generally led from divisions down to companies by officers experienced at their ranks, used to working with the units on either side of them. It was at the corps level, however, that the French stood out. Napoleon's operational system depended heavily, indeed essentially, on corps commanders able to cooperate in both maneuver and combat; able to react independently to immediate situations, but not usually given to thinking too much beyond those situations. And in 1806 he had arguably the finest corps command team for his kind of system ever assembled. Davout of III Corps, Soult of IV Corps, Lannes of V, Ney of VI – all could maneuver men and lead them. All had the sense of terrain and situation called *coup d'oeil* that enabled them to exploit opportunities and minimize contretemps. Augereau of VII Corps suffered primarily by comparison. The weakest link, Bernadotte of I Corps, was directly under Napoleon's eye and thumb. And, with Joachim Murat commanding the army's cavalry, there was no question that the troopers would be employed with skill and energy.

None of these men was as yet burned out by too many battles and too much responsibility. Their corps, ranging from 16,000- to 30,000-strong, were large enough to function independently and small enough to be controlled by one commander: a single intelligence, a single will, and a single voice. This was a sharp contrast to later campaigns, when a corps might count more than 70,000 men, like Davout's in 1812: at best a bludgeon, certainly not a rapier. The limited strengths meant as well that Napoleon could use his corps as chess pieces. At this stage none of his chief subordinates had the sense of being great captains

---

18   For a recent perspective on the Grande Armée, see Michael J. Hughes, *Forging Napoleon's Grande Armee: Motivation, Military Culture, and Masculinity in the French Army, 1800–1808* (New York, 2012); see also Jean-Claude Damamme, *Les soldats de la Grande Armée* (Paris, 1998).

themselves. They could fight independently – fight brilliantly and win decisively, as Davout would demonstrate in a few days. But thinking was Napoleon's province; only he saw over the entire board, whether operational or tactical.

The emperor's failure to develop generals able, consistent, and effective to command the field armies that emerged as the dominant higher formation in the Napoleonic Wars remains controversial. Did his ego reject even a possibility of possible competition? Did he fear cultivating potential rivals for power? Did he simply lack the time for systematic mentoring? Napoleon Bonaparte and Frederick the Great both wrote extensively on the art of war, but their approaches are fundamentally different. Frederick is a schoolmaster, endlessly explaining both principles and details to readers he does not expect to understand fully. Napoleon is a magician, laying out in detail the tricks – but reserving to himself the keys to their success. The respective approaches arguably reflect the fundamental difference between a hereditary monarch and a self-legitimating usurper.[19]

A simpler response may be the most accurate. Napoleon, who was nothing if not a good judge of men, may well have recognized that the team he had formed since his early days in Italy had a collective low ceiling. His marshals had learned war by making war – and making war in contexts that stressed immediate problem-solving as opposed to more abstract reasoning. British engineers in the Industrial Revolution, American generals in the Civil War, Red Army commanders in the Russian Civil War: these are only some examples of the limitations of experience as a teacher. Napoleon observed in retrospect that his marshals wanted a strong hand. Wanted or needed? Did the marshals reflect the Grande Armée's command dynamic, or was that dynamic tailored to the marshals?[20] In any case the system of strong hand and short leash worked in 1806 – worked better than it ever did again in any theater of the emperor's wars.

IV   The Tools of War

The French broke out quickly. Napoleon made war with men's legs, and after three days the Grande Armée was through the Thuringian Forest without facing any opposition. That reflected the fact that the Prussians and their new

---

19   See the anthologies edited by Jay Luvaas, *Frederick the Great on the Art of War* (New York, 1966), and *Napoleon on the Art of War* (New York, 1999).

20   The relevant chapters in Chandler, *Napoleon's Marshals*, can be consulted for the beginning of an answer to this very open question.

Saxon allies were scattered all over the zone of operations. Prussia had by no means ignored the metastasizing fighting power of Revolutionary/Napoleonic France. Its response was an emphasis on developing a "high-quality army," able to counter French mass and skill with even greater fighting power of its own. The military qualities admired in the French army could be replicated by institutional reform, underpinned by social changes well short of revolution. Tactical doctrine remained a subject of debate. Enthusiasts advocated infusing formal training with appeals to the soldiers' goodwill and natural enthusiasm. Institutionally oriented officers favored synthesizing the open-order tactics of the Revolution with the linear formations that had continued to prove their worth when appropriately handled. That still-unresolved debate was rendered moot by the declaration of war. The army did, however, benefit from a series of administrative reforms. Regulations were simplified. The logistical system was overhauled. Baggage and supply trains were reduced: the 4,000 vehicles with which the army took the field represented a genuine improvement over earlier standards. The Prussian army of the Jena campaign was a good deal leaner than it had been since the Seven Years War. It was also better articulated – at least on paper. After years of discussion, a divisional system along French lines was finally introduced at the beginning of the 1806 campaign. Unsurprisingly, in addition to the normal problems afflicting improvised formations with inexperienced commanders, the divisions were badly balanced; deficient alike in fire power and shock power. They were, however, in place and better than nothing.

The Prussian army of 1806 can reasonably be described as well into the process of adapting to the new ways of war developed in the previous decade. In comparative terms, it was about where the Austrians stood three years later at Wagram. Not until at least 1810 would Britain's principal field army reach the structural and administrative levels at which the Prussian army stood immediately before Jena–Auerstedt. But in October 1806 that level would prove uncompetitive – above all on the operational level.[21]

Perhaps the best thing an army and its commanders can have in their favor is an obliging enemy. An obliging enemy is not one who makes mistakes. In war those are inevitable, and even egregious ones can be overcome. An obliging enemy makes the kind of decisions the opponent would make if its headquarters were preparing the orders. The Prussians came sufficiently close to that

---

21　Dennis E. Showalter, "Hubertusberg to Auerstedt: The Prussian Army in Decline?" *German History* 12 (1994), 308–333; and Olaf Jessen, "Eingeschlafen auf den Lorbeeren Friedrichs des Grossen? Das Altpreussische Heer 1786–1806", in Tullner, *1806: Jena, Auerstedt*, 110–129, address specifics. Peter Paret's dazzling *The Cognitive Challenge of War: Prussia 1806* (Princeton, NJ, 2009), synergizes war, society, and culture.

standard that Napoleon remained puzzled alike by their locations and intentions as late as 10 October.²² Yet that very "obligingness" was confusing. Prussian movements might be muddled, as Mack's had been in the Ulm campaign the previous year. Or the Prussians might be more percipient than Napoleon had accepted. Confused policy did not necessarily translate into confused planning.

Every league the French advanced extended their lines of supply. Rapid lateral communication in the still near-primeval Thuringian Forest was difficult. To compensate, Napoleon had established lines and times of march so that his three columns were advancing at about the same rate. Once they emerged from the forest, however, either flank might come under attack. French advance guards won skirmishes around Hof and Schleiz. At Saalfeld, Lannes's V Corps took the measure of a mixed Saxon–Prussian detachment whose commander, Prince Louis Ferdinand of Prussia, was killed in a hand-to-hand fight with a French sergeant of hussars.²³

Dramatic in itself, the encounter might be described as an amalgam of old order and new. Neither Saalfeld nor the other skirmishes, however, did anything to clarify the operational situation: where the Prussians were; where they might be going. Nevertheless nothing remained further from Napoleon's mind than halting in place to develop his intelligence. The fragments of information available by 8:00 AM on 10 September indicated that the Prussians intended to attack in two columns, one advancing through Jena–Saalfeld–Coburg, the other through Meiningen and Fulda. His response was to push his right column toward the road junction at Gera as the first step toward the Grande Armée's concentration there. This would threaten both the Prussians' operational line of retreat toward Leipzig and their strategic connection with their Russian allies. The probable result, Napoleon reasoned, would be that the Prussians would – obligingly – concentrate at Gera for a major battle.

Once on the ground, "things would clarify themselves," the emperor wrote on the evening of the 10th.²⁴ The eventual "clarification" was that Gera proved empty – demonstrating that even Napoleon could be completely wrong at the top of his voice. For the rest of 11 October, no useful intelligence on Prussian whereabouts or intentions surfaced. Around midnight, however, two crucial dispatches reached imperial headquarters. One, from Murat, stated that a captured Saxon officer had declared the Prussian main army was at Erfurt. Another

---

22 *CN*, No.10977, 13:332–334.
23 For the engagement at Saalfeld, see the text and after-action reports in Bressonnet, *Apogee*, 10–64.
24 *CN*, No.10980, 13:335–336.

from Soult asserted that the Prussians had retreated from Gera toward Jena.[25] Both reports were as fresh as possible in an age of literal horsepower: advancing French cavalry left small detachments behind on the main roads so that messengers could replace exhausted horses. Napoleon consulted his updated maps, took counsel from the only advisor he respected, himself, then summoned Berthier and began dictating. From 2:30 to 6:00 AM a series of orders went out to the corps. Their sum was a left turn at a right angle: 90 degrees in the direction of the Saale River. Lannes and Augereau were to march directly on Jena. Bernadotte and Davout would continue north, reach Auerstedt–Naumburg, then swing left and approach Jena from the northeast, in the direction of Lannes's right. In the riskiest shuffle of all of them, Soult and Ney were to turn west, cross the original center column's lines of communication and advance on Jena from the east. Once in position they, along with the Guard, would be the center and reserve, with Bernadotte and Davout now forming the Grande Armee's right flank. This was the *bataillon carré*, the "battalion square" able as required to face to the front or either flank with its elements remaining mutually supporting. Murat and the cavalry reserve were ordered to "flood the countryside" in the direction of Leipzig; even if they found nothing, that would still be a positive sign of enemy intentions. Expect, Napoleon declared, a battle on the 16th, probably around Erfurt.[26]

The process of preparing this elaborate movement in the middle of the night highlights another fundamental aspect of Napoleon's operational art: his staff system. Berthier's principal initial function that night was secretarial: taking notes from Napoleon's rapid, often allusive speech. Berthier's secretarial functions could become even more subordinate; he was reputedly the only one at headquarters who could consistently decipher the emperor's tortured handwriting. But Berthier was no mere amanuensis. The focus of his skill – arguably of his genius – lay in translating Napoleon's general intentions into specific orders – and then clarifying those orders to the junior staff officers who wrote them out for the emperor's final perusal and approval.[27]

An interesting aspect of military writing is its tendency to present as optimal for troop staffs, as opposed to planning staffs, the Prussian-German structure. Ideally – and often in fact – this was a synergy amounting to a

---

25 Van Creveld, "Napoleon and the Dawn of Operational Warfare," 28.
26 See *CN*, Nos. 10981, 10982, 10984, 13:336–338; and Colonel Jean-Baptiste Vachée, *Napoleon en campagne* (reprint, Paris, 2012), 45–46.
27 Martin van Creveld, *Command in War* (Cambridge, MA, 1985), 65–78, summarizes Napoleon's headquarters and staff system. Hermann Giehrl, *Der Feldherr Napoleon als Organisator. Betrachtungen über seine Verkehrs- und Nachrichtenmittel, seine Arbeits- und Befehlsweise* (Berlin, 1911), is more detailed.

symbiosis between the commander and his chief of staff: one providing the will and the other the mind, each able to comprehend and internalize the other's perspective. Napoleon's model of a field staff as a subaltern institution, essentially responsible for translating the commander's will and mind into orders and actions, emerges as at best second-best.[28] In fact, the Prussian model was realized for only about a half-century: 1866 to 1918. During the Second World War, the German army was commanded by its commanders. It requires careful investigation to unearth any staff officers who at troop levels were anything more than Berthiers *aprés la lettre*. The United States as well adopted in the First World War, and has retained since, the structure and the mentality of the troop staff as introduced by Napoleon.[29]

Parenthetically, Berthiers have proven no easier to develop than Napoleons. The team of Napoleon and Berthier was personal, not institutional; Berthier was often described as Napoleon's wife.[30] It was best adapted to a focused campaign rather than one conducted along far-flung lines. Even then it was limited in the size of the forces it could effectively maneuver and control. All three factors came together on the night of 11 October 1806 to give the French the beginnings of a vital edge.

Napoleon's intention was to force the Prussians into a decisive battle by threatening their lines of supply, communication – and retreat. Its implementation required 200,000 men, plus guns, horses, and wagons, to defy fog and friction. The average time to deliver an order was between two and three hours: remarkable in itself given that the aides de camp had to negotiate broken, unfamiliar terrain in darkness. Even more impressive was the time between the orders' delivery and their initial implementation. That was about two hours – further proof of a system thoroughly worked in and accustomed to surprises.[31]

The real proof of the Grande Armée's effectiveness as an instrument of operational art was, however, the smoothness with which its corps completed their arabesques. That in great part reflected minimal supply lines, vulnerable neither to traffic jams nor enemy raids. Intendant-General Pierre Antoine Noël Bruno Daru is by all odds the most overlooked senior member of Napoleon's military household. Distinguished by his organizing capacity, his diligence,

---

28 Trevor Dupuy, *A Genius for War: The German Army and General Staff, 1809–1945* (Englewood Cliffs, NJ, 1977), is a good example of this genre.
29 See the twenty-eight capsule case studies in David T. Zabecki, ed., *Chief of Staff: The Principal Officers Behind History's Great Commanders*, 2 vols (Annapolis, MD, 2008).
30 And a regularly abused spouse he was, to the point of physical violence. See Samuel J. Doss, "Louis-Alexandre Berhtier", ibid., 32.
31 Van Creveld, *Command in War*, 87–88.

THE JENA CAMPAIGN: APOGEE AND PERIHELION   263

and his honesty – that last an unusual, if not a unique, characteristic in his milieu – Daru had demonstrated a repeated ability to produce enough logistical straw to make operational bricks. This time he had almost nothing to work with: no reserves of food; few wagons and most of those owned by a private company of dubious competence. The numbers had to be made up by requisitioning: a process that involved a good deal of theft between units and violence against civilians.[32]

At first glance, this need for wagons seems to challenge a dominant myth about Napoleonic logistics. The French army was legendary as a force of matchless, ruthless foragers. This time, it took the field at the end of harvest season in a year when yields had been good, in an area that had never been subjected to fine-tooth combing by men in uniform. Population increases, improved agricultural methods, and acceptance of the potato as a food crop further improved prospects for living off the land. But foraging produced high wastage and was notoriously bad for discipline. It was designed to complement, not replace, basic issued rations such as hardtack biscuits and salted meat. The French army traveled light. It eschewed tents for greatcoats, which saved time making and breaking camp. But soldiers often abandoned the coats as superfluous weight on a long march. An army needed shoes and clothing – replacements from France were arriving barefoot. It needed sundries, everything from salt to medical supplies.

Daru, the marshals, the colonels and the captains, coped. As the advance began, one corps reported two days' bread – but enough salt for fifteen days, two days' worth of beef on the hoof, and not least two rations of brandy. This was Soult's outfit, and he had a reputation for keeping his men supplied whatever it took. An average provision was four days' bread and two pairs of shoes per man. That meant that a corps of the Grande Armée usually had a train of around 300 wagons – Spartan by 18th-century standards but still not exactly self-regulating. Daru established commissions to administer supplies of meat and forage, and to oversee the hospitals. Corps lines of communication were divided into districts patrolled by units of the Gendarmerie Nationale. Compared to the ad hoc provost forces of other contemporary armies, they provided a level of traffic control that kept roads open and supplies moving even as the marching columns intersected.[33]

---

32   For his career, see Bernard Bergerot, *Daru, Intendant-Général de la Grande Armée* (Paris, 1991).
33   Telp, *Evolution of Operational Art*, 86–87, and Elting, *Swords Around a Throne*, 563–564.

v   Closing the Net

Prussia's troop movements in the previous week had been the consequences of a council of war held at Erfurt on 5 October by Frederick William and his inner circle of civilian and military advisors. One faction, dominated by General Friedrich Ludwig zu Hohenlohe-Ingelfingen and Colonel Christian Karl August Ludwig von Massenbach, advocated an immediate offensive: crossing the Saale River in force and striking Napoleon while he was still in Franconia. Long-time foreign minister Christian August Heinrich Kurt von Haugwitz spoke for those believing Napoleon's strategy would be defensive: that what he most wanted was to lure Prussia into a premature attack that would favor a defensive posture. The army's nominal commander, the duke of Brunswick, also believed Napoleon would initially assume the defensive. In the middle stood General Ernst von Rüchel, who expected a French advance but considered crossing the Saale to meet it an excessive risk.

Gerhard Johann David Waitz von Scharnhorst, Brunswick's chief of staff and one of the army's rising stars, declared that in war what was done mattered less than acting with unity and energy. His point was as intelligent as it was irrelevant. "Council of war" is by definition a near-synonym for "indecision." This particular debate degenerated into chaos, and concluded with compromises. Brunswick's main army remained north of Erfurt. The next largest body, Prussians and Saxons under Hohenlohe, was around Rudolstadt and Stadtroda. Rüchel's contingent provided the right-flank guard at Eisenach; the left was covered by a smaller force posted around Hof, under the relatively junior Prussian general Bogislav Friedrich Emanuel von Tauentzien. When the advance guards are included, the Allied army had been divided, or better said fragmented, into no fewer than seven distinct parts in the face of Napoleon's sledgehammer.[34]

Reality began emerging when Tauentzien's detachment, which had already withdrawn from its badly exposed position at Hof, was forced back toward Hohenlohe by Murat's vanguards. Any doubt vanished when on 12 October a report arrived that Davout's III Corps had reached Naumburg. From Brunswick's perspective, it seemed that the French were moving into position to bypass his left flank, indeed his entire army, and strike directly for the heart of the newly formed Prusso-Saxon alliance: Halle, Magdeburg, Dresden, and ultimately Berlin. This, moreover, was only a beginning: Napoleon's ultimate aim was the

---

34   Chandler, *Campaigns of Napoleon*, 455–459, effectively summarizes this pattern of "idea, counteridea, no idea." See also Olaf Jessen, *"Preussens Napoleon"? Ernst von Rüchel. Krieg im Zeitalter der Vernunft 1754–1823* (Paderborn, 2007), 279–281.

destruction of the Prussian army itself. "God help us!" Brunswick allegedly cried. "It's a question of our very existence."[35] Frederick William summoned another council of war early on 13 October. A minority favored moving eastward and making a stand at Jena. The weight of opinion, however, was that the army should immediately retreat north, toward Halle–Magdeburg and the 15,000 troops posted there as a strategic reserve. The debate was lengthy and acrimonious. Brunswick finally responded with his major decision to date: a general retreat on Leipzig via Apolda and Auerstedt, with the intention of forming a new defensive line further to the north, protecting Berlin and Magdeburg. Hohenlohe was to hold position around Jena while avoiding a battle, with Rüchel now in support around Weimar. Once the retreat was successfully under way, Rüchel would fall back and Hohenlohe would become the army's rearguard.[36]

All was by the book – the 18th-century book Napoleon had been rewriting for a decade. The emperor had arrived in Gera around 8:00 PM on 12 October. In a note to Josephine, he asserted that things were going very well, quite as hoped.[37] But at 4:00 AM he expressed his underlying concerns to Lannes and Murat: "I need information on what [the enemy] intends to do."[38] Continuing along the current axes of advance meant pointlessly moving away from the Prussians, enabling them either to withdraw behind the Saale or fall back on Weimar and Erfurt and begin a general retreat north. Expecting – or hoping – his marshals and their light cavalry would clarify the situation expeditiously, Napoleon issued preliminary orders to Murat and Lannes to hold in place on the 13th and rest men who had been marching as much as twelve and fifteen miles a day.

Losing time for a second successive day was not an optimal first choice. The decision to halt surprised, when they learned of it, even the Prussians. Another possible explanation is provided by a junior aide de camp, whose memoir describes the emperor sending him directly to Frederick William with an offer of peace that the battle-seeking Hohenlohe kept him from delivering.[39] Unsupported elsewhere and implausible on its face, the story nevertheless merits repeating as an extreme example of Napoleon's power to move at will

---

35   C.L.A. von Massenbach, *Historische Denkwuerdigkeiten zur Geschichtee des Verfall des preussischen Staates ...*, 2nd edn., edited Hanne Witte, et al. (Frankfurt, 1984), 269–276.
36   Jessen, *"Preussens Napoleon,"* 285.
37   *CN*, No.11000, 13:348.
38   Ibid., Nos. 10982 and 10983, 13:336–337.
39   Anatole de Montesquieu, *Souvenirs de Révolution, l'Empire, la Restauration et la règne de Louis-Philippe*, ed. by Robert Burnand (Paris, 1961), 75.

up and down the four stages of war-making, in this case seeking a political resolution of a tactical situation.

In the same time frame, Napoleon catechized Lannes and Davout, requesting what news they had. Around 9:00 AM on 13 October, messengers arrived from Murat, Davout, and Augereau. Composed at different times during the night, their dispatches had taken from eight to ten hours to deliver. The combined contents added up to establishing the Prussian main body in the area of Weimar–Erfurt; closer to Weimar but far enough east to suggest a general retreat northwards. Davout reported that his corps had faced no opposition in its advance; that only pickets had been observed around Jena. Even more significantly, Davout's cavalry had captured an entire pontoon train on the road to Naumburg. These bulky artifacts, guaranteed road-blockers, were never moved without an objective – in this case moving the Prussians across the rivers around Naumburg.[40]

The deciding piece of information came from a major of hussars. Passing as Saxons, he and his troopers had arrived in Weißenfels, a dot on the map northeast of Naumburg. He found only stragglers. Questioning passengers on the stagecoaches from Erfurt and Leipzig, he was "fairly positive" that the "terrorized" enemy army was hastily withdrawing toward Merseburg, Halle, and Magdeburg.[41]

It was as neat a piece of light cavalry work as any during two decades of war. And it led Napoleon to assert that "the veil [was] torn at last:" The Prussians were retreating, and retreating toward Magdeburg. This assurance may have been at least in part for public consumption; the emperor had a way of stimulating morale among his marshals by speaking more positively than his available information really justified. Nothing had arrived from Lannes, whose V Corps, near Jena, was now closest to the enemy. Napoleon therefore ordered Murat to move Bernadotte's I Corps plus his dragoons and cavalry to Dornburg, between Jena and Naumburg, in position to support Lannes should he come under attack. Napoleon also dispatched the army's heavy cavalry to Jena, and started Augereau's VII and Soult's IV Corps in the same direction, intending them to arrive on Lannes's left and right flanks respectively. Napoleon himself proposed to reach Jena around 2:00 PM.[42]

En route with a small escort, and running slightly late, the emperor finally encountered a courier from Lannes around 3:00 PM. The message was sufficiently detailed to compensate for its delayed submission. Lannes stated that

---

40   Bressonnet, *Apogee*, 73–74.
41   Ibid., 76.
42   *CN*, No. 11000, 13:348.

he had arrived at Jena on the 12th, and the 12,000 or 15,000 Prussians facing him had retreated toward Weimar. Rather than launch a pursuit in the dark over "abominable" terrain, Lannes had buttoned up and hunkered down. Available intelligence indicated that the Prussians were in "great disorder," but left him uncertain whether they would attack him or retreat. Lannes declared himself nevertheless ready to advance on Weimar – but not without knowing Napoleon's intentions. Subaltern initiative in the Grande Armée had its limits: approximately where operational art began.

Lannes's information convinced Napoleon that the decision he sought might come not on the 16th, but as early as the next day. He responded by dictating new orders literally from the saddle. The emperor's general intention was to advance toward Weimar and be prepared for battle anywhere along the way. Soult, Augereau, and the Imperial Guard, a *bataillon carré manqué*, would join Lannes, fix the Prussians in place, and do the heavy lifting. Ney was ordered to force-march to complete the concentration. Should Lannes be attacked on the evening of the 13th, Davout was to support him on the left. Otherwise the emperor would forward plans for the 14th when he developed them.[43]

Originally Napoleon had conceived of both Bernadotte and Davout operating tactically: coming in from Dornburg and Naumburg directly against the Prussian left flank and immediate rear. But if this information on Prussian positions and movements were reasonably correct, it was growing clear that the eventual main line of march, communication, and retreat of the enemy directly in front ran through Apolda and southwest of Naumburg. That made them even more vulnerable at what can be considered an operational level. Napoleon's first set of orders reached Davout's headquarters around 7:30 PM – another credible performance by imperial aides under the circumstances – with a notation that an updated version would arrive that night. These arrived about 3:00 AM. According to the III Corps war diary, Davout then informed his senior subordinates that the next day's objective was Apolda. How Davout got there was up to him, as long as he participated in the battle. Berthier had added a codicil. The emperor hoped Bernadotte was at Dornburg as ordered. Should he be with Davout, however, the two corps could march together against the enemy rear.[44]

Bernadotte, never one to push himself unnecessarily, was in fact at Naumburg, where he had halted his corps to await further orders when Davout

---

[43] The communications are excerpted in Brissonet, *Apogee*, 77–78. See also Chandler, *Campaigns of Napoleon*, 475.

[44] Bressonnet, *Apogee*, 249. The operations of III Corps are presented in detail in Davout's report of the 1806–1807 campaign, elaborately published as *Napoleon's Finest: Marshal Louis Davout and His III Corps*, ed. by Scotty Bowden, et al. (Remington, VA, 2006).

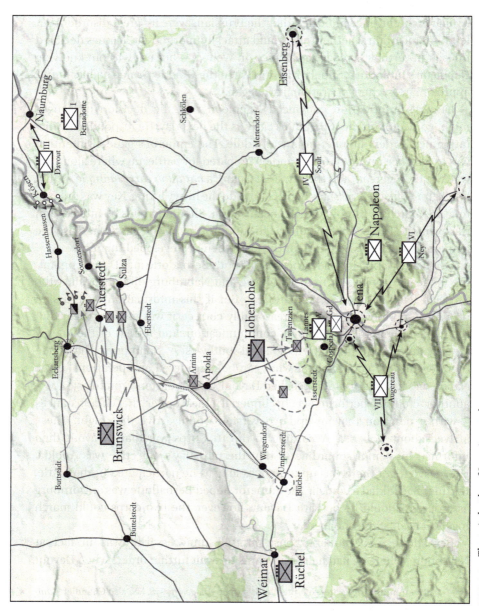

MAP 7.2 The twin battles of Jena-Auerstedt

stopped.⁴⁵ At 4:00 AM Davout handed him a written précis of the emperor's communication. As often noted, Napoleon's marshals were anything but a band of brothers. A more appropriate metaphor might be streetwalkers competing for a favorable corner – or the favorable attention of their pimp. Bernadotte was an insecure prima donna. Davout was brusque under almost any circumstances. The upshot of their interaction was that Bernadotte, in the absence of new direct orders from Napoleon himself, refused to accept de facto subordination to Davout. Instead he insisted on moving to Dornburg as originally instructed.⁴⁶

"*Tant pis*," Davout was heard to murmur as he left. That phrase can mean "never mind" or "too damn bad." On 14 October both applied. Napoleon's preferred option was Bernadotte striking the Prussian left from Dornburg – but the marshal took his own time in moving south – enough time that I Corps spent the day on the road, missing the opportunity of putting the finishing touch on Jena and the chance of winning glory alongside Davout at Auerstedt. One might, indeed, consider Bernadotte's pique-generated misfortune as oddly paradigmatic for French performances on the tactical level that day. At Jena the Prussians fought so well at the regimental level, and some of Napoleon's subordinates (Ney in particular) encountered enough difficulties, that the emperor was constrained to manage the battle at the tactical level – to the point where he lost contact with other formations. Soult, perhaps Murat, received no orders at all during the day. And Davout, far from intercepting a broken-spirited retreat, ran headlong into the main Prussian army at Auerstedt: more than 60,000 against fewer than 30,000. In some of the finest fighting ever done on a smoothbore battlefield Davout's corps took 25 per cent casualties and broke an army. ⁴⁷

VI   No Escape

French historian François-Guy Hourtoulle aphorizes Jena–Auerstedt as Napoleon winning a battle he could not lose and Davout winning a battle he could not win.⁴⁸ It can also be interpreted as a battle structured operationally and decided tactically. Napoleon may have misinterpreted details of the limited intelligence he received, but on the whole he evaluated and processed the

---

45   Bernadotte to Berthier, 13 October 1806, 8:00 PM, cited in *Napoleon's Finest*, 122–123.
46   Chandler, *Jena 1806*, 24.
47   See the analysis in Pierre Charrier, *Le maréchal Davout* (Paris, 2005), 165–208.
48   A major subtext of Hourtoulle, *Jena–Auerstedt*.

information perceptively enough to impel his enemies to retreat without first giving battle, and then to bring his whole force to bear on their flank and rear. Certainly Davout's men performed beyond reasonable expectations in winning their commander the title "Duke of Auerstedt" (though only in 1808: Napoleon jealously hoarded that kind of recognition). It may be said as well, however, that had Bernadotte acted according to Napoleon's clear intentions, Auerstedt might have been much less near-run. Fifteen thousand muskets would have substantially lessened the odds, and Bernadotte himself was no mean battle captain.

In the event, Napoleon had to come to grips with the fact that he had engaged only the lesser part of the Prussian–Saxon army. On receiving Davout's initial report from Auerstedt Napoleon incredulously – or sarcastically – asked whether the shortsighted marshal had been seeing double. But in the bulletin of the Grande Armée published on the 15th, Davout was lauded handsomely for "bravery and firmness of character" which had "performed wonders."[49] In another housekeeping matter, Napoleon prepared the documents for Bernadotte's court-martial – then changed his mind. He may have been mellowed as he processed the double victory. He may have remembered Bernadotte was married to Napoleon's one-time fiancée, whom he had abandoned for Josephine. Perhaps Napoleon reasoned that his practice of encouraging rivalry and friction among his marshals must inevitably produce this kind of fallout, yet all had ended well. And perhaps the emperor saw the advantages of having to hand an entirely fresh corps with a commander who had a good deal to prove to the rest of the army – and perhaps himself.[50]

Certainly Bernadotte played a leading role in the pursuit that confirmed the Jena campaign as an early example and an enduring masterpiece of operational art. At Auerstedt, 14 October ended around 4:30 PM with Davout ordering a halt to a pursuit clearly beyond the capacities of his exhausted men. At Jena, Murat led his troopers in a final charge, and a pursuit that by 6:00 PM brought them to the gates of Weimar and garnered 6,000 prisoners. Ney's vanguard reached Apolda and linked up with Bernadotte's lethargic advance from Dornburg – too late to cut the Prussian–Saxon line of retreat, able only to round up stragglers. Thus far, it was a more or less typical follow-up of even a one-sided victory. Sustained pursuits were no less rare in the Napoleonic era than in the 18th century. Black-powder battles were fought at ranges close enough that winners were usually as exhausted as losers, without the

---

49 Chandler, *Campaigns of Napoleon*, 488–489.
50 Ibid., 485–497; Bernadotte to Napoleon, 14 October 1806, in Foucart, *Campagne de Prusse, 1806*, 1:697.

adrenalin rush of fear to fuel activity. Denouements usually occurred toward evening; dusk and dark invited "own-goal" accidents. Casualties disrupted organization. Aside from the human desire to find out who was still alive and unwounded, the question of exactly "who commanded what" often took sorting out. Nor could commanders expect prompt and precise reports. Emperors were not exempt from the effects of stress and fatigue. Napoleon spent the immediate aftermath of Austerlitz riding more or less aimlessly across the battlefield. At Jena he fell asleep studying his maps. Not until 5:00 AM on 15 October did orders for a general pursuit emerge from imperial headquarters.

And what a pursuit it became. The Prussian and Saxon armies were already beginning to unravel – less because, as often alleged, their "unreformed" nature rendered them fragile than because they had given all they had on the 14th. Officers lost touch with their men, and men with their officers. Straggling and desertion became endemic, with companies and regiments dissolving into an undifferentiated mass.

Napoleon's orders assigned Soult, Ney, and Murat's light cavalry to keep up direct pressure on the Allies. Augereau and Lannes on the left, Davout and Bernadotte on the right, were to forge ahead, occupying Halle, Dresden, and the Elbe River crossings before the Saxons and Prussians reached them. This proved overoptimistic. Murat rounded up as many as 14,000 demoralized prisoners at Erfurt by nightfall on the 16th. But the sorely tried infantry were slower off the mark – except for Bernadotte. His corps not only reached Halle on the 16th, but scattered the 15,000 troops originally left there as a reserve: the last substantial organized Prussian force in the field.[51]

Napoleon simultaneously moved a piece on his policy chessboard by treating Saxony as a neutral state and releasing its army on parole without benefit of a peace treaty.[52] It was the first step in developing Saxony as a client-cum-ally that, as a kingdom in the Confederation of the Rhine, would provide some of Napoleon's best and most reliable troops for the next seven years. It was Saxon cuirassiers who led the way into the Great Redoubt at Borodino in 1812. The emperor made a strategic decision as well, rerouting the line of communication to his rear base at Mainz directly to Erfurt. This one was less obviously successful. Soult, in particular, denounced the increased plundering that fostered indiscipline sufficiently extreme to endanger the lives of officers seeking to enforce discipline and that, more seriously, destroyed resources wantonly. Nevertheless – or perhaps in consequence – with Bernadotte setting the pace

---

51   The following account's military aspects are based on Chandler, *Campaigns of Napoleon*, 497–502, and Petre's more extended narrative in *Napoleon's Conquest of Prussia*, 181–300.
52   Blaschke, "Sachsen zwischen Preussen und Napoleon," 145–146.

the other corps followed on, caught up, and reached the Elbe on 20 October. Davout crossed the next day at Wittenberg. Lannes got his vanguard across a repaired bridge that evening. Bernadotte was trying to improvise a bridge as Ney and Soult closed in on Magdeburg. Though the Prussians had managed to run faster than they were being chased, the way to Berlin – and presumably the end of the war – was wide open. By the evening of the 24th, French cavalry had entered the city. Davout's corps received the honor of leading the next day's victory march.

Yet victory remained incomplete. The most effective element of the Prussian army, now under Hohenlohe (Brunswick had been mortally wounded at Auerstedt), had withdrawn toward the Pomeranian fortress of Stettin on the Oder River in the hope of getting support from the Russians. That was now Napoleon's major concern as well; he sent Lannes's V and Bernadotte's I Corps and the ubiquitous light cavalry of Murat in pursuit. On 28 October, the French advance guard overtook Hohenlohe at Prenzlau. Murat, a Gascon to rival Cyrano de Bergerac himself, blithely informed Hohenlohe on his word of honor that he was surrounded by 100,000 men. After brief dithering, the Prussian surrendered his command, by now only 10,000 strong, to half that number. Stettin and its garrison of 5,000 capitulated the next day – without firing a shot, and to a brigade of light cavalry(!). Twenty thousand more Prussian bits and pieces, rallied around General Gebhard Leberecht von Blücher, headed for the Hanseatic city of Lübeck in the hope of being evacuated by the Royal Navy. Instead Bernadotte caught up with him, and on 5 and 6 November the last and largest force of fugitives from Jena–Auerstedt downed its arms. Magdeburg and its 22,000 ostensible defenders surrendered to Ney on the 8th.[53] With further resistance seeming futile and pointless, smaller forces and lesser fortresses followed suit like beads pulled from a string. Well might Murat have informed his master that the fighting was over because no enemy remained.

VII Aftermath

The Jena campaign stands as the first masterpiece of operational art. In less than two months, Napoleon crushed the army and overran the territory of a great power. Prussia, however, was humiliated but not destroyed. Napoleon's seemingly total victory instead generated a sense of nothing left to lose. The

---

53 Wilfried Luebeck, "8. November 1806. Die Kapitulation von Magdeburg, die feige Tat des Governeurs von Kleist?" in Tullner, *1806: Jena, Auerstedt*, 140–152.

war party, inspired by Queen Marie Louise, whom Napoleon called "the best man in Prussia," kept the field in company with Russia. And the next eight months demonstrated a paradox. The same factors that had enabled operational art had also expanded war's scope and scale beyond operational art's capacity to decide. At Friedland on 14 June 1807, after almost twenty-four hours of fighting, Napoleon gained a tactical victory that directly led to political triumph: a negotiated peace with Russia, and a dictated one on far harsher terms to Prussia. Tilsit brought Napoleon to the peak of his power and influence. But neither the Grande Armée nor its commander had been able to replicate the operational mastery of the Jena campaign, or the mastery of France's enemies that it produced.

Over half a year in Poland and East Prussia dulled the Grande Armée's edge – and arguably Napoleon's as well. The weather was much worse, marching distances much further, and foraging prospects much less than in the compact west. Logistic and replacement systems were overstretched. The Russians proved consistently unobliging enemies, neither readily outmaneuvered nor readily outfought. The fighting took place far from Muscovy's heartland and on other peoples' ground. No serious possibilities existed of breaking the enemy army, much less the enemy country, in the operational context Napoleon was developing.[54] The result was not peace but a heavily armed, mutually suspicious truce between France and Russia that lasted no more than five years – and a domestic reform movement that set Prussia on the path toward a primacy in Europe that proved no less ephemeral than Napoleon's.

In a final irony, both of those empires were founded upon operational art, and both fell because they failed to understand its limitations. Let it never be said that Clio and Bellona lack a sense of humor.

Bibliography

Bowden, Scott, et al., eds. *Napoleon's Finest: Marshal Louis Davout and His III Corps*. Remington, VA, 2006.

Bressonnet, Pascal. *Études tactiques sur le campagne de 1806 (Saalfeld–Iéna–Auerstedt)*, trans. by Scott Bowden as *Napoleon's Apogee*. Berkeley, CA, 2009.

---

54 Chandler, *Campaigns of Napoleon*, 507ff., and F.L. Petre, *Napoleon's Campaign in Poland, 1806–1807: A Military History of Napoleon's First War with Russia* (London, 1907), are standards. C.J. Summerville, *Napoleon's Polish Gamble: Eylau and Friedland, 1807* (Barnsley, UK, 2005), is recent and readable.

Chandler, David G. *The Campaigns of Napoleon: The Mind and Method of History's Greatest Soldier.* New York, 1966.

Chandler, David G. "Napoleon, Operational Art, and the Jena Campaign." In Michael D. Krause and R. Cody Philips, eds, *Historical Perspectives of the Operational Art.* Washington, DC, 2007.

Elting, John R. *Swords Around a Throne: Napoleon's Grande Armée.* New York, 1988.

Epstein, Robert M. "Patterns of Change and Continuity in Nineteenth-Century Warfare." *Journal of Military History* 56 (1992), 375–388.

Foucart, Paul Jean, ed. *Campagne de Prusse, 1806: d'apres les archives de la guerre*, 2 vols. Paris, 1887.

Fresser, Gerd and Reinhard Jonscher, eds. *Umbruch im Schatten Napoleons. Die Schlachten von Jena und Auerstaedt und ihre Folgen.* Jena, 1998.

Paret, Peter. *The Cognitive Challenge of War: Prussia 1806.* Princeton, NJ, 2009.

Telp, Claus. *The Evolution of Operational Art, 1740–1813: From Frederick the Great to Napoleon.* London, 2005.

Van Creveld, Martin. "Napoleon and the Dawn of Operational Warfare." In John Andreas Olsen and Martin van Creveld, eds, *The Evolution of Operational Art: From Napoleon to the Present.* New York, 2011.

CHAPTER 8

Napoleon's Operational Warfare during the First Polish Campaign, 1806–1807

Alexander Mikaberidze and John H. Gill

The campaigns during the winter of 1806–1807 and the spring of 1807 provide further opportunities to examine Napoleon's practice of the operational art and the intersection of his operational actions with his larger strategic considerations. This period of the War of the Fourth Coalition encompasses three campaigns (or "maneuvers" as they were termed in the nineteenth century), each of which resulted in a major engagement or battle. The first two, Pultusk in December 1806 and Eylau in January–February 1807, ended indecisively despite great exertion and bloodshed. The third, Friedland in May–June 1807, led to one of the French emperor's great battlefield triumphs and a favorable conclusion to the war. Whether initiated by Napoleon or in reaction to Russian moves, each of the three offers valuable insights into Napoleon's art of war and the limitations he encountered in attempting to fight his style of campaign in the geographic and climatic conditions of Poland and eastern Prussia.[1]

The Jena campaign of October–November 1806 lasted just four weeks, but it precipitated the military and political collapse of Prussia, which in turn had immense and immediate ramifications on the war. In contrast to his victory over Austria in 1805, Napoleon insisted on organizing a victory parade in Berlin, where the prisoners from the Prussian Gardes du Corps, who just weeks before had sharpened their swords on the French embassy's steps, were prominently featured. The war not only destroyed Prussia's martial reputation but also ended Berlin's claim to be a great power. In return for an armistice, Napoleon demanded vast concessions from Prussia's King Frederick William III: all Prussian territory, except for Magdeburg and Altmark, on the left bank of the Elbe and a debilitating war indemnity. Napoleon gave the king one week to comply, but as more and more Prussian cities and fortresses surrendered, the emperor increased his demands, adding the requirement that Prussia

---

1 Note that no Polish state existed at this time as Russia, Prussia, and Austria had partitioned the former Kingdom of Poland out of existence by 1795. Napoleon revived a Polish political entity called the Duchy of Warsaw as part of the Treaties of Tilsit in July 1807, but this became a source of serious friction with Russia.

surrender all territory east of the Vistula. Frederick William rejected the terms and fled, along with his family and court, to the fortress of Königsberg in East Prussia, where he desperately grasped at the straw of salvation proffered by Russia.

March to Contact (November–December 1806)

Technically, Russia and France remained at war after the collapse of the Third Coalition in 1805. Although Austria had signed the Treaty of Pressburg on 26 December 1805 that formally ended the Third Coalition, Tsar Alexander I had refused to submit to the French emperor. Consequently, a state of hostility persisted between his empire and Napoleon's (albeit with few active combat operations) as Russia recovered from the disaster at Austerlitz. Russia and Prussia reached an accommodation in the summer of 1806, and Russian promises of support had helped convince Frederick William III to embark on the calamitous Jena campaign in October of that year. Apparently hoping to bloody Napoleon's nose before the onset of winter and to buy time for their allies to enter the lists (see Chapter 6), the Prussians advanced before the tsar's troops had even approached the Russo-Prussian border more than 640 kilometers to the east. Frederick William and his army were thus alone when they encountered Napoleon and the Grande Armée at Jena–Auerstedt. In the aftermath of that debacle, all that remained of the Prussian army were scattered fortress garrisons and a small remnant field force numbering only some 20,000 men. This meant that Russia would face Napoleon almost entirely on its own during the winter and spring campaigns in Poland.

Napoleon had no interest in carrying his successful war into Russia proper. Indeed, he had hoped for an accommodation with Alexander so he could pursue his struggle with Great Britain, but the tsar had rejected his offer in July 1806. Therefore, Napoleon's strategic aim in the late fall/early winter of 1806 was to end the war rapidly with a decisive military victory that would capitalize on the triumph at Jena and open a path to a political settlement with Alexander. The tsar, however, was determined to support his Prussian ally despite Frederick William's desperately weakened condition. This decision left the French emperor no choice but to continue the war against the Russian armies now entering Poland. Russia had learned valuable lessons at Austerlitz and had used the lull in hostilities during 1806 to reorganize and reform its military forces. The Russians recruited more than 600,000 men from 31 provinces to create new regiments and divisions.² These vast human resources allowed Alexander to establish three armies for the campaign in Poland. Two of these, marching generally toward the area north of Warsaw, would form the principal force committed to contending with Napoleon's Grande Armée: General Levin (Leontii Leontievich) von Bennigsen (70,000 men with 276 guns) and General Friedrich Wilhelm (Fedor Fedorovich) von Buxhöwden (55,000 men with 216 guns). A smaller, third force under General Magnus Gustav (Ivan Nikolaevich) von Essen (37,000 men, 132 guns) was approaching from Moldavia to guard the Russian strategic left flank and shield Russian territory from any French forays to the east.³

Following the victory at Jena–Auerstedt, Napoleon split the Grande Armée into two large, ad hoc groups.⁴ The first, consisting of VI, I, and IV Corps with much of the Reserve Cavalry, remained preoccupied with the pursuit and destruction of the Prussian units that had escaped Jena–Auerstedt. Thus, VI Corps besieged the fortress of Magdeburg while I and IV Corps with the Reserve Cavalry pursued Prussian forces under General Gebhard Leberecht von Blücher north toward the Baltic coast. The second part of the French army moved into cantonments: Lannes's V Corps in and around Stettin, Davout's III Corps at Frankfurt-an-der-Oder, and Augereau's VII Corps, the Imperial Guard, and the remainder of the Reserve Cavalry billeted in Berlin; the Bavarian corps camped near Crossen. As soon as the first group completed the task of subduing the remaining Prussians, Napoleon intended to concentrate his army and march east to face the approaching Russians. The emperor was still unaware of the Russian army's strength and positions. Therefore, he instructed the commanders of the corps closest to the Oder River to conduct forceful reconnaissance.⁵ Marshal Davout, who had established his headquarters at Frankfurt-an-der-

---

2 Alexander Mikhailovsky-Danilevsky, *Opisanie vtoroi voiny Imperatora Aleksandra s Napoleonom v 1806–1807 godakh* (St. Petersburg, 1846), 47–53.

3 Order of Battle of Bennigsen's, Buxhöwden's and Essen's Corps, ibid., 63n, 69n, 71–72. See also Army Rosters, RGVIA, f. 846, op. 16, d. 3164, ll. 25–33. Essen is often termed "Essen I" to distinguish him from other officers with the same name such as Peter Kirillich von Essen ("Essen III"), who commanded the Russian 8th Division in this campaign.

4 For a general discussion of the operations in late 1806, see Eduard von Höpfner, *Der Krieg von 1806 und 1807* (Berlin, 1850), 3:1–157; Mathieu Dumas, *Précis des événemens militaires, ou, Essais historiques sur les campagnes de 1799 à 1814* (Paris, 1826), 27:99–205; Karl Ritter von Landmann, *Der Krieg von 1806 und 1807: auf Grund urkundlichen Materials sowie der neuesten Forschungen und Quellen* (Berlin, 1909), 300–327; Carl von Plotho, *Tagebuch während des Krieges zwischen Russland und Preussen einerseits, und Frankreich andrerseits, in den Jahren 1806 und 1807* (Berlin, 1811), 1–43; F. Lorraine Petre, *Napoleon's Campaign in Poland, 1806-7* (London, 1901), 59–118.

5 CN, Nos 11141, 11151, and 11160, Napoleon to Berthier, Davout, and Lannes, 2–3 November 1806, 13:454, 460–461, 467.

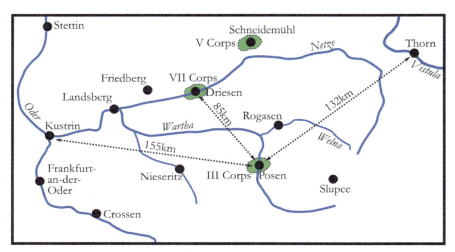

MAP 8.1 Napoleon's forward corps deployment, early November 1806

Oder, received overall command of these reconnaissance missions, which involved the light cavalry from III, V, and VII Corps as well as the Bavarian contingent crossing the Oder River and operating as far away as Landsberg and Posen, some 160 kilometers from his headquarters. As the reconnaissance revealed that the Russians had yet to reach Warsaw, Napoleon instructed his corps to move their main forces across the Oder: on 8–9 November, III Corps marched toward Posen, VII Corps to Driesen, and V Corps to Schneidemühl.

Napoleon's instructions demonstrate the flexibility inherent in his operational art. His orders for Davout stressed that, should the Russians attack III Corps, the marshal would reconnoiter "all crossing points on the Wartha River" and take up "a strong position" near Posen, where the other corps (V and VII) would converge. If forced to retreat, the marshal would select a second position where all three French corps (III, V, and VII) could unite west of the Wartha and maintain a direct line of operation with Stettin. Furthermore, new intelligence reports indicated that the Russians had some 50,000 men, who, Napoleon reasoned, could not reach any important objective all at the same time. He assumed that the enemy's lead units (5 columns of 5,000 men each, according to Napoleon's calculation) would reach Thorn by 8 November but that the rest would not arrive until the 20th, which meant that Napoleon could easily mass his forces and achieve numerical superiority: by having his available forces unite near Posen, he would have some 80,000 men. If, despite these calculations, the Russians managed to unite their forces and attack Davout before I, IV, and VI Corps completed the destruction of the Prussian forces currently retreating north toward the Baltic coast, Napoleon intended for Davout to withdraw to the western bank of the Wartha and hold his positions until additional forces arrived. If the enemy advanced northward, III, V, and VII Corps would serve as the screening force while I, IV, and VI Corps would become the *masse de manoeuvre* with which Napoleon could strike one of the enemy's flanks.

Fortune favored the French. By the second week of November, the remnants of the Prussian army had surrendered, with Blücher capitulating near Lübeck on 7 November and the fortress of Magdeburg falling the following day. Napoleon thus regained additional corps to send eastward to support Davout against the slowly advancing Russians. In accordance with the new imperial instructions, Davout moved his headquarters to Posen and pushed his light cavalry outposts further east, with some French scouts venturing as far as Kalisch and Thorn (110 kilometers east of Posen). As the Russians were still far away, Napoleon ordered III, V, and VII Corps to converge on Thorn, which the French occupied on 18 November.[6] By the end of the month, Napoleon had concentrated the rest of the Grande Armée around Posen, where the emperor arrived on 27 November. Threatened by the French advance, the Russians evacuated Warsaw on 1 December and retreated behind the Bug and Narew Rivers, destroying the local bridges to delay the French pursuit. Napoleon learned of the Russian retreat on 5 December and urged his corps commanders to reach the Vistula River. Assuming that the Russians would continue to fall back, Napoleon directed VI Corps to Thorn and ordered III Corps to seize Sierock (20 kilometers north of Warsaw), where it would control the confluence of the Narew and Vistula Rivers and thus safeguard the northern approaches to Warsaw. He sent VII Corps to Zakroczin and Wyszogrod while tasking V Corps with occupying Warsaw and its suburbs. Surprised that his forces encountered only modest resistance while crossing the Vistula, the emperor sent letters to his marshals explaining his operational concept in the event of a Russian counteroffensive. If the Russians counterattacked along the Pultusk–Sierock route, V and VII Corps would maintain positions around Zakroczin and support III Corps as it conducted a holding action near Sierock, where Davout would "defend with all his strength a bridgehead on the Narew." Believing that III Corps would halt the Russian advance near Sierock, Napoleon planned to move V and VII Corps in a flanking maneuver against the Russian right flank while Murat would sweep behind the enemy lines with all of the army's

---

6 CN, Nos 11251, 11257, and 11258, Napoleon to Davout and Lannes 13–14 November 1806, 13:529–530, 537–538. See also 32nd Bulletin, 16 November 1806, ibid., 545–546.

cavalry. Should the Russians move north and threaten Ney's VI Corps, the emperor instructed the marshal to avoid a pitched battle, move across the Vistula, and hold his ground long enough to allow the Grande Armée's right flank (three army corps strong) to make a flanking maneuver against the Russian left.[7] Whether on the offense or defense, this was Napoleon's preferred course of action at the broadest level: hold the opposing force in place with one part of his army while the other portion maneuvered to strike the flank or rear of an enemy that had already committed its reserves.

The Maneuver of Pultusk (December 1806)

On entering Poland, Napoleon's fundamental objective was to occupy a position on the Vistula with suitable bridgeheads at Thorn and Warsaw from which he could launch a spring offensive. Thus ensconced, he could rest his weary army, reduce the Prussian fortresses in his rear, and rally the restive Poles to his side. In total, the emperor could count on more than 120,000 men in six corps, the reserve cavalry (now split into two formations), and his elite Guard.[8] Additional forces, mainly from his German allies of the Confederation of the Rhine, conducted rear-area duties such as blockading and besieging Prussian fortresses.[9] Given the absence of intelligence regarding Russian movements and the surprising ease with which the French had seized the crossings over the Vistula, Napoleon continued to press forward. By mid-December, he deployed the Grande Armée along a 160-kilometer front extending from Strasburg to Warsaw. While I Corps and the Guard remained at Thorn, Napoleon again split the rest of the army into two groups: the right wing consisted of Augereau's VII Corps at Zakroczin, Davout's III Corps near Nowy Dwor at the confluence of the Narew and the Vistula, and V Corps at Warsaw; the left wing included Ney's VI Corps at Strasburg and Marshal Nicolas Jean-de-Dieu Soult's IV Corps stretched between Rippin and Dobrzyn. Murat's cavalry maintained communication between the two wings. As before, the French deployment underscores the simple yet effective nature of Napoleon's operations. If the Russians decided to move toward Warsaw, III and V Corps supported by VII

---

7 *CN*, Nos 11422 and 11430, Napoleon to Murat and Ney, 9–10 December, 14:55–56, 61–62. Napoleon underscored the important role cavalry played in his operational plan: to explore the countryside, maintain communication between the army's flanks, and to constantly harass and push "the Russian cavalry back on to its infantry."

8 Strengths from Paul-Jean Foucart, *Campagne de Pologne* (Paris, 2006), 2, Organization Tables.

9 Saxony, a foe on the field of Jena by way of Prussian coercion, joined the Confederation of the Rhine (or Rheinbund) on 11 December 1806 under the Treaty of Posen.

Corps would pin them down while the rest of the army attacked from the northwest; if the enemy chose a northern route toward Thorn (via Soldau/Strasburg), VI and IV Corps would pin them down while the right wing attacked from the south.

Napoleon's dispositions also facilitated the offensive operations that he formulated in mid-December from his headquarters at Posen. Baffled by the seemingly incomprehensible Russian movements, the emperor sought an opportunity to retain the initiative and end the war immediately rather than waiting for spring.[10] A quick conclusion to the conflict would have the additional bonus of quashing any thoughts Austria might entertain of interfering in the war to avenge its defeat at Austerlitz the previous year. Napoleon thus commenced operations in an effort to catch the Russians between the Wkra and Narew Rivers, an operation known as the "maneuver of Pultusk." His broad concept was to push north from the Warsaw/Zakroczin area with III, V, and VII Corps and part of the cavalry ("I CC" on Map 8.2) while Marshal Bernadotte advanced on Beizun with a wing comprising I and VI Corps and the remainder of the cavalry ("II CC" on Map 8.2); Soult's IV Corps would connect the two wings.[11] In addition to driving the Russians back and, he hoped, precipitating a decisive battle, this maneuver would separate the Russian corps from the remnant of the Prussian forces around Soldau and the Prussian royal court at Königsberg. Although his complex operation required close coordination over great distances in a poorly mapped region under execrable weather, Napoleon, underestimating the difficulties, hoped for a decisive outcome before the end of December.

Internal squabbles in the Russian camp facilitated Napoleon's operations. The Russian army commanders, Generals Buxhöwden and Bennigsen, disliked each other and refused to cooperate. Exasperated by their bickering and lamenting that he had "not a single good general with the talent of being a commander-in-chief," Tsar Alexander chose Field Marshal Count Mikhail Fedotovich Kamensky to lead Russian forces.[12] This was a poor choice. The ailing sixty-nine-year old Kamensky had not commanded an army since the death of Catherine the Great in 1796. In one letter to Alexander, for example, he bemoaned that he was "too old to lead an army; I cannot see much and I

---

10 Frédéric Naulet, *Eylau: La campagne de Pologne, des boues de Pultusk aux neiges d'Eylau* (Paris, 2007), 58–62.
11 For the evolution of Napoleon's concepts, see Georges Germain Félix Lechartier, *La manoeuvre de Pultusk* (Paris, 1911), 487–491.
12 Alexander to Tolstoy, date not indicated, in Mikhailovsky-Danilevsky, *Opisanie vtoroi voiny Imperatora Aleksandra*, 72–73. General Mikhail Kutuzov, one of the few able Russian commanders, was disgraced after the defeat at Austerlitz.

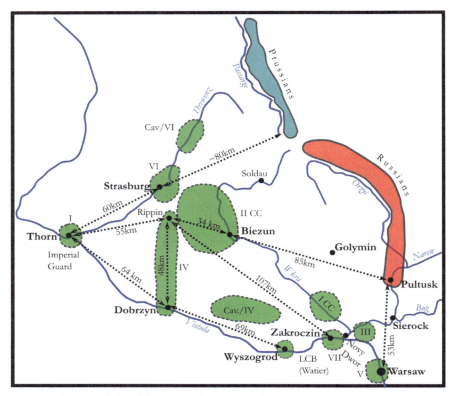

MAP 8.2 The Grande Armée's corps deployments, mid-December 1806

cannot I ride a horse ... I am unfamiliar with this region and cannot locate sites on a map ... I am signing [orders] not knowing what they prescribe."[13] Unmoved, the tsar named him commander-in-chief in December. Initially wanting to concentrate his forces, Kamensky ordered Bennigsen to fall back from the Vistula to the line of the River Wkra, where he could unite with Buxhöwden's forces, which were about ten days away. However, with Napoleon advancing, Kamensky belatedly realized his mistake of conceding the Vistula and allowing the French to cross the river unhindered. Consequently, he instructed Bennigsen to advance in an attempt to regain the line of the Vistula but the corps commander demurred, correctly pointing out that the French had already taken positions along both the Vistula and the Narew Rivers. As a result, Bennigsen retreated east to hold the line of the Wkra.

---

13   Kamensky to Alexander, 22 December 1807, ibid., 76.

In worsening weather, the Grande Armée marched deeper into Poland to engage the Russians in accordance with Napoleon's operational concept.[14] This advance resulted in two bloody yet inconclusive engagements as the French, slogging north between the Wkra and the Narew, intersected with the Russians retreating east. Unfortunately for the French, Napoleon had misread the enemy situation. With no time to establish a reliable spy network, and cavalry reconnaissance hampered by bad roads and omnipresent Cossack patrols, Napoleon assumed the Russian main body was withdrawing north through Golymin. In fact, Bennigsen and the bulk of his command had slipped away east to Pultusk, while French pressure forced only a disparate collection of Russian detachments to retreat via Golymin.

Confusion and misperceptions in both headquarters resulted in the exhausted armies fighting two brutal but disconnected engagements on 26 December under dreadful weather conditions. At Golymin, three French columns (Augereau, Murat, and Davout) caught an assortment of Russian units more or less under the command of General Dmitry Vladimirovich Golitsyn, whose troops were too exhausted to march further. Despite the muddled Russian command arrangements, the various generals succeeded in supporting one another while the three French columns failed to coordinate their attacks. Furthermore, although they enjoyed a manpower superiority of some 31,000 against the 16,000–18,000 Russians of Golitsyn's ad hoc force, the French were at a distinct disadvantage in artillery, having only a handful of guns to post against the three dozen available to their foes. Murat opened the fight in the center around 2:00 p.m., but his cavalry struggled painfully in the mud and his attack soon stalled. Meanwhile, on the French left, Augereau proved excessively tentative and failed to press Golitsyn with sufficient vigor. He and Murat had largely exhausted themselves by the time one of Davout's divisions approached from the south on the French right late in the day. Largely due to Golitsyn's skill in deploying his slender reserves, the Russians parried each French advance separately during the brief winter afternoon. In fact, Murat reported to Napoleon that he faced 50,000 Russians at Golymin.[15] Sporadic fighting continued well beyond sunset, but the desperate Russians retained their hold on the town and conducted an orderly withdrawal to the northeast under the cover of darkness. Each side lost some 800 men in the fighting.

---

14 "Snow, rain and thaw ... we sunk down to our knees ... and our shoes would stick in the wet mud," recalled Jean-Roch Coignet, in *The Narrative of Captain Coignet, Soldier of the Empire, 1776–1850* (New York, 1890), 138. For the Russian perspective, see Alexander Mikaberidze, ed., *Russian Eyewitness Accounts of the Campaign of 1807* (London, 2015), 27–108.

15 Höpfner, *Der Krieg von 1806 und 1807*, 3:126.

On the same day, about 20 kilometers to the southeast, another bloody battle raged throughout the day at Pultusk on the Narew River. Here the numerical advantage was reversed. Lannes, with approximately 19,000 men, was advancing to seize the town and establish a bridgehead on the east bank of the river. Believing he faced only a retreating Russian rearguard of 8,000 to 10,000, he attacked immediately upon reaching Pultusk around 10:00 a.m. In reality, he struck Bennigsen's main body of 45,000 in a well-contrived defensive position; his V Corps soon found itself fighting for its existence. Lannes, aggressive and audacious, continued his assaults on the strong Russian position even when it should have been obvious that he was both badly outnumbered and badly outgunned: Bennigsen possessed at least 120 pieces whereas the French had only been able to move 5 or so through the all-consuming mud. Although the French demonstrated great élan in repeatedly driving back the Russians, their foes were equally courageous, consistently restoring their positions and shattering French attacks. By afternoon, Lannes faced the real possibility of a crushing defeat. He was saved by the unexpected arrival of the 3rd Division of Davout's III Corps under General Joseph Augustin Daultane (Gudin, its regular commander, was ill). Davout had sent Daultane south toward Pultusk while the rest of his corps slogged north to Golymin on the morning of the 26th. Daultane, hearing the rumble of battle to his front late in the afternoon, honorably marched to the sound of the guns to appear on Lannes's left flank in the nick of time with his 5,000 men. He attacked at once. Such a small force could not turn the tide of the struggle in favor of the French but, by surprising Bennigsen and forestalling a Russian counterstroke against Lannes, he was able to gain enough time for night to bring the fighting to an end. It had been a vicious battle. The French suffered 3,000 to 4,000 casualties and the Russians probably more. Lannes, who was lucky to avoid a severe repulse, wrote on the following day: "in all my years of war, I have never seen a more bitter combat."[16] Bennigsen, who claimed that he had defeated 50,000 French under Napoleon himself, recognized that his position was perilous and chose to retreat after the battle despite the censure he faced from other Russian officers.

The battles at Pultusk and Golymin demonstrated that Napoleon could not hope for the swift and brilliant victories that had crowned his previous campaigns. Poland, one of the poorest regions in Europe, contained scarce resources for man and horse, and an inferior communication network; decent maps were practically non-existent. Miserable weather further complicated the situation, turning the roads into sloughs of cold, cloying mud. "It rained or snowed incessantly," complained one French officer. "Provisions became very

---

16   Lannes to Napoleon, 27 December 1806, in Foucart, *Campagne de Pologne*, 4:465.

scarce – no more wine, hardly any beer, and what there was – exceedingly bad; muddy water, no bread, and quarters for which we had to fight with the pigs and the cows."[17] Under such conditions, comprehensive intelligence, operational coordination, and rapid movement – the hallmarks of Napoleon's campaigns – were rarely attainable. He was "strategically blind," his army "lost in a sea of mud."[18] Present at neither Golymin nor Pultusk, Napoleon remained at Lopacin, 20 and 30 kilometers from the battlefields respectively, waiting in vain for definitive information; he did not learn of the combat at Pultusk until 27 December – twenty-four hours after the engagement. The gamble represented by the maneuver of Pultusk thus failed in the execution and led only to costly stalemates in the engagements of 26 December. In Clausewitz's terms, Napoleon's campaign had reached its culminating point. Nonetheless, the emperor had at least succeeded in stalling any possible Russian advance, in isolating the great fortress of Danzig on the Baltic, and in securing for himself large parts of Poland that would supply thousands of new recruits for the next campaign.[19]

With the Russians retreating northward, Napoleon decided to move his army into winter quarters.[20] After the grueling campaign, he hoped to rest the troops and improve his overstretched and inadequate logistical system.[21] Accordingly, he established a series of supply depots along the Vistula and instructed each corps to forage within a carefully allotted area. A quick glance at the map of French cantonments indicates that Napoleon employed his preferred operational formation, the *bataillon carré*, which underpinned French strategic flexibility and mobility in the early campaigns of the Napoleonic Wars. In case of a Russian attack, VI Corps would concentrate at Mlawa, IV Corps at Golymin, III Corps at Pultusk, V Corps at Sierock, and VII Corps at

---

17   Jean-Baptiste-Antoine-Marcelin Baron de Marbot, *The Memoirs of Baron de Marbot* (New York, 1903), 1:193. Conditions for the Russians, of course, were no better; see Sacken's diary notes from 27 December in Mikaberidze, ed., *Russian Eyewitness Accounts*, 96.
18   Lechartier, *La manoeuvre de Pultusk*, 337, 473. Lechartier faults Bernadotte for failing to move aggressively to contribute to the fighting on 26 December.
19   Naulet, *Eylau*, 93; Stéphane Béraud, *La révolution militaire Napoléonienne* (Paris, 2007), 286; Lechartier, *La manoeuvre de Pultusk*, 473–502.
20   For a discussion of the operations in late 1806, see Höpfner, *Der Krieg von 1806 und 1807*, 3:1–157; Dumas, *Précis des évènemens militaires*, 17:99–205; Landmann, *Der Krieg von 1806 und 1807*, 300–327; Plotho, *Tagebuch*, 1–43; Petre, *Napoleon's Campaign in Poland*, 59–118.
21   For vivid descriptions of the privations endured by both sides, see the collection of memoir extracts in Natalia Griffon de Pleineville and Vladimir Chikanov, *Napoléon en Pologne: la campagne de 1806–1807* (Paris, 2008), 133–158; for a technical analysis of the Grande Armée's logistics during these campaigns, see Georges Germain Félix Lechartier, *Les services de l'arrière à la Grande Armée en 1806–1807* (Paris, 1910).

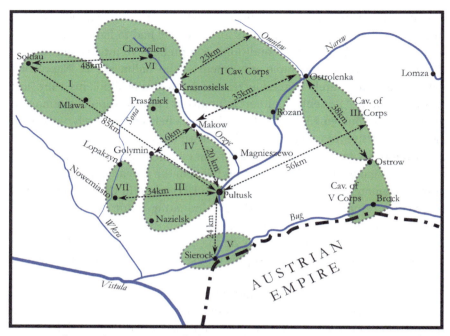

MAP 8.3   The Grande Armée's corps deployments, late-December 1806

Plonsk. Thus, these five corps would form a diamond-shaped formation, with two forward corps separated by a distance of less than 25 kilometers while the rear corps remained one day's march away, allowing Napoleon to concentrate his forces wherever the enemy threatened and "once the desired battle situation came within the realm of possible attainment."[22]

The Eylau Campaign (January–February 1807)

Meanwhile, the Russians changed commanders again. As the first shots fell at Pultusk on 26 December, Kamensky decided that he was too old for such active campaigning and forthwith resigned his post. Bennigsen, who had nominally assumed command during the lull after Pultusk, held a council of war at Nowogrod, where the Russians approved a plan for a winter offensive on 2 January 1807. According to this concept of operations, Bennigsen and Buxhöwden would assemble their respective armies on the Narew and then

---

22   David Chandler, *The Campaigns of Napoleon* (New York, 1966), 154.

make a flanking maneuver through the Johannisburg Forest into East Prussia, from where they would be in a position to threaten the French left. Reconnaissance operations revealed that the French left wing – Bernadotte's I Corps and Ney's VI Corps – was in a precarious position, stretched too far north and separated from the rest of the army. Marshal Ney had exacerbated his vulnerability by extending elements of his VI Corps toward Königsberg in search of rations and fodder despite Napoleon's orders prohibiting any forward movement that could provoke the Russians.[23] Observing Ney's dispositions, Bennigsen concluded that the French were vulnerable to surprise and defeat in detail. Therefore, he decided to attack the French left wing, drive Ney and Bernadotte back to Thorn, and force the rest of the Grande Armée to retreat to the Vistula. This offensive would also serve to protect Königsberg, where the Prussian court and huge Russian supply magazines were located. At the same time, the 37,000 men commanded by Essen I deployed between the Bug and the Narew Rivers to monitor the French right wing.

The Russian army advanced on 6 January, with Bennigsen marching along the Narew via Lomza to Tykoczin, where he arrived on 8 January. There, the long-simmering tensions between Bennigsen and Buxhöwden finally erupted. The latter left the army, but not before challenging his rival to a duel; fortunately for the Russian cause, it never took place. Assuming overall command of the army, Bennigsen led some 70,000 Russians across the ice-covered Bobra River and marched north under the cover of the vast forests to Biala, where they arrived on 14 January.[24]

---

23   Although sufficient provisions were available in Prussia, bad weather and terrible roads complicated their transport to the front. Thus, by mid-January, Ney had dispersed his troops over a vast territory between Bartenstein, Bischofsburg, and Guttstadt: Ney to Berthier, circa January 1807, in Henri Bonnal, *La vie militaire du Maréchal Ney, duc d'Elchingen, prince de la Moskowa* (Paris, 1910), 2:365–366; Marquis de Colbert-Chabanais, *Le général Auguste Colbert (1793–1809): traditions, souvenirs et documents touchant sa vie et son temps* (Paris, 1888), 3:1–11; Colbert to Mme. de Colbert, Colbert to Josephine de Colbert, 15–18 January 1807, in Jeanne A. Ojala, *Auguste de Colbert: Aristocratic Survival in an Era of Upheaval, 1793–1809* (Salt Lake City, 1979), 132–133; Raymond-Aymery-Philippe-Joseph de Montesquiou Fezensac, *Souvenirs militaires de 1804 à 1814* (Paris, 1863), 133–134. Part of the problem arose because of poor communications, specifically the long delay in delivering Napoleon's instructions to Ney; for two different interpretations, see James R. Arnold and Ralph R. Reinertsen, *Crisis in the Snows. Russia Confronts Napoleon: The Eylau Campaign 1806–1807* (Lexington, VA, 2007), 198–206, and Naulet, *Eylau*, 112–117.

24   On paper, Bennigsen commanded some 70,000 men with 276 guns and Buxhöwden's corps numbered 55,000 men with 216 guns. Along with Essen I's 37,000 men and 132 guns, Russian forces amounted to 160,000 men with 624 cannon. However, due to attrition and battle casualties, many units were undermanned. As early as mid-December, Kamensky had complained that Buxhöwden's corps numbered fewer than 40,000 men; its strength

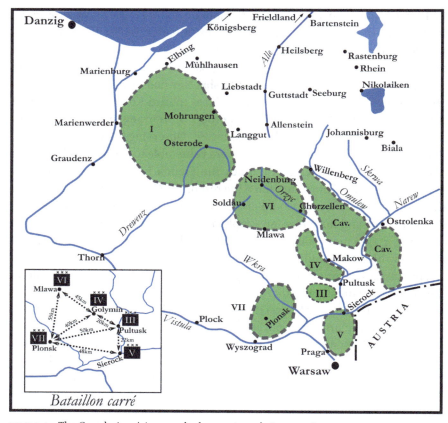

MAP 8.4 The Grande Armée's corps deployments, early January 1807

Meanwhile, French headquarters had yet to collect any detailed information on Russian movements as bad weather, the ubiquitous Cossacks, and unfamiliarity with the region made it difficult to conduct reconnaissance. In early January, Napoleon received little useful intelligence on enemy movements; he remained uncertain about the precise location of the Russian army until the last week of January. On the 18th, he learned that Ney's units had moved closer to Königsberg. The displeased emperor immediately fired off a sharp rebuke to the marshal: "Such individual measures interfere with the

---

was further reduced by the events at Golymin. The situation was equally dire in Bennigsen's corps. See Order of Battle of Bennigsen's, Buxhöwden's and Essen's Corps, in Mikhailovsky-Danilevsky, *Opisanie vtoroi voiny Imperatora Aleksandra*, 63n, 69n, 71–72. See also Army Rosters, RGVIA, f. 846, op. 16, d. 3164, ll. 25–33.

general plan of operations, and are capable of compromising an entire army."[25] Ney complied with orders to fall back to Mlawa but his withdrawal coincided with the start of the Russian offensive that targeted him. Hidden from French reconnaissance, Bennigsen had managed to march his army north from Biala before turning west to appear in Ney's sector unexpectedly. On 19 January, a surprised Ney learned of Russian patrols reconnoitering the roads from Rhein toward Liebstadt, to where the Russian army, with the Prussian corps of General Anton von L'Estocq on its right flank, was advancing in three columns.[26] Ney quickly extricated his forces and, by 22 January, succeeded in concentrating his corps between Soldau and Neidenburg, where he could be covered by Soult's IV Corps on his right and Bernadotte on his left. Supported by the Prussians, the Russian army continued to push west. On 22–23 January, they attacked the French positions around Liebstadt and Mohrungen, where Bennigsen halted the offensive to concentrate his forces.[27]

Although receiving some reports on the Russian movements, Napoleon could not believe that Bennigsen would undertake a winter campaign so soon after Pultusk.[28] Thus, he initially dismissed these reports, insisting that the Russians were simply redeploying their forces in response to Ney's movements. The emperor remained certain that the Russians would take winter quarters as soon as they completed this repositioning. Reports from Ney, Soult, and others all claimed that a large number of Russian troops were concentrating to the north in preparation for an advance between Mühlhausen and Liebstadt.[29]

---

25 Berthier to Ney, 18 January 1807, in Dumas, *Précis des évènements militaires*, 3:324–325. See also Victor-Bernard Derrécagaix, *Le maréchal Berthier, prince de Wagram et de Neuchâtel* (Paris, 1905), 2:193–194.

26 *Zhurnal Voennykh Deistvii Imperatorskoi Rossiiskoi Armii* [hereafter cited as *Journal of Military Operations of the Russian Imperial Army*] (St. Petersburg, 1807), 59 (this journal records all army movements and operations); "Deistvia Russkikh voisk v kampaniu 1806–1807 godov," RGVIA, f. 846, op. 16, d. 3161, ll. 25–26; Höpfner, *Der Krieg von 1806 und 1807*, 3:183–185; Landmann, *Der Krieg von 1806 und 1807*, 330–331; Plotho, *Tagebuch*, 49–51.

27 *Journal of Military Operations of the Russian Imperial Army*, 61–63; Sir Robert Wilson, *Brief Remarks on the Character and Composition of the Russian Army, and a Sketch of the Campaigns in Poland in the Years 1806 and 1807* (London, 1810), 85–86; "Extract of the Reports received from General Bennigsen," St. Petersburg, 7 February 1807, ibid., 237.

28 Davout, for example, interrogated deserters and captured Russian soldiers, informing the emperor that the two Russian corps had united and had been marching to Johannisburg since 15 January.

29 According to Ney, "trustworthy information derived from merchants agrees with the stories of deserters and prisoners in stating that there is a considerable mass of Russian troops assembled at this moment between Mühlhausen and Preußisch Eylau, and that the united army under the command of General Bennigsen is 80,000 men strong": Ney to Berthier, 24 January 1807, in Colbert-Chabanais, *Général Auguste Colbert*, 3:257–258.

Regardless, it took the whole week of 20–27 January to convince the emperor that the Russians had in fact launched a general offensive. Despite this slow start, Napoleon perceived a chance to encircle and defeat his opponent. As usual, once he had made his decision, Napoleon acted with characteristic energy and determination to convert the enemy's unexpected advance into an opportunity: "the emperor does not wish to return to winter quarters until he has annihilated the enemy," wrote Berthier to Ney on 27 January.[30] He anticipated that, by proceeding further westward, Bennigsen would inevitably expose his left flank and rear to the French main army. Accordingly, Napoleon conceived a brilliant *manoeuvre sur les derrières*.[31] Keeping X Corps (16,000 men) at Thorn, Napoleon instructed Bernadotte to fall back to lure Bennigsen further west and into a trap. Bernadotte's retrograde movement would cover Napoleon's real intention of launching a *bataillon carré* along the Chorzellen–Willenberg axis to turn Bennigsen's left flank, drive the Russian army into a narrow spot between the Lower Vistula and the Frisches-Haff (or Vistula Lagoon), and destroy it. Thanks to his previous dispositions, Napoleon could concentrate some 115,000 men against the Russians for his counteroffensive.[32]

Yet, in the words of one Russian officer, "the Russian God was too great" to allow Napoleon's scheme to unfold as he had hoped.[33] By the end of January, Bennigsen's advance guard reached Deutsch Eylau, pushing patrols to Allenstein and Osterode, and between Langgut and Drewenz. General Nikolay Alexeyevich Tuchkov's corps assembled between Mohrungen and Liebemühl while General Fabian Gottlieb von der Osten-Sacken's corps deployed between Guttstadt, Deppen, and Seeburg. General Andrey Andreyevich Somov's 4th Division stood in reserve at Guttstadt; L'Estocq's small Prussian corps reached Freystadt.[34] With Bennigsen still at Mohrungen, a Cossack patrol intercepted a

---

30   Cited in Naulet, *Eylau*, 132.
31   For details, see Höpfner, *Der Krieg von 1806 und 1807*, 3:193–194; Pierre Grenier, *Étude sur 1807: manoeuvres d'Eylau et Friedland* (Paris, 1901), 51–53; Oscar von Lettow-Vorbeck, *Der Krieg von 1806 und 1807* (Berlin, 1896), 4:31–49; Colmar von der Goltz, *From Jena to Eylau: The Disgrace and the Redemption of the Old-Prussian Army: A Study in Military History* (London, 1913), 197–203.
32   V Corps received the separate task of containing Essen's corps between the Bug and the Narew Rivers: CN, Nos 11778 and 11780, Dispositions générales de la journée, Allenstein, 3 February 1807; 56th Bulletin, Arensdorf, 5 February 1807, 14:354–355; Höpfner, *Der Krieg von 1806 und 1807*, 3:193–194; Grenier, *Étude sur 1807*, 51–53.
33   Denis Davydov, "Vospominaniya o srazhenii pri Preussisch-Eylau 1807 goda yanvarya 26-go i 27-go," in *Russkaya voennaya proza XIX veka* (Leningrad: Lenizdat, 1989), <http://www.museum.ru/1812/Library/Davidov7/index.html>.
34   Wilson to Lord Hutchinson, 2 February 1807, in Herbert Randolph, ed., *Life of General Sir Robert Wilson: From Autobiographical Memoirs, Journals, Narratives, Correspondence* (London, 1862), 2:403; RGVIA, f. 846, op. 16, d. 3161, ll. 28–29; Mikhailovsky-Danilevsky,

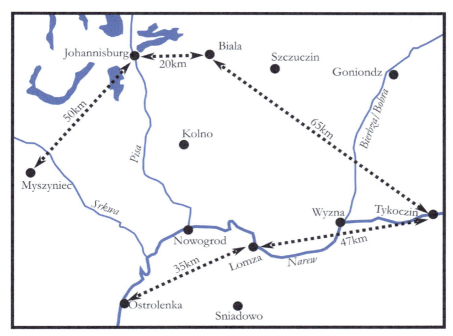

MAP 8.5   Russian Movements, early January 1807

French courier who had become lost in the bad weather. Unfortunately for the French, the orderly had failed to destroy an imperial dispatch to Bernadotte containing the details of Napoleon's plan of operations.[35] Realizing that he was "rushing blindly on to his destruction," Bennigsen immediately ordered his army to withdraw.[36] Pursuing vigorously, Napoleon's forces almost trapped Bennigsen at Allenstein between 2 and 4 February. However, as in the December campaign, bad weather, short days, and the difficulties of coordinating multiple French columns combined with tenacious Russian resistance to thwart Napoleon's plans. As the Russian retreat continued, the two sides clashed in a series of hard-fought rearguard actions on 6 and 7 February, ending with the French in possession of the small town of Preußisch Eylau after a costly strug-

---

      Opisanie vtoroi voiny Imperatora Aleksandra, 157–159; Höpfner, *Der Krieg von 1806 und 1807*, 3:189–190; Plotho, *Tagebuch*, 57–59.

35   Berthier to Bernadotte, 31 January, in Dumas, *Précis des événemens militaires*, 18:380. For detailed discussion of the correspondence between Berthier and Bernadotte, see Petre, *Napoleon's Campaign in Poland*, 148n.

36   Antoine Jomini, *Vie politique et militaire de Napoléon, racontée par lui même* (Paris, 1827), 2:355.

gle. Here, Bennigsen decided to make a stand. Further retreat would have meant the loss of Königsberg and its depots, as well as its political significance as the Prussian court's capital in exile. Seeking refuge in the old fortress was not an option, as this would have left the Russian army trapped and neutralized with no prospect of relief. Therefore, Bennigsen held his ground. As Napoleon examined the terrain north of the ruined town on the morning of 8 February, he could see the entire Russian army, some 67,000 men, arrayed on a range of low, snow-covered hills to the east. With only 50,000 troops immediately available (IV and VII Corps, Reserve Cavalry, and Guard), he would have to await Davout's III Corps to launch his main attack and hope that Ney's VI Corps would march to the sound of the guns and arrive on the Russian right in a timely fashion.

One of the grimmest battles of the age, the French and Russians fought at Eylau in bitter cold, deep snow, and sporadic blizzard-like snow squalls. Napoleon planned to crush Bennigsen's unsupported left flank with Davout's corps. While awaiting Davout, he sent Augereau's two divisions forward to pin the Russians in place and force Bennigsen to commit his reserves. The result, however, was a debacle for the French as Augereau's men lost their way in a sudden snow squall and marched parallel to the Russian front. As the snow cleared, a storm of lead from Bennigsen's massed batteries and battalions engulfed VII Corps. In just a few minutes, VII Corps was wrecked and a lively Russian counterattack pushed into Eylau itself before being repulsed by the French Imperial Guard. With his center shattered and little formed infantry available, Napoleon turned to his sole remaining resource to restore the situation: the 10,000 troopers of the Cavalry Reserve. In one of the great charges of history (actually a series of charges), Murat's men broke the Russian counterattack and penetrated Bennigsen's center before charging back through the Russian lines to resume their former position near Eylau. The crisis was averted and Davout's men started to arrive, slowly driving back the Russian left until it formed a ragged 'L' at right angles to the center. Just as the French started to threaten Bennigsen's line of retreat, General Gerhard von Scharnhorst led L'Estocq's 8,000 Prussians into position on the Russian left in time to repulse Davout's advance and save the Russian army. Marshal Ney, who had been chasing L'Estocq, did not reach the battlefield on the Russian right flank until evening, too late to alter the outcome.[37] By the end of the day, tens of thou-

---

37   For the most recent study, see Arnold and Reinertsen, *Crisis*, 268–376. See also Pleineville and Chikanov, *Napoléon en Pologne*, 221–312; Naulet, *Eylau*, 145–177; Mikhailovsky-Danilevsky, *Opisanie vtoroi voiny Imperatora Aleksandra*, 161–217; Höpfner, *Der Krieg von 1806 und 1807*, 3:201–258.

sands of corpses littered the frozen fields around Eylau, causing one participant to describe it as "the bloodiest day, the most horrible butchery of men that had taken place since the beginning of the Revolutionary wars."[38] Each commander claimed he had won a great victory, but the Battle of Eylau is best described as a costly draw, with losses estimated to be more than 25,000 Russians and some 20,000–30,000 French. The Grande Armée was in such a state of exhaustion that it was unable to pursue the enemy. Bennigsen was equally battered, and soldiers of both sides welcomed the return to winter quarters to recover from this bloodletting and from the endless marching on meager rations in cruel weather. The campaign closed, however, with a clear expectation of renewed fighting in the spring.[39]

As the second operational phase of the war concluded, Napoleon had again failed to trap and destroy the Russian army. Instead of resting and recuperating, his army had been forced to respond to the abortive Russian offensive only to suffer considerable losses at Eylau and the associated smaller engagements. As Ney remarked on viewing the grim fields at Eylau: "What a massacre, and without results!"[40] However, from an operational perspective, several aspects of this winter campaign stand out. In the first place, the same factors that had hampered Napoleon's maneuvers in December remained major obstacles in January and February: bad roads, inclement weather, brief hours of daylight, poor maps, scanty logistical support, and seemingly omnipresent bands of patrolling Cossacks, not to mention a dogged and tactically skillful enemy. Under these conditions, Napoleon managed to repel the Russian offensive and maintain his position east of the Vistula. This strategic position was important, as it allowed him to utilize his existing line of communications through Thorn. Moreover, it permitted him to isolate the fortress of Danzig at the mouth of the Vistula. A strategically important Prussian fortress on the Baltic, Danzig posed a direct threat to the French left and could thus serve as a potential landing point for Allied forces seeking to threaten the French army's rear. Eliminating this danger, of course, would also free French troops for Napoleon's principal objective: the struggle with the Russian field army.

Perhaps even more significant for Napoleon was the symbolic value of remaining both in possession of the sanguinary field at Eylau and establishing his winter quarters east of the Vistula. The two sides waged an active public relations war in the aftermath of Eylau, each trying to convince potential

---

38 Jean Baptiste Barrès, *Memoirs of a Napoleonic Officer* (London, 1925), 101.
39 CN, Nos 11816, 11822, and 11827, A l'Armée and Napoleon to Berthier, 60th–61st Bulletins, 16–19 February 1807, 14:381–391; Mikhailovsky-Danilevsky, *Opisanie vtoroi voiny Imperatora Aleksandra*, 233–234; Petre, *Napoleon's Campaign in Poland*, 215–237.
40 Fezensac, *Souvenirs militaires*, 464.

belligerents that it was the undisputed victor in this gruesome affray. Napoleon was especially keen to keep Austria neutral, but he also hoped to invigorate the Ottomans in their war with the tsar and to engage Persia in an alliance to create a distraction on Russia's southern frontiers. As the physical occupation of Eylau was seen as emblematic of victory, he kept much of his army encamped there for one week before withdrawing to cantonments further west. In addition, he positioned the army along the west bank of the Passarge River rather than retreating west of the Vistula or even to the Oder. Finally, although his effort to ensnare Bennigsen did not succeed, it is noteworthy that his careful disposition of his corps after Pultusk facilitated the rapid switch to an offensive that came close to cutting off and crushing the Russians. Forced to react to the unexpected Russian advance, he immediately turned the tables on his foe, swiftly responding to changes in the operational situation, seizing the initiative, and exercising psychological dominance throughout this brief but brutal winter campaign.

The Friedland Campaign (May–June 1807)

Despite occasional small engagements and constant skirmishing between outposts, the next three months passed in relative quiet as the two field armies settled into winter quarters to recover from the rigors of the preceding campaigns. Bennigsen placed most of his troops in bivouacs and billets around Heilsberg on the Alle River, where he had a series of strong earthworks constructed. On his right along the east bank of the Passarge stood a Russo-Prussian corps under the Prussian general L'Estocq. Altogether, Bennigsen commanded a combined field force of approximately 119,000 men. An additional Russian corps of 16,000 covered the area east of Warsaw. Other Prussian troops garrisoned Königsberg, Pillau on the Frisches-Haff, the blockaded fortress of Graudenz, and a number of besieged fortresses in Silesia. A Prussian garrison of some 15,600 men commanded by General Friedrich Adolf von Kalkreuth held Danzig.[41] Outside Danzig's formidable walls, the French X Corps, consisting of two Polish divisions under General Jan Henryk Dąbrowski, one Saxon division, one contingent from Baden, two Italian divisions, and about 10,000 French troops, in total about 45,000 men, formally besieged the city in the middle of March.[42] Other French forces continued the sieges of Prussian for-

---

41   James R. Arnold and Ralph R. Reinertsen, *Napoleon's Triumph. La Grande Armée versus the Tsar's Army: The Friedland Campaign, 1807* (Lexington, VA, 2011), 45. Strength figures are from Pleineville and Chikanov, *Napoléon en Pologne*, 356.
42   Rothenberg, *The Art of Warfare in the Age of Napoleon*, 219.

NAPOLEON'S OPERATIONAL WARFARE DURING THE FIRST POLISH CAMPAIGN   295

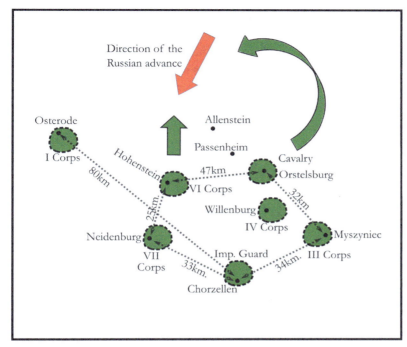

MAP 8.6   The Grande Armée's positions, late January 1807

tresses in Silesia and guarded the coasts along the North and Baltic Seas. The bulk of the Grande Armée – I, III, IV, and VI Corps with the Guard and Cavalry Reserve (approximately 114,000 men) – cantoned along the west bank of the Passarge from Braunsberg on the left to Allenstein on the right. Two new formations totaling 31,000 men – a Reserve Corps under Marshal Lannes and VIII Corps commanded by Marshal Adolphe Édouard Mortier – would join this central group by the start of the spring campaign in June. Finally, V Corps (26,000 men), now under Marshal Masséna, held the army's far right flank from Warsaw to Ostrolenka with a division of 10,000 raw Polish recruits situated at Neidenburg to link V Corps with the main army.

In late March, Tsar Alexander personally visited his troops in Poland, boosting their morale in expectation of a new campaign. He held military reviews, inspected the entrenchments at Heilsberg, and brought strong reinforcements, including the Russian Imperial Guard.[43] Alexander and Frederick William III also held discussions on the future of the war at Bennigsen's headquarters in

---

43   Levin Bennigsen, "Zapiski grafa L.L. Bennigsen o voine s Napoleonom 1807 goda" [hereafter referred to as "Memoirs"], ed. by P. Maikov, *Russkaya starina*, 100 (December

Bartenstein, concluding that it was "indispensably necessary to continue the war in the most vigorous manner." They established expansive war aims, expressing the hope that Austria, Britain, and Sweden would soon be actively involved as allies.[44] Bennigsen, however, was not so optimistic. He remained concerned that Napoleon would concentrate the Grande Armée and overwhelm the Russian army and its Prussian allies as soon as the weather improved. He thus sought a spoiling attack (in modern parlance) to preempt Napoleon and gain an advantage before the French were ready. He again focused his attention on Ney's VI Corps, which, as in January, was deployed ahead of the rest of the French army. With luck, he would destroy the seemingly isolated VI Corps before Napoleon could react. By the middle of May, Bennigsen had assembled his army around Heilsberg and Migehnen but, despite the best efforts of the Russian cavalry screen, French scouts detected Russian movements and alerted Ney to the impending attack.[45] Furthermore, rumors spread in Russian headquarters that Napoleon himself was marching with his main army to reinforce Ney. As a result, Bennigsen postponed his offensive, which the Russian troops, exasperated by their futile marches, derogatively called "The First of May Promenade."[46] The Russian army remained idle for the next two weeks, suffering from lack of supplies.

In the meantime, the French successfully concluded the siege of Danzig on 24 May.[47] This discouraging news reached Russian headquarters on 30 May, prompting a renewed study of plans for a preemptive offensive. The fall of Danzig meant that Napoleon would be able to secure his rear and divert reinforcements to the Passarge front. To anticipate French moves, the Russo-Prussian command returned to the idea of attacking the seemingly vulnerable VI Corps before the rest of the French army arrived. However, the resulting plan

---

1899): 700; Wilson, *Brief Remarks*, 128–129; "Ob uchastii gvardii v kampaniu 1807 g.," RGVIA, f. 846, op. 16, d. 3163, ll. 1–13.

44 Hardenberg's Notes on Alexander's Meeting with Friedrich-Wilhelm III, in *Vneshnaya politika Rossii XIX i nachala XX veka: dokumenti Rossiiskogo Ministerstva Inostrannikh del* (Moscow, 1961), 3:546; Landmann, *Der Krieg von 1806 und 1807*, 388–389; Bennigsen, "Memoirs," *Russkaya starina*, 100 (October 1899), 226–228; 100 (December, 1899), 697–700; Fedor Fedorovich de Martens, *Recueil des traités et conventions conclus par la Russie avec les puissances étrangères* (St. Petersburg, 1883), 6:408–418.

45 Davout to Ney, circa 2 June, in Bennigsen, "Memoirs," *Russkaya starina*, 101 (January 1901): 261–262.

46 Mikhailovsky-Danilevsky, *Opisanie vtoroi voiny Imperatora Aleksandra*, 276.

47 On the other hand, the Prussian commander in blockaded Graudenz refused all calls to capitulate and the fortress remained in Prussian hands until the end of the war.

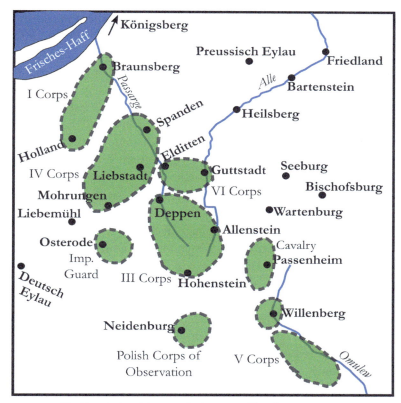

MAP 8.7   The Grande Armée's corps deployments, May 1807

contained serious flaws.[48] Mainly, it divided Allied forces into six columns that would attack along a wooded front of 30 kilometers in an attempt to trap Ney's corps between several converging thrusts. To divert French attention elsewhere, Bennigsen instructed L'Estocq's corps to attack Bernadotte's I Corps at Spanden while Lieutenant General Dmitry Sergeyevich Dokhturov's Russian column pinned Soult's IV Corps at Lomitten. Unfortunately for the Allies, the plan ignored the experiences of the previous two campaigns and neglected the flexibility of the French corps system. Although it did seek to exploit the apparent dispersal of the enemy army, the Allies did not realize that Napoleon had carefully cultivated an appearance of disunity. Far from leaving his corps iso-

---

48   For the Russian deployment, see Dispositions, 3–4 June 1807, RGVIA, f. 846, op. 16, d. 3163, ll. 18–19; Disposition for Attack, 5 June 1807, in Bennigsen, "Memoirs," *Russkaya starina*, 101 (January, 1901): 262–263; *Journal of Military Operations of the Russian Imperial Army*, 155–158; Mikhailovsky-Danilevsky, *Opisanie vtoroi voiny Imperatora Aleksandra*, 294–295.

lated, Napoleon had deployed the army along a line of operations that allowed his forces to achieve a rapid concentration within the space of twenty-four to forty-eight hours.

Thus, instead of concentrating some 40,000 men against Ney's 16,000, the Russian command divided its forces. As the offensive unfolded on 2 June, only one Russian column engaged Ney's corps while the remaining five struggled to find their routes and arrive in time. One British observer lamented the fact that "the different columns were directed to connect operations ... instead of having orders to press vigorously and reach the Passarge with all possible expedition so as to anticipate the arrival of [Ney's corps] who, pursued by superior forces, could not deviate to undertake any operations that might delay his retreat."[49] The Prussian corps made a series of probes on the French positions at Spanden but did not press its attack because, according to the plan, it was only to serve as a diversion. Meanwhile, Ney conducted a brilliant rearguard action at the battle of Guttstadt–Deppen on 5 and 6 June. Although the marshal lost his baggage train and 2,042 men, he successfully withdrew VI Corps to the west bank of the Passarge.

By 7 June, the Russian "offensive had expended its force and come to a standstill."[50] In contrast, as soon as he received news of the Russo-Prussian attack, Napoleon prepared his forces for a counteroffensive, encouraged by reports that the "enemy is constantly marching to and fro on the plateau of Deppen ... revealing great indecision in his actions; he seems to be rather confused."[51] Napoleon immediately gained and held the initiative for the remainder of this brief campaign. On 9 June, Soult crossed the Passarge on the French left while Murat's cavalry, supported by Ney and closely followed by Lannes's Reserve Corps and the Guard, advanced between Deppen and Guttstadt on the right, forcing the Russians to fall back to their fortified positions at Heilsberg.[52] Napoleon perceived Bennigsen's intention to fight a battle around Heilsberg and decided to annihilate the Russian army through yet

---

49   Bennigsen, "Memoirs," *Russkaya starina*, 101 (January, 1901), 272; Mikhailovsky-Danilevsky, *Opisanie vtoroi voiny Imperatora Aleksandra*, 298–302; Höpfner, *Der Krieg von 1806 und 1807*, 3:583; Wilson, *Brief Remarks*, 137.
50   Petre, *Napoleon's Campaign in Poland*, 284.
51   Berthier to Davout, 7 June 1807, in *Correspondance du maréchal Davout, prince d'Eckmühl*, ed. by Charles de Mazade (Paris, 1885), 1:459.
52   *CN*, No. 12741, Napoleon to Davout, 6 June 1807, 15:321–322; Berthier to Ney, in Dumas, *Précis des événemens militaires*, 19:326; Louis Nicolas Davout, *Opérations du 3e corps, 1806–1807. Rapport du de maréchal Davout, duc d'Auerstaedt* (Paris, 1896), 192; Grenier, *Étude sur 1807*, 115–118.

another *manoeuvre sur les derrières*. According to his plan, one part of the Grande Armée would attack and pin the enemy at Heilsberg while III and VIII Corps executed a flanking maneuver and blocked the road to Königsberg.

On 10 June, the two sides clashed at Heilsberg in a sanguinary but ultimately inconclusive battle. As noted, Bennigsen had constructed a ring of earthworks around Heilsberg that included six redoubts and more than one dozen entrenched batteries on both sides of the Alle River. Three of the six redoubts were located on the Russian right flank and served as the keys to Bennigsen's position. Now, after his own offensive had failed, he hoped to win a defensive battle by luring the French into attacking his army in its entrenched position. The first hours of the battle were fought in the hills and ravines outside the Russian fortifications as Murat's cavalry, advancing on the west (left) bank of the Alle River, encountered the Russian rearguard about 4 kilometers outside Heilsberg at 10:00 that morning. A vicious back-and-forth struggle ensued for the next several hours during which the Russians inflicted heavy losses on Murat, whose rash cavalry charges accomplished nothing beyond exhausting and disordering his troopers. Infantry from Soult's IV Corps and part of the Guard succeeded in seizing two of Bennigsen's three redoubts late in the day at heavy cost, but they could not retain their prizes in the face of counterattacks by numerically superior Russian forces. Arriving with his Reserve Corps during the evening, the impetuous Marshal Lannes launched a wasteful final assault around 10:00 p.m., only to see his men blasted by Russian artillery. Accounts of losses during the day vary but clearly favor the Russians, who probably lost 6,000 to 9,000 men compared to approximately 12,000 French casualties. Bennigsen held his fortified position against a force less than half his number, and he had wisely refused advice to depart his entrenchments and attack the temporarily outnumbered French. The following day saw no fighting, but the Russian situation grew perilous as French reinforcements arrived, threatening to outflank Bennigsen on his right and cut him off from Königsberg.[53] Concerned about Napoleon's flanking maneuver and the imminent prospect of attack by superior forces, Bennigsen abandoned his fortified positions on

---

53 Höpfner cites French losses at 1,398 killed, 10,069 wounded, and 864 captured. As for the Russian losses, Plotho acknowledges 9,000 killed and wounded, while Mikhailovsky-Danilevsky claims 6,000 casualties. Landmann estimates 8,000–9,000 men lost on the Russian side and 10,000–11,000 on the French. See Höpfner, *Der Krieg von 1806 und 1807*, 3:615; Plotho, *Tagebuch*, 162; Mikhailovsky-Danilevsky, *Opisanie vtoroi voiny Imperatora Aleksandra*, 315; "Relation de la Bataille de Heilsberg le 10 Juin 1807," RGVIA, f. 846, op. 16, d. 3204, l. 18; Bennigsen, "Memoirs," *Russkaya starina* 101 (February 1901): 511.

the night of the 11th and withdrew north along the east (right) bank of the Alle River.[54]

Finding the Russian earthworks abandoned on the morning of 12 June, Napoleon again faced the challenge of nailing down and destroying an enemy who had repeatedly escaped his grasp. After his cavalry lost track of the Russians, Napoleon could only speculate on their route of retreat: due north toward Königsberg via the grisly field of Eylau or along the Alle to its confluence with the Pregel? In either case, the emperor resolved to exploit his position west of the Alle and place himself between Bennigsen and Königsberg. The Russians would then have to retreat east and away from their Prussian allies or be forced into a fight Napoleon was sure he would win. Sending reconnaissance in all directions, he marched north, seeking battle.

Conversely, Bennigsen sought to avoid another engagement. Weary and suffering from kidney stones that had caused him to faint from exhaustion during the Battle of Heilsberg, the Russian commander had barely received any rest when his cavalry informed him of the presence of French outposts on the west bank of the Alle near the town of Friedland on the afternoon of 13 June. Under heavy pressure from the tsar's court to "do something" besides retreating, and once again thinking he had an opportunity to destroy an isolated French corps, Bennigsen sent most of his army across the Alle during the night and into the morning of 14 June. This proved to be a grave error. His intended victim was Lannes's newly constituted Reserve Corps. Although the Russians enjoyed at least a 3:1 numerical advantage between 6:00 a.m. and 9:00 a.m., the marshal conducted an exemplary holding action, tying down the Russians as Napoleon rushed reinforcements to the battlefield.[55]

As more French troops (I, VI and VIII Corps, the Guard and substantial cavalry) and then the emperor himself arrived, Bennigsen's situation became dire. His army had its back against an unfordable river that could be crossed only by several bridges that connected Friedland to the east bank. In effect, the location of these bridges made the little town a funnel that would quickly clog with troops advancing or retreating. Furthermore, a stream flowing through a deep, unbridged ravine divided the battlefield and considerably limited the ability to shift troops laterally. Napoleon immediately perceived the vulnerability of the Russian position. Reminding his men that 14 June was the anniversary of Marengo, he made quick but careful adjustments to the French dispositions.

---

54 "Relation de la Bataille de Heilsberg le 10 Juin 1807," RGVIA, f. 846, op. 16, d. 3204, ll. 9–10; Mikhailovsky-Danilevsky, *Opisanie vtoroi voiny Imperatora Aleksandra*, 307–308; Höpfner, *Der Krieg von 1806 und 1807*, 3:602–622; Landmann, *Der Krieg von 1806 und 1807*, 412–415.

55 Hubert Camon, *Le système de guerre de Napoléon* (Paris, 1923), 103; Frédéric Naulet, *Friedland: la campagne de Pologne, de Danzig aux rives du Niémen* (Paris, 2007), 116, 201.

Around 5:30 p.m., a salvo of twenty French guns signaled the attack. Despite great courage on the part of the defenders, the assault on the Russian left by Ney and Victor proved unstoppable as the advancing French skillfully employed their artillery to maintain devastating fire on the tightly packed masses of Russian infantry. Around 8:00 p.m., with its ranks decimated and its flanks threatened, the Russian left wing started to withdraw through the narrow streets of Friedland and the congested bridges over the Alle River. Many drowned in the attempt to escape. The situation on Bennigsen's right was equally critical and only the last-minute discovery of a previously unknown ford and the exhaustion of the French cavalry saved the Russian right wing from total destruction. As it was, the army suffered some 20,000 killed and wounded as well as a severe blow to its morale and discipline. French losses totaled some 12,000 casualties. The Battle of Friedland was another soaring military triumph for Napoleon.[56]

The Friedland campaign was brief; its principal military activity lasted only twelve days from the opening Allied advances on 5 June to the French entry into Königsberg on the 16th. Nevertheless, Napoleon's mastery of the operational art is clearly evident even in this short period. The first facet to note is his constant evaluation of the enemy's options. He almost instinctively considered the moves open to the Russians and positioned his forces to be able to respond to all possible contingencies whether during the winter lull or during the short but intense period of active operations. He always intended to take the offensive in the spring, and his supple dispositions allowed him to transition rapidly to the attack and seize the initiative even after his adversary moved first. Second, he aimed for decisive results. For example, at Heilsberg on 10–11 June, he was not satisfied to simply drive the Russians from their entrenched position. Instead, he sought to block Bennigsen's road to Königsberg, thereby threatening the Prussian court, endangering a major Allied supply source, and driving a military and political wedge between the Russian and Prussian forces by pushing the Russians east toward their own borders. Thus, the bloody draw of Heilsberg earned Napoleon both material and psychological advantages. Although Napoleon could not foresee the precise circumstances under which next battle would occur, Heilsberg established the conditions for a decisive victory. Third, he fixed his priority on the enemy's main army and accepted the carefully calculated risk to his rear by assigning second-line troops to guard the

---

56   Harold T. Parker, *Three Napoleonic Battles* (Durham, NC, 1983), 17–18; Petre, *Napoleon's Campaign in Poland*, 304–309; Höpfner, *Der Krieg von 1806 und 1807*, 3:652–653; Plotho, *Tagebuch*, 163; Maurice Girod de L'Ain, *Grands artilleurs: Drouot–Sénarmont–Eblé* (Paris, 1895), 180–181, 224–226; Pleineville and Chikanov, *Napoléon en Pologne*, 472–475. For the most recent English-language account, see Arnold and Reinertsen, *Napoleon's Triumph*.

coasts and neutralize the numerous Prussian fortresses, a function that also served to train and harden these contingents. Even the siege of Danzig, an essential component of Napoleon's plan for the spring, unfolded with a judicious allocation of resources. Although he sent siege guns and key technical experts from the army's staff to assist the besieging force, he neither detached troops from the main field army nor went himself to oversee the reduction of the fortress.

The fruits of Napoleon's planning, energy, and leadership were reaped with the Battle of Friedland, which indeed proved to be a decisive military and diplomatic victory. It demonstrated the fullest extent of his ability to quickly evaluate a situation and exploit the enemy's mistakes, tailoring his tactics according to circumstances. In the aftermath of the battle, the battered Russian army retreated toward the Niemen River, which marked the boundary of the Russian Empire; there they were joined by the dispirited remnants of the Prussian army, forced to evacuate Königsberg on 16 June after the Prussian court fled to Memel. On 19 June, five days after Friedland, the French received Bennigsen's letter seeking an armistice. "After the torrents of blood which have lately flowed in battles as sanguinary as frequent," the letter read, "[the Russians] desire to assuage the evils of this destructive war, by proposing an armistice before we enter upon a conflict, a fresh war, perhaps more terrible than the first." The offer was accepted, and on 25 June Alexander met Napoleon on a decorative raft anchored in the Niemen River to discuss peace. Although the military defeats lay heavily on Alexander's mind as he stepped onto the raft, so did his bitterness with Britain, which seemed to have been set on consolidating its interests in the wider world rather than supporting its allies in Europe. Meeting with the British minister one week before, Alexander had vented his frustration that "the whole burden of the war [had] fallen upon his armies ... that hopes had been held out that a British force would be sent to ... Germany – month after month however passed, and no troops were even embarked."[57] As they met on the raft, Alexander supposedly greeted Napoleon with the words, "Sire, I hate the English as much as you do." To which Napoleon replied immediately, "In that case, the peace is made ...."[58]

The Treaties of Tilsit, signed in July 1807, marked the culmination of Napoleon's campaigns that had reshaped the European balance of power in a mere two years. These wars "inordinately extended the range of Napoleon's

---

57 Leveson-Gower to Canning, 17 June 1807, cited in Herbert Butterfield, *The Peace Tactics of Napoleon, 1806–1808* (Cambridge, 1959), 197–198.
58 Louis Pierre Bignon, *Histoire de France depuis le 18 Brumaire jusqu'à la paix de Tilsit* (Paris, 1830), 6:316; Armand Lefebvre, *Histoire des cabinets de l'Europe pendant le Consulat et l'Empire* (Paris, 1847), 3:102.

enterprises, and so made the French Empire merely the core of the 'Grand Empire' which itself began to evolve," notes the great French historian Georges Lefebvre.[59] Indeed, French hegemony now stretched from the snowy fields of Poland to the rugged Pyrenees and from the sun-swept hills of Calabria to the misty shores of Prussia. "All the German speaking lands were either under Napoleon's direct control, or under the control of a German vassal loyal to Napoleon, or part of a state conquered by or surrendered to Napoleon."[60] Returning to Paris in late July, Napoleon received almost universal public acclaim. The French capital celebrated his birthday on 15 August with a splendor that evoked the era of Louis XIV.[61] The emperor's speech at the opening session of the Legislative Corps was one of his proudest: it spoke of humiliating defeats inflicted upon Austria and Prussia, the collapse of the Holy Roman Empire, and a profound territorial and structural reorganization of Central Europe. France's "new triumphs and peace treaties have redrawn the political map of Europe," Napoleon informed the legislators.[62] Not since the days of Charlemagne had one ruler exercised such vast power on the continent, deciding the fates of rulers and millions of their subjects.

Bibliography

Arnold, James R. and Ralph R. Reinertsen. *Crisis in the Snows. Russia Confronts Napoleon: The Eylau Campaign 1806–1807*. Lexington, VA, 2007

Arnold, James R. and Ralph R. Reinertsen. *Napoleon's Triumph. La Grande Armée versus the Tsar's Army: The Friedland Campaign, 1807*. Lexington, VA, 2011.

Barrès, Jean Baptiste. *Memoirs of a Napoleonic Officer*. London, 1925.

Bennigsen, Levin. "Zapiski grafa L.L. Bennigsen o voine s Napoleonom 1807 goda," ed. by P. Maikov, *Russkaya starina*, 100 (December 1899).

Béraud, Stéphane. *La révolution militaire Napoléonienne*. Paris, 2007.

Bignon, Louis Pierre. *Histoire de France depuis le 18 Brumaire jusqu'à la paix de Tilsit*. Paris, 1830.

Bonnal, Henry. *La vie militaire du Maréchal Ney, duc d'Elchingen, prince de la Moskowa*. Paris, 1910.

Butterfield, Herbert. *The Peace Tactics of Napoleon, 1806–1808*. Cambridge, 1959.

---

59 Lefebvre, *Napoleon*, 249.
60 Sam A. Mustafa, *Germany in the Modern World: A New History* (New York, 2011), 95.
61 Claire Élisabeth Jeanne Gravier de Vergennes, Comtesse de Rémusat, *Memoirs of Madame de Rémusat, 1802–1808*, ed. by Paul de Rémusat (London, 1880), 2:341–343.
62 CN, No. 13034, Discours de S.M. L'Empereur et Roi à l'ouverture du Corps Législatif, 16 August 1807, 15:498–500.

Camon, Hubert. *Le système de guerre de Napoléon*. Paris, 1923.
Chandler, David. *The Campaigns of Napoleon*. New York, 1966.
Coignet, Jean-Roch. *The Narrative of Captain Coignet, Soldier of the Empire, 1776–1850*. New York, 1890.
Colbert-Chabanais, Marquis de. *Le général Auguste Colbert (1793–1809): traditions, souvenirs et documents touchant sa vie et son temps*. Paris, 1888.
Davout, Louis Nicolas. *Correspondance de maréchal Davout, prince d'Eckmühl*, ed. by Charles de Mazade. Paris, 1885.
Davout, Louis Nicolas. *Opérations du 3e corps, 1806–1807. Rapport du de maréchal Davout, duc d'Auerstaedt*. Paris, 1896.
Derrécagaix, Victor-Bernard. *Le maréchal Berthier, prince de Wagram et de Neuchâtel*. Paris, 1905.
Dumas, Mathieu. *Précis des événemens militaires, ou, Essais historiques sur les campagnes de 1799 à 1814*. Paris, 1826.
Fezensac, Raymond-Aymery-Philippe-Joseph de Montesquiou. *Souvenirs militaires de 1804 à 1814*. Paris, 1863.
Foucart, Paul-Jean. *Campagne de Pologne*. Paris, 2006.
Girod de L'Ain, Maurice. *Grands artilleurs: Drouot–Sénarmont–Eblé*. Paris, 1895.
Goltz, Colmar von der. *From Jena to Eylau. The Disgrace and the Redemption of the Old-Prussian Army: A Study in Military History*. London, 1913.
Grenier, Pierre. *Étude sur 1807: manoeuvres d'Eylau et Friedland*. Paris, 1901.
Höpfner, Eduard von. *Der Krieg von 1806 und 1807*. Berlin, 1850.
Jomini, Antoine. *Vie politique et militaire de Napoléon, racontée par lui même*. Paris, 1827.
Landmann, Karl Ritter von. *Der Krieg von 1806 und 1807: auf Grund urkundlichen Materials sowie der neuesten Forschungen und Quellen*. Berlin, 1909.
Lechartier, Georges Germain Félix. *Les services de l'arrière à la Grande Armée en 1806–1807*. Paris, 1910.
Lechartier, Georges Germain Félix. *La manoeuvre de Pultusk*. Paris, 1911.
Lefebvre, Armand. *Histoire des cabinets de l'Europe pendant le Consulat et l'Empire*. Paris, 1847.
Lettow-Vorbeck, Oscar von. *Der Krieg von 1806 und 1807*. Berlin, 1896.
Marbot, Jean-Baptiste-Antoine-Marcelin Baron de. *The Memoirs of Baron de Marbot*. New York, 1903.
Martens, Fedor Fedorovich de. *Recueil des traités et conventions conclus par la Russie avec les puissances étrangères*. St. Petersburg, 1883.
Mikaberidze, Alexander, ed. *Russian Eyewitness Accounts of the Campaign of 1807*. London, 2015.
Mikhailovsky-Danilevsky, Alexander. *Opisanie vtoroi voiny Imperatora Aleksandra s Napoleonom v 1806–1807 godakh*. St. Petersburg, 1846.

Mustafa, Sam A. *Germany in the Modern World: A New History*. New York, 2011

Naulet, Frédéric. *Eylau: la campagne de Pologne, des boues de Pultusk aux neiges d'Eylau*. Paris, 2007.

Naulet, Frédéric. *Friedland: la campagne de Pologne, de Danzig aux rives du Niémen*. Paris, 2007.

Ojala, Jeanne A. *Auguste de Colbert: Aristocratic Survival in an Era of Upheaval, 1793–1809*. Salt Lake City, 1979.

Parker, Harold T. *Three Napoleonic Battles*. Durham, NC, 1983.

Petre, F. Lorraine. *Napoleon's Campaign in Poland, 1806–7*. London, 1901.

Pleineville, Natalia Griffon de and Vladimir Chikanov, *Napoléon en Pologne: la campagne de 1806–1807*. Paris, 2008.

Plotho, Carl von. *Tagebuch während des Krieges zwischen Russland und Preussen einerseits, und Frankreich andrerseits, in den Jahren 1806 und 1807*. Berlin, 1811.

Randolph, Herbert, ed. *Life of General Sir Robert Wilson: From Autobiographical Memoirs, Journals, Narratives, Correspondence*. London, 1862.

Rémusat, Claire Élisabeth Jeanne Gravier de Vergennes, Comtesse de. *Memoirs of Madame de Rémusat, 1802–1808*, ed. by Paul de Rémusat. London, 1880.

Rothenberg, Gunther E. *The Art of Warfare in the Age of Napoleon*. Bloomington, IN, 1978.

Vneshnaya politika Rossii XIX i nachala XX veka: dokumenti Rossiiskogo Ministerstva Inostrannikh del. Moscow, 1961.

Wilson, Sir Robert. *Brief Remarks on the Character and Composition of the Russian Army, and a Sketch of the Campaigns in Poland in the Years 1806 and 1807*. London, 1810.

CHAPTER 9

An Ulcer Inflamed: Napoleon's Campaign in Spain, 1808

Huw J. Davies

> I shall find in Spain the Pillars of Hercules, but not the limits of my power.
> NAPOLEON BONAPARTE, *31 July 1808*

∴

The war in the Iberian peninsula was the war Napoleon did not want. The injection of 120,000 French troops into Iberia was a means to an end, not the end itself. Originally, the intention had been threefold: to seal off the few remaining ports open to British markets on the European continent; to take the corrupt and inefficient Spanish government in hand, thereby securing for France access to the riches of the Spanish empire; and, ultimately, to give Napoleon access to Gibraltar and the Barbary coast – the so-called Pillars of Hercules – in an effort to deprive the Royal Navy of access to the Mediterranean. If successful, such a strategy might lead to a combined Franco-Russian attack on the Levant and the East Indies, dealing Britain that crippling blow that would finally force it out of the war.[1] "Nothing but peace with that country can make me sheathe the sword and restore tranquillity to Europe," Napoleon had written to his brother in April 1808.[2] Indeed, the British were worried. Facing the prospect of a French invasion of India, no matter how outlandish such a prospect might be, the governor-general, Gilbert Elliot-Murray-Kynynmound, Lord Minto, wrote of his fear that "we are not warranted in deeming it in the present situation of affairs to be altogether chimerical and impracticable under the guidance of a man whose energy and success appear almost commensurate with his ambition ... What would have seemed impossible had become scarcely improbable, since we have seen one State after another in

---

1 Chandler, *Campaigns of Napoleon*, 593–601.
2 Napoleon Bonaparte, *The Confidential Correspondence of Napoleon Bonaparte with His Brother Joseph, Sometime King of Spain...* (hereafter cited as CC) (New York, 1856), Napoleon to Joseph, Bayonne, 12 April 1808, 1:319.

Europe, among them those we deemed most stable and secure, fall like a house of cards before the genius of one man."[3]

Key to Napoleon's strategy against the British was his Continental System, which in 1807 extended across Europe with the exception of Portuguese ports. Napoleon sought to undermine British power by either forcing the Portuguese regency to accept French terms and declare war against Britain, or invade Portugal and depose the monarchy. On 19 July 1807, Napoleon instructed his foreign minister, Charles Maurice de Talleyrand, to order Portugal to close its ports to British trade, arrest all British subjects in Portugal, and confiscate all British property in the country. This, Napoleon claimed, was in response to Britain's Orders in Council, which effectively gave the Royal Navy carte blanche to search and detain neutral shipping. "The English declare that they will no longer respect neutrals at sea," wrote an enraged Napoleon; "I will no longer recognise them on land."[4] The failure of the Portuguese to acquiesce to all of Napoleon's demands gave the French emperor the pretext he needed to order the invasion force he had prepared in the south of France – the First Corps of Observation of the Gironde under General Jean-Andoche Junot – to begin its march through Spain to the Portuguese frontier.

But the invasion of Portugal was a useful means of preparing for an eventual military occupation of Spain. "Send me descriptions of the provinces through which you pass, of the roads and the nature of the terrain," Napoleon wrote to Junot in October 1807. "Let me know distances between villages, the nature of the countryside and its resources."[5] Clearly, from the outset, Napoleon had grander plans than the occupation and subjugation of Portugal.

As the Portuguese government recognized the inevitability of French domination they agreed to Napoleon's demands, seeking only a guarantee of the Bragança dynasty. Napoleon would not back down, however, and ordered Junot to accelerate his march, fearful that the British would send an army to defend Lisbon. Junot's army, ruined and bedraggled after a forced march through inhospitable terrain in appalling weather conditions, entered Lisbon on 30 November 1807 having covered 300 miles in 14 days. Their victory was muted, however, by the sight of the Portuguese fleet, supported by the Royal Navy, escaping the Tagus estuary at the last moment, transporting the Portuguese royal family, the treasury, and the majority of Lisbon's political elite to Brazil.

---

3 Gilbert Elliot-Murray-Kynynmound, Lord Minto, *Lord Minto in India, Life and Letters of G. Elliot from 1807 to 1814* (reprint. London, 2013), Secret and Separate General Letter, 2 February 1808, 102–103.
4 D.A. Bingham, *A Selection from the Letters and Despatches of Napoleon* (London, 1834), 2:324.
5 *CN*, No. 13267, 16:98.

Spain, meanwhile, had supported the French invasion of Portugal, but the Spanish first minister, Manuel de Godoy, had for the last few years been working to extricate Spain from its alliance with France – an alliance that had seen Spanish power devastated in the war with Britain, both militarily, at the Battle of Trafalgar, and economically, its ports blockaded by the Royal Navy, and its vital supply line with the colonies in Central and South America cut. In 1806, as Napoleon went to war against Prussia, Godoy saw an opportunity to break with France, but the overwhelming French victory at Jena–Auerstedt in October that year, and the resultant dismemberment of the Prussian state, caused Godoy to backtrack. He claimed the mobilization of Spanish forces had been against Britain rather than France, but Napoleon smelled a rat. He remained convinced that administrative, economic, and military incompetence within the Spanish state was preventing it from benefiting from the untold wealth that the Central and South American colonies were providing. All that was needed was the strong hand of France, and Spain would be restored to its previous imperial glory, with France, of course, being the primary beneficiary.

Three corps were assembled in southwestern France, in preparation for military intervention in Spain. Initially, at least, it seemed to Napoleon that what was required was a wholesale reordering of the Spanish government, leaving the Bourbon dynasty on the throne. But infighting between the king, Charles IV, and his son Ferdinand, resulting in the eventual forced abdication of the former in favour of the latter, convinced Napoleon that the Bourbons would have to go. The 60,000 French troops waiting on the border were ordered into Spain, ostensibly in support of the invasion of Portugal, and to guard against a British counterattack from Gibraltar. Marshal Murat was appointed on 20 February 1808 to command them and began a gradual approach to Madrid. Charles and Ferdinand sought Napoleon's mediation in order to settle their dispute and were both invited to Bayonne. There, Napoleon finally revealed his hand. On 5 May 1808, both were forced to concede the throne of Spain to Napoleon, who offered it to his older brother Joseph. Napoleon had apparently subjugated the peninsula in one fell swoop. He was warned by his security chief, Joseph Fouché, that Spain might yet prove a difficult nut to crack. "The rabble," Napoleon believed, would only require "a few cannon shots [to] disperse them."[6] Events were to prove this analysis to be devastatingly inaccurate.

Already Spain was in revolt. Fearful that the monarchy was about to be usurped, a large and rowdy crowd gathered outside the royal palace at Aranjuez

---

6 Cited in Charles Esdaile, *The Peninsular War* (London, 2002), 30.

on 2 May. Murat sought to disperse the crowd, and in the process ten Spaniards were killed in a volley of musket-fire. The crowd fled, but word quickly spread through Madrid of the French brutality, and bands of lightly armed civilians started to coalesce throughout the city. At the end of the day, and after a series of skirmishes with French troops, 300 Spaniards lay dead and a further 200 were executed overnight. The French suffered 31 dead and 114 wounded. This was the famous *dos de mayo*, and news of the rebellion against the French quickly spread throughout Spain's regions. Over the next few weeks and months, a large-scale, but regionally focused rebellion broke out. *La guerrilla* had begun.

It is worth noting at this point, however, that *la guerrilla* was a complicated insurgency, which was motivated as much by resistance to the reforms of the government of Charles IV as by the French invasion. Thus, the first months of the insurrection were marked by bloody reprisals visited upon the representatives of these reforms, as well as by traditional guerrilla tactics against the French. The insurrection was overwhelmingly regional, with little national cohesion or overall strategy. In some ways, this was a weakness, but in others it was a strength. Napoleon would have to subjugate the whole of Spain to defeat *la guerrilla*. He ordered that "Marshal [Jean-Baptiste] Bessières ... should fall on any ... village that rises in revolt or mistreats any soldier or courier ... In a campaign one terrible example ... is sufficient," and that "retrograde movements ... must never be adopted in people's wars."[7] On 5 June, two squadrons of French dragoons were ambushed at a pass in the Sierra Morena. In response, Napoleon ordered a series of "flying columns," which would move rapidly, in order to secure key strategic towns and, where necessary, wreak terrible, punitive destruction, in the hope that this combination of tactics would cow the population and nip the rebellion in the bud.

Underestimating the determination, if not the military ability, of their opponents, the French spread themselves too thinly throughout Spain. Initially, 80,000 troops held the vital terrain between the French border and the Spanish capital, where Marshal Murat had established his headquarters. In the south General Dupont commanded 24,000 men along the Upper Tagus, and was soon ordered to occupy Seville and Córdoba and then move on to Cádiz. In the north, Bessières had 13,000 men in Old Castile and 14,000 in Aragón. Not only was Bessières to prevent the rebellion from intensifying, he was also expected to hold the critical highway between Madrid and Bayonne, as well as seize Santander and secure the Cantabrian coastline against a possible British amphibious incursion. The whole plan of operations was wildly ambitious.

---

7   Cited ibid., 61.

Where irregular resistance was encountered, the French regularly received a bloody nose, as at Valencia and Zaragoza. The unexpectedly hardy resistance of the Spaniards shocked the French, but Napoleon appeared to refuse to accept the reality of the situation, despite repeated warnings from his brother, who entered Spain on 9 July, and saw for himself the magnitude of the difficulties the French faced. Initially, Joseph called for more troops. "To get through this task quickly, so hateful to a sovereign," wrote Joseph melodramatically shortly after entering Spain, "to prevent further insurrections, to have less blood to shed and fewer tears to dry, enormous force must be employed."[8] But, once in Madrid, he learned that the depredations of French troops were inflaming the problem. For example, General Auguste-Jean-Gabriel de Caulincourt had sacked Cuenca on 20 July. "Every sensible person in the government and in the army says that a defeat would have been less injurious," Joseph wrote seeking castigation for Caulincourt.[9] But Napoleon was having none of it. "Caulincourt did what was perfectly right at Cuenca," the emperor replied in irritation. "The city was pillaged: this is one of the rights of war, since it was captured while the defenders were still in arms." More generally, Napoleon wanted the rebels, rather than his generals, punished. "No measures are to be kept with ruffians who assassinate our wounded, and commit every kind of horror: the way in which they are treated is quite right."[10] Joseph, whose temperament was less belligerent than his brother's, foresaw what such an approach would entail: "Your glory will be shipwrecked in Spain," Joseph wrote frantically, but to no avail.[11] Napoleon was convinced that Spain would be subjugated once its armies were defeated. "Have no fears concerning war," Napoleon wrote in an attempt at reassurance, "and do not be uneasy about the success of my armies in Spain."[12]

Where French forces encountered regular Spanish armies, though, they met with higher levels of success. The Spanish armies were composed principally of raw recruits, who had received very little training, and in some cases did not even know how to use the weapons they carried. Unsurprising, then, that at Medina de Rioseco in Old Castile, the first battle of the Peninsular War on 14 July 1808, the French obtained a total victory, the Spaniards fleeing the field in disarray. Thereafter, Napoleon believed that a success for Dupont in Andalucía would extinguish the flame of resistance. "It is now necessary to support General Dupont," the emperor wrote insistently on 17 July. "It is of great

---

8   cc, Joseph to Napoleon, 18 July 1808, 1:334.
9   Ibid., Joseph to Napoleon, 22 July 1808, 1:340.
10 Ibid., Napoleon to Joseph, 31 July 1808, 1:341–342.
11 Ibid., Joseph to Napoleon, 24 July 1808, 1:341.
12 Ibid., Napoleon to Joseph, 18 July 1808, 1:331.

consequence that General Dupont should beat the Army of Andalucía ... General Dupont is now the principal object."[13]

But any pretence that the French were on course for the immediate and complete subjugation of the peninsula was dispelled on 19 July, when Dupont, instead of achieving a decisive victory, was forced to surrender 17,000 French troops to General Francisco Javier Castaños, having sustained 2,200 casualties and been cut off from retreat during the hard-fought Battle of Bailén. The defeat was devastating for the French; Joseph, having only just arrived in Madrid, promptly abandoned the capital and retreated with his whole force behind the Ebro River, in the northeast of Spain. "Dupont has dishonoured our flag. What incapacity!" wrote an enraged Napoleon. "What cowardice!"[14] In any event, Bailén had two effects. In the first instance, it convinced the Spanish that they were capable of defeating the French without support or, more tellingly, any significant political or military reform, thus lulling them into a false sense of security. In the second instance, it prompted Napoleon to send massive reinforcements, consisting of elite French troops, to the peninsula.

In this atmosphere, delegates from Asturias arrived in England seeking assistance from the British government. Ordinarily, the Spanish delegates might have encountered apathy upon arrival in London. The Iberian peninsula was of peripheral strategic relevance in Britain's war effort. Instead, Britain traditionally focused its military efforts on liberating the Low Countries or the Mediterranean, while diplomatic and financial resources were centered on building a coalition of powers to enable a decisive victory over France.[15] But between 1806 and 1807 that strategy had foundered badly. First Austria in 1805, then Prussia in 1806, and finally Russia in 1807, one by one the great powers of Europe had all succumbed to Napoleon's military skill. Realizing that an invasion of the British Isles was perhaps unfeasible in the short term, Napoleon elected instead to impose the Continental System, and the British reaction – designed to isolate France from any global trade – only antagonized the neutral European powers, and eventually led to war with the United States in 1812. So desperate had Britain's position become that the government genuinely considered abandoning Europe and the Mediterranean and focusing its efforts on

---

13   Ibid., Napoleon to Joseph, 17 July 1808, 1:330.
14   Ibid., Napoleon to Joseph, Bordeaux, 3 August 1808, 1:344.
15   See Huw J. Davies, *Wellington's Wars: The Making of a Military Genius* (London, 2012), ch. 4, for an in-depth discussion of British strategic thinking at the beginning of the Peninsular War.

building a new empire in South America after a successful British incursion there in 1806.[16]

Such a policy would have been madness, however, because the Mediterranean was a bastion against French expansion in the Near and Middle East. With no allies on the continent, and no obvious way of exerting its limited military power on land, Britain looked for alternative strategies. The Franco-Russian alliance that emerged in 1807 in the aftermath of the War of the Fourth Coalition forced London's hand. British intelligence on the negotiations seemed to indicate that Napoleon planned to seize one of the last remaining viable navies in Northern Europe by either reaching an agreement with the Danes or invading Denmark. Such a coup would have been disastrous for Britain, with the Danish navy representing at least a local threat to the Royal Navy's command of the sea.

In response to this intelligence, the British organized a preemptive strike on Copenhagen harbor in July 1807. Although the attack caused a rupture in Anglo-Danish relations, it nevertheless successfully deprived Napoleon access to a key resource. A new strategy thus presented itself to the British. If one decisive blow against Napoleon was currently impossible, then Britain could use its tiny army to deprive the French access to key resources. When the delegates of the Galician and Asturian juntas arrived in London in 1807, then, the British government recognized another opportunity to deny Napoleon access to a useful navy. While military aid could be provided to the Spaniards in the form of arms, ammunition, materiel, and advisors, Britain's main interest could be met in seizing and securing the Spanish navy in Cádiz. This explains why Britain became interested in the Iberian peninsula from a strategic point of view.

Given the absence of other continental military opportunities, combined with the chance to deny Napoleon access to naval resources in Spain and Portugal, as well as key resources in their colonies, Britain enthusiastically delivered. Within two months of the outbreak of the rebellion, 12,000 swords, 30 guns, large amounts of ammunition, and £500,000 had been sent.[17] Spain, though, did not want military intervention, despite the British government offering armed support. For a foothold on the continent, Britain would have to look to Portugal. Spurred on by news of French brutality in Lisbon, and of the rebellion in Spain, similar nationalist movements developed in northern Portugal. A new government coalesced around rebel leaders in Porto, and it is

---

16   See Martin Robson, *Britain, Portugal and South America in the Napoleonic Wars: Alliances and Diplomacy in Economic Maritime Conflict* (London, 2011).
17   Esdaile, *Peninsular War*, 89.

from there that the British received requests for assistance. Supporting the Portuguese was enticing for the British for a number of reasons, but primarily because of the opportunity the intervention offered of neutralizing French and Russian naval forces that were harbored in the Tagus.[18]

A small military force commanded by a junior lieutenant-general named Arthur Wellesley, which had been preparing for deployment to Venezuela, was instead diverted to Portugal. Napoleon was dismissive of the British intervention. "The English are of little importance," he wrote to Joseph after hearing of Wellesley's deployment. "They have never more than a quarter of the troops that they profess to have."[19] Wellesley landed at Mondego Bay on 1 August 1808. Three weeks later, having marched his army toward Lisbon, Wellesley won an important victory over Junot's forces at the Battle of Vimeiro. Initial intelligence had indicated that Junot commanded only 4,000 men but, when it was discovered that French strength was closer to ten times that number, the British government reacted quickly and dispatched thousands of reinforcements. Wellesley was too junior a general to command such a vast force, however, and at the climax of his victory he was superseded in command by Sir Harry Burrard, who was in turn superseded by Sir Hew Whitefoord Dalrymple. Both generals were weak and indecisive and refused to follow up Wellesley's victory. Instead, when Junot offered terms, Dalrymple and Burrard accepted without question. The terms were too generous and, when news of them broke in London, all three were recalled to account for their actions in a court of inquiry. This left Sir John Moore in command of the British army, which was by now in Lisbon.

Moore was a superb general, considered to be a future commander in chief, but he had some serious personality defects that had perhaps hampered his rise. Among them was the impression he gave of aloofness and disdain, and a permanent sense of disgruntlement. These were to manifest in a devastating fashion throughout the autumn. Following Castaños's victory over Dupont at Bailén, and with Junot's force evacuated from Portugal, the new alliance

---

18   Robson, *Britain, Portugal and South America*, 220–222; The National Archives (TNA) WO 1/228, Castlereagh to Wellesley, 21 June 1808; J. Gurwood, *The Dispatches of Field Marshal the Duke of Wellington During His Various Campaigns in India, Denmark, Portugal, Spain, the Low Countries and France*, 13 vols (hereafter cited as *WD*) (London, 1852), 4:8–9. In the wake of the Treaty of Tilsit, a Russian naval squadron under the command of Admiral Dmitry Nikolayevich Senyavin, was withdrawn from the Mediterranean and was sheltering in the Tagus when the Royal Navy began its blockade of the harbor following the flight of the Portuguese royal family. In reality, Senyavin was an Anglophile who refused to support Junot against the Portuguese or British when they landed, but his presence remained a cause of concern to the British government.

19   *CC*, Napoleon to Joseph, Niot, 9 August 1808, 1:346.

between Spain, Britain, and Portugal seemed to be bearing unusually ripe fruit, unusually quickly. Spain appeared all but liberated, and a short decisive campaign with Spanish forces capitalizing on their gains in the south, and a British supporting drive to the north of Madrid, might deal a fatal blow to the short-lived Bonapartist monarchy in the peninsula. Moore remained unsure of the nature of the terrain beyond the Portuguese border, and was even less convinced of the durability of the Spanish victory. He waited until he could be sure that a British advance deep into northwestern Spain would reap sufficient rewards.

After the humiliating defeat at Bailén, Joseph withdrew his forces behind the Ebro River, an unnecessarily cautious move, and one that annoyed Napoleon. "The country which suits your army is a flat country, and you have entangled yourself in a mountainous one, without reason or necessity. In so precipitate a retreat," he continued, "how many things must have been lost or forgotten! The army retiring in this manner cannot but have been exceedingly demoralized." Calming down a little, Napoleon tried to assuage his brother's concerns. "In your position, one sees enemies everywhere, and sees them immensely strong. Your army, organized as it is, is capable of beating all the insurgents; but it wants a head."[20] Herein lay the primary difficulty Joseph would face throughout his reign. While he was nominally commander in chief of French forces in Spain, there was little he could do to make the marshals follow his orders, and Napoleon would in any case continue to direct the campaigns remotely. In this particular instance, though, Napoleon had decided that he had to intervene personally to retrieve the deteriorating French position in the peninsula.

Meanwhile, the French retreat behind the Ebro was greeted with universal joy throughout Spain. The effect of this retreat was to confirm in the Spanish mind that victory against France was not only possible, but also could be obtained with relatively little effort: conscription was implemented only half-heartedly, limited reforms were made to the armed forces, and the government, what there was to speak of, entered a state of paralysis. The population, on the other hand, turned on itself, and the violence that ensued was directed as much against the enlightened absolutism of Charles IV's regime as it had been against the French.

Only after two months was a central junta created (23 September 1808), and even then it refused to appoint a commander in chief with the authority to unite the military efforts of the armed rebellions throughout the regions of Spain. The central junta, meanwhile, attempted to reinforce the war effort by

---

20   Ibid., Napoleon to Joseph, Saint-Cloud, 16 August 1808, 1:348.

imposing a variety of emergency war contributions on the regional juntas, but in so doing it represented a serious threat to the independence of those regions, not least because the British switched all aid from the regional to the central junta.[21] On top of this, the army was in a parlous state. Overstocked with inexperienced officers and recruits, undertrained and -equipped, the army could stand well on the defensive, but was frequently outmaneuvered. When put to flight, there was no possibility of rallying the troops. The inevitable defeat was likely to be heavy, as the absence of any significant cavalry arm left the infantry unprotected and vulnerable to horse-borne attack. This threat was compounded by the open terrain of much of Spain, devoid of natural defensive positions to shelter from such an attack.

In the absence of a supreme commander, a war council was convened with the remit to reform the Patriot forces in Spain. On 5 September, they agreed to a major reorganization of the Spanish armies, into four principal forces, named the Armies of the Left, Center, Right, and Reserve. The dispositions of these forces were ill conceived, and their command and control abysmal, while infighting among the leading generals rendered cooperation between the armies nearly impossible. All in all, then, the Spanish were comprehensively underprepared to meet the shock and awe Napoleon was preparing across the Pyrenees.

Napoleon responded to Bailén with a vengeance unseen before during his reign in France. Securing his rear by offering Russia concessions in Finland and Poland, and threatening complete destruction on Austria and Prussia, he also offered peace to Britain. Into Spain he poured 130,000 reinforcements from the Grande Armée, including the elite Imperial Guard, and raised a further 80,000 new recruits. The Army of Spain was reorganized into six *corps d'armée*, half of which were transferred from Germany in a "masterpiece of planning and administration," with troops setting out on the long journey on 22 August, and arriving at Bayonne no later than the middle of November.[22] Napoleon's concern lay primarily in the belief that defeat at the hands of the mob in Spain would incite similar rebellions across Europe. In this analysis, he was correct, although a crushing military response was not necessarily the most effective means of response. His plan of operations consisted of a major offensive against the Spanish center, based around Burgos, followed by a drive on Madrid, before launching a series of turning maneuvers to destroy the remaining Spanish forces. His principal tactic of concentration of strength on vulnerable parts of the enemy line was likely to yield rapid results against the

---

21 Esdaile, *Peninsular War*, 121.
22 Chandler, *Campaigns of Napoleon*, 630.

disorganized Spanish, while his superior organization ensured startlingly rapid movements.

Napoleon ordered several shaping operations to "prepare for those which will take place when the reinforcements arrive, and will afford an army of 60,000 men the room, the activity, and the confidence which it ought to have."[23] Desperate, perhaps, to act before his brother's arrival, and recoup some of his lost prestige and independence, Joseph suggested collecting as many troops as possible and marching on Madrid. "I shall beat the large bodies, and I shall spread terror among the inhabitants of Madrid," Joseph wrote exuberantly. "They will fling away their arms and their pens when they know that 50,000 French are marching on them."[24] This was an uncharacteristically violent proposal from Joseph, who had until now advocated conciliation and negotiation, rather than retribution. In any event, Napoleon rubbished the suggestion: "The proposal is to march with 50,000 men on Madrid, keeping them together, and abandoning all communication with France," he wrote matter-of-factly in response. "The art of war is an art founded on principles which must not be violated. To change one's line of operation is an operation which only a man of genius ought to attempt." The implication was clear: he was a man of genius; Joseph was not. But Napoleon was not finished; "to lose one's line of operation is so dangerous that to be guilty of it is a crime." He continued:

> There is no doubt that with the number of troops which from the Army of Spain you may march to Madrid, and you ought to do so, but only after having destroyed all the enemy's corps by combined movements on Palencia and Zaragoza, if the enemy commits the fault of approaching you in force. But to do this, one must have one's army in hand, understand one's art, and act on the spur of the moment. I can only repeat what I have said again: attack the enemy if he comes within two marches. If you obtain a decisive victory over his united force, or several victories over his separate corps, those victories will point out what is to be done. But all these battles must be fought according to the rules of war; that is to say, with the lines of operation secure.[25]

In essence, Napoleon had outlined his plan of attack when he arrived in Spain.

To meet Napoleon's counteroffensive, the Spanish deployed their six provincial armies in two defensive lines. On the right of the first line, immediately

---

23   CC, Napoleon to Joseph, Saint-Cloud, 14 September 1808, 1:358.
24   Ibid., Joseph to Napoleon, Miranda de Ebro, 14 September 1808, 1:360.
25   Ibid., Napoleon to Joseph, Châlons-sur-Marne, 16 September 1808, 1:362.

opposite Joseph's 75,000 on the Ebro, was General José Rebolledo de Palafox y Melci who commanded a force that on paper measured some 42,000 men, but in reality barely managed to deploy 25,000 in the field. In the center, meanwhile, the victor of Bailén, General Castaños, commanded 31,000 infantry and 3,000 cavalry, to the south and east of Logroño, while on the left, General Joaquín Blake y Joyes commanded 43,000 Galicians and Asturians, only 32,000 of which were at the front line around Reinosa, with the remainder at Astorga. Two other smaller armies were in reserve: that commanded by José Galluzo y Páez supported Castaños near Burgos with 13,000 troops, while 20,000 troops were in Catalonia, besieging Barcelona. The second defensive line – more truthfully, a ragged assortment of badly trained or invalid troops – saw 15,000 troops at Granada, 13,000 at Madrid, 13,000 scattered in various garrisons from Asturias to Extremadura, 22,000 militiamen at Zaragoza, and 12,000 reserves in Andalucía. Altogether, the first line was composed of 125,000 troops, with perhaps 80,000 available at a push in the second line.[26] Setting aside the relative weakness and poor quality of the Spanish force, the plan of operations developed in the early autumn was a recipe for disaster. The left and right wings were to push forward in an attempt to envelop the French forces east of the Ebro. Blake would march along the Biscay coastline toward Bilbao, while Castaños and Palafox would push forward toward Pamplona, turning the French flank as they did so. The plan left the Spanish center completely exposed, creating a gap of some 200 miles between the two wings of the Spanish force.

There were significant misgivings about the Spanish plan. Moore called it a "sort of gibberish,"[27] while a British liaison officer, Samuel Whittingham, at Castaños's headquarters feared "the result of this action. The French are concentrated, and we are considerably scattered. Their troops are all equal; ours, some bad and some good. They have the advantage of unity of command; we are directed by three generals, all independent of each other ... We are not yet organised, and ... I cannot help entertaining some doubts of the issue of the first battle ... For the first time in my life," Whittingham concluded, "my heart misgives me, and forebodes no good."[28]

In truth, the Spanish were playing straight into Napoleon's hands. In an operational plan that exhibited characteristic boldness and simplicity, Napoleon planned to wait until the two wings of the Spanish armies had

---

26   Chandler, *Campaigns of Napoleon*, 626–627.
27   Ibid., 629.
28   F. Whittingham, ed., *A Memoir of the Services of Lieutenant-General Sir Samuel Ford Whittingham* (London, 1868), 48–50.

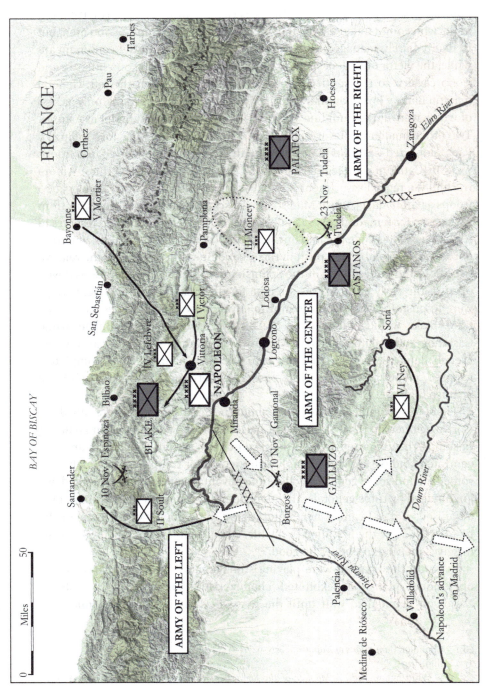

MAP 9.1 Napoleon's advance to the Ebro

advanced far enough from their supply bases, and then strike both simultaneously by encircling them and cutting off their line of retreat, while he himself advanced in overwhelming force on the weak Spanish center at Burgos. The assault against Blake's Army of the Left on the Biscay coast was to be led by Marshals François Joseph Lefebvre (IV Corps) and Victor (I Corps), while Ney (VI Corps) and Moncey (III Corps) would attack Castaños and Palafox on the right. However, at Pancorbo on 31 October, Lefebvre was unable to contain himself and attacked Blake prematurely. The Spanish sustained 600 dead and wounded, the French fewer than 200, but Blake was alerted to the coming French onslaught and began a precipitate retreat.

Napoleon was understandably furious. If he was to crush Spanish resistance, he had to first wipe out the regular Spanish armies. His plan of action was entirely dependent on his ability to destroy Blake, Castaños, and Palafox. If their armies escaped, they would continue to pose a threat to the French, and give the insurrection the breathing space it needed to flourish and take hold. Lefebvre's rash action posed a serious threat to the main objective of the whole plan. Meanwhile, Napoleon was experiencing supply problems as the Spanish winter began to take hold. "I have only ... 7,000 great-coats instead of 50,000; 15,000 pairs of shoes instead of 129,000 ... My army will begin the campaign naked: it has nothing," he raged at his Director of Administration of War, Jean François Aimé Dejean. "The conscripts are not clothed. Your reports are waste paper."[29] The Spanish, meanwhile, were in a similar predicament. More than a third of their force was unable to join the front line because of similar shortages of clothing.[30]

Despite these shortcomings, which were clearly exaggerated, Lefebvre's premature attack forced Napoleon's hand, and he ordered the three-pronged advance to commence on 6 November. He gave explicit orders to Victor to move as quickly as possible, as there was still a chance Blake could be cut off. Perhaps continuing to underestimate Blake's generalship, however, Victor and Lefebvre advanced with little urgency, allowing their columns to become strung out along the rain-swept Cantabrian mountains. At the same time, Blake's strength had increased, with the arrival of Pedro Caro y Sureda, marqués de la Romana, smuggled out of Denmark by the Royal Navy, to 24,000 all arms. On 5 November, Blake turned around and attacked Victor's vanguard under the command of General Eugène-Casimir Villatte, at a tiny village called Valmaçeda. The French were taken completely by surprise and Villatte was

---

29 *CC*, Napoleon to Dejean, Director of Administration of War, Bayonne, 4 November 1808, 1:369.
30 Whittingham, *Memoir*, 48–50.

forced to withdraw, forming his infantry into square to facilitate his retreat. Napoleon was once more furious: "His Majesty is severely displeased," wrote Berthier to Victor, "that you left General Villatte at grips with the enemy without moving to his aid."[31]

Blake recommenced his withdrawal until he reached Espinosa on 10 November. There he deployed his army in a strong defensive position, and Victor took the opportunity to attack with his three divisions, but he would again be surprised by the quality of the Spanish resistance. "Their arrogance came to grief in the face of the valour and serenity of our division," recounted Juan Manuel Sarasa, one of the Spanish defenders. "Letting our opponents approach to within ten paces, with every volley we brought down an entire column. The enemy repeated their attacks with fresh troops, but each time ... they were beaten back, leaving mountains of corpses in front of our lines."[32] The following day, Victor renewed the attack, but this time followed a more determined and considered plan. This time, he sent forward a thick skirmish line that, as it advanced against the weakly held Spanish center, targeted officers and NCOs. Eventually, the Spanish line collapsed, and Blake was forced to withdraw. This time, there would be no sudden rearguard actions. The remains of his army struggled through freezing rain and snow, across some of the highest mountain ranges in Spain. Less than half his original fighting force of 43,000 made it to the relative safety of León. Blake's army had not been destroyed as Napoleon would have wished but, for the time being at least, it was no longer a credible fighting force.

At the same time, the Spanish were dealt an even more serious and crippling blow in the center of their defensive line. Napoleon himself commanded a 67,000-strong force in the main attack directed against Burgos. Against him was the Spanish Army of Extremadura, now under the command of the inexperienced General Ramón Fernando Patiño y Osorio, conde de Belveder. Napoleon had halted his army at the small village of Gamonal and, as soon as the first corps of his army had arrived, he deployed the "three infantry divisions, a division of dragoons and half of the Guard ... not in line," recalled one participant, Dezydery Chlapowski, one of Napoleon's aides de camp, "but in battalion column with skirmishers in front. The skirmishers went into line, and the artillery must have fired about 500 rounds at the enemy."[33] The impact was devastating and immediate. Confusion swiftly broke out in the Spanish ranks

---

31 Quoted in Chandler, *Campaigns of Napoleon*, 633.
32 Sarasa, *Vida y hechos*, 11, quoted in Charles Esdaile, *Peninsular Eyewitnesses: The Experience of War in Spain and Portugal 1808–1813* (London, 2008), 52.
33 T. Simmons, ed., *Memoirs of a Polish Lancer: The Pamietniki of Dezydery Chlapowski* (Chicago, 1992), 43.

and, as the skirmishers found their marks, discipline broke down completely. Passing through the scene of the battle the following day, André Miot de Melito, a close aide of Joseph Bonaparte's, recounted a field "still strewn with corpses," while Burgos had suffered a terrible fate. "Almost all the houses had been pillaged and their furniture smashed to pieces ... part of the city was on fire ... and the streets were encumbered with the dead and dying."[34]

With the Spanish center in tatters and the left fleeing to León, the final attack against the Spanish right, led by Marshals Lannes (who had replaced Moncey) and Ney was to commence. Castaños and Palafox had been quarreling between themselves as to who was in overall command on the right, and as a result were in a state of confusion when Lannes's attack commenced on 21 November. Castaños ordered a partial withdrawal to Tudela. Badly handled, his army by the evening of the 22nd was split in half by the Ebro, occupying two hills, which, in the view of one officer in the French army who arrived the following day, "were perhaps too steep as artillery on such heights cannot fire downwards effectively."[35]

Napoleon had ordered Lannes to make a frontal assault in the direction of Tudela, forcing the Spanish to give battle, while Ney took a circuitous route to the south and west in order to cut off Castaños's line of retreat. Lannes attacked Castaños's 45,000-strong army on 23 November with 29,000 infantry and 5,000 cavalry. "Before dawn, two infantry divisions set off up the hillside in four columns with skirmishers out in front," recalled Chlapowski, now aide de camp to Marshal Lannes. "The Spanish outposts half-way up fired at them and retired to the summits, from which the artillery opened a heavy fire. For two hours, the French columns did not stop, and their skirmishers duly reached the ridgeline."[36]

The Battle of Tudela was marked by appalling incidents of Spanish incompetence. First, Castaños failed to utilize his cavalry in a reconnaissance role in order to identify the French line of attack; then, entire Spanish units refused to engage in the fight, watching as the French took a remorseless toll on the center of the Spanish line. Indeed, one observer commented that fewer than half the French attacking force was engaged during the battle, which raged "sometimes this way, sometimes that, from morning to night, but none of our troops were engaged for more than two hours at any one time."[37] This gave rise to criticism from Napoleon that Lannes might have more effectively utilized his forces

---

34   A. Miot de Melito, *Mémoires du Comte Miot de Melito* (Paris, 1858), 3:22, quoted in Esdaile, *Peninsular Eyewitnesses*, 51.
35   Simmons, *Memoirs of a Polish Lancer*, 43.
36   Ibid.
37   J. North, ed., *In the Legions of Napoleon: The Memoirs of a Polish Officer in Spain and Russia, 1808–1823* (London, 1999), 46.

to achieve the total destruction of Castaños's army. In the course of the day, 4,000 Spaniards were killed or wounded, and 26 guns were lost, but the Spaniards were able to limp back to Zaragoza with their force damaged but intact.[38] Ney, meanwhile, was too far to the southwest to be able to complete the enveloping maneuver that Napoleon had prescribed for him. Although he marched his force at an astonishing rate, 120 miles of poor roads still lay between him and Tudela on the evening of the 23rd, and he was able to bring his force into position only on the 26th.

Napoleon now took the opportunity to make one final advance to recapture Madrid. The advance began on 28 November, and was formed once more in three columns, the main central column led by Napoleon, with flanking columns commanded by Lefebvre and Ney. In total, 130,000 French troops began the march south. Lefebvre, on the right, would march via Palencia, Valladolid, and Segovia, while Ney advanced via Guadalajara. Napoleon himself would take 45,000 men, composed principally of the Imperial Guard and two heavy cavalry divisions, and march down the main route to Madrid across the Sierra de Guadarrama mountains, immediately north of Madrid.

There, at Somosierra, a 1,500-meter-high pass, Napoleon encountered the last remaining obstacle to his reconquest of Madrid, a scratch-force of Spanish troops under the command of General Benito de San Juan, who had divided his 13,000 troops in two. One branch occupied the outlying village of Sepulveda, while a second occupied the highest and narrowest part of the pass. This force had dug entrenchments across the pass, some of them with artillery batteries, making the road virtually impassable. Napoleon ordered an immediate reconnaissance, which revealed the extent of the Spanish defences, although the pass was shrouded in heavy fog. On 29 November, Napoleon attacked the 3,500 Spaniards occupying Sepulveda, but suffered a bloody repulse. Unfortunately for San Juan, facing odds of more than ten to one, the occupants of Sepulveda abandoned their position that night.

Napoleon had been informed by his reconnaissance that the road would need to be repaired, but that the Spaniards had deployed their infantry poorly, failing to protect their flanks. Rather than wait, however, Napoleon ordered Louis-Pierre Montbrun to make an immediate assault with Captain Jan Leon Hipolit Kozietulski's 3rd Squadron of the Polish 1st Light Cavalry Regiment of the Imperial Guard in spite of the fact that the reconnaissance and attack on Sepulveda the previous day had given away the French position and the Poles would be charging into the mouths of sixteen artillery pieces. The road was so narrow that Kozietulski was forced to deploy his unit four abreast, and

---

38   Chandler, *Campaigns of Napoleon*, 637.

commence what would become one of the most gallant charges of the Peninsular War.

The "Polish cavalry galloped up the mountain, fell upon the Spanish entrenchments and sabered some of the artillerymen at their posts," recalled Louis-François Lejeune, Napoleon's aide de camp, "but the roughness of the ground, combined with the volley of grapeshot which met him, compelled [them] to retreat and rally ... beyond the range of the guns."[39] Witnessing what he perceived to be a second reverse, Napoleon reputedly flew into a rage. "My Guard must not be stopped by peasants, by mere armed brigands!"[40] He ordered the charge to recommence but, according to Lejeune, "in the thick of the hail of shot, the Poles recognized the emperor himself and ... returned to the charge, overcame all the obstacles which had deterred them at first, carrying everything before them and penetrating into the very heart of the formidable position of the Spaniards who were unable in the fog to see how very small the attacking column was. The cavalry of the guard followed the movement [and] every one of the Spanish gunners ... was cut down."[41]

Lejeune was exaggerating the success of the cavalry charge. The Poles had suffered sixty casualties out of the eighty-six men in Kozietulski's squadron, and was no longer an effective fighting force. Napoleon now ordered in a combined-arms attack. Infantry penetrated the unguarded hillsides on each Spanish flank, while the 96th Regiment capitalized on the damage done by the cavalry charge, and finally secured control of the pass. With the Spanish units now wavering, a third cavalry charge was ordered, and only then, as Lejeune had recorded, were all the Spanish guns finally captured, and did San Juan's army disintegrate. Napoleon praised the gallantry of his Polish cavalry and, as a reward, promoted the squadron "straight from the Young to the Old Guard, and ... also ordered the whole Guard to present arms to the squadron as it passed by."[42]

The following day, the French army reached the suburbs of Madrid, where 20,000 citizens had been armed to supplement the remaining 2,500 regular soldiers. The defence would not last long. On 4 December, Napoleon ordered a devastating bombardment and storming of the makeshift defences at the Retiro Heights. By midday, the Spanish capital had surrendered. Thus ended Napoleon's counteroffensive. Bailén had been categorically avenged. Madrid, Burgos, Santander, and Bilbao were all recaptured. Although not the complete

---

39 Lejeune, *Memoirs*, 1:87–90.
40 Quoted in Chandler, *Campaigns of Napoleon*, 641.
41 Lejeune, *Memoirs*, 1:87–90.
42 Simmons, *Memoirs of a Polish Lancer*, 45.

annihilation of the Spanish forces that Napoleon had hoped for, the three-pronged attack on the Spanish defensive lines was outstandingly successful. All three Spanish armies had been dealt blows of varying degrees of severity. The conde de Belveder's force had been all but destroyed outside Burgos, and Blake's army had been so badly damaged by its encounter with Victor and its subsequent retreat through the Cantabrian mountains that it would no longer play a role in the 1808 campaign. Only Castaños had escaped and, although some of his men would fight again at Somosierra, the rout suffered by San Juan on 30 November had effectively destroyed the Spanish reserve forces as well.

Yet all around were grim forebodings of the nature of the war that the French were now engaged in. Following the victory at Gamonal, for instance, the French had quickly set about pillaging Burgos, including the cathedral, where a small group of horse grenadiers had paused to feed their horses. "At the foot of a small stairway there appeared a little boy of eleven or twelve," recalled one observer, Jean-Roche Coignet. "As soon as one of them saw him, he ran back up the stairway, but the grenadier caught up with him at the top of the steps. As soon as he reached the landing, the little boy entered with him. The door closed, and the ... little boy came down again." The scene repeated itself several more times, each time a grenadier disappeared into the room at the top of the stairway in the tower of the cathedral. Becoming suspicious that none of their comrades had returned, the remainder of the grenadiers stormed up the stairs, "burst open the door, and found their comrades lying there with their heads cut off and bathed in their own blood." Enraged, the soldiers slaughtered the monks and threw "the little boy out of the windows and into the garden."[43]

Elsewhere, the French encountered eerie silence and deserted towns where they expected bustling communities. "We no longer saw those clouds of smoke, which, constantly rising through the air, form a second atmosphere over inhabited and populous cities," observed French officer Albert Jean Michel de Rocca. "The houses, now empty, served only to re-echo tardily and discordantly the deep sounds of the drum or the shrill notes of the trumpet."[44] Villages and towns, even parts of Madrid, were deserted, the populace fleeing before the arrival of the French. Some fled in fear of their lives, others to join growing bands of resistance in the countryside. Soon, the French were unable to communicate easily, with unguarded couriers snatched from the road, horribly tortured and mutilated, before being left as grisly portents of what awaited their comrades should they too be captured. The failure of Napoleon's marshals

---

43 J. Fortescue, ed., *The Notebook of Captain Coignet* (London, 1989), 165–166.
44 P. Haythornthwaite, ed., *Memoirs of the War of the French in Spain* (London, 1990), 32–33.

to execute his plan properly had allowed the Spanish armies to escape, albeit in tatters. The Spanish army has been criticized for its performance in the Peninsular War, but its survival instinct, to flee a battle already lost, before the French could exact the complete annihilation of the force allowed Spanish resistance to continue.

Alongside the presence of a small army of British redcoats, the combination of regular and irregular Spanish resistance could pose a major threat to the French war effort. However, Napoleon now appeared convinced that Moore's redcoats posed no serious threat to his northwestern flank, and he instead turned his attention to reforming the Spanish state and preparing forces for the conquest of southern Spain and Portugal. In order to effect this set of objectives, Napoleon began to collect huge numbers of troops in the vicinity of Madrid. In the capital itself, Napoleon remained in command of 40,000 troops while Junot marched across the border with a further corps. Marshal Mortier with V Corps was to engage in the ongoing – and soon to be bloody – siege of Zaragoza. General Laurent de Gouvion Saint Cyr, with VII Corps consisting of 30,000 troops, was on his way to Barcelona to commence the subjugation of Catalonia. Soult was given 17,000 troops to quell the rebellious provinces of León and Old Castile. Finally, Lefebvre and Victor received orders to prepare to march on Lisbon and Seville respectively.[45] It appears as though Napoleon had not given a second thought to Moore's army. It was something of a shock, then, to discover that, rather than fleeing headlong for a safe evacuation from Lisbon, Moore had, in fact, commenced an advance from Salamanca up the Douro valley.

Since succeeding to the command of Britain's only field army in early September, Moore had begun preparations for an advance into northern Spain, in coordination with Blake and Belveder. The British war effort in the peninsula was dogged throughout by poor cartography. In 1808, Moore was incorrectly informed that the quickest route from Lisbon to Salamanca, via Coimbra, was impassable for cavalry and artillery. As a result, Moore sent half his army on an unnecessary 130-mile detour through Badajoz and Talavera before it could join him at Salamanca. It was not until late November that Moore had collected his whole army, including the reinforcements under the command of General Sir David Baird, who had arrived from Coruña.

Halted at Salamanca, Moore now encountered a dearth of information on events in the Spanish capital and beyond, a situation somewhat exacerbated by the Spaniard's refusal to report reality. "The difficulties of information of the enemy's movements is very great, and you are by no means to believe what you

---

45   Chandler, *Campaigns of Napoleon*, 644.

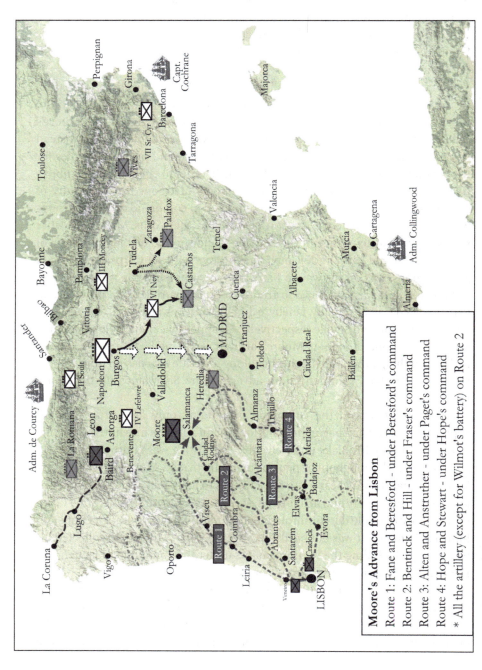

MAP 9.2 Moore's advance from Lisbon

see in the Papers of their total evacuation of Old Castile &c &c," complained Baird's aide de camp, Alexander Gordon. "On the contrary, we have received accounts of their having pushed forward some small parties to within a few leagues of Burgos."[46] This was extremely frustrating for Moore, who now perceived the opportunity to strike on the French flank slipping from his grasp.

After news reached his headquarters of the Spanish rout at Tudela, Moore elected to retreat to Lisbon but, a week later, startling news reached him that the people of Madrid were heroically resisting French attempts to capture their city. With this in mind, then, Moore decided to march into Old Castile, in an effort to draw off the French forces attacking Madrid. Soon after he marched, news arrived of the capitulation of Madrid, but the logic of Moore's movement still remained. A surprise strike into Old Castile might prevent further encroachment of French forces into Andalucía, allow the defeated Spanish forces to regroup, and also protect Portugal. Inevitably, the British would have to retreat, but a considerable delay could be imposed on the French advance, reinvigorating the Spanish resistance.

Moore's staff was by no means confident that their commander had made the correct decision. His second in command, Baird, was unconvinced. "I must say this Spirit is too late," wrote Captain Gordon, "the French are now too strong."[47] Moore had also been warned that the French advance was likely to force the Spanish to fall back on Valladolid.[48] Nevertheless, he clearly felt a certain amount of political pressure to advance to support the Spanish allies: "They have been buoyed up in England by the false information transmitted by the officers sent to the various Spanish armies," Moore recorded anxiously in his diary, "who had neither sense nor honesty to tell the truth, so that Lord Castlereagh has very little idea of the situation in which we are here."[49] To some degree this was true: the British minister in Lisbon, John Hookham Frere, had taken a view through somewhat rose-tinted spectacles of the entire Spanish position, but it was also an attempt to justify Moore's vulnerable position in central Spain.

The truth of the matter was that Moore had fallen between two stools representing British strategic values in 1808: namely supporting allies and not risking the army. Aware that he had to advance to justify the British deployment to Spain, he was also undoubtedly aware that to do so carried with it enormous

---

46 Gordon to Aberdeen, Coruña, 30 October 1808, in R. Muir, ed., *At Wellington's Right Hand: The Letters of Lieutenant-Colonel Sir Alexander Gordon, 1808–1815* (Stroud, 2003), 7.
47 Gordon to Aberdeen, Villa Franca, 7 December 1808, ibid., 12.
48 National Library of Scotland, Edinburgh (hereafter cited as NLS), MS 21261, Stuart to Moore, Aranjuez, 27 October 1809.
49 J.F. Maurice, ed., *The Diary of Sir John Moore*, 2 vols (London, 1904), 2:281.

risk. That said, intercepted French dispatches captured by Spanish guerrillas gave Moore excellent local operational intelligence.[50] He was thus well informed of the French dispositions, and also knew that the French did not know of his dispositions. The opportunity to strike a blow was too great to ignore. Therefore, aware of the risk of having his "communication with the Galicias interrupted, but from a wish to do something I took my chance."[51] On 11 December 1808, Moore commenced his advance northeast from Salamanca with 22,500 infantry, 2,500 cavalry, and 66 guns.[52]

On 13 December, Moore received another intercepted dispatch. This one was from Berthier instructing Soult to move north against La Romana's forces at Leon. If Soult followed the instruction, it would leave him badly exposed. "The letter states," recorded Moore in his diary, "that Madrid was quiet, that the troops were on their march to Badajoz," while Soult would find "nothing Spanish could oppose his two divisions, and the English had retreated into Portugal."[53] On the 17th, Moore received word from La Romana that the latter was prepared, with his 22,000 troops, to cooperate with the British, but Moore "placed no dependence on him or his army."[54] Moore had no time to wait for the Spanish, and instead pressed on in an effort to catch Soult while the latter was isolated. A British victory would rip a hole in the French flank and jeopardize Napoleon's communications with Bayonne.

On the 20th, however, these plans were dealt a blow when Moore received word that Soult had not moved north as instructed. Moore had marched north needlessly and, if he was to catch Soult, he would now need to march south to Saldanha. Nevertheless, the following day, the British cavalry distinguished themselves at Sahagún de Campos, where two regiments of hussars attacked a 700-strong brigade of Soult's cavalry, consisting of the 1st Provincial Chasseurs and the 9th Dragoons.

Posted near the road to Carrión de los Condes, the French squadrons proved a tempting target, and the British cavalry commander, General Henry William, Lord Paget (the future marquess of Anglesey), ordered an immediate attack. "The French, upon our coming in sight, made a flank movement, apparently with the intention of getting away," recalled Gordon, a captain in the 15th Hussars, "but the rapidity of our advance soon convinced them of the futility of

---

50 Esdaile, *Peninsular War*, 148. Moore also received intercepted dispatches from Stuart. See NLS MS 21261, correspondence between Stuart and Moore, autumn 1808.
51 B. Brownrigg, *The Life and Letters of Sir John Moore* (Oxford, 1923), 241.
52 Chandler, *Campaigns of Napoleon*, 646.
53 Maurice, *Diary of John Moore*, 2:285.
54 Ibid., 286.

such an attempt." Instead they formed a close column, six deep, and began firing at the advancing British:

> The interval between us was perhaps 400 yards, but it was so quickly passed that they had only time to fire a few shots upon us before we came upon them ... The shock was terrible: horses and men were overthrown, and a shriek of terror, intermixed with oaths, groans and prayers for mercy, issued from the whole extent of their front. Our men pressed forward until they had cut their way quite through the column. In many places the bodies of the fallen formed a complete mound of men and horses, but very few of our people were hurt.

On the left, Gordon found the French "broken and flying in all directions ... Notwithstanding this, there was a smart firing of pistols and our lads were making good use of their sabres." In total, "the mêlée lasted about ten minutes ... There was not a single man of the 15th killed in the field, [although] we had about thirty wounded, five or six severely, two of whom died the next day."[55] French casualties were much higher, with 13 officers and 140 men captured.[56]

An immediate exploitation of this victory might have delivered a crushing blow to Soult, achieving the delaying objective of Moore's advance, and allowing the British to get off in good order before Napoleon could counterattack. As it was, Moore opted to rest his weary troops for forty-eight hours. "It was necessary to halt ... after the hard marches the troops had in very cold and bad weather, the ground covered with snow," Moore wrote in his diary. "I was also obliged to stop for provisions ... Next night I mean to march to Saldanha so as to arrive and attack at daylight."[57] As he began to advance against Soult, though, Moore learned that the French were advancing from the south.

Moore's actions had gone largely unnoticed by the French until this point, but one officer, General Guillaume-Mattieu Dumas, based in Burgos, had recognized the danger from the British march. "We were badly informed of the rendezvous and the line of march of the British army, for General Moore was careful to cover his tracks," Dumas later recalled in his memoirs. The latter point was more luck than design on the part of the British, as the operations of the guerrillas meant that the French were denuded of information, while Moore could operate with relative impunity. "The object of his bold march

---

55   H. Wylly, ed., *A Cavalry Officer in the Corunna Campaign: The Journal of Captain Gordon of the Fifteenth Hussars* (London, 1913), 352.
56   Maurice, *Diary of John Moore*, 2:286.
57   Ibid.

appeared to be an attack upon Marshal Soult's corps," continued Dumas, "then a move on Burgos to sever our line of operations and at the same time excite and aid a revolt in Navarre, Aragón, and the Basque Provinces, and to combine these moves with those of the land and sea forces which the allies were then assembling in Catalonia and along the lower reaches of the Ebro."[58] Dumas was spot on, but he had great difficulty convincing the various corps commanders of the severity of the danger the British posed. At length he convinced Generals Jean-Thomas-Guillaume Lorge, Jean-Louis Fournier, Maximilien-Sébastien Foy, and Henri-François Delaborde to move to Palencia in an effort to secure the French flank and curtail the worst impact of Moore's action. When he learned from Dumas of the presence of British troops on his northern flank, Napoleon immediately saw the danger they represented. He canceled all other operations including Lefebvre's and Victor's on Lisbon and Seville. In a short space of time, 80,000 troops were assembled and sent to encircle Moore.

The VI Corps, Imperial Guard, and General Pierre Bellon Lapisse de Saint-Hélène's 2nd Division of I Corps were set in motion from Madrid, along with the cavalry from Ney's corps. Soult was given immediate command of the dragoons under General Lorge's command, as well as elements of Victor's I Corps originally destined for Seville. Joseph was left with 36,000 troops from Lefebvre's IV Corps to hold Madrid. The operational plan was simple. Soult would pin down Moore in the vicinity of Saldanha, while Napoleon himself would encircle the British. By 22 December, Napoleon was crossing the Guadarrama Pass in appalling weather conditions, so much so that the Dragoons of the Guard advised that it was impossible to pass.[59] Napoleon refused to heed this advice and wanted to press on, determined that the British should not escape. "Men and horses were hurled over precipices," recalled Jean Baptiste Antoine Marcellin de Marbot. Napoleon "ordered that the members of each section should hold one another by the arm. The cavalry, dismounting, did the same. The staff was formed in similar fashion, the emperor between Lannes and Duroc ... and so, in spite of wind, snow and ice, we proceeded, though it took us four hours to reach the top."[60]

Meanwhile, at Sahagún, Moore received word from a spy that "the French were marching from Madrid in this direction." This was confirmed "by information ... received that a quantity of provisions and forage was prepared for the enemy in the villages in front of Palencia," he wrote. "I also knew that the

---

58 Quoted in Chandler, *Campaigns of Napoleon*, 649.
59 Ibid., 650.
60 A.J. Butler, ed., *The Memoirs of Baron Marbot, late Lieutenant-General in the French Army* (London, 1892), 352.

march of the French on Badajoz was stopped. Having therefore no doubt that all their disposable troops were turned against me, I had no option but to give up all idea of an attack on Soult and to get back to secure my communications with the Galicias."[61]

Realizing that he was in danger of being encircled, Moore reversed course and began what became an infamous retreat to Coruña. Moore justified his decision because his plan to attack Soult had "never been undertaken with any other view but that of attracting the enemy's attention from the armies assembling in the south, and in the hope of being able to strike a blow at a weak corps whilst it was thought the British army was retreating into Portugal." Although he had failed to deliver a significant blow to Soult's II Corps, Moore had indeed succeeded in distracting Napoleon from the conquest of Andalucía and Portugal. "I was aware that I risked infinitely too much," he wrote, "but something, I thought, was to be risked for the honour of the service and to make it apparent that we stuck to the Spaniards long after they themselves had given up their cause as lost."[62]

Nevertheless, the decision to retreat was greeted in the British army with despair. "To the sensible mortification of the whole army," recorded Henry Clinton in his journal, "the following morning commenced a retreat which in point of fatigue and privation and hardship stands almost without a parallel in the military annals of Britain."[63] Unfortunately, whatever political capital Moore had accumulated by his march to Sahagún was squandered as the discipline of the army deteriorated through the course of an arduous and unplanned retreat through appalling weather conditions in inhospitable terrain. "There was nothing to sustain our famished bodies or shelter them from the rain or snow," recalled Thomas Howell of the 71st Foot. "The road was one line of bloody foot-marks from the sore feet of the men, and on its sides lay the dead and dying ... There was nothing but groans mingled with execrations, to be heard between the pauses of the wind."[64] In the final entry in his diary, Moore acknowledged that the retreat would be difficult "at this season of the year, in a country without fuel, it is impossible to bivouac."[65] From the beginning, Moore marched his men hard – at one point he forced them to march for

---

61 Maurice, *Diary of John Moore*, 2:286.
62 Ibid., 286–287.
63 Beinecke Rare Books and Manuscript Library, New Haven, CT (hereafter cited as BRBML), OSB MS 168/18/5 Journal of Henry Clinton 1808–1809, Entry: Sahagun, 22 December 1808.
64 C. Hibbert, ed., *A Soldier of the Seventy-First: The Journal of a Soldier in the Peninsular War* (London, 1975), 28–32.
65 Maurice, *Diary of John Moore*, 2:287.

thirty-six hours without a break.[66] "If we can steal two marches upon the French we shall be quiet; if we are followed close, I must close and stop and offer battle."[67] In reality, Moore had escaped Napoleon's clutches early on. The storm that had delayed the French advance through the Guadarrama Pass had allowed Moore to gain the two-day advantage he thought was necessary to ensure his escape. Having served him well up to this point, the intelligence from French dispatches intercepted by the guerrillas now dried up, so much so that Gordon commented that the army's "want of information is distressing."[68]

Despite being clear of his pursuers, as Moore's army began to disintegrate in the terrible conditions, so more and more were picked off or taken prisoner by the French advance guard. "The road all the way was strewed with men unable to proceed," recalled one British soldier, Stephen Morley. "Discipline was forgotten, none commanded, none obeyed … Seeing smoke issue from a large building off the road, I crawled rather than walked to it. It was something like a barn, and full of our men who had made a fire. I found a spare corner, and, putting my pouch under my head, fell into a sound sleep … When I awoke, I was told the army … had gone on."[69] Morley's ragtag assortment of stragglers put up fierce resistance to the oncoming enemy, a story that was repeated throughout the retreat, but the result was inevitable, and Morley was taken prisoner.

If the British soldiers were suffering in the horrendous conditions, the experience of the Spaniards whose villages they marched through was at least equal to it, if not worse. Many bore witness to acts of barbarity and incivility on numerous occasions. Bembibre, for example, "exhibited all the appearance of a place lately stormed and pillaged. Every door and window was broken, every lock and fastening forced,"[70] while another village was completely gutted by fire, "the wretched inhabitants … sitting amidst the trifling articles of property they had been able to seize from the flames, contemplating the ruins of their homes in silent despair."[71] In short, British actions had significantly undermined relations with Spain. The marqués de la Romana believed that "the

---

66 Esdaile, *Peninsular Eyewitnesses*, 65.
67 Maurice, *Diary of John Moore*, 2:287.
68 Muir, *At Wellington's Right Hand*, Gordon to Aberdeen, Lugo, 6 January 1809, 32.
69 S. Morley, *Memoirs of a Sergeant of the Fifth Regiment of Foot Containing an Account of his Service in Hanover, South America and the Peninsula* (London, 1842), 61–64.
70 J. Sturgis, ed., *A Boy in the Peninsular War: the Services, Adventures and Experiences of Robert Blakeney, Subaltern of the Twenty-Eighth Regiment* (London, 1899), 49–50.
71 Wylly, *Journal of Captain Gordon*, 149.

AN ULCER INFLAMED: NAPOLEON'S CAMPAIGN IN SPAIN, 1808

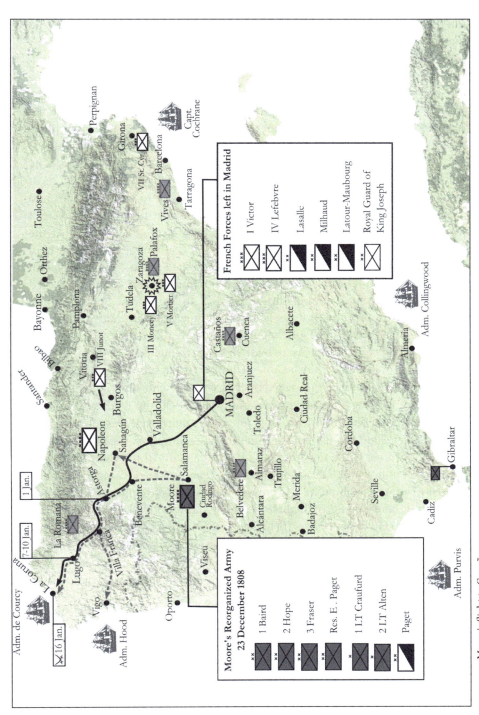

MAP 9.3 Moore's flight to Coruña

French themselves could not have found agents better calculated to whip up hate of the British than the army commanded by General Sir John Moore."[72]

The British retreat to Coruña marked the first in a string of crises in Anglo-Spanish relations, and while the Spanish at times could claim justly to be unable to discern their enemies from allies, given the depredations of the British soldiery, for their part, the British were as much aggrieved at the Spanish. When Moore's army briefly rendezvoused with La Romana's force, there was for a brief time consideration given to offering the French battle. "It is difficult to conjecture how such an absurd report could have gained credit," wrote Gordon. "The Spanish force amounted to about 6,000 men in the most deplorable condition. They were ill-clothed; many were without shoes and even without arms; a pestilential fever raged amongst them; they had been without bread for several days and were quite destitute of money."[73] At the same time, irritation grew in the British ranks at the failure, as they saw it, of the Spanish population to offer any resistance to the French. "The apathy with which the inhabitants ... have witnessed our misery is revolting," recalled August Schaumann, a commissary in the British army, "Not only did these puffed-up patriots ... give us no assistance, but they also ... murdered and plundered our own men who fell out left and right along the road."[74]

The pursuers were faring just as badly, battling though snow storms that left, in the words of Joseph de Naylies, one of Soult's cavalry officers, their troops "in a deplorable condition ... oppressed by cold, covered with snow ... many of our riders were fainting from exhaustion and want."[75] On top of this, where the French encountered the British, they found an enemy that was far from broken. General Charles Lefebvre-Desnouettes, for example, was captured at the end of December while in command of the Chasseurs of the Guard, much to Napoleon's annoyance. "I had sent him ... to reconnoiter, desiring him to take no risks," wrote the emperor. "He crossed the river [Esla] opposite Benavente, and found there 3,000 British horse, he charged them, killed a great many, but was forced to yield to numbers."[76] In fact, Lefebvre-Desnouettes's initial attack against the weak rearguard had been successful, but Paget had managed to smuggle a sizable force through the streets of Benavente unnoticed by the French, and then proceeded to attack the chasseurs in the flank. Outnumbered,

---

72   Cited in Esdaile, *Peninsular Eyewitnesses*, 153.
73   Wylly, *Journal of Captain Gordon*, 145–147.
74   A. Ludovici, ed., *On the Road with Wellington: The Diary of a War Commissary in the Peninsular Campaigns* (New York, 1925), 127–128.
75   J.J. de Naylies, *Mémoires sur la guerre d'Espagne pendant les années 1808, 1809, 1810 et 1811* (Paris, 1817), 37–38.
76   CC, Napoleon to Joseph, Benavente, 31 December 1808, 1:386.

Lefebvre-Desnouettes ordered a general retreat.[77] "In attempting to recross the river, his horse was wounded," wrote Napoleon. "He was drowning, when two of the English saved him." Four squadrons were virtually destroyed, and at least seventy chasseurs were taken prisoner, compared to fifty British casualties.[78] Meanwhile, at the beginning of January, Chlapowski was with the advance guard of Soult's II Corps, commanded by General Auguste-François-Marie Colbert de Chabanais, as it passed through Astorga. "A little beyond Cacabellos [Colbert] encountered some Scottish infantry in a good defensive position," Chlapowski later recounted. "He rode through the village with one platoon, for, while he was waiting for his infantry to come up, he wanted to study the ground. The enemy fired a few shots, and a musket ball hit Colbert square on the forehead, and he fell dead on the spot."[79]

In all, then, the retreat of the British army to Coruña, amid the deteriorating Spanish army of La Romana, followed by the French is more complex than the usual account suggests. Rather than a one-sided precipitate retreat, Moore's command ensured that the British stayed ahead of the French, and maintained enough cohesion to pose delays to the French that exacerbated those already caused by the harsh weather. At the same time, Moore forced his men to march faster and longer than was strictly necessary, and the disintegration of the British force as it neared its objective caused scenes of horrendous brutality and depravity to the Spanish population. Napoleon, though, recognized that the chance to inflict a crippling defeat on the British had escaped him. "I have been pursuing the English for some days, but they are fleeing in a terrified fashion," he wrote to Josephine on New Year's Eve.[80]

David Chandler argues that Napoleon, not wishing to be personally associated with failure, determined to remove himself from the pursuit and hand over command to Soult, which he did so on 1 January. But, in truth, the pursuit had cost the French as much as it had the British. Both armies had experienced the same persistent freezing conditions; both were outstripping their supply lines which were getting bogged down in muddy or frozen roads; and the French were suffering not insignificant casualties at the hands of well-organized British rearguard actions. Having failed to catch Moore, Napoleon now realized that the British were going to escape, but to assume that Napoleon wanted to destroy the British army to prevent further support of the Spanish resistance is to foreshadow events still to come. In early January 1809, with the

---

77   Chandler, *Campaigns of Napoleon*, 652.
78   CC, Napoleon to Joseph, Benavente, 31 December 1808, 1:386.
79   Simmons, *Memoirs of a Polish Lancer*, 47–49.
80   Chandler, *Campaigns of Napoleon*, 652.

British army in tatters and flying headlong to the coast for evacuation, Napoleon's new priority would have been the subjugation of the remainder of Spain. There was no indication the British would return to the peninsula. Indeed, every aspect of British strategy in the war thus far had suggested they would not return after achieving a limited aim and suffering such a bloody nose. Napoleon's decision to leave the pursuit to Soult and return to issues of greater importance was a sensible strategic and operational judgement.

Moore's army reached Coruña on 12 January 1809, pursued by Soult, whose command was now badly strung out over the Cantabrian mountains. He recognized that Moore was a competent general, whose army, even in its battered condition, was not to be taken lightly. While the British endured an agonizing two-day delay caused by contrary winds, which prevented the British transport fleet from entering Coruña harbor, Soult took four days to bring up his army. By now, Moore had been able to replenish his command from the depots at Coruña and select a suitable defensive position from which he could fight a delaying action while his army embarked. On 13 January, he blew up the remaining stocks. "The whole town was thrown into considerable alarm at about 9:00 AM by a tremendous explosion, which shook the buildings like a earthquake," wrote Alexander Gordon. Moore had blown up 1,500 barrels of gunpowder but "there was another depot of nearly 5,000 barrels in an adjoining building, but that this circumstance was concealed ... by the Spanish officer in charge of the magazine. The consequence was ... an explosion infinitely more violent in its effects than had been calculated." The explosions killed several British soldiers employed in destroying the provisions and razed a village close by, killing most of the inhabitants.[81]

On the 14th, the winds changed and the transport fleet was able to get into harbor. The evacuation commenced immediately. Seeing this, Soult decided on an attack on the 16th, forcing Moore to fight the delaying action he had anticipated. He posted 15,000 troops on the ridges of Monte Mero, overlooking Coruña, south of the town. If he was to break through, Soult had to capture this ridge. He first decided to bring up artillery on a ridge adjacent to Moore's position, as guns "placed there could enfilade the English line." Pierre Le Noble, part of the team charged with bringing guns to the position recalled that "we did not control any road that led to the position, and, given ... the nature of the terrain, the obstacles that had to be overcome to get artillery up there can easily be imagined. However, our gunners again proved that there was nothing

---

81 Wylly, *Journal of Captain Gordon*, 197–199.

they could not do."[82] Soult's positioning of artillery had an immediate effect. "Such was the advantage of their position," recalled Henry Clinton, "that almost every shot took effect and claimed a heavy loss to the right of the British Army."[83]

Soult then attacked the British right, where, among others, the 42nd Black Watch were posted, perceiving a weakness in the line that would allow him to trap the British on the coastline while he cut off their access to the harbor. In this estimation he was mistaken. A captured picket gave away the attack on the British right, and reserves were thrown in to counter the assault:

> The enemy were ... seen advancing in two very large compact columns down on our brigade ... Sir John was soon on the ground where the attack was expected to be made. Our artillery fired a few shots, and then retreated for want of ammunition. Our flankers were sent out to assist the pickets. The French soon formed their line and advanced, driving the pickets and flankers before them, while their artillery kept up a close cannonade on our line with grape and round shot. A few of the 42nd were killed, and some were wounded ... We had not then moved an inch in advance or retreat. Sir John came in front of the 42nd. He said, "There is no use in making a long speech, but, 42nd, I hope you will do as you have done before." With that he rode off the ground in front of us ... This ground ... was very bad for making an engagement, being very rocky and full of ditches, and a large valley between the two positions. The French army did not advance very rapidly on account of the badness of the ground. Our colonel gave orders for us to lie on the ground at the back of the height our position was on, and, whenever the French were within a few yards of us, we were to start up and fire our muskets, and then give them the bayonet. They came up the hill cheering as if there were none to oppose them, we being out of their sight. When they came to the top of the hill, all the word of command that was given was "42nd: charge!" In one moment, every man was up ... and every shot did execution. They were so close upon us we gave them the bayonet the instant we fired ... and many of us skewered pairs, front and rear rank. To the right-about they went, and we after them ... When we had driven them in upon their other columns, we ourselves retreated ... and took the advantage of a

---

82   P.M. Le Noble, *Mémoires sur le operations militaires des français en Galice, Portugal el le vallée du Tage en 1809 sous le commandement du Maréchal Soult* (Paris, 1821), 38–39.
83   BRBML OSB MS 168/18/7 Journal of Henry Clinton 1808–1809, Entry: Corunna, 16 January 1809.

ditch that was in the valley from which we kept up a constant fire on the enemy until dark.[84]

Through intense fighting, the British managed to cling onto their positions on the right, thwarting Soult's attempt to capture the ridge and cut off Moore's final line of retreat to the port. On the British left, attempts to capture the village of Piedralonga were defeated in an intense close-order combat, involving a bayonet charge "which struck consternation into the enemy (tho' it is supposed they imagined it a general attack)."[85] The memory of the brutality and misery of the retreat urged many British soldiers on, and accounts frequently evinced passionate hatred of the French. "We painfully recollected the wanton carnage committed on … defenceless stragglers," recalled Robert Blakeney, "and the many cold nights we passed in the mountains of Galicia … The haughty and taunting insults, too, of our gasconading pursuers were fresh in our memory."[86]

Moore was fatally wounded directing the reserves in the battle, after a cannonball tore away his left shoulder and mangled his chest. The wound was so severe that his military secretary John Colborne thought "from the profuse gushing out of the blood … he would have instantly expired," but Moore survived long enough to learn that his army had held the French off, and had been able to embark in safety.[87] The Coruña campaign had cost the British army in the peninsula a fifth of its strength: 5,000 men had died during the retreat, and another 800 were killed and wounded in the battle at Coruña, compared with 1,500 French casualties. Worse was the loss of huge numbers of guns, ammunition, gunpowder, and stores, not to mention the heart-breaking slaughter of the cavalry's horses. Unable to embark them on the transports, they were killed by their riders to prevent them falling into French hands, with one commissary in the Royal Artillery overseeing the destruction of 400 horses.[88] This had a devastating effect on the cavalry, who had barely three weeks earlier ridden their horses to success at Sahagún. Thus, "the destruction of these irrational companions of their toils, the hearts of the soldiers were more affected with

---

84   Anon., *The Personal Narrative of a Private Soldier who served in the Forty-Second Highlanders for Twelve Years during the Late War* (London, 1821), 114–117.
85   National Army Museum, London (hereafter cited as NAM), MS 6807/148, Papers and Correspondence of Ensign Augustus Dobree, 14th Regiment, 16 January 1809.
86   Sturgis, *A Boy in the Peninsular War*, 114–117.
87   NAM MS 6807/452, Colbourne to his sister, Mrs. Duke Yonge, February 1809.
88   NAM MS 8009/50, Journal of Captain Commissary John Charlton, Corps of Royal Artillery Drivers.

pity and grief than by all the calamities they had witnessed during their retreat."[89]

What had the campaign achieved for the British? It is perhaps too much to say that Moore's actions saved Andalucía and Portugal from a decisive invasion by Napoleon, thereby preventing the French from a swift victory and extinguishing the spark of insurrection before it had a chance to ignite properly. However, it is fair to say that the French advance was stalled and that Moore had given the Spanish valuable breathing space. Arguably, he could have been more decisive in his movements, and dealt Soult a more decisive blow after Sahagún. His actions are unsurprising given the difficult position he found himself in, with contending political pressures undermining his military judgement. In the event, the British army had been saved and could be reconstituted and sent back to Lisbon, or elsewhere, depending on the strategic prerogatives of the government.

More generally, what had Napoleon's campaign in Spain achieved? Everywhere the French had borne arms, they had succeeded. Napoleon had defeated three Spanish armies on his way to Madrid, and routed a fourth outside the capital. The pacifying operations he had sent his marshals on in the weeks between his arrival in Madrid and receiving the news of Moore's advance from Salamanca had begun to bear partially ripe fruit. The strategy of governmental, economic, and military reform ushered in a reactionary Spanish government in Cádiz that harbored similar liberal motives. In all likelihood, the strong French hand he believed was necessary to bring the chaotic Spanish state to efficiency would probably have reaped enormous rewards for the country in the long term.

But his policies disenfranchised middle-class property-owners through rigorous tax and property law reforms, while he simultaneously alienated the peasantry by imposing reform on the Catholic Church. The rebellion that exploded in Napoleon's face was as much a reaction to Spanish absolutism as it was to Napoleonic reform, and his failure to understand this merely added fuel to the flames. Napoleon's forces never captured Cádiz and with it the remnants of the Spanish navy. Even though French arms triumphed wherever they fought, they did not succeed in totally eliminating the Spanish regular army. Napoleon was right from the outset that the utter destruction of the Spanish army was the first step in the key to subduing the peninsula. Without a regular threat from the Spanish army, and then after 1811, the Anglo-Portuguese army under the command of Lord Wellington, Napoleon's marshals, divided and uncooperative though they were, would have been able to focus on pacifica-

---

89 Wylly, *Journal of Captain Gordon*, 146–147.

tion. Instead, they had two enemies to fight, a regular and an irregular, the one requiring concentration, the other dispersal of force. As a result the Peninsular War sucked in hundreds of thousands of high-quality French soldiery. The final mixed success – kicking the British out of Spain, but allowing their army to survive – gave Britain the opportunity, unexpected even in Whitehall, to open up a continental military campaign against Napoleonic France that, while accurately described as a sideshow, gave Perfidious Albion the ability to forge new alliances with the continental great powers, this time with the added assurance that Britain too was paying its fair share, not just in treasure, but blood as well.

Napoleon's operational art was never better on display than in his campaign to subdue Spain. Simple and clear, his plans had the ability to deal decisive and crippling blows to his enemy. But they failed in their ultimate execution: his marshals and generals, with the exception of a few, proved unequal to the task allotted them and, despite repeated success, the Spanish army, and with it, Spanish resistance survived.

Bibliography

Black, Jeremy. *Britain as a Military Power, 1688–1815*. London, 1999.
Bonaparte, Napoleon, *The Confidential Correspondence of Napoleon Bonaparte with his Brother Joseph, sometime king of Spain...* New York, 1856.
Broers, Michael. *Europe Under Napoleon, 1799–1815*. London, 1996.
Brownrigg, B. *The Life and Letters of Sir John Moore*. Oxford, 1923.
Chandler, David G. *The Campaigns of Napoleon: The Mind and Method of History's Greatest Soldier*. London, 1995.
Collins, Bruce. *War and Empire: The Expansion of Britain, 1790–1830*. London, 2010
Connelly, Owen. *Blundering to Glory: Napoleon's Military Campaigns*. Wilmington, DE, 1987.
Coss, Edward J. *All for the King's Shilling: The British Soldier Under Wellington, 1808–1814*. Norman, OK, 2010.
Davies, Huw J. *Wellington's Wars: The Making of a Military Genius*. London, 2012.
Elting, John R. *Swords Around a Throne: Napoleon's Grand Armée*. New York, 1997.
Esdaile, Charles. *Napoleon's Wars: An International History*. London, 2008.
Esdaile, Charles. *Peninsular Eyewitnesses: The Experience of War in Spain and Portugal 1808–1813*. London, 2008.
Esdaile, Charles. *The Peninsular War*. London, 2002.
Fortescue, J.B. *A History of the British Army*, 19 vols. London, 1906–1920.

Gurwood, J. *The Dispatches of Field Marshal the Duke of Wellington During His Various Campaigns in India, Denmark, Portugal, Spain, the Low Countries and France*, 13 vols. London, 1852.

Hall, Christopher. *British Strategy in the Napoleonic War*. Manchester, 1992.

Knight, Roger. *Britain Against Napoleon: The Organisation of Victory, 1793–1815*. London, 2013.

Maurice, J.F., ed. *The Diary of Sir John Moore*, 2 vols. London, 1904.

Moon, Joshua. *Wellington's Two-Front War: The Peninsular Campaigns at Home and Abroad, 1808–1814*. Norman, OK, 2010.

Muir, Rory, ed. *At Wellington's Right Hand: The Letters of Lieutenant-Colonel Sir Alexander Gordon, 1808–1815*. Stroud, 2003.

Muir, Rory, ed. *Britain and the Defeat of Napoleon, 1806–1815*. London, 1996.

Muir, Rory, ed. *Tactics and the Experience of Battle in the Age of Napoleon*. London, 1998.

Nosworthy, Brent. *Battle Tactics of Napoleon and His Enemies*. London, 1995.

Robson, Martin. *Britain, Portugal and South America in the Napoleonic Wars: Alliances and Diplomacy in Economic Maritime Conflict*. London, 2011.

Schroeder, Paul W. *The Transformation of European Politics, 1763–1848*. Oxford, 1994.

Severn, John. *Architects of Empire: The Duke of Wellington and His Brothers*. Norman, OK, 2007.

Snow, Peter. *To War With Wellington: From the Peninsula to Waterloo*. London, 2010.

Uffindell, Andrew. *The National Army Museum Book of Wellington's Armies: Britain's Campaigns in the Peninsula and at Waterloo, 1808–1815*. London, 2003.

CHAPTER 10

1809: The Most Brilliant and Skillful Maneuvers

John H. Gill

The Franco-Austrian War of 1809 provides an ideal framework in which to examine Napoleon as a commander at the tactical, operational, and strategic levels of war.[1] On the tactical battlefield, his *coup d'oeil*, leadership skills, and personal example were key to the outcomes of the Battles of Aspern–Essling and Wagram: mitigating defeat in the first instance and assuring victory in the second. At the operational level, he orchestrated the actions of multiple corps in a series of campaigns that seized the initiative from the attacking Austrians, captured their capital, and brought about a set of decisive battles to end the war on his terms. Strategically, in his unique position as head of state as well as commander in chief, he not only coordinated the actions of armies from the Baltic to the Adriatic, but also ensured that these military actions were designed and sequenced to achieve his evolving political goals. Although the principal theme of this chapter is Napoleon's actions at the operational level, these different levels of war are points on a spectrum, not hermetically sealed categories, and all three need to be considered in order to assess the French emperor's performance. His operational decisions, for instance, make sense only if evaluated within the context of his strategic vision, itself supple rather than static. Similarly, his operational maneuvers were intended to set the stage for decisive tactical engagements that would deliver strategic results. The intermingling of these levels of war and their fusion into a single conceptual whole in Napoleon's mind will be evident through the pages that follow. Indeed, as will be discussed below, Napoleon's personal qualities as a commander were arguably more important in the 1809 war with Austria than during previous imperial campaigns.[2]

Given the aim of this volume, this chapter will focus on operations in the Danube valley, the principal theater of war in 1809 and the one in which Napoleon was personally present. Operations on the banks of the great river conveniently divide into three discrete campaigns. The first began with the

---

[1] Consistent with the leitmotif of this volume, this chapter focuses on Napoleon. A similar study of the Austrian command structure, of course, would also yield interesting results. For an introduction, see Gill, *Thunder on the Danube*.

[2] Much of this chapter is drawn from the three volumes ibid.; see subsequent notes for specific citations.

1809: THE MOST BRILLIANT AND SKILLFUL MANEUVERS 343

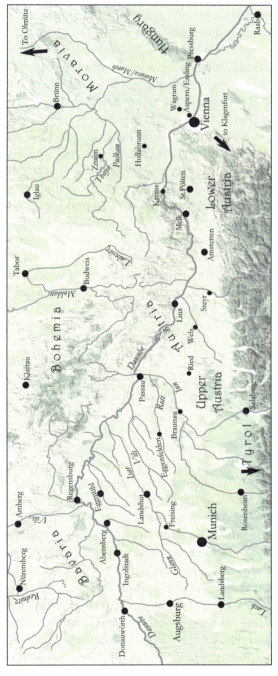

MAP 10.1 The Danube Valley theater of war in 1809

Austrian invasion of Bavaria on 10 April and ended with the Battle of Regensburg on the 23rd and the Austrian retreat into Bohemia. In the second, Napoleon drove his army down the Danube toward Vienna, hoping to draw the Austrians into a grand battle before the Habsburg capital. This campaign concluded with the horrific bloodletting at the Battle of Aspern–Essling where the Austrians repelled the first French attempt to cross the Danube (21–22 May). An operational pause ensued in the primary theater of war following Aspern: both sides remained in place near Vienna, warily eyeing each other across the Danube's waters and preparing for the next contest, while flanking armies grappled in secondary theaters. These subsidiary actions largely turned out to French advantage, and the third campaign opened when Napoleon, bolstered by forces from his strategic flanks, crossed the Danube for a second time. Defeating the Austrians at Wagram (5–6 July), he pursued his retreating foes to a final encounter at Znaim (10–11 July). An armistice signed at Znaim on 12 July effectively brought the war to an end even though the ultimate peace treaty would not be concluded until 14 October. Napoleon and his Habsburg opponents also devoted considerable time and effort to the other theaters of war, and these operations will be covered as appropriate to construct the war's strategic context. Both sides knew, however, that the outcome of their contest depended on the actions of their main armies along the Danube, and it is to these battles that we now turn our attention.

The Regensburg Campaign (10–23 April 1809)

The 1809 war had its origins in the revanchist attitudes of key leaders in the Habsburg hierarchy including Foreign Minister Johann Philipp Stadion, Empress Maria Ludovica, and several of the imperial archdukes. Constituting an informal "war party" in Vienna, they convinced themselves that Napoleon purposed the destruction of the Habsburg monarchy. During the spring and summer of 1808, they created an atmosphere of desperation and impending doom, perceiving their dynasty's fate in Napoleon's dethronement of the Spanish Bourbons. A gleam of opportunity appeared on this bleak horizon, however, as Napoleon dissolved the Grande Armée in Germany and took himself and tens of thousands of his veteran troops across the Pyrenees into Spain in October 1808. Fears of an imminent French attack transformed into hopes for an Austrian offensive war that would not only preempt Napoleon's presumed plans to break up the Habsburg Empire, but would also right the perceived injustices Austria had suffered at the hands of revolutionary and imperial France since 1792. Popular Spanish resistance to the French, unfounded hopes of military support from other countries, and wildly exaggerated expectations that "all of Germany" would rise up against the Napoleonic imperium reinforced the sense of a now-or-never opportunity. In this hothouse environment, the war party succeeded in gaining Kaiser Francis's approval for a new war with France despite the reluctance of Archduke Charles, the empire's senior military commander and one of the emperor's younger brothers. On 10 April 1809, therefore, the white-coated Habsburg battalions crossed the border to invade the territory of Napoleon's German ally Bavaria.[3] That same day, an Austrian army under Archduke John marched into northern Italy while smaller forces entered the Grand Duchy of Warsaw (Poland) and Dalmatia (then part of Napoleon's Kingdom of Italy) several days later.[4] A special column was detailed to invade Bavarian-ruled Tyrol where Habsburg agents had been actively stoking rebellion. The war was on.

Napoleon did not want war with Austria in 1809. Indeed, he did not want war with Austria at all and exerted himself to avoid confrontation through a mixture of threats and blandishments during late 1808 and early 1809. As Austria moved to arm itself, however, he took prudent preparatory measures: ordering up thousands of new conscripts, reinforcing his remaining forces in Germany, calling upon his German allies of the Confederation of the Rhine (Rheinbund) to mobilize their armies, and drafting a comprehensive contingency plan in case Austria attacked. Perhaps the most important of these measures was his decision to return to Paris from Spain in January 1809. Having no intention of launching an offensive himself, he remained at his capital and did not travel to Germany. He hoped thereby to demonstrate his peaceful intentions and to avoid provoking Vienna. Through the first months of 1809, he entertained the comfortable illusion that his actions would deter the Austrians. Only in late March did it become clear that war was unavoidable but, even so, the emperor believed the Habsburg host would not move before 15 April at the earliest. By that time, he hoped that his own military preparations would be complete to meet the Austrian invasion and launch an immediate counteroffensive. The Austrian attack on 10 April was thus a tactical surprise for

---

3 Although the Austrian Main Army crossed the Inn River into Bavaria on 10 April, a detachment in the Tyrol had already entered Bavarian sovereign territory on the 9th.
4 The Grand Duchy of Warsaw comprised a portion of historically Polish territory, mainly taken from Prussia as a result of the Treaty of Tilsit that ended the War of the Fourth Coalition. It had been created by Napoleon in 1807, but had been placed under the king of Saxony's scepter to mollify Russia.

Napoleon: his army was still gathering, and he himself was still in Paris at least four or five days distant from the principal theater of war.[5]

Before the war began, Napoleon had already reached the strategic decision that Germany would be the main theater of operations. He by no means neglected other fronts, but his intelligence network clearly showed that most Austrian forces were disposed along the monarchy's borders with Bavaria. The force that Napoleon was cobbling together as the "Army of Germany" to meet this threat, however, was an ad hoc creation. Though founded on a solid core of veteran units and excellent officers, it was not the Grande Armée of the 1805, 1806, and 1807 campaigns and was still very much a "work in progress" when the 1809 war began. The Imperial Guard and many key senior officers had not yet arrived from Spain, the constituent elements of the Cavalry Reserve were not assembled, thousands of conscripts were still en route to their regiments, and the army as a whole was plagued by numerous equipment shortages. Two additional deficiencies compounded these serious problems. First, the army was scattered in dispersed cantonments to ease the logistical burden on France's Rheinbund allies. It would thus take several days for the Army of Germany's components to reach the positions Napoleon intended them to occupy. The second deficiency was the absence of an overall commander. The emperor immediately dispatched his able chief of staff, Marshal Berthier, from Strasbourg to serve as his representative until he could arrive in person but, given the personalities and ranks of the marshals commanding corps in the Army of Germany, this was a position only Napoleon himself could fill. He hastened from Paris as soon as he learned of the Austrian invasion, departing on the night of 13 April but, as a result of the early Austrian advance, he would be absent for the first few days of the war and would have to conduct the opening campaign with an ad hoc army that was assembling itself on the march.

Facing Napoleon's Army of Germany (c. 160,000 men) was the Austrian Main Army or *Hauptarmee* (171,000), probably the best force fielded by the old empire during the entire revolutionary and Napoleonic period. The product of several years of reform initiated by Archduke Charles, it had been trained under the guidelines of a new drill manual, was for the first time organized into French-style *corps d'armée* and embodied a new spirit for what was, at least initially, a relatively popular war. A large force of national militia called *Landwehr* supplemented the regular army with the intention of providing some limited expression of national enthusiasm. Mindsets and institutional

---

5 The surprise was "tactical" in that Napoleon knew "strategically" that an Austrian invasion was possible, but he did not think "tactically" that the Austrians would move as early as 10 April.

culture, however, remained deeply conservative, especially among senior officers, and the army had had no chance to exercise in its new corps structure. Charles thus maintained that the army was not ready in the spring of 1809 and was profoundly skeptical about the prospects for the war he was called upon to launch that April. Nonetheless, if the Austrians could move with sufficient celerity and determination, they had a real chance, albeit slim, to inflict a serious defeat on the French before Napoleon could arrive and marshal his new Army of Germany.

Fortunately for the French, Charles's reforms had done little to ameliorate the ponderously methodical Habsburg approach to war. Buffeted by bad weather and nagged by logistical shortfalls, the archduke declared a rest day on 13 April, only three days into the invasion and before any combat had occurred. Moreover, the Austrians were already experiencing extreme difficulty coordinating the two wings of their invasion force. Charles had elected to send two corps (I and II, 49,000 men) southwest from Bohemia in the general direction of Amberg north of the Danube while personally leading the remainder of the Main Army (roughly 122,000 men in four regular and two reserve corps) out of Austria south of the Danube.[6] Indecision, lassitude, and poor communication, however, would mean that the two corps north of the Danube would not play a role commensurate with their numbers in the coming campaign.

Although Napoleon was surprised at the early date of the Austrian advance, he had considered this possibility in his prewar contingency planning. If the Austrians waited until late April or early May before opening hostilities – which he assessed to be their most likely course of action – he intended to dispose his troops in four general groups: Marshal Davout with his III Corps on the left at Nuremberg, Lannes (II Corps) and Bessières (Cavalry Reserve) at Regensburg, the Bavarian army (embodied as VII Corps under Lefebvre) covering the right flank from Munich to the Danube near Straubing east of Regensburg, and Masséna along the Lech River north of Augsburg with his IV Corps. With Regensburg as his army's pivot, Napoleon would be master of the key Danube crossing and could respond to an enemy advance from either Bohemia or along the Danube. Should Charles, contrary to expectations, invade before 15 April, Napoleon planned to concentrate his army to the rear between Donauwörth, Ingolstadt, and Augsburg. The emperor unfolded these two options and explained the rationale behind each in a long missive for

---

6   These figures and all others in this chapter, unless otherwise indicated, count infantry and cavalry only (not artillery, engineers, etc.).

Berthier dated 30 March.[7] Berthier, however, misunderstood, and his confusion, combined with delays in the transmission of several key instructions, resulted in a great deal of marching and countermarching to no apparent purpose under wretched weather on mud-filled roads. The French army was thus disheartened, disarrayed, and vulnerable when Napoleon stepped down from his carriage in Donauwörth in the early morning hours of 17 April.

The morning of the 17th found Masséna with IV Corps and General Nicolas Charles Oudinot with II Corps (Lannes had not yet arrived) just beginning to collect their dispersed troops around Augsburg, the small Württemberg army (VIII Corps under General Dominique René Vandamme) gathered at Donauwörth and the VII Corps on the Abens River falling back toward Ingolstadt in accordance with Berthier's orders. Isolated and alone at Regensburg was Davout's III Corps. Charles with the bulk of the Austrian army was south of Regensburg and about to interpose his forces between Davout and Lefebvre's VII Corps while the other two Habsburg corps hemmed in Regensburg north of the Danube. The situation could hardly have been worse for Napoleon.

Poring over recent dispatches while waiting for Berthier in Donauwörth that morning, Napoleon quickly gained a general appreciation of the army's peril and acted with alacrity to turn the tables on the slowly advancing Austrians. His understanding of the overall situation was flawed in several respects, but the broad contours were accurate enough, and he rapidly devised a general concept of operations that would guide his thinking for the next several days. In the first place, Davout's III Corps would retire from Regensburg, leaving a garrison in the city to hold the crucial bridge and prevent the Austrians north of the Danube from cooperating with those to the south. Confident in Davout's skills and the torpor of the Habsburg commanders, Napoleon boldly directed the marshal to withdraw south of the river to join with the Bavarians of VII Corps on the Abens. Second, he sent VII Corps back to the Abens to form the hinge of his intended maneuver. Third, Masséna, commanding Oudinot's II Corps as well as his own IV Corps, would strike for the Austrian line of communication through Landshut on the Isar. Thus cut off from his base in Austria and squeezed into the bend of the Danube south of Regensburg, Charles would be hard pressed to escape a disastrous defeat.

The army's morale soared with Napoleon's arrival. Compared with the hesitancy of the preceding days, officers and men alike noticed at once that the orders now streaming out of imperial headquarters exuded Napoleon's unmistakable energy and iron will. "The purpose of your march is to combine with

---

7 "Instructions pour le Major Général," in Charles Saski, *Campagne de 1809 en Allemagne et en Autriche* (Paris, 1899–1902), 1:421–435.

1809: THE MOST BRILLIANT AND SKILLFUL MANEUVERS 349

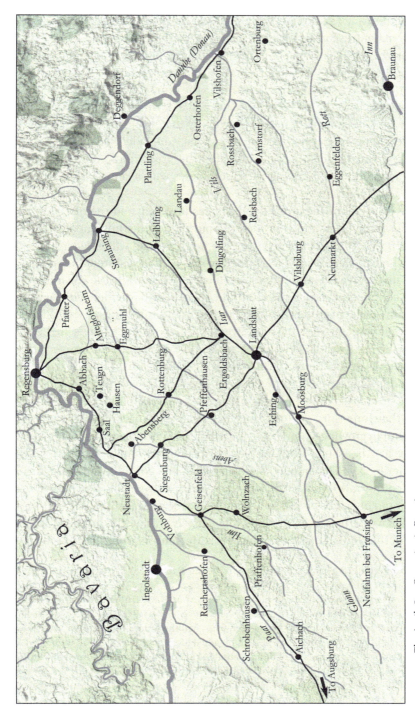

MAP 10.2 The April 1809 Campaign in Bavaria

that of the army to catch the enemy *en flagrant délit* and destroy his columns," he wrote to Masséna on the 17th, scrawling "Activity! Activity! Speed! I rely on you," in the margins of a note to the marshal the following day.[8] In addition to the driving urgency and determination in these practical instructions, the emperor issued a stirring proclamation to the army informing the men that he had arrived "with the speed of an eagle" and assuring them that "our past successes are a certain guarantee of the victory that awaits us." "March now, and let the enemy know their conquerors!" he concluded.[9] The psychological aspects of his leadership style animated the army, reinforcing his practical operational moves and filling his subordinates with a sense of urgency and a desire to triumph.

The dispersal of the army, the distances involved, and the often-appalling weather (rain, sleet, and cold) delayed but did not disrupt Napoleon's plans. The 18th was a day of maneuver, but the next five days witnessed a succession of five French victories. On the 19th, Davout's III Corps bested the Austrian III Corps in a savage encounter battle at Hausen–Teugn while the Bavarians of VII Corps contained Austrian forces on the Abens. The day ended with Davout no longer in danger of being cut off and the Austrians tumbling back in confusion. From that point forward, the initiative was firmly in French hands. In the Battle of Abensberg the following day, French, Bavarian, and Württemberg troops smashed in the Austrian left wing, throwing it back more than a dozen kilometers and driving a wedge between it and the remainder of Charles's army. The archduke, focused on his successful capture of Regensburg, did not know that more than one-third of his army had been defeated and was retiring on Landshut in growing disorder. On the other hand, Napoleon overestimated the victory at Abensberg, thinking he had beaten the Austrian main body in "another Jena."[10] The emperor's misapprehension continued through the 21st as he led the bulk of his army in pursuit of the Austrian left wing, throwing the shaken enemy across the Isar at Landshut just as Masséna appeared on the Austrian western flank south of the river. It was only at 2:00 on the morning of 22 April that Napoleon realized his error. Messengers from Davout – who had

---

8   Napoleon to Masséna, 17 April 1809, 1300, and Napoleon to Masséna, 18 April 1809, in Saski, *Campagne de 1809*, 2:206–208 and 240–242.

9   Proclamation to the Army, 17 April 1809, ibid., 2:201. For reactions among the French and German troops, see Gill, *Thunder on the Danube*, 1:175–179, 223–225. A late 19th-century Bavarian officer observed: "His subordinates had the proper concepts, his soldiers were outwardly and inwardly superior. All breathed life, zeal, and activity, all were filled with the will to victory, the will of the emperor." See Rudolf von Xylander, "Zum Gedächtnis des Feldzugs 1809 in Bayern," *Darstellungen aus der Bayerischen Kriegs- und Heeresgeschichte* 18 (1909), 1923.

10 Napoleon to Davout, 21 April 1809, 5:00 AM, in Saski, *Campagne de 1809*, 2:304.

been holding and even advancing against Charles and the Habsburg main body all day – finally convinced the emperor that the principal enemy force was still intact. Reacting with characteristic speed, Napoleon left a small detachment to pursue the disordered Austrian left and headed north with the bulk of his army by forced marches to strike the unsuspecting Charles on the flank at Eggmühl. The Battle of Eggmühl (22 April) left the stunned archduke and his disheartened troops no option but retreat. Fortunately for Charles, the capture of Regensburg had provided him with a secure bridge. Using this and a pontoon span, he and his wounded army escaped over the Danube on 23 April despite a successful French assault on the city and the eventual capture of the pontoon bridge late in the day.

Although the Austrians escaped, they had been severely handled, losing 44,700 men, 73 guns, their entire pontoon train, and a multitude of other vehicles as compared to French losses of approximately 16,300 soldiers. Only the possession of Regensburg and its vital bridge prevented a greater calamity from befalling the Habsburg forces and their demoralized commander. A mere two weeks after the opening of hostilities and one week after Napoleon's arrival in the theater of war, the Austrian army was in full retreat and the French emperor was poised to invade the Habsburg heartland.

To the end of his days, Napoleon regarded the Regensburg campaign as his greatest.[11] Within twenty-four hours of stepping down from his coach in Donauwörth, he had turned his retreating army around and, within forty-eight hours, he and his troops had wrested the initiative from the uncertain hands of their Austrian opponents. They never loosened their grip thereafter. Much of the credit for this remarkable turn of events, of course, goes to the French and German soldiers of the Army of Germany. Two divisions of Davout's III Corps, for instance, accompanied by the Württemberg Light Brigade, covered some 150 kilometers in execrable weather between 19 and 23 April, fighting in significant engagements on four of those five days. Many of Masséna's regiments, though involved in less fighting, marched even farther.

The army, therefore, was an apt instrument, but it was the commander who fired its ardor and directed its actions. Several aspects of Napoleon's leadership are worth highlighting here. First, he evaluated the situation, developed a course of action, and initiated operations with terrifying swiftness and a degree of resolution that left his opponents breathless. "Thus," wrote Charles, "were those enemies overpowered who were not possessed of a similar

---

11   Napoleon repeatedly remarked that "the Battle of Abensberg, the maneuvers of Landshut, and the Battle of Eggmühl were the most brilliant and most skillful maneuvers" of his career: quoted in Gill, *Thunder on the Danube*, 1:300.

decisiveness."[12] Second, the astonishing tempo of his operations kept the Austrians in a constant state of uncertainty and anxiety. As an admiring French staff officer wrote: "Napoleon's activity doubled the time available, devouring space and obstacles, multiplying thereby the means of victory."[13] Nor did he relent once the armies were engaged. The steady hammering applied to the Austrian left wing on the 20th and 21st or the blows directed against Charles on the 22nd are examples of this, although it is likely that an earlier start on 23 April would have garnered still greater laurels.[14] Third, whenever possible he struck in depth against the enemy's lines of communication as exemplified by Masséna's drive toward Landshut. The results in this case would have been more satisfying had the marshal appeared a few hours earlier, but the concept was sound and the emperor was thus able to outflank the enemy's defenses and unite his army at one stroke. Fourth, he had the measure of his foe and accepted risk to concentrate against the enemy's center of gravity, in this case the heart of the *Hauptarmee*. He did not hesitate, for instance, to leave a tiny force of 1,700 men north of the Danube to observe two Austrian corps (49,000 men) in order to concentrate the weight of his force south of the river where he knew that the campaign would be decided. Finally, his own skills and the quality of his army granted Napoleon a valuable margin for error. With men who could march like Masséna's or fight like Davout's, he could redeem Berthier's missteps and recover from his own miscalculations (erring regarding the opening date for the Austrian invasion, for instance, or inflating the scale of victory at Abensberg).

Although the Regensburg campaign did not end the war and although the Austrian army escaped shaken but intact, Napoleon's achievement during this seven-day period in April 1809 was remarkable, reaffirming French and German assumptions of martial superiority and casting a pall over all subsequent

---

12 Archduke Charles, "Ein Beitrag zur Geschichte des Krieges zwischen Oesterreich und Frankreich im Jahre 1809," in *Ausgewählte Schriften* (Vienna, 1893–1894), 6:357.
13 Jean Jacques Pelet, *Mémoires sur la guerre de 1809 en Allemagne* (Paris, 1824–1826), 2:61. In a study of 1809, Prussian field marshal Helmut von Moltke (the Elder) wrote: "Bavaria was cleared, the war was carried back into the heart of the Austrian monarchy. The enemy stood nearer to Vienna than the archduke. And this turnabout had occurred fourteen days after the opening of the campaign, four days after the beginning of real operations, and without a major battle being fought" ("Der Feldzug 1809 in Bayern," *Moltkes Militärische Werke* (Berlin, 1899), III/2, 46). Similarly, Xylander ("Zum Gedächtnis des Feldzugs," 21) praised the "rapid change ... the ruthless turnabout ... the exemplary distribution of forces."
14 Fearing the confusion of a night action, Napoleon had called a halt to the pursuit after Eggmühl late on the night of 22/23 April and the army lost several hours organizing itself for combat the following morning.

Austrian calculations. An Austrian participant provided an apposite summary in his 1811 history of the war: "The 23rd of April is one of the most important in the history of our times; it brought the war into the heart of the Austrian monarchy, dashed or changed the moral and political dispositions that could have turned in its favor, deranged the general plan of that war and decided it, despite the opportunities that later offered themselves to the Austrians."[15]

From Regensburg to Aspern (24 April to 23 May 1809)

The fall of Regensburg and Charles's withdrawal toward Bohemia concluded the first campaign along the Danube. The next phase of the war – from late April to late May – affords us an opportunity to examine the emperor's thinking as he addressed a new set of challenges, specifically his integration of strategic and operational concerns as he evaluated his options in the wake of his successes in the Regensburg campaign. The following section will focus on two enduring controversies during this period of the war to illustrate Napoleon's approach to operational art: first, whether to pursue Charles or march on Vienna after the victory in Bavaria; and, second, whether and when to cross the Danube on reaching the Habsburg capital.

On 24 April, with the Austrian army on its way out of Bavaria, Napoleon had to decide his next move.[16] He could either take his army north over the Danube in the hope of crushing the retreating *Hauptarmee* or he could drive down the Danube valley to Vienna as he had in 1805. This was a decision that clearly went beyond military operational issues and Napoleon, surveying the political-military horizon from his headquarters in a Carthusian convent outside Regensburg, had to incorporate several strategic factors into his planning. Although the opening campaign had concluded in a fairly satisfactory fashion, his larger concerns included the possibility of Prussian military collaboration with Austria, the outbreak of popular discontent in parts of Germany, and the potential for a British descent along the Channel or North Sea coast. The Tyrol was already in open rebellion, severing his direct communications with his forces in Italy. He knew that a large Austrian army had invaded Italy, and he was worried that he did not yet have any news on developments south of the

---

15 Karl von Stutterheim, *La guerre de l'an 1809 entre l'Autriche et la France* (Vienna, 1811), 283. See also Xylander ("Zum Gedächtnis des Feldzugs," 23): "the brief campaign ... must fill us with admiration for the emperor's achievements. Almost nowhere else in military history has it been possible to reverse such unfavorable circumstances so rapidly and comprehensively."
16 This section is largely drawn from Gill, *Thunder on the Danube*, 2:3–7.

Alps. Similarly, he had heard nothing from Poland, but knew that substantial Habsburg forces had been committed to that front as well. All of these strategic considerations argued for bold new advances that would capitalize on the string of recent victories in Bavaria to keep the initiative firmly in his hands, transmit that initiative to the other theaters of war, and produce a psychological impact favorable to his interests on the international stage. He decided to march on Vienna.

At first glance, this decision to push for Vienna rather than launching a direct pursuit of the battered *Hauptarmee* seems inconsistent with one of the central features of Napoleonic strategy: that the first aim of military operations should be the elimination of the opponent's armed forces, so that the adversary would be incapable of resisting the victor's political demands. Many commentators, benefiting from hindsight, thus regard the focus on Vienna as a major strategic error and a violation of Napoleon's own principles of war. General Henry Bonnal and Commandant Edmond Buat, two of the most articulate French critics, argue that Napoleon, succumbing to pride, chose "an essentially geographic objective" when he should have pursued the injured *Hauptarmee* to destruction.[17] In common with many other observers, they contend that the Austrian Main Army and its commander would have collapsed if Napoleon had pushed vigorously after Regensburg. With the principal pillar of the Habsburg state thus removed, Napoleon would have been able to dictate terms to Kaiser Francis.

Napoleon, however, was thinking more broadly in April 1809. Viewed through the lens of subsequent events – the costly repulse at Aspern–Essling and the sanguinary but incomplete victory at Wagram – the emperor's decisions can seem questionable if not outright mistaken. He reportedly later mused that objections could be raised to his actions as a commander, but that he "contemplated the situation in Europe and the impression it would make if I would enter Vienna rapidly."[18] An analysis based on the larger political-military situation and on what Napoleon knew at the time, therefore, leads to a conclusion different from that suggested by Bonnal and Buat.

In the first place, the Habsburg capital was not an end in itself. Napoleon's objective remained the destruction of the Austrian army, but it was by no means clear that this could be achieved by pursuing Charles north of the

---

17 See Henry Bonnal, *La manoeuvre de Landshut* (Paris, 1905), 260, 345–351; and Edmond Buat, *1809: de Ratisbonne à Znaim* (Paris, 1909), 1:16–22. See also F.L. Petre, *Napoleon and the Archduke Charles* (London, 1909), 201–206. The quote is from Buat, *1809*, 1:22.

18 Napoleon's remark as recalled by an Austrian general from a conversation in September 1809 during the armistice in Friedrich M. Kircheisen, ed., *Gespräche Napoleons* (Stuttgart, 1912), 2:73.

Danube. Indeed, this course of action involved considerable risk. The Austrians already had a lead of at least one day, perhaps two, and the pursuit would be slowed by the exhaustion of the French troops and commanders (including Napoleon himself). Getting the Army of Germany over the Danube would occasion additional delays, especially because the stone bridge at Regensburg was the only immediately available crossing point. By the time sufficient French forces were across the river and concentrated for a decisive battle, Charles could have either settled himself into a formidable defensive position in the rugged terrain on the Austro-Bavarian frontier or escaped over the Bohemian mountains. If the Austrians succeeded in evading battle, the French would be drawn into a potentially protracted pursuit over poor mountain roads deep into Bohemia. Rather than adopt this risky course of action, Napoleon aimed for the capital, a target he believed the archduke would have to defend. The odds would then be high that the Austrian army would be crushed in a grand battle somewhere between Passau and Vienna on the south bank of the Danube.[19] If Charles left the way to Vienna open, the emperor might be able to repeat the maneuver of 1805: seizing the city, passing over the Danube, and finding his decisive engagement on the north bank in what General Hubert Camon called a "vast operation *sur les derrières*." In either case, as Camon observes, Vienna was "only one point on his trajectory toward the archduke's army."[20]

Second, by advancing directly on Vienna Napoleon would place himself advantageously in a central strategic position from which he could deal with either the *Hauptarmee* in Bohemia or Archduke John's army in Italy as circumstances required.[21] In the process, his drive down the Danube valley would force John to abandon his gains in Italy. If the archduke were not ordered to withdraw to protect Vienna, he would certainly have to pull back for fear of being strategically outflanked.[22] Meanwhile, Napoleon's presence south of the Danube would protect his line of communication through Bavaria and induce caution if not submission in the rebellious Tyrol.

Third, a strike for Vienna would likely have meaningful political-strategic impact. Although capture of the Habsburg capital was unlikely to decide the war, it would reinforce Prussian fears of French power, dampen potential unrest in Germany, and reassure Napoleon's German allies. This was, above all, a war that Napoleon wanted to finish quickly. Pursuit of Charles under the

---

19 Napoleon to Davout, 26 April 1809, 3:00 PM, and Napoleon to Davout, 27 April 1809, 9:00 AM, in Saski, *Campagne de 1809*, 3:33–34 and 44–45.
20 Hubert Camon, *La manoeuvre de Wagram* (Paris, 1926), 5, 75.
21 Ibid.
22 *CN*, 18:509.

existing conditions, however, could easily result in extended operations in Bohemia – a campaign that could drag on for weeks, prolonging the conflict and creating opportunities for the resentful Prussian court or various discontented Germans (or both) to intervene.[23]

Logistical and administrative considerations were major factors in Napoleon's calculations as well. In contrast to the rich Danube valley, Bohemia was poor in resources, and the river was far superior as a line of communication when compared to the second-class roads that snaked through the snow and rugged forests of the Bohemian mountains. Napoleon had focused close attention on fortifying the city of Passau for just this reason in the weeks prior to the war, and he continued to stress the importance of the river as a supply route.[24] In addition to benefiting Napoleon, of course, occupation of the Danube valley and Vienna would drastically reduce Austria's ability to wage war. Loss of the capital and the rich agricultural lands south of the Danube would disrupt the Habsburg administrative apparatus, interrupt logistical connections, and sever communications, thereby seriously hampering the empire's ability to raise new troops, shift forces, and conduct operations. Vienna was also a critical Habsburg arsenal, so its seizure would at once deprive Austrian forces of significant resources while adding its stores of clothing, shoes, food, wine, ammunition, artillery, and other supplies to Napoleon's list of assets.

In selecting Vienna as his immediate goal, therefore, Napoleon was not traducing his own principles by aiming solely for a geographic objective, nor was he imagining that Austria would sue for peace upon the city's fall (though he doubtless would have welcomed such an outcome). On the contrary, he founded his decision on an array of persuasive considerations completely congruent with his own military philosophy and with every expectation that the war would continue until he had broken the *Hauptarmee*. He had not yet defined his own war aims (specifically, the level of punishment he would want to impose on Austria), but his strategic eye was firmly fixed on the destruction of Austrian military power as the first order of business. Entering the seat of Habsburg authority on 13 May – one month to the day after departing Paris – he could be well satisfied with the damage done to Austria's military potential and the salutary political effect in Prussia, Germany, and elsewhere. He had not, however, achieved his principal goal of bringing the Austrian *Hauptarmee* to battle. Charles had not obliged Napoleon by coming south of the Danube to offer battle before Vienna. The French emperor would now have to find a way

---

23   Ibid., 18:519.
24   Ibid., 18:296–297.

to move his army across the great river and force the archduke into a decisive engagement.

Unfortunately for Napoleon, the Austrians had thoroughly burned the great span over the Danube at Vienna and, as one French staff officer later explained, "for the emperor who wanted, above all, to terminate the war, it meant little to have the city without the bridges."[25] Determined to exploit his operational momentum, however, Napoleon lost no time in seeking viable crossing sites as soon as Vienna was in his hands. Indeed, Marshal Lannes directed an abortive crossing on the very day the city fell. The failure of this initial attempt rendered the best potential site useless (the Austrians, now alerted, immediately bolstered their defenses) and, to the emperor's intense frustration, several days passed before a suitable alternative was identified. Further days were consumed in gathering sufficient material to construct an improvised bridge across the main channel of the Danube and two smaller branches. The fragile span that finally came into use on 19 May connected the south bank of the Danube with a large island called Lobau on the northern fringe of the river. From Lobau Island, French troops painstakingly constructed yet another bridge to grant access to the *Marchfeld*, a vast plain stretching along the Danube's northern shore. A full week had passed, however, by the time French troops finally debouched onto the *Marchfeld* on 20 May.

These riverine proceedings were the prelude to the bloody Battle of Aspern–Essling on 21–22 May. The French unexpectedly found the entire *Hauptarmee* arrayed on the *Marchfeld* and it seemed Napoleon would have the decisive battle he had so earnestly sought. His army, however, depended on the series of uncertain bridges that tied it from the *Marchfeld* to Lobau and thence to the south bank. This tenuous link, pounded by rising water levels and flaming rafts shoved into the river upstream by the enterprising Austrians, broke repeatedly, leaving the French forces on the northern shore bereft of reinforcements and resupply.

On the first day (21 May), the French had only been able to bring across three divisions of Masséna's IV Corps, part of the Imperial Guard, and elements of the Cavalry Reserve – some 32,000 infantry and cavalry – when the bridge broke for the first time. Facing 98,000 Austrians, Napoleon thus had little choice but to ensconce his infantry in the villages of Aspern and Essling (from which the battle draws its name) on his flanks and launch his cavalry in daring but costly charges to protect his center with a "shield of blows." Skillfully executed, these desperate tactics sufficed to protect the tenuous bridgehead, but the emperor wanted a decisive victory. He therefore held his ground and, with

---

25   Pelet, *Mémoires sur la guerre*, 2:255.

the bridge repaired, pushed II Corps, the rest of the Guard, the final division of IV Corps, and additional cavalry across the Danube during the night. Thus reinforced to approximately 80,000 men, Napoleon launched Lannes with II Corps in a powerful assault on the Austrian center early on 22 May. When the main bridge suffered a devastating rupture that morning, however, Napoleon was denied the additional troops (principally Davout's III Corps) and ammunition he needed to press his attack. He was forced to call off the advance and restrict himself again to a tenacious defense of the two villages for the remainder of the day. The aggressive defense of the villages and a thin but intimidating line of cavalry and Guardsmen in the center kept the Austrians at bay. Having suffered 20,000 casualties (including the invaluable Lannes), the French withdrew to Lobau during the evening more or less undisturbed. The withdrawal was so adroitly conducted that the French lost only three guns during the entire battle despite being badly outnumbered on both days and forced to retreat over a single shaky bridge. The Austrians, who had lost 23,000 men, contented themselves with enjoying their defensive success, but Napoleon's first attempt to cross the Danube thus ended in bloody repulse.

As with his decision to push for Vienna after Regensburg, Napoleon's hasty crossing of the Danube and the resulting carnage at Aspern–Essling have occasioned no little controversy.[26] The standard interpretation is to treat this initial attempt to leap the Danube as reckless and foolish, the result of Napoleon's overweening pride and arrogance.[27] In part, this is an accurate assessment. He certainly held a low opinion of the Austrian army in general and particularly denigrated its performance during the Regensburg campaign. Overstating Austrian losses in men, material, and morale during the first two weeks of the war, he also underestimated his foe's powers of resilience and failed to appreciate the improvements the Austrian army had instituted since 1805. This deprecation of Habsburg military prowess contributed to Napoleon's willingness to take risks and clearly informed his decision to cross the Danube and bring Charles to battle as quickly as possible once he had reached Vienna.

However, his decision to cross was not so unreasonable if we take into consideration what he knew at the time. In the first place, he had little useful intelligence regarding Charles and the *Hauptarmee*. They were in enemy territory where he had few if any spies and on the far side of a great river inaccessible to his cavalry. Intelligence, which often appears so pellucid after the fact, is usually much less precise and unmistakable when evaluated in the welter of other information leaders have to sift in making crucial decisions. Such was

---

26   The following two paragraphs are largely drawn from Gill, *Thunder on the Danube*, 2:197.
27   Buat, *1809*, 1:280–286; Petre, *Napoleon and the Archduke Charles*, 298.

the case here. Napoleon had hints but nothing definitive regarding Charles's location and the state of his army. Indeed, one of the first tasks he assigned his subordinates on crossing the Danube was to "flood the plain" with cavalry to locate the enemy.[28] Second, he had the initiative and wanted to exploit it to bring the war to a swift close. As soon as he had occupied Vienna, therefore, he began searching for crossing options, and he was deeply frustrated that a week had elapsed between his entry into the Habsburg capital and the completion of the bridge. Moreover, we must consider the alternatives he must have weighed. If not now, when? The Austrians were reeling, Europe was intimidated, and his own army was psychologically ascendant. Waiting additional days or weeks to allow spring flood waters to recede and to gather more reliable bridging materials would have granted the Austrians additional time to recover from the drubbing they had received in Bavaria and might have encouraged his adversaries in Prussia and elsewhere to reconsider their neutrality. Endeavoring to capitalize on his army's momentum, Napoleon gambled and lost, but it is important not to lose sight of how close he came to success. He returned to his rooms in the Habsburg summer palace at Schönbrunn with a revised opinion of the Austrian soldiery and an adamantine determination that the next crossing would be prepared with infinite care and executed with every available musket, saber, and gun.

From Aspern to Wagram and Znaim (23 May to 12 July 1809)

A six-week operational pause followed the Battle of Aspern–Essling in the principal theater of operations. Recuperating and rebuilding after their exertions thus far in the war, the main armies watched each other across the Danube, but engaged in no combat action beyond pinprick raids and patrols. Operations on the strategic flanks, however, continued apace and would have significant implications for the outcome of the next clash along the Danube.

Although Austria invested most of its resources and hopes in the *Hauptarmee*'s advance into Bavaria, other Habsburg forces had invaded the Grand Duchy of Warsaw (Poland) and Dalmatia in April. Both efforts, however, soon came to naught. Along the Vistula, Austrian forces captured Warsaw only to be outmaneuvered by the inexperienced but enthusiastic Polish army. By early July, as Napoleon was preparing to cross the Danube for the second time, the Poles had evicted the Austrians from almost every corner of the Duchy and were advancing into Austrian Poland (Galicia). Distance made timely imperial

---

28   Berthier to Davout, 19 May 1809, 4:00 PM, in Saski, *Campagne de 1809*, 3:328.

management of the campaign on the Vistula nearly impossible, but operations in this theater were well aligned with Napoleon's desires as expressed in the broad guidance he had provided to the Polish commander: tying down a significant number of Habsburg troops and posing a distant but unmistakable threat to the Austrian strategic rear. Similarly, the French Army of Dalmatia under General Marmont repelled the Austrian incursion into the Balkans. Here Napoleon's principal concern was that Marmont rapidly neutralize the Austrian invaders and then bring his small but veteran force to Vienna as quickly as possible. Marmont did not move as expeditiously or as skillfully as Napoleon had expected, but here too the emperor's plans came to fruition when Marmont's Army of Dalmatia arrived in time for the Battle of Wagram and the subsequent pursuit.

Napoleon also turned his attention to rear-area security, particularly the threat posed by the Tyrolian uprising, the danger of serious insurrection in Rheinbund Germany, and the possibility of a British amphibious attack in Holland or northern Germany. These considerations had been incorporated in his planning even before the war began, so he had already communicated a conceptual outline to his commanders and erected an organizational framework when the Austrians invaded Bavaria. His guiding principle was to employ no regular forces in rear-area duties if at all possible. Instead he would rely on second-line formations of Allied troops and provisional French units often composed of men who were wearing uniforms and holding muskets for the first time. He supplemented these sketchy forces with a shield of deception: inflating troop numbers, designating formations with exaggerated titles (labeling a division-size force an "army," for instance), assigning renowned senior officers to command small units, and exploiting the aura of French military prowess.[29] Above all, he accepted risk in the rear areas as well as on the flanks in order to concentrate the greatest number of first-line troops for his main effort against the Austrian *Hauptarmee*.

As far as illuminating Napoleon's practice of the operational art is concerned, the most significant secondary theater and the one in which he exercised the greatest direct influence involved the Army of Italy under his stepson, Eugene de Beauharnais. The war there had begun badly for the French, with John defeating Eugene at Sacile on 16 April and pushing the Army of Italy back almost 150 kilometers to the west. By the end of April, however, the

---

29 See John H. Gill, "Impossible Numbers: Solving Rear Area Security Problems in 1809," in Donald D. Horward, Michael F. Pavkovic, and John Severn, eds, *The Consortium on Revolutionary Europe, Selected Papers 2000* (Tallahassee, FL, 2000). Note that the title given in that volume is a misprint: it should read "Imaginary Numbers."

Austrians had reached their culminating point, Eugene had recovered his poise and Napoleon had thrown Charles out of Bavaria. Turning to the offensive, Eugene harried John out of Italy and deep into Habsburg territory, inflicting several punishing defeats on the increasingly disorganized Austrians in the process. To Napoleon's considerable satisfaction, Eugene's army established contact with the Army of Germany southwest of Vienna on 26 May.

On the other hand, John, though depleted, remained at large in southern Hungary. To remove this threat to his strategic right flank, Napoleon reinforced Eugene and sent his stepson into Hungary in pursuit of John. His instructions were to shatter John's "army" (actually corps-size by this time) and disperse the slowly assembling Hungarian militia while remaining close to Vienna so that Napoleon could call upon Eugene's troops on short notice. Eugene accomplished these tasks in a brief campaign that ended with a victory over John and the Hungarian militia at Raab on 14 June, the anniversary of Marengo and Friedland. Although John's army was not destroyed, it was badly damaged and withdrew in disorder north of the Danube.

By the time Eugene was running John to ground at Raab, Napoleon's preparations to cross the Danube were well underway.[30] This time, the emperor would leave as little as possible to chance or to Austrian intervention. Broadly speaking, his operational planning consisted of two elements. First, he wanted a secure base from which to launch his assault. The emperor therefore transformed Lobau Island, previously placid and insignificant, into a gigantic fortified camp crisscrossed with orderly roads and equipped with powder magazines, bakeries, food stores, and a hospital. Workshops of every description sprang up to construct the numerous bridges and boats he would need to carry the army across the final arm of the Danube and onto the *Marchfeld*. To protect this crucial base, he established 14 batteries armed with 109 guns and mortars; this armament would also provide a formidable base of fire for the coming crossing, suppressing Austrian artillery and destroying Austrian entrenchments on the north bank. His engineers and artillerymen connected Lobau to the south bank with two sturdy bridges and drove pilings into the riverbed upstream from the bridging site to ward off the fire rafts and floating debris the Austrians had employed so effectively to break the lone bridge in May. He also had a small flotilla of gunboats built from scratch under command of a navy captain to patrol the river, fend off Austrian efforts to interrupt the crossing, and bombard enemy positions on the far shore. Of course, his concept also included a series of bridges to link Lobau to the *Marchfeld*. These, constructed on the island, were marvels of ingenuity in themselves, designed to be pushed

---

30   For the following, see Gill, *Thunder on the Danube*, 3:155–159.

into the river channel and clamped together as soon as the assault troops had secured a lodgement on the farther shore. In all, these herculean preparations represented one of the greatest military engineering achievements in history and Napoleon could justly boast that "the Danube no longer exists for the French army."[31]

The second element in Napoleon's planning was overwhelming numbers. Leaving only the thinnest screen to guard his lines of communication, he had his staff prepare detailed instructions to bring every possible soldier and gun to Vienna, sequencing their arrival to give the Austrians little time to react to the vast numbers he planned to assemble. The rebellious Tyrol was to be cordoned off and simply contained by second-line Bavarian and Italian troops; the IX Corps (Saxon troops) and one Bavarian division were called in from security duties along the Danube west of Vienna; Eugene's Army of Italy marched up from Hungary; and Marmont's Army of Dalmatia arrived from southern Austria. As examples of what these measures meant in numbers, Eugene brought 29,000 infantry and cavalry to the coming battle, leaving only 5,700 men to secure 130 kilometers on the army's southern flank; likewise, a mere 3,700 men stood on the main road from Vienna south to Klagenfurt, a distance of some 300 kilometers. Although some of these formations would not arrive until 6 July, Napoleon would have a tremendous force of 172,000 infantry and cavalry with 475 guns at his disposal for the coming struggle, a physical manifestation of his single-minded focus on the strategically decisive action.

The Habsburg leadership, on the other hand, remained strategically indecisive, incapable of exploiting the success its army had gained at Aspern. Among the factors that help explicate the Austrian inaction, two stand out. The first was the lack of consensus on Austria's larger strategy. In basic terms, the question was: should Austria seek to continue the war to some kind of larger military victory or should it use the promising moment offered by Napoleon's discomfiture to seek a relatively tolerable peace? The members of the war party at court, reinvigorated by the recent battle, favored energetic pursuit of a military solution (without defining that option beyond uttering the most vague and airy bellicosities), while Charles saw this as the moment for peace. Here was another example of the advantage Napoleon enjoyed by embodying army commander and monarch in one person. In contrast, the divided Austrian government deliberated and bickered endlessly, each side growing increasingly frustrated with the other. In the end, the question was never really resolved. The second major factor for Austria was its extremely awkward strategic

---

31 CN, 19:212–224.

situation. Its best opportunity for an offensive was in the days immediately after Aspern–Essling, when the French were exhausted, low on ammunition, and cut off from the south bank. Any such operation (attacking Lobau, crossing elsewhere, etc.), however, was fraught with risk and Charles let it pass. Thereafter, the odds of a successful Austrian attack across the Danube against Napoleon's main army grew worse with each passing day. The French rapidly rearmed, reorganized, and regained their poise. Charles, who had just witnessed his army's clumsiness as an offensive instrument, did not relish the prospect of crossing a major river against a large French army under Napoleon's direct command: "a gamble where all probability is against success" (note that in all of the Habsburg vacillations and recriminations, it is not difficult to detect Napoleon's psychological domination of his adversary).[32] With the leadership unable to decide on a move in the primary theater, Austrian strategy devolved into a frantic search for some action on the fringes of the war: trying to draw in the Prussians, launching forays into central Germany, even considering the detachment of a significant portion of the *Hauptarmee* to oppose the Russians in Galicia.[33] These either failed (Prussia), were irrelevant (central Germany), or never came to fruition (Galicia). After six weeks of painful waiting, therefore, Charles was left to use his courageous but cumbersome army as he thought best: on the defensive on the favorable terrain of the *Marchfeld* in the hopes of repeating the success of Aspern–Essling.[34]

In early July, the French obliged him. Napoleon's meticulous preparations and the skills of his subordinates resulted in the French putting more than 150,000 men, thousands of horses, 400 guns, and countless other vehicles across the final arm of the Danube in the space of 24 hours starting on the night of 4 July. It was an astonishing achievement by any standard, made all the more impressive considering that the assault began at night under a violent thunderstorm and was conducted against Austrian opposition. The ensuing

---

32 The quotation is from a 23 June 1809 memorandum Charles prepared for Kaiser Franz, in Oskar Criste, *Erzherzog Carl von Österreich* (Vienna, 1912), 3:177. See Gill, *Thunder on the Danube*, 3:154.

33 Russia, allied with France but sympathetic to Austria, sent an army into Austrian Galicia in accordance with the letter of its agreement with Napoleon. The invasion was largely a sham, intended to make a show of supporting the French while avoiding all combat with the Austrians. Nonetheless, the steady advance of the Russian troops, peacefully gobbling up Austrian territory, worried and angered the Habsburg leadership. In hopes of intimidating or even attacking the intruding Russians, therefore, Charles was forced to issue orders to detach 12,000–15,000 men to Galicia from the Main Army. Fortunately for the Habsburg Empire, these orders were drafted in early July just as Napoleon was preparing to cross the Danube. They were, of course, forgotten once the French crossing began.

34 This paragraph condenses the discussion in Gill, *Thunder on the Danube*, 3:148–55.

Battle of Wagram was a struggle of titanic proportions with the two sides deploying well over 300,000 men and nearly 1,000 guns along a 22-kilometer firing line for two long, hot days (5–6 July). The gargantuan dimensions of the struggle, however, were easily within the scope of Napoleon's abilities at the grand tactical level, and the French army maneuvered, as one officer remembered, "like a regiment responding to the voice of its commander." Even the often-skeptical Buat observed that, "on the French side, a single will, in effect, directed the general and specific movements of a mass of almost 200,000 men ... in the brilliant period of the imperial epic, one is unlikely to find a more vivid and striking example of the preponderant influence exercised in battle by a supreme commander."[35]

Much of the first day (5 July) was consumed in bringing the bulk of the French army across the Danube and winning space to deploy on the vast *Marchfeld*. Cavalry engagements flared and artillery boomed, but there was little major fighting as the French and their German allies flooded the plain. By evening, the French right and center faced a formidable Austrian defensive position on a low rise called the Russbach Heights with, from right to left, III Corps (Davout), II Corps (Oudinot), the Army of Italy (Eugene), and IX Corps (Saxons under Bernadotte) opposite the town of Wagram at the pivot of the line. To Bernadotte's left was Masséna's IV Corps covering the long stretch of open ground to the Danube. The Guard and Cavalry Reserve were under Napoleon's direct command in the center and additional reinforcements were on the way. The emperor, evidently wanting to test Austrian determination and make sure his quarry did not escape into the night, launched a poorly managed assault on the Russbach Heights that evening. Somewhat surprisingly, French tactical skill almost brought success, but the lack of coordination meant that the attacking battalions were eventually repelled, streaming back down the slopes in disorder. The Saxons in particular were badly mangled after an abortive assault on Wagram itself.

The second day (6 July) opened with Austrian attacks on both French wings. This time, it was the Austrians who failed to orchestrate their efforts, and the attack on the French right was quickly repulsed. Stolidly advancing against the outnumbered Masséna and the shaken Saxons, however, the Austrians on the French left gained enough ground to threaten the French bridges from Lobau

---

35 Pelet, *Mémoires sur la guerre*, 4:166; and Buat, *1809*, 1:ii; see Gill, *Thunder on the Danube*, 1:xii. Assessing the opening campaign seventy years later, a Bavarian officer remarked that there are "few examples in military history where the influence of the top leadership is evident with more *éclat* than in the engagements of Abensberg, Eggmühl and Regensburg" (Hermann Hutter, "Die Operationen Napoleons in den Tagen vom 16. bis 24. April 1809," *Neue Militärische Blätter* 20 (1882), 209).

Island. Though his center was in confusion and his left in retreat, Napoleon remained calm. He placed his faith in Marshal Davout on his right. He had ordered III Corps to outflank the Austrians on the heights, knowing that this move would lever the entire Austrian army out of position. To gain time for this flank attack to take effect and to prepare a strike at the Austrian center, he "made military history" in the words of a modern Austrian historian.[36] Masséna turned 90 degrees to his left and boldly marched across the front of the Austrian advance to retrieve the situation along the Danube; three divisions of the Army of Italy under General Étienne Jacques Joseph Alexandre Macdonald also turned 90 degrees to the left to launch the central attack; and a massed battery of more than 100 guns was formed to cover the gap left by Masséna and prepare the way for Macdonald's assault. Meanwhile, Oudinot would charge the Russbach Heights as Davout redoubled his efforts on the right flank. Envisaged, ordered, and implemented on the spot, in crisis and under fire, these actions are the ones that occasioned the praise cited above and many other expressions of admiration for the emperor as a battlefield commander. At the same time, these astonishing maneuvers were possible only because the army he had created and inspired was capable of executing them. This fundamental dynamic between leader and led, of organizational culture, unit cohesion, and a tradition of triumph, were crucial to the victory at Wagram.

The success, however, was dearly purchased and incomplete. Casualties were enormous: 38,870 Austrians and 35,060 French and Germans were dead, wounded, missing, or captured as night fell on 6 July. This immense expenditure of blood, however, did not deliver the stunning triumph Napoleon had desired. He had an undeniable victory, but "the emperor was indifferently content with the Battle of Wagram; he wanted a second representation of Marengo, Austerlitz, or Jena and he had taken great care to obtain such a result; but far from this, the Austrian army was intact; it was departing to throw itself into some position that would necessitate new planning efforts to bring about an engagement followed by better results."[37]

Napoleon now had to take up the pursuit of the defeated but unbroken Austrians. Pursuit, however, presented an immediate problem because the exhausted French had lost touch with the enemy on the night of 6/7 July. The emperor, therefore, was not certain which direction Charles and the bulk of his army had taken after Wagram: due north toward Brünn or northwest toward Znaim? Furthermore, while focused on the Austrian Main Army, he could not

---

36 Manfried Rauchensteiner, *Die Schlacht bei Deutsch Wagram am 5. und 6. Juli 1809* (Vienna, 1977), 28.
37 Anne-Jean-Marie-René Savary, *Mémoires du duc de Rovigo* (Paris, 1828), 4:182–183.

totally ignore Archduke John and the Hungarian militia troops east of Wagram at Pressburg. He thus decided to send strong pursuit forces to the north and northwest along the two principal routes Charles may have taken, assigned Eugene to contain John in the east, and remained in the center of this array with a powerful reserve, ready to act in any of these directions.

The decision to wait has occasioned criticism of Napoleon for supposed "indecision" or "inactivity" during the days immediately after Wagram.[38] Viewed from imperial headquarters, however, the post-Wagram panorama looked rather different. With French formations already probing the most likely avenues of retreat, choosing one path or the other too soon would have placed the force on the other route in unacceptable jeopardy. Likewise, moving his central reserve to some point more or less equidistant between these two avenues might have left his rear area and Vienna vulnerable to Austrian forces in the south and east. Until he was certain of Charles's location, therefore, he kept this reserve and the Army of Italy on the edges of the *Marchfeld*. On the evening of 9 July, when he finally learned that the *Hauptarmee* was retreating north through Znaim, he acted at once, and a flurry of urgent orders from imperial headquarters placed some 50,000 men on the road by forced marches to intercept the fleeing Austrians. Napoleon's decision to wait from 7 to 9 July, therefore, was not a case of imperial indecision or lethargy, but lack of information on the enemy. Under the circumstances, it is hard to see how he could have justified moving any earlier than he did.

Although Napoleon acted as quickly as could be reasonably expected to catch Charles's retreating army, most of his men could not possibly reach Znaim until 12 July. In the meantime, a vicious battle had erupted around this walled Moravian town. Fought on 10 and 11 July, the battle represented an effort by the French pursuit force to tie Charles down until the emperor could arrive with the reinforcements he had set in motion on the evening of the 9th. Though outnumbered by more than three to one, Marmont intrepidly – perhaps rashly – engaged Charles on 10 July as the Austrian baggage train was attempting to negotiate a difficult defile on the road north. Napoleon himself and part of Masséna's corps arrived on the 11th reducing the numerical ratio to two to one in favor of the Austrians, but the troops the emperor needed to seal a decisive victory would not be available until the morning of the 12th at the very earliest. On the evening of 11 July, however, he accepted a ceasefire and signed a

---

38   For example, Buat, *1809*, 2:330–341. For a detailed political-military account of Znaim see John H. Gill, *The Battle of Znaim: Napoleon, the Habsburgs and the End of the War of 1809* (London, 2020).

temporary armistice with Charles the following day.[39] Repeatedly extended, this armistice set the stage for peace negotiations that ended with the Treaty of Schönbrunn on 14 October. The war thus effectively came to an end outside this ancient town late on 11 July.

Napoleon's decision to accept the ceasefire and armistice at Znaim affords us another opportunity to examine his strategic and operational thinking in 1809.[40] For him, acceptance of the ceasefire and armistice was a logical move for both operational – military and political – strategic reasons. From an operational perspective, his formations were not yet in position to launch any kind of serious attack, let alone the sort of decisive blow he would need if he wanted to destroy the *Hauptarmee*. On the afternoon of the 11th, he had only some 36,000 infantry and cavalry to face the approximately 64,000 Austrians available on the battlefield. The bulk of his reinforcements, the men and guns he needed to impose his will on Charles, were strung out along the roads to the east and south, wearily but urgently moving to join him by forced marches. He could not expect to gain numerical ascendancy until sometime on 12 July at best. The prospects for a conclusive victory would then be high, but there was also a good possibility that the Austrians would escape beforehand. If Charles slipped away during the night of 11–12 July (unknown to Napoleon, the archduke had indeed issued orders for just such a move), he would deprive the French of an immediate triumph and drag the war yet further north into Moravia and Bohemia.[41] Such a delay would strengthen the hand of the Habsburg war faction and could incite additional unrest in Germany, perhaps even motivate Prussia to join the conflict as Austria's ally. For Napoleon, who above all wanted to end the war quickly, any such prolongation was highly undesirable. Acceptance of the local ceasefire, on the other hand, would cost

---

39   Charles proposed the ceasefire and accepted the harsh conditions of the armistice because he believed his army, the final shield of the dynasty, was in danger of being destroyed. Were the army to be broken, he feared, Napoleon would be free to dissolve the empire and dethrone the House of Habsburg. He was personally exhausted and was reading reports from his corps commanders that suggested their soldiers were equally close to physical and psychological collapse. At the same time, he overestimated French strength, and he knew that Napoleon was already present on the field. All of these conditions argued for securing an agreement while the army was still intact. Moreover, Charles probably believed that he had to act fast. He held plenipotentiary power as the supreme army commander, but his enemies at court were busily undermining his authority. Were he to wait, he might lose the opportunity, as he saw things, to save the army and thus save the empire. See Gill, *Thunder on the Danube*, 3:287–288.
40   The following section is drawn from ibid., 3:288–289.
41   See "Über die Benutzung der in der Schlacht von Aspern erfochtenen Vortheile und über den Waffenstillstand von Znaym," *Pallas* 1 (1810), 412–433; and Savary, *Mémoires*, 4:196.

him nothing and might lock Charles in place for the night.[42] Then, on the 12th, he would be in a position to eliminate the Austrian army if the archduke rejected his armistice terms.

In addition to these immediate military considerations, Napoleon faced a larger political question with regard to the general armistice: what terms did he want to impose on Austria? If he wanted the war to conclude with the disintegration of the monarchy, he would need to destroy the Austrian army utterly. If, however, he could be satisfied with a weakened but intact Habsburg Empire, then an immediate cessation of hostilities was acceptable, even preferable. The former course might have seemed more appealing to Napoleon the general, but Napoleon the statesman selected the latter. He knew Russia would not suffer the destruction of the Habsburg monarchy, and he wanted no additional trouble in the east while still involved in Spain. Furthermore, many Austrian and French interests were compatible, and conserving the Danubian monarchy as a major European power, albeit under a French shadow, might also allow him to build on these mutual interests in the future. There may have been a personal aspect in his thinking as well. Like his army, Napoleon was physically tired (he had also been seriously indisposed on the 9th). As noted above, he was dissatisfied that Wagram, despite the huge effort involved and vast effusion of blood, had not been the culminating battle in this unwanted war. Although he had not as of yet determined the final shape of the peace settlement, his military, political, and perhaps personal concerns thus made an armistice attractive. He held an extempore council in his tent on the afternoon of the 11th and listened thoughtfully to various viewpoints from his subordinates, but terminated the discussion by stating that, "enough blood has flowed."[43] He thereupon ordered Berthier to sign the agreement, and the active phase of the war came to a close.

The Franco-Austrian War in 1809 presented serious challenges to Napoleon's skills as a commander and reigning monarch. In the first place, the French Army of Germany of 1809 was not the Grande Armée of 1805 to 1807. Though not as fragile as sometimes portrayed, it was a raw and untested instrument with a higher proportion of conscripts than its predecessors and far from complete in structure, equipment, or manpower when hostilities opened. The difficulties presented by the Army of Germany's organizational uncertainties were compounded by its operational dispersal when the Austrians crossed

---

42 In fact, Charles did modify his instructions to keep the army at Znaim for the night after agreeing to the ceasefire: "Operations Journal der Haupt-Armee vom 6ten bis 16ten July," Austria, Kriegsarchiv, Alte Feldakten, *Operationsjournale der Hauptarmee und Korps*, Karton 1381.

43 Pelet, *Mémoires sur la guerre*, 4:278.

Bavaria's borders on 10 April as well as by the disarray and discouragement introduced by Berthier's blunders during his brief tenure in de facto command.[44] Where Napoleon's forces were on the defensive, scattered, unprepared, and vulnerable during the first week of operations, the enemy was concentrated and had the initiative. Moreover, that enemy had improved. The Austrian army of 1809 was superior to its antecedents and, in Archduke Charles, it had an experienced, competent commander of no little renown. The situation facing Napoleon as he hurried east from Paris was thus daunting indeed.

Using an operational lens to analyze the way in which Napoleon dealt with these challenges in 1809 illuminates his mastery of his craft. His understanding and his execution were not, of course, by any means flawless, but the key decisions examined here demonstrate his ability to overcome significant obstacles by rapidly fusing information, developing comprehensive plans, and integrating actions across the strategic, operational, and tactical levels of war. Although he had misjudged when the Austrians would attack, for instance, he quickly made himself master of the operational battlefield. In a week of constant activity, he and his newly hammered-together army seized the initiative, mauled the Austrian *Hauptarmee* in five separate engagements, and forced Charles to hastily retreat back into Habsburg territory. Determined to capitalize on his success in this first campaign, Napoleon decided on a rapid thrust to Vienna in the hopes of creating an operational situation that would force Charles to accept battle while simultaneously paralyzing his other potential opponents and reassuring his array of allies. This was a sound decision that balanced his strategic concerns (Prussia, Germany, Italy, etc.) with his unwavering focus on destroying the enemy Main Army. It thus supplies a good example of Napoleon making operational decisions within the larger political and strategic framework. At the same time, Napoleon erred in overestimating the amount of physical and psychological damage he had inflicted on Charles and the *Hauptarmee* in the fighting around Regensburg. The combat at Aspern–Essling showed him that the Austrian army had acquired an unanticipated degree of durability, but the revival of his adversary does not necessarily invalidate his decision to conduct a hasty crossing of the Danube after the fall of Vienna. From what he knew at the time, the crossing was a reasonable gamble, bold but not rash, and the ensuing battle could have had a very different outcome under slightly different circumstances. With his offensive blunted and the momentum that had sustained him since Regensburg gone, Napoleon exploited June's operational pause to ensure that the next attempt on the

---

44 Berthier was not the actual "commander" of the Army of Germany, but he essentially functioned as such while Napoleon was on the road from Paris.

Danube would not go awry. Relatively untroubled by the Austrians, he orchestrated his distant forces to set the strategic and operational stage for a second strike at Charles. The brilliant success of the crossing operation brought victory at Wagram, but the resilience of the Austrian army again denied him the replica of Austerlitz or Jena he had so earnestly sought. Nonetheless, Charles and his men, despite stout fighting at Znaim, were at the end of their tether and the emperor was able to dictate stiff terms for the armistice and subsequent peace. With an ad hoc army that had been caught before it was fully assembled and in the face of a substantially improved foe, Napoleon had again defeated the Habsburg Empire. The improvements in the Austrian army and the erosion of his own forces limited the scale of victory on the war's various battlefields, but the emperor's skills across all levels of war sufficed to place him once more in occupation of Habsburg palaces and to bring this unwanted conflict to a successful conclusion only three months after the Austrian invasion.

Bibliography

Arnold, James. *Crisis on the Danube*. New York, 1990.

Arnold, James. *Napoleon Conquers Austria*. London, 1995.

Binder von Kriegelstein, Christian Freiherr. *Der Krieg Napoleons gegen Oesterreich im Jahre 1809*, 2 vols. Vienna, 1906.

Blin, Arnaud. *Wagram 5–6 Juillet 1809*. Paris, 2010.

Bonnal, Henry. *La manoeuvre de Landshut*. Paris, 1905.

Buat, Edmond. *1809: de Ratisbonne à Znaim*, 2 vols. Paris, 1909.

Camon, Hubert. *La manoeuvre de Wagram*. Paris, 1926.

Charles, Archduke. *Ausgewählte Schriften*. Vienna, 1893–1894.

[Charles, Archduke.]. "Über die Benutzung der in der Schlacht von Aspern erfochtenen Vortheile und über den Waffenstillstand von Znaym." *Pallas* 1 (1810).

Criste, Oskar. *Erzherzog Carl von Österreich*. Vienna, 1912.

Epstein, Robert. *Napoleon's Last Victory and the Emergence of Modern War*. Lawrence, KS, 1994.

Gill, John H. *1809: Thunder on the Danube – Napoleon's Defeat of the Habsburgs*, 3 vols. London, 2008–2010.

Gill, John H. *The Battle of Znaim: Napoleon, the Habsburgs and the End of the War of 1809*. London, 2020.

Gill, John H. "Impossible Numbers: Solving Rear Area Security Problems in 1809," in Donald D. Horward, Michael F. Pavkovic, and John Severn, eds, *The Consortium on Revolutionary Europe, Selected Papers 2000*. Tallahassee, FL, 2000.

Gill, John H. *With Eagles to Glory: Napoleon and His German Allies in the 1809 Campaign*, 2nd edn. London, 2011.

Hutter, Hermann. "Die Operationen Napoleons in den Tagen vom 16. bis 24. April 1809." *Neue Militärische Blätter* 20 (1882).

Kircheisen, Friedrich M., ed. *Gespräche Napoleons*. Stuttgart, 1912.

Krieg 1809, ed. by Austrian War Archives staff, 4 vols. Vienna, 1907–1910.

Mayerhoffer von Vedropolje, Eberhard. *Österreichs Krieg mit Napoleon I*. Vienna, 1904.

Mikaberidze, Alexander. "Non-Belligerent Belligerent: Russia and the Franco-Austrian War of 1809." *Napoleonica: La Revue* 10/1 (2011) <http://www.cairn.info/revue-napoleonica-la-revue-2011-1-page-4.htm>.

Moltke, Helmut von. *Moltkes Militärische Werke*. Berlin, 1899.

Naulet, Frédéric. *Wagram*. Paris, 2009.

Pelet, Jean Jacques. *Mémoires sur la Guerre de 1809 en Allemagne*, 4 vols. Paris, 1824–1826.

Petre, F.L. *Napoleon and the Archduke Charles*. London, 1909.

Rauchensteiner, Manfried. *Die Schlacht bei Deutsch Wagram am 5. und 6. Juli 1809*. Vienna, 1977.

Rothenberg, Gunther E. *The Emperor's Last Victory*. London, 2004.

Rothenberg, Gunther E. *Napoleon's Great Adversaries: The Archduke Charles and the Austrian Army 1792–1814*. Bloomington, IN, 1982.

Saski, Charles. *La campagne de 1809 en Allemagne et en Autriche*, 3 vols. Paris, 1899–1902.

Savary, Anne–Jean–Marie–René. *Mémoires du Duc de Rovigo*. Paris, 1828.

Stutterheim, Karl Freiherr von. *La guerre de l'An 1809 entre l'Autriche et la France*. Vienna, 1811.

Welden, Ludwig Freiherr von. *Der Krieg von 1809*. Vienna, 1872.

Xylander, Rudolf von. "Zum Gedächtnis des Feldzugs 1809 in Bayern." *Darstellungen aus der Bayerischen Kriegs– und Heeresgeschichte* 18 (1909).

CHAPTER 11

The Limits of the Operational Art: Russia 1812

Alexander Mikaberidze

Even two centuries later, the great tragedy of 1812 continues to excite considerable interest and wonder. Napoleon's decision to invade Russia in the summer of 1812 was his last and greatest effort to secure the French imperium in continental Europe. It resulted in war on a colossal scale and produced results diametrically opposite to those the French emperor wished to attain. This six-month long campaign furnished numerous episodes of triumph and hardship, transcendent courage and wanton depravity, but it offered many military lessons as well. In the grandeur of its conception, its execution, and its abysmal end, this war had no analogy until the German invasion of the USSR in 1941.

The conflict between Russia and France began without an official declaration of war but it did not come as a surprise to contemporaries as relations between the two states had become increasingly tense after the signing of the Treaty of Tilsit in 1807.[1] Although both rulers occasionally sought to placate each other, each was disappointed and antagonized by the conduct of the other; this feeling contributed significantly to the outbreak of the war. For its part, Russia remained disgruntled by diplomatic setbacks suffered at the hands of Napoleon and deeply concerned by his dominance over Europe. Crucially, Napoleon's economic war with Britain (the so-called Continental System), which Alexander was obliged to join under the terms of Tilsit, proved disadvantageous as Russia lost lucrative trade with Britain, a major destination for wheat, timber, hemp, tallow, and other resources. Without compensation for lost revenue, Russian merchants faced financial ruin. The Polish Question further strained relations. The old Kingdom of Poland had been partitioned and swallowed up by Russia, Prussia, and Austria between 1772 and 1795. Napoleon's creation of the Grand Duchy of Warsaw, "a splinter in the body of Russia" as Alexander described it, awakened Russian fears of a full reconstitution of Polish lands and national identity. In addition, Franco-Russian interests clashed over the Germanic states and the future of the Ottoman Empire. Alexander's ambition of acquiring Constantinople through conquest appeared to be a move that Napoleon – fearing Russian interference in the Mediterranean

---

[1] For an interesting overview of the Franco-Russian relations, see Dominic Lieven, *Russia Against Napoleon* (London, 2010); Michael Adams, *Napoleon and Russia* (London, 2006).

– was determined to block. On the other hand, Napoleon's reorganization of the Confederation of the Rhine affected many German princes who were related to the Russian imperial house. Alexander's sister, Catherine, was married to the son and heir of the duke of Oldenburg, so the French annexation of that principality in 1810 looked like a deliberate insult to Alexander.[2]

By 1810–1811, it was apparent that the political arrangement of Europe that had been reached at Tilsit had outlived its usefulness and that a new European war would soon ignite in Eastern Europe. In March 1810, French foreign minister Jean-Baptiste de Nompère de Champagny's "Report on Continental Affairs" argued that France's alliance with Russia had run its course and that war was inevitable. France should, therefore, return to its traditional reliance on the Ottoman Empire, Sweden, and Poland to contain the "Russian imperial colossus."[3] A month later, Napoleon approved Champagny's proposal for the creation of an alliance between France, Sweden, Denmark, and the Grand Duchy of Warsaw, which, however, did not materialize due to Swedish and Danish reluctance to participate.[4] At the same time, Alexander and his advisors also reached the conclusion that war with France was imminent and so sought to entice Berlin and Vienna to turn against Napoleon. But the French presence in the Germanic states and the recent defeat of Austria in 1809 left little choice for these countries other than to submit to Napoleon.[5]

---

2   The duke of Oldenburg agreed to join the Continental System, but he permitted British products to be smuggled into the Duchy in violation of this agreement. Napoleon was therefore able to justify the annexation of the principality.

3   This report, dated 16 March 1810, is reproduced in full (in French) in Nikolai Shilder, *Imperator Aleksandr pervyi* (Saint Petersburg, 1898), 3:471–483.

4   *CN*, 20:305. Champagny wrote to the French envoy to Denmark, Charles-François-Luce Didelot that "Sweden already fears Russia. Does Denmark feel the same fear? Common interests must force Sweden, Denmark, and the Duchy of Warsaw to unite in a secret alliance, which can absolutely and really be guaranteed by France." Denmark eventually agreed to a treaty with France. On 7 March 1812, Napoleon shored up his northern territories by inducing King Frederick VI of Denmark to mobilize 10,000 troops on the Holstein and Schleswig frontier to deter a possible landing there by British, Swedish, and/or Russian troops. The Military Convention between France and Denmark of 7 March 1812 can be found in Jules de Clercq, ed., *Recueil des traités de la France* (Paris, 1864), 2:363–365.

5   Throughout 1810 and 1811, the Prussian court was haunted by the dread that Napoleon might attempt to carry out his oft-repeated threat to dispossess the Hohenzollern dynasty. Consequently, King Frederick William III pursued a dual policy of appeasing France in public while secretly seeking help against Napoleon. In this, he was influenced by his chancellor Karl August von Hardenberg and the head of the Prussian General Staff, General Gerhard Johann David Waitz von Scharnhorst. On 18 October 1811, Russian foreign minister Nikolai Petrovich Rumyantsev and Scharnhorst actually signed a treaty of mutual support in the event of a war with France. But the Prussian king refused to ratify that deal unless Austria joined the effort as well – a step that Austrian emperor Francis I was not yet willing to make.

According to a treaty signed on 24 February 1812, Prussia agreed to allow French and allied forces free passage through its territory and to supply 20,000 troops for the invasion of Russia; Prussia would also provide the French military with necessary supplies.[6] France likewise negotiated an alliance with Austria. Having suffered four defeats at Napoleon's hands in the preceding fifteen years, Austria was not particularly interested in defying France and supporting Russia; the memories of Russia's support of France against Austria in 1809 remained fresh. In 1810–1812, Napoleon endeavored to tie Austria closer to France. His marriage to Austrian archduchess Marie Louise was the first step in this direction, followed by overtures to convince Austrian emperor Francis I to accept an alliance with France. Austrian chancellor Klemens Wenzel Nepomuk Lothar von Metternich also pursued a more conciliatory, yet pragmatic policy, seeking to maintain good relations with France while Napoleon was on top of his game. In the new Treaty of Paris (14 March 1812), France and Austria pledged mutual support and Austria agreed to raise an auxiliary corps 30,000-strong that would report to Napoleon's supreme command in case of a war against Russia.[7] Austria, however, was playing a duplicitous game, since just one month later Metternich assured Tsar Alexander that Austria would not pursue this war aggressively.

Although Napoleon's overall strategy for the war against Russian considered the use of Sweden and the Ottoman Empire to form his extreme flanks, he was unable to exercise influence over either power. Sweden, though led by a former French marshal,[8] formed an alliance with Russia.[9] This treaty secured Russia's

---

6 The Franco-Prussian Treaty of Paris of 24 February 1812 can be found in Clercq, *Recueil des traités de la France*, 2:356–363.

7 The Franco-Austrian treaty of 14 March 1812 can be found ibid., 2:369–372.

8 In a coup on 13 March 1809, Swedish king Gustav IV had been assassinated and replaced by the more complacent Charles XIII. The childless king was forced to adopt as his son and successor Christian Auguste d'Augustenborg, a Danish prince, who eventually died on 28 May 1810. With Sweden's Riksdag (national assembly) facing a problem of succession, Napoleon interfered to suggest a French candidate as the new crown prince. On 6 January 1810, a treaty was signed binding France to return Swedish Pomerania and Rügen Island to Stockholm, while Sweden would join the Continental System; it should be noted that Napoleon lived up to his end of the bargain but Stockholm did not. The Swedes then agreed to take a French candidate and chose Marshal Bernadotte as crown prince on 21 August 1810. Although uneasy with the choice, Napoleon accepted it as a way of advancing French interests in the region.

9 In the 5 April 1812 Treaty of Saint Petersburg, Sweden and Russia agreed to form an alliance to "ensure safety of their possessions and the independence of the North, which are equally threatened by the ambitious and predatory plans of France." The two sides pledged to create a combined force to land in Swedish Pomerania, which had been seized by France, and Russia obligated itself to aid Sweden in annexing Norway either by

northern territories and freed military forces deployed in Finland. As for the Ottomans, their traditional alliance with France made them a natural ally for Napoleon but their six-year war against Russia had been a failure, with their armies defeated and finances exhausted. In May 1812, Russia managed to achieve a significant diplomatic success by concluding that war with the signing of the Treaty of Bucharest,[10] which secured Russia's southern regions and allowed the Army of the Danube to participate in the military operations against Napoleon. As the war with France began, Russia also scored two more diplomatic successes. On 18 July 1812, the Treaty of Orebro ended the state of war between Britain and Russia and pledged their mutual support against France.[11] Two days later, in the Treaty of Velikiye Luki, Russia became the first great power to officially recognize the representatives of the Spanish *cortes*, which was waging a bloody guerrilla war against Napoleon, and both sides agreed to coordinate their struggle against France.[12]

French War Preparations

Amidst his growing disagreements with the Russians, Napoleon launched preparations for war. New levies of conscripts were called from the 1811–1812 classes and French garrisons in North Germany, particularly at Danzig and Hamburg, were reinforced; by 15 November, 115,839 French troops were in the region, with tens of thousands of German troops in the process of mobilization.[13] The Grande Armée slowly formed around Marshal Davout's well-disciplined "Corps of Observation of the Elbe." In January 1811, Napoleon

---

negotiations with Denmark or by rendering military assistance until the beginning of joint actions in Germany. The Treaty of Saint Petersburg was later augmented with additional conventions signed in Vilna on 3 June and Åbo on 30 August, and effectively laid the foundation for the establishment of the Sixth Coalition that fought Napoleon in 1813–1814. See *Vneshnyaya politika Rossii XIX i nachala XX veka* (Moscow, 1967), 6:318–328.

10   Russia received Bessarabia and most of western Georgia, but surrendered Moldavia and Wallachia, which its armies had occupied since 1807. For the text of the treaty, see *Vneshnyaya politika Rossii*, 6:406–417.

11   Peace Treaty of Orebro, 18 July 1812, in Fedor Martens, *Recueil des traités et conventions conclus par la Russie avec les puissances étrangères* (Saint Petersburg, 1895), 11:162–165.

12   Treaty of Velikiye Luki, 20 July 1812, in *Vneshnyaya politika Rossii*, 6:495–497.

13   Tableau de la force de l'Armée Francaise au Nord de l'Allemagne, 15 Novembre 1811, *Otechestvennaya voina 1812 goda: materialy Voyenno-Uchenogo Arkhiva Generalnogo Shtaba* (hereafter cited as *General Staff Archives*) (Saint Petersburg, 1905), 6:302–303. Napoleon's letter of 30 October, however, refers to 120,000 men: CN, No. 18215, 24:538. Major French garrisons in North Germany included Hamburg (6,375 men), Magdeburg (8,851), Danzig (20,464), and Stettin (8,491).

reorganized his forces into four corps: Davout's I Corps of Observation of the Elbe (five infantry divisions and two light cavalry brigades); Oudinot's II Corps of Observation of the Elbe (three infantry divisions and two light cavalry brigades); Ney's Corps of Observation of the Ocean (four infantry divisions and two light cavalry brigades); and Eugene's Corps of Observation of Italy (three infantry divisions and two light cavalry brigades).[14] In addition, the mobilization of military forces began in the Netherlands and the Confederation of the Rhine.

Early in 1811, the emperor informed Davout of the intention to expand his corps to "a force of 80,000 men," that would "form *the advance guard* and move where necessary."[15] This decision was in response to Russia's military preparations. Napoleon's letters to King Frederick I of Württemberg and King Frederick Augustus I of Saxony provide insight into the emperor's thinking. For example, he wrote that, "if the emperor of Russia wishes war, the direction of public sentiment is consistent with his intentions; if he does not want it and does not stop this momentum quickly, he will be led there next year in spite of himself, and thus the war [will take] place in spite of me, despite himself, despite the interests of France and of Russia. I have seen it arise so often in my past experience that it reveals to me that future. All of this is just an opera scene, and it is the English who direct it."[16]

In addition, Napoleon viewed the expansion of I Corps as a means to counter a potential Russian incursion into Polish territory. Napoleon was concerned that as soon as the Russians "[had] finished their war with the Turks and their army [was] back in force and on the borders of Poland, they [would] become more demanding, and by then it [would] be too late for us to make preparations to counter an invasion of [the Grand Duchy of] Warsaw." Throughout 1811, Davout displayed remarkable administrative skills as Napoleon increasingly relied on him to carry out military preparations "spontaneously, secretly, and as soon as possible."[17] Fortifications were repaired and reinforced at Danzig, Thorn, Modlin, and Warsaw. To secure the French rear and maintain Prussia under tight control, French garrisons were placed at Berlin, Spandau, Küstrin, Pillau, and Königsberg.[18]

---

14 The Cavalry Reserve was divided into three parts, each containing one light and two cuirassier divisions, except for III Corps, where one division of cuirassiers was replaced by one division of dragoons.
15 CN, No. 17289, 21:365 (emphasis added).
16 Ibid., Nos. 17553 and 17612, 22:16, 67–68.
17 Ibid., No. 17516, 21:506; see also No. 17621, 22:75.
18 Kolberg and Graudenz remained garrisoned by Prussian troops but under French command.

Contrary to the popular belief that he underestimated the difficulties that lay before him, Napoleon was well aware of challenges he would face in Russia. The sheer size of the army Napoleon gathered and the meticulous preparations that he undertook bear testimony to this. Together with a study of the history and geography of Russia,[19] his previous campaigns in Poland provided him with personal experience of fighting in underpopulated areas that lacked supplies and good roads. In December 1811, Napoleon warned his stepson, Eugene, that "war in Poland [Russia] in no way resembles war in Austria; without means of transport, everything is useless."[20] "We can hope for nothing from the countryside," he cautioned Davout on 26 May 1812, "and accordingly must take everything with us."[21] Knowing the vast scope of the Russian Empire, he planned to engage the Russians as soon as possible and had every confidence that he could achieve the desired victory within three weeks by waging decisive battles in frontier regions. Consequently, in 1811 and early 1812, he made extensive logistical preparations for war.

The military issues that dominated the first six months of Napoleon's correspondence in 1812 provide perfect demonstration of his organizational talent. Over the course of this period, Napoleon coordinated the redeployment of the twelve corps that made up his Grande Armée, meticulously supervised the organization, movements, and outfitting of tens of thousands of troops and the establishment of vast supply and ammunition depots to support them. The valley of the Vistula River became a logistical base for the Grande Armée. French artillery parks were deployed at Danzig, Glogau, Küstrin, and Stettin while a vast arsenal was created at Warsaw. Napoleon established major ammunition and supply depots at Warsaw, Modlin, Thorn, Marienburg, and Danzig;[22] the last one alone contained a fifty-day supply of provisions for some

---

19   Thus, on 19 December 1811, Napoleon's private secretary, Claude François de Méneval, informed the emperor's librarian, Antoine-Alexandre Barbier: "I request that you send me for his Majesty a few good books, most suitable for studying the nature of the soil of Russia, and especially of Lithuania, with respect to its marshes, rivers, forests, and roads. His Majesty also desires to obtain works that describe, in detail, the campaign of Charles XII in Poland and Russia. In addition, send any books on military operations in this region that might be useful." See *CN*, No. 18348, 23:95. A month later, Méneval again asked for books concerning the "history of Courland, as well as all that can be obtained regarding the history, geography, and topography of Riga, Livonia, etc.": ibid., No. 18423, 23:162.
20   Ibid., No. 18402, 23:143.
21   Ibid., No. 18725, 23:432.
22   Additional supply depots were formed at Breslau, Plock, and Wyszogrod. Vast quantities of grain were milled for flour which was delivered to Thorn, where some 60,000 rations of biscuits were produced each day. Napoleon also established two transport flotillas at Danzig and Elbing that could carry eleven days of supplies. As the army advanced into Russia, the former flotilla sailed from Frische-Haff to Königsberg and then proceeded via the

400,000 men.²³ In addition, two siege trains were organized at Danzig and Magdeburg,²⁴ and twenty-six pontoon and engineer companies were raised as well.²⁵ Major hospitals were also established at Warsaw, Thorn, Breslau, Marienburg, Elbing, and Danzig. The French left flank was anchored on the Danzig fortress (with Thorn and Modlin as support bases) but the right flank, which extended to Warsaw, was not well provided for and some supplies were eventually moved to Modlin. Furthermore, twenty train battalions were formed to keep the army well supplied.²⁶ In early June 1812, Napoleon gave further orders for the formation of auxiliary convoys, using transports acquired in East Prussia. Having arrived at the Niemen River with some 500,000 men, the emperor expected to lead an army of about 300,000 into the Russian interior. He planned to be able to feed this army by transporting with it forty days' worth of supplies and utilizing the resources of the country.

Yet, despite such vast preparations, the French army quickly encountered logistical problems at the start of the war. In previous campaigns, Napoleon's troops had normally dispersed to subsist off the land and frequently remained on the move to avoid exhausting a region's resources. The Russian campaign would have been no exception to this practice, and the very timing of the invasion points to Napoleon's intention to take full advantage of the harvest cycle

---

channel of Deime and Kurisches-Haff to the Niemen River. The latter sailed up the Pregel (Pregolya) River and assisted in establishing depots at Tapiau (now Gvardeisk), Insterburg (now Chernyakhovsk), and Gumbinen (Gusev).

23   In terms of food reserves, Napoleon maintained a strict rule that, until crossing into the Russian territory, his troops were expected to live off the surrounding country's resources: *CG*, No. 30, 12:301.

24   By early 1812, the siege train at Danzig contained 130 heavy cannon; that at Magdeburg, 100 cannon. Danzig held 300,000 pounds of gunpowder; Magdeburg stored 462 cannon, 2,000,000 cartridges, and 300,000 pounds of gunpowder; Stettin: 263 guns, 1,000,000 cartridges, and 200,000 pounds of gunpowder; Küstrin: 108 guns, 1,000,000 cartridges, and 100,000 pounds of gunpowder; and Glogau: 108 cannon, 1,000,000 cartridges, and 100,000 pounds of gunpowder. See Décret du 21 Décembre 1811, in Louis Joseph Margueron, ed., *Campagne de Russie: préliminaires de la campagne de Russie, ses causes, sa préparation, organisation de l'armée du 1 Janvier 1810 au 31 Janvier 1812* (Paris, 1899), 3:427–430. For the Polish fortresses, see *CN*, No. 18614, 23:344.

25   There were nine pontoon companies, two marine companies, nine sapper companies, and six companies of miners. In addition, the army possessed three pontoon trains (two of them featuring one hundred pontoons each) and one engineer park.

26   Of these train battalions, twelve battalions contained 3,024 four-horse wagons (each battalion had 771 men, 1,227 horses, and 252 wagons, each loaded with 1,500 kg); four battalions comprised 2,424 one-horse *chars à la comtoise* (each battalion included 606 carts, each loaded with 600 kg); and the final four battalions featured 2,400 carts drawn by oxen, which were to be later eaten (each battalion consisted of 600 ox carts, each loaded with 1,000 kg). In total, these trains could transport 8,390 tons of supplies.

THE LIMITS OF THE OPERATIONAL ART: RUSSIA 1812 379

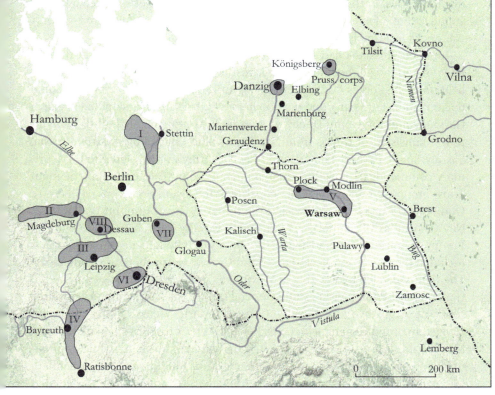

MAP 11.1   Napoleon's supply depots in 1812

as late summer would have provided fresh crops of hay and oats to replenish his stocks. However, Napoleon's earlier campaigns had been mostly conducted in Central Europe, a densely populated and well-developed region where the agricultural revolution and the nascent industrial revolution of the late 1700s had created favorable environments for the mobile style of warfare that Napoleon preferred. Furthermore, this region featured numerous well-built (in many cases even paved) roads that connected towns and cities and provided efficient means of transporting troops. In comparison, Russia's western provinces were among the poorest and most underdeveloped regions in Europe that suffered from inadequate overland transport links. With the start of the campaign, Napoleon and his commanders realized that the heavy four-horse caissons could not, for the most part, be used in Russia because of their weight and the poor roads, forcing them to utilize vehicles of smaller size that they seized from the locals. This, however, resulted in delays, supply losses, and disorder. Thus, in the first few weeks of the war, it was not so much a lack of supplies that affected so many of Napoleon's men as the inability to transport the stocks in a timely fashion to where they were needed.

After the Russians had scored a decisive victory over the Turks at Ruse in late 1811 and forced them to sign an armistice, Napoleon accelerated the mobilization of his forces and, by late spring of 1812, the Grande Armée of some 608,000 men, 1,372 guns, and 180,000 horses had gradually assembled in North Germany and the Grand Duchy of Warsaw.[27] Approximately half of its manpower consisted of troops from Napoleon's allies, including Austria, Prussia, Saxony, Spain, Bavaria, Poland, and Italy. The army was divided into three primary commands deployed in an area ranging from Tilsit to Lublin. The main army group, led by Napoleon, consisted of Davout's I Corps (Pillwiski), Oudinot's II Corps (near Pillwiski), the Imperial Guard (around Wilkowiski), Ney's III Corps (Marienpol), and I, II, and III Cavalry Corps between Kovno and Prenny. A central command, led by the viceroy of Italy, Eugene de Beauharnais, included the IV Corps (Olecko) and Saint Cyr's VI Corps (both at Czimochen). The right wing, led by the king of Westphalia, Jerome Bonaparte, consisted of General Jozef Poniatowski's V and General Dominique Vandamme's VIII Corps (both at Avgustovo); IV Cavalry Corps of Marie Victor Latour-Maubourg (Avgustovo); and General Jean Louis Reynier's VII Corps (Ostrolenka). Marshal Macdonald's X Corps (Tilsit) protected the extreme left flank while approximately 34,000 Austrians under General Karl Philipp zu Schwarzenberg (Lukow) covered the extreme right.[28] Although the Grande Armée was divided into three groups, the center and right wing possessed not a shadow of autonomy and remained closely controlled by the emperor, who, despite the enormous size of his forces and the vastness of the theater of war (his forces were scattered over some 450 km) in which he would operate, stayed true to his principle of unity of command.

Theater of War

By 1812, Russia's imperial border in the west ran from the shores of the Baltic Sea, along the Niemen, Narew, Bug, and Pruth Rivers to the Black Sea. This vast

---

27 The army consisted of about 492,000 infantry, 96,000 cavalry, and some 20,000 auxiliary forces. On 3 March, Napoleon settled the organization of the Grande Armée, which consisted of eight army corps (four French and four foreign) and four cavalry corps. See CN, No. 18544, 23:277–278.

28 Behind the main forces, Napoleon also formed reserves consisting of IX Corps under Victor, now a marshal, and XI Corps under Marshal Augereau.

territorial expanse was intersected by numerous natural obstacles, the most important of which was the Polesye – the vast area of marshes along the Pripyat River – that divided western Russia into two theaters of operations. The northern theater spread from the Baltic shoreline to the Polesye Swamps, while the southern extended from the marshes to the Black Sea. The northern theater was by far the more important because there lay the shortest routes to Russia's political, economic, and cultural centers. It contained some 630 km of the imperial border from Polangen (via Kovno and Grodno) to Brest-Litovsk which, naturally, posed a tremendous challenge for a defending army.[29] The area presented a vast plain that lay north of the Carpathian Mountains and, opening out almost infinitely to the east, made up most of western Russia. These rolling plains were studded with dense woods of pine, birch, and beech[30] and were intersected everywhere by water courses. On its way into Russia, the Grande Armée's first natural obstacle consisted of the frontier rivers: the Niemen, Bobr, and Bug. The broad and slow flow of these rivers had cut deep into soft soil, creating steep banks and abrupt ravines but the rivers did not pose a serious hurdle to the invasion and offered multiple crossing points – between Kovno and Brest-Litovsk alone were six major sites.[31] Further east, the next obstacle in the direction of Saint Petersburg was the Western Dvina, and toward Moscow the Upper Dnieper, both wide and strong rivers that could have posed considerable difficulties if not for a sixty-mile gap that existed in between them.[32] Aside from major waterways, numerous smaller rivulets and lakes intersected the area. Advancing through the northern Belorussian provinces, the Grande Armée had to cross the Berezina, Viliya, Shara, Serguch,

---

29 As one Russian historian justly observed, "If Napoleon aimed at complete subjugation of Russia to his power, he would have set the conquest of our southern, prosperous provinces as his initial task. But because he only wanted to force [Russia] to abide by his policies, he chose to direct his attention to north of the Polesye which was closer to our political centers." See Arkadii Skugarevskii, *1812 god ot nachala voiny do Smolenska* (Kazan, 1898), 14.

30 In 1797, a government survey described the basin of the Berezina and Ulla Rivers as "full of dense woods, rocky terrain, and relatively high hills": Ivan Herman's Survey, 9 [20] February 1797, *Arkhiv gosudarstvennago soveta* (Saint Petersburg, 1888), II:269–270.

31 These locations were Kovno, Grodno, Khorosh, Tsekhanovets, Drogochin, and Brest-Litovsk. The width of the Niemen above Kovno was between 250 to 300 paces, and below Kovno some 350 to 400 paces.

32 The Western Dvina river was bridged only at Riga, Dunaburg, Vitebsk, and Surazh. The width of the river between Vitebsk and Dunaburg was between 180 to 200 paces, but at Riga some 800 paces. The Upper Dnieper flows east to west and was thus parallel to invasion routes.

Druts, Ulla, Nacha, Skha, and Obol Rivers, to name just a few.[33] Generally, Russia's western provinces had a great many roads that intersected one another in every direction. However, the quality of these roads was far inferior to the great roads of Central Europe, where Napoleonic armies had previously campaigned. The road conditions depended on weather and the time of year and prevented continued employment of heavy transport. In the wooded and marshy areas the number of roads was strictly limited, and communication remained difficult, especially in spring and autumn, when rainy weather made existing roads almost impassable.

The Russian high command expected Napoleon to choose the northern theater of war, in which case he could target either of Russia's political centers. In the case of Saint Petersburg, which was located some 800 km from the border, Napoleon would have two possible directions: Kovno–Dunaburg–Saint Petersburg or Tilsit–Riga–Saint Petersburg. However, both of these directions presented considerable difficulties since the northern provinces were relatively poor in resources and more topographically challenging; the northern bank of the Dvina was covered by innumerable lakes, marshes, forests, small hills, and streams. On the other hand, Moscow, which stood about 900 km from the border, was located in the heart of ancient Russia and surrounded by thriving provinces with rolling terrain that favored military operations. For an advance on Moscow, Napoleon could select one of three major operational directions:

1. Kovno–Vilna–Glubokoe–Vitebsk–Smolensk–Moscow
2. Kovno–Vilna–Minsk–Smolensk–Moscow
3. Bialystok–Slonim–Bobruisk–Mogilev–Smolensk–Moscow

All three Moscow routes converged at Smolensk, one of the most valuable and historic cities in Russia that had formerly been an important frontier fortress and the site of a bloody Russo-Polish contest just two centuries earlier. The city was surrounded by a massive 17th-century brick wall[34] but its fortifications

---

33   Naturally, these rivers differed in size. The Ulla was a minor river and its width averaged 25–40 meters while the Berezina, some 600 km long, was one of the major rivers in Belorussia. Rising in the marshes of the northwest, it flowed southeast into the Dnieper, averaging a width of 10–30 meters upstream and some 80–100 meters downstream. Even as late as 1838, the river had only two major bridges (at Borisov and Bobruisk) and its flat banks were notoriously marshy, prone to flooding in the spring and freezing solid in winter.

34   The city walls were 6.5 km long, 19 m high and 5 m wide, with seventeen towers: I. Smirnov, *Smolensk – gorod russkoi slavi* (Smolensk, 1982), 38–49.

were decrepit. In general, the northern theater had limited artificial buttresses; of the existing ones, the most important was the fortress of Riga, which controlled the Dvina's estuary. Demographically, both theaters presented potentially grave danger to Russia. Much of the region had been annexed to the Russian Empire just a few decades prior as the result of the infamous Polish Partitions. The Polish residents had little love for the Russians, and their nobility certainly looked longingly to the Grand Duchy of Warsaw which provided them with a glimmer of hope for the eventual restoration of the Polish state.

Napoleon's Planning

Napoleon did not intend to advance as deep into Russia as he eventually did, and the Dvina River was the farthest point he had anticipated reaching.[35] Neither did he anticipate a prolonged campaign, which could not begin before June because of Russia's typical poor spring weather and the accompanying lack of sufficient grass in the field to feed the horses. Conversely, the campaign could not extend beyond November when the snows would begin to fall. Napoleon hoped that the Russians would accept battle and be defeated within several weeks, which would allow him to dictate peace before winter arrived.[36]

---

35 Klemens Wenzel Lothar Metternich, *Mémoires, documents et écrits divers* ... (Paris, 1880), 1:121–123.

36 Napoleon's belief that the Russian armies would fight him in the borderlands might have been bolstered by Russian counterintelligence. Although this subject is rarely discussed in the Western historiography, Russian historians have long considered it in their own analysis. France and Russia both engaged in active espionage operations and the exploits of Colonel Alexander Chernyshev, who successfully infiltrated the French ministry of war, are quite well known. But less well known is the success of Russian counterintelligence in dealing with French spies and agents throughout the western provinces of the Russian Empire. In 1811, Russian counterintelligence pulled off its greatest coup against its French counterparts when a retired Russian officer, David Savan, knocked on the doors of the Russian military headquarters in Vilna. Savan was employed by Polish intelligence, directed by Stanislaw Fiszer, chief of staff of the Grand Duchy of Warsaw, which had tasked him with crossing the Russian border to gather information on the deployment of Russian units, their numerical strengths, leaders, and location of headquarters as well as public opinion in the western provinces of the Russian Empire. Unbeknownst to Fiszer, Savan was motivated not by pecuniary rewards but by his desire to serve his adopted motherland once more. The first thing Savan did upon crossing into Russia was to go directly to Russian military headquarters in Vilna and inform the Russian authorities of his mission. Russian counterintelligence quickly exploited this chance to turn Savan into a double agent. They supplied him with precious but fabricated information on the Russian military. Fiszer was impressed with the quality of intelligence Savan had procured for him, rewarded him with a monthly pension, and then gave him several more missions which

In a conversation with Metternich at Dresden, Napoleon speculated that the campaign would probably end at Minsk or Smolensk, and that he would make a halt there, fortify both places, take up winter quarters at Vilna, organize conquered Lithuania, and feed his army at the expense of Russia. If this did not result in peace, the next year he would press on to the interior and, just as patiently as in the first campaign, wait for the submission of Alexander. The Swiss-born French staff officer and future military theorist Antoine-Henri Jomini relates a table conversation in Vilna after the campaign commenced in which the emperor stated his plans exactly as he had expressed them to

---

Savan, naturally, successfully accomplished. His success soon garnered the attention of Louis Pierre Bignon, the French diplomat who coordinated French intelligence operations in the Grand Duchy of Warsaw. Bignon recruited Savan into French intelligence and, after training, dispatched him as a spymaster to Vilna.

Over several months Savan found himself at the heart of unfolding political and intelligence intrigues as France and Russia gradually moved towards war. He proved essential to the Russian efforts to uncover more than half a dozen French agents and to shut down the funding for the remaining infiltrators. All the while he fed misinformation to his handlers in the Grand Duchy of Warsaw and thereby influenced French preparations for the campaigns. He played a particularly important role in late spring of 1812 when Napoleon dispatched his aide de camp Louis Narbonne-Lara on a mission to Vilna. Officially this mission was styled as Napoleon's last-ditch effort to avert the war, but the French emperor well knew that war was unavoidable, and his instructions urged Narbonne to keep his eyes open while in Russia for everything concerning the Russian army, popular mood, and opinion in Russia's western provinces. Russian counterintelligence anticipated that Narbonne would seek to gather military intelligence and closely observed every move the French delegation made on the Russian soil. It also used Savan to further deceive his opponent. The Russian double agent made contact with Narbonne's delegation, explaining that he was a French intelligence officer who had lost contact with his handlers in Warsaw. Savan's documents, signed by Bignon, convinced the members of the French delegation of his sincerity, and they organized several meetings between Narbonne and the agent who delivered detailed information on the deployment of Russian forces, their leaders, and overall conditions in the army. The documents disclosed that the Russian armies were preparing to vigorously contest the French crossing of the Niemen and would engage the Grande Armée once it was across the Russian border. For Narbonne, this information was priceless, and he immediately conveyed it to his superiors. Yet, all of these details had been carefully vetted by Russian counterintelligence that sought to misinform the French on the eve of the war. It is unclear if this information reached Napoleon but, if it did, it would have certainly reinforced his belief that the Russian armies would fight him in the borderlands. For details, see the transcript of Savan's questioning in *General Staff Archives*, II, 296–299; "Zapiski Yakova Ivanovicha de Sanglena," *Russkaya starina* 1888, vol. 37, 543–544; K. Voyenskii, "Priyezd general-adjutanta Napoleona I grafa Narbonna v Vilnu v maye 1812 goda," *Russkaya starina* (1907), vol. 131, 219–235 (contains excerpts from the journal of police surveillance); A. Popov, "Epizody iz istorii dvenadtsatogo goda," *Russkii arkhiv* 3 (1892), 351–352; V. Bezotosnyi, *Razvedka i plany storon v 1812 godu* (Moscow, 2005).

Metternich at Dresden. "If Barclay [de Tolly] supposes I would run after him to the Volga, he is mightily mistaken. We shall follow him as far as Smolensk and the Dvina, where a good battle will provide us with cantonments. I shall return with headquarters to Vilna to spend the winter, and will send for a troupe of the Paris Opera and the *Théâtre français*. The next May the business will be finished, unless we make peace during the winter."[37]

On the eve of war, Napoleon believed that the Russian armies would invade the Grand Duchy of Warsaw, with Bagration's 2nd Western Army seeking to turn the French right flank. In early March 1812, Napoleon stated that the "principal goal is to prevent [the Russians] from ravaging the Grand Duchy." Three weeks later, as he dictated orders to reinforce the Polish fortresses of Thorn, Modlin, Zamosc, and others, the emperor stressed that "it is very important that Zamosc is abundantly supplied because it is very likely to be besieged [by Bagration's troops]." On 26 March, Napoleon again reiterated his concern that the Russians might declare war and "invade the Grand Duchy."[38]

Thus, the initial deployment of the Grande Armée revealed Napoleon's effort to address this possibility. If the Russians indeed attacked, Jerome Bonaparte's four corps had instructions to slowly retreat toward the Vistula River, where the fortresses of Modlin, Thorn, and others had been already reinforced. By luring the enemy deeper into the Grand Duchy, Napoleon's main force (five corps and the Imperial Guard) would be able to strike at the right flank of Russia's 1st Western Army and, by driving it into the 2nd Western Army, destroy both Russian forces. Even late in the spring of 1812, when it became clear that the Russians would not risk invading the Grand Duchy and the Grande Armée would have to cross the border instead, Napoleon still expected the Russian armies to act offensively. He considered two possibilities: once the war was underway, the Russians would either counterattack in direction of Warsaw or unite their forces to fight a decisive battle close to the border. The Grande Armée was already prepared for the first scenario and Napoleon now considered the latter possibility. He envisioned carrying out a strategic envelopment maneuver, similar to the one he had conceived and brilliantly executed in the 1805 Ulm campaign. Due to the flawed disposition of the Russian armies (see below), Napoleon expected that as soon as hostilities commenced Barclay de Tolly's 1st Western Army would be separated by more than 100 miles from Bagration's 2nd Western Army. He intended to use Jerome's army group to pin

---

37 Antoine-Henri Jomini, *Précis politique et militaire des campagnes de 1812 à 1814* (Lausanne, 1886), 1:72.

38 For details, see a series of instructions (particularly Nos. 18584 and 18587) Napoleon dictated to Berthier on 16 March 1812 in CN, 23:314–319; No. 18614, 23:344. See also Nos. 18545, 18604–18608, 23:278–280, 335–340.

down Bagration while the pivoting central group of the Grande Armée would swing from the north, seize Vilna, and pressure both the 1st and 2nd Western Armies into the pocket formed by the Pripyat, Bug, and Narew Rivers, where the Russians would be forced to fight a battle. "Make sure that the enemy believes that you are aiming for the Volhynia," Napoleon instructed Jerome, "and keep the enemy engaged in this region for as long as you can. In the meanwhile, I will turn the [Russian] extreme right flank and gain twelve or fifteen marches in the direction of Saint Petersburg. I will, thus, find myself on the right wing ... and occupy Vilna, *which is the first objective of this campaign* ... Once this operation is underway and revealed, the enemy will choose one of two possibilities: either he will concentrate his forces to fight a battle in the interior, or he will launch a [counter]offensive [toward Warsaw]. In the latter case ... as the enemy would approach the ramparts of Praga [suburbs of Warsaw] and the banks of the Vistula ... I will launch a movement to the right with the whole of my army, which will overwhelm the enemy and throw him into the Vistula."[39]

This plan of operations was as bold and breathtaking as any Napoleon had previously conceived. Writing to his brother less than three weeks before the war, Napoleon stressed that, "in such an extended theater of war, success may be gained only through a well-conceived plan in which all the components are in full harmony. It is, therefore, important to [carefully] consider your orders and do neither more nor less than what you are told, especially when it comes to combined movement."[40] But the French emperor faced major challenges. The vast theater of war dramatically differed from Central Europe in availability of resourses and basic infrastructure. Furthermore, the nature of this new theater of war posed immense practical problems in directing and controlling forces scattered over hundreds of miles. The sheer size of the Grande Armée sapped its leadership's ability to cope with challenges. Men who were accustomed to commanding corps and divisions found themselves entrusted with what can be termed "army groups," and very few of them had any experience of or potential to command at this level.[41] Neither was the Grande Armée that which had triumphed in 1805. Although it was the largest land force ever assembled in Europe up to that point, its quality left much to be desired. An influx of new recruits had diluted the quality of French forces, and many units,

---

39 Ibid., No. 18769, 23:470 (emphasis added). Macdonald's X Corps and Schwarzenberg's Austrian Corps formed the extreme flanks and covered possible Russian threats via East Prussia and Galicia respectively. For details, see ibid., No. 18781, 23:480–481.
40 Ibid., No. 18769, 23:469.
41 For example, Jerome Bonaparte received command of an "army group" consisting of three army corps, even though he was woefully unprepared for such a task.

especially from Germany and the Netherlands, were insufficiently trained and lacked motivation to fight.[42] The army's size and polyglot nature – it included at least dozen nationalities from across Europe – posed major challenges for the officer corps.

Russian War Preparations

Russia began preparing for the seemingly inevitable war in 1811. By then a number of Russian officers had been already assigned as attachés to the Russian missions in Germany and France to gather intelligence on French preparations; the most important of these intelligence centers were at Berlin (headed by Christophe Andreyevich Lieven) and Paris (led by Aleksandr Ivanovich Chernyshev). By cultivating their relations with senior officers or bribing officials, these agents produced a steady stream of precious reports on Napoleon's habits, the political situation in various regions of Europe, French military recruitment, troop movements, and logistics as well as official documents stolen from the French ministries. Alexander himself considered war against Napoleon as early as late 1810–early 1811.[43] In instructions to his embassy at Vienna dated 25 February 1811, Alexander underscored the necessity of occupying Poland and was willing to transfer Wallachia and Moldavia to mollify Austria.[44] But these preparations were halted after Józef Poniatowski, who was approached with a request that he switch allegiance to the Russian emperor and support a Russian invasion of the Grand Duchy, informed Napoleon about Russian intentions.[45] In late October 1811, Russian corps that had been deployed along the Polish border received orders to be in full readiness to initiate the

---

42   Training consisted of more than drill alone. Many recruits had yet to acquire foraging and field craft skills that were crucial to the French way of war – much of the speed and mobility of the French could be ascribed to their practice of living off the land. Yet the new recruits, whether French, German, or Italian, were not properly trained in foraging techniques nor were they accustomed to grueling marches and deprivation. Consequently, many of them succumbed to the war's physical demands or were stricken by demoralization.

43   His sentiments are well expressed in a letter to Prince Adam Czartorisky on 25 December 1810/6 January 1811 in *Besedi i chastnaya perepiska mezhdu imperatorom Aleksandrom i knyazem A. Chartorizhskym* (Moscow, 1912), 147–154.

44   Imperial instruction of 25 February 1811, in F. Martens, *Sobraniye traktatov i konventsii zaklyuchennykh Rossiyei s inostrannimi derzhavami* (Saint Petersburg, 1876), 3:78–80.

45   For a good discussion, see Albert Vandal, *Napoléon et Alexandre Ier: l'alliance russe sous le Premier empire. La rupture* (Paris, 1897), 3:140–146.

invasion of the duchy,[46] but Prussia's alliance with France compelled the Russians to abandon any thought of offensive operations and turn to defensive strategy. As it lacked alliances with Poland, Prussia, and Austria, any attempt by the Russian army to wage offensive war against France was doomed.

In case of enemy invasion, one of Russia's main concerns was the improvement of existing fortifications. The Russians therefore conducted major inspections to examine the area between the Niemen, Western Dvina, and Dnieper Rivers, to determine repairs that needed to be made to existing fortifications, and to designate places for new ones.[47] Throughout 1811, fortifications at Riga and Kiev were repaired and construction on new fortresses began at Bobruisk and Dunaburg; the former, largely completed by June 1812, was expected to withstand a siege while the latter was still in its early stages and only a bridgehead had been completed on the left bank of the Dvina.[48] In April 1812, the Russians began constructing a fortified camp near Drissa on the left bank of the Dvina and a bridgehead near Borisov on the right bank of the Berezina (both were only partially completed by July). Additional bridgeheads were built at Mosty and Belitsy on the Niemen River to protect communication between the Russian forces.

Considerable efforts were made to establish new supply depots and magazines. Looking at the supply depot allocation, it becomes clear that the Russian command focused on the northern operational line where most of the resources were stored. Along this line, central supply depots were established at Novgorod, Trubchevsk, and Sosnish; major magazines were built at Riga, Dunaburg, Drissa, Disna, and Bobruisk and smaller depots at Libava, Shavli, Vilkomir, Sventsyany, Vilna, Koltynyani, Grodno, Slonim, Slutsk, Pinsk, and Mozyr. In the southern theater of war, a central depot was formed at Kiev, with additional depots at Velikiye Luki, Dubno, Ostrog, Starokonstantinov, Zhitomir, and Kovel. In June 1812, Barclay de Tolly issued an order instructing his corps

---

46   See the secret instructions to Peter Ludwig Adolf von Wittgenstein, Karl Fedorovich Baggovut, Ivan Nikolayevich Essen, Dmitry Sergeyevich Dokhturov, and Bagration, 24–29 October 1811, in *General Staff Archives*, 5:268–270, 302–304, 313–315.

47   Karl von Oppermann, who supervised these missions, reported that "such vast engineering works have not been attempted or carried out since the days of Peter the Great": Oppermann to Barclay de Tolly, 13 November 1810, ibid., 1:271. This report contains a detailed overview of the repair and construction work conducted on fortifications in western Russia.

48   These works seem to have been conducted rather hastily, which affected their quality. In mid-June, the Guard Lieutenant Kashintsev informed Barclay de Tolly that the main supply depot at Dunaburg was "not properly built: the bricks were of poor quality and the building's walls already showed cracks, some half an inch wide": Kashintsev to Barclay de Tolly, 15 June 1812, ibid., 13:21.

commanders to identify every district official who had access to information about land resources and ownership and should be deported during the war to prevent the French from recruiting these men for the purposes of collecting requisitions and taxes.[49]

Three Russian armies would deploy along the western borders and be supported by a network of recruitment and artillery depots. The first reserve line, itself arranged in three tiers, consisted of recruitment/training depots that had first been established in 1808 and reorganized in 1811.[50] In addition, three lines of fifty-eight artillery parks (containing complete caissons, musket ammunition, etc) were established throughout western Russia; the parks of the 1st Line were mobile and contained caissons, ammunition, and repair stock while the 2nd and 3rd Lines were immobile depots and supplied the 1st Line with necessary resources.[51]

Russian strategic deployment, however, was flawed on several counts. To begin with, the 1st and 2nd Western Armies, commanded by Barclay de Tolly and Bagration respectively, stood too far away from each other and neither was capable of independently engaging a superior enemy force. Together they covered a front of some 300 km, and if forced to retreat they would have to first concentrate at different locations that were some 170 km away from each and separated by the Niemen River.[52] Bagration was too weak to halt the enemy advance from Grodno and, if pushed back, he would be forced to retreat along the south bank of the Niemen, thus further separating himself from Barclay. General Dmitry Sergeyevich Dokhturov's corps, deployed between the two armies, was also too weak to operate independently, while its isolation could

---

49 Shuvalov to Barclay de Tolly, No. 50 (Secret); Platov to Barclay de Tolly, No. 2; Tormasov to Barclay de Tolly, 13–17 June 1812, ibid., 13:3, 5, 41–42.

50 Each recruitment depot was assigned to regiments in one of twenty-four divisions. Recruits received initial training (without weapons) at the depots of the 2nd Line and were then dispatched for thorough training and full equipment to the 1st Line, where they were assigned to fourth (reserve) battalions (6 battalions per depot; each some 500 men strong) for infantry, and the sixth (cuirassier/dragoon) or eleventh and twelfth squadrons for light cavalry (each 150 men strong). In 1811, the 81st Levy produced some 130,000 recruits, with 87,500 sent to the 1st Line and 43,000 to the 2nd Line. Of the 87 fourth battalions from the recruitment depots, 12 joined the Riga garrison and six fought under Wittgenstein; the rest were incorporated into the retreating 1st and 2nd Western Armies on the march. General Mikhail Andreyevich Miloradovich joined Kutuzov's forces on the eve of the Battle of Borodino with most of the remaining battalions, some 13,500 men. All men of the fourth battalions were distributed to replenish the ranks of regiments.

51 Each park of the 1st Line contained 534 horses provided by recruitment districts in western provinces. Parks of the 2nd and 3rd Line had no horses, and resources had to be transported on rented civilian transports.

52 Vilna for the 1st Western Army and Slonim for the 2nd.

be easily exploited by the enemy. The deployment of the 3rd Reserve Army of Observation in the southern theater was a major mistake since all evidence suggested that Napoleon was planning to invade north of the Polesye. The southern provinces could have been easily defended by a single corps (supported by the Army of the Danube) left to face the Austrians while the rest of General Aleksandr Petrovich Tormasov's forces (some 30,000 men) should have been moved northwards and placed at the disposal of Bagration.

The question of Russian strategy is still debated since Russian military planning in 1810–1812 represents a complicated and confusing picture. Mistrustful of his generals, Alexander concealed much military intelligence from them, and the planning was conducted in utmost secrecy.[53] In the two years leading up to the war, plenty of ink was wasted in drafting various plans, and one Russian scholar, in fact, counted as many as thirty submitted by various officers.[54] Many of these officers had studied the operations of Arthur Wellesley, the future duke of Wellington, in Spain and those of Peter the Great against King Charles XII of Sweden in the 1700s, while Prussian officers, including Scharnhorst, advised the Russians to pursue "a defensive war."[55]

Several of these plans are worthy of discussion. In March 1810, the minister of war, Barclay de Tolly, submitted a memorandum to the tsar that argued that Russia's western border was particularly vulnerable because it covered a wide expanse and was poorly defended, both by nature and by man. Unlike most of

---

53   Even the chief of staff of the 1st Western Army, General Aleksey Petrovich Yermolov, had little information about the strategy discussed by the emperor and his staff. In late spring of 1812, he still believed in the offensive and remarked, "In 1812, it seemed everything was ready for us to wage an offensive war: armies were deployed on the borders, enormous magazines were established in the Bialystok district and in the Grodno and Vilna provinces." See Aleksey Yermolov, *The Czar's General: The Memoirs of a Russian General in the Napoleonic Wars*, trans. and ed. by Alexander Mikaberidze (Welwyn Garden City, UK, 2005), 108. General Levin Bennigsen also complained that the tsar "did not show me any [approved] operational plans and I do not know of any person who had seen any": Bennigsen, "Zapiski grafa L.L. Bennigsena o kampanii 1812 goda," *Russkaya Starina* 6 (1909), 517.

54   V. Pugachev. "K voprosu o pervonachalnom plane voiny 1812 g.," in *1812 god: sbornik statei* (Moscow, 1962), 32–34. Among those who submitted plans were P. Bagration, Allonville, K. Toll, P. Volkonskii, L. Wolzogen, K. Pfuel, L. Bennigsen, E. Kankrin, A. Württemberg, Ya. Gawerdowski, Ch. Dumorierz, M. Magnitskii, R. Lilienstern, E. Saint-Priest, I. Barclay de Tolly, G. Armfeldt, F. d'Auvray, F. Uvarov, F. Driezen, I. Crossard, A. Polev, V. Crone, I. Diebitsch, etc.

55   Prussian reformer Scharnhorst advised the Russians, "Une guerre défensive ⍰comme Wellington et d'autres grands généraux l'ont conduite, adoptée aux projets et à la manière d'agir des chefs des partis présence, au théâtre de la guerre et aux qualités distinctives des armées, semble être, pour la Prusse comme pour la Russie, le parti plus convenable": quoted in Gabriel Joseph Fabry, *Campagne de 1812* (Paris, 1912), 1:i.

Russia's other borders, the western provinces lacked defensive lines or fortifications and constructing them would be prohibitively expensive, not to mention the prolonged time that such an undertaking would require. Thus, Barclay proposed the establishment of a single defensive line along the Western Dvina and Dnieper Rivers. He maintained that, if a strong enemy force invaded the territories Russia had annexed from Poland in 1772–1795, the Russian army would have to stage a fighting withdrawal to this defensive line, "leaving the enemy in a scorched countryside, without bread, cattle, or any other means of supplying himself." Then, after the enemy had exhausted his forces, the Russian armies would launch a counteroffensive. Barclay believed that the enemy's main attack would be directed either southeast toward Kiev or northeast into Courland and Livonia. "We cannot expect that the enemy would dare to advance in the center," he noted, referring to the direction toward Minsk and Smolensk, but if it did so then the small "Reserve Army" deployed there would delay the enemy advance while the two main Russian armies attacked Napoleon's flanks and rear.

As for force allocation, Barclay assumed that peace would be concluded with the Ottomans while Austria would remain disinterested. In this case, of Russia's twenty-three existing divisions, he envisioned eight remaining in Finland, the Caucasus, and the Danube regions, leaving fifteen divisions for the western front. Of these, seven would form an army deployed in the south to cover direction on Kiev, four divisions would protect the right in Courland, and four divisions (deployed between Vilna and Minsk) would cover the vast territory in between these two armies.[56] Alexander approved this plan later that year and by December 1811 considerable preparations had been made based on it.

In early 1812, many senior Russian officers, including Bagration, Bennigsen, and Alexander of Württemberg, opposed this defensive strategy and called for an offensive one.[57] They argued that a defensive strategy gave the enemy the initiative and ability to exploit the geography of the western borderlands to divide the Russian forces, and defeat them in detail. Bagration reflected the opinion of these hardline officers when he called for a more aggressive stance toward the French. He proposed establishing a demarcation line along the Oder River, and its violation, "even by a single French battalion," would be considered a *casus belli*. The Russian army would then invade the Grand Duchy of Warsaw and Prussia to raise "national" movements against the French and "to

---

56 Barclay de Tolly to Alexander, March 1812, *General Staff Archives*, I, part II, 1–6.
57 Bennigsen's plan of military operations can be found ibid., 2:83–93; Alexander of Württemberg's plan is ibid., 10:253–275.

move the theater of war from the boundaries of the [Russian] Empire." The purpose of such a preemptive offensive into the Grand Duchy of Warsaw was to move the "scorched-earth" zone, where the Russians wanted to engage Napoleon, as far west as possible. If this were achieved, the entire burden of the war would be removed from the shoulders of the Russian nation and placed on its neighbours. Indeed, should Napoleon invade Russia, he first would have to prepare massive amounts of supplies in the Grand Duchy of Warsaw and East Prussia to sustain the invading army. These resources would be vulnerable to a Russian preemptive attack.[58]

Even bolder plans were proposed. French *émigré* count d'Allonville submitted an interesting memorandum in January 1811. He proposed establishing a close alliance with Britain and making common cause with Spain, with a guarantee that its independence would be closely tied to the outcome of the Russian war. Allonville urged a quick peace with Turkey, even if that meant making generous concessions to them, and diverting Ottoman attention to the fact that Austria, their ancient enemy, was now allied to Napoleon. He hoped the Turks would enter the war, launch a powerful diversion to Illyria, and harass France's Mediterranean coastline. Austrian neutrality would be sought; if Vienna refused, Russia would attack Austria together with the Turks. A Russian observation corps would be dispatched through Prussia to threaten Westphalia and cause agitation in North Germany for an insurrection against the French. Local German ports would be opened to the British. To secure its northern borders, Russia should negotiate with Sweden, threatening to blockade its coastline with the support of the British navy should Stockholm refuse an alliance offer; furthermore, in case of *coup d'état*, Russia had to ensure that the Swedish crown passed to "*héritiers légitimes de la maison royale*" who were related to Russian imperial family. Russia and Britain would revive the royalist movement in France and exploit it to divert Napoleon's attention. Finally, Allonville urged the Russian army to make as many diversions as possible, attacking French interests in Illyria, Naples, Calabria, Pomerania, Hanover, Holland, Brittany, Bayonne, and other places.[59]

Yet considerable support for a purely defensive strategy also surfaced. For example, a plan proposed by another French *émigré* in Russian service, General Guillaume Emmanuel Guignard de Saint-Priest, called for: "(1) [The Russian] army should be supplied at the expense of the enemy; (2) [we should try] to

---

58 Bagration to Alexander, circa March 1812, in Sergei Golubov, ed., *General Bagration: sbornik dokumentov i materialov* (Leningrad, 1945), 134–136.

59 *Mémoires politique et militaire sur les circonstances presentes par d'Allonville*, in Fabry, *Campagne de 1812*, 1:ii–iv.

prevent the enemy from using any supplies during the offensive, to cut his lines of communication, and to always follow a 'scorched-earth' policy during our retreat; (3) if separated from our base and reinforcements, we must avoid any decisive actions, and engage the enemy only in the places advantageous to us; (4) we must prolong the war for as long as possible; (5) if the enemy retreats, we should always pursue him with all available forces; (6) if one of our armies retreats in front of superior forces, the other army... should attack them in the flank and rear."[60]

Most notably, Ludwig Adolf Friedrich von Wolzogen, a Prussian officer who joined the Russian army in 1807, proposed deploying two armies along the western frontier. If the French attacked, one of them would withdraw to a special line of well-supplied fortresses organized along the Dvina, Dnieper, and other rivers, where it would make a stand. The second army would operate against the enemy's lines of communication.[61] Wolzogen's ideas proved to be particularly influential as they caught the attention of General Karl Ludwig August Friedrich von Pfuel, another former Prussian officer who advised the Russian tsar.[62] Pfuel believed that Napoleon could not have more than 250,000 men and would keep them divided in two groups. He proposed countering them with two Russian armies. The first, the "Army of the Dvina," would retreat to the "Drissa camp," which would be fortified in the style of Wellesley's Lines of Torres Vedras,[63] on the Western Dvina River and hold the enemy there. The second army, the "Army of the Dnieper," would then operate on the enemy's flanks and rear, destroying lines of supply and communication. Once this was achieved, the Army of the Dvina would counterattack in the direction of Memel–Tilsit–Insterburg.

Pfuel's assistant, Wolzogen, spent several months examining the area around Riga, Vilna, Dinaburg, Vitebsk, Drissa, and Mogilev before selecting a

---

60 Saint-Priest's plan is in *General Staff Archives*, 13:408–415.
61 Wolzogen to Barclay de Tolly, 3 October 1811 (with the plan of operation attached to the letter), ibid., 5:107–111; a French translation is in Fabry, *Campagne de 1812*, 1:ii–xxviii.
62 After the collapse of the Prussian army in 1806, Pfuel joined the Russian army and soon became one of the tsar's confidantes. Pfuel lived secluded at imperial headquarters in Vilna. He had no official position, no authority, and no office. He received no reports nor any information regarding the status or situation of the army or that of the enemy; he rarely communicated with Barclay. Pfuel admired Frederick the Great and his system of warfare and, despite fighting Napoleon for almost a decade, he failed to grasp the new French tactics and strategy. He was a good theoretician, but his ideas were worthless in practice.
63 A contemporary wrote that Pfuel had closely watched the operations in Iberia and "wanted to imitate the English actions at Torres Vedras in setting up a fortified camp at Drissa": N. Bozherianov, *Graf E.F. Kankrin* (Saint Petersburg, 1897), 16.

site near Drissa on the Western Dvina River.[64] However, the building of the camp did not begin until April 1812, and it was not completed when the war began. It also became obvious that the defense works constructed during the previous two years in accordance with Barclay's designs were useless; the depots and warehouses with their vast amounts of supplies had to be abandoned because the lack of logistical support complicated transportation of supplies to new warehouses. As a result, during the first weeks of the war in June–July, the retreating Russian armies were compelled either to leave huge magazines to the French or destroy them.

Pfuel's plan was flawed for several reasons. First, it greatly underestimated the size and strength of the Grande Armée and therefore its capacity to engage both armies at once. The limited strength of the second army made an attack on the flank and rear of the superior enemy unrealistic since Napoleon only had to oppose it with an equivalent force to halt its advance. Furthermore, Russian forces would be divided and isolated by long distances and difficult terrain. Pfuel failed to grasp the essence of Napoleonic warfare, which aimed at the destruction of the enemy army. By confining the Russian troops to the Drissa camp, Pfuel in fact would have facilitated the achievement of Napoleon's goals. Besides, the plan suffered from too much theoretical thought and detailed instructions that specified the number of marches, provisions, and ammunition necessary for the operations and even indicated where each Russian unit should be on a given day and what supplies it should have. Nevertheless, Alexander accepted Pfuel's ideas and some elements of this plan were carried out by June 1812.[65]

Thus, Russian strategic plans at least on the surface revolved around Pfuel's ideas. But it is also clear that Pfuel's plan had only a limited impact on Barclay de Tolly's thinking. Neither Barclay in 1810 nor Pfuel in 1811 had anticipated that Russia would be invaded by an army of some half a million men. In principle their plans had much in common as both relied on strategic retreat and fortified camps and called for Russian forces striking Napoleon's flanks and rear. But, unlike Barclay's, Pfuel's plan placed the Russian army unsupported at

---

64   For Wolzogen's detailed reports, see Wolzogen to Barclay de Tolly, 23 July 1811, in *General Staff Archives*, 3:342–346; Wolzogen to Barclay de Tolly, 10 August 1811, ibid., 4:89–96; Wolzogen to Barclay de Tolly, 21 August 1811, ibid., 4:203–206; Wolzogen to Barclay de Tolly, 4 September 1811, ibid., 4:277–283.

65   Carl von Clausewitz, who served in Barclay de Tolly's army, studied the position at Drissa shortly before the 1st Western Army retreated and declared that, "if the Russians had not voluntarily abandoned this position, they would have been attacked from the rear and, regardless of whether they numbered 90,000 or 120,000 men, they would have been driven into the semicircle of trenches and forced to capitulate": Carl von Clausewitz, *The Campaign of 1812 in Russia* (Hattiesburg, MS, 1970).

Drissa where it could be easily destroyed. Tsar Alexander seemed to have genuinely believed his advisor but Dominic Lieven raises a very good point when he notes that "Alexander did not want Napoleon to penetrate into the Russian heartland, though he feared that he might do so. Any open admission that Napoleon might reach Great Russia in his initial campaign, let alone the circulation of plans based on such an idea, would have destroyed the emperor's credit. If Napoleon was to be stopped short of the Great Russian border, Pfuel's plan seemed the only one currently available. Should it fail, Alexander knew that Pfuel would be the perfect scapegoat. A foreigner without protection, Pfuel was despised by the Russian generals as the epitome of a German pedantic staff officer who knew nothing about war."[66]

Barclay de Tolly's thinking was more in line with an April 1812 memorandum submitted by Lieutenant-Colonel Pyotr Chuikevich of the secret chancellery of the ministry of war. It argued that Napoleon would seek a decisive battle since his whole system of war depended on rapid and decisive victories. Therefore, for the Russians, the key to victory was "to plan and pursue a war exactly contrary to what the enemy wants." Referring to the Spanish example, Chuikevich contended that "it is necessary to conduct a war that [Napoleon] is not accustomed to," meaning retreating, raiding enemy communications, and wearing down his forces. Chuikevich anticipated that the Russians would have to abandon vast territories to Napoleon but that this would only weaken the enemy: "The loss of a few provinces must not frighten us because the state's survival depends on the survival of its army."[67] In addition to retreat, Chuikevich also advocated a number of ways in which Europe might be incited to rise against Napoleon, including landing Russian, Swedish, or British forces in North Germany or Pomerania, or sending flying columns on deep raids into the Grand Duchy of Warsaw and Prussia. Although Chuikevich's memo lacks details and tends to be of broad nature, it certainly indicates that the "Scythian Plan" was seriously discussed in its various aspects by the Russian high command on the eve of war. In the month preceding the start of the war, Barclay de Tolly and Bagration were already discussing evacuating large supply depots and laying waste to the countryside to create obstacles for the enemy to overcome. The minister of war's instructions specified that "we should prevent the enemy from using any of our supplies during the offensive, cut his lines of communication, and always employ a 'scorched-earth' policy during our

---

66 Lieven, *Russia Against Napoleon*.
67 For the full text of Chuikevich's memo, see the Napoleon Series website <http://www.napoleon-series.org/research/russianarchives/c_Chuikevich.html>. See also V. Bezotosny, "Analiticheskii proyekt voyennikh deistvii v 1812 g. P.A. Chuikevicha," *Rossiiskii arkhiv*, 7 (1996): 43–49.

retreat."⁶⁸ Such a Scythian plan, however, was limited in nature and contemplated retreating only as far as the Western Dvina. The intendant general of the 1st Western Army, General Georg Ludwig von Kankrin, agreed that, "at the start of the war, no one anticipated retreating beyond [the] Dvina, and certainly not as far as Smolensk; as a result, very few supply magazines were established beyond that river."⁶⁹

Intelligence did provide the Russians with much food for thought. French officers who disliked Napoleon revealed to Chernyshev that, because Napoleon would seek decisive battles and rapid victories, the Russians should avoid engaging him at all costs. On 20 February 1812, Chernyshev reported that he often spoke "to officers who are of great merit and knowledge and who have no affection for [Napoleon]. I have asked them about what strategy would be best in the coming war, taking into account the theater of operations, the strength, and the character of our adversary." These officers all assured Chernyshev that Napoleon would seek a decisive battle at the start of the campaign and therefore the Russians should avoid giving him what he wanted. "The system we should follow in this war," Chernyshev wrote, "is the one in which Fabius [Cunctator] and indeed Lord Wellington offer the best examples."⁷⁰

On 30 May 1812, an unknown Russian intelligence agent submitted a rather revealing report that summarized prevailing attitudes and concerns at French headquarters. The agent resided in Warsaw and seems to have been well connected, for he possessed valuable information. With regard to Napoleon's plans, the agent reported that the French emperor had no intentions of invading deep into Russia. "He fully understands the dangers such an enterprise poses; besides, it is far from his desire to finish the war as soon as possible. The sole goal that he pursues at this moment is to reverse the everlasting accomplishment [*l'immortel ouvrage*] of Catherine the Great and to revive Poland which will serve as a new obstacle for us. By driving us beyond the Dvina and the Dnieper, he would be able to despotically govern the rest of Europe, which we would be unable to protect."⁷¹

---

68 Instructions to Saint-Priest, n.d. [June 1812]; Bagration to Alexander, No. 283, 18 June 1812; Bagration to Barclay de Tolly, No. 294 (secret), 18–22 June 1812, all in *General Staff Archives*, 13:49, 96–97, 414.

69 I. Bozheryanov, *Graf Yegor Frantsevich Kankrin* (Saint Petersburg, 1897), 20.

70 Chernyshev's reports to Alexander, Barclay de Tolly, and Rumyantsev have been published in the massive volumes of *Sbornik Imperatorskogo Rossiiskogo Istoricheskogo Obshchestva* (hereafter cited as SIRIO), 1905–1906, vols 121–122. The quote is from Chernyshev to Barclay de Tolly, 20 February 1812, ibid., 1906, 121:208.

71 *General Staff Archives*, 12:287–288.

From the Niemen to Smolensk

After months of intensive preparations, Napoleon crossed the Niemen on 23–24 June. Due to the vastness of the theater of war, this discussion will concentrate on the central group to the exclusion of the flanks. As it became clear that the Russians had no intention of invading the Grand Duchy of Warsaw, Napoleon sought to envelop them in a sweeping flanking maneuver through Vilna.[72] If successfully executed, this maneuver would turn the right flank of Barclay de Tolly's 1st Western Army and drive it into Bagration's 2nd Western Army, with both Russian armies being enveloped and crushed by Napoleon's numerically superior forces. However, neither Napoleon's advance to Vilna, designed to envelop the 1st Western Army, nor Jerome's effort to pin down the 2nd Western Army fully succeeded and both Russian armies were able to withdraw eastward. On 28 June Napoleon reached Vilna where the city's Polish populace received him with acclamation, but he knew better than to celebrate. The operation at Vilna was Napoleon's first major operation of the war and proved to be a failure that largely set the tone for the next two and half months of the war. The Russian armies avoided direct confrontation with superior enemy forces and embarked upon a continuous retreat that eventually brought them to the gates of Moscow. As they withdrew, the Russians turned to a scorched-earth policy destroying supplies and provisions to deny resources to the enemy. The searing heat and rains further complicated the task at hand as they led to unexpected attrition in the Grand Armée; by 1 July, hundreds of decomposing human and animal corpses choked the road from Kovno to Vilna. The Vilna operation is interesting also because it showed how the sheer mass of the Grande Armée sapped its leadership's ability to cope with challenges. The vast increase in size of units produced numerous vacancies for commissioned and noncommissioned officers that were filled with less than suitable candidates. Just eight days into the war, Napoleon himself condemned the work of his staff officers by complaining that "nothing gets done."[73] Indeed, internal reports and correspondence reveal the fog of war in which Napoleon's headquarters operated. Despite having experienced military intelligence and strong cavalry forces, the French headquarters had rather limited knowledge about enemy positions, and virtually nothing of their intentions, not to mention of local terrain and routes. Only one day into the campaign Berthier

---

72 The term "Vilna Maneuver" is rarely used in Anglophone studies but it has a long history in Russian and French historiography. Thus, General H. Bonnal published his *La manoevre de Vilna* (Paris) in 1905.
73 Napoleon to Berthier, 2 July 1812, in *CN*, 24:7.

complained to Davout that "the maps we are currently using are not sufficiently detailed and we do not really know where you are located."[74] A day later Napoleon himself expressed his exasperation that "our maps are so deficient that they are practically unusable."[75]

The Grande Armée's stay at Vilna is also noteworthy for an extraordinary weather pattern that had a significant impact on the army's performance. In late June, a storm broke over Vilna and the surrounding countryside, extending for several hundred miles north and south of the city. For hours, torrential rains drenched the ground and the tens of thousands of imperial soldiers, who were forced to spend the night exposed to the elements as their campfires were extinguished and tents blown away by strong wind and hail. Writing their memoirs, some participants confessed that they had never experienced anything like it. The storm was particularly savage on the animals which, already fatigued from long marshes, became panic-stricken at each lightning flash and suffered from a sudden spell of cold during the night. After the storm, hundreds of horses were dead while some surviving animals "were shivering so violently that they broke everything once hitched, rearing up wildly in their harness collars and kicking out in frantic fits of rage." Murat's chief of staff estimated that more than 8,000 horses perished during the two days of fiendish weather.[76] The storm also had a profound effect on morale as hundreds of soldiers despaired and turned to plundering, swarming the countryside in search of food and booty.

With the 1st Western Army retreating toward the Drissa camp, Napoleon realized that the gap between the two Russian armies had increased and so he sought to isolate Bagration by surrounding him with Jerome's forces from the west and Davout's from the north. Bagration demonstrated good judgement in these difficult circumstances (which required him to defy orders from Tsar

---

74 Berthier to Davout, 8 PM, 24 June 1812, in Fabry, *Campagne de 1812*, I, 4.
75 Napoleon to Berthier, 5:00 AM, 25 June 1812, ibid., 1:9. Bordesoulle's report to Murat shows that complaints about cartographic deficiencies were not limited to senior command. For example, at 8:00 AM on 25 June, he laments, "I beseech you, Sire, to provide me with a map and have one or two Polish officers, who speak French or German, sent from the 9th Polish Regiment, since otherwise it is absolutely impossible to lead a vanguard. I grope about as if I am blind and it is rather detrimental to operate in such a manner." Murat's solution to the problem was to approach a local Jew, "who promised to provide me with accurate information while I promised him a lot of money": Murat to Napoleon, 4:00 PM, 25 June 1812, ibid., 1:18.
76 Heinrich von Brandt, *Aus dem Leben des Generals der Infanterie z. D. Dr. Heinrich von Brandt* (Berlin, 1870), 339; Jean-Roch Coignet, *Les cahiers du capitaine Coignet (1799–1815)* (Paris, 1883), 295–296; Victor Bernard Derrécagaix, *Les États-Majors de Napoléon: le Lieutenant Général Comte Belliard, Chef d'État-Major de Murat* (Paris, 1980), 488.

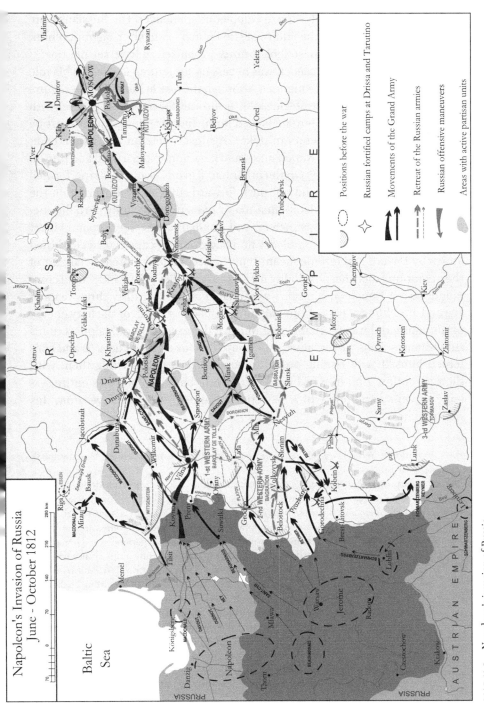

MAP 11.2 Napoleon's invasion of Russia

Alexander) and successfully eluded Napoleon's maneuver. The Russians were greatly assisted in this by the failure of the French leadership; Bagration himself acknowledged that "these fools [*duraki*] themselves have set me free."[77] For Napoleon's plan to succeed, it was necessary for Jerome to execute his role in an energetic and effective manner. Although the task at hand did not require extraordinary tactical or strategic skills, it did call for an active general with experience and initiative. Jerome lacked both, and his appointment must be regarded as one of Napoleon's mistakes. Against a veteran and active commander such as Bagration, Napoleon should have appointed a tried and proven professional military man.[78] On the other hand, even Davout underperformed during this operation and did not push forward sufficiently, lingering on the road to Minsk. Thus, Napoleon's first major maneuver was only partially successful: the Russian line was pierced and Russian forces were separated. Yet Barclay de Tolly's retreat to Smolensk and Bagration's escape from a combined attack by Davout and Jerome meant that the second and more crucial part of the operation failed. Responsibility for this partially lies on the individual commanders, but Napoleon himself was culpable as well. At forty-three years of age and after fifteen years of campaigning, he had lost much of the fiery energy of his youth and was more inclined to leave the execution of his plans to his subordinates. Thus, he remained quietly at Vilna for eighteen days (!) and contented himself with issuing orders to subordinates and trusting them with their execution. And further blame can be ascribed to Napoleon's entire system of centralization, which effectively sapped the initiative from his subordinates.

---

77 Bagration to Yermolov, 7 July 1812, in *K chesti Rossii: iz chastnoi perepiski* (Moscow, 1988), 50.

78 It is surprising that Napoleon gave Jerome command of four corps considering his criticism of the manner in which the king of Westphalia had handled x Corps in 1809: Jerome Bonaparte, *Memoires et correspondance du roi Jerome et de la reine Catherine* (Paris, 1861–1863), 4:210–211. Many Russian contemporaries were perplexed by Jerome's appointment. One officer observed, "We cannot but wonder why Napoleon, experienced and perceptive in choosing people, appointed his inept brother to command one of his armies with the most important and decisive mission of pinning down our armies": A. Muravyev, *Sochineniya i pisma* (Irkutsk, 1986), 93. Jerome struggled to deal with mounting challenges even before the war began in earnest as his troops lacked basic resources. Once across the Niemen, he faced more difficulties and continued criticism not just from his brother, but from staff members as well. "Tell [Jerome] that it would be impossible to maneuver in worse fashion," wrote Napoleon to Berthier on 5 July while at Vilna. "Tell him he has robbed me of the fruit of my maneuvers and the best opportunity ever offered in war – all because of his extraordinary failure to grasp the basic principles of warfare." See *CN*, No. 18905, 24:19–20. See also John G. Gallaher, *Napoleon's Enfant Terrible: General Dominique Vandamme* (Norman, OK, 2008).

Thus, one month into the war, Napoleon's initial plan to destroy Russia's armies in a decisive battle had been frustrated: instead, his army suffered considerable losses from combat, strategic consumption, and desertion. Weather proved to be, according to Baron Lejeune, "a veritable disaster for our troops," who suffered from the extraordinary heat in the early days of July.[79] As noted above, it was preceded by torrential rains that had a great impact on Napoleon's cavalry and were among the causes of the slowness of the army's movements. Owing to the state of the rain-soaked roads, the wagon trains laden with provisions and ammunition could not keep pace with the troops, who were constantly pushed forward by forced marches.

On 8 July, the 1st Western Army reached the fortified camp at Drissa but quickly found it untenable. Following a council of war on 13 July, the Russian high command made the decision to abandon the camp and completely reject Pfuel's strategy. Instead, it planned to pursue the junction of the 1st and 2nd Western Armies.[80] On 14 July, Barclay de Tolly abandoned the Drissa camp and marched in the direction of Vitebsk, leaving Wittgenstein with some 20,000 men to protect the roads leading to Saint Petersburg. The Russian withdrawal to the Drissa camp was in itself a major mistake. Instead of moving closer to effect a junction, the two Russian armies had in fact retreated along divergent lines. Barclay de Tolly was not entirely to blame for this since Tsar Alexander had imposed this strategy on him. To his credit, Barclay rectified this error by quickly abandoning the camp and moving to Vitebsk as soon as he found Drissa both strategically and tactically unacceptable. Had he lingered there, Napoleon undoubtedly would have closed on him and destroyed the 1st Western Army.

After learning about the Russian movement toward Vitebsk, Napoleon responded with a new operational plan. Murat's II and III Cavalry Corps, together with II and III Corps and three divisions of I Corps, received orders to pursue Barclay de Tolly while the Imperial Guard and IV and VI Corps launched a flanking maneuver to turn the Russian left by first moving toward Dokshitsy-Glubokoe and then to Polotsk or Vitebsk, depending on the circumstances. Davout, who now commanded Jerome's forces, was tasked with defending the Borisov–Orsha line and preventing Bagration from moving north to join Barclay. Napoleon intended to force Barclay to accept battle or, at the least, to prevent the junction of the two Russian armies in the vicinity of Vitebsk.

---

79   Louis François Lejeune, *Memoirs of Baron Lejeune, Aide-de-Camp to Marshals Berthier, Davout and Oudinot* (New York, 1897), 2:155.

80   Urged by his advisers, Tsar Alexander left the army without appointing a commander in chief, thereby prolonging the crisis of command that the Russian military experienced.

On 23 July, the 1st Western Army approached Vitebsk, where Barclay de Tolly planned to wait for Bagration and, if necessary, accept battle with Napoleon. The following day, he designated General Aleksandr Ivanovich Osterman-Tolstoy's IV Infantry Corps as a rearguard to delay the advance of the enemy army along both banks of the Western Dvina River. On 25–26 July, the two sides fought a series of actions near the villages of Ostrovno and Kakuvyachino, with the Russians successfully delaying the French advance for two days.

Meanwhile, after escaping Napoleon's envelopment near Minsk, Bagration continued to retreat hastily toward Mogilev, where he intended to cross the Dnieper River and join Barclay de Tolly. However, Davout beat him to the town. Arriving at Mogilev on 21 July and unaware of the enemy's strength, Bagration decided to attack Davout with only the VII Infantry Corps under General Nikolai Nikolayevich Rayevskii. If only Davout's vanguard could hold Mogilev, Rayevskii's corps was strong enough to recapture the town and open the route to Smolensk. However, if Davout was there in force, Rayevskii would have to fight a delaying action to keep the French on the right bank of the Dnieper while Bagration's engineers built a bridge south of Mogilev at Novyi Bykhov. Unbeknownst to Bagration, Davout's forces were reduced by fatigue and attrition, and the French marshal commanded only 28,000 men, whom he deployed on a strong position near the village of Saltanovka. The Battle of Saltanovka commenced on the morning of 23 July when the Russian VII Infantry Corps attacked Davout's positions. Despite repeated Russian charges, the French repelled all of them and inflicted considerable losses. The battle thus ended with the French maintaining their positions and the Russians unable to break through. However, by then, Bagration's bridge at Novyi Bykhov was complete, and he led his army across the Dnieper toward Smolensk. The Battle of Saltanovka, sometimes referred to as the Battle of Mogilev in Western literature, is often considered a French victory, though in reality it must be viewed as a Russian strategic success because Bagration managed to break through to Smolensk, where the Russian armies eventually united.[81]

Returning to Barclay de Tolly, encouraged by the performance of his army at Ostrovno and Kakuvyachino and in pursuance of his intention to give battle, he took a position before Vitebsk. However, during the night of 27 July, he received news from Bagration that the 2nd Western Army had failed to break through at Mogilev and so had proceeded to Smolensk. This news drastically changed the situation and forced Barclay de Tolly to abandon his original plan

---

81 For details, see Alexander Mikaberidze, "The Lion of the Russian Army: Life and Military Career of General Prince Peter Bagration" (PhD dissertation, Florida State University, 2003), 694–712.

and retreat with this army to Smolensk. His rearguard held its ground throughout 27 July, gaining one day for the rest of army to retreat. During the night, the Russians maintained large bivouac fires burning on the site of the army encampment, which convinced Napoleon that the Russians would at last hold the ground and fight. He spent the afternoon on horseback, reconnoitering positions and preparing for battle. "Until tomorrow, at 5:00, the sun of Austerlitz," were his parting words to Murat that night. Instead, the morning sun illuminated a heart-wrenching sight: the Russians had slipped away under the cover of darkness.

Napoleon could not conceal his frustration. His response was to spend two weeks at Vitebsk (28 July–12 August) to deal with a host of immediate problems. In the five weeks since the passage of the Niemen, he had failed to bring the enemy to battle and succeeded only in occupying some territory. The lack of provisions caused widespread disorder in the army and the countryside was already filled with bands of marauders who had abandoned their units. There had been a vast loss of transport animals and of cavalry horses. The scarcity of drinking water in the hot midsummer season forced Napoleon's men to consume polluted water from swampy streams and lakes, which naturally resulted in an outbreak of dysentery that affected tens of thousands of troops. According to a Württemberger physician at a camp southeast of Vitebsk, diarrhea "assumed such violent scope that it was impossible to ensure normal service, let alone indulge in any kind of drill. The houses were all filled with sick men, and in the camp itself there was such a continuous running back and forth behind the front that it was as though purgatives had been administered to entire regiments."[82] Attrition rates due to malnutrition, disease,[83] and other factors were uncommonly high; some units had already lost up to half of their strength, causing some unit commanders to cover up their losses. Napoleon seems to have not been fully aware of the army's actual circumstances because of these deceptions. For example, when Dutch general Anton Gijsbert van Dedem discovered that his brigade had lost nearly 40 per cent of its men (1,500 of 4,000), his superior, General Louis Friant, insisted on reporting an effective brigade strength of 3,280.[84]

---

82   Heinrich von Roos, *Avec Napoléon en Russie: souvenirs d'un médecin de la Grande Armée* (Paris, 1913), 51–53.

83   For details, see Stephan Talty's *The Illustrious Dead: The Terrifying Story of How Typhus Killed Napoleon's Greatest Army* (New York, 2009), although it tends to exaggerate the role of disease in shaping the outcome of the campaign.

84   Anton Gijsbert van Dedem de Gelder, *Un général hollandais sous le Premier empire: mémoires du général Bon de Dedem de Gelder* (Paris, 1900), 225–227.

After the armies of Barclay de Tolly and Bagration united at Smolensk in early August, the Russians faced a crisis of command. This conflict stemmed from discord between the old Russian aristocracy and the "foreigners" who had gained influence at court and army headquarters. The specific reason for this tension was the difference in views regarding strategy, evident among senior officers, who represented opposing parties. Barclay de Tolly, the nominal commander in chief, was surrounded by a group of officers (many of German extraction) who supported his defensive plans. Opposing them was the much larger "Russian party," led by Bagration (ironically a Georgian), which urged an immediate counteroffensive. Anti-Barclay sentiments were so strong among the senior officers that they openly loathed the commander in chief and intrigued for the appointment of Bagration as supreme commander. Some even encouraged Bagration to replace Barclay by force. Bending under pressure, Barclay de Tolly agreed to an offensive from Smolensk in an attempt to break through the French center and destroy the remaining French corps piecemeal. But due to differences among the commanders – made worse by Barclay's vacillation – precious time was lost in futile marches, which allowed Napoleon to recognize Russian intentions and seize the initiative.

Napoleon's response, the maneuver at Smolensk, was masterfully conceived and reveals his operational skill. His cantonment of corps had been designed to enable 180,000 men to assemble on a short front line in just two days. After forming a formidable *bataillon carré*, the emperor launched it across the Dnieper along a fifteen-mile front between Orsha and Rosasna. He formed two massive columns. The Rosasna column, commanded by Napoleon himself, would consist of Murat's cavalry, the Imperial Guard, and III and IV Corps. The second column, under Davout, was composed of I, V, and VIII Corps, while Latour-Maubourg's cavalry made a diversion southward from the Dnieper. After crossing the Dnieper, the Grande Armée would advance along the left bank of the river, and either occupy Smolensk or engage the Russian armies there. On 10 August, Napoleon commenced his maneuver. Covered by a heavy cavalry screen, his movements remained concealed from the Russians. During the night of 13–14 August, General Jean-Baptiste Éblé completed pontoon bridges over the Dnieper at Rosasna and by daylight almost the entire Grande Armée was advancing on Smolensk.

By marching on Smolensk, Napoleon hoped to master Russian communications with Moscow, as he had done in the case of the Austrians at Marengo in 1800. Yet a resolute rearguard action at Krasnyi on 14 August enabled the Russians to delay the Grande Armée and prepare Smolensk for defence as Bagration and Barclay de Tolly rushed their commands back to the city. On 15–16 August, the Russians repulsed French assaults on Smolensk but were nonetheless forced to abandon the city. As the Russians withdrew toward Moscow, a perilous gap opened between the 1st and 2nd Western Armies, which Napoleon recognized and exploited. He dispatched his main forces along the northern bank of the Dnieper in pursuit of Barclay de Tolly's army while General Junot's VIII Corps marched on the southern side toward Lubino, where it was to sever the Russian line of retreat. Remarkably, Bagration's rearguard left the important crossroads near the village of Lubino unprotected and the 1st Western Army was at risk of being intercepted and potentially destroyed. Had Junot acted more forcefully, events at Lubino would have unfolded quite differently, but he failed to rise to the occasion. It took several hours for Junot to find his way over the Dnieper and then, in a drunken stupor, he refused to advance despite the repeated pleas of his colleagues.[85] This proved to be fatal to any hopes of destroying Barclay de Tolly's army, which successfully escaped.

The maneuver at Smolensk was the last great operation Napoleon undertook in 1812. Like his previous attempts at Vilna, Minsk, and Vitebsk, it too had failed. Several reasons that account for its miscarriage can be identified. The maneuver itself was brilliantly conceived, and this was indeed one of the finest movements Napoleon had executed during his many campaigns. But tactical failures doomed the entire operation. First, Murat's inability to overwhelm the small Russian rearguard at Krasnyi resulted in the loss of precious time. Next, the failure to locate fords over the Dnieper in good time resulted in a bloody head-on collision before the walls of Smolensk that produced heavy losses. Junot's inaction at Lubino then contributed to Barclay de Tolly's escape when he should have been cut off. Oddly enough, an important factor in Napoleon's setback at Smolensk was the differences that arose between the two Russian commanders, who could not agree on a course of action.

Napoleon spent several days at Smolensk as he vacillated over the course to take: whether to advance farther or remain in Smolensk until the next year. He had already considered this issue at Vilna and had told one of his officers that his intention was to advance as far as Smolensk and then return to Vilna and establish winter quarters closer to the border. But he based this plan on the understanding that the Russians would already have been defeated. As it stood, Napoleon had little to show after almost two months of campaigning. Furthermore, several new factors had appeared to complicate his circumstances. He expected the Russian forces on either flank to follow the movements of their main armies, but Tormasov held ground and even scored a victory over Schwarzenberg in the south while Wittgenstein held his own against Oudinot

---

85 See Charles H. MacKay, "The Tempest: The Life and Career of Jean-Andoche Junot, 1771–1813" (PhD dissertation, Florida State University, 1995), 427–435.

and Saint Cyr. The conclusion of peace between Russia and the Ottoman Empire allowed Russian admiral Pavel Vasiliyevich Chichagov's Army of the Danube to threaten the right wing of the Grande Armée, while the signing of the Russo-Swedish Åbo Treaty on 30 August promised to do the same in the north, where Macdonald's X Corps was already occupied with the blockade of Riga. Battles and strategic consumption had reduced the strength of the central army group to fewer than 180,000 men, who continued to be greatly affected by the difficulties of supply and transport.

In such circumstances, advancing into the Russian interior promised only to extend lines of communication. Aside from logistical concerns, there was also a political dimension, since Napoleon was not just the commander-in-chief but also the head of state presiding over a vast empire that stretched from Spain to Poland. On the other hand, Napoleon could not simply turn back from Smolensk and halt his forces in cantonments while the enemy had not been defeated in a decisive battle. More importantly, political considerations rendered any retrograde movement unthinkable since it would appear tantamount to failure in the eyes of Europe and might jeopardize the French imperium. Thus, for Napoleon, the only course was to continue the advance in the hope of forcing the Russians to accept a decisive battle, which would allow him to dictate peace terms. With at least two months of good weather still ahead of him, Napoleon thought he had sufficient time to accomplish this.

The surrender of Smolensk further aroused general discontent in the Russian army and society at large. Tsar Alexander replaced Barclay de Tolly with General Mikhail Kutuzov, who took command on 29 August at Tsarevo Zaimische. Kutuzov withdrew the troops still further to the west, deploying them for battle near the village of Borodino. After receiving reinforcements, Kutuzov commanded some 155,000 troops, of whom 115,000 were regulars, supported by 636 guns. Napoleon fielded approximately 135,000 men with 587 guns. The Battle of Borodino took place on 7 September, with Napoleon opting for frontal attacks on fortified Russian positions instead of flanking maneuvers that might have prompted another Russian withdrawal. In a savage and bloody struggle, both sides displayed great bravery and steadfastness, but the French remained in possession of the battlefield and claimed victory, while the Russian army withdrew in good order toward Moscow. At Borodino, French losses numbered around 35,000 men, including 49 generals, while Russian losses were 45,000–50,000 men, including 29 generals.[86]

---

86 For an in-depth discussion, see Alexander Mikaberidze, *Napoleon Versus Kutuzov: The Battle of Borodino* (London, 2007); Christopher Duffy, *Borodino and the War of 1812* (New York, 1972); Digby Smith, *Borodino* (Moreton-in-Marsh, UK, 1998).

During his retreat to Moscow, Kutuzov still considered engaging the enemy in front of the capital. But after a military council at Fili on 13 September, he ordered Moscow to be abandoned without a fight. The following day, Napoleon's troops entered the city. Later that same day, fires started by the Russians spread throughout Moscow and continued to burn until 18 September, destroying two-thirds of the city. The fiery devastation of the Russian capital had a profound effect on the troops of the Grande Armée, as they were forced to billet amid the ruins, lacking proper provisions and shelter. Discipline became lax and many troops turned to pillaging.

Meanwhile, Wittgenstein continued to hold ground on the northern flank and made preparations for an offensive that culminated in an important victory at Polotsk on 20 October, which secured the northern approaches to Saint Petersburg. In the south, Tormasov and Chichagov guarded the southwestern Russian provinces and prepared to move north to help the main Russian army. In the Baltic provinces, Russian forces continued to thwart Marshal Macdonald's attempts to seize Riga.

The Moscow Sojourn

Napoleon spent thirty-six days in Moscow.[87] It is impossible to explain "his pertinacity in prolonging the stay of the army in the center of Russia, amidst the smoking ruins of the ancient capital, except by supposing that he was nearly certain of the speedy conclusion of peace," a French general later opined.[88] Simply abandoning Moscow and retreating was not an option since, in Napoleon's opinion, this would be tantamount to acknowledging defeat. Yet staying in the burnt-out city held only bleak prospects for ending the war. Signing a peace treaty, on the other hand, offered a way out of this complicated situation. Napoleon made several peace proposals to Alexander but all were rejected. Like many of his contemporaries, Napoleon had misread Alexander's character. British historian Dominic Lieven recently pointed out that "most European statesmen and much of the Russian elite shared some of the doubts on Alexander's strength of will."[89] Napoleon believed that Alexander would not hesitate to make peace as soon as he received a letter offering it. He "nourished his hopes [for peace] with the recollections of Tilsit and Erfurt," believing

---

87 For details, see Alexander Mikaberidze, *Napoleon's Trial by Fire: The Burning of Moscow* (London, 2014); Vladimir Zemtsov, *1812 god: pozhar Moskvy* (Moscow, 2010).
88 Mathieu Dumas, *Souvenirs...* (Paris, 1839), 3:454–455.
89 Lieven, *Russia Against Napoleon*, 251.

that the Francophiles in the Russian court would push Alexander in that direction.[90] Thus, Napoleon failed to understand how profoundly his relationship with Alexander, as well as the sentiments of Russian society, had changed since 1807. The Russian tsar was well aware of the widespread displeasure that prevailed in Russia about the Franco-Russian alliance. Such sentiments only intensified in the wake of the continual withdrawal of the Russian armies and loss of Russian provinces. Just days after the fall of Moscow, Grand Duchess Catherine informed her august brother that "the taking of Moscow has put the finishing touches on the exasperation of the people. Discontent is at its highest and your person is far from being spared. If such news reaches me, you can imagine the rest. You are openly accused of having brought disaster upon your empire, of having caused general ruin and the ruin of private individuals, lastly, of having lost the honor of the country and your own personal honor. I leave it to you to judge the state of affairs in a country whose leader is despised."[91] Even if he desired it, Alexander could not afford to compromise with the man who had invaded and despoiled his realm. Public opinion was against it and any sign of weakness on Alexander's part might have led to tragic consequences. A second Tilsit would have sealed the condemnation of his reign and Alexander knew only too well what happened to unpopular monarchs in Russia – the preceding eighty years had witnessed a number of palace coups and murders of reigning sovereigns, including Alexander's own father.

With a Russian response to his peace overtures not coming, Napoleon once again found himself facing two choices: he could take the army back to Lithuania and Poland, where it would take up comfortable winter quarters; or he could follow the advice of Secretary of State Pierre-Antoine-Noël-Bruno Daru – which Napoleon called "the lion's advice" – of rallying his troops, collecting provisions, and hunkering down for the winter in Moscow. Daru argued that it would be easier to feed the army at Moscow than to risk marching back. The city still offered sufficient means of subsistence, including plenty of corn, rice, vegetables, alcohol, and salted provisions. But remaining in Moscow entailed several major challenges. While troops could be sufficiently well fed, the army was desperate for forage for the horses which were dying of starvation. Such losses had already weakened cavalry, artillery, and transport in a season which was far from being the least favorable of the year. Furthermore, Moscow was hundreds of miles away from the heartlands of the French Empire

---

90   Philippe-Paul Ségur, *History of the Expedition to Russia Undertaken by the Emperor Napoleon in the Year 1812* (London, 1825), 77.

91   Grand Duchess Catherine to Emperor Alexander, 18 September 1812, in *Correspondance de l'Empereur Alexandre Ier avec sa soeur la Grande-Duchess Catherine* (Saint Petersburg, 1910), Letter XXXIII.

and maintaining communications over such vast distances was a challenging task. Facing attacks from the hostile local populace and roaming Cossack and partisan detachments, Napoleon would have to commit considerable resources to guarding his lines of communication. By late September, French convoys were already so threatened that he had to specify that no convoy should leave Smolensk without being escorted by 1,500 men of infantry and cavalry. The thought of what would happen in Paris or the rest of Europe if, despite all his efforts, there should be some week in which no news of his whereabouts was received no doubt preoccupied Napoleon. "One must not be away from home too long," he told his companion. "I feel Paris calling me even more than Saint Petersburg tempts me."[92] More importantly, what advantage would he gain by being at Moscow at the commencement of the succeeding spring? Tsar Alexander had already rebuffed his repeated attempts to open negotiations and there were no signs of Russian willingness to compromise.

Napoleon was well aware of these challenges and understood the benefits that a departure from Moscow could offer. Withdrawing toward Vitebsk, if not all the way back to the Grand Duchy of Warsaw, would bring the Grande Armée closer to its reinforcements and supply depots in Prussia and Poland, and shorten communication lines that could be better defended. It could spend the next few months in winter cantonments, regrouping and preparing for the next stage of the war in the spring. But, besides purely military considerations, the emperor also had to consider political implications of his actions and, in this regard, he was convinced that leaving Moscow without any tangible gains, not even an armistice, would have the appearance of acknowledging defeat. This could seriously undermine his standing in Europe. "As if I do not know that in a military point of view Moscow is of no value!" he had told his secretary of state in October. "But Moscow is not a military position, it is a political position ... and in political measures we ought never to recede, never to back down, never to admit ourselves to be wrong, as it lessened our consideration; that, even when in error, we should persist in it, in order to have the appearance of being in the right."[93]

While the Grande Armée remained at Moscow, Kutuzov skillfully maneuvered from the Ryazan road east of Moscow to the Kaluga road southwest of Moscow, where he established a fortified camp at Tarutino. Through this maneuver, the Russian commander covered the southern provinces, which were abundant with supplies and manufacturing enterprises. Kutuzov also

---

92   Abel Francois Villemain, *Souvenirs contemporains d'histoire et de littérature* (Paris, 1854), 1:230.
93   Ségur, *History of the Expedition to Russia*, 1:80.

began intensive preparations for future operations, receiving reinforcements that increased his army to 110,000–120,000 men, with additional forces to come. He encouraged guerrilla operations against the invaders and organized cavalry detachments to harass French communications and supply lines. In mid-October, Napoleon began probing Russian positions southwest of Moscow. On 18 October, Murat's forces suffered a sudden defeat on the River Chernishnya, north of Tarutino.[94] This proved to be a wake-up call for Napoleon, who realized the need to abandon the devastated ruins of Moscow before winter arrived and the Russians descended upon him.

Departure from Moscow: Retreat or Strategic Withdrawal?

After spending just over one month in Moscow, Napoleon finally departed from the city on 19 October 1812. His forces had dwindled to about 115,000 men, accompanied by thousands of noncombatants and an enormous baggage train laden with loot.[95] French officer Pierre-Armand Barrau lamented about the state of the army: "Anyone who did not see the French army leave Moscow can only have a very weak impression of what the armies of Greece and Rome must have looked like when they marched back from Troy and Carthage." Traffic on this scale not only slowed the army's movements but also distracted the troops, many of whom were more concerned about securing their portion of booty than about maintaining discipline. But looks can be deceiving: the Grande Armée was still a potent tool of war. While the cavalry was significantly reduced, the infantry was rested and eager to leave the hostile land.

Napoleon planned to move his forces to the western provinces of Russia, where supplies and magazines had already been prepared. "We are going to withdraw to the frontiers of Poland," he told a trusted aide de camp. "I shall take good winter quarters and hope that [Tsar] Alexander will make peace." For Napoleon, it was a strategic withdrawal, not a retreat, a point he tried to reinforce in the memoirs he dictated at Saint Helena.[96] The route from Moscow to Smolensk, via Gzhatsk, was devastated after the allied forces had fought their way to the Russian capital from July through September. Therefore, Napoleon decided to advance by the Kaluga road, toward the intact southwestern regions, before veering north. Initially, he successfully deceived the

---

94   The best study of this battle is Vitalii Bessonov, *Tarutinskoye srazheniye* (Moscow, 2008).
95   The number of vehicles accompanying the army was truly staggering and, depending on sources, is estimated at between 15,000 and 40,000.
96   Jean Rapp, *Mémoires ...* (Paris, 1823), 221–222; Charles Tristan Montholon, *Mémoires pour server a l'Histoire de France sous Napoleon, écrits a Sainte-Hélène* (Paris, 1823), 2:104.

THE LIMITS OF THE OPERATIONAL ART: RUSSIA 1812   411

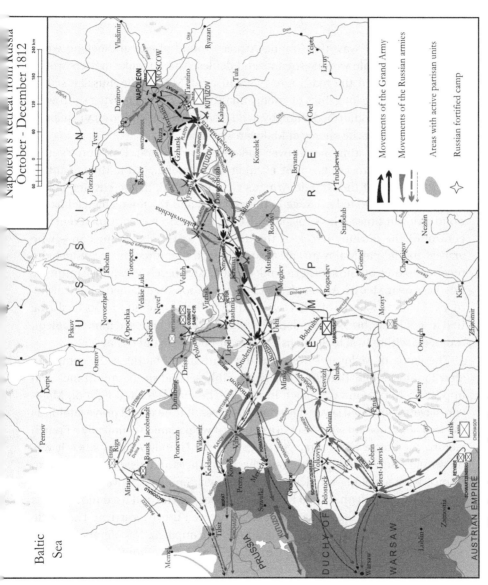

MAP 11.3   Napoleon's retreat from Russia

Russians. Despite the Cossack outposts and Russian flying detachments around Moscow, the Grande Armée filed from the capital in such secrecy that Kutuzov did not learn of its departure for two days. Secrecy was crucial to the success of Napoleon's plan for, if alerted, Kutuzov could have barred the Kaluga road with ease.

Burdened as it was, the Grande Armée ground along, gridlocking when obliged to negotiate various streams and defiles. And, to make matters worse, heavy rains turned the roads into rivers of mud. Meanwhile, Russian scouts soon observed the long lines of enemy infantry and cavalry moving southwest and immediately informed Kutuzov, who dispatched Dokhturov's VI Infantry Corps to intercept the enemy at Maloyaroslavets.

After an exhausting march over bad roads and in rain, Dokhturov's men arrived at Maloyaroslavets on the evening of 23 October, just in time to anticipate the arrival of the Grande Armée's advance guard. In the ensuing battle, the fighting proved to be savage in the extreme, and the town changed hands up to a dozen times. The struggle ended around 11:00 PM with the French in control of the burning wreck of the town. On 25 October Napoleon – who arrived too late at Maloyaroslavets to influence the outcome – conducted a reconnaissance on the southern bank of the Lusha, barely escaping capture by Cossacks near Medyn. Although the emperor's troops had gained a tactical victory at Maloyaroslavets, his effectives had dwindled to around 70,000. Realizing that he could not break through the Russian force that opposed him, Napoleon ordered a withdrawal to Smolensk by way of Borodino and Gzhatsk.[97]

The Battle of Maloyaroslavets was the third-largest battle of the campaign after Smolensk and Borodino but is probably second in its importance and impact on Napoleon's campaign in Russia. The march to, and fight at, Maloyaroslavets consumed seven days – and this loss of time would prove fateful, as the ferocious Russian winter set in a couple of weeks later. Technically a French victory, the battle was a strategic defeat for the Grande Armée, since it was prevented from reaching the rich southern provinces and instead was forced to retrace its steps along the devastated route via Smolensk. Given the battle's importance, Napoleon should have taken direct control and used more troops to flank and defeat the Russian defenders before Kutuzov's arrival. The battle also signaled a change in the character of the campaign. Napoleon's strategic withdrawal from Moscow now turned into a retreat. From this point, the

---

97   For details, see I. Bezsonov, *Bitva v Maloyaroslavtse, 12 oktyabrya 1812 goda* (Kaluga, 1912); Aleksei Vasiliyev, "Srazheniye za Maloyaroslavets, 12 oktyabrya 1812 goda," in *Yubileinyi sbornik: k 190-letiyu Maloyarslavetskogo srazheniya* <http://www.museum.ru/1812/library/Mmnk/2002_9.html>.

Grande Armée ceased offensive operations and sought to withdraw from the occupied provinces as fast as possible. The Russians, on the other hand, assumed a more aggressive stance, which many Russian/Soviet historians described as the start of the "counteroffensive" stage of the war, following Joseph Stalin's famous postulation. But in truth Russian actions hardly constituted a "counteroffensive." Despite significant numerical superiority, Kutuzov avoided open confrontation with Napoleon at Maloyaroslavets and chose to withdraw, despite the objections of his lieutenants. Nevertheless, Maloyaroslavets was the starting point for Kutuzov's "parallel-march" strategy, designed to dog Napoleon's footsteps without risking costly clashes, thereby reducing unnecessary losses. This strategy would play an important part in the events leading up to the Berezina.

From Maloyaroslavets to Smolensk

After the Battle of Maloyaroslavets, Kutuzov spent a couple of days regrouping his army before launching the pursuit. The main Russian army moved along the Kuzovo–Suleika–Bykovo route while the advance guard, led by Miloradovich, operated between Kutuzov and the old Smolensk road, and Ataman Matvei Ivanovich Platov's Cossacks pressed the enemy along the old Smolensk road. In addition, the flying detachments were always at hand to harass the enemy.

In the meantime, Napoleon directed his army to Mozhaisk, where he returned to the old Smolensk road, which had been devastated during the August–September fighting. The morale of the army, already undermined by the retreat, was further lowered when the troops marched across the Borodino battlefield still covered with corpses, half-eaten by wolves or pecked at by carrion crows. To move faster, Napoleon ordered the wounded to be evacuated on wagons and carriages but the troops who were forced to give up their places were angered by the decision, and this led to abuses. On 29 October, the Grande Armée reached Vyazma, a major town in Smolensk province, and occupied it after a few minor skirmishes with local forces. The three-day march from Maloyaroslavets had exhausted Napoleon's troops. The weather was becoming colder, and the nights of 27 and 28 October saw temperatures plunge to as low as −4 °C. Competition among the troops for the quickly diminishing supplies began, while lack of forage weakened the horses. In fact, in order to transport artillery, horses were taken from nonessential wagons, which were abandoned along with the wounded men and loot they contained. The march of tens of thousands of men and animals on earthy roads soon created a muddy morass, causing further delays and exacerbating the suffering of the troops.

In early November, Napoleon led the Grande Armée toward Smolensk. Ney's III Corps and Davout's I Corps remained behind as rearguard. On 3–4 November, Russian forces under Miloradovich and Platov attacked the French and captured Vyazma. While a Russian victory, the battle also represents a missed opportunity. Despite being in proximity, Kutuzov's main army did not participate but continued its march to Bykov. Kutuzov was probably concerned that an attack on his part would oblige Napoleon to turn back, thus leading to a major battle, which Kutuzov was not willing to risk at Vyazma. In response to Miloradovich's pleas for support, Kutuzov dispatched cavalry reinforcements which arrived too late to take part in the fighting. Many Russians criticized Kutuzov's actions and one contemporary noted that "had our [main] army, located nearby, joined the advance guard, the enemy would have been routed from its initial position, [and] its remaining forces would have been pursued and destroyed piecemeal." Robert Wilson, the British commissioner to the Russian army, wrote to Lord William Cathcart, British ambassador at Saint Petersburg, asking him to lobby for Kutuzov's dismissal.

The battle, however, had a disruptive impact on the retreat of the Grande Armée and accelerated the demoralization of its troops, especially in rear units, where chaos spread in a chain reaction. "Here at Vyazma we witnessed for the last time the actions of the enemy forces that had spread horror with their victories and earned our respect," wrote one Russian officer. "We could still see the skill of their generals, the obedience of their subordinates, and their energy. But, no orderly enemy troops were left; the experience and abilities of their generals were of no use now, discipline had disappeared and the soldiers seemed to have lost their last strength, each of them now a victim of hunger, exhaustion, and the cruelty of [the] weather."[98]

On 5 November, Napoleon received reports of the action at Vyazma and decided to halt to concentrate his forces. He initially considered turning on the pursuers but soon abandoned the idea. As snow began to fall, the countryside turned a monotonous white contrasting with the dark procession of sniveling stragglers creeping onward, hoping to reach their native lands. Friedrich Klinkhardt, a Westphalian officer, recalled that "snow fell heavily and severe cold immediately froze it so the horses could move on the hard crust without sinking. It did not last for long but I managed to freeze my nose, ears, hands, and feet and could move around and get on a carriage only with assistance." Claude François de Méneval recounted that in "one night the thermometer

---

98   Yermolov, *The Czar's General*, 192.

went down to twelve degrees below zero [−15 °C] and two days later to eighteen degrees [−22 °C]. From that time forward the cold grew worse and worse."[99]

Grievously lacking provisions as well as proper clothing or footwear, the soldiers suffered terribly. The number of stragglers – most of them unarmed – rapidly increased as morale declined, and discipline gave way to the instinct of self-preservation. Everyone looked to Smolensk and its large supply stores as if it were the promised land. Napoleon entered Smolensk on 9 November and the army poured into the city over the next four days. Cold and hungry, the soldiers – many of whom had subsisted on horseflesh for the past few days – ravaged the magazines, leaving virtually no provisions for those who arrived after them. Meanwhile, Napoleon ordered the Imperial Guard to be furnished with all necessary supplies, which only increased the antagonism felt by regular units toward the privileged Guardsmen.

While at Smolensk, Napoleon received news from France informing him that a false report of his death had led to a failed coup by General Claude François Malet in Paris. This event deeply affected Napoleon and made him sensible to the necessity of quitting the army as soon as he could and returning to Paris to consolidate his control over the empire. As his forces concentrated at Smolensk, Napoleon weighed his options. The strategic situation had turned against him. During the fourteen days since the Grande Armée had left Moscow, it had suffered staggering losses. With each passing day, the number of men under arms diminished, while those of the stragglers swelled. Remaining at Smolensk appeared pointless, since the city was untenable and the stores were nearly exhausted. The army had already been reduced to a fragment of its original strength; the remaining troops were tired, hungry, and cold. With Russian forces closing from the north, south, and east, the French emperor believed his only chance of escape was to quit Smolensk, beat the Russian converging forces to the Berezina, and seek better winter quarters further west.

On the cold morning of 14 November, Napoleon left Smolensk with his Imperial Guard and proceeded along the main road through Krasnyi followed by the remaining corps. This movement made the army vulnerable to attack. By 13 November, the main Russian army had already approached Smolensk from the south and, having bypassed it, made a direct thrust to Krasnyi, threatening to cut the French line of retreat. On 14–16 November, Russian forces made repeated attacks on Napoleon's I, III, and IV Corps while they marched

---

99 Friedrich Klinkhardt, *Feldzugs-Erinnerungen des Königlich Westfälischen Musikmeisters Friedrich Klinkhardt: aus den Jahren 1812 bis 1815* (Braunschweig, 1908), 61; Claude Francois de Méneval, *Memoirs Illustrating the History of Napoleon I from 1802 to 1815* (New York, 1894), 3:71.

from Smolensk to Krasnyi. Each corps was temporarily cut off, and Ney's III Corps even surrounded, but none was forced to lay down their arms: a testament to the strength of French organization and leadership. Separated from the main army, Ney conducted a heroic retreat across the Dnieper River. Still, Napoleon's main army proceeded pellmell to Orsha on the right bank of the Dnieper.

The Battle of Krasnyi was not a battle on the scale of Borodino or Maloyaroslavets but rather a series of isolated engagements spread over three days. Yet, as at Borodino, the victor at Krasnyi seems to be in the eye of beholder. Many Francophile historians claim it as a French success, although it is hard to accept this conclusion. Although Napoleon escaped the Russian encirclement, he lost up to 30,000 men including some 10,000 killed. His IV and I Corps suffered heavy casualties and III Corps effectively ceased to exist. Napoleon's combat-ready core of troops was now reduced to about 30,000 men with perhaps 40 guns. Crucially, the Grande Armée lost a large portion of its artillery (up to 200 guns) during the retreat, making it vulnerable to Russian artillery in future combat. While the army still nominally counted "corps" and "divisions," in reality these were all but skeletons, with many of the latter reduced to regimental strength. Meanwhile, the army remained heavily burdened by tens of thousands of stragglers.

The Russian army, having left the Tarutino camp with about 100,000–110,000 men, numbered some 60,000–65,000 men at Krasnyi. This attrition is explained by strategic consumption, which required the Russian command to divert forces, but also by losses due to combat, weather, and lack of supplies.[100] Until recently, Russian and Soviet historians tended to exaggerate the importance of this battle, largely because Kutuzov described it as a decisive victory in his reports.[101] In reality, the Russians launched disjointed attacks against the separate French corps (IV, I, and III). A more vigorous attack would have produced decisive results and potentially changed the course of the Napoleonic Wars. But Kutuzov effectively withheld his forces, and his motives for restraining continue to be debated. Some suggest that Kutuzov's age and poor health

---

100   Thus, on 12 November, III Corps mustered 8,286 men (with 90 cannon) but more than 5,700 men were in the hospitals. The 12th Division was reduced to 2,611 men after more than 4,200 men fell sick. The cavalry fared no better, with the 1st Cuirassier Division reporting 1,908 men present and 300 sick, and the 2nd Cuirassier Division having 1,261 men present and 679 sick.

101   Russian historians such as Buturlin, Mikhailovsky-Danilevsky, Garnich, and Beskrovnyi call it the "decisive battle" brilliantly won by the Russians, while Pavel Zhilin goes as far as to claim that "the three-day-long battle at Krasnyi ended with a complete rout of Napoleon's army": Zhilin, *Gabel napoleonovskoi armii v Rossii* (Moscow, 1968), 258.

had some effect on his judgement, and that he did not want to jeopardize his place in posterity by risking open combat with Napoleon. Kutuzov's documents certainly reveal his concern regarding Napoleon's whereabouts, and he repeatedly requested his commanders to 'use all means necessary to locate the exact position of the [Imperial] Guard," noting that, without such information, "the field-marshal does not intend to attack."[102] Kutuzov wanted to preserve his forces and let starvation, exhaustion, and the elements complete the destruction of the enemy. As he told a captured French chief commissary officer: "I was convinced of your defeat [due to starvation and weather] and had no desire to sacrifice a single soldier to achieve this. This is how we barbarians of the North conserve our men."[103]

Instead of pitched battles, he preferred using Cossacks and flying detachments to harass the retreating enemy and capture stragglers by the thousands. Napoleon's defeat could no longer be doubted, and winning one more battle was not as important as future political developments in Europe and Russia's role in them. When a British commissioner pressed him for a more vigorous pursuit of Napoleon, Kutuzov bluntly told him that "I am by no means sure that the total destruction of the Emperor Napoleon and his army would be such a benefit to the world. His succession would not fall to Russia or any other continental power, but to that which already commands the sea [Britain], and whose domination would then be intolerable." According to Prince Eugen of Württemberg, Kutuzov told him that "our young hot-heads are angry at me, for I restrain their frenzy; but they do not realize that circumstances are more effective than our weapons. We cannot reach the frontiers with empty hands [without an army]."[104]

As Napoleon retreated westward, the Russians received a unique chance of trapping him at the Berezina River. The main Russian army under Kutuzov pursued Napoleon's forces while Wittgenstein's corps converged from the northeast and Chichagov's army from the southwest to surround the enemy near Borisov on the Berezina. However, in desperate fighting, Napoleon extricated part of his army, but suffered 25,000 battle casualties and the loss of

---

102   Kutuzov to Ozharovsky, No. 438; Kutuzov to Seslavin, No. 442, 16 November 1812, Rossiiskii Gosudarstvennyi Voyenno-istoricheskii arkhiv (hereafter referred to as RGVIA), f. VUA, op. 16, d. 3521, ll. 63b–64.

103   Louis-Guillaume Puibusque, *Lettres sur la guerre de Russie en 1812, sur la ville de Saint-Pétersbourg, les moeurs et les usages des habitans de la Russie et de la Pologne* (Paris, 1816), 146–147.

104   Eugen of Württemberg, "Vospominaniya o kampanii 1812 g. v Rossii," *Voyennii zhurnal*, 3 (1849), 131; Robert Wilson, *Narrative of Events During the Invasion of Russia by Napoleon Bonaparte* (London, 1869) 234; A. Voyeikov, "General Graf Leontii Leontiyevich Bennigsen," *Russkii Arkhiv*, 59 (1868), 1857.

some 30,000 noncombatants. But the success was not due to Napoleon's genius but rather a combination of dedicated and skilled troops, sound leadership on corps and regimental levels, and, most crucially, the lack of Russian military initiative and coordination.[105]

The retreat from the Berezina to Vilna contains little of military interest. Much of the Grande Armée was gone, its divisions reduced to battalion and company strengths. Although the chain of command remained intact, relations between officers, especially corps commanders and marshals, deteriorated; thus Marshal Ney was on bad terms with Marshals Davout and Victor while Murat and Davout quarreled every time they met. Having led the Grande Armée across the Berezina – its last major obstacle before the Polish frontier – Napoleon considered his job as a military leader largely done, and he decided to return to Paris to assume the mantle of political leader that had been shaken by the recent coup attempt. On 5 December, he appointed his brother-in-law, Murat, commander of the army and left for France.[106] By 10 December, Russian forces had captured Vilna, where some 14,000 enemy soldiers, including 7 generals, surrendered. By the end of month, the last remnants of the Grande Armée, including the corps of Macdonald[107] and Schwarzenberg,[108] crossed the Niemen.

So ended the "severest campaign of six months on record in the annals of the world."[109] It had disastrous consequences for the Napoleonic imperium in Europe. Napoleon's power had been previously tested on several occasions in Spain but none of the setbacks in the Peninsular War approached the devastation of the Russian defeat. The most immediate result of the campaign was all but the total destruction of Napoleon's army, with the loss of up to a half mil-

---

105   For in-depth discussion, see Alexander Mikaberidze, *Napoleon's Great Escape: The Battle of the Berezina* (London, 2010).
106   For an excellent discussion of French leadership at this period, see Frederick C. Schneid, "The Dynamics of Defeat: French Army Leadership, December 1812–March 1813," *Journal of Military History*, 63, 1 (Jan. 1999), 7–28.
107   Macdonald received his orders to retreat on 18 December and started the next day in two columns. He moved largely unimpeded by the Russians, who focused on Napoleon's main body. On reaching Tauroggen along the Russo-Prussian border, Prussian general Hans David Ludwig von Yorck concluded the famous convention by which the Prussians were declared neutral.
108   By December, Schwarzenberg was still preoccupied with the Russian forces in the Volhynia region. On learning of the catastrophe of the Grande Armée, he retreated to Bialystok between 14 and 18 December; General Jean Louis Ebénézer Reynier's Saxon corps followed him behind the Bug. The Austrian corps eventually reached its own territory while Reynier moved into Saxony. Poniatowski's Polish corps was interned by the Austrians until the summer armistice of 1813.
109   Wilson, *Invasion*, 368.

lion men and huge amounts of materiel. The cavalry arm was virtually wiped out – approximately 200,000 trained horses had been lost – and never fully recovered during the subsequent campaigns in 1813–1814. As for the artillery, it also suffered enormous losses; the Russians captured more than 920 of some 1,300 cannon. In politics, the direct result of the Russian victory in 1812 was the general uprising of northern Germany against Napoleon and the complete overthrow within one year of the French imperium in Central Europe.

The basic factor in Napoleon's failure in 1812 was the very magnitude of the war. No previous campaign of the Revolutionary or Napoleonic Wars involved such enormous forces, vast distances, long-drawn-out lines of communication, or logistical challenges. Furthermore, the fact that the French emperor was engaged in a two-front war against Russia in the north and the British and their allies in Iberia rendered the concentration of his resources and political, military, and diplomatic effort impossible. Thus, 1812 was not just the year of French military defeats but of diplomatic setbacks as well. The failure of French diplomacy to prevent Russia's treaties with the Ottoman Empire and Sweden had an important impact on the campaign as it resulted in the ability of two Russian armies to operate on the wings of the Grande Armée.

Additional factors also made success unattainable. To prevail in this conflict, the Russians committed immense human and material resources. Consequently, the Grande Armée was not defeated by winter but rather the brave Russian troops led by devoted leaders.[110] Despite their infighting, Bagration and Barclay de Tolly must be credited for the solid leadership of their troops during the retreat. Starting in August, Kutuzov demonstrated his operational and strategic skills that further contributed to the Russian triumph.

The Grande Armée, half-composed of foreigners, had neither the high standard of discipline nor the unfaltering devotion that it had demonstrated in previous campaigns. Troops from more than a dozen nationalities were bound to lose cohesion and discipline under the vicissitudes of failure. Although Napoleon made extensive logistical preparations, his supply system failed to function properly as major depots were established at too great a distance from the army while the lack of transport infrastructure within Russia prevented the timely delivery of available supplies to the troops. The countryside, meanwhile, provided few provisions, especially in forage, which led to immense losses in cattle, transport animals, and horses.

---

110 By the time freezing temperatures set in November, the outcome of the war had been largely decided, as the Grande Armée was in disarray and hastily retreating from Russia.

Throughout this campaign Napoleon demonstrated glimpses of his military genius. His operations at Vilna, Minsk, Vitebsk, and Smolensk were brilliantly conceived and could have delivered the decisive victory he so desired. Yet time and again, the emperor failed to bring them to fruition. His subordinates frequently showed lack of initiative or made poor tactical choices that had effects on the operational level. Jerome should not have held such a prominent command while the troops of Macdonald, Oudinot, Saint Cyr, and Victor should have been placed under one commander instead of being subordinated to four marshals; through more coordinated and rigorous action, they could have easily crushed Wittgenstein or been of more assistance during the retreat of Napoleon's main body. The emperor himself showed signs of apathy and vacillation, lingering too long at Vilna (eighteen days), Vitebsk (twelve days), and Moscow (thirty-five days), failing to exploit Russian strategic errors in July–August and subordinating military considerations to political goals in September–October.

At the start of the war, he had hoped for a decisive battle but, when the Russians finally accepted the challenge at Borodino, Napoleon resorted to rather unimaginative tactics that failed to deliver a second Austerlitz or Jena. Napoleon's failure to maintain a vigorous pursuit of the enemy to and beyond Moscow meant that the Russians had successfully performed a flanking maneuver and placed themselves in an advantageous position to threaten his extended line of communication. During the retreat from Moscow, the emperor rarely demonstrated his customary resolution or leadership and neither Smolensk and Borodino, nor Maloyaroslavets and Vyazma, bear imprints of his martial genius. The Battle of the Berezina is sometimes lauded as an example of Napoleon's military brilliance but it is hard to accept such wholehearted admiration. One can certainly agree with one French historian's assessment that it was "*une victoire militaire*" but we must also consider another historian's opinion that, "if getting the remnant of the Grande Armée across the Berezina with very heavy loss" is to be viewed as "a masterpiece, what epithets are to be attached to Austerlitz and Friedland?"[111]

Bibliography

Beskrovnyi, Lyubomir, ed. *M.I. Kutuzov: sbornik dokumentov*, vol. 4. Moscow, 1954.
Beskrovnyi, Lyubomir, ed. *Otechestvennaya voina 1812 goda*. Moscow, 1968.
Bessonov, V. *Tarutinskoye srazheniye*. Moscow, 2008.

---

111 Book review, *English Historical Review*, 24 (1909), 413.

Bezotosnyi, Victor, gen. ed. *Otechestvennaya voina 1812 goda: entsiklopediya.* Moscow, 2004.
Bezotosnyi, Victor, gen. ed. *Razvedka i plany storon v 1812 godu.* Moscow, 2005.
Bogdanovich, Modest. *Istoriya Otechestvennoi voiny 1812 g. po dostovernym istochnikam*, 3 vols. Saint Petersburg, 1859–1860.
Britten Austin, Paul. *1812: Napoleon's Invasion of Russia.* London, 2000.
Buturlin, Dmitri. *Istoriya nashestviya Imperatora Napoleona na Rossiyu v 1812 godu*, 2 vols. Saint Petersburg, 1823.
Cappello, Girolamo. *Gli italiani in Russia nel 1812.* Città di Castello, Italy, 1912.
Cate, Curtis. *The War of the Two Emperors. The Duel Between Napoleon and Alexander: Russia 1812.* New York, 1985.
Chambray, Georges de. *Histoire de l'expédition de Russie: avec un atlas, un plan de la bataille de la Moskwa, et une vue du passage du Niémen*, 2 vols. Paris, 1823.
Dzhevegelov, Aleksei and N. Makhnevich, et al., eds. *Otechestvennaya voina i Russkoye obshchestvo*, 7 vols. Moscow, 1911–1912.
Fabry, Gabriel Joseph, ed. *Campagne de 1812*, 5 vols. Paris, 1900–1912.
Foord, Edward. *Napoleon's Russian Campaign of 1812.* London, 1914.
Helme, R. "Pribalticheskii teatr voyennykh deistvii Otechestvennoi voiny 1812g." PhD diss., University of Tartu (Estonia), 1987.
Holzhausen, Paul. *Die Deutschen in Russland, 1812.* Berlin, 1912.
Josselson, Michael. *The Commander: A Life of Barclay de Tolly.* Oxford, 1980.
Kharkevich, Vladimir. *Voina 1812 goda: ot Nemana do Smolenska.* Vilna, 1901.
Kukiel, Mariel. *Wojna 1812 roku*, 2 vols. Kraków, 1937.
Lieven, Dominic. *Russia Against Napoleon: The True Story of the Campaigns of War and Peace.* New York, 2010.
Maag, Albert. *Die Schicksale der Schweizer-Regimenter in Napoleons I. Feldzug nach Russland, 1812.* Biel, Switzerland, 1890.
Mikaberidze, Alexander. *The Battle of Borodino: Napoleon versus Kutuzov.* Barnsley, UK, 2007.
Mikaberidze, Alexander. "'The Lion of the Russian Army': Life and Military Career of General Prince Peter Bagration 1765–1812," 2 vols. PhD diss., Florida State University, 2003.
Mikaberidze, Alexander. *Napoleon's Great Escape: The Battle of the Berezina.* Barnsley, UK, 2007.
Mikaberidze, Alexander. *Napoleon's Trial by Fire: The Burning of Moscow, 1812.* Barnsley, UK, 2007.
Mikaberidze, Alexander. "Napoleon's Lost Legions. The Grande Armée Prisoners of War in Russia," *Napoleonica. La Revue* 2014/3 (21): 35–44.
Nafziger, George. *Napoleon's Invasion of Russia.* Novato, CA, 1988.
Popov, Aleksandr. *Otechestvennaya voina 1812 goda.* Moscow, 2008.

Popov, Andrei. *Velikaya armiya v Rossii: pogonya za mirazhem*. Samara, Russia, 2002.
Popov, Andrei. *Pervoye Polotskoye srazheniye*. Moscow, 2010.
Otechestvennaya voina 1812 goda: materialy Voyenno-Uchenogo Arkhiva General'nogo Shtaba, 21 vols. Saint Petersburg, 1910–1917.
Riehn, Richard. *1812: Napoleon's Russian Campaign*. New York, 1991.
Ségur, Philippe-Paul. *Histoire de Napoléon et de la Grande-armée pendant l'année 1812*. Paris, 1824.
Tarle, Eugene. *Nashestviye Napoleona na Rossiyu, 1812 god*. Moscow, 1938.
Thiers, Adolphe. *Histoire du Consulat et de l'Empire*, vol. 14. Paris, 1845–1862.
Thiry, Jean. *La campagne de Russie*. Paris, 1969.
Troitskii, Nikolai. *1812: velikii god Rossii*. Moscow, 1988.
Troitskii, Nikolai. *Fel'dmarshal Kutuzov: mify i fakty*. Moscow, 2002.
Vandal, Albert. *Napoléon et Alexandre Ier: l'alliance russe sous le Premier empire. La rupture*. Paris, 1891–1897.
Voronovskii, V. *Otechestvennaya voina 1812g. v predelakh Smolenskoi gubernii*. Saint Petersburg, 1912.
Welden, Ludwig von. *Der Feldzug der Oesterreicher gegen Rußland im Jahre 1812*. Vienna, 1870.
Zamoyski, Adam. *Moscow 1812: Napoleon's Fatal March*. New York, 2004.
Zemtsov, Vladimir and A. Popov. *Borodino: severnyi flang*. Moscow, 2008.

CHAPTER 12

Prometheus Chained, 1813–1815

Michael V. Leggiere

This chapter will explore the reasons behind Napoleon's downfall by examining the campaigns and operations of the Wars of the Sixth and Seventh Coalitions. The first crack in Napoleon's imperial system came with Russia's defection from the Continental System and the resulting war between the two empires in 1812. After Napoleon's monumental defeat in Russia, Prussia broke its alliance with France in March 1813. That same month, Russia and Prussia formed the Sixth Coalition. Britain joined, followed by Sweden and Austria later in the year. By mid-August 1813, Napoleon faced the combined strength of Europe's four other great powers. After his Fall Campaign ended in disaster at the Battle of Leipzig, he retreated across the Rhine River with the survivors of the Grande Armée of 1813. The Allies pursued, while in Spain the duke of Wellington's Anglo-Portuguese-Spanish army drove the French across the Pyrenees. Throughout November and December, Allied forces moved into the Low Countries as the two main Allied armies prepared to invade France. Crossing the Rhine River in late December 1813 and early January 1814, the two Allied armies quickly closed on Paris. In February 1814, Napoleon launched a brilliant counteroffensive that nearly led to the destruction of one Allied army. Yet numbers favored the Coalition. Reinforced by two army corps that invaded France from the Low Countries, the Allies pressed Napoleon in March. Following a general advance, Coalition forces captured Paris on 31 March 1814. On 11 April, Napoleon abdicated and the Allies restored Louis XVIII to the French throne.

Exiled to the tiny Mediterranean island of Elba, Napoleon escaped with his personal guard of 1,000 men and four cannon in late February 1815, landing in southern France on 1 March 1815. After the French forces sent to apprehend the emperor of Elba defected to Napoleon's cause, Louis XVIII fled to Belgium. Reaching Paris on 20 March, Napoleon restored the empire. Despite his attempts to secure peace with the Allied powers, all diplomatic channels remained closed. The Allies branded him an "Enemy and Disturber of the Tranquility of the World." On 25 March, Britain, Russia, Prussia, and Austria formed the Seventh Coalition against France. Three months later, Napoleon met his final defeat on the fields of Waterloo on 18 June 1815. Four days later, on 22 June, Napoleon abdicated a second time. He spent the rest of his life in exile on the rock of Saint Helena in the South Atlantic, where he died in 1821 at age fifty-one.

War of the Sixth Coalition

In January 1813, Eugene de Beauharnais, the viceroy of Italy, assumed command of all imperial forces east of the Elbe River. Initially, this force numbered a mere 44,110 men and 81 guns. By February 1813, he possessed 80,000 men for field operations. One month later, this figure had increased to 113,360 men and 185 guns to confront the smaller, exhausted, disorganized Russian army that was slowly approaching Prussia. Additional French reinforcements between the Rhine and the Elbe amounted to 142,905 men and 320 guns. French garrisons that had become stranded on the Elbe, Oder, and Vistula, and in the Grand Duchy of Warsaw, totaled 69,250 men.[1] To stop the Russians, Napoleon planned for Eugene's force – the Army of the Elbe – to hold the Elbe River from Hamburg to the Austrian frontier. Behind the Army of the Elbe, the emperor would form his new force: the Army of the Main.

Led by Tsar Alexander I, the Russians carried the war westward in a great effort to drive the French from Central Europe. The destruction of the Grande Armée of 1812 offered an opportunity to build a Russian-dominated coalition to liberate Europe. Russian pressure forced the French to fall back from the Vistula River and then across the Oder to Berlin by mid-February 1813. While Eugene surrendered land for time, direct negotiations between the Russians and Prussians commenced. Their talks culminated on 28 February with the signing of the Treaty of Kalisch: the much-anticipated Russo-Prussian military alliance. The Prussians agreed to field an army of 80,000 men to assist a Russian contingent of 150,000; both states pledged not to make a separate peace with Napoleon. Alexander promised to restore Prussia's pre-Jena material strength and Frederick William acknowledged that he would lose most of his Polish territory to a Polish kingdom under Russian hegemony. Prussia would be compensated by Allied conquests in Germany, specifically Saxony. On 19 March 1813, the Russians and Prussians signed the Treaty of Breslau – the diplomatic supplement to the military alliance forged at Kalisch. According to its terms, the Russians affirmed their agreements to restore Prussia's pre-Jena material

---

1 "Situation," 13 March 1813, Archives nationales, Paris, France (hereafter cited as AN), AF IV, Carton 1651. At Stettin were 7,715 men and 148 guns; Küstrin 3,372 men; Spandau 2,926 men; Glogau 4,501 men; Thorn 3,908 men; Danzig 27,328 men; Modlin 4,300 men; Zamosc 4,000 men; Czenstochau 1,200; Magdeburg 5,000 men; Wittenberg 3,000 men; and Torgau 2,000 Saxons.

strength.² The British did their part to bolster the new coalition by promptly dispatching 54 cannon along with arms and ammunition for 23,000 men to the Baltic for use by the Russians and Prussians.³ Both the Russians and Prussians hoped Austria would join the alliance in early 1813 but Austria's foreign minister, the adroit Klemens von Metternich, feared Russian success would be accompanied by Russian territorial expansion. With Alexander's armies approaching Central Europe, the Austrians declared neutrality.⁴

For Napoleon, 1813 brought a fresh series of challenges. As French forces in the east steadily retreated, his political situation likewise deteriorated. Failure in Russia not only resulted in the loss of the Grand Duchy of Warsaw, but also threatened French control of the Confederation of the Rhine. While Napoleon's prestige plummeted, German nationalists called for a *Befreiungskrieg*, a war of liberation. Prussia's declaration of war only added to the complex set of problems that confronted Napoleon. Austria stood as an armed neutral, endeavoring to mediate between Napoleon and his enemies. Despite the dynastic ties between France and Austria due to the marriage of Napoleon and Marie Louise, the daughter of Emperor Francis I, the Austrians could not be trusted.

Opposing Forces

The burden of waging war in Central Europe fell on Tsar Alexander in the early stages of the contest. On crossing the Prussian frontier in January 1813, Russia's frontline army, likewise devastated by the winter campaign in 1812, consisted of 51,745 tired soldiers, 12,283 Cossacks, and 439 guns. Reinforcements, not expected to reach the front until the beginning of April, amounted to 12,674 men, 2,307 Cossacks, and 48 guns. Russian second-line troops – 56,776 men, 9,989 Cossacks, and 319 guns – besieged French-controlled fortresses on the Oder and the Vistula Rivers.⁵ A reserve of 48,100 men had yet to depart from Russia. As for the Russian high command, it had been divided for some time.

---

2 Enno Kraehe, *Metternich's German Policy*, vol. 1, *The Contest with Napoleon* (Princeton, NJ, 1963), 1:156–157.
3 In 1813, the British sent more than £1,000,000 in military stores to the Baltic for use by the Prussians and Russians; in all £11,294,416 of the 1813 military budget went to Great Britain's allies as advances, while an additional £11,335,412 was distributed as direct loans. See Philip J. Haythornthwaite, *The Napoleonic Sourcebook* (New York, 1990), 195; Rory Muir, *Britain and the Defeat of Napoleon, 1807–1815* (London, 1996), 248.
4 Henry Kissinger, *A World Restored: Metternich, Castlereagh and the Problems of Peace, 1812–1822* (Boston, 1957), 24, 48–49.
5 The siege corps of Stettin, Küstrin, and Glogau totaled 2,280 men, 1,570 Cossacks, and 16 guns. The siege corps of Danzig and Thorn numbered 21,289 men, 3,687 Cossacks, and 155 guns.

While Tsar Alexander fashioned himself as the liberator of Germany, Russian commander in chief General Mikhail Kutuzov opposed carrying the war into Central Europe to emancipate the same countries that had supported Napoleon's bid to conquer Russia. Other Russian commanders expressed concerns over their tenuous lines of communication. Therefore, crushing the Russian army on the field of battle amid so much disagreement would certainly put the Russians to flight, similar to the 1805 campaign.

Several factors hampered Prussian mobilization in January and February 1813. French troops still occupied half of the country and held all of Prussia's significant fortresses. Tedious negotiations with the Russians also slowed the process. Concentration of the field army, scheduled to begin on 12 February, had to be postponed until the formation of the coalition. After creating the alliance at Kalisch, the mobilization continued at an accelerated pace and culminated with the 17 March 1813 decrees creating a national *Landwehr* (militia). Aside from a few battalions, the militia would not be ready for field service until August. At the beginning of the war, the Prussian regular army consisted of 127,394 men and 269 guns. Of this figure, only 65,675 men had received sufficient training to be utilized in the field; only half of Prussia's armed forces were trained regulars or reservists. Nevertheless, Napoleon would find that the Prussian army of 1813 was far superior to the one he had humiliated and crushed in 1806.

Of the 600,000 men and 1,300 guns of the Grande Armée of 1812, only 93,000 men and 250 pieces returned.[6] Undaunted by such catastrophic and unprecedented losses, Napoleon planned to have a new army numbering 656,000 men by June of 1813. General mobilizations occurred in France, the Confederation of the Rhine, and Italy to replace the men lost in Russia. As early as September 1813, Napoleon had ordered the conscription of 140,000 men in France and 30,000 in Italy. Despite their growing bitterness, Napoleon's vassals obeyed. He still possessed powerful weapons to employ against his satellites: outright terror; control of propaganda and information; the threat of force; their persistent belief in his military superiority; and the fact that many princes owed their political existence to him. As a result, most of the recruits had already reached their depots by the time Napoleon returned to Paris in December; they completed their training as they marched to the front. For leadership, the emperor transferred experienced noncommissioned officers from his armies in Spain to

---

A third group, which operated in the Grand Duchy of Warsaw, included the siege corps of Modlin, Zamosc, and the Warsaw garrison – a total of 27,115 men, 4,250 Cossacks, and 148 guns.

6 Of the survivors, the Prussian and Austrian contingents that had served Napoleon in 1812 accounted for at least 60,000 men.

the new units. In a little more than four months, Napoleon's unrivaled organizational skills produced the 140,000-strong Army of the Main. Including Eugene's Army of the Elbe, imperial forces amounted to almost 200,000 men by the end of April.

After it had lost 180,000 horses in Russia, critical deficiencies remained in the cavalry; this robbed the army not only of its shock tactics, but also its eyes and ears. The French adequately replaced the losses sustained in Russia, but draft horses remained in short supply. Reflective of the army itself, the French officer corps in 1813 contained strengths and weaknesses. In the senior ranks, the Russian campaign had taken its toll on the aging marshalate. One asset, however, remained the army's field-grade officers, most of whom were battle-hardened veterans. As one historian notes, the Grande Armée of 1813 provided Napoleon with an effective fighting force, "but one that suffered from the internal germs of weakness." Consequently, the Grande Armée of 1813 lacked many of the tactical attributes of previous French armies, which in turn placed strategic and operational limitations on Napoleon.[7]

With an army that raised more questions than it answered, Napoleon needed a brilliant strategy to produce another Ulm, Austerlitz, Jena–Auerstedt, or Wagram. His operational planning in 1813 strongly suggests that he believed a strategy of maneuver in North Germany would produce victory. He envisioned a drive across the North German plain to Danzig in order to reconquer Prussia and relieve the Oder and Vistula garrisons. Liberating Danzig became an important strategic objective, which had to be achieved quickly.

In view of this goal, Napoleon planned to lead his army from the Main River to the Elbe, unite with Eugene south of Magdeburg, and cross the lower Oder. Relying on a *manoeuvre sur les derrières*, he hoped to strategically envelop the Russians as he had done so brilliantly to the Prussians in 1806. In the least, the offensive would force the Russians to abandon the Oder and retreat beyond the Vistula. After the Russians withdrew behind the Vistula, the emperor could reestablish control over the Grand Duchy of Warsaw and draw on Polish resources. Also, an operation in North Germany would keep the war far from Austria's borders. Prussia's declaration of war in March followed by the Coalition's invasion of Saxony in April 1813 forced Napoleon to delay this initial operation, which historian David Chandler labels as the emperor's "master plan of 1813." Most commentaries agree with Chandler's assessment that

---

7 Chandler, *Campaigns of Napoleon*, 866–867, 869–870. For a discussion of the problems of the Grande Armée of 1813, see 867–869.

"although circumstances made it impossible to put it into execution ... the emperor never forgot it."[8]

French operations can be analyzed in four phases. Napoleon's first phase of planning, concluded on 11 March, envisioned the drive across the North German plain to Danzig. His second phase of strategic planning, which culminated in the Battles of Lützen and Bautzen and ended with the Grande Armée deep in Silesia, concluded with the Armistice of Pläswitz. August ushered in the third phase of campaign planning as the emperor had to choose between offensive or defensive operations for the resumption of hostilities. Although Austria joined the Coalition, a degree of success again appeared to be offered by an operation against Berlin and North Germany. The plan adopted by Napoleon refused to sacrifice the offensive but again ignored the principle of mass. Bonaparte planned to open the Fall Campaign with another operation against Berlin, while the bulk of his forces remained echeloned between Dresden and the Katzbach River in Silesia. The fourth and most controversial phase of strategic planning culminated in Napoleon's 30 August *"Note sur la situation générale de mes affaires"* in which he considered either an offensive against Prague or another march on Berlin as his next step. Both projects ignored the objective of annihilating the main enemy army, which would have provided the most direct means of achieving total victory. Absent from either is discussion of a decisive battle with any one of the three Allied armies. Geographic points dominate the emperor's objectives, similar to the 18th-century wars of maneuver.

Although the first phase of strategic planning ended with the postponement of the "master plan," its key objectives can be found in Napoleon's subsequent planning and operations. First and foremost was the suppression of Prussia through a morale-breaking conquest of Berlin. In the event of an offensive against Berlin, he believed the Prussians would abandon their allies and race northward. In this case, Napoleon planned to destroy the Prussians as they marched to defend their capital. Should the Prussian army remain in Saxony, a weakly defended Berlin would fall and presumably disrupt Prussian mobilization. Control of the plain between the Elbe and the Oder Rivers provided another consideration. If he transferred his base of operations northward to Hanover, Brandenburg, or Pomerania, the Elbe and Oder fortresses would protect his right flank. Napoleon's desire to relieve the besieged garrisons on the Oder and the Vistula formed another objective. Lastly, a drive through North Germany to the Vistula would threaten Russian communications that stretched across Silesia and Poland.

---

8 Ibid., 875.

Spring Campaign

During initial operations, the Allies liberated Berlin with their northern army of 30,000 Prussians and 18,000 Russians commanded by the Russian general Wittgenstein, while the Prussian general Blücher's 26,000 Prussians and 10,500 Russians took the Saxon capital of Dresden with the Coalition's smaller southern army. Behind these two armies followed Kutuzov – now Allied commander in chief – with the Russian main army and reserve. After clearing Berlin, Wittgenstein drove southwest through a detachment of the French Army of the Elbe at Möckern near Magdeburg on 5 April, allowing for his union with Blücher east of the Saale River in the vicinity of Leipzig. Following Kutuzov's death on 28 April 1813, Tsar Alexander named Wittgenstein Allied commander in chief.

The appearance of Allied forces in Saxony in late March prompted Napoleon to concentrate his forces on the left bank of the Saale River throughout April. The emperor began his counteroffensive on 30 April by leading 120,000 men across the Saale to confront the Allied army near Leipzig. Reports of French movements indicated that the emperor would converge on Leipzig in two columns: Eugene's Army of the Elbe southeast from Magdeburg and Napoleon's Army of the Main due east from Weißenfels. The Allies resolved to attack. For the war's first major engagement, Wittgenstein marshaled approximately 88,000 Russians and Prussians and 552 guns. Napoleon's army of 145,000 men and 372 guns outnumbered the Allies in infantry but faced a threefold superiority in cavalry and double the artillery. Although Napoleon possessed fewer total guns, he had more heavy batteries than the Allies, which granted the French artillery an advantage in range and effectiveness. Early on 2 May 1813, the Allied army advanced southeast to northwest in the hope of smashing through the imperial armies as they moved east.

Wittgenstein opened the 2 May 1813 Battle of Lützen by having the Prussian II Corps attack a supposed French rearguard holding the quadrilateral of villages immediately north of the Allied army: Großgörschen, Kleingörschen, Rahna, and Kaja. This French force turned out to be Napoleon's massive III Corps. Although surprised by the Allies, Napoleon ordered a double envelopment but needed time for his IV and XI Corps to arrive. At the start of the battle, the Prussians drove the French from Kleingörschen toward Kaja, where Napoleon himself arrived around 2:30 with the Imperial Guard not far behind. With III Corps reeling, Napoleon quickly adjusted thanks to his practice of moving corps along parallel roads within mutual supporting distance known as the *bataillion carré*. Around 4:00 PM, IV Corps arrived to threaten Wittgenstein's left flank. One hour later, the artillery of XI Corps – sixty cannon

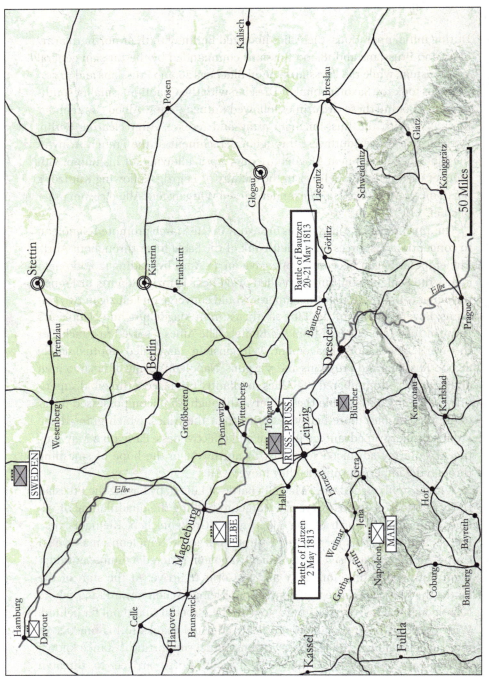

Map 12.1 Theater of war, spring 1813

and howitzers – opened fire against his right flank. Napoleon recognized that the time was right to deliver the *coup de grâce*. While artillery pulverized the quadrilateral, sixteen battalions of Young Guard formed in four brigade columns. Behind them, six battalions of Old Guard followed by the Guard Cavalry moved up. As the emperor rode past the Guard's position, he issued his order in classic form: "*La garde au feu!*" Although Russian reserves managed to stop the progress of XI Corps, the Guard overwhelmed the Allied center. After eight hours of brutal fighting, Napoleon's enveloping forces reached their positions. With both flanks threatened, Wittgenstein assembled his corps commanders to determine if the Allied army could renew the battle on 3 May. All reported that the condition of the infantry did not appear favorable: confusion, dissolution, and extreme exhaustion. Moreover, the Russian ammunition parks had not followed the army and little chance existed for timely resupply. All the advantages the Allies had enjoyed at the start of the battle gradually eroded and Napoleon clearly enjoyed numerical superiority. Wittgenstein ordered a general retreat.

The 2 May 1813 Battle of Lützen proved extremely bloody. The Prussian army shouldered the weight of the engagement and paid dearly in its debut, losing 8,400 men. Russian losses are not known but can be estimated at 3,000 casualties. According to Wittgenstein's report to the tsar, the Allies "retained the battlefield and captured 16 guns and 1,400 men, many of them officers. We did not lose a single cannon. The enemy lost up to 15,000 men. Our losses amount to some 10,000 men, most of them lightly wounded." Imperial forces lost some 22,000 combatants and 5 guns.[9] Neither side lost a flag or standard. Operationally, the Battle of Lützen again demonstrated Napoleon's supremacy. His ability to move units to the battlefield where and when they were needed to deliver maximum combat power remained unrivaled. Indeed, on 2 May, the Sixth Coalition came within hours of being destroyed by a double envelopment that would have been so crushing it would have ended the war. The experience of the Russians and the zeal of the Prussians only serve to accentuate the brilliance of Napoleon's victory. Not the inexperienced Austrians of 1796 or 1805 overwhelmed by his highly mobile, destructive form of warfare, the Allied commanders have no excuse for falling victim to Napoleon's proficient generalship.

Yet, tactically, the battle provides further proof of the parity in terms of combat-effectiveness between the imperial soldiers of the Grande Armée and their adversaries, a situation that had existed since the 1805 struggle at Austerlitz. Without doubt, Lützen proved that the young imperial soldiers,

---
9 Wittgenstein to Alexander, 3 May 1813, RGVIA, f. VUA, op. 16, d. 3926, ll. 77–79b.

who in no way rivaled the *grognards* of the 1805–1807 Grande Armée, provided a capable instrument in the hands of their master. Nevertheless, the Allies in general, but mainly the Prussians, impressed Napoleon with their tactical and organizational improvements. His oft-quoted statement that "the animals have learned something" indicates the emperor's reluctant admission that his adversaries had closed the gap in terms of tactical proficiency.

Following Lützen, the shortage of cavalry prevented Napoleon from unleashing a deadly pursuit to annihilate the Allies and make his victory decisive. Although his weak cavalry arm and inexperienced infantry could not maneuver the Allies into accepting battle under conditions favorable to him, numerically superior French forces would create strategic opportunities. Thanks to the resources of the empire, Napoleon could place an army in North Germany that would be considerably larger than anything the Allies could muster in opposition, while the army under his personal command still outnumbered the principal Allied forces in Saxony. Thus on 4 May Napoleon directed Marshal Ney to the Elbe fortress of Torgau, which, along with Wittenberg, provided the gateway to Berlin and North Germany. He believed that Ney's movement toward Berlin would induce the Prussians to separate from the Russians and march with all possible speed to cover their capital. Napoleon would then mask the Russians, reunite with Ney, and lead 175,000 men to destroy what he believed to be between 60,000 and 80,000 Prussians as they marched to Berlin. Napoleon instructed Ney that it was "natural" for the Prussians to separate from the Russians, who were retreating toward Silesia, and advance to Berlin to defend their capital. Should the Allied army remain united and decide to again confront Napoleon in Saxony, Ney would still be within supporting distance. In the last scenario, if a united Allied army continued to retreat, Napoleon planned to drive it out of Saxony, through Silesia, and as far as Poland. Should Ney enjoy success in North Germany, he might reach the Vistula before the Allies, in which case they would be caught between two numerically superior French armies. Although these calculations appeared sound, success could have been attained only by diverting French forces to North Germany and away from the pursuit of, and possible battle with, the Allied main army in Saxony. Ney's army eventually numbered 84,300 men while Napoleon commanded 119,000.[10] Napoleon knew that Ney's march to Torgau would signal to the Allies the start of an offensive against the Prussian

---

10 *CN*, Nos. 19956, 19958, and 20006, 25:264–266, 292–293; Jean-Jacques Pelet, *Des principales opérations de la campagne de 1813* (Paris, 1826–1828), 1:54; Rudolf Friederich, *Die Befreiungskriege, 1813–1815* (Berlin, 1913), 1:249; C.L.M.L. Lanrezac, *La manoeuvre de Lützen 1813* (Paris, 1904), 177–178, 185–186.

capital. He hoped this would force the Allies to split their army, with the Prussians marching north toward Berlin and the Russians continuing east along their line of operations. Similar to his First Italian Campaign, he would then execute a *manoeuvre sur la position centrale* to destroy the Prussians and Russians in succession.

Napoleon viewed Ney's operation as the best means to achieve three main objectives by month's end: occupy Berlin; relieve the fortress of Glogau on the Oder River; and take Breslau, the provincial capital of Silesia. Consequently, he ordered Ney to Luckau, halfway between Berlin and Bautzen, in order to either strike the Prussian capital or move into a position to support the Grande Armée in Saxony. Twenty-four hours later, confirmed reports arrived that the entire Allied army had marched to Bautzen. Napoleon believed the Allies would continue their retreat eastward perhaps as far as Silesia rather than stand at Bautzen. For this reason, he wanted Ney to continue to march east, parallel to Napoleon's march, in order to prevent the Allies from making a stand at the Spree, Neiße, Queis, or Bober Rivers. In addition, Ney could proceed as far as Glogau and sever Russian communications through Poland. Consequently, Ney received orders to move III and V Corps in the direction of Spremberg – one day's march from Bautzen. As for the other units of Ney's army, the emperor wanted Marshal Victor to lead II and VII Corps and II Cavalry Corps against the Prussian capital.[11]

Meanwhile, Wittgenstein had retreated east to the Spree River, where he placed the Allied army in a commanding position just east of the river and the town of Bautzen. The imperials followed slowly and cautiously, engaging in almost daily combats with Wittgenstein's rearguard. Instead of effecting a split among the Allies, Napoleon found his adversaries in a fortified position around Bautzen and along the Spree River. Although the emperor intended to engage the Allies at Bautzen and still move against Berlin with a portion of Ney's army, the marshal mistakenly brought his entire army south to join the battle.

Napoleon issued orders to attack the Allied left wing and center on 20 May. While his Guard, IV, VI, XI, and XII Corps fixed the Allies, Ney's III, V, VII, and II Corps marched southeast to envelop the Allied right. By nightfall on the 21st, he planned to have 144,000 combatants on the battlefield facing 96,000 Coalition soldiers. To facilitate Ney's operation against the Allied right, Napoleon sought to deceive the Allies into thinking he intended to turn their left. He spent the morning of 20 May 1813 moving his pieces around the board to increase Allied concern over the left wing. Although Wittgenstein did not fall for the ruse, Alexander did. Ignoring Wittgenstein's objections, Alexander

---

11 *CN*, Nos. 20006–20008, 25:292–294.

transferred his few reserves to the left wing. Wittgenstein walked away and fell asleep under a tree after the tsar assumed full control over the battle. Around noon, French artillery blasted the Allied positions while IV, VI, XI, and XII Corps advanced east across the Spree. Combat lasted until 8:30 that night. Altogether the Allies lost some 1,400 Russians and 500 Prussians; French losses are not known. The engagement on the 20th won Napoleon the keys to Wittgenstein's forward position: the town of Bautzen and the crossings over the Spree. By pinning the Allies and deceiving them over the point of his attack, the emperor attained basic objectives through the simplest of means.

Napoleon resumed the offensive by attacking the Allied left at dawn on 21 May. General Miloradovich's Russian corps held Wittgenstein's left while Russian units and the Prussian I Corps formed the Allied center; the Prussian II Corps on the Kreckwitz Heights anchored the right. Informed of Ney's approach, Wittgenstein posted Barclay de Tolly's Russian corps on the extreme right wing. Around 9:00 AM, Ney's III and V Corps smashed through Barclay's outnumbered Russians and turned south. Napoleon succeeded in fixing the Allied left with his XI and XII Corps, prompting the gullible tsar to commit the last of his reserves. Not much else occurred on Napoleon's right for the rest of the battle. Instead, focus shifted to his center and left.

At 11:00 AM, Napoleon directed his VI Corps to move against the Allied center. Around 2:00 PM, two divisions of IV Corps crossed the river and prepared to assault the Allied right on the Kreckwitz Heights. Confused by Napoleon's instructions, Ney did not know whether he should march *southeast* to Weißenberg in accordance with the emperor's orders to sever the Coalition's line of operations. On seeing the Kreckwitz Heights to the *southwest*, Ney became enthralled with the idea that the hills formed the key to the Allied position. Dismissing the advice of his chief of staff, Henri Jomini, Ney decided to await the arrival of his rearward divisions and then storm the Kreckwitz Heights. Had Ney advanced according to his instructions, two army corps would have reached a position directly east of the Allied position before noon. One hour later, Ney turned southwest to storm the Kreckwitz Heights instead of proceeding southeast to sever Wittgenstein's only line of retreat. As imperial forces closed on his right from the west, north, and east, Tsar Alexander reluctantly agreed to break off the battle.

Allied losses on the second day of Bautzen are estimated to be 10,850 men. By comparison, French losses reached 22,500 men including 3,700 missing. Napoleon could not interpret the Battle of Bautzen as anything but a disappointment. Fortunately for the Allies, the compulsive Ney could not turn away from the Kreckwitz Heights. The war quite conceivably could have ended with both Alexander and King Frederick William III of Prussia being taken prisoner.

Ney's blunder could not have been more fortuitous for the Allies and therefore disappointing for Napoleon. Not only was the operation against Berlin postponed at a time that offered the optimal chance of success, but Ney's confusion, resulting from Napoleon's less than clear instructions, would cost the emperor the manpower of his II Corps, approximately 25,000 men, which failed to reach Bautzen in time for the battle. Consequently, this blunder provides the first and most crucial censure of Napoleon's obsession with the "master plan." The operation failed to achieve its objective and prevented Napoleon from concentrating all of his available forces at Bautzen. Both Ney and Napoleon have received their due share of criticism for their roles in this miscarriage, and Ney committed grave tactical errors during the Battle of Bautzen that cost Napoleon a decisive victory.[12]

Summer Armistice

The inability to exploit his success at Lützen and Bautzen because of the severe shortage of cavalry denied Napoleon the decisive victory he needed to end the war. The Allied army retreated into Silesia but Napoleon failed to maneuver it

---

12 Pelet, who notes that Napoleon "reserved for Ney the most beautiful gem of the victory – the march on Berlin," defends Napoleon's strategy and concludes that not enough documentary evidence exists to prove that Napoleon actually intended for Ney to march on Berlin. He argues that, although the emperor informed both his ambassador in Austria and Marshal Davout that Ney was marching on Berlin, these letters were destined to be shown to the Allies or fall into enemy hands. Moreover, Pelet maintains that such letters did not contain the real objective of the operations. "It was also important to communicate with the Saxon garrison in Torgau," wrote Pelet, "and, (if events allow it) with those of Küstrin and Stettin." Pelet believes that these concerns probably influenced Napoleon's calculations and thus the directions given to Ney. Again, in these plans the march on Berlin, "which writers hurry to criticize as having no motive," is secondary. "Thus," concludes Pelet, "the question of Berlin and its occupation prior to the armistice has never been answered, at least correctly. The order that was supposedly given to Marshal Ney was never given, even for a part of his corps; while the march from Torgau to the battlefield, prepared since 14 May, was issued and executed day by day ... from this moment all [of Ney's army] marched rapidly to the great operation [at Bautzen]. This beautiful maneuver, which has been presented as a grave error, was on the contrary, a masterpiece of strategy." Lanrezac counters that "the emperor committed a grave fault [*une faute très grave*] by dividing his army to operate against the main Allied army and against the corps that covered Berlin. He committed this error when he ordered Ney to divide his army and send Victor with II and VII [Corps] and Sébastiani's cavalry to take Berlin and relieve the Oder fortresses. He should have summoned all [of his forces] to Bautzen." See Lanrezac, *La manoeuvre de Lützen*, 238; Pelet, *Des principales opérations de la campagne de 1813*, 51, 54, 60.

into a third battle.[13] By late May 1813, marauding and straggling in Napoleon's army had increased to epic proportions. With 90,000 men on the sick list, the emperor realized he had pushed his army beyond exhaustion. Although not the ultimate factor in Napoleon's decision to accept an Austrian proposal for an armistice, these ugly indicators as well as the realization that he simply could not substitute infantry for cavalry and expect to destroy the enemy coalition led him to open negotiations with the Prussians and Russians. An Austrian proposal to extend a temporary armistice to 20 July was signed at Pläswitz in Silesia on 4 June.

Following Bautzen, Napoleon had instructed Marshal Oudinot to resume the operation against Berlin with XII Corps. In contrast to the 84,000 men that Ney had assembled a few weeks earlier, Oudinot commanded fewer than 25,000 men. Nevertheless, Napoleon believed that Oudinot possessed sufficient combat power to take Berlin and drive the Prussians across the Oder. Oudinot marched *northwest* toward Berlin while the Grande Armée pursued the Allies eastward. After the main Allied army retreated to Silesia, only one corps of 30,000 men commanded by the Prussian general Friedrich Wilhelm von Bülow stood between Oudinot and Berlin. On 4 June, Bülow defeated Oudinot in a hard-fought combat at Luckau. Operations ceased after both commanders learned of the armistice.

Eventually extended to 17 August, the Armistice of Pläswitz saw the failure of Austria's attempt to mediate a peace between Napoleon and the Allies. After Austria declared in favor of the Coalition, the Allies finalized their plans to field three multinational armies. The 42-year-old Schwarzenberg received command of all Allied forces, including the main army – the Army of Bohemia – which consisted of 220,000 Austrians, Prussians, and Russians. The controversial Prussian general, Blücher, commanded the Army of Silesia – 105,000 Russians and Prussians, while former French marshal Bernadotte took command of the Army of North Germany – 140,000 Prussians, Russians, Swedes, and North Germans. The Army of Bohemia, including its reserves and guard units, numbered 127,435 Austrians, 78,200 Russians, and 44,907 Prussians; the Army of Silesia – 66,401 Russians and 38,484 Prussians; and the Army of North Germany, including the brigades blockading Küstrin and Stettin, 91,318 Prussians, 29,357 Russians, and 23,449 Swedes. A fourth Allied army, Bennigsen's Army of Poland, was expected to reach Silesia in September. The Allies created

---

13   CN, No. 20037, 25:312–313; Michael Leggiere, *Napoleon and Berlin: The Franco-Prussian War in North Germany, 1813* (Norman, OK, 2002), 70–88.

these multinational armies both to prevent Napoleon from defeating them piecemeal, and to limit politically motivated acts of national self-interest.[14]

For operations, the Coalition devised the Reichenbach Plan. According to it, the three Allied armies would form a wide arc around French forces in Saxony and Silesia and only engage detached enemy corps: pitched battles with Napoleon would be avoided. Should the emperor concentrate against any one army, it would retreat, while the other two attacked his flanks and communications. As Napoleon could personally command only one army at a time and thus could directly challenge only one Allied army at a time, the other two Allied armies would attack his flanks and lines of communication, while the threatened army would refuse battle but induce the emperor to pursue, thus extending and exposing his line of communication.[15] The plan aimed to split and exhaust French forces. Although Napoleon had the advantage of interior lines, he would be forced to fight against armies advancing simultaneously against his center, flanks, and communications.

The Allies assumed Napoleon would evacuate Silesia, unite all his forces on the left bank of the Elbe, and turn against either Schwarzenberg in Bohemia or Bernadotte in Brandenburg. Based on this supposition, Allied strategists assigned the Silesian Army a secondary role based on the conviction Napoleon would withdraw his forces from Silesia for a general offensive into either Bohemia or Brandenburg. As enemy forces presumably retreated from Silesia to join the main effort against either Schwarzenberg or Bernadotte, Blücher should delay and continuously harass them with his light troops, but always avoid a battle with superior forces. At the same time, his army should protect Silesia and, in unison with Bennigsen's Army of Poland, guard Russian communications to Poland. Should Napoleon advance into Silesia, which turned out to be the case, Blücher would withdraw his main body toward the Neiße River and his respective wings along the Silesian mountains and the Oder. His task would be to draw the French deep into eastern Silesia and away from Saxony. Should Blücher thus facilitate Schwarzenberg's advance into Saxony, Blücher had to pursue the imperial army in Silesia as soon as it broke off the chase and turned west to confront Schwarzenberg in Saxony. If Napoleon allocated his main force to operations in Saxony or Brandenburg, Blücher would advance. If Napoleon directed his main strength against the Army of North Germany, which was rumored to be likely, the Bohemian Army would pursue

---

14   Barthold von Quistorp, *Geschichte der Nord-Armee im Jahre 1813* (Berlin, 1894), 3:1–60.
15   See Gordon Craig, "Problems of Coalition Warfare," in Craig, *War, Politics, and Diplomacy; Selected Essays* (New York, 1966), 28–29.

along the left bank of the Elbe, while the Silesian Army moved down its right bank.

To cover his base of operations at Dresden, maintain his mastery of the Elbe River, and capitalize on the enemy's mistakes, Napoleon assembled his forces in three groups. In the center, the Grande Armée (I, IV, and V Cavalry Corps, Guard, and I, II, VI, and XIV Corps) stood between Bautzen and Görlitz. On his left in Silesia, he posted III, V, XI Corps and II Cavalry Corps under Ney's command. After the expiration of the armistice, he wanted these forces to march west to Bunzlau. This would allow the emperor to concentrate his left and center – almost 270,000 infantry and 30,000 cavalry – between Görlitz and Bunzlau to oppose what he believed to be the Coalition's main army of 200,000 Russians and Prussians in Silesia. Based on the actions of the Allies in May, Napoleon counted on their accepting battle in Silesia, where he planned to decisively defeat them before the Austrians could launch a serious operation against Dresden.

As for the Austrians, after they had detached forces to Italy and the Bavarian border, Napoleon did not think they could assemble more than 100,000 men in Bohemia to oppose him. He initially expected that the Russo-Prussian army he pursued to the Oder in May would advance west from Silesia toward Saxony while the Austrian army in Bohemia invaded Saxony either along the right bank of the Elbe or through Zittau. He knew of the Reichenbach Plan but did not think the Allies would dare expose Silesia by sending considerable forces to Bohemia. Due to the fortifications around Dresden, he had little concern about an Allied operation along the left bank of the Elbe. The Coalition's decision to form its main army in Bohemia as opposed to Silesia caught Napoleon by surprise, thus paralyzing him at the commencement of the campaign on 17 August.[16]

Meanwhile, on Napoleon's right wing, the IV, VII, and XII Corps and III Cavalry Corps of Oudinot's "Army of Berlin" supported by Marshal Davout's XIII Corps coming from Hamburg would conduct an offensive against the Prussian capital. After defeating the Coalition's Army of North Germany, Napoleon planned for the Army of Berlin to liberate the besieged imperial garrisons along the Oder River and advance to the Vistula, wheeling behind the Allied army in Silesia, which itself would be retreating eastward after being defeated by the emperor. Should Bernadotte somehow check the Army of Berlin, Napoleon could easily shift forces from the Silesian theater to Brandenburg to finish the job.

---

16   *CN*, No. 20360, 26:35.

Napoleon's most feasible strategy in the Fall Campaign of 1813 would have been to exploit his central position. Similar to the Roßbach–Leuthen phase of Frederick the Great's autumn campaign of 1757, had Napoleon maintained a defensive posture, utilized his central position to its fullest advantage, and practiced economy of force on his flanks, he could have exploited a few key characteristics that had governed previous coalitions. First and foremost, the Allies needed a decisive victory. Eventually, they had to come to him in order to liberate Central Europe. A prolonged war of attrition and maneuver would have deflated Allied enthusiasm. Moreover, such a war might have encouraged the subordination of the military goal of defeating Napoleon to traditional foreign policy objectives, the bane of previous coalitions. During their councils of war in July, at which time the Allies had formulated the Reichenbach Plan, the Russians and Prussians understood that the collective fate of Central Europe hung in the balance. Despite Napoleon's setbacks in Russia and Iberia, only an unprecedented cooperative effort could liberate Central Europe from French control. Although the Austrians limited Allied war objectives and preferred caution in order to avoid another Ulm, a combination of prudence and calculated aggression characterized the Allied war effort in 1813. Finally, the continental allies certainly had to consider their British paymaster. In view of Great Britain's tremendous financial investment in the Sixth Coalition, London would not subsidize a prolonged war of attrition in Central Europe, particularly since Wellington was brilliantly executing the new "continental strategy" in Iberia.

Fall Campaign

After learning that the Allied main army had actually assembled in Bohemia, Napoleon still planned to destroy their forces in Silesia (Blücher's army), thus removing the threat they posed to the rear of both his Grande Armée in Saxony and Oudinot's Army of Berlin. Although he did not know where Schwarzenberg would lead the Army of Bohemia, Napoleon decided to march against Blücher, defeat him, and then rush back to Dresden.[17] As for Blücher, from 15 to 20 August 1813 he chased Ney's forces westward from the banks of the Katzbach River to Bunzlau on the Bober River. Napoleon likewise reached the Bober on the 20th, attacking Blücher on the 21st. Complying with the Reichenbach Plan, Blücher retreated eastward for the next four days. Meanwhile, Schwarzenberg led the Bohemian Army across the Saxon frontier on 22 August en route to

---

17 Ibid., No. 20421, 26:103–104.

Dresden. With Blücher running, Napoleon's attention immediately switched to Bohemia. On the night of 22–23 August, he issued orders for the Guard, VI Corps, and I Cavalry Corps to return to Görlitz as the preliminary measure of massing the Grande Armée at Dresden. With the forces that remained in Silesia (III, V, and XI Corps and II Cavalry Corps – 100,000 men according to Napoleon's calculation), he formed the Army of the Bober commanded by Marshal Macdonald.[18]

Always seeking a decisive victory, Napoleon welcomed Schwarzenberg's advance on Dresden as an opportunity rather than a setback. He planned to concentrate 200,000 men at Dresden to confront the Army of Bohemia.[19] Little did Napoleon know that, as he made these plans, Bernadotte's Army of North Germany was holding its ground eleven miles south of Berlin at Großbeeren on 23 August 1813. The Prussians again shouldered the brunt of the combat: their losses amounted to more than 1,000 killed, wounded, and missing. Imperial casualties numbered more than 3,000 men and 14 guns. Despite the low body count, Oudinot ordered a headlong retreat that did not stop until his army reached the safety of Wittenberg on the Elbe. The Coalition's victory at Großbeeren saved Berlin and provided much-needed confidence for the Prussians.

Back in Silesia, Macdonald eagerly prepared to move against Blücher's suspected position east of the Katzbach River on 26 August. Meanwhile, Blücher, suspecting Napoleon had departed for Dresden, likewise ordered his army to resume the offensive. On that day, the Army of the Bober collided with the Army of the Silesia along the banks of the Katzbach River. In a heavy downpour, the Allies repulsed the imperials, losing fewer than 1,000 men. Macdonald's losses on the 26th are not known but his army suffered acute attrition during the ensuing retreat west to Saxony. By 1 September 1813, the Army of the Bober had lost 30,000 men and 103 guns.

Meanwhile, the Bohemian Army moved across the Saxon frontier on 22 August and stormed the imperial camp at Pirna on the 23rd. As the Silesian Army engaged the Army of the Bober on the 26th, Schwarzenberg assailed Dresden. In the midst of the engagement, Napoleon unexpectedly arrived with the Guard to repel Schwarzenberg's assault. During the night, II and VI Corps came up, increasing Napoleon's combatants to 135,000 men against 215,000 Allied soldiers. Continuing the battle on the 27th, Napoleon enveloped Schwarzenberg's left, crushing two Austrian corps. With the French also

---

18   Ibid., No. 20442, 26:115–116. Napoleon summoned Ney to join the imperial entourage, thus transferring command of III Corps to General Joseph Souham.

19   Ibid., Nos. 20445 and 20446, 26:118–120.

PROMETHEUS CHAINED, 1813–1815

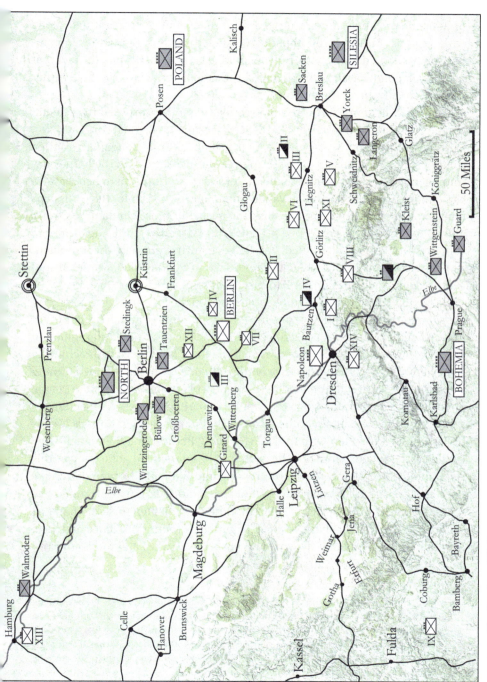

MAP 12.2 Theater of war, fall 1813

steadily working around his right, Schwarzenberg ordered a retreat. The Army of Bohemia withdrew after losing 38,000 killed, wounded, and captured, along with 40 guns. Although the imperials sustained far fewer casualties in comparison (10,000), decisive victory again evaded Napoleon. Despite the fact that he had adequate cavalry, illness forced the emperor to leave the field rather than personally direct the pursuit.

General Vandamme's I Corps followed by XIV and VI Corps led the pursuit. On the 29th, Vandamme caught one of Schwarzenberg's Russian corps at Kulm, thirty-five miles south of Dresden and just inside the Bohemian frontier. Neither side gained an advantage despite savage fighting. With the battle continuing on the 30th, Schwarzenberg's Prussian II Corps marched east to Nollendorf, directly north of Vandamme's position. While the Prussians attacked the rear of I Corps, the Russians pushed against Vandamme's front, and an Austrian corps enveloped his left. With XIV and VI Corps too distant to support, Vandamme attempted but failed to drive through the Prussians. Imperial losses on 29 and 30 August amounted to 25,000 killed, wounded, and captured along with 82 guns; Allied casualties numbered 11,000 men.[20]

Following the defeats at Großbeeren, the Katzbach, and Kulm, Napoleon considered either an offensive against Prague or another march on Berlin for his next step. Both projects sacrificed the principle of annihilating the main enemy army, which would have provided the most direct means of achieving total victory. Rather than a decisive battle with one of the three Allied armies, geographic objectives dominated the emperor's planning. Rejecting the Prague offensive, Napoleon returned to the capture of Berlin. Napoleon's objections to a march on Prague contain both reasonable military considerations as well as his continued obsession with the "master plan." Because the Bohemian Army would reach Prague before him, he could not be guaranteed possession of this geographic objective. Moreover, by crossing into Bohemia, he would sacrifice his central position and place himself at the end of a line that extended 346 miles northwest to Hamburg – a line that the same lieutenants who had just suffered defeats would have to hold in order to secure his flank and rear. Another concern was that he would be pushed westward and forced to campaign between the Elbe and the Rhine.

---

20 After surrendering, Vandamme met with Tsar Alexander, who accused the French general of being a brigand and plunderer. The Frenchman supposedly retorted: "I am neither a plunderer nor a brigand but, in any case, my contemporaries and history will not reproach me for having murdered my own father" – a reference to the widespread belief that Alexander had conspired in the murder of his father, Tsar Paul I. See Jean Baptiste Antoine Marcellin, baron de Marbot, *Mémoires du général baron de Marbot*, 3 vols (Paris, 1891), 2:375.

As for his subordinates, Napoleon judged the condition of Macdonald's army to be far more favorable than it actually was, and he did not want to leave Oudinot's army completely isolated at Wittenberg. It appeared exceedingly risky to leave these two army groups so far north of the Bohemian mountains for any length of time. The Prague operation also meant the certain loss of his garrisons in the Oder fortresses because his army "would not be on the way to Danzig." Lastly, although in his "Note" Napoleon does not evaluate the Prague option as an offensive against Schwarzenberg, it can be inferred that the emperor had convinced himself of the dangers of seeking a decisive battle in Bohemia. At the most, he would be able to assemble only 160,000 men for such an operation – not enough to achieve numerical superiority over Schwarzenberg. Consequently, he could not be guaranteed success in a second battle with the Army of Bohemia. Moreover, should the Allies avoid a confrontation, both the emperor and his main army would be further removed from the center of his operations. Although these considerations would have certainly prevented a commander schooled in the 18th-century art of war from conducting such an operation, it is hard to believe that the same man who had executed the maneuvers of the First and Second Italian Campaigns, as well as those that led to Austerlitz, Jena, and Friedland, shirked from such a challenge. Hugo Freytag-Loringhoven adds that, if he chose Berlin over Prague, "success could be far more easily attained if the emperor appeared in the north, reinforced the Army of Berlin with his Guard, and personally assumed command. If he could decisively defeat the North German Army and take Berlin, he could relieve Küstrin and Stettin, and even Danzig. Should the Allied army again invade Saxony, he hoped to return there within fourteen days to deliver a decisive blow."[21]

To Napoleon, a victory over the Army of North Germany and the timid Bernadotte appeared certain. Moreover, a northern offensive would allow him to maintain his central position close to his magazines. He deemed that the fall of Berlin would produce a moral victory that would erase the memory of Großbeeren and the Katzbach, and make a huge impression on the German princes of the Confederation of the Rhine. The Oder fortresses could be relieved by Davout's XIII Corps as it cleared the way to Danzig. Furthermore, by taking Berlin and driving to the Vistula, Napoleon envisioned the ultimate dissolution of the Bohemian Army. After the loss of their capital, he thought the Prussian contingent of Schwarzenberg's army would depart from Bohemia and make for Brandenburg. As for the Russians, they would fall back on their lines of communication as soon as a French army threatened Poland. Should Allied

---

21 H.F.P.J. Freytag-Loringhoven, *Kriegslehren nach Clausewitz aus den Feldzügen 1813 und 1814* (Berlin, 1908), 90.

resolve prove stronger and should Schwarzenberg hold his army together to lead a new offensive against Dresden, Napoleon would have a force of four corps commanded by his brother-in-law, Joachim Murat, to slow the Allied advance. As for Blücher's Army of Silesia, Napoleon underestimated the dissolution of Macdonald's Army of the Bober after its defeat on the Katzbach and so hoped the marshal could hold the line of the Neiße River. Should his lieutenants succeed, Napoleon predicted that fourteen days would suffice for him to take Berlin, resupply Stettin, and return to the Saxon theater to confront either Blücher or Schwarzenberg. Thus, the emperor decided to allow the Army of Bohemia to recover after its drubbing at Dresden, while he personally commanded the march on Berlin. He planned to lead 30,000 men from Dresden, unite with the Army of Berlin, and resume the operation against the Prussian capital.[22]

Despite these hopes, Napoleon never executed the Berlin offensive as planned. Due to events in southeast Saxony, he neither marched north nor provided reinforcements for the Army of Berlin. Blücher's pressure on Macdonald's beleaguered Army of the Bober required Napoleon's personal intervention. Ney, who replaced Oudinot as commander of the Army of Berlin on 3 September, never received word of the emperor's change of plans. Therefore, when he began his operation on the 4th, he ordered the Army of Berlin to march eastward to unite with Napoleon, who, according to Ney's information, would reach Luckau on 6 September. Instead of his emperor, Ney found the Prussian III and IV Corps of the Army of North Germany at Dennewitz on the 6th. Ney's losses amounted to 21,500 dead, wounded, and captured along with 53 guns. Prussian casualties numbered 9,700 killed and wounded. After this

---

22 "*Note sur la situation général de mes affairs*," in *CN*, No. 20492, 26:153–157. Pelet again defends Napoleon's decision: "Napoleon saw the failure of his main project, namely that on Berlin and on the lower Oder, which would have rendered him the master of North Germany and the arbiter of Europe. Oudinot and Macdonald, who had cooperated in its execution, had been beaten. The disaster of Kulm negated the victory at Dresden. Meanwhile, Oudinot's army was neither defeated nor broken; it could have continued. It was protected by the indecision of the victor. Napoleon hoped that a daring chief could take Berlin. He wanted to support the operation personally. Placing himself between Bernadotte and Blücher, he prepared to defeat the former and to stop the progress of the latter. During the month of September, the emperor sought to resume the execution of this plan; all intelligence indicated increasing advantages. The Poles and even the Lithuanians awaited us. In Austria, the party that had declared war would be easily shaken if the Russians and Prussians were forced to defend their lands. Middle Germany would remain all the more faithful. Finally, our blockaded fortresses needed to be revictualized." See Pelet, "Des principales opérations de la campagne de 1813," 344–345.

victory, the Army of North Germany pursued the wreck of the Army of Berlin to Wittenberg and Torgau on the Elbe.[23]

Napoleon's situation had become critical after less than one month of campaigning. The success of the Reichenbach Plan had depleted the ranks of the Grande Armée. Since the expiration of the armistice, the imperials had lost 150,000 men and 300 guns – an additional 50,000 names filled the sick rolls.[24] While French commanders suffered defeats at Großbeeren, the Katzbach, Kulm, and Dennewitz, the emperor raced back and forth between the Elbe and the Bober Rivers in futile attempts to achieve a decisive victory. Under normal conditions, the constant marches and countermarches would have exhausted his conscripts both mentally and physically. Yet the conditions remained far from normal. Heavy rains had washed out the roads and Cossacks menaced the lines of communication. Although the poor conditions forced Napoleon to grant his men plenty of rest, the slow starvation of the army could not be ignored. Supply shortages and the exhaustion of the Saxon countryside prompted Napoleon to write: "The army is no longer fed; to view it in any other way would be mere self-deception."[25]

The Battle of Dennewitz provided a crucial turning point in the Fall Campaign. In its aftermath, both sides changed strategy. Blücher led his Army of Silesia down the Elbe to Wartenburg, where it crossed the river on 3 October and defeated the French IV Corps. Based on an agreement with Blücher, Bernadotte also ordered his Army of North Germany to cross the Elbe and move into the Saxon theater. Blücher's decisions in early October and the efficient work of the Prussian General Staff throughout the campaign made the Battle of Leipzig possible. For his part, Napoleon made one final attempt to catch Blücher and Bernadotte south of Wittenberg. On 9 October, Napoleon and 150,000 imperial soldiers stood ready to destroy the two Allied armies in the region of Bad Düben and Dessau. Yet, both Blücher and Bernadotte escaped by retreating west across the Saale River, thus exposing Berlin and their own communications. Only a small corps of mostly Prussian militia stood between Napoleon and Berlin, and the long-awaited execution of the "master plan." Moving north over the Elbe would have certainly saved the garrisons in Torgau, Wittenberg, Magdeburg, Küstrin, and Stettin, as well as Davout's corps at Hamburg. Murat's four corps would have been able to escape eastward from Leipzig to Torgau. In a virtual *coup de théâtre*, Napoleon could have exchanged places with the Allies, stranding the Bohemian, Silesian, and North German

---

23   See Leggiere, *Napoleon and Berlin*, 189–228.
24   Chandler, *Campaigns of Napoleon*, 916.
25   *CN*, No. 20619, 26:236–238.

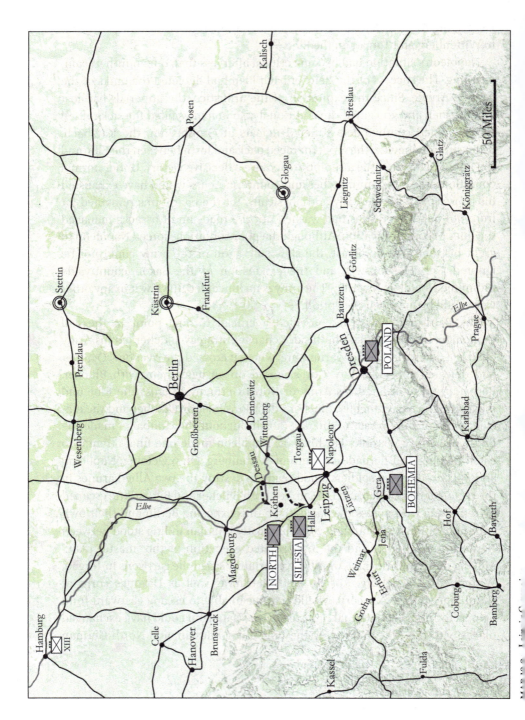

Armies in the depleted Saxon countryside, and holding the right bank of the Elbe against them from Hamburg to Dresden. Yet, at this juncture, Napoleon decided to draw the Allies to Leipzig for an epic struggle: the Battle of Nations. Knowing that Schwarzenberg was slowly advancing on this city, the emperor accepted the fact that he would soon be surrounded. After months of chasing an elusive enemy who had smashed his lieutenants, Napoleon welcomed the prospect of a showdown.

Leipzig

As Blücher's Army of Silesia approached Leipzig from the northwest, and Schwarzenberg steadily advanced from the south, Bennigsen's Army of Poland marched from the southeast with 50,000 men. Bernadotte planned to concentrate his army northwest of Leipzig at Landsberg on the 16th. Due to his phlegmatic habits, which included sleeping until noon, his staff did not issue orders until 11:00 AM on the 16th. As a result, the concentration did not occur until that evening. Napoleon concentrated 177,000 men around the Saxon city by the evening of the 14th. Planning for the opportunity that had eluded him since his victory at Dresden six weeks earlier, Napoleon no longer worried about keeping the Allied armies apart. Both sides spent much of the 15th probing and planning for battle on the 16th. Napoleon did not intend to fight a defensive battle. Instead, he planned to destroy Schwarzenberg's army between the Pleiße and the Parthe Rivers. The Allies also planned to launch their main attack in the southern sector as Blücher's army advanced on Leipzig from the northwest. A small operation also would be conducted against the west side of Leipzig by an Austrian corps of 19,000 men.

On the 16th, the Silesian and Bohemian Armies attacked Leipzig. Heavy combat ensued along the northern, western, and southern sectors of the front with struggles centering on Möckern, Lindenau, and Wachau. Blücher's unexpected arrival and the ensuing confusion robbed Napoleon of the forces he planned to employ against Schwarzenberg. Had the 30,000 men of XIV Corps that Napoleon had left at Dresden been present, he most likely would have crushed Schwarzenberg. By the end of the fighting on the 16th, the Allied attacks in the Wachau and Lindenau sectors had failed, but Blücher's Prussian I Corps had fought a savage battle to achieve victory at Möckern. French losses for the 16th neared 25,000 men, while the Allies lost 30,000: an ominous ratio as Napoleon's reinforcements would only increase the Grande Armée to 200,000 men and 900 guns, while the Allies would reach 300,000 men and 1,500 guns with the arrival of the North German and Polish Armies.

After the fighting ended on the 16th, Napoleon considered a retreat to the Rhine. Although he issued preliminary orders to secure the bridge over the Saale, he should have done more. Rather than throw additional bridges over the Elster and the Pleiße Rivers, the emperor opted for a retreat over a single bridge through the west side of the city. Moreover, a shortage of ammunition became a factor; dwindling reserves would not support another day of intense fighting. Further discouraging news made a retreat inevitable. A force of 30,000 Bavarians posted on the Inn River and commanded by General Karl Philipp von Wrede had made common cause with the Austrians and were preparing to march against Napoleon's lines of communication with France. Despite this consideration, Napoleon postponed the retreat until the 18th in the hope that the Allied forces surrounding Leipzig might blunder. He also attempted to divide the Allies by offering an armistice to his father-in-law, Emperor Francis of Austria. The peace initiative not only failed, but also served to strengthen the Coalition's resolve by convincing the Allies that Napoleon was spent. The heavy fighting of the day – particularly the events at Möckern – should have convinced Napoleon to retreat but, as historian F.L. Petre notes, "the Emperor Napoleon was now, to a great extent, the master of General Bonaparte, and the Emperor could not bear to yield what practically meant his dominion in Germany, though the General saw that to do this was the only hope."[26]

Minimal fighting occurred on the 17th as both sides rested to renew the struggle on the following day. On the morning of the 18th, 295,000 Coalition soldiers supported by 1,466 cannon prepared to assault Leipzig. The Allies planned to launch six massive attacks along the entire front. Napoleon stood in the middle with 160,000 men. Early on the 18th, he contracted his southern front by a few miles in preparation for the retreat. The French position catered solely to the defensive, and allowed Napoleon to quickly bolster weak spots. The Allies facilitated the French defensive by attacking concentrically along the entire front, rather than concentrating their superior combat power on one point.[27] Casualty figures vary for both sides on the 18th. The Coalition probably sustained another 20,000 casualties, while the French suffered approximately

---

26 F.L. Petre, *Napoleon's Last Campaign in Germany* (London, 1912; reprint, London, 1993), 353.

27 Blame for this can again be attributed to Bernadotte's refusal to accelerate his march. "Provided the French are beaten," he supposedly sneered, "it is of no difference to me whether I or my army take part and, of the two, I had much rather we did not." Petre notes that "for days past he had been hanging back; even on the 18th he might easily have been up three or four hours before he was. Then there would have been an overwhelming force against Napoleon's left on the Parthe. Even when he did arrive, Bernadotte acted very feebly. His Swedes did practically nothing": ibid., 370.

10,000 killed and wounded. Realizing that he could no longer hold Leipzig, Napoleon ordered the retreat to commence late on the 18th. Germany was lost.

Napoleon's dwindling ammunition reserves and the overall weight of Allied numerical superiority decided the issue. That night, the baggage and part of the Reserve Cavalry departed over the Lindenau causeway and crossed the Elster River en route to the Rhine. At 2:00 AM on the 19th, the Reserve Artillery followed by the Guard, IV Cavalry Corps, X Corps, II Corps, and II Cavalry Corps began the retreat. A rearguard of 30,000 troops remained behind to hold Leipzig until the rest of the army escaped. The French lines thinned before sunrise, but the departing troops left numerous campfires to deceive the Allies. Napoleon himself eventually made his way out of Leipzig around 11:00 AM on the 19th. Napoleon also dispatched orders for the garrisons of Torgau and Wittenberg to capitulate as long as the men were granted free exit. The garrison at Dresden had to escape if it could. To the west, IV Corps had already reached the Saale with orders to build additional bridges. Napoleon also dictated orders to summon the French National Guard to defend the country.[28]

As the sky began to grey on the morning of the 19th, Coalition forces prepared to storm Leipzig. Schwarzenberg's unimaginative orders called for his four armies to concentrically advance on Leipzig from the north, east, southeast, and south. Although the remaining defenders withdrew into Leipzig's suburbs, the Allies did nothing to stop the Grande Armée's westward retreat to the Rhine. Rather than annihilate the enemy army, Schwarzenberg remained fixated on capturing Leipzig. According to estimates, the 30,000 defenders held a perimeter of 6,500 yards, or four men per yard. Regardless, resistance collapsed in all sectors of the city by noon. Just before 1:00 PM, a tremendous explosion rocked the city and shattered the hopes of escape for the remaining defenders. Napoleon had ordered the bridge over the Elster mined and destroyed once the last French units had cleared the city. In a fit of confusion, the unfortunate corporal who had been left behind to execute the orders became alarmed by the approach of some Russian skirmishers and lit the fuse. Soldiers, horses, and wagons lined the bridge when it blew. Once the charges detonated, "the air was filled with flying fragments of the bridge, with broken parts of wagons, and with the limbs of horses and men, which descended in a ghastly shower on the whole neighborhood." Thousands of French soldiers found themselves stranded in Leipzig. Some tried to swim to safety and drowned in the process.[29] The battle ended after staggering losses. Allied

---

28   Chandler, *Campaigns of Napoleon*, 935; Petre, *Napoleon's Last Campaign*, 368, 373–375, 378.
29   Petre, *Napoleon's Last Campaign*, 380.

casualties totaled an estimated 54,000 men. The Russians suffered the highest casualty rate at 22,605 men, followed by 16,033 Prussians, and 14,958 Austrians – the Swedes sustained 178 casualties. Napoleon lost approximately 73,000 men, including 30,000 prisoners and 5,000 German deserters, as well as 325 guns and 40,000 muskets. Of the marshals, Prince Josef Anton Poniatowski drowned in the Elster just twelve hours after receiving his baton on the battlefield, while Ney, Macdonald, and Marmont were wounded. The Allies also captured thirty-six French generals.

For the remainder of October 1813 and into early November, the Coalition's Bohemian and Silesian Armies pursued Napoleon to the middle Rhine, but the Army of North Germany split. One Russian and one Prussian corps insured the collapse of the Confederation of the Rhine by marching through the heart of Germany, while Bernadotte led the rest of his forces north to contend with Davout's XIII Corps at Hamburg. Reaching the Rhine in the second week of November, the Allies convened a council of war at Frankfurt to plan the invasion of France. Deliberations lasted for the better part of the next six weeks. In the midst of the military planning, the Allies offered Napoleon a conditional peace based on the "Frankfurt Proposals." Accordingly, Napoleon would have remained ruler of a France that included the natural frontiers of the Rhine, Alps, and Pyrenees. Although these terms offered France territory which generations of Frenchmen had died in vain attempting to secure, Napoleon rejected the offer. Napoleon himself wrote: "Europe seems to offer peace, but she does not sincerely wish it. You believe that by humiliating ourselves we shall disarm her; you are mistaken. The more yielding we are, the more exacting she will become, and from demand to demand she will lead us on to terms of peace that we cannot accept. She offers the line of the Rhine and the Alps, and even some part of Piedmont. These certainly are favorable conditions; but if we appear willing to accept, she will soon propose the frontiers of 1790. Well, can I accept them – I, to whom the natural frontiers have been entrusted by the Republic?"[30]

During a council of war on 7 December 1813, the Austrians suggested that the majority of the Bohemian Army cross the upper Rhine at Basel, Switzerland, to bypass the sources of the Moselle and the Meuse Rivers, and then advance northwest between the Vosges and Jura Mountains to the plateau of Langres. Essentially, this plan would allow the Bohemian Army to avoid most of the French fortresses that guarded the Rhine. In addition, by making for the gap

---

[30] Quoted in Adolphe Thiers, *History of the Consulate and the Empire of France Under Napoleon* (Philadelphia, 1893–1894), 9:282–283; Napoleon to Caulaincourt, 4 January 1814, in CN, No. 21062, 27:10; Kissinger, *A World Restored*, 101.

between the Jura and Vosges Mountains, the majority of the army would not have to cross difficult terrain in the midst of winter. By extending his left wing south, Schwarzenberg could sever French communication with Italy through the Simplon and Mt. Cenis Passes. Such a threat could even induce the French to withdraw from Italy, thus allowing the Austrian army to pursue across the Alps, invade southern France, and link Schwarzenberg's left with Wellington's right. Regarding logistics, the troubling prospect of feeding 200,000 men in hostile territory during the winter influenced the campaign plan considerably. "It was emphasized," explains one contemporary, "that the weakest point of the French frontier always had been acknowledged to be on the side of Switzerland; that Austria had suffered too much in the first years of the Revolutionary War by operating from the Netherlands and the Lower Rhine; that the natural line for her to adopt was the one proposed, receiving her supplies from her own provinces by the Danube, and the direct communications [with Austria] through Bavaria."[31]

In the meantime, elements of the Army of North Germany would liberate the Low Countries, while the Army of Silesia would cross the middle Rhine and proceed through Metz to attract the enemy's attention and facilitate Schwarzenberg's march. The estimated timetables called for Blücher to arrive at Metz by 15 January – the same day that the Army of Bohemia should reach Langres. The Austrian General Staff claimed that the plateau of Langres dominated France and would allow the Allies to gain control of the entire country. The Meuse, the Marne, and the tributaries of the Seine all flowed from Langres to the North Sea, while the tributary of the Saône flowed from the plateau to the Mediterranean. An army that crossed the upper Rhine could skirt the Vosges and the Moselle, and circumvent the Meuse and the Marne at their sources. By taking a position at Langres to threaten the French interior, the Austrians hoped to avoid a bloody battle and force Napoleon to the peace table. Both contemporaries and historians have passed judgement on the Allied invasion plan and the objective of Langres. Paris became the goal of further operations, but the details of these operations would be determined at a later date. Based on this plan, the Allies invaded France across a front that stretched from the North Sea to Switzerland.

---

31   John Fane, *Memoir of the Operations of the Allied Armies, Under Prince Schwarzenberg and Marshal Blücher, During the Latter End of 1813 and the Year 1814* (London, 1822), 65–66.

Invasion of France 1814

Following Leipzig, the remnants of the Grande Armée of 1813 retreated across the middle Rhine at Mainz to defend France's natural frontiers. Fewer than 60,000 soldiers returned in early November 1813. Although the emperor continued on to Paris, he left his shattered army on the left bank of the historic river in the hands of his equally shattered marshals, who received the impossible task of defending the eastern frontier from Switzerland to the North Sea. Missives containing absurd promises and calculations flowed from the emperor's headquarters throughout November.[32] A mixture of threats, verbal abuse, encouragement, and twisted logic followed after the Allies crossed the Rhine on 20 December. Regardless of the method of persuasion, Napoleon failed to bolster the resolve of his chief lieutenants. By 24 January 1814, the forces he had entrusted to his marshals in early November stood on the Marne River after a headlong retreat that resulted in the abandonment of Alsace and Lorraine, as well as Franche Comté, Holland, and Belgium.

Historians have heaped much blame on the marshals and deservingly so. While arguments of strategic and operational incompetence are closer to the mark at this stage of the campaign rather than self-serving desires to retain titles and wealth, the marshals clearly failed at almost every turn in the crucial first month of the Allied invasion. Accepting the premise that the marshals did fail raises the question of whether they had a chance to succeed in the first place and, if not, where the blame lies. Ultimately, the answer is that the marshals did not have a chance to succeed, and blame must be attributed to Napoleon. The sheer size of the two Allied armies that overran Alsace and Lorraine – the Bohemian Army and the Silesian Army – offers an oversimplified and incomplete answer as to why the marshals failed. The two marshals charged with the defense of Alsace and Lorraine – Victor and Marmont – were placed in an impossible situation before the first Allied soldier crossed the Rhine in their respective sectors. Specifically, the reasons for the loss of Alsace and Lorraine can be found in Napoleon's preoccupation with the Low Countries. It mattered little what Victor and Marmont did or failed to do, the emperor tied their hands by ignoring the concentration of Allied forces on

---

32 CN, No. 20878, 26:418: "Tell him [Macdonald]," Napoleon instructed Berthier, "that 600,000 conscripts, almost all men thirty years of age, are in movement; numerous detachments already have arrived in the depots and the armies will be promptly formed." See also Berthier to Macdonald, 13 December 1813, SHAT, C¹⁷ 183: "The moment of crisis has passed, 80,000 uniformed, armed, and equipped conscripts are on the march to reinforce the regiments of the various army corps; 300,000 other conscripts are heading to the regimental depots."

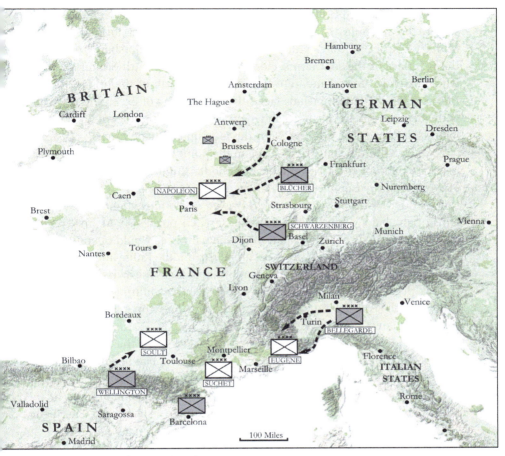

MAP 12.4   Invasion of France 1813–1814

the upper Rhine and directing his precious reserves to the lower Rhine. Consequently, the mistakes that cost Napoleon control of the eastern provinces were made before the invasion began.

To oversee the mobilization of France, Napoleon remained at Paris during the Allied invasion but formed a cordon mainly along the left bank of the Rhine with the remains of his army. He divided his frontier from Switzerland to the North Sea into three sectors and placed a marshal in command of each.[33] Macdonald held the 25th Military District, which stretched 185 miles from

[33]   CN, No. 20858, 26:497; Berthier to Marmont, Macdonald, Victor, Clarke, and Kellermann, 5 November 1813, SHAT, C¹⁷ 182.

Koblenz to Zwolle in Holland, with XI Corps.[34] Marmont received the middle sector: the 110 miles between Koblenz and Landau that formed the 26th Military District. Victor established his headquarters at Strasbourg to oversee the 138 miles of the southern sector of the frontier: the 5th Military District, which extended from Landau to Huningue, just north of the bridge over the Rhine at Basel.[35] The marshals faced the grim reality of executing their task with effectives amounting to 56,000 men; the absolute number of French combatants in France and the Low Countries is estimated to be a mere 154,000.[36]

Napoleon's initial concern focused on the point where the Allied pursuit of his army had halted in November: the middle Rhine between Koblenz and Mainz. For this reason, he placed II, IV, V, and VI Corps and II, III, and V Cavalry Corps under Marmont's command. However, Allied movements all along the entire right bank of the Rhine kept the French puzzled.[37] At first, reports strongly indicated that the Coalition's principal forces would operate against Holland while the Austrian army occupied the middle Rhine and the Russian army moved up the Rhine to establish a cordon as far as the Swiss border. These reports, provided by both civilian and military sources, affirmed the emperor's belief that the Allies planned to mask the middle and upper Rhine to operate against the Low Countries.

Napoleon certainly had good reason for concern over the Low Countries. Behind Macdonald, the cauldron of nationalist unrest had begun to bubble in the German, Dutch, and Belgian *départements* of the empire. In early November popular revolt against French rule fomented in Holland's major cities as the cries "*Vive Orange*" and "*Orange boven*" spread from Amsterdam to The Hague. Unfortunately for Macdonald, the 14,000-man French occupation force in Holland could neither man the Dutch forts nor quell the growing insurrection. To make matters worse, Prussian and Russian forces detached from the Army of North Germany were approaching the Dutch frontier. Aided by Dutch insurgents and Belgian smugglers, Russian light troops and Cossacks moved

---

34 Berthier to Macdonald, 1, November 1813, and Orders, 7 November 1813, SHAT, C¹⁷ 182; *CN*, Nos. 20845 and 20869, 26:392–393, 411.

35 Berthier to Nansouty, Kellermann, Sorbier, and Clarke, 3 November 1813, SHAT, C¹⁷ 182; Auguste Frédéric Louis Viesse de Marmont, duc de Raguse, *Mémoires du maréchal Marmont, duc de Raguse de 1792 à 1841: imprimés sur le manuscrit original de l'auteur*, 9 vols (Paris, 1857), 6:11; *CN*, No. 20857, 26:406–407.

36 Approximately 36,000 troops held the fortresses along the Rhine and facing the Swiss frontier. Eleven divisions of Imperial Guard numbering 28,000 men were spread among Paris, Brussels, Liège, Luxembourg, and Thionville. An additional 20,000 men occupied the fortresses of Holland and Belgium, where French field units amounted to 14,000 men.

37 Berthier to Marmont, 12 November 1813, SHAT, C¹⁷ 183; Marmont to Napoleon, 14 November 1813, AN, AF IV 1663A plaquette 2.

unopposed into central Holland. News that Russian forces had crossed the frontier sparked a revolt in Amsterdam on the night of 14–15 November; the Russians arrived nine days later.

In response, Napoleon transferred II Cavalry Corps (2,500 sabers) from Marmont's army group to Macdonald's command and shifted Marmont's III Cavalry Corps (2,000 sabers) and V Corps (3,000 bayonets) north to Koblenz.[38] Despite these measures, the mobile forces at Macdonald's immediate disposal to cover a front of almost 125 miles amounted to only 3,300 cavalry, 3,500 infantry, and 40 guns of XI Corps and II Cavalry Corps. Consequently, Napoleon also transferred command of V Corps from Marmont to Macdonald.[39] More transfers followed as Napoleon's concern over Holland increased. On the same day that V Corps departed, Marmont received instructions to turn over command of III Cavalry Corps to Macdonald.[40]

At the end of the cordon, Victor initially had nothing more than a handful of National Guards and conscripts to defend the region where Schwarzenberg's 200,000 men would eventually cross the Rhine. Although that remained several weeks away, Allied troops besieged Kehl opposite Strasbourg; daily skirmishing around the bridgehead ensued from 3 November.[41] On 11 November

---

38   Berthier to Sébastiani and Arrighi, 6 November 1813, and Berthier to Charpentier and Albert, 7 November 1813, SHAT, C¹⁷ 182.

39   Berthier to Sébastiani, Macdonald, and Marmont, 18 November 1813, SHAT, C¹⁷ 183; Napoleon to Marmont, 18 November 1813, in Marmont, *Mémoires*, 6:77–78; CN, Nos. 20917, 20921, and 20927, 26:445, 449, 451. By 1 December Marmont had 19,777 infantry, 10,129 cavalry, and 66 guns at his disposal. Unless reinforcements arrived quickly, this number could be expected to decline rapidly due to the army's horrible health: the sick list numbered 17,058. See François Armand Édouard Lefebvre de Béhaine, *Campagne de France*, 4 vols (Paris, 1913–1934), 2:121–127.

40   CN, No. 20943, 26:468–469. The V and XI Corps and II and III Cavalry Corps now formed Macdonald's "army." Moreover, the emperor wanted even more combat power shifted toward Macdonald. He pulled back the Young Guard divisions from the Rhine to Kaiserslautern. On 25 November he directed the 12th and 13th Guard Voltigeur Regiments (1,600 men each) in Metz to depart for Brussels as soon as General Philibert-Jean-Baptiste-François Curial completed their organization, which included removing all native Belgian and Dutch soldiers. At Brussels the 2 regiments would unite with the 12th and 13th Guard Regiments to form General François Roguet's 3rd Young Guard Tirailleur Division, which Napoleon projected would consist of 6,000 infantry, 200 cavalry, and 1 battery of 8 guns. He also ordered General Charles Lefebvre-Desnouettes 2nd Guard Cavalry Division to immediately depart for Brussels. Clarke was instructed to ensure that a battery of horse artillery left Metz to join this division in Brussels.

41   On 2 November 1813 General Jean-Baptiste Broussier was named *commandant supérior* of Strasbourg and Kehl, which were connected by a pontoon bridge. The French successively defended Kehl against Bavarian, Württemberger, Badenese, and finally Russian troops.

Victor warned the master of an enemy mass of 50,000 men moving toward Mannheim.[42] Napoleon, however, remained convinced that the main Allied attack would come from the north across the lower Rhine and through the Low Countries. Several days before learning of the Dutch revolt and of the arrival of Prussian and Russian forces in Holland, Napoleon informed Marmont: "It appears that our movement must be made toward Holland, and that the enemy has intentions in this direction."[43]

The march of the Bohemian Army to the southern districts of the Grand Duchy of Baden did not go unnoticed by the French marshals. Both Marmont and Victor received an overwhelming number of reports from civil and military officials. Between 16 and 24 November they provided Napoleon persuasive evidence regarding the movement of considerable Allied forces up the Rhine. On the 18th, the emperor read Marmont's report from 15 November which should have considerably influenced his views. The brief contained critical news of Allied troop movements provided by French prisoners returning to France via Frankfurt. "The general rumor in Frankfurt is that the Russians will ascend the Rhine to Basel and that the tsar himself will go to this city," relates the marshal; "it appears that the troops are in full march toward this objective. In my opinion, if the enemy wants to cross the Rhine at this time of the year, the city of Basel appears to be of the greatest importance to him."[44] Regardless, this crucial report, as well as Marmont's statements regarding an enemy corps of 15,000 to 20,000 men that passed Kehl and continued toward the upper Rhine, did little to change the emperor's convictions.[45] "The enemy probably will not attempt to cross the Rhine," responded Napoleon on the 20th, "so allow your troops some rest and do not torment yourself; if the enemy crosses the Rhine, he will cross the lower Rhine."[46] On 24 November Marmont reiterated his belief that possession of the Basel bridge appeared to be a principal Allied objective.[47] On 9 December he again reported that the general movement of the Allied army continued in the direction of the upper Rhine.[48] This letter appears to be Marmont's last attempt to persuade Napoleon. Subsequent reports indicate that the marshal had finally accepted the emperor's

---

42   Victor to Berthier, 11 November 1813, SHAT, C² 301.
43   *CN*, No. 20900, 26:433.
44   Marmont to Napoleon, 15 November 1813, AN, AF IV 1663^A plaquette 2; Lefebvre de Béhaine, *Campagne de France*, 2:91, 307.
45   Marmont to Napoleon, 19 November 1813, AN, AF IV 1663^A plaquette 2.
46   *CN*, No. 20927, 26:451.
47   Marmont to Napoleon, 24 November 1813, AN, AF IV 1663^A plaquette 2.
48   Marmont to Napoleon, 9 December 1813, AN, AF IV 1663^A plaquette 2.

assumption that the Allies probably would not attempt to cross the Rhine.[49] According to his summary report of 14 December, in which he noted the departure of a siege train destined for the Austrian army at Basel, the marshal showed little concern about the security of his own front. In fact, he no longer mentioned the forces before him and evidently did not know the Silesian Army had received considerable reinforcements.[50]

In Victor's sector, the intelligence he forwarded to Paris of Allied troop movements toward Switzerland likewise failed to influence the emperor.[51] Despite the marshal's requests for manpower, Napoleon insisted on employing II Corps and V Cavalry Corps on the middle Rhine and closer to Macdonald. To Marmont he reiterated his belief that Victor should be content with the National Guard to defend Alsace.[52] Yet throughout November, the marshal received numerous reports of Allied movements and intentions. By the end of the month, Allied columns accompanied by siege and bridging equipment could be seen on the main highway leading to the Swiss frontier. Unlike Marmont, no letter from Paris could convince Victor that the main Coalition armies intended to invade the Low Countries, especially after French intelligence confirmed Schwarzenberg's march up the Rhine toward the Swiss frontier.[53]

---

49 CN, No. 20927, 26:251.
50 Lefebvre de Béhaine, *Campagne de France*, 2:95–96.
51 Victor to Napoleon, 14 November 1813, AN, AF IV 1663^A plaquette 1^{II}. On 14 November the commandant of the Bas-Rhin Departement, General Jean-Adam Schramm, informed Victor that Bavarian troops from a corps of 20,000 men, which formed part of the Austro-Bavarian army, had occupied Plittersdorf on the right bank of the Rhine opposite Seltz. According to Schramm's intelligence, this corps had billeted in and around Rastatt on the 13th before continuing its march that morning on the road to Offenburg, where the surrounding hills offered a dominating position to observe Kehl or launch an operation against the French bridgehead. Another corps of similar size was expected to arrive that evening in Rastatt; bridging equipment would supposedly reach the town around the 17th or 18th. Shramm expressed his belief that the Allies intended to cross the Rhine at Ft. Vauban. From Landau, Colonel Jean-François Verdun warned that enemy movements appeared to have Ft. Vauban as the immediate objective. Victor forwarded this information to the emperor, who received it on the afternoon of the 16th.
52 CN, No. 20921, 26:449. "Unless it is absolutely necessary," wrote Napoleon to Marmont, "the division of II Corps must remain under your command. The duc de Bellune would like to have it for himself, but he has no reason to fear for Strasbourg. The enemy would be crazy if he attacked from this direction. It is more natural to think the enemy will turn at Cologne, Wesel, and Koblenz."
53 Lefebvre de Béhaine, *Campagne de France*, 2:309–311. Since the 17th spies had revealed preparations in and around Mannheim to accommodate a large troop mass as well as the headquarters of the Russian tsar. Construction of pontoon bridges on the Neckar River, which joined the Rhine at Mannheim, made it apparent that an Allied crossing would be

On learning that a functionary from the war ministry, Colonel Jacques-Henry Baltazar, was traveling from Worms to Paris, Victor met with him at Strasbourg. Baltazar informed the marshal that, according to a reliable spy, Schwarzenberg had left Mannheim on 1 December en route for Karlsruhe. From there the Austrian commander and the troops accompanying him would proceed to Freiburg-im-Breisgau. Meanwhile, on the other side of the Black Forest, large enemy columns were moving toward eastern Switzerland. Victor then met with Louis-Pierre-Édouard Bignon, the former French minister in Warsaw, who was returning to France with diplomatic immunity. Traveling between Rastatt and Kehl, Bignon observed what he described as seemingly endless columns of Austrian troops, artillery, and bridging equipment en route to Freiburg-im-Breisgau to join the Austro-Bavarian corps, whose forward units already had reached Huningue.

The information gleaned from Baltazar and Bignon provided Victor with compelling evidence to present Napoleon. In a 5 December letter to the emperor, Victor claimed that strong Austrian columns were en route to Freiburg-im-Breisgau with bridging equipment to cross the Rhine between Neuf-Brisach and Huningue. He also believed the Allies intended to violate Swiss territory in order to occupy Franche-Comté. Possession of Basel's stone bridge would be indispensable to the Allies since drift ice on the Rhine would render pontoons unreliable and risky. The marshal warned Napoleon that the Swiss would open their borders to the Allies and that he had no troops to spare to defend Switzerland.[54] On the next day, the head of Napoleon's intelligence service, Élisabeth-Louis-François Lelorgne d'Ideville, forwarded the emperor a summary of the reports from the Rhine frontier. According to D'Ideville, Austrian and Russian troops with contingents from Baden and Württemberg, preceded by thousands of Cossacks, were continuing to march toward

---

attempted near that city. Other sources claimed the tsar would continue upstream from Mannheim to Karlsruhe and that a corps of approximately 40,000 men would assemble at Rastatt and attempt to cross the Rhine between Landau and Strasbourg. Moreover, it was no secret that the tsar of Russia, kaiser of Austria, king of Prussia, their ministers, and Schwarzenberg remained at Frankfurt; neither the Russo-Prussian Guard and Reserve nor the Austrian Reserve had moved. Newspapers from Basel appeared to answer why the Allied high command remained at Frankfurt. According to the media, Schwarzenberg's army would cross the Rhine at Oppenheim and attack Mainz along both banks of the Rhine, while Blücher's army moved to Koblenz. The Austro-Bavarian army supported by 20,000 Cossacks would make a diversion in Upper Alsace.

54 Victor to Napoleon, 5 December 1813, AN, AF IV 1663^A plaquette 1^II; Lefebvre de Béhaine, *Campagne de France*, 2:314–315. "They know the weakness of our resources," declared Victor, "and they do not expect to encounter any difficulties other than those presented by the river."

Switzerland along the highway that ran parallel to the Black Forest. With all this information at his disposal, it is difficult to determine why General Bonaparte ignored Allied preparations to cross the upper Rhine.[55]

On 10 December Victor warned Paris that the Allies appeared poised to immediately cross the Rhine between Neuf-Brisach and Huningue.[56] Two days later travelers arriving from Lörrach informed the marshal that the enemy army intended to cross the Rhine near Huningue, probably at Basel. As this news confirmed his suspicions, the marshal doubled his efforts to draw Napoleon's attention to the upper Rhine.[57] The rumors that reached Strasbourg on 13 December placed the Allied sovereigns at Rastatt awaiting the result of the passage of the Rhine, which would be "effected in a few days between Huningue and Basel." According to Victor, the 9 December newspapers from Karlsruhe indicated that the 60,000-man "Russian Reserve Army" had started marching through Germany toward the Rhine five days earlier.[58] His reports finally forced the emperor to consider the upper Rhine and the defense of Alsace. Realizing that Victor required more than National Guard units to defend his sector, Napoleon transferred command of 11 Corps and v Cavalry Corps from Marmont to Victor.[59] Indicative of the extent to which Marmont's reports ignored Blücher's Silesian Army, the emperor no longer considered the middle Rhine threatened. Conversely, the situation in the Low Countries also robbed Marmont of his reserve. On 20 December he learned that the emperor had ordered the Guard divisions to move from Trier to Namur.[60] With the

---

55   Lefebvre de Béhaine, *Campagne de France*, 2:94–95.

56   Vieuville to Victor, 9 December 1813, and Victor to Napoleon, 10 December 1813, AN, AF IV 1663^A plaquette 1^{II}. Also on the 10th Victor received a letter from the Prefect Auguste-Joseph de la Vieuville of the Haut-Rhin Department that contained several details. According to Vieuville, the Allies had received considerable reinforcements on the right bank including numerous pieces of artillery. Support personnel could be seen assembling bridging equipment at Muhlheim, opposite Chalampé, described by Vieuville as one of the easiest points of passage. "He has severely prohibited all communication between the inhabitants on the right bank with those on the left," wrote the prefect, "which makes one suppose that he is thinking of an attempt to cross. He has started establishing batteries all along the line ... The enemy troops are composed almost exclusively of Austrian infantry and Russian cavalry. This hostile demonstration spreads fear all along the left bank." Victor included Vieuville's letter with his report to Napoleon on the following day: Victor to Berthier, 10 December 1813, SHAT, C^2 164.

57   Victor to Napoleon, 12 December 1813, AN, AF IV 1663^A plaquette 1^{II}.

58   Victor to Berthier, 13 December 1813, SHAT, C^2 164: "The news I received today indicates the concentration of a large enemy army on the upper Rhine and its plan to immediately cross this river, [which] confirms all that I have reported up until now."

59   Berthier to Marmont, 7 December 1813, SHAT, C^{17} 183.

60   Berthier to Marmont, 17 December 1813, SHAT, C^{17} 183. This included the 1st Old Guard Division, the Old Guard Cavalry Division, and the Reserve Artillery. In addition, the 2nd

Guard's departure, no troops remained near the middle Rhine to support Marmont's forces in case of an attack in his sector.

On 21 December Victor's reports and incessant admonitions regarding the threat to Alsace produced more results in Paris; Napoleon finally conceded the real possibility that the Allies would attempt to cross the upper Rhine. Unaware that Schwarzenberg's army was in the midst of crossing the river that very day, Napoleon issued a long series of directives entitled "Orders," which should be viewed as preliminary measures for the *eventual* defense of Alsace and Franche-Comté. He wanted Marmont to shift VI Corps and I Cavalry Corps south to Landau, leaving IV Corps to guard Mainz and his line of communication.[61] Nevertheless, the majority of these "Orders" concerned the ongoing reorganization of the army. Regarding Victor, Napoleon offered nothing further that can be interpreted as a response to the marshal's numerous warnings of a massive Allied operation along the upper Rhine.[62]

News that an Allied army of 160,000 men was crossing the Rhine at Basel reached Paris late on the 24th in the form of a report dated 20 December from the French minister in Switzerland. Later that same night, Marshal Berthier reiterated the emperor's instructions from the 21st for Marmont to establish his headquarters at Landau and to move VI Corps and I Cavalry Corps up the Rhine. "It is true that the enemy has taken Basel and will cross to the left bank there," confirmed Berthier.[63] On 26 December, Berthier sent Marmont another grave missive: the enemy had reached Mulhouse on the 23rd. "You will march to support the duc de Bellune [Victor]. His Majesty believes you have started your movement to Landau. It is of the utmost importance to support the duc de Bellune." Berthier also requested an update of Marmont's musters: the emperor wanted to know how many men the marshal could move into upper Alsace. The hint of desperation in Berthier's letter reveals the importance Napoleon placed on Marmont's intervention in Alsace. Incredibly, the emperor paid little heed to Blücher. Willing to denude the middle Rhine of VI Corps and I Cavalry Corps, Napoleon placed the defense of the 26th Military District solely in the hands of the disease-ridden IV Corps at Mainz.[64]

Old Guard Division and the 1st and 2nd Young Guard Divisions were instructed to move deeper into the French interior.

61 Berthier to Marmont, 21 December 1813, SHAT, C^{17} 183.

62 *CN*, No. 21,024, 26:521; Berthier to Victor, 25 December 1813, SHAT, C^{17} 183. Two days later, and before he received Victor's report of the Allied movement across the Rhine, the emperor focused his attention on the possibility of military operations in Franche-Comté and Alsace.

63 Berthier to Marmont, 21 and 24 December 1813, SHAT, C^{17} 183.

64 Berthier to Marmont, 26 December 1813, SHAT, C^{17} 183.

At Mainz on the night of the 27th, Marmont received Berthier's letter of the 24th directing VI Corps and I Cavalry Corps to Landau. The marshal issued the corresponding orders, but timing became an issue. Marmont could do nothing until the divisions of IV Corps and 1st Honor Guard Regiment relieved the divisions of VI Corps and I Cavalry Corps along the left bank. He figured that at least eight days were needed to assemble his corps at Landau and reach Strasbourg.[65] On the morning of the 29th, Marmont received the letter Berthier penned at 3:00 AM on the 26th containing the stirring cry: "It is of the utmost importance to support the duc de Bellune." Marmont informed Victor that relief was on the way.[66] Delaying his general movement to conduct reconnaissance on the 30th, Marmont finally commenced his march on the 31st. Early on 1 January the Silesian Army crossed the Rhine at Koblenz, Kaub, and Mannheim. Blücher's offensive across the middle Rhine caught Marmont in the midst of moving his two corps south to assist Victor. The old Prussian shattered Marmont's command and control, forcing the marshal to fall back consecutively to the Saar, the Moselle, the Meuse, and ultimately the Marne.

On the evening of 2 January news reached Strasbourg that the Silesian Army had crossed the Rhine at three points further downstream and severed Victor's communication with Marmont. This shocking news brought the realization that he would not be able to unite with Marmont's forces.[67] Just four days later and after claiming to have "examined all the disadvantages," Victor decided to immediately turn west, cross the Vosges through the Donon Pass, and forsake Alsace. To prevent being cut off from the French interior and believing he could better defend the mountain passes from the western slopes, Victor issued orders at 1:00 AM for II Corps and V Cavalry Corps to evacuate Alsace.[68] The final stage of this inglorious drama occurred eight days later. Unable to hold the passes through the Vosges, Victor retreated to Nancy, where he arrived on the 14th. Believing that Marmont's retreat from the Saar to the Moselle rendered his position at Nancy untenable by threatening his line of retreat, Victor abandoned the capital of Lorraine and likewise fell back to the Moselle.

Although the threat to Alsace had increased with each day, the emperor remained convinced that upper Alsace, Franche-Comté, and the Juras at most could become a secondary theater due to the region's inability to support the strategic and tactical operations of large armies. Moreover, he counted on Swiss resistance to provide time for him to organize his defenses. This suggests

---

65 Marmont to Berthier, 28 December 1813, SHAT, C² 166.
66 Marmont to Berthier, 29 December 1813, SHAT, C² 166. The actual letter to Victor is lost; Marmont informed Berthier of his correspondence with Victor.
67 Victor to Berthier, 3 January 1814, SHAT, C² 169.
68 Victor to Berthier, 6 January 1814, SHAT, C² 170.

that Napoleon planned to use the Swiss, natural obstacles, fortresses, and the National Guard to defend Alsace and Franche-Comté. The remains of the Grande Armée of 1813 augmented by new recruits would guard the middle Rhine. For the lower Rhine, Napoleon allocated his elite troops: the Imperial Guard. Grand strategic and political motivations abound in this decision to commit the finest soldiers of the French army to the Low Countries. Control of the mouth of the Scheldt allowed France to regulate the trade flowing to and from the greatest port on the continent. By annexing Holland and Belgium, the French had theoretically added the colonial empires of these states to France's global possessions. The conquest of the Low Countries handed the French control of the Dutch fleet – so necessary for France to challenge the Royal Navy. Finally, Holland and Belgium provided Napoleon with staging areas from which he could launch an invasion of Britain.

Such considerations, as weighty as they appear, no longer had any bearing on the European state of affairs by the end of 1813. British naval supremacy, the failure of Napoleon's Continental System, and the destruction of imperial armies in 1812 and 1813 had voided the grand strategic advantages of controlling the Low Countries. At most, the Low Countries represented the first conquests of the Revolution, and Napoleon felt the solemn obligation to conserve them for France. Besides, his pride and lack of diplomatic tact would not permit him to surrender any territory unless it was ripped from his empire. At most Napoleon sought to hold the Low Countries for as long possible in order to use them as bargaining chips in future negotiations. He also may have hoped for a rift to occur among the Allies as they debated the structure of postwar Europe and the details of France's boundaries. Strategically, the emperor possibly viewed the Low Countries as the soft underbelly of France and envisioned the same wheeling movements that the Germans would execute in the First and Second World Wars. Above all, he feared that, by separating the Dutch and Belgians from the empire, the Allies would trigger a chain reaction that would unravel his hold over the French. Consequently, he moved his best troops to Belgium, regardless of the reports that poured in from Alsace.

Combined with the Dutch revolt, the arrival of Prussian and Russian forces appeared to land a heavy blow square on Napoleon's chin.[69] Indeed, the

---

69 Berthier to Macdonald, 13 December 1813, SHAT, C^{17} 183. Following the emperor's instructions, Berthier informed Macdonald that the Prussians had only 8,000–9,000 men at Utrecht. He added the British could not have more than 4,000 troops, and made no mention of either the Russians or the Dutch insurgents. See CN, No. 21091, 27:37: "The enemy is in three groups. It does not seem that this group coming from Breda [the Prussians] ... can be more than 9,000 men." Although Napoleon purposefully underestimated the size of the Allied forces operating in the Low Countries, the Prussians, Russians, British, and

emperor responded as if enemy legions had been spotted only a few leagues from Paris. Rather than concern for the Low Countries, Napoleon became so obsessed about events there that he paid little heed to the situation along the middle and upper Rhine until it was too late. He persisted in his belief that the Allied invasion was unfolding in the Low Countries. Forgetting that the Allied sovereigns had accompanied the operations of the Bohemian Army in the previous campaign, he ignored reports that the monarchs and Schwarzenberg had remained at Frankfurt until departing for destinations on the middle and upper Rhine to join this same army. Finally, as the 200,000 men of the Bohemian Army approached the Alsatian frontier, Napoleon's attention remained fixed on the Low Countries. He planned to assemble a significant force – the Army of the North – to deny the Allies any gains in Belgium and to eventually drive them from Holland. On 21 December the emperor appointed General Nicholas-Joseph Maison commander of all French forces in Belgium.[70] He received instructions to build an entrenched camp at Antwerp that could hold a Guard corps of approximately 30,000–40,000 infantry and 6,000 cavalry.[71] Napoleon planned to have a Guard corps of 30,000 men in this camp by early January.[72] Despite the clear indications that Schwarzenberg's massive army was preparing to drive across the upper Rhine, the emperor allocated more forces in the opposite direction in the hopes of holding Belgium and retaking Holland.

Dutch numbered at most 45,000 men in December and the first half of January, but almost half were either blockading or occupying forts and fortresses on the lower Rhine (Wesel) and in the Dutch interior. The number of Allied soldiers available for mobile operations was far fewer than the masses of the Bohemian Army.

70 Clarke to Maison, 21 December 1813, SHAT, C² 316; *CN*, No. 21024, 26:607; Agathon-Jean-François Fain, *Manuscrit de mil huit cent quatorze, trouvé dans les voitures impériales prises à Waterloo, contenant l'histoire des six derniers mois du règne de Napoléon* (Paris, 1824), 41.

71 Napoleon allocated considerable reinforcements to the Guard in the Low Countries and based the figure of 30,000–40,000 men on the following unit strengths he expected to achieve by 15 January, the actual musters as of 15 December are in parentheses: Guard Cavalry: 6,000 men (4,790); 1st Tirailleur Division: 9,600 men (600); 3rd Tirailleur Division: 8,000–9,000 men (650); 3rd Voltigeur Division: 6,000 men (294); 1st Old Guard Division: 6,000 men (4,800). See *CN*, No. 21033, 26:528.

72 Ibid., Nos. 21005 and 21023, 26:509, 520; Berthier to Oudinot, 14 December 1814, SHAT, C¹⁷ 183. The emperor appointed Marshal Oudinot to command this corps as soon as his health permitted. Although undesignated, the corps itself would consist of the 4th, 5th, and 6th Young Guard Divisions, which were already at Antwerp and together mustered 10,000 men. On 17 December Mortier led the 4,800 men of the 1st Old Guard Division from Trier to Namur, where they arrived on the 26th; the 2,400 troopers of the 1st Guard Cavalry Division likewise proceeded to Namur.

Few excuses can be found to absolve the French emperor of his failure to correctly interpret Allied intentions. In this case, his marshals are not to blame. Both Marmont and Victor provided enough information to correctly orient Napoleon toward the true direction of the Allied invasion. They correctly assessed the value of Basel and warned that the Allies would violate Swiss neutrality to gain its bridge. Both waged a letter campaign in an effort to demonstrate the danger to Alsace. By mid-November exceptional French intelligence provided General Bonaparte with the most essential information regarding the impending Allied invasion, but Emperor Napoleon did little to prepare the defense of the upper Rhine. By no means could Marmont and Victor have held Alsace and Lorraine in the face of almost 300,000 Allied soldiers. However, it is important to note that Blücher had been chained to the right bank of the Rhine awaiting Schwarzenberg's summons to cross the river and commence the invasion. This directive came after ten days as a result of Schwarzenberg's panic over the brave but brief defense of upper Alsace by V Cavalry Corps. Had Napoleon heeded the intelligence concerning the Basel bridge and provided Victor with adequate manpower, particularly the Guard divisions that had been sent to Belgium, the marshal (or one of his more aggressive generals of division) would have had an excellent opportunity to stop the Allies on the banks of the Rhine. For a coalition still so fragile and so extremely divided over the very issue of invading France and for a general as cautious as Schwarzenberg, the consequences could have changed history. Such an Allied setback indeed could have provided Napoleon with the time he so desperately needed to mobilize another Grande Armée. As it stood, Napoleon left Paris on 25 January to join the marshals. His operations in February mainly sought to stall the Allied advance and buy time to complete the mobilization.

Meanwhile, after crossing the middle Rhine near Mainz on New Year's Day 1814, the much smaller Silesian Army forced one river line after another to reach the Marne. During the course of January, the two Allied armies gradually approached each other as Schwarzenberg moved west from Basel toward Langres, and Blücher advanced southwest, eventually crossing the Marne and reaching Brienne, the place where Napoleon had attended military school as a youth. After spending one week in the region of Langres, the Bohemian Army started moving northwest between the Marne and the Aube Rivers in the direction of Paris. As Schwarzenberg's army lumbered forward, the Allied commander received the surprising news that the 27,000 men of the Silesian Army stood on the same road only one march north of him. After leaving 34,000 Russians to besiege Mainz, and the 21,500 men of the Prussian I Corps among the fortresses on the Moselle River, Blücher, now a field marshal, turned south with a single Russian corps of 27,000 men to seek a union with Schwarzenberg and propel the Bohemian Army into a battle with Napoleon or an accelerated march on Paris.

Napoleon made his first appearance in the field just in time to strike the rear of Blücher's sole corps as it followed the course of the Aube northward on 29 January. Blücher accepted battle at Brienne, engaging the French as they assaulted from the northeast. Unable to move all of his forces to the battlefield in time, Napoleon mustered only some 30,000 soldiers against an equal number of Blücher's Russians – Schwarzenberg's lead elements remained too distant to support. Both sides sustained approximately 3,000 casualties, and both sides claimed victory. Although he conceded the field by withdrawing seven miles south to Trannes, Blücher considered Brienne a personal victory over Napoleon. The two armies remained in this position on 30 and 31 January. To appease the tsar and the Prussians, Schwarzenberg finally authorized Blücher to deliver a battle on 1 February at La Rothière, halfway between Trannes and Brienne. He placed III and IV Corps of the Bohemian Army under Blücher's direct command. Furthermore, the 34,000 men of Barclay's Russo-Prussian Guard and Reserve would support from Trannes and Bar-sur-Aube, but Blücher received no direct authority over these units. In addition, Schwarzenberg ordered the 26,000 men of his V Corps to advance west toward Brienne. Not only did he make approximately 85,000 men available to support Blücher's own 27,000, but Schwarzenberg also relinquished command of the upcoming battle in favor of the Prussian. Nevertheless, he rejected the notion of a battle of annihilation that would interfere with Austrian politics. To avoid the suspicion of his allies, he transferred command to Blücher but did not place all of the troops committed to the battle at the Prussian's disposal. Because the Austrians did not desire a decisive victory, Schwarzenberg provided Blücher only enough manpower to drive Napoleon from his position but not to destroy him. Should the operation fail, the corps of the Bohemian Army that did not participate in the battle would take an *Aufnahmestellung* (receiving position) to cover Blücher's retreat.

Napoleon mustered all the forces he could: 45,100 men and 128 guns. Fortunately for the French, the terrain forced Blücher to take a narrow approach march that prevented him from deploying his superior numbers. Combat lasted long into the cold night. Napoleon vigorously led his troops in several counterattacks. Late in the evening, Allied cavalry advanced through gaping holes in the French center and left, forcing the emperor to commence a general retreat. French losses amounted to 6,000 men, including 2,400 prisoners and 54 guns, while the Allies claimed to have captured 3,000–4,000 men and 73 guns. The battle cost the Allies approximately 6,000 men – more than half being Russian – mainly due to the effectiveness of French artillery. Although a victory, the outstanding feature of the Battle of La Rothière is that the Allies achieved no decisive results. Blücher scored a tactical victory over Napoleon on French soil, routed a majority of his forces, inflicted more casualties proportionately although not numerically, and captured a considerable portion of French artillery, but much more could have been achieved. Several reasons contributed to the squandering of the opportunity presented at La Rothière, and blame falls on Allied Headquarters. Approximately 125,000 Allied soldiers could have been committed to the battle, but only 80,000 actually saw action on 1 February. Rather than destroy the enemy, Schwarzenberg limited the objective to driving the enemy from Brienne. A general pursuit could have ended the war but Blücher lacked fresh reserves and Schwarzenberg's rearward units remained too distant to participate. Napoleon's stand at La Rothière should have been a monumental defeat for the emperor. Unless the two Allied armies separated, another confrontation could result in a French disaster. Fortunately for Napoleon, Schwarzenberg decided to separate the two armies.

The Struggle for France

Allied success at La Rothière healed longstanding rifts in the Coalition caused by fierce debates over strategy. In the aftermath of this victory, Tsar Alexander managed to seize the reigns of the Coalition from Metternich's hands. Austrians, Prussians, and Russians all agreed that Paris should be the objective of the Coalition's armies. Blücher's army would advance to Paris along the Marne, where it would reunite with Yorck's Prussian I Corps and be reinforced by the Prussian II Corps. Meanwhile, Schwarzenberg's forces would approach the French capital by way of the Seine. Of the dangers entailed, the two Allied armies initially would not advance in mutual supporting distance. Instead, they would be separated by almost forty miles, which amounted to a march of three days due to the conditions of weather and terrain. Schwarzenberg and Blücher did not view this as problematic, as the two highways that led west to Paris would gradually bring the Allied armies closer together as they converged on the enemy capital. In addition, Schwarzenberg assigned the task of maintaining communication between the two armies to his VI Corps and to General Aleksandr Seslavin's Cossack corps. Yet, for the plan to achieve complete success, *both* armies had to march on Paris, while contact with Napoleon's army had to be maintained on a daily if not hourly basis.

With his army in need of rest, Schwarzenberg halted operations at Troyes until 10 February. Tragically for Blücher's soldiers, the Allied commander in chief summoned VI Corps to Troyes rather than Arcis-sur-Aube. Seslavin, whose Cossacks should have maintained communication between VI Corps and Blücher, received orders to raid as far as possible westward toward the Loire River. Thus, communication between the Bohemian and Silesian Armies no longer existed. Only 100 Cossacks from the small Vlasov Regiment roamed the wide space between the Seine and the Marne. Schwarzenberg's decision allowed Napoleon to use his superior generalship to radically alter the situation. Although considering an attack on Schwarzenberg's left wing at Bar-sur-Seine, the need to defend Paris kept Napoleon's attention focused on Blücher. In response to Macdonald's evacuation of Châlons-sur-Champagne, he decided to move the army twenty-two miles north-northeast to Sézanne and from there fifteen miles north-northwest to Montmirail. He planned to unite with Marmont and Macdonald, and then maneuver the army into a position to block Blücher's advance. Napoleon acknowledged the possibility that Schwarzenberg could conduct an offensive against Paris or Nogent-sur-Seine, but counted on the Austrian's notorious lethargy. In any event, the master would be close at hand should the Bohemian Army advance. Napoleon believed he would make short work of Blücher and then be able to turn against the Bohemian Army with all his forces. Leaving a holding force to mask the slow-moving Schwarzenberg, Napoleon launched his famous "Six Days Campaign." From 9 to 15 February 1814, the emperor defeated Blücher's Prussians and Russians in four battles at Champaubert, Montmirail, Château-Thierry, and Vauchamps. Casualties during the combats amounted to an overwhelmingly lopsided 18,000 Allied soldiers to only 3,400 French.

Fortunately for Blücher, Schwarzenberg finally continued his drive on Paris, which commenced with a general crossing of the Seine. This prompted Napoleon to disengage from the Silesian Army and fly south to secure his marshals. Blücher ordered the remains of his army to retreat eighteen miles east to Châlons-sur-Champagne, where ample supplies awaited the exhausted survivors. Protected by the Marne, the Silesian Army reunited and reorganized. While another commander may have sat idle for a prolonged period, Blücher had his army marching in just two days to answer Schwarzenberg's call for help. With reinforcements already en route, Blücher filled the gaping holes in his ranks so that the Army of Silesia numbered 53,000 men and 300 guns on 21 February. Failing to finish off Blücher's army would cost Napoleon the war and his crown.

Meanwhile, Schwarzenberg ordered Blücher to move the Silesian Army closer to his own.[73] The very next day, 17 February, Napoleon stopped

---

73   Schwarzenberg to Blücher, Bray-sur-Seine, 17 February 1814, Österreichisches Staatsarchiv Kriegsarchiv, FA 1606, 434 and Add. Mss. 20,112.

Schwarzenberg's advance at Mormant, some thirty miles southeast of Paris. Concentrating the corps of Victor, Macdonald, Oudinot, and Ney as well as the Guard and reinforcements that arrived from Spain, Napoleon commanded some 55,000 men including 20,000 cavalry. An Allied council of war at Schwarzenberg's headquarters decided on a general retreat to Troyes, where the two Allied armies could unite and accept battle. Pursuing the Army of Bohemia in three columns on the 18th, the French closed on Schwarzenberg's IV Corps at the crossing over the Seine at Montereau, inflicting some 6,000 casualties. Napoleon's troops starting crossing the Seine at Montereau on the morning of the 19th. During the next few days, the French army concentrated at Nogent-sur-Seine, while Schwarzenberg assembled the Bohemian Army at Troyes and Blücher reached Méry-sur-Seine.

Intending to advance against Schwarzenberg, Napoleon abandoned the offensive because of Blücher's flank position.[74] Nevertheless, the emperor's constant pressure convinced Schwarzenberg to retreat across the Aube and return to Langres. Although Alexander and Frederick William objected, an absurd report from Seslavin dated 10:00 AM on 21 February stated that Napoleon was seeking a major battle and commanded over 180,000 men, including 82 cavalry regiments. Schwarzenberg used this outrageous report as a virtual weapon to force Alexander and Frederick William to approve the retreat. Schwarzenberg also ordered Blücher's army to withdraw some 117 miles east of Nancy. After learning of the decision to retreat, Blücher feared the next step would be a withdrawal across the Rhine. To prevent this, he requested and received permission for the Silesian Army to march north and cross the Marne. He planned to unite with the two corps of the Army of North Germany that had recently liberated the Low Countries and then advance along the right bank of the Marne against Paris. Approving, Schwarzenberg decided that the Bohemian Army would retreat only to Bar-sur-Aube for the moment.

Schwarzenberg commenced his retreat on 23 February, while Blücher's advance began on the 24th. Napoleon initiated the pursuit of the Silesian Army on the 25th. Leaving 33,000 men under Macdonald to mask Schwarzenberg, the emperor took scrupulous measures to give the impression that he remained at the Seine facing the Bohemian Army. As he was stopped at the Marne and forced to build bridges on 1 March 1814, the loss of time allowed Blücher to escape across the Ourcq River. Napoleon complained bitterly, claiming that, if the pontoons had arrived from Paris in time, he would have caught the Silesian Army in full retreat on 2 March and "the army of Blücher would be no more."[75]

---

74   Maximilian Yorck von Wartenburg, *Napoleon as a General* (London, 1902), 2:398.
75   *CN*, No. 21421, 27:278.

By the evening of 2 March, Napoleon found himself at a crossroads: did he need to continue the pursuit of Blücher or should he contend with Schwarzenberg?[76] His plan for defeating the Bohemian Army entailed the operation Schwarzenberg feared most. "I am prepared to transfer the war to Lorraine," he informed his brother, Joseph, "where I will rally my troops that are in my fortresses on the Meuse and the Rhine."[77] Thus, he planned a *manoeuvre sur les derrières* to turn Schwarzenberg's right flank and operate against his rear.

Knowing that Allied headquarters dreaded such an operation, Napoleon should have implemented this plan immediately. Schwarzenberg would have conducted a headlong retreat to the Rhine. The evidence to support this assumption speaks clearly. At Troyes, with Blücher merely eighteen miles to the north at Méry-sur-Seine, Schwarzenberg convinced Alexander of the necessity to retreat to Langres. With Blücher now north of the Marne, an envelopment of the Bohemian Army's right wing and Napoleon's appearance on the Rhine would be viewed as a monumental disaster. But instead of terrorizing Schwarzenberg, whose retreat would eventually have forced Blücher to renounce his own operations, Napoleon changed his mind, opting to continue the pursuit of the Silesian Army. He based this decision on his overwhelming concern for the security of Paris. Napoleon furiously drove his men after Blücher, who retreated further to the Aisne River. There, he united with the two corps from the Army of North Germany, which fortuitously convinced the commandant of Soissons to surrender on 3 March. Utilizing the city's stone bridge as well as its own pontoons, the Army of Silesia miraculously escaped across the Aisne with Napoleon closing from the east and the marshals from the west.

Faced with the choice of continuing the pursuit of Blücher or turning against Schwarzenberg, Napoleon again chose the former. He intended to envelop Blücher's left wing, cut his lines of communication, and drive the Silesian Army northward.[78] On 6 March, Blücher learned that the French had crossed the Aisne at Berry-au-Bac. At Craonne on 7 March, Russian infantry held Blücher's center on the height while a Russian cavalry force of 10,000 troopers and 60 horse guns took a position at Filain. After the cavalry failed to wheel around the French rear, a bloody encounter occurred at Craonne. Fighting a defensive action, the Russians suffered 5,000 casualties thanks to the cavalry's inactivity. Blücher's three Prussian corps could not arrive in time

---

76 Ibid., No. 21419, 27:276–277.
77 Ibid., No. 21420, 27:277.
78 Ibid., Nos. 21432, 21434, 21436, 21438, and 21439, 27:284–287, 288–289.

to support. After suffering this tactical defeat at Craonne on the 7th, Blücher withdrew to a defensive position at Laon, where he concentrated his army of more than 100,000 men. He did not have to wait for long before the French arrived. Napoleon opened the assault on the evening of 8 March.

During the course of the three-day battle that saw the rout of Marmont's VI Corps on the 9th, Napoleon could muster only 48,000 combatants. Ney's failure to dislodge the Allies on the 10th finally convinced the emperor that he could not break Blücher's formidable position without sustaining significant losses.[79] He withdrew during the night of 10–11 March in the direction of Soissons after losing 6,500 men and exacting 4,000 Allied casualties. With 20,000 men, Napoleon overwhelmed the Allies at Reims on 13 March, taking 12 guns and inflicting 1,500 casualties on the Russians. Saint-Priest, the native Frenchman, received a mortal wound. The Prussian *Landwehr* fared worse, losing 1,877 casualties and 11 guns. At 3:00 AM on 14 March, the French entered Reims after losing 800 men. Aside from exaggerating the extent of his victory for propaganda purposes, Napoleon believed he had succeeded in severing communication between Blücher and Schwarzenberg. While a tactical victory that again demonstrated his endless energy and denied Blücher some reinforcements, Napoleon's success at Reims had no bearing on the strategic situation. In the end, this victory, the emperor's penultimate on French soil, meant little.[80] Uncertainty over Napoleon's next move along with Blücher's illness had kept the Silesian Army in place until 18 March, when it marched south and crossed the Aisne.

To Schwarzenberg's credit, the Army of Bohemia advanced as soon as Allied headquarters received confirmation that Napoleon had departed in pursuit of Blücher. On 27 February, the Bohemian Army took Bar-sur-Aube and commenced a general offensive, driving Macdonald from Troyes on 4 March. Two days later, the marshal withdrew across the Seine at Méry and did not stop until he reached Provins.[81] News of Macdonald's collapse stunned and outraged Napoleon. "I cannot believe this stupidity," he wrote to Joseph. "There is no better position than Troyes, where the enemy has to maneuver on both banks of the river. They cannot be any worse off than I am. At Troyes, I left a fine army and a beautiful cavalry, but it lacks soul. In battle, this army is certainly stronger than anything Prince Schwarzenberg can oppose it with."[82] After his failure at Laon, Napoleon turned south to confront the Bohemian

---

79 Ibid., No. 21461, 27:301.
80 *CN*, No. 21478, 27:311; August von Janson, *Geschichte des Feldzuges 1814 in Frankreich*, 2 vols (Berlin, 1903–1905), 2:203–204; Yorck von Wartenburg, *Napoleon as a General*, 2:405.
81 Yorck von Wartenburg, *Napoleon as a General*, 2:405.
82 *CN*, No. 21449, 27:293–294.

Army. On 20 March 1814, he drove Schwarzenberg's V Corps from Arcis-sur-Aube and crossed the river. During the night, the Bohemian Army's IV and VI Corps arrived, increasing Allied forces to 80,000 men, while Napoleon received a mere 8,000 reinforcements. On the 21st, Napoleon yielded to Schwarzenberg's masses and retreated behind the Aube after losing 3,000 men and inflicting 4,000 casualties on Coalition forces.

At this juncture, Napoleon decided to attempt the *manoeuvre sur les derrières* and reach the Rhine. Following the Battle of Arcis-sur-Aube, he marched east. Not only were the two Allied armies on the verge of uniting for a third time, they both stood closer to Paris than Napoleon did. Alexander believed that the Allies should not pursue Napoleon, but instead march on Paris. Frederick William and Schwarzenberg agreed. Only 10,000 Russian cavalry, commanded by General Ferdinand von Wintzingerode, followed Napoleon. On 26 March 1814, Napoleon defeated Wintzingerode at Saint-Dizier: the emperor's last victory before his abdication. Nevertheless, Wintzingerode achieved his purpose – Napoleon could not recover the lost time to reach Paris before Blücher and Schwarzenberg.

Allied unity, which started to crumble during January and February, was restored in March thanks to Napoleon's intransigence. His refusal to come to terms drove the Allies together and even convinced Metternich that only Napoleon's complete overthrow would bring peace to Europe. Therefore, on 9 March 1814, the representatives of Russia, Austria, Prussia, and Britain signed Treaty of Chaumont, binding the four powers to unconditionally defeat Napoleon and creating the Quadruple Alliance for a stipulated twenty years to prevent France from ever again threatening the balance of power in Europe.

After defeating Marmont at Fère-Champenoise on 25 March, both Allied armies pursued the marshal to Paris. An intense struggle for control of the French capital occurred on the 30th. Late that afternoon, Tsar Alexander concluded a ceasefire with Marmont, who agreed to evacuate his positions. On the following day, 31 March, the ceremonial entry of the Allied sovereigns into the French capital occurred. Rushing west from Saint-Dizier, Napoleon learned of the surrender of his capital. Three days later, on 3 April, a provisional French government deposed him, but Napoleon refused to relinquish power. Finally, after Ney and some of the other marshals mutinied, he agreed to abdicate in favor of his son on 6 April, signing the formal act of abdication at Fontainebleau on the 11th. Regardless, the Allies restored the Bourbons under King Louis XVIII, and Napoleon went into exile on the tiny Mediterranean island of Elba.

The Seventh Coalition

Napoleon escaped from Elba with his personal guard of 1,000 men and 4 cannon in late February 1815. Landing in France on 1 March, he reached Paris and restored the empire nineteen days later. To ease the public's increasing fear of another coalition war, Napoleon issued a statement claiming peace with Austria and a twenty-year truce with the other Allies. He confidently declared to the French people that the Allies would not mobilize. Regardless, the Seventh Coalition against France formed with Britain, Russia, Prussia, and Austria each agreeing to furnish an army of 150,000 men and to not lay down arms "until Bonaparte shall have been put absolutely beyond the possibility of exciting disturbances and of renewing his attempts to seize the supreme power in France."

Napoleon found fewer than 200,000 Frenchmen under arms.[83] Such swift and obstinate Allied opposition forced him to create a much bigger army. With an unstable political position, he could not enact radical measures such as a *levée en masse* to increase his armed forces. Instead, the emperor recalled thousands of furloughed men and deserters. Due to hopeless negotiations with the Coalition, French authorities did not post the summons until 9 April. Nevertheless, by the end of May, he had organized 224,000 men into 7 corps and armies of observation. The emperor's main force, the Army of the North, numbered 120,000 men. Napoleon divided his remaining troops among the Armies of the Rhine, Loire, Alps, and Pyrenees. Should the Allies invade France, Paris and Lyon would serve as rallying points for the French armies. The mobilization of 375,600 National Guards strengthened the frontier fortresses.

The Coalition planned to mobilize five armies for the invasion of France. Preliminary plans called for the Army of the Lower Rhine – 117,000 Prussians led by Blücher – and an Anglo-Dutch force of 93,000 men commanded by the duke of Wellington to operate in Belgium. With an Austrian army of 210,000 men, Schwarzenberg would take a position on the upper Rhine while a Russian army of 150,000 men under Barclay de Tolly would deploy to the middle Rhine. From Italy, an Austro-Italian force of 75,000 men under General Johann Frimont would invade southeastern France. The Allies planned to defeat Napoleon through numerical superiority. Blücher, Wellington, and Schwarzenberg would then march directly on Paris with Barclay de Tolly's army in support; Frimont's force would advance on Lyon. All Allied armies

---

83 The general estimate of the Royal Army on 15 January 1815 was 192,675 men. This number does not include veterans, the gendarmerie, and household troops. Napoleon's estimate of the effective strength of the army on 20 March was 149,000 men.

would cross the French frontier between 27 June and 1 July. This timetable enabled Napoleon to seize the initiative before the Allies could reach French territory.

Blücher met with Wellington at Brussels from 28 to 30 May. Although the Prussian commander pressed for operations to commence as soon as possible to relieve his supply woes, Wellington refused to cross the frontier until Schwarzenberg's army reached the upper Rhine. Wellington did agree to commence the invasion on 1 July, the timeframe in which Schwarzenberg would be ready to cross the upper Rhine. In the event Napoleon attacked first, presumably to win Brussels, Blücher would concentrate the Army of the Lower Rhine at Sombreffe. From there, he would either support Wellington's left flank if Napoleon targeted the Anglo-Dutch army, or hold fast until Wellington arrived should the emperor aim his blow at the Prussians. In this latter case, Wellington would concentrate his army at Quatre-Bras and march to support Blücher's right.[84]

Secretly, Napoleon concentrated the Army of the North's 120,000 men along the Sambre River within a twelve-hour march of the border town of Charleroi. He planned to strike the Anglo-Dutch and Prussian armies in turn. Much like his 1796 Campaign, he faced two armies that operated from different bases. Once separated, they would be forced to fall back in different directions. This meant Wellington would be forced to withdrew northwest through Brussels to the English Channel, while Blücher retreated northeast through Liège to the Rhine. To defeat each enemy army in turn, Napoleon had to pierce the center of the Allied front at Charleroi. From there, he had to *simultaneously* drive along both of his adversaries' lines of communication. Wellington's line, the Charleroi–Brussels road, ran north through Quatre-Bras, Genappe, Belle-Alliance, La Haye Saint, Mont-Saint-Jean, and Waterloo. Blücher's ran northeast through Fleurus and Sombreffe to Liège. The east–west-running Nivelles–Liège road, the main artery over which the two Allied armies could support each other, intersected Wellington's line at Quatre-Bras and Blücher's at Sombreffe. Should both armies be forced to retreat, they could still communicate with each other until passing the Nivelles–Quatre-Bras–Sombreffe–Liège road. Thus, after piercing the enemy's front, Napoleon's second objective had to be gaining Quatre-Bras and Sombreffe *simultaneously*. His third step would be to mask one of the enemy armies using economy of force and overwhelm the other. Thus, Napoleon counted on both Allied armies falling back on their

---

84   Karl von Damitz, *Geschichte des Feldzuges von 1815 in den Niederlanden und Frankreich* (Berlin, 1837), 1:37–39; Yorck von Wartenburg, *Napoleon as a General*, 2:428.

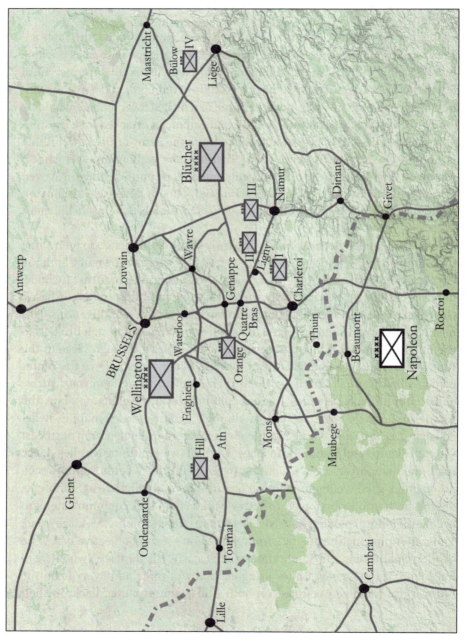

MAP 12.5 Theater of war, 1815

respective lines of communication to push them further apart and eliminate their chances of mutual support.[85]

At 4:30 AM on 15 June 1815, French cavalry drove the Prussian I Corps from Charleroi toward Fleurus. The Army of the North poured into Belgium. With the Prussians withdrawing northeast along their line of communication and away from Wellington's army, Napoleon's offensive could not have started much better. On 16 June, Ney fixed elements of Wellington's army at Quatre-Bras while Napoleon engaged Blücher further southeast at Ligny. Assuming only one Prussian corps stood at Ligny, Napoleon ordered Marshal Emmanuel Grouchy to advance against it on the 16th with III and IV Corps and I, II, and IV Cavalry Corps. Ney, commanding I and II Corps and III Cavalry Corps, received orders to drive through Quatre-Bras. With the Guard and VI Corps, Napoleon would follow as the reserve, supporting either Ney or Grouchy depending on the situation. If possible, Ney would swing northeast and behind the Prussians at Ligny to isolate and destroy this single corps, which Napoleon estimated to be no more than 40,000 men.[86]

By 2:30 on the afternoon of the 16th, Napoleon had concentrated 62,882 men and 204 guns against Blücher's 83,417 men and 224 guns. Although denied the support of his IV Corps, which could not reach the battle in time, as well as the reinforcements promised by Wellington, Blücher countered each of Napoleon's assaults. Between 6:00 and 7:00 PM, the Prussians maintained their center and left while their right gained ground. Had he been facing a commander other than Napoleon, Blücher probably could have counted on victory. Yet, as with the majority of the battles he waged, Napoleon brilliantly managed his resources. While Blücher's fresh units consisted of his 8th and 12th Brigades as well as six cavalry regiments, Napoleon still possessed his Regular Reserve – VI Corps – as well as his Grand Reserve: sixteen Guard battalions as well as the Guard's heavy cavalry. By 8:30, the Prussian line still held but Napoleon himself reached Ligny and directed the final eight battalions of the Guard – 1st and 2nd Grenadier and Chasseur Regiments – to punch through the Prussian center. French losses at Ligny are unclear, with estimates ranging from 8,000 to 12,000 men. Nevertheless, Napoleon mauled the Prussian army, inflicting some 12,000 casualties, including Blücher himself, taking 15 guns, and providing opportunity for 8,000 men to desert. That few prisoners were taken by either side indicates bitter fighting. Nevertheless, Blücher's Army of the Lower Rhine rallied thanks to the durability of the corps system.

---

85 Yorck von Wartenburg, *Napoleon as a General*, 2:424–425.
86 *CN*, Nos. 22058 and 22059, 28:289–292.

Blücher and his chief of staff, August Wilhelm Antonius Neidhardt von Gneisenau, remained determine to cooperate with Wellington and so ordered the army to retreat north to Wavre instead of east along its line of communication. A student of Napoleon's wars, Gneisenau recognized the similarities between the current situation and that of the Austrians and Sardinians in 1796. By retreating eastward, he would create the conditions for Napoleon to defeat each army in turn. Even if Gneisenau disagreed with the decision to retreat north rather than east as is famously depicted in both literature and film, he honored Blücher's wishes to continue cooperating with Wellington. After a stalemate at Quatre-Bras on the 16th, Wellington likewise retreated north to Waterloo on the 17th. He notified Blücher that he would make a stand if supported by one Prussian corps. Blücher resolved to send three. From Wavre, only a lateral march of ten miles separated the Prussians from Wellington's position.

On the evening of the Battle of Ligny, Napoleon did not think it feasible to pursue the Prussians any further than the Brye–Sombreffe line. The orderly withdrawal of the Prussian right and left wings, their occupation of Brye and Sombreffe, and concerns that Blücher could receive reinforcements contributed to this conclusion. At dawn on the 17th, the emperor ordered I and II Cavalry Corps to pursue eastward on the road to Namur. Around 4:00 on the morning of the 17th, the commander of I Cavalry Corps, General Claude Pierre Pajol, reported to the emperor from Balâtre that the enemy appeared to be in full retreat eastward toward Namur and Liège. Napoleon, having transferred his headquarters to Quatre-Bras, received this report at 7:00 AM. One hour later, he still remained uncertain, but believed Blücher would withdraw in this direction and along his line of communication. Not long after commencing their hunt, the light horse of I Cavalry Corps captured a Prussian battery belonging to III Corps as it retreated toward Namur, despite being ordered to Gembloux. Pajol sent the thirty prisoners to headquarters, and his report strengthened Napoleon's conviction that Blücher would flee to Namur. Soon, however, the reports of Pajol's forward units cast doubt that the Prussians had retreated eastward. Pajol left the Nivelles–Namur highway and proceeded northeast to Saint-Denis where he found signs of the retreating Prussians.

At imperial headquarters, Napoleon tasked Grouchy with leading the pursuit of the Prussian army. While the Prussians beat a retreat early on the 17th, the French followed late. Having already conceived the idea of driving the Prussians east toward Namur, and the British north toward Brussels, the emperor still needed to work out the details. Around 11:00 AM, he finally gave Grouchy verbal instructions to pursue the Prussians with 33,000 men and 96 guns – one-third of the Army of the North. "Pursue the Prussians, complete their defeat by attacking them as soon as you catch up with them, and never let them out of your sight. I will unite the remainder of this portion of the army with Marshal Ney's corps, march against the English, and fight them should they hold their ground." Napoleon decided to clarify in writing the verbal instructions. He directed Grouchy to Gembloux with I and II Cavalry Corps, the light cavalry of IV Corps, 21st Division from VI Corps, and III and IV Corps. "You will send scouts in the direction of Namur and Maastricht, and you will pursue the enemy. Reconnoiter his march and tell me of his movements, so I can divine his intentions."[87]

Grouchy's force sufficed to observe Blücher's movements but not accept battle with the Army of the Lower Rhine. Regardless, Napoleon's newest marshal failed to recognize that Blücher had maneuvered his army to Wavre to unite with Wellington's. At Wavre, the entire Prussian army already stood between Wellington and Grouchy; nothing could stop Blücher's advance. To prevent the Allied armies from uniting, Grouchy needed to threaten Blücher by taking positions at Saint-Géry and Mousty. Instead, Grouchy believed the Prussians would withdraw to Brussels. To fulfill Napoleon's orders, he planned to pursue them through Walhain or Corbais. Facing Wellington, Napoleon desperately needed Grouchy to march parallel to the Prussians and arrive at Waterloo. Grouchy's decision to follow the Prussians proved a costly error and greatly contributed to Napoleon's defeat at Waterloo.[88]

At 4:00 AM on 18 June 1815, Blücher's IV Corps commenced the march to Waterloo followed by II and I Corps. Meanwhile, Wellington positioned his army on the road to Brussels with its right wing at Braine-l'Alleud, the center near Mont-Saint-Jean and its left beyond La Haye Sainte. Due to heavy rains on the 17th and the muddy condition of the battlefield, Napoleon delayed his attack on Wellington until 11:30 AM. Shortly after 1:00 PM, he observed the Prussians marching on the hills near Saint-Lambert. At this time, he interrogated a captured Prussian hussar who bore a letter informing Wellington of Bülow's arrival at Saint-Lambert. The hussar claimed that the troops seen in the distance belonged to Bülow's advance guard. At 1:30, imperial headquarters dispatched orders for Grouchy to move closer to Napoleon's right flank and engage Bülow. As the Prussian IV Corps neared Saint-Lambert, Napoleon

---

87   Emmanuel Grouchy, *Relation succincte de la campagne de 1815 en Belgique, et notamment des mouvements, combats et opérations des troupes sous les ordres du maréchal Grouchy, suivie de l'exposition de quelquesunes des causes de la perte de la bataille de Waterloo* (Paris, 1843), 19; Henry Houssaye, *1815: Waterloo* (London, 1900), 130.
88   Houssaye, *1815*, 164–165.

opened the battle. Receiving these orders around 5:00 PM, Grouchy still decided to commit his entire force to attack the Prussian rearguard at Wavre.[89]

Although it was largely a stalemate, Napoleon wore down Wellington's forces during the course of four long hours. Blücher's arrival at 3:30 PM provided tremendous assistance for Wellington. Instead of utilizing his entire force to break Wellington's center, Napoleon detached 7,000 infantry from his VI Corps and 2,300 light cavalry to protect his flank and rear. Blücher's front ran parallel to Napoleon's main line of operations. His own line was well supported on both flanks and commanded the French right and rear. It became clear to Napoleon that Blücher expected more troops to arrive. Sensing the threat to his line of retreat, Napoleon sought to accelerate the pace of the battle by finishing off Wellington. In one last gamble, he decided to launch a massive assault against Wellington's center with the Imperial Guard.

Blücher responded to the advance of the Guard against Wellington by committing freshly arrived brigades against the village of Plancenoit and the French VI Corps. Around 8:30 PM, the Prussians gained full control of Plancenoit, but the French VI Corps rallied and advanced as part of the general surge of the French right wing. Also at this time, the Imperial Guard advanced between La Haye Sainte and Hougomont against Wellington's center but was rejected. French forces took Papelotte and La Haye Sainte. At the same time, Blücher's 1st Brigade of I Corps reached Wellington's extreme left wing, retaking Papelotte and La Haye Sainte in conjunction with four of Wellington's battalions. Broken on all fronts, the French evacuated the field in a general retreat. French casualties exceeded 30,000 men killed, wounded, and captured, while Wellington lost some 15,000 men and Blücher 7,000.

At 9:15 PM, Blücher met Wellington at Belle-Alliance, where he gave the reserved duke a bear-hug. The Prussian field marshal volunteered to execute the pursuit. His joy in seeing the rout of Napoleon's army produced an intoxicating effect on the old hussar, who claimed to be "pregnant with an elephant." Fifteen minutes later he met with his corps commanders, ordering them to "pursue the enemy as long as they had a man and horse able to stand." No quarter would be given. Unable to coordinate resistance on the Belgian side of the frontier, Napoleon proceeded to Philippeville, where he hoped to receive news of Grouchy. Remaining there for four hours, Napoleon directed the remains of the Army of the North to Laon. In the meantime, the wreck of the French army continued its retreat across the frontier. Some units struggled to reach Avenes and Philippeville but coordination remained difficult. Many men simply disregarded their arms and returned to their homes. A few officers managed to

---

89   Ibid., 190–191, 258–259.

collect some units and lead them to Laon. Napoleon himself left Philippeville at 2:00 PM and reached Laon later in the afternoon. His conviction to remain near the frontier to rally the army soon changed and he departed for Paris. French units continued the retreat to Laon as late as the 22nd.

After a fierce battle at Wavre with Blücher's III Corps on the 18th, Grouchy withdrew to Reims. Napoleon hoped to unite the remains of his army with Grouchy to stop that Allied advance. At Paris, he went before the legislature to plead for a *levée* that would furnish the manpower he needed to destroy the invading Allied armies. Lack of support from the legislature prompted him to abdicate a second and final time on 22 June 1815. On 24 June, Blücher received a letter from the commissioners of the French government that revealed Napoleon's second and final abdication. They requested an armistice but Blücher refused unless they surrendered Napoleon. Following Napoleon's abdication, Grouchy received command of the entire Army of the North. His right stood at Reims with the left at Soissons. Viewing this force as a threat to the crossings over the Oise River, Blücher ordered I and III Corps to hasten to Compiègne while IV Corps secured the bridges over the Oise at Pont Saint-Maxence and Creil. Blücher's rapid advance thwarted Grouchy's attempt to secure the Oise's passages and forced the marshal to retreat on Paris. French resistance was ebbing. Increased desertions indicated the failing effort to reorganize the army. Realizing that his troops could not confront the Prussians, Grouchy hoped to reach Paris by forced marches. Blücher's determined measures to destroy Grouchy's army misfired as the marshal skillfully evaded his traps.

By late evening on the 28th, the Prussian army succeeded in closing the French line of retreat along the main Soissons highway. Blücher's outposts stood five miles north of Paris and the sound of his cannon could be heard in the city. By the night of 28 June, his IV Corps reached Marly-la-Ville with detachments at Le Bourget and Stains; I Corps camped at Nanteuil with detachments at Le Plessis, Belleville, and Dammartin; III Corps reached Crespy. Wellington placed his right wing at Saint-Just and his left at La Taulle, with units at Roye, Antheuil, Petit-Crevecoeur, Ressons, and Couchy. The remains of the French I and II Corps reached the Parisian suburbs; III and IV Corps continued the retreat through Lagny and Vincennes, with the Guard and VI Corps following from Meaux. Blücher's old nemesis, Davout, the Iron Marshal, had assembled 65,000 men and 300 guns to defend Paris. Events at Paris ended the struggle before Blücher could. Davout, aware of the approaching Austrian and Russian armies, viewed further resistance as pointless. Negotiations with Wellington opened on 2 July. After Wellington declared he would not agree to an armistice while Davout's army still occupied Paris, the French representatives withdrew from the peace talks. Blücher's determined advance to Paris on 2 July forced the marshal to plan a counterstrike the next day. At 3:00 AM on 3 July, two columns debouched from Vaugirard to assault Blücher's I Corps at Issy-les-Moulineaux. After both sides sustained heavy losses, the Prussians repulsed the French, pursuing them to Paris's outer wall. A ceasefire followed and Davout opened negotiations with Blücher and Wellington. Later on the 3rd, the Military Convention of Paris ended hostilities. The next day, Davout led the French army out of Paris to the Loire. After three weeks of combat, the two Allied armies entered Paris on 7 July 1815 and Louis XVIII was restored. As for Napoleon, the British exiled him to the south Atlantic island of Saint Helena, where he died on 5 May 1821.

Conclusion

Decisive Allied victories in 1814 and 1815 raise the question: did Napoleon's skills deteriorate over time? The answer is intertwined with the quality of the Grande Armée, which peaked in 1805–1807 following the intense training it received in the years prior to the War of the Third Coalition. After sustaining irreplaceable losses in 1807, Napoleon then committed many of the survivors to Iberia, from where they would never return. After exhausting this invaluable, highly trained force, he became increasingly dependent on German, Italian, and Polish manpower that had not received training on par with the original Grande Armée.

The imperial forces that waged Napoleon's wars from 1809 onward simply could not rival the performance of the Grande Armée that had won the Wars of the Third and Fourth Coalitions. Coinciding with this qualitative decline is a marked change in Napoleon's tactics. Instead of continuing the progression of his tactical innovations for battlefield problem-solving, Napoleon became increasingly dependent on the weight of massed batteries, huge formations, and unimaginative frontal assaults as illustrated by the Battles of Aspern–Essling, Wagram, Borodino, and Waterloo.

After losing the Grande Armée of 1812 in Russia, Napoleon commenced the War of the Sixth Coalition with young conscripts – both French and foreign – who lacked all but rudimentary training. With the exception of Bautzen and the Six Days Campaign, he rarely sought to achieve victory through operational maneuver. In itself, the absence of a progression on the operational level reflects three important considerations concerning Napoleon's generalship during the last years of the empire. First, he understood that the qualitative decline of his army placed limitations on his operations and tactics. Second, he increasingly viewed his adversaries with utter contempt. Lacking respect for his enemy's capabilities, Napoleon waged war with a false sense of infallibility that stifled his novel approach to battlefield problem-solving.[90] Third, Emperor Napoleon increasingly placed emphasis on securing geographic objectives such as Berlin as opposed to General Bonaparte's maxim of annihilating the enemy army and destroying his ability to resist. Carl von Clausewitz insists that "the grand objective of all military action" should be the destruction of the enemy's armed forces.[91] In 1805, Napoleon had conquered two-thirds of Austria and gained Vienna, but it was the decisive victory at Austerlitz that brought Francis to terms. By November of the following year, the Grande Armée controlled Berlin and one-half of Prussia, yet met resistance in Silesia and East Prussia where the remnant of Frederick William's army held on until the Russians arrived. That conflict did not end until Napoleon broke the tsar's military might at Friedland in 1807. Conversely, the capture of Moscow in 1812 did not force Alexander to the peace table since the Russian army, although badly mauled, had marched away from Borodino. Compounding these developments, the aging marshalate and incompetent divisional generals often rendered "out-of-the-box" thinking impractical.

Defeat in 1813, 1814, and 1815 can in part be attributed to the marshals whom Napoleon selected to conduct independent operations. While Davout, perhaps the greatest of Napoleon's lieutenants, languished in Hamburg in 1813 and 1814 and then Paris in 1815, Marshals Ney, Oudinot, Victor, Macdonald, Marmont, and Grouchy commanded French forces in critical campaigns. In particular, his failure to appoint officers capable of independent army command symbolizes the lapse in judgement that plagued the emperor's last campaigns. Particularly after the defection of his chief of staff, Jomini, Ney simply could not coordinate independent operations. The fact that the marshals consistently failed to meet their master's expectations underscores Napoleon's failure to grasp the importance of an adequate General Staff system. Lastly, Napoleon's instructions, which at times lacked clarity, did not help his lieutenants. French

---

90 When Soult suggested that Grouchy should be recalled to join the main force, Napoleon purportedly responded: "Just because you have all been beaten by Wellington, you think he's a good general. I tell you Wellington is a bad general, the English are bad troops, and this affair is nothing more than eating breakfast." Later, after his brother, Jerome, told him of some gossip overheard by a waiter between British officers at lunch at the King of Spain Inn at Genappe that the Prussians were to march over from Wavre, Napoleon supposedly declared that the Prussians would need at least two days to recover and would be dealt with by Grouchy. See Elizabeth Longford, *Wellington: The Years of the Sword* (London, 1971), 547.

91 Clausewitz, *On War*, ed. and trans. by Howard and Paret, 577.

commanders were impeded by the emperor's fatal tendency to underestimate the numbers of his adversaries and overestimate his own.

Yet is it fair to condemn Napoleon's brave and loyal lieutenants? It should be noted that Oudinot, Macdonald, and Ney never possessed the same resources as did Napoleon. Wherever Napoleon went so did his Imperial Guard. Not only did the Guard serve as the epitome of the period's most elite fighting force, but it provided Napoleon the ultimate trump card. As we have seen, Napoleon favored having both a Regular Reserve and a Grand Reserve – the Guard, infantry, cavalry, and artillery. In numerous battles, he committed the Guard to deliver the *coup de grâce* after expending his regular reserve. None of the marshals who commanded independently in 1813 enjoyed the luxury of being able to commit the bearskins. Moreover, as the Army of Berlin and the Army of the Bober each consisted of three army corps and one cavalry corps, their commanders would have been hard pressed to mimic the master's practice of assigning the role of Regular Reserve to an entire army corps, or one-third of the combined-arms forces. Admittedly, although the Guard probably would not have helped Macdonald all that much at the Katzbach, Oudinot and Ney certainly could have benefitted from the use of these crack troops.

Napoleon's thoughts on his subordinates' failures are best seen in a long conversation he had on the evening of 8 September 1813 while dining with Murat and Saint-Cyr. During the course of the dinner, Napoleon's aide de camp, General Anne-Charles Lebrun, arrived with a detailed account of Ney's defeat at Dennewitz. With "unshakable composure," the emperor listened to every detail and then asked a few questions. On finishing, Napoleon clearly and correctly explained the reasons for Ney's failure but showed not the slightest dissatisfaction with Ney or his subordinates. In Napoleon's view, the cause lay in the difficulty of the art of war, which had not yet been brought to light. "If," he concluded, "time will allow me, I will produce a book in which I will develop all the rules of war with such clarity that it will be accessible to all military men like any other science." Then the discussion turned to the question of how much practice influenced a commander's skill in the art of war. Napoleon opined that only Louis XIV's general, Henri de La Tour d'Auvergne, vicomte de Turenne, had succeeded in perfecting his own innate talent through experience. In his opinion, only Turenne had obtained what he hoped to explain in his future teachings on the art of war.[92]

In operations, Napoleon suffered no rival; the enemy's commanders, including Wellington, could not match him. In strategy, however, the Reichenbach

---

92 Laurent de Gouvion Saint Cyr, *Mémoires pour servir à l'histoire militaire sous le Directoire, le Consulat et l'Empire*, 4 vols (Paris, 1831), 4:148–150.

Plan exhausted both the emperor and his army, keeping him off-balance and robbing him of one of his greatest maxims – initiative. Just as important as the Reichenbach Plan was the "community of interest" that solidified the Sixth Coalition in 1813 and the Seventh Coalition in 1815. Political unity had not been a characteristic of the previous coalitions that France faced. However, in 1813 and 1815, Napoleon confronted a coalition marked by an unprecedented degree of unity. Although badly shaken in 1814, the Allies did resolve their differences to decisively defeat Napoleon.[93] Lastly, the adoption of many French innovations, especially the corps system that allowed for distributed maneuver on the operational level, enabled the Allies to meet Napoleon head on. As his own army declined in quality, Napoleon faced much improved adversaries.

In 1813, Napoleon's presence on the field of battle sufficed to maintain the advantage in favor of the French and their allies. However, his subordinates met with disaster in situations of independent command. After the loss of the Grande Armée of 1813 in Germany, not even Napoleon's mastery of operations could offset the Coalition's vast numerical superiority in 1814.

With 500,000 Allied soldiers ready to cross the middle and upper Rhine in 1815, a French victory at Waterloo would have meant little in the end.

Bibliography

An Account of the Battle of Waterloo, Fought on the 18th of June, 1815, by the English and Allied Forces, Commanded by the Duke of Wellington, and the Prussian Army, Under the Orders of Prince Blücher, Against the Army of France, Commanded by Napoleon Bonaparte. By a British Officer on the Staff. With Appendix Containing the British, French, Prussian and Spanish Official Reports. London, 1815.

Anon. *Précis militaire de la campagne de 1813 en Allemagne.* Leipzig, 1881.

Aster, Heinrich. *Die Gefechte und Schlachten bei Leipzig im October 1813 Grossentheils nach neuem, bisher unbenutzten archivarischen Quellen dargestellt,* 2 vols. Dresden, 1852–1853.

Bantysh-Kamenskii, Dmitrii. *Slovar dostopamyatnikh lyudei russkoi zemli.* Saint Petersburg, 1847.

Barker, Henry A. *Description of the Field of Battle, and Disposition of the Troops Engaged in the Action, Fought on the 18th of June, 1815, near Waterloo.* London, 1816.

Batty, Robert. *An Historical Sketch of the Campaign of 1815.* London, 1820.

---

[93] This community of interest almost collapsed in 1814. Only Tsar Alexander's threat to continue the war with the armies of Russia and Prussia kept the Austrians from retreating across the Rhine.

Beauchamp, A. *Histoire des campagnes de 1814 et de 1815, ou histoire politique et militaire des deux invasions de la France, de l'entreprise de Bounaparte au mois de mars, de la chute totale de sa paissance, et de la double restauration du trône, jusqu'à la seconde paix de Paris, inclusivement. Seconde partie, comprenantle récit de tous les événemens survenus en france en 1815. Rédigée sur des matériaux authentiques au inedits*, 3 vols. Paris, 1817.

Becke, A.F. *Napoleon and Waterloo: The Emperor's Campaign with the Armee du Nord 1815*. London, 1946.

Beitzke, Heinrich. *Geschichte der deutschen Freiheitskriege in den Jahren 1813 und 1814*, 3 vols. Berlin, 1854–1855.

Bernhardi, T. *Denkwürdigkeiten aus dem Leben des Kaiserlich Russischen Generals von der Infanterie Carl Friedrich Grafen von Toll*, 4 vols. Leipzig, 1856–1866.

Blaise, Jean François and Édouard Lapène. *Campagnes de 1813 et de 1814 : sur l'Ébre, les Pyrénées et la Garonne, précédées de considérations sur la dernière guerre d'Espagne*. Paris, 1823.

Blücher, Gebhard Leberecht von. "Aus Blüchers Korrespondenz," ed. by Herman Granier. *Forschungen zur brandenburgischen-preußischen Geschichte* 26 (1913), 149–178.

Blücher, Gebhard Leberecht von. *Blücher in Briefen aus den Feldzügen, 1813–1815*, ed. by Wilhelm Günter Enno von Colomb. Stuttgart, 1876.

Blücher, Gebhard Leberecht von. *Blüchers Briefe*, ed. by Wilhelm Capelle. Leipzig, 1915.

Blücher, Gebhard Leberecht von. *Blüchers Briefe: Vervollständigte Sammlung des Generals E. von Colomb*, ed. by Wolfgang von Unger. Stuttgart, 1912.

Blücher, Gebhard Leberecht von. "Zwölf Blücherbriefe," ed. by Herman Granier. *Forschungen zur brandenburgischen-preußischen Geschichte* 12 (1900): 479–496.

Bogdanovich, Modest Ivanovich. *Geschichte des Krieges 1814 in Frankreich und des Sturzes Napoleon's I. Nach den zuverläßigsten Quellen*, trans. by G. Baumgarten. Leipzig, 1866.

Bogdanovich, Modest Ivanovich. *Geschichte des Krieges im Jahre 1813 für Deutschlands Unabhängigkeit. Nach den zuverläßigsten Quellen*, 2 vols. Saint Petersburg, 1863–1868.

Bouvier, F. *Les premiers combats de 1814. Prologue de la campagne de France dans les Vosges*. Paris, 1895.

Bowden, Scott. *Napoleon's Grande Armée of 1813*. Chicago, 1990.

Boyen, Hermann von. *Erinnerungen aus dem Leben des General-Feldmarschalls Hermann von Boyen*, ed. by Friedrich Nippold, 3 vols. Leipzig, 1889–1890.

Boyen, Hermann von. *Erinnerungen aus dem Leben des General-Feldmarschalls Hermann von Boyen*, ed. by Dorothea Schmidt, 2 vols. Berlin, 1990.

Brett-James, Antony. *Europe Against Napoleon: The Leipzig Campaign, 1813, from Eyewitness Accounts*. London, 1970.

Buckland, C.S.B. *Metternich and the British Government from 1809 to 1813*. London, 1932.

Bunbury, Henry. *Memoir and Literary Remains of Lieutenant-General Sir Henry Edward Bunbury, bart*. London, 1868.

Caemmerer, Rudolf von. *Die Befreiungskrieg, 1813–1815: Ein Strategischer Überblick*. Berlin, 1907.

Calmon-Maison, J.J.R. *Le général Maison et le 1er corps de la grande armée: campagne de Belgique décembre 1813–avril 1814*. Paris, 1913.

Campana, I.R. *La campagne de France 1814*. Paris, 1922.

Cathcart, George. *Commentaries on the War in Russia and Germany in 1812 and 1813*. London, 1850.

Caulaincourt, A.A.L. *Mémoires du general de Caulaincourt, duc de Vicence, Grand Écuyer de l'empereur*, ed. by J. Hanoteau, 3 vols. Paris, 1933.

Caulaincourt, A.A.L. *No Peace with Napoleon: Concluding the Memoirs of General de Caulaincourt, Duke of Vicenza*. New York, 1936.

Chandler, David G. *The Campaigns of Napoleon: The Mind and Method of History's Greatest Soldier*. New York, 1966.

Charras, Jean Baptiste Adolphe. *Histoire de la campagne de 1815*. Brussels, 1857.

Charras, Jean Baptiste Adolphe. *Histoire de la guerre de 1813 en Allemagne. Derniers jours de la retraite, insurrection de l'Allemagne, armements, diplomatie, entrée en campagne*, 2nd edn. Paris, 1870.

Chessney, C. *Waterloo Lectures: A Study of the Campaign of 1815*. London, 1868.

Chuquet, A. *L'Alsace en 1814*. Paris, 1900.

Clausewitz, C. *La campagne de 1813 et la campagne de 1814*. Paris, 1900.

Clausewitz, C. *Der Feldzug 1812 in Rußland und die Befreiungskriege von 1812–1815*. Berlin, 1906.

Clausewitz, C. *Historical and Political Writings*, trans. and ed. by P. Paret and D. Moran. Princeton, NJ, 1992.

Clausewitz, C. *Hinterlassene Werke des Generals Carl von Clausewitz über Krieg und Kriegführung*, 10 vols. Berlin, 1832–1837.

Clausewitz, C. *On War*, ed. and trans. by Michael Howard and Peter Paret. Princeton, NJ, 1986.

Clercq, Jules de and Alexandre J.H. de Clerq. *Recueil des traités de la France*, 23 vols. Paris, 1864–1917.

Conrady, Emil von. *Leben und Wirken des Generals Carl von Grolman*, 3 vols. Berlin, 1933.

Craig, Gordon A. *The Politics of the Prussian Army: 1640–1945*. Oxford, 1956.

Craig, Gordon A. "Problems of Coalition Warfare: The Military Alliance Against Napoleon, 1813–1814." In *War, Politics, and Diplomacy: Selected Essays by Gordon Craig*. London, 1966.

Crusius, A. *Der Winterfeldzug in Holland, Brabant, und Flandern, eine Episode aus dem Befreiungskriege 1813 und 1814*. Luxembourg, 1865.

Damitz, Karl von. *Geschichte des Feldzuges von 1814 in dem östlichen und nördlichen Frankreich bis zur Einnahme von Paris: als Beitrag zur neueren Kriegsgeschichte*, 3 vols. Berlin, 1842–1843.

Damitz, Karl von. *Geschichte des Feldzuges von 1815 in den Niederlanden und Frankreich als Beitrag zur Kriegsgeschichte der neuern Krieg*. Berlin, 1837.

Droysen, Johann. *Das Leben des Feldmarschalls Grafen Yorck von Wartenburg*, 2 vols. Leipzig, 1851.

D'Ussel, Jean. *Études sur l'année 1813: la défection de la prusse, décembre 1812–mars 1813*. Paris, 1907.

Esposito, Vincent and John Elting. *A Military History and Atlas of the Napoleonic Wars*. New York, 1964.

Fabry, Gabriel Joseph. *Étude sur les opérations de l'empereur, 5 septembre au 21 septembre 1813*. Paris, 1910.

Fabry, Gabriel Joseph. *Étude sur les opérations du maréchal Macdonald du 22 août au 4 septembre, 1813: La Katzbach*. Paris, 1910.

Fabry, Gabriel Joseph. *Étude sur les opérations du maréchal Oudinot du 15 août au 4 septembre: Groß Beeren*. Paris, 1910.

Fabvier, C.N. *Journal des opérations du sizième corps pendant la campagne de 1814 en France*. Paris, 1819.

Fain, A.J.F. *Manuscrit de mil huit cent quatorze, trouvé dans les voitures impériales prises à Waterloo, contenant l'histoire des six derniers mois du regne de Napoléon*. Paris, 1824.

Fane, J. [Lord Burghersh]. *Memoir of the Operations of the Allied Armies, under Prince Schwarzenberg, and Marshal Blücher, During the Latter End of 1813, and the Year 1814*. London, 1822; reprint, London, 1996.

Fezansac, Raymond. *Souvenirs militaires de 1804 à 1814*. Paris, 1870.

Fleury, A. *Reims en 1814 pendant l'invasion*. Paris, 1902.

Fleury, É. *Histoire de l'invasion de 1814 dans les départments du nord-est de la France*, 2nd edn. Paris, 1858.

Foucart, P. J. *Bautzen: 20–21 mai 1813*, 2 vols. Paris, 1897.

Fournier, A. *Der Congress von Châtillon. Die Politik im Kriege von 1814*. Vienna and Prague, 1900.

Freytag-Loringhoven, Hugo Friedrich Philipp Johann von. *Aufklärung und Armeeführung dargestellt an den Ereignissen bei der Schlesischen Armee im Herbst 1813: Eine Studie*. Berlin, 1900.

Freytag-Loringhoven, Hugo Friedrich Philipp Johann von. *Kriegslehren nach Clausewitz aus den Feldzügen 1813 und 1814*. Berlin, 1908.

Friccius, C. *Geschichte des Krieges in den Jahren 1813 und 1814 mit besonderer Rücksicht auf Ostpreußen und das Königsbergische Landwehrbattalion*, 2 vols. Berlin, 1848.

Friederich, Rudolf. "Die Aufassung der strategischen Lage seitens der Verbündeten am Schlusse des Waffenstillstandes von Poischwitz 1813." *Militair-Wochenblatt* (1902), 1–36.

Friederich, Rudolf. *Die Befreiungskriege, 1813–1815*, 4 vols. Berlin, 1911–1913.

Friederich, Rudolf. *Geschichte des Herbstfeldzuges 1813*, 3 vols. Berlin, 1903–1906. In *Geschichte der Befreiungskriege, 1813–1815*, 9 vols. Berlin, 1903–1909.

Friederich, Rudolf. "Die strategische Lage Napoleons am Schlusse des Waffenstillstandes von Poischwitz." *Militair-Wochenblatt* (1901), 1–36.

Gallas, L. *Les invasions autrichiennes de 1814 et 1815 à Chalon-sur-Saône et en Bourgogne*. Chalon-sur-Saône, 1938–1940.

Gardner, D. *Quatre-Bras, Ligny, and Waterloo*. London, 1882.

Gérôme, Auguste Clementé. *Campagne de 1813*. Paris, 1904.

Giraud, P.F.F.J. *Campagne de Paris en 1814, précédée d'un coup-d'oeil sur celle de 1813, ou précis historique et impartial des événemens, depuis l'invasion de la France*. Paris, 1814.

Gneisenau, August von. *Briefe August Neidhardts von Gneisenau. Eine Auswahl*, ed. by Koehler and Amelang Verlagsgesellschaft mbH. Munich, 2000.

Gneisenau, August von. *Briefe des Generals Neidhardt von Gneisenau: 1809–1815*, ed. by Julius von Pflugk-Harttung. Gotha, 1913.

Gneisenau, August von. *Gneisenau: Ein Leben in Briefen*, ed. by Karl Griewank. Leipzig, 1939.

Gneisenau, August von. *The Life and Campaigns of Field Marshal Prince Blücher*. London, 1815.

Gneisenau, August von. *Neithardt von Gneisenau: Schriften von und über Gneisenau*, ed. by Fritz Lange. Berlin, 1954.

Grouard, A. *Stratégie Napoléonienne: la critique de la campagne de 1815*. Paris, 1904.

Grouchy, E. *Mémoires du maréchal de Grouchy, par le marquis se Grouchy*. Paris, 1873–1874.

Grouchy, E. *Relation succincte de la campagne de 1815 en Belgique, et notamment des mouvements, combats et opérations des troupes sous les ordres du Maréchal Grouchy, suivie de l'exposition de quelquesunes des causes de la perte de la bataille de Waterloo*. Paris, 1843.

Hassenkamp, H. *General Graf Bülow von Dennewitz in den Feldzügen von 1814 und 1815*. Leipzig, 1843.

Haythornthwaite, Philip J. *The Napoleonic Sourcebook*. New York, 1990.

Hellwald, F.J.H. and Karl Schöhals. *Der k.k. österreichische Feldmarschall Graf Radetzky: eine biographische Skizze nach den eigenen Dictaten und der Correspondenz des Feldmarschalls von einem österreichischen Veteranen*. Stuttgart, 1858.

Henckel von Donnersmarck, W.L. von. *Erinnerungen aus meinem Leben*. Leipzig, 1846.

Hennequin, É. *Les opérations de 1814 dans l'Aube*. Troyes, 1921.

Hiller, F. *Geschichte des Feldzuges 1814 gegen Frankreich unter besonderer Berücksichtigung der Anteilnahme der Königlich württembergischen Truppen*. Leipzig, 1894.

Hofmann, Georg Wilhelm von. *Die Schlacht bei Leipzig*. Posen, 1835.

Hofmann, Georg Wilhelm von. *Zur Geschichte des Feldzuges von 1813*. Berlin, 1843.

Hofmann, Georg Wilhelm von. *Zur Geschichte des Feldzuges von 1815 bis nach der Schlacht von Belle-Alliance*. Koblenz, 1849.

Hofschröer, Peter. greatestbattles.iblogger.org/GB/Liebertwolkwitz/Liebertwolkwitz PartIII-ByHofschroer.htm.

Holleben, A. von and R. von Caemmerer. *Geschichte des Frühjahrsfeldzuges 1813 und seine Vorgeschichte*, 2 vols. Berlin, 1904–1909. In *Geschichte der Befreiungskriege, 1813–1815*, 9 vols. Berlin, 1903–1909.

Höpfner, Eduard von and Eduard von Fransecky. "Darstellung der Ereignisse bei der schlesischen Armee im Jahre 1813, mit besonderer Berücksichtigung des Antheils der preussischen Truppen." *Militair-Wochenblatt*, 1843–1847.

Houssaye, H. *1814*. Paris, 1888.

Houssaye, H. *1815: Waterloo*. Paris, 1900.

Janson, August von. *Geschichte des Feldzuges 1814 in Frankreich*, 2 vols. Berlin, 1903–1905.

Jany, Curt. *Geschichte der königlichen preußischen Armee*, 4 vols. Berlin, 1929.

Jomini, Antoine Henri de. *Lettre du général Jomini à M. Capefigue sur son histoire d'Europe pendant le Consulat et l'Empire*. Paris, 1841.

Jomini, Antoine Henri de. *Précis politique et militaire des campagnes de 1812 à 1814*. Lausanne, 1886.

Jomini, Antoine Henri de. *Vie politique et militaire de Napoléon*, 4 vols. Paris, 1827.

Jones, George. *The Battle of Waterloo with Those of Ligny and Quatre-Bras, Described by Eye-Witnesses and by the Series of Official Accounts Published by Authority. To Which Are Added the Memoirs of F.M. The Duke of Wellington, F.M. Prince Blücher, and The Emperor Napoleon*. London, 1852.

Kerchnawe, H. and A. Veltze. *Feldmarschall Karl Fürst zu Schwarzenberg: der Führer der Verbündeten in den Befreiungskriegen*. Vienna, 1913.

Kissinger, Henry. *A World Restored: Metternich, Castlereagh, and the Problems of Peace, 1812–1822*. Boston, 1990.

Klinkowström, A., ed. *Österreichs Theilnahme an den Befreiungskriegen. Ein Beitrag zur Geschichte der Jahres 1813 bis 1815 nach Aufzeichnungen von Friedrich von Gentz nebst einen Anhang: "Briefwechsel zwischen den Fürsten Schwarzenberg und Metternich." Herausgegeben von Richard Fürst Metternich-Winneburg*. Vienna, 1887.

Koch, Frédéric. *Mémoires pour servir à l'histoire de la campagne de 1814*. Paris, 1819.

Kraehe, Enno. *Metternich's German Policy*, 2 vols. Princeton, NJ, 1963.

Lachouque, H. *Napoleon en 1814*. Paris, 1959.

Langeron, Alexandre Louis Andrault. *Mémoires de Langeron, général d'infanterie dans l'armée russe: campagnes de 1812, 1813, 1814.* Paris, 1902.

Lanrezac, C.L.M. *La manoeuvre de Lützen 1813.* Paris, 1904.

Lefevbre de Behaine, F. *La campagne de France,* 2 vols. Paris, 1913.

Leggiere, Michael V. *Blücher: Scourge of Napoleon.* Norman, OK, 2014.

Leggiere, Michael V. *The Fall of Napoleon,* vol. 1, *The Allied Invasion of France.* Cambridge, 2007.

Leggiere, Michael V. *Napoleon and Berlin: The Franco-Prussian War in North Germany, 1813.* Norman, OK, 2002.

Lettow-Vorbeck, Oscar von. *Napoleons Untergang 1815,* 2 vols. Berlin, 1904–1906.

Lieven, Dominic. *Russia Against Napoleon: The True Story of the Campaigns of War and Peace.* New York, 2010.

Macdonald, Etienne-Jacques-Joseph-Alexandre, duc de Tarente, and Camille Rousset. *Souvenirs du Maréchal Macdonald, duc de Tarente.* Paris, 1892.

Marmont, A. de. *Mémoires du Duc de Raguse,* 9 vols. Paris, 1857.

Martens, F.F. *Recueil des traités et conventions, conclus par la Russie avec les puissances étrangères,* 15 vols. Saint Petersburg, 1874–1909.

Martens, G.F. *Recueil de traités d'alliance, de paix, de trêve, de neutralité, de commerce, de limites, déchange, etc., et plusieurs autres actes servant à la connoissance des relations étrangères des puissances et états de l'Europe depuis 1761 jusqu'à présent,* 16 vols. Göttingen, 1817–1842.

Mathieu, M.R. *Dernières victoires, 1814: la campagne de France aux alentours de Montmirail.* Paris, 1964.

Maude, F.N. *The Leipzig Campaign, 1813.* London, 1908.

Mauguin, G. *Ney et Blücher en Nancy en 1814.* Paris, 1930.

Maycock, F.W.O. *The Invasion of France, 1814.* London, 1914.

Meinecke, Friedrich. *Das Leben des Generalfeldmarschalls Hermann von Boyen,* 2 vols. Stuttgart, 1896–1899.

Metternich, C.L.W. *Memoirs of Prince Metternich, 1773–1815,* edited by R. Metternich, trans. by A. Napier, 5 vols. New York, 1970.

Mikhailovsky-Danilevsky, Aleksandr Ivanovich. *Denkwürdigkeiten aus dem Kriege von 1813,* trans. by Karl Goldhammer. Dorpat, 1837.

Mikhailovsky-Danilevsky, Aleksandr Ivanovich. *Opisaniye voiny 1813 goda,* 2 vols. Saint Petersburg, 1840.

Müffling, Friedrich Karl Ferdinand von. *Aus meinem Leben.* Berlin, 1851.

Müffling, Friedrich Karl Ferdinand von. *Betrachtungen über die großen Operationen und Schlachten der Feldzüge von 1813 und 1814.* Berlin, 1825.

Müffling, Friedrich Karl Ferdinand von. *Passages from My Life; Together with Memoirs of the Campaign of 1813 and 1814,* trans. and ed. by Philip Yorke. London, 1853.

Müffling, Friedrich Karl Ferdinand von. *Zur Kriegsgeschichte der Jahre 1813 und 1814. Die Feldzüge der schlesischen Armee unter dem Feldmarschall Blücher von der Beendigung des Waffenstillstandes bis zur Eroberung von Paris.* Berlin, 1827.

Muir, Rory. *Britain and the Defeat of Napoleon, 1807–1815.* London, 1996.

Napoleon I. *La correspondance de Napoléon Ier: publiée par ordre de l'empereur Napoléon III*, 32 vols. Paris, 1858–1869.

Natzmer, Gneomar Ernst von. *Aus dem Leben des Generals Oldwig von Natzmer: ein Beitrag zur preußischen Geschichte.* Berlin, 1876.

Nicolson, Harold. *The Congress of Vienna: A Study in Allied Unity.* New York, 1946.

Nostitz, August Ludwig Ferdinand von. *Das Tagebuch des Generals der Kavallerie, Grafen von Nostitz*, 2 vols. Pt. 1 of *Kriegsgeschichtliche Einzelschriften*, 6 vols. Berlin, 1885.

Norvins, Jacques Marquet de. *Portefeuille de mil huit cent treize, ou tableau politique et militaire renfermant: avec le récit des événemens de cette epoque, un choix de la correspondance inéd. de l'empereur Napoléon*, 2 vols. Paris, 1825.

Odeleben, E.O. von. *A Circumstantial Narrative of the Campaign in Saxony, in the Year 1813.* London, 1820.

Odeleben, E.O. von. *Napoleons Feldzug im Sachsen im Jahre 1813.* Dresden, 1816.

Oechscli, W. *Le passage des Allies en Suisse, 1813–1814*, trans. by F. Borrey. Paris, 1912.

Oncken, Wilhelm. *Österreich und Preußen im Befreiungskrieg: urkundliche Aufschlüsse über die politische Geschichte des Jahres 1813*, 2 vols. Berlin, 1876–1879.

Osten-Sacken und Rhein, Ottomar von. *Militärisch-politische Geschichte des Befreiungskrieges im Jahre 1813*, 2 vols. Berlin, 1813.

Pelet, Jean-Jacques. *Des principales opérations de la campagne de 1813.* Paris, 1826.

Pertz, G.H. and Hans Delbrück. *Das Leben des Feldmarschalls Grafen Neithardt von Gneisenau*, 5 vols. Berlin, 1864–1880.

Petre, F.L. *Napoleon at Bay: 1814.* New York, 1914.

Petre, F.L. *Napoleon's Last Campaign in Germany, 1813.* London, 1912; reprint, London, 1993.

Philippart, J. *Campaign in Germany and France*, 2 vols. London, 1814.

Philippart, J. *Memoirs and Campaigns of Charles Jean, Prince Royal of Sweden.* Baltimore, 1815.

Pierer, H.A. *Der Feldzug des Corps des Generals Grafen Ludwig von Wallmoden-Gimborn an der Nieder-Elbe und in Belgien in den Jahren 1813 und 1814.* Altenburg, 1848.

Plotho, Carl von. *Der Krieg in Deutschland und Frankreich in den Jahren 1813 und 1814*, 3 vols. Berlin, 1817.

Pougiat, F.E. *Invasion des armées étrangères dans le Départment de l'Aube.* Troyes, 1833.

Prittwitz, Karl Heinrich. *Beiträge zur Geschichte des Jahres 1813. Von einem höheren Offizier der Preußischen Armee*, 2 vols. Potsdam, 1843.

Quistorp, Barthold von. *Geschichte der Nord-Armee im Jahre 1813.* Berlin, 1894.

Radetzky von Radetz, J.J.W.A.F.K. *Denkschriften militärisch-politischen Inhalts aus dem handschriftlichen Nachlaß des k.k. österreichischen Feldmarschalls Grafen Radetzky.* Stuttgart and Augsburg, 1858.

Régnault, J.C.L. *Le maréchal Macdonald et la défense du Bas-Rhin, novembre–décembre 1813.* Nancy, 1931.

Roloff, G. *Politik und Kriegführung während des Krieges von 1814.* Berlin, 1891.

Ropes, John. *The Campaign of Waterloo: A Military History.* New York, 1893.

Ross, S. *European Diplomatic History, 1789–1815: France Against Europe.* New York, 1969.

Roux, X. *L'invasion de la Savoie et du Dauphiné par les Autrichiens en 1813 et 1814.* Grenoble, 1892.

Sauzey, Jean-Camille-Abel-Fleuri. *Les allemands sous les aigles françaises: essai sur les troupes de la Confédération du Rhin, 1806–1814.* Paris, 1902.

Schroeder, Paul. *The Transformation of European Politics, 1763–1848.* Oxford, 1994.

Schwartz, Karl. *Leben des generals Carl von Clausewitz und der Frau Marie von Clausewitz geb. Gräfin von Brühl.* Berlin, 1878.

Schwarzenberg, K. zu. *Briefe des Feldmarschalls Fürsten Schwarzenberg an Seine Frau, 1799–1816.* Leipzig, 1913.

Sherwig, John. *Guineas and Gunpowder: British Foreign Aid in the Wars with France, 1793–1815.* Cambridge, 1969.

Siborne, W. *History of the War in France and Belgium in 1815.* London, 1845.

Stanhope, P.H. *Notes of Conversations with the Duke of Wellington, 1831–1851.* London, 1888.

Steenackers, F.F. *L'invasion de 1814 dans la Haute-Marne.* Paris, 1868.

Steffens, H. *Adventures on the Road to Paris, during the Campaigns of 1813–1814.* London, 1848.

Stewart, R., Viscount Castlereagh. *The Correspondence, Dispatches and Other Papers of Viscount Castlereagh*, ed. by Charles William Vane, 12 vols. London, 1848–1853.

Stewart, Lord Londonderry, Lieutenant General Sir Charles William Vane. *Narrative of the War in Germany and France in 1813 and 1814.* London, 1830.

Saint Cyr, Laurent de Gouvion. *Mémoires sur les campagnes des armées du Rhin et de Rhin-et-Moselle: Atlas des cartes et plans relatifs aux campagnes du Maréchal Gouvion St-Cyr aux armées du Rhin et de Rhin et Moselle pendant les années 1792, 1793, 1794, 1795, 1796 et 1797.* Paris, 1828.

Thielen, M.F. *Der Feldzug der verbündeten Heere Europas 1814 in Frankreich unter dem Oberbefehle des k.k. Feldmarschalls Fürsten Karl zu Schwarzenberg.* Vienna, 1856.

Thiers, Adolphe. *History of the Consulate and the Empire of France Under Napoleon*, 12 vols. London, 1893–1894.

Thiry, J. *La chute de Napoléon I.* Paris, 1938.

Uffindell, A. *The Emperor's Last Triumph: Napoleon's Victory at Ligny, June 1815,* London, 1994.

Valentini, Georg von. *Der grosse Krieg*, 2 vols. Berlin, 1833.
Valentini, Georg von. *Lehre vom Kriege*, 2 vols. Berlin, 1835.
Varnhagen von Ense, Karl August. *Leben des Fürsten Blücher von Wahlstatt*. Berlin, 1933.
Varnhagen von Ense, Karl August. *Das Leben der Generals Gräfen Bülow von Dennewitz*. Berlin, 1853.
Vaudoncourt, Guillaume. *Histoire de la guerre soutenue par le Français en Allemagne en 1813*. Paris, 1819.
Vaudoncourt, Guillaume. *Histoire des campagnes de 1814 et 1815 en France*, 5 vols. Paris, 1826.
Venturini, Carl. *Rußlands und Deutschlands Befreiungskriege von der Franzosen-Herrschaft unter Napoleon Buonaparte in den Jahren 1812–1815*, 4 vols. Altenburg, 1816–1818.
Wagner, C.A. von. *Plane der Schlachten und Treffen von der preußischen Armee in den Feldzügen der Jahre 1813, 1814 und 1815*, 4 vols. Berlin, 1821.
Webster, C. *British Diplomacy, 1813–1815: Select Documents Dealing with the Reconstruction of Europe*. London, 1921.
Weil, Maurice-Henri. *La campagne de 1814*. 4 vols. Paris, 1892.
Wilson, Robert. *General Wilson's Journal, 1812–1814*, ed. by Antony Brett-James. London, 1964.
Wilson, Robert. *Private Diary of Travels, Personal Services, and Public Events: During the Mission Employed with the European Armies in the Campaigns of 1812, 1813, 1814*. London, 1861.
Woynar, Karl. *Österrikes förhållande till Sverige och Danmark under åren 1813–1814 hufvudsakligen dess politik vid Norges förening med Sverige*. Stockholm, 1892.
Yorck von Wartenburg, Hans Ludwig David Maximilian Graf. *Napoleon as a General*, ed. by Walter H. James, 2 vols. London, 1897–1898.

CHAPTER 13

Napoleon's War at Sea

Kenneth G. Johnson

Napoleon's assumption of power in France in 1799 placed him at the head of the second most powerful navy in the world. Challenged with the colossal task of revivifying a navy weakened by the neglect of the Bourbon monarchy and battered by the turbulence of the French Revolution, Napoleon plunged into the minutiae of naval affairs with the same vigor as he did for the army and every other matter of the state. As commander-in-chief, Napoleon personally devised much of France's naval strategy and designed many naval operations with the advice of several trusted naval officers. Over the course of his fourteen and one-half years as ruler of France, Napoleon developed an astute understanding of sea power. At the outset, he routinely launched risky operations that promised prodigious results if successful, but which ultimately decimated his navy. Constantly tinkering with his naval strategy, Napoleon eventually formulated a robust "fleet-in-being" strategy aimed at draining British coffers while he reconstituted his enervated navy. The French navy was on the verge of renewing its challenge to Britain's control of the seas just as his empire was collapsing in 1813.

After assuming control of the French state on 9 November 1799, Napoleon became the commander-in-chief of the French navy. Despite having no formal naval training, he would use his navy in four particular ways. First, he viewed sea power predominantly as a means of power projection: transporting men and materiel across the globe. Second, while Napoleon never abandoned the hope of using his navy to extend French power across the globe, in the latter half of his reign he resorted to the *guerre de course* or commerce raiding. Third, at the same time that Napoleon decided to pursue the *guerre de course*, he adopted the parallel strategy of a "fleet-in-being." Fourth, he continued to seek opportunities to engage the British navy in large fleet actions, but such battles could be attempted only in a very calculated manner to minimize risk.

While Napoleon's first priority was to send reinforcements to his beleaguered Army of the Orient in Egypt, he sought offensive operations to strengthen his position at the negotiating table after peace with Britain became a possibility in 1801.[1] In general, he hoped to force the British to evacuate the

---

1 After becoming First Consul in November 1799, Napoleon immediately focused on the Levant, where the Army of the Orient and the garrison of Malta urgently required reinforcements,

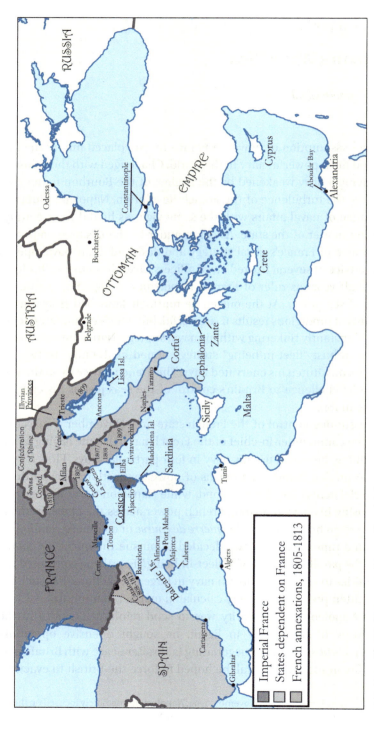

MAP 13.1   The Mediterranean Sea as a French lake

entire Mediterranean by expanding the French and Spanish fleets and blocking British access to the ports of Sicily and Naples. Concurrently, he planned for the Franco-Spanish fleet at Brest, the Dutch fleet, and squadrons of the League of Armed Neutrality to fix a large contingent of the British navy in the Atlantic and Baltic.[2] However, his attempt to assemble a large Franco-Spanish fleet at Cádiz was frustrated when the British captured a French seventy-four-gun ship, and two Spanish 112-gun ships accidently fired upon each other during the night until they both exploded. Finally, he sought to build a flotilla in his northern ports for an invasion of Britain, a staple of French strategy since the 1740s. The commander of this flotilla, *Contre-amiral* Louis-René Latouche-Tréville, received orders to prepare for a possible expedition to Britain, although his initial primary mission was to protect coastal shipping and prevent any incursions by the British. While Latouche-Tréville and Napoleon continued to discuss plans for the invasion during the summer, Napoleon received the news that the British were interested in peace negotiations. He responded by pressing the preparations for a possible invasion as a means to influence the negotiations. Although the French flotilla continued to expand, the progress of the peace negotiations eventually rendered them unnecessary, and Napoleon issued orders for most of the boats to be disarmed.

With the conclusion of the Anglo-French Peace of Amiens in March 1802, Napoleon turned his attention to reestablishing control over several wayward colonies. In the Caribbean, the colonies of Guadeloupe and Saint-Domingue had repulsed British invasions thanks to the fierce resistance of both free black and freed slave populations. However, black leaders had grown increasingly worried about the inclusion of many proponents of slavery in Napoleon's new

---

fresh supplies, and munitions. A small squadron left from Toulon with 3,000 troops but the British intercepted it near Malta and captured one ship of the line. Napoleon also had hoped to dispatch a Franco-Spanish fleet from Brest to operate in the Mediterranean, but he was unable to secure Spanish cooperation before a larger British fleet appeared off the French coast in March. After several months of delays, *Contre-amiral* Honoré Joseph Antoine Ganteaume sailed out of Brest with squadron of seven ships and two frigates, carrying 5,000 soldiers and extra munitions for Egypt in January 1801. After putting into Toulon to make repairs in February and delayed by winds for several months, Ganteaume's squadron finally left for Egypt in late April. With disease forcing him to send three ships back to Toulon, Ganteaume reached the North African coast in June. Spotted by a superior British fleet, Ganteaume raced back to Toulon without having landed any reinforcements. In the end, the last remaining French garrison of Alexandria held out just long enough for the news of their surrender to arrive too late to affect peace negations. Napoleon's efforts to sustain his forces in Egypt, came at a heavy cost. See *CN*, Nos 4393 and 5097, 6:10–11, 578–579; Louis Edouard Chevalier, *Histoire de la marine française sous le consulat et l'empire* (Paris, 1886), 6–8, 10, 39–47; James, *Naval History of Great Britain*, 3:14–15; Troude, *Batailles navales*, 3:197–200, 228–232.

2 *CG*, Nos 5991, 6018, 3:549, 562–563.

administration and so expelled their islands' colonial administrators. France's colonies had always been an important cog in its economy. The export of colonial goods and the connected slave trade not only generated vast sums of wealth and tax revenue, but had also led to the development of the ports of Nantes, Bordeaux, La Rochelle, and Le Havre.[3] While the loss of Saint-Domingue would later dampen Napoleon's colonial ambitions, the remaining Caribbean colonies of Martinique and Guadeloupe were still valuable.[4] Comparatively, the value of the French colonies in the Indian Ocean emanated primarily from their strategic location along the trade route between Europe and the Orient.[5] While much of the tax revenue would be consumed by local administration in times of war, the economic activity generated by these colonies was important for France's economy.

Furthermore, the colonies were important military assets. These islands were ideally situated to facilitate military operations against British commerce. While each colony possessed a number of commercial ports, the island of Martinique was naturally endowed with one of the greatest harbors in the Caribbean.[6] Thus, Martinique served as the hub of Napoleon's naval campaigns of 1805 and 1806. The colonial trade also served as a precious nursery for training seamen.[7] Reestablishing this colonial trade would allow Napoleon to replenish France's lists of trained seamen, which had suffered after nearly ten years of debilitating war.[8]

---

3   Pierre-Francois Page, *Traité d'économie politique et de commerce des colonies* (Paris, 1801), 15, 18–19, 45, 142.
4   Pierre-Clément Laussat, *Mémoires sur ma vie à mon fils* (Pau, 1831), 193, 282; see Table 8 in Eugène-Édouard Boyer-Peyreleau, *Les Antilles Françaises, particulièrement la Guadeloupe depuis leur découverte jusqu'au 1er Janvier 1823* (Paris, 1823), vol. 2.
5   Located 680 km off the eastern coast of Madagascar, the French Mascarene Islands consisted of three islands: Île de France (Mauritius), Île Bonaparte (Réunion), and the much smaller island of Rodrigues, which lay 600 km further east.
6   Not only was the immense bay of Fort-de-France able to contain a massive fleet, it was also one of the best shelters from hurricanes. Nestled within a semi-circle of mountains that protected ships from the winds, the westward-facing harbor was also less prone to the storm surges that accompanied hurricanes: Alexandre Moreau de Jonnès, *Aventures de guerre au temps de la République et du Consulat* (Paris, 1858), 153.
7   *Discours de Villaret-Joyeuse sur l'importance des colonies & les moyens de les pacificier*, 12 Prairial an 5 (31 May 1797), 2.
8   It is estimated that more than 15,000 French sailors served aboard merchant vessels traveling to the Caribbean during the late 1780s, while another 20,000 sailors served in French coastal shipping, which relied heavily on colonial goods. See Michael Duffy, *Soldiers, Sugar, and Seapower: The British Expeditions to the West Indies and the War against Revolutionary France* (Oxford, 1987), 22.

The Caribbean was Napoleon's initial priority due to its relative value and the imminent threat of the increasingly independent behavior of local black leaders. Even before the preliminaries of the peace had been ratified, Napoleon ordered 17,000 troops to Saint-Domingue and another 1,700 soldiers to Guadeloupe.[9] This initial wave consisted of the forces assembled at Brest, Lorient, and Rochefort. Additional squadrons followed from other French ports, the Batavian Republic, Spain, and Italy. The main body of the expedition (8,200 troops) and the future *Capitaine-général* Charles Leclerc sailed from Brest with the Franco-Spanish fleet. Under the commands of *Vice-amiral* Louis Thomas Villaret-Joyeuse and *Jefe de escuadra* Federico Carlos Gravina y Nápoli, this fleet consisted of ten French ships, five Spanish ships, and nine frigates. A smaller small division of six ships, six frigates, and one corvette loaded with 3,500 troops assembled at Rochefort. Led by Latouche-Tréville, the Rochefort squadron would join the Franco-Spanish fleet at sea, before heading on to Saint-Domingue. *Contre-amiral* Jean-Louis Delmotte's squadron brought another 900 men from Lorient aboard one ship, one frigate, two corvettes, and one transport.[10] Unlike preceding French agents who often had to rely on the support of local black leaders, Leclerc would have a significant military force at his command to reassert French control.

The Saint-Domingue expedition encountered difficulties at the outset. Unable to rally at sea, the three fleets eventually gathered in late January 1802 at the final rallying point of Samaná Bay, located on the northeastern side of the island of Hispaniola. Not only did sea power enable Napoleon to dispatch such a large expedition to this colony, but it also played an important role in the subsequent operations. Unsure of François-Dominique Toussaint Louverture's reaction and hoping to establish control quickly to avoid bloodshed and resistance, Napoleon had ordered Leclerc to divide his forces, thereby securing nearly all major coastal cities almost simultaneously. The main body under the command of Villaret-Joyeuse and Leclerc sailed directly for the principal port of Le Cap Français.[11] While Toussaint Louverture's subordinates at Santo-Domingo and Jérémie surrendered without a fight, the garrisons of Port-au-Prince and Le Cap offered sharp resistance. With Le Cap and other towns burnt to the ground, Leclerc's expedition continued to face determined resistance during the subsequent campaign into the interior.[12] The second wave of

---

9   *CN*, Nos 5785, 5786, 7:273–279; *CG*, No. 6544, 3:802–803.
10 Chevalier, *Marine française consulat et l'empire*, 78–79; Troude, *Batailles navales*, 3:269.
11 Paul Roussier, ed., *Lettres du général Leclerc, commandant en chef de l'armée de Saint-Domingue en 1802* (Paris, 1937), 264–269.
12 Thomas Ott, *The Haitian Revolution, 1789–1804* (Knoxville, 1973), 151–153.

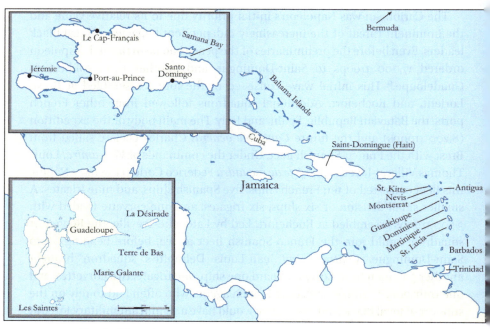

MAP 13.2   The Caribbean Sea

the invasion arrived as Leclerc conducted his campaign inland.[13] After these shipments, frigate squadrons or individual ships that had not been prepared in time to sail with the aforementioned fleets transported reinforcements to Saint-Domingue. In summary, the operation against Saint-Domingue was an exceptional example of both strategic and tactical sealift in the Age of Sail.

Although on a much smaller scale, Napoleon also sent similar expeditions to Guadeloupe, Martinique, and the Mascarene Islands. *Contre-amiral* François Joseph Bouvet transported 3,500 troops aboard his squadron of two ships, four frigates, one flute, and three transports to Guadeloupe in May 1802. Villaret-Joyeuse returned to the Caribbean with a small squadron of two ships, one frigate, and six smaller vessels to retake possession of Martinique from the

---

13   On 12 February, another 2,300 troops arrived aboard Ganteaume's fleet of four ships, one frigate, and one corvette from Toulon. Two days later, Linois arrived with another 2,000 troops from Cádiz aboard his three ships and three frigates. Having departed from Vlissingen on 4 January 1802, a Dutch squadron reached Saint Domingue only in April 1802 with another 1,500 men. Vice-Admiral Pieter Hartsinck with the *Brutus* (76), *Neptunus* (68), *Joan de Witt* (68), and the brig *Ajax* were accompanied by the French frigate *Poursuivante*. See Chevalier, *Marine française consulat et l'empire*, 79; Troude, *Batailles navales*, 3:270–271.

British. With an ever-increasing number of troops diverted to Saint-Domingue, an expedition to the Indian Ocean did not sail until March 1803. *Contre-amiral* Charles-Alexandre Léon Durand Linois ferried 1,350 soldiers to the Mascarene Islands on two transports escorted by one ship and three frigates. With his primary mission complete and facing greater numbers of British ships, Linois initially wanted to return to France, but the new *Captaine-général* of Île de France, General Charles Mathieu Isidore Decaen, persuaded him to conduct a commerce-raiding campaign.[14]

Plying the seas, even unopposed, had its dangers. As numerous French vessels crossed the Atlantic, the French lost a total of two ships of the line, two frigates, and three corvettes and brigs either sunk or wrecked on shore due to weather or enemy action.[15] In addition to decimating the Army of Saint-Domingue, the outbreak of yellow fever in 1802 killed nearly 8,000 sailors. While most of the ships quickly returned to France after unloading their cargoes, Napoleon maintained a small squadron at Saint-Domingue under the command of Latouche-Tréville. After the collapse of the Anglo-French Peace of Amiens in 1803 and the resurgent slave revolt, these remaining ships soon sought refuge back in France or in neighboring colonies. Often undermanned and loaded with frightened refugees, many of these French ships fell prey to the British navy, which circled offshore. The British captured one ship of the line, six frigates, fourteen corvettes and brigs, and scores of other smaller vessels, many of which would later enter into British service.[16] Thus, in total, the colonial operations of 1801–1803 cost the French navy three ships of the line, eight frigates, and fifteen corvettes or brigs. More importantly, the capture of an estimated 2,000 sailors, coupled with the 8,000 sailors who died from disease, proved a serious blow to Napoleon's aspiration of reconstituting his beleaguered navy. Continually denied access to the sea during the war, Napoleon had hoped to profit from the Peace of Amiens by providing his sailors with crucial experience.

While Napoleon had always anticipated that the Peace of Amiens would be temporary, Britain's decision to declare war on 18 May 1803 left him in a quandary. The abbreviated peace proved insufficient to rejuvenate his navy, as the nearly fourteen-month cession of hostilities did not provide much opportunity for training or ship construction. Already by mid-March, Napoleon had forbidden the departure of any ships of the line or frigates for the Americas.[17]

---

14 C. Northcote Parkinson, *War in the Eastern Sea, 1793–1815* (London, 1954), 198–201, 204–206, 214.
15 Ships – *Banel* (64), *Desaix* (74); frigates – *Cocarde* (40), *Consolante* (40).
16 Troude, *Batailles navales*, 3:270, 277, 296, 298–299.
17 *CG*, No. 7523, 4:75.

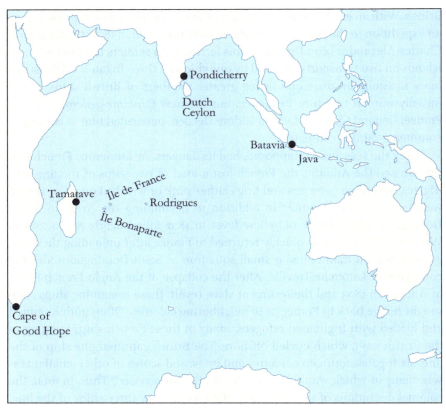

MAP 13.3   The Indian Ocean

Despite this measure, the French navy was dangerously dispersed with twenty-five ships and twenty-five frigates at sea. Furthermore, many of the ships in French ports were in dire need of repairs after several trans-Atlantic voyages. Even an optimistic report by Admiral Denis Decrès, the French minister of the navy and colonies, estimated that Napoleon would only have twenty-one ships at his disposal by September 1803.[18] The French navy thus emerged from the Peace of Amiens even more weary and unprepared for a renewed naval war with Britain.

As the resumption of hostilities with Britain becoming increasingly probable, Napoleon revisited his earlier plans to invade the British Isles. At the end of February 1803, he inquired about the state of the flotilla built in 1801. Less than two weeks later, he ordered an additional 500 gunboats built by September

---

18   Report by Decrès, 25 March 1803, in Desbrière, *1793–1805*, 3:36–40.

1806. At the end of March, the First Consul further ordered all available commercial vessels, both large and small, gathered in Atlantic ports to serve as impromptu transports.[19] Although it is difficult to determine Napoleon's true intent, it is very likely that these early preparations were meant to influence negotiations.

After Britain declared war in May 1803, the invasion flotilla evolved from being merely a political tool into a genuine effort to conquer the country. Napoleon ordered almost every available facility to construct boats for the flotilla, assuring Decrès that "money is no object."[20] Over the course of the summer, the configuration of the invasion flotilla continually underwent revision. Similar to 1801, the flotilla of 1803 relied heavily upon relatively flat-bottomed boats. By September 1803, Napoleon called for 1,675 flat-bottomed boats of various sizes, supported by 81 fishing corvettes armed for war, another 220–270 fishing vessels as transports, and 108 fishing vessels converted to horse transports.[21] Shortages of funds and Napoleon's frequent adjustments contributed to delays in construction that left the invasion flotilla at two-thirds of the projected required strength by June 1804. The entire country of France and many of its satellite states were eventually involved in this project.[22]

Crossing the Channel with the flotilla still presented the greatest challenge, particularly as the vigilant British navy would contest their passage. While some admirals less familiar with the flotilla boats critiqued their capabilities, those admirals who had worked directly with these boats did not question their stability.[23] Instead, their primary concern was the British navy. While initial plans called on crossing during a calm that would deprive Britain of most of its maritime defense, launching so many boats from Channel ports, which were heavily dependent upon the tides, rendered this plan infeasible. By the fall of 1803, Napoleon began to entertain ideas of combining operations of the flotilla with the regular French navy.

---

19   CG, Nos 7498, 7548, 4:60, 86–87; Order, 11 March 1803, in Desbrière, *1793–1805*, 3:22–25.
20   Note for Decrès, 17 June 1803, in Desbrière, *1793–1805*, 3:84.
21   Napoleon issued various orders calling for 54 *prames* (prams), 324 *chaloupes canonnieres*, 432 *bateaux canonniers*, 756 *peniches* (barges), and 108 *caiques*: Decrès to Berthier, 14 September 1803, ibid., 3:107–109.
22   In support of this operation, the Dutch had built another 200 gunboats by May 1804. These landing craft were bolstered by a fleet of more than 600 fishing vessels in both French and Dutch ports. Although it is difficult to obtain an accurate figure, this momentous endeavor cost France in excess of 37,000,000 francs just in the construction and purchasing of boats. Napoleon spent another 3,000,000 to 4,000,000 francs improving Boulogne and the other Channel ports to enable them to house and launch so many boats: ibid., 3:90–91, 132, 174, 355–356, 380, 411, 452, 463.
23   M.A. Thiers, *Histoire de l'Empire* (Paris, 1865), 1:52.

Weakened by losses in men and materiel during the expeditions to Saint-Domingue, the French navy was a shadow of its strength at the onset of peace in 1801. In early June 1803, Napoleon ordered Decrès to push the construction and repair of ships and frigates in Antwerp and French ports. He hoped to have a large fleet of twenty-one ships at Brest with smaller fleets ready in Toulon, Rochefort, and the Scheldt by November. Coupled with the flotilla, these fleets were to threaten "the isles of Jersey and Guernsey and every point of the continent of [Great Britain]."[24] By prioritizing the invasion flotilla, however, Napoleon deprived the port of Brest of the adequate funds, ship-builders, and sailors needed to rapidly rearm the fleet.[25] The French fleets would not reach his projected strengths until the summer of 1804.

Meanwhile, Britain took the first overt action to broaden the Anglo-French conflict. Based on faulty intelligence that Spain was preparing for war, the British launched an audacious preemptive attack by sending a frigate squadron to intercept a Spanish frigate squadron laden with gold from the Americas. Unprepared for action yet unwilling to surrender to the British, the Spanish ships resisted. During the resulting engagement on 5 October 1804, one of the Spanish frigates exploded and the other three Spanish frigates eventually surrendered.[26] In response to this blatant violation of its neutrality, nonaligned Spain declared war on Britain in December, thereby providing Napoleon with an ally of significant maritime strength.

While the specifics of a Franco-Spanish alliance were not solidified until January 1805, Napoleon began to formulate operations in December 1804 based on the assumption that the Spanish navy would be at his disposal. The plans made by Napoleon in December 1804 called for the French fleets at Rochefort and Toulon to assemble in the Caribbean, return to Europe to unite with additional French and Spanish ships, and then sail to the English Channel. Whichever fleet reached the Caribbean first would assail British-held colonies while it awaited the arrival of the other. After some time in the Caribbean, the fleets would rally in Martinique under Villeneuve's command, and disembark troops and munitions before heading back to European waters. The combined fleet would free the French and Spanish ships blockaded in the northern Spanish port of Ferrol, and then head to Rochefort, where they would be joined by twelve Spanish ships coming from Cádiz. Meanwhile, *Contre-amiral* Honoré

---

24   CG, No. 7691, 4:154–155; Instructions to Bruix, 21 July 1803, in Desbrière, *1793–1805*, 3:295–299.
25   Joseph Averous, *Marie-Joseph Caffarelli (1760–1845): préfet maritime de Brest sous le Consulat et l'Empire* (Paris, 2006), 81–88.
26   Moore to Cornwallis, 6 October 1804, No. 354, in Leyland, *Blockade of Brest, 1803–1805*, 2:87–90.

Joseph Antoine Ganteaume's Brest fleet would continue to serve as a diversion, sailing an expeditionary force of more than 21,000 soldiers to "Ireland or elsewhere," with India also a potential target. With the campaign underway, Napoleon ordered all officers of the invasion flotilla and the Army of England to return to their posts to prepare for the crossing.[27]

To deceive the British of his ultimate objective, Napoleon undertook a variety of measures to spread false intelligence to British spies. As Villeneuve was "to spare nothing from the first moment to lead others to believe that [his] mission is directed against the East Indies," Decrès ordered him to provide a copy of *Neptune Orientales*, a navigational atlas for the East Indies, to every ship in the Toulon fleet. Moreover, Villeneuve was to conduct official inquiries on the conditions of the Cape of Good Hope. While preparing for their eventual departure, Villeneuve and General Jacques Lauriston secretly were to reduce the size of the expeditionary force in such a way that the other officers did not suspect anything until long after the fleet had sailed. Meanwhile, Napoleon continued to consider an expedition to India if the invasion of Britain suffered any reversals.[28] While Napoleon contemplated alternative plans, Villeneuve's fleet set sail.

Success relied almost completely on Villeneuve, who had grown increasingly despondent. Starting in early January, his reports demonstrated growing pessimism. On 4 January, he complained that Nelson was surely aware of his impending departure and would have all avenues of escape covered. His fear of Nelson was compounded further by his negative opinion of his own fleet's capabilities, which would make it "all the more difficult for me to succeed in this mission." Nelson's vigilant blockade led Villeneuve to believe that the British would intercept his fleet before it could reach Gibraltar. Although he overestimated Nelson's abilities, the poor handling of ships by his subordinates during the operation validated his fears. After returning to port, Villeneuve wrote a frank report to Decrès attesting the depth of his despair. Reminding Decrès that he had not wanted command of the squadron in the first place, he vehemently expressed his desire not to see his career ruined by an operation that he believed was doomed to fail and requested that he be replaced. As Villeneuve was his protégé, Decrès apparently hid Villeneuve's desire to be relieved of command from Napoleon. Aware only of Villeneuve's "lack of

---

27 *CN*, Nos 8206, 8209, 8231–8232, 10:63–67, 69, 78–81, 83; *CG*, Nos 9445, 9509–9510, 9539, 9541–9542, 4:975–976, 5:34–37, 52–53.

28 Decrès to Villeneuve, 27 February 1805, SHD, Marine BB⁴ 230, f. 32; *CG*, Nos 9621, 9828, 9932, 5:94–95, 198, 247–248.

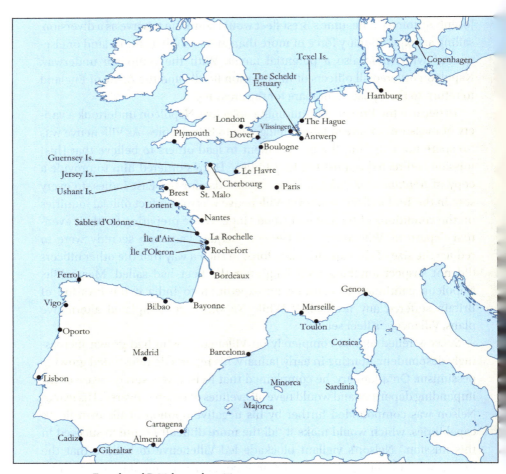

MAP 13.4 French and British naval positions

resolve" thanks to Lauriston's report, Bonaparte left the increasingly fragile Villeneuve in command.[29]

Napoleon still hoped to gather a massive fleet to secure temporary command of the Channel. While he had originally wanted to do this through careful maneuver, Napoleon accepted the inevitability of a battle, openly referring to the future "Battle of Ouessant [Ushant]."[30] He continued to modify his

---

29   SHD, Marine BB⁴ 230, f. 101, 107, 109, 117; CG, No. 9547, 5:55–56.
30   CG, Nos 10140, 10152, 10238, 5:349, 353–354, 395–396. A battle of Ushant (*bataille d'Ouessant*) between the French and British fleets had taken place on 27 July 1778 some 160 km west of Ushant, an island at the mouth of the English Channel off northwestern

plans as he received new intelligence regarding the movements of the British fleets and his own forces. Based on reports from the Caribbean that he had received in June, Napoleon began to doubt Villeneuve's suitability for the important mission. Once again, he turned to Ganteaume to take command of the combined fleet when Villeneuve appeared off the coast of Brest. Napoleon ordered Ganteaume not to make any sorties as his "intention [was to] lull [the British] into a false sense of security as much as possible regarding the Brest fleet." Napoleon hoped to lure more British ships away from Brest by spreading false news of his own departure to Utrecht coupled with corresponding troop movements. To further distract the British, he ordered the Dutch fleet at Texel to make a quick sortie, while troops were loaded aboard the transports in Holland.[31] Thus, Bonaparte prepared an alternative means of obtaining command of the Channel in case Villeneuve did not prove up to the task.

The pace of the campaign accelerated quickly in July. As Napoleon secretly raced back to Paris from Italy in mid-July, the British received reports of Villeneuve's impending arrival. In response, the British fleet abandoned the blockade of Rochefort and joined Admiral Robert Calder off the coast of Ferrol on 15 July. With his fleet now increased to fifteen ships, Calder set sail to intercept Villeneuve. Taking advantage of their departure, the new commander of the Rochefort fleet, Captain Zacharie Allemand, sailed with five ships, three frigates, and two brigs.[32] When Allemand opened his secret orders at sea, he learned that he was already supposed to be raiding Ireland. As his second mission was to link with Villeneuve off Ferrol between 29 July and 3 August, Allemand headed west to wait until the designated time. Receiving reports that the blockade of Rochefort had been lifted and the British fleet guarding Brest was out of sight, Napoleon accurately assessed that the British had learned of Villeneuve's approach. Upset that Ganteaume had not taken advantage of this situation per his orders, Napoleon ordered him out to sea. If he encountered fewer than sixteen British ships, he was to engage. If the passages were clear, he was to sweep into the Channel. If the British left a small squadron to shadow the Brest fleet, then he was to race to Ferrol to link with Villeneuve.[33] Unfortunately for Napoleon, this window of opportunity had already passed as Admiral Samuel Cornwallis had resumed command of the

---

France. The first major naval engagement between the French and British fleets in the American Revolutionary War, the battle ended indecisively.

31 CG, Nos 10243, 10333, 10356, 10359, 5:458–459, 461–462.
32 Calder to Cornwallis, 15 July 1805, No. 555, and Martin to Decrès, 17 July 1805, No. 556, in Leyland, *Blockade of Brest*, 2:304–306.
33 CG, Nos 10419, 10429, 5:492, 496–497.

Channel fleet, raising its strength to eighteen ships.[34] With Ganteaume bottled in Brest, Napoleon's hopes of commanding the Channel lay solely on Villeneuve.

Villeneuve's return to European waters proved troublesome. With its voyage delayed, first by contrary winds and later by threats of a storm, his Franco-Spanish fleet finally approached the coast of Spain on 22 July, where it encountered Calder's fleet. During the ensuing battle, often obscured by fog, the British captured two Spanish ships. While Calder secured his prizes, Villeneuve abandoned any efforts to continue the battle and sailed for Ferrol. Hampered by continually changing winds, the already irresolute Villeneuve changed his course several times, as he alternated between heading to Ferrol, Cádiz, and Vigo over the next couple of days. Eventually, the Franco-Spanish fleet anchored in Vigo Bay on 27 July. Although the loss of two Spanish ships was unwelcome, many opportunities remained as the Rochefort fleet of five ships was at sea, the Franco-Spanish fleet of fourteen ships at Ferrol was no longer blockaded, and Villeneuve was anchored nearby at Vigo. Leaving behind 1,200 sick men and three of his slowest, worn-out ships, Villeneuve departed from Vigo with thirteen French ships and two Spanish ships on 31 July. Reaching Ferrol on 2 August, Villeneuve received Napoleon's orders of 16 July. Forbidden from anchoring in Ferrol, Villeneuve instead was instructed to free the fleets of Brest and/or Rochefort. However, if Villeneuve suffered some sort of misfortune that "considerably changed [his] situation," he was to rally the fleets from Rochefort and Ferrol and head to Cádiz.[35] Having already twice expressed to Decrès his intent to sail for Cádiz if the winds impeded his approach to Ferrol, Villeneuve probably believed that these orders reinforced his eventual decision to head for Cádiz. In the meantime, he anchored in Coruña and set about preparing his fleet for a long voyage by conducting necessary repairs and stocking provisions and water. Delayed by contrary winds for three days, the admiral eventually set sail with a massive Franco-Spanish fleet of twenty-nine ships (eighteen French, eleven Spanish), six frigates (four French, two Spanish), and four smaller ships on 13 August. Napoleon's chances for invading Britain now rested on this substantial force commanded by an increasingly despondent Villeneuve.

Uncertainty reigned amongst the British fleets scattered across the Bay of Biscay in the summer of 1805. Unaware of Napoleon's plans and Allemand's location, the British navy began to concentrate off the coat of Brest. After waiting several days for Nelson, Calder joined Cornwallis and the Channel fleet at Ushant on 13 August. Having sailed to Gibraltar in the belief that Villeneuve

---

34   Cornwallis to Marsden, 7 July 1805, No. 549, in Leyland, *Blockade of Brest*, 2:300.
35   Maine, *Trafalgar*, 143–146; CG, No. 10412, 5:489–490.

was heading to the Mediterranean, Nelson eventually reached the Channel fleet with another eight ships on 15 August. Although Cornwallis sent six ships back to Britain due to an immediate need for repairs and provisions, he still possessed a formidable force of thirty-four ships to block Villeneuve. On 16 August, Cornwallis made the potentially disastrous decision to split his forces. Calder sailed with eighteen ships to join two other ships in a blockade of Ferrol.[36] Had Villeneuve managed to slip past Calder, Cornwallis would have faced the dangerous prospect of being caught between Villeneuve's twenty-nine ships and Ganteaume's twenty-one ships with only sixteen ships at his disposal.

Already apprehensive about his mission, Villeneuve's fraying resolve was quickly tested. Upon his departure from Ferrol, lookouts spotted several unknown ships and frigates. Although it was actually only a single ship and two frigates left by Calder to observe Ferrol, their presence troubled Villeneuve. The following day, lookouts sighted a large number of sails on the horizon. Despite his superior numbers, Villeneuve did not approach the unknown sails. After he received false reports of twenty-five ships being in the area on 15 August, he lost all remaining courage and opted to sail for Cádiz the next day. The strange sails, however, were not a British fleet as Villeneuve feared, but rather Allemand's squadron en route for Vigo. Unfortunately for the French, Villeneuve proved correct Napoleon's assessment of him: "a poor man, who sees double, and who has more perception than character."[37] After chasing away the three British ships blockading Cádiz, Villeneuve and the Franco-Spanish fleet dropped anchor on 17 August, thereby ending the campaign to invade Britain.

Uncertain of Villeneuve's progress and encountering growing trouble with Russia and Austria, Napoleon faced a difficult strategic decision. By late July, he had already received reports that Austria was preparing for war. On learning of Villeneuve's departure from Ferrol, Napoleon believed that "there [was] still time" to invade Britain but also prepared for the possibility that he would have to delay the operation and contend with Austria. After reading Villeneuve's pessimistic letters, Napoleon deduced that the admiral was no longer sailing for the English Channel. On 25 August, Napoleon decided to postpone the invasion and strike at Austria.[38] While he dashed eastward to conduct his

---

36 Cornwallis to Marsden, 13 and August 1805, Nos 578, No. 580, Cornwallis to Calder, 16 August 1805, No. 581, in Leyland, *Blockade of Brest*, 2:341, 343–345.
37 CG, No. 10556, 5:562–563.
38 CG, Nos 10645, 10664, 5:607–608, 622–623.

campaign against Austria, several of his final orders regarding the naval campaign would have disastrous effect.

The postponement of the invasion also marked a major shift in Napoleon's naval strategy. After dictating a series of orders directing the Grande Armée to Germany, Napoleon developed new plans for his scattered fleets before setting out to wage the War of the Third Coalition. Already anticipating the possibility that Cádiz was Villeneuve's destination, Napoleon asked Decrès for his opinion on the manner to proceed. Citing the potential both to strike Britain and to develop the French navy, Decrès advocated the use of the fastest ships to conduct raids against British commerce while the slower ships remained armed in port "to occupy the enemy." On 1 September, Napoleon adopted Decrès's suggestion and ordered him to develop plans for eleven various cruises that would employ around thirty ships and eleven frigates from Brest and Cádiz.[39] Unlike the traditional *guerre de course*, the emperor's new naval strategy relied on small squadrons of ships rather than privateers or frigates.

Napoleon had only occasionally dabbled with the *guerre de course*, as he had been mainly preoccupied with efforts to reestablish control over his colonies and later to invade Britain. He had contemplated this idea as early as January 1800, when he issued instructions for five ships and two frigates to raid commerce between Portugal, the island of Madeira, the Caribbean, Newfoundland, and the Azores.[40] Napoleon eventually scrapped these plans due to the growing demand for reinforcements in Egypt. In early 1803, the French raided British commerce in the Indian Ocean, but it had not been Bonaparte's original plan. Now, commerce raiding was to become a central part of his strategy.

By mid-September, Napoleon and Decrès had drafted plans for a series of expeditions that crisscrossed the Atlantic. According to Napoleon, "it is these bizarre and incalculable cruises that will do the greatest harm to the enemy." The Brest fleet was to divide into two separate squadrons once it had made it out to sea. *Contre-amiral* Corentin de Leissègues's division of five ships, two frigates, and one corvette would transport 1,000 soldiers and much-needed provisions to the besieged town of Santo Domingo, the principal city on the Spanish half of Hispaniola and the last remaining French foothold on the island. Leissègues would then raid British commerce in the Caribbean before heading back to the waters off Britain. Meanwhile, *Contre-amiral* Jean-Baptiste Willaumez would lead the other half of the fleet consisting of six ships and two frigates on a cruise in the South Atlantic and then the Caribbean. Another

---

39   Decrès to Napoleon, 23 August 1805, AN, AF IV 1196; *CG*, Nos 10618, 10730, 5:594, 659–660.
40   *CN*, No. 4495, 6:64–65.

small squadron of one ship and a few smaller vessels would raid the African coast. Pairs of frigates and other smaller vessels would attack the British from the Caribbean to Ireland. "English commerce is everywhere," Napoleon observed; "we must strive to be everywhere possible to hurt it."[41] The apparent ease with which his fleets had evaded the British navy may have enticed Bonaparte to focus on smaller squadrons.

Allemand was adeptly demonstrating the potential of this system of war. After failing to unite with Villeneuve and the Franco-Spanish fleet, Allemand cruised to intercept British commerce off Britain and later the Canaries. Persistently eluding detection by the British, Allemand's "Invisible Squadron" captured the fifty-six-gun HMS *Calcutta*, three smaller vessels, and more than forty merchant ships, estimated to be worth 8,000,000 francs, before returning unmolested to Rochefort on 24 November. Allemand's exploits thrilled Napoleon, but they also compounded his growing irritation with the delayed departures of his other cruises. "You see the damage that Allemand is causing," he complained; "think of what our cruisers would be doing if they wanted to leave; but they do not leave for one reason or another."[42] In recognition of his brilliant campaign, Napoleon "wholeheartedly" promoted Allemand to the rank of *contre-amiral* in January 1806, even antedating his promotion to the date when his fleet had sailed in mid-July 1805. Subsequent operations, however, did not fare so well, as the British navy was not as preoccupied as it had been during Allemand's cruise, thanks to the defeat of Villeneuve and the Franco-Spanish fleet at the Battle of Trafalgar.

Impatient to see the Franco-Spanish fleet return to Toulon, Napoleon inadvertently pushed the erratic Villeneuve to set a course that ultimately led to the disastrous Battle of Trafalgar. Already frustrated by Villeneuve's lack of resolve, Napoleon did not wish to see the Franco-Spanish fleet languish in Cádiz, which had already exhausted its supplies arming and outfitting the Spanish ships. On 15 September, Napoleon issued his final orders for Villeneuve to head for Naples, where he was to disembark the soldiers on board to support General Gouvian St. Cyr's planned invasion. This operation, however, was of only minor importance as Napoleon's essential wish was for the massive Franco-Spanish fleet to reach Toulon. According to the emperor, "the existence of such a considerable fleet at Toulon will have incalculable results; it will be a strong diversion." More importantly, Napoleon had also decided to relieve Villeneuve of command. Yet his fatal mistake was ordering Villeneuve to the Mediterranean even as he simultaneously sent *Contre-amiral* François Étienne de

---

41 *CG*, No. 10822, 5:703–704.
42 *CG*, No. 11063, 5:827–828; Chevalier, *Marine française consulat et l'empire*, 240–241.

Rosily-Mesros to assume command of the Franco-Spanish fleet. Spurred by news that Rosily was on his way to replace him, the once-hesitant Villeneuve quickly ordered the Franco-Spanish fleet to sail for the open sea as soon as he believed that the British had weakened their blockading force. During the resulting Battle of Trafalgar, subsequent minor engagements, and storms, the Franco-Spanish fleet was almost completely annihilated. Seven French and eight Spanish ships ultimately floundered, wrecked on shore, or were burned, while the British managed to secure five French ships and three Spanish ships as prizes. The remaining five French and five Spanish ships escaped to the safety of Cádiz. Due to the chaos of the battles and the subsequent storms, it is impossible to account accurately for the loss in personnel but, based on letters and official estimates, in excess of 6,000 French and Spanish died in combat or drowned, while more than 6,000 were taken prisoner.[43] By inadvertently pushing his unstable admiral, Napoleon lost a significant portion of his sea power.

Undeterred by the defeat at Trafalgar, Napoleon expedited his commerce-raiding campaign. After learning of the disastrous results of Trafalgar, he assured Decrès that "nothing has changed regarding my projects for cruises." Rather, the emperor chastised the latter, stating, "I am upset that everything is not ready. They must leave without delay."[44] The subsequent cruises during the winter of 1805/1806 inflicted significant economic losses on the British, but also came at a considerable cost to the French. Although not all of the planned cruises sailed, twelve ships, fifteen frigates, and nine smaller vessels took part in eight expeditions. *Capitaine de vaisseau* Jean-Marthe-Adrien Lhermitte set sail from Lorient for the African coast with a small division of one ship, two frigates, and two brigs on 31 October.[45] Although Lhermitte seized or destroyed commercial shipping estimated to be worth 10,000,000 francs, the British captured one of his frigates and one of his brigs.[46] A pair of frigates and a pair of brigs leaving separately from Vlissingen in November had less success as a storm drove one of the frigates into port, while the British eventually captured the other ships before they could inflict much damage on British commerce.[47] As Napoleon dealt with a defeated Austria, the Brest fleet finally sailed on 13

---

43 CN, No. 9220, 11:204–205; Chevalier, *Marine française consulat et l'empire*, 187–223; James, *Naval History*, 4:22–117; Troude, *Batailles navales*, 3:368–412.
44 CG, No. 11120, 5:860.
45 Ship – *Regulus* (74); frigates – *President, Cybèle*; brigs – *Surveillant, Diligent*.
46 Chevalier, *Marine française consulat et l'empire*, 263–264; Maurice Dupont, *L'amiral Decrès et Napoleon* (Paris, 1991), 203; Troude, *Batailles navales*, 3:434, 471–472.
47 "Chroniques Maritimes d'Anvers de 1804 à 1814: histoire d'une flotte du temps passé," *Revue Maritime et coloniale* (Paris, 1890), 104: 194–95; Troude, *Batailles navales*, 3:433, 466–467.

December 1805. After thirty-six hours at sea, the fleet separated into two divisions with Leissègues heading for the Caribbean and Willaumez steering for the south Atlantic.

Damaged by tropical storms while en route, Leissègues's scattered command reached his initial destination of Santo Domingo on 20 and 25 January. After unloading troops and supplies, Leissègues faced an unenviable decision. His orders directed him to Havana, where significant port facilities would ensure that repairs could be completed in absolute safety. Fearing either an encounter with a superior British fleet or finding himself subsequently blockaded in Havana and unable to continue his mission, Leissègues made the fatal decision to conduct hasty repairs at anchor in the unprotected harbor of Santo Domingo. None of the ships was prepared for battle when a British fleet of seven ships and two frigates under the command of Vice-Admiral John Thomas Duckworth appeared on 6 February.

Duckworth's presence was a testament to the extent that the Atlantic had become crowded as French and British squadrons crisscrossed the ocean during the winter of 1805/1806. Having actually started his cruise chasing Allemand's "Invisible Squadron," Duckworth received reports of a French squadron attacking a British convoy. Unaware that the Brest fleet had reached the open sea and that Leissègues was the true culprit, Duckworth sailed in pursuit, assuming that it was Allemand. Ten days later, Duckworth stumbled on Willaumez's squadron, which he continued to believe was Allemand's. After chasing Willaumez into the south Atlantic, Duckworth called off the pursuit to gather his scattered squadron. Taking advantage of the trade winds, Duckworth sailed to the Caribbean to resupply before making the return trip to European waters. While sitting at anchor in Barbados, Duckworth learned that a French squadron had been spotted at Santo Domingo.

The ensuing Battle of Santo Domingo resulted in the complete destruction of Leissègues's division before it could undertake its commerce-raiding mission in earnest. A vigorous melee erupted as the British ships opened fire on the French ships that were slowly getting underway. Succumbing to the superior British firepower, three French ships lowered their flags in surrender. Leissègues drove his two remaining, battered ships onto the shore to avoid capture. While Leissègues extricated most of the crews of his two beached ships, British boats eventually secured the ships and set fire to them. Due to the chaotic nature of the engagement, it is difficult to assess French losses accurately. Most estimates point to around 1,500 French sailors killed or wounded, and another 1,850 taken prisoner. News of this disaster infuriated Napoleon, who bitterly complained that "these imbecile sailors have come to take part in another unprecedented scuffle. ... That is not bad luck, but unexampled stupidity and fatality."[48] Disappointing reports regarding his winter cruises continued to reach the emperor.

After evading Duckworth, Willaumez cruised the south Atlantic and the Caribbean. Battered by storms, his scattered command sought refuge in various ports of the United States. He inflicted damage on British shipping estimated between 12,000,000 and 15,000,000 francs, but his division was shattered in the process. The British had captured one ship and one frigate while the damage to another ship and frigate was so extensive that the French sold them to the United States for scrap. Only a single ship reached France safely as scheduled. The other three ships required extensive repairs, eventually returning to France one by one over the course of the next three years.[49] Although these ships returned to service, Napoleon had effectively lost five of his ships.

Survivors of the Battle of Trafalgar were also incorporated into these winter cruises as many of the frigates and brigs had emerged from the battle unscathed. Although the winter cruises succeeded in capturing or burning around sixty British merchant vessels, these losses proved negligible to British commerce and came at a heavy cost. Despite carrying cargo estimated to be worth 27,500,000 francs, these sixty ships represented a tiny fraction of the more than 19,000 British merchant ships traversing the globe. Furthermore, more than half of the French vessels participating in these cruises never returned to France. In total, the winter cruises cost the emperor seven ships, six frigates, and seven brigs or corvettes, coupled with 1,700 men killed or wounded, and 4,800 men captured. Thus, on the heels of the losses of Trafalgar, Napoleon's naval strategy had suffered an additional significant reverse.

Ceasing to focus on invading Britain, Napoleon developed a more nuanced naval strategy over the course of the next few years, which would persist until the end of his reign. Although he initially envisioned a renewed *guerre de course* in the Atlantic during the winter of 1806, he eventually abandoned the idea in December 1806. Seeking to rebuild his navy, he began to shift to a "fleet-in-being" strategy. As he acquired additional ships through construction or conquest, he kept his fleets armed and ready to sail, thereby forcing the British to maintain their own fleets at sea. Coupled with embargoes on British products, known as the Continental System, Napoleon sought to drain British coffers through increased expenditures, maintaining an extensive navy across the globe. In support of this strategy, he dispatched frigates to the Indian Ocean to wage a commerce-raiding campaign. Unable to abandon his Caribbean

---

48   CN, No. 10035, 12:246–247; Chevalier, *Marine française consulat et l'empire*, 251–255; James, *Naval History*, 4:190–203; Troude, *Batailles navales*, 3:446–454.

49   Troude, *Batailles navales*, 3:440–446.

colonies, the emperor relied on frigates and other smaller vessels to reinforce the Caribbean garrisons.

Losses suffered during the previous six months did not quell Napoleon's desire to strike at Britain as he continued to devise commerce-raiding expeditions for the next winter season. Based on reports of his various squadrons encountering British convoys, Napoleon believed that small squadrons of two ships and one frigate would achieve the best results. By dispatching a total of nine ships and nine frigates in six small squadrons from Rochefort, Lorient, and Brest, the emperor believed that they "would do great harm to the enemy. Every convoy seen would be a convoy lost."[50] By mid-May 1806, he had expanded this plan to "ten good cruises which will cover every sea." For the future Atlantic campaign, he wanted a "vast new system" with cruises predominantly attacking enemy commerce along the coasts of Spanish America, Brazil, and the coasts of North America. Only a single expedition would be dispatched to the Lesser Antilles with reinforcements, while additional frigates would reinforce the emperor's Indian Ocean campaign.[51]

While Napoleon planned for the upcoming naval campaign, he also pursued peace negotiations with Britain to end the war at sea during the summer of 1806. At the center of negotiations was the fate of Sicily, an island strategically situated to bisect the Mediterranean. Villeneuve's ill-fated sortie from Cádiz in October 1805 had the ultimate aim of seizing this key island. After the Neapolitan court had fled to Sicily due to the French invasion in February 1806, possession of the island assumed additional importance because it represented a threat to Joseph Bonaparte's legitimacy as the new king of Naples. To create a staging area for a later expedition to Sicily, Napoleon also contemplated an expedition to Sardinia in April 1806.[52] Unable to launch an expedition from Toulon and with his forces in Naples busy suppressing an uprising in Calabria, Napoleon had no alternative other than to turn to diplomacy to secure this important prize.

Although Napoleon's diplomatic maneuvers nearly brought about peace with Britain, his desire to expand his naval power greatly contributed to the diplomatic rupture with Prussia. In June 1806, a British envoy, Francis Seymour-Conway, Lord Yarmouth, arrived in Paris to negotiate a peace treaty. Although the British were willing to recognize Napoleon's brother as king of Naples, they would not relinquish Sicily. While negotiating with the British, the emperor

---

50 Three squadrons of two ships and one frigate from Rochefort and three squadrons of one ship and two frigates from Lorient and Brest: in total, nine ships and nine frigates. See CG, No. 11989, 6:368.
51 CG, No. 12134, 6:435–436.
52 CG, Nos 11976, 12147, 6:363, 442–444.

pushed his brother to prepare an expedition to seize the island. With the British refusing to budge on Sicily, Napoleon called for them to relinquish Malta as an alternative. Although this was partly a diplomatic maneuver to divide Britain and Russia, Bonaparte could not afford to leave both islands in British hands, as they would create "an impenetrable barrier that [would block] communication between the Adriatic and Constantinople." Despite Napoleon's efforts, the British refused to budge on Sicily. With Sicily remaining the "stumbling block" for peace, the emperor confided to Joseph that, "I would prefer ten years of war than leave your kingdom incomplete and Sicily in contention." By building a Neapolitan fleet of six ships, nine frigates, and some brigs, Joseph would aid Napoleon "to be master of the Mediterranean, the principal and constant goal of my politics." Thus, his aspirations of being a maritime power in the Mediterranean thwarted his attempt to negotiate a separate peace with Britain. While pushing his brother to suppress the Calabrian revolt and capture coastal islands to prepare for the eventual invasion of Sicily, Napoleon even considered venturing to Naples himself in September as long as "affairs on the continent do not call me elsewhere."[53] However, trouble was brewing on the continent. Already bristling at the creation of the Confederation of the Rhine, Prussia mobilized for war in August 1806 after learning of Napoleon's offer to return Hanover to Britain in exchange for Sicily.

Over the course of the campaign against Prussia, Napoleon altered his grand strategy as he combined economic measures and his maritime strategy to undermine Britain's financial system. Before marching east, the emperor formulated naval operations with the principal goals of seizing territory or attacking British merchant shipping. Scraping together the few remaining ships available, Napoleon thought of dispatching small squadrons from Rochefort, Brest, and Cádiz independently to Brazil; these would race back to the Mediterranean to join the Toulon squadron to facilitate an invasion of Sicily. Meanwhile, since July the emperor had been pressuring his brother Louis, the king of Holland, to prepare an expedition to retake the Dutch colonies of Suriname or the Cape of Good Hope. Preoccupied with his campaign against Prussia, Napoleon did not return to his grand strategy until late November, after his corps had chased down the scattered remnants of the vaunted Prussian army that had been routed at Jena and Auerstedt. From the Prussian capital, the emperor issued his famous Berlin Decree, which declared all British goods contraband, allowing him to seize British ships and merchandise present in the various Germanic ports that he had just occupied.

---

53   CG, Nos 12347, 12381, 12427, 12453, 12499, 12551, 12612–12613, 6:538, 555–556, 578–579, 589, 613–614, 639, 666–668, 668–670.

While moving further eastward into Poland, Bonaparte continued to wrestle with his naval strategy. As he slowly formulated his grand strategy of a "fleet-in-being," he still could not resist the temptation of planning grandiose commerce-raiding expeditions that would have his ships of the line at sea for as long as ten months. Begging Napoleon to postpone these operations, Decrès summarized the bleak conditions facing the French navy:

> the difficulties of maritime operations have never been as great as on this occasion! The enemy has never had as many ships available and we have never had fewer ports of call and greater shortages in our distant ports. All of these expeditions of nine or ten months at sea appear to me to have no chance of success, and especially no parity between their probable advantages and the nearly inevitable dangers that are associated with it.[54]

Convinced by Decrès's frank assessment, the emperor ceased planning any future commerce-raiding expeditions with his ships of the line. Based on a recommendation from Decrès, he directed his fleets at Rochefort and Cádiz to Toulon, thereby giving him a fleet of eighteen ships in the Mediterranean. By threatening Sicily or posing the possibility of sailing into the Adriatic or to Constantinople in support of the Ottomans, he hoped to draw the British fleet to Toulon, thereby freeing up the passage from Naples for an invasion of Sicily. In support of this deception, he wanted to name Ganteaume as commander of the Toulon fleet, thereby leading the British to believe he would sail for Egypt or Constantinople. Orders were issued to the Rochefort and Cádiz fleets, but persistent British blockades prohibited their departure. Preoccupied with battling the Russian army during the Eylau campaign, Napoleon did not return to naval affairs until the end of March 1807. After learning about a failed British attack on the Ottoman fleet in the Dardanelles in mid-March, the French emperor wanted the Toulon fleet increased to ten ships and sent to Naples to "give the enemy trouble off of Sardinia and Sicily." A few days later, the emperor canceled these plans as it was no longer the season for naval operations. Instead, Decrès was to prepare for the next season (September 1807) with plans to gather thirty ships in the Mediterranean or send an expedition to resupply the Caribbean islands. To achieve thirty ships, Napoleon pushed Decrès to accelerate naval construction, claiming that "there is not a moment to lose."[55]

Although Napoleon tentatively adjourned naval operations until September, he did not wish to give the British any respite as he shifted to a fleet-in-being

---

54 Decrès to Napoleon, 23 December 1806, AN, AF IV 1196.
55 CG, Nos 14043, 14167, 14170, 14173, 14699, 14805, 14915, 15391, 7:76, 130–132, 134, 362–363, 411, 464, 676–677.

strategy during the summer of 1807. First, the French emperor sought to use deception to force the British to maintain large fleets on station. While the Brest fleet openly prepared for an expedition to Ireland, the Rochefort fleet would "to do everything possible" to make the British believe that it was heading for the Cape of Good Hope. Napoleon also wanted Decrès to refer openly to three other "secret expeditions." However, this did not mean that he wanted his fleets to remain passive. After receiving reports in June 1807 that only three British ships were observing the Toulon fleet of five ships, Napoleon instructed them to attack under such favorable circumstances, even if it required stripping sailors from the frigates. To the north, the progress of construction pleased the emperor as the Franco-Dutch fleet continued to grow. "The English cannot help but be worried by this squadron," noted Napoleon.[56]

With the signing of the Treaties of Tilsit in July 1807 and the end of the Fourth Coalition, Napoleon was able to turn his attention back to Perfidious Albion, his incessant foe across the Channel. He reached the conclusion that naval success against the British depended on "France, Spain, and Holland uniting." Although the combined naval power of these states should have rivaled the Royal Navy, the British had inflicted a series of severe reversals on the French and Spanish navies from 1803 to 1806. By 1808, Napoleon believed that the problem was that France and its allies "were disunited; England had fought their navies separately." Thus, he shaped his grand strategy and strategy to bring the naval assets of as many European states as possible under his direct control. First, he annexed the entire Adriatic coastline of the Papal States to the Kingdom of Italy in August 1807. Not only did this maneuver connect the two vassal states of Italy and Naples, but this region also contained the port of Ancona, whose value Napoleon had first noticed in 1797. He subsequently annexed the Kingdom of Etruria in May 1808. By incorporating this prior client state of France, Napoleon sought to increase the number of sailors at his disposal and provide him with more direct control over the coastline.[57] While these measures improved his access to ports and recruits, they did not address the emperor's immediate need for ships.

The most expeditious solution available to Napoleon was the acquisition of preexisting navies of Denmark, Portugal, and Spain. In the summer of 1807, he hoped to pressure Denmark into joining his alliance to contest Britain for control of the Baltic. Cognizant of the danger, the British navy launched a preemptive strike on the Danish fleet at Copenhagen in August. Not only did

---

56   CG, Nos 15455, 15514, 15750, 15826, 15903, 7:706, 736–737, 840, 873–874, 908.
57   CN, Nos 1497, 5968, 13000, 13292, 13718, 13846, 13855, 2:332–334, 7:395–396, 15:478, 16:114, 470–474, 17:87–88, 94.

the British capture all fifteen Danish ships, they also absconded with nearly 20,000 tons of naval stores that Napoleon desperately needed to expand his navy. The desire to acquire warships quickly was also a primary instigator for Napoleon's invasions of both Portugal and Spain. Although Portugal had a small navy of only eleven ships of the line, their quality was "equal, if not superior, to the British." In nearly every order issued to the commander of the invasion of Portugal, General Jean-Andoche Junot, Napoleon stressed the need to secure the Portuguese fleet. The slow pace of the French army through the mountains of Portugal, however, enabled the Portuguese royal family to flee to Brazil aboard all of their serviceable vessels, leaving Junot only two ships and three frigates that needed repairs. Meanwhile, Napoleon believed that the lack of activity in Spanish ports "compromised the security of France and the fate of the war against England." Tired of the antics of the Spanish royal family, the emperor decided to remove them from power. Once this was accomplished, he could then use all of Spain's resources to reestablish its once-proud navy. His instructions to Marshal Murat emphasized the need to secure Spain's major ports of Cádiz, Cartagena, and Ferrol. Faced with unexpected stiff popular resistance, Napoleon's attempt to invade Spain failed to secure any of the Spanish ports or their fleets. Furthermore, the squadron of five French ships trapped in Cádiz surrendered after the Spanish turned their artillery against them. While the French did succeed in capturing the arsenal of Ferrol and the Spanish fleet of five ships and six frigates, the British recovered the Spanish ships when the French evacuated Galicia in July 1809. Ultimately, the quest to secure the fleets of other states and their respective ports not only failed, but it also embroiled France in a protracted and brutal war in the Iberian Peninsula that would sap its strength and that of its armies.

Thwarted in his efforts to appropriate the ships of other states, Napoleon had to rely on building his own ships. Even before the 14 June 1807 Battle of Friedland, he had informed Decrès that "everything leads me to believe that the war on the continent is over. Every effort must now be given to the navy." Already expecting to have twenty-nine ships in September 1807, Napoleon hoped to have forty-one French ships by September 1808. As of May 1808, he planned to launch thirty ships by September 1809. In conjunction with this effort, the emperor also expanded his system of ports. To maximize efficiency, he designated certain responsibilities to various ports. While some ports would specialize in ship-building, other ports would be used only for repairs and armament.[58]

---

58   CN, Nos 12448, 12848, 13698, 14005, 15:133–134, 382, 454–455, 17:218–220; CG, No. 18190, 8:689.

In the Mediterranean, Napoleon looked to his Italian ports to bolster France's existing maritime facilities. Toulon was to serve as a port of armament, its basins and slipways to be used only for repairs. Almost all French ships for the Mediterranean were to be built at Port-de-Bouc, 80 km northwest of Toulon. Connected to the major waterways of France through canals, this port had the capacity to build several ships of the line at once. Additional ships for the Toulon fleet would be built in the Italian port of Genoa, which had been annexed in 1805. However, as Genoa's facilities were situated beyond the port's fortifications, Napoleon looked for another locale in Italy. One hundred kilometers southeast of Genoa lay the natural gulf of La Spezia, which the emperor wanted to turn into "a military port like Toulon." Yet establishing such a massive complex required enormous expenditures that he could not immediately afford. Therefore, he opted to build La Spezia gradually to spread the expense over a number of years. Meanwhile, as he needed all major facilities churning out as many ships as possible, he continued to build ships at Genoa. Furthermore, these ship orders had the added benefit of serving as an economic stimulus that helped keep the people of Genoa happy.[59] The combined production of these ports would eventually reestablish the French Mediterranean fleet that had been lost at the Battle of Trafalgar in 1805.

On the eastern Italian coast, Napoleon reinvigorated the ports of Venice and Ancona in the Kingdom of Italy to provide him with a fleet to command the Adriatic Sea. Having taken Venice and part of the Dalmatian coast after defeating Austria in 1805, Napoleon had quickly ordered the construction of "a squadron of six ships and as many frigates" in Venice to "protect commerce from the Levant, either against Turks or Russians." Napoleon wanted these ships to have drafts shallow enough to allow them to enter the port of Alexandria, thereby demonstrating his continued interest in Egypt. In August 1806, he expanded the construction project to ten seventy-four-gun ships in Venice. As the deepening of Venice's shallow canals would have been an expensive project, he opted for a cheaper alternative: Dutch "sea camels." Attached to the sides of the ship, these external tanks provided extra buoyancy, thereby decreasing the ship's draft enough to allow it to pass through the shallow Venetian channels. The slow progress of ship construction, however, disappointed Napoleon, who eventually asked Decrès to help reorganize his Italian navy in May 1807.[60] Despite these efforts, production in Venice continued to

---

59 Unable to afford the estimated 20,000,000 francs needed to establish the fortifications necessary to completely protect La Spezia, Napoleon prioritized defending the roadstead, port, and maritime arsenal: CG, Nos 15391, 16472, 18208, 22272, 7:676–677, 1165–1166, 8:695–696, 8:1306; CN, Nos 13846, 13848, 13977, 14004, 14079, 18257, 17:87–89, 193–194, 217–218, 290–291, 23:13.
60 CG, Nos 11353, 12720, 13450, 15041, 6:71–72, 718, 1088, 7:525–526.

remain sluggish. Of the ten ships ordered in August 1806, the first was finally completed in September 1810, followed by two more in 1811, and another two in 1812; the remaining five ships were still incomplete by the end of the Napoleonic Wars.

Napoleon also envisioned the satellite kingdom of Naples augmenting his sea power in the Mediterranean. As Ferdinand IV had fled to Sicily with the majority of the small Neapolitan navy in 1806, the French managed to capture only two frigates, four smaller craft, and a score of gunboats, as well as the naval facilities around the city of Naples. To the south, Naples also possessed the port of Taranto, whose impressive roadstead had led Napoleon to occupy it since 1803. Heavily fortified, it could provide shelter to a fleet against superior forces. When the French emperor made Joachim Murat the king of Naples on 15 July 1808, the treaty required Murat to build a fleet of two eighty-gun ships, four seventy-four-gun ships, six frigates, and six brigs or corvettes. Although paid for by the Kingdom of Naples, Napoleon envisioned this small navy as an extension of his own naval power. Regardless, despite Napoleon's continued prodding, by 1812 Murat had established only one-third of this fleet.[61]

Along the Atlantic coast, Napoleon focused his attention on the combined facilities of Antwerp and Vlissingen instead of France's port of Brest. In April 1804, he had declared that "it is Antwerp that ought to be our grand dockyard." While the emperor wanted most of the ships built at Antwerp, Vlissingen would serve as a port of armament, where he eventually hoped to have thirty warships. The emperor knew that the expanding fleet would become "progressively more worrisome for England," being situated directly across the Channel. Brest would still serve as an important port of armament with only a limited amount of resources dedicated to ship-building, while most of the ships would be built in the dockyards of Cherbourg and Lorient. Similarly, the port of Rochefort was to be used primarily for repairs, although ships were still built there. These facilities were supplemented with additional dockyards at Bayonne and Le Passage, upriver of Bordeaux.[62]

While pushing for the construction of warships, Napoleon also understood the importance of building proper transport ships. Although he had routinely relied on improvised transports for his earlier expeditions, he started building transport ships in 1808. After ordering the construction of twenty fluyts at Vlissingen in March 1808, he called for eight more to be added to the five already anchored at Toulon. In May, he added ten horse transports to various

---

61   CG, No. 16292, 7:1086; Article 12 of the treaty concluded at Bayonne, 15 July 1808, No. 3408 in Paul Le Brethon, *Lettres et documents pour server a l'histoire de Joachim Murat* (Paris, 1912), 6:219–224; CN, Nos 16490, 16851, 16920, 16980, 20:365–366, 21:79, 125–126, 166.
62   CG, Nos 8851, 17600, 18190, 4:695, 8:371, 689; CN, Nos 14095, 17452, 17:306–307, 21:462–464.

ports along the Mediterranean coast. The emperor later set aside an additional 2,500,000 francs to increase the number of available transport ships in the ports of Lorient and Nantes. In 1810, he continued this trend, dedicating millions of francs to accelerate the construction of large fluyts and horse transports. A few fluyts also were built in Channel ports such as Le Havre and Cherbourg.[63] Although Napoleon continued to formulate expeditionary plans that relied on the use of warships as transports, an increasing amount of sealift capability was shifted to ships specifically designed for that purpose.

Having expressed interest in the Adriatic since his invasion of Italy in 1797, the annexation of Venice to the Kingdom of Italy gave Napoleon the opportunity to establish a naval force in the Adriatic Sea. Routinely in his correspondence with Eugène de Beauharnais, the viceroy of Italy, and Decrès, the emperor emphasized becoming "masters of the Adriatic." As it would take time to build ships in Adriatic ports, he wanted to dispatch four frigates to the Adriatic in 1807 "to keep this sea free or require the enemy to keep considerable forces there." A key component to controlling the Adriatic was the island of Corfu, whose strategic location, known as the Strait of Otranto, commanded the entrance of the Adriatic. In accordance with the secret articles of the Treaty of Tilsit, French troops occupied the island of Corfu in August 1807. While Corfu possessed significant fortifications that rendered it difficult to assault, reinforcements and provisions had to be delivered by sea. After the British navy intercepted these crucial convoys, Napoleon dispatched a fleet to establish temporary control of the Ionian Sea. Pursuing his desire to amass nearly all of his ships in the Mediterranean, he told Decrès to send the squadrons from Brest, Lorient, Rochefort, and Cádiz to Toulon. Although Decrès acknowledged that "one squadron could evade enemy surveillance *with good luck (and a lot of skill)*," he viewed four or five squadrons having the same luck "*as impossible!*" While instructing the other fleets to stand ready, Decrès ordered the Rochefort fleet to sail. Slipping out of Rochefort on 17 January 1808, Allemand led his five ships to the Gulfe Juan, near Antibes. Joined by Ganteaume's five ships from Toulon on 10 February, they sailed for Corfu accompanied by three frigates and eight transports. Damaged and scattered by storms, the French fleet still managed to facilitate the convoy's crossing and return to Toulon on 10 April without encountering the British.[64] This operation succeeded primarily due to timing

---

63   Using warships as a method of transportation, although expedient, was very inefficient as it required around two sailors for every soldier. In comparison, dedicated transports, known as fluyts, could carry around 300 troops while needing only around 100 sailors to crew the ship. See *CN*, Nos 13708, 13737, 13997, 14078, 16602, 16664, 16:461–463, 492–493, 17:207–212, 289–290, 20:439, 494–495.

64   *CG*, Nos 15951, 16716–16717, 16880, Article 2 of the secret articles of the Treaty of Tilsit, No. 17151, 7:928, 1277–1278, 1351–1352, 1413, 8:135–136; Decrès to Napoleon, 20 December

and chance, as it was not until early March that the British could gather a sizable fleet, which narrowly missed Ganteaume's fleet as it sailed back to Toulon.

As shipwrights around Europe labored to expand the navies of France and its satellite states, Napoleon sought to use his port-bound ships and transports as a means of economic warfare in support of his Continental System. Initially conceived as a means of seizing British goods, the Continental System evolved into a direct attack on British commerce. In November and December 1807, the emperor issued the Milan Decrees to broaden confiscatory measures to include neutral ships carrying British goods. While supervising the invasion of Spain from Bayonne, he formulated the naval component of the Continental System. More ships would be armed across Europe, thereby forcing "the English to spend a lot and disseminate their forces, because they are obliged to have ships in the seas around Spain, Portugal, America, Baltic, etc." Napoleon wanted his fleets to "sail frequently, to head out and present combat to [enemy cruisers] who are inferior to them, and to keep themselves in a state of continual mobility."

At the same time, Napoleon completed the conceptual basis of his fleet-in-being strategy. According to his calculations, the British would have to maintain four ships for every French ship that sat in port ready to sail, as the British would have to rotate their ships on station. Thus, Napoleon's "system of war" was to "harass [the British] with expenses and fatigue." Aware that an immobilized fleet posed little threat, he ordered small squadrons to sail frequently in order to "pass the summer playing tag" with the British. Anticipating that he would secure the Portuguese and Spanish fleets, Napoleon estimated that the British would need 126 ships to blockade his fleets and escort their convoys. Therefore, the British would "need to double their navy, leading to the expenditure of money, the pressing of sailors, and increasing risk of disasters." The importance that Napoleon placed on his fleet-in-being strategy can be seen in his decision to depose his own brother, Louis, and annex Holland in 1810 to better manage its naval resources.[65]

Although Napoleon could not afford to risk his precious ships of the line as he strove to reach parity with the British navy, he could not resist the temptation to plan offensive naval operations. Already contemplating an expedition to Sardinia or Sicily in September 1807, he began organizing several major overseas expeditions in the spring of 1808. Possibly inspired by Ganteaume's successful mission to revitalize Corfu, Napoleon and Decrès began planning

---

1807, in "L'Amiral Duc Decrès d'après sa correspondance" *Correspondant* (10 October 1911), 963; Chevalier, *Marine française consulat et l'empire*, 282–284; James, *Naval History*, 5:3–9.

65 *CG*, Nos 17918, 18129, 21973, 8:541–542, 651, 9:1117–1118; *CN*, Nos. 13829, 13853, 13873, 15991, 16455, 16467, 16616, 17:75, 91–92, 107–109, 20:24–25, 341, 348–349, 450.

for an expedition to Egypt, Tunis, or Algiers in April 1808. Napoleon also expanded his plans for the upcoming winter season to include a dual strike to the east. While the Toulon fleet delivered 19,000 troops to Egypt, the Brest and Lorient fleets would transport 15,000 troops to the Indian Ocean. To preoccupy the British, the Vlissingen fleet and the flotilla at Boulogne would mobilize to "menace Ireland." Napoleon believed that the combination of these operations would strike such fear in the British that London would "have no means of bothering us [in Europe] or bothering the Americas." Furthermore, the emperor believed that these operations would "ruin the English colony from top to bottom," thereby striking "a mortal blow to England's affairs." To maintain tight security, he withheld the destination from his commanders, even asking for reports on different locations in order to spread false rumors.

Yet, as the invasion of Spain met unexpected popular resistance and Austria was becoming increasingly belligerent, Napoleon eventually postponed his ambitious plans. He instructed Decrès to continue buying and building ships. However, he used naval preparations as strategic feints as he shifted additional units to the Iberian front in the fall of 1808. While Murat's Neapolitan troops captured the island of Capri and prepared for an invasion of Sicily, Napoleon had the Toulon fleet maintain a state of preparedness and began moving two infantry divisions toward Toulon. He had envisioned that the capture of Capri would signal his interest in Sicily, thereby "causing the British to fear for the safety of Sicily, which would be very useful." To facilitate this diversion, Bonaparte had his minister of police, Joseph Fouché, plant indications for his plans to invade Sicily throughout dozens of articles in Dutch, German, and French newspapers. In response to the capture of Capri, the British dispatched three additional ships to Palermo.[66] Increasingly, however, French attention turned to the Caribbean, where the remaining colonies were under increasing threat.

Unwilling to risk ships of the line in the Caribbean after the disastrous Battle of Santo Domingo, Napoleon had turned to his frigates and smaller vessels to continue reinforcing his colonies.[67] While this decision mitigated any risk to the precious ships of the line, it placed considerable pressure on the various frigates, brigs, and corvettes scattered across the French empire. Between 1806 and 1808, Napoleon directed more than fifty frigates, brigs, and corvettes, either individually or in small squadrons, to his Caribbean colonies. Their success depended primarily on avoiding British cruisers. In total, the British captured seven frigates, while four others had to be wrecked or scuttled. The smaller

---

66   CG, Nos 18432, 18496, 18955, 19133, 19294, 19295, 19297, 19333, 8: 811, 839–840, 1092, 1166, 1236–1237, 1251; Desmond Gregory, *Sicily: The Insecure Base* (London, 1988), 72–73.

67   CN, Nos 9662, 9725, 10364, 10703, 11:531–532, 567–569, 12:467–468, 13:114.

ships also suffered dramatic losses with the capture of eighteen brigs and corvettes, with three others burnt. As part of these smaller actions, around 300 French sailors were killed and another 4,100 ended up as prisoners. Due to the strengthening British blockade of the colonies, only 60 percent of all ships actually reached their intended or alternate destinations. Moreover, only half of these ships returned safely to France. While the reinforcements and provision provided helped sustain French garrisons, the fate of the colonies depended on larger relief efforts.

Cognizant that the British navy had tightened its blockade of the Caribbean, Napoleon abandoned his long-standing directive to avoid deploying ships of the line to the colonies. In June 1808, he contemplated sending a small squadron from Rochefort to take around 3,000 tons of flour, biscuits, and wine to Martinique, but this plan was eventually dropped in favor of dispatching additional frigates. In August, Napoleon and Decrès began to formulate a plan to dispatch the Vlissingen fleet with around 2,000 troops on board to reinforce the garrison on Guadeloupe, retake the neighboring islands of Marie-Galante and Désirade that had fallen to the British in March, cruise the Caribbean for British commerce, and then sail for Toulon. Abandoning this plan the next month, the emperor ordered Missiessy to take the Vlissingen fleet to Cherbourg, Brest, Lorient, Rochefort, or Toulon.[68] Whether this was a strategic feint as Napoleon prepared to personally direct the Spanish campaign or an attempt to gather a large fleet in the Mediterranean for future operations mattered little as Missiessy remained bottled in the port by the British blockade.

With news that the British were preparing an expedition to the Caribbean, Napoleon drafted new plans to relieve his colonies. Just before leaving Paris to lead the second invasion of Spain in late October 1808, he ordered two small squadrons to the Caribbean in the hope of rescuing his colonies. With neither expedition able to sail and the situation in the Caribbean growing more dire, the emperor ordered the Brest fleet of nine ships and four frigates to embark 3,000 troops and as many provisions as possible for the besieged town of Santo Domingo or Martinique if the town had fallen.[69]

The Caribbean expedition soon became linked with Napoleon's plans for the Mediterranean. Keenly interested in gathering a large fleet in the Mediterranean, he reiterated his desire for the Vlissingen fleet to sail for Toulon on 31 December 1808. This junction would provide him with sixteen ships at Toulon. From Brest, Willaumez would sail with eight ships provisioned with six months of food and four months of water so that his squadron would not need to enter the port of Toulon. Meanwhile, Ganteaume was to be ready to sail at

---

68   *CG*, Nos 18296, 18549, 18726, 18882, 19107, 8:748–749, 867, 966–967, 1060–1061, 1155.
69   *CG*, Nos 19128, 19129, 19641, 8:1163–1164, 1385.

the head of a massive expedition by 1 March. With his seventeen ships, nine frigates, nine corvettes and brigs, twenty transports and twenty smaller vessels, Ganteaume would carry 32,000 troops "to some point in the Mediterranean." Napoleon quickly dispatched engineers and artillery to Toulon and had them board their respective ships. In order to deceive the British about his intentions, Napoleon pushed the Neapolitans to prepare for an invasion of Sicily without ever letting them know that it was a diversion. Although he never explicitly stated the ultimate destination of this expedition in any of his correspondence or orders, most evidence points to Algiers.[70]

With the reinforcements destined for the Caribbean blockaded by superior British forces, Napoleon sought to use his Mediterranean operation to facilitate their departure. On 7 February 1809, he ordered Willaumez to sail as soon as possible from Brest with his fleet of eight ships to lift the blockades and free the squadrons at Lorient and Rochefort. Willaumez would escort these two squadrons to the Caribbean and then sail for Toulon.[71] Taking advantage of favorable winds, Willaumez slipped out of Brest undetected early on the morning of 21 February.

This complex operation soon suffered a series of reversals. A British ship cruising nearby spotted Willaumez and reported his presence to the British squadron blockading Lorient, thereby eliminating any chance he had of surprising the isolated squadron. After Willaumez reached Lorient, calm weather and the tides stalled the departure of *Capitaine de vaisseau* Amable Troude's division (three ships, three frigates, two transports). While Willaumez sailed for Rochefort the next day, a light breeze enabled the three frigates of Troude's division to get underway, but a changing tide and the fickle wind impeded the departure of the remaining ships. The senior captain, Pierre Roch Jurien de la Gravière, sailed the three frigates in search of Willaumez's fleet per Napoleon's orders, but was soon spotted by a small British squadron that was returning to its station off Lorient. Fleeing before this superior opponent, Gravière sought refuge in the port of Les Sables d'Olonne. While his frigates successfully repulsed the attack of three British ships of the line and two frigates, they suffered such significant damage that they were either scrapped or removed from active service.[72]

Back at Lorient, the wind increased on 26 February, allowing Troude to sail with his three ships and two frigate transports. After learning of the capitulation of Martinique, he steered directly for Guadeloupe. As the two major

---

70 CG, Nos 19642, 19725, 19755, 19763, 19764, 19768, 19932, 8:1385, 1427, 1439, 1442–1447, 1537.
71 CN, No. 14763, 18:254–256.
72 Troude, *Batailles navales*, 4:16–23; Chevalier, *Marine française consulat et l'empire*, 318–323.

anchorages of Guadeloupe were only lightly protected, he opted to sail for the Saintes, a small archipelago located 15 km to the south of Guadeloupe. Although his ships reached the Saintes safely on 29 March, a larger British squadron learned of their presence and established a blockade. After the British ships moved to capture some of the neighboring islands, Troude decided to take his chances at sea. Setting sail with his three ships during the evening of 14 April, he hoped to attract the British squadron as the two frigate transports made their way to Guadeloupe. Chased by the majority of the British ships, he eventually had to abandon one of his ships, the seventy-four-gun *D'Hautpoult*, whose slowness endangered the other two ships. Overwhelmed by massive firepower, the *D'Hautpoult* soon lowered her flag.[73] Taking advantage of this diversion, the two frigate transports slipped into the harbor of Guadeloupe to unload some 560 conscripts and much-needed provisions. Nevertheless, both frigates succumbed to British cruisers during their attempt to return to France one month later.[74] Napoleon paid a high price for such fleeting results, as these reinforcements were only sufficient to protect Guadeloupe from a quick strike.

Back in France, the naval campaign of 1809 continued its disastrous run. Willaumez arrived off the coast of Rochefort on 24 February, where his signals for Lhermitte's division of three ships and an old fifty-four-gun ship converted to a transport to set sail went unanswered. An outbreak of disease had ravaged the crews of the Rochefort fleet, including Lhermitte, leaving many ships without enough sailors to man them.[75] Although six British ships were coming into view, Willaumez still had time to evade them and head directly to Toulon per his standing orders. *Capitaine de vaisseau* Jacques Bergeret, Lhermitte's replacement, promised to sail three more ships in support, so Willaumez opted to wait. Mobilizing even just these three ships took hours as their crews had to be cobbled together from the other ships, and they remained 20 percent short of their respective crews when they sailed. During these precious hours, the British fleet had steadily grown to sixteen ships, thereby increasing the likelihood that any attempt to slip out of Rochefort would end in a battle. Unwilling to risk combat with superior forces, especially given the weakened state of some of his ships, Willaumez opted to shift his fleet to Rochefort's inner roadstead near Île d'Aix. During the maneuver, the seventy-four-gun *Jean Bart* ran aground on a nearby shoal and was eventually wrecked once every effort to clear the shoal had failed.[76] While awaiting a favorable moment to slip out to

---

73 Troude, *Batailles navales*, 4:23–34; Chevalier, *Marine française consulat et l'empire*, 345–349.
74 Troude, *Batailles navales*, 4:69–72.
75 Ibid., 4:34–54; James, *Naval History*, 5:99–122; Chevalier, *Marine française consulat et l'empire*, 323–341.
76 Dupont, *Willaumez*, 331–334.

sea, Willaumez arranged his remaining ships in a defensive line of the southern edge of Île d'Aix. After learning of Willaumez's situation, Napoleon ordered 3,600 troops to the area to protect Île d'Aix in case of attack, along with additional supplies for the coastal batteries.[77] In April, the British launched fireships at the French fleet. During the resulting panic, four French ships and one frigate were destroyed while the remaining ships suffered severe damage.[78] The winter campaign of 1808–1809 had proven costly, with the loss of six ships and six frigates, coupled with the deaths of nearly 300 sailors and the capture of nearly 1,700 more.

Exigencies of the Peninsular War soon led Napoleon to call upon the Toulon fleet. Despite Spain's proximity to France, the Pyrenees presented a significant obstacle for overland supply trains. Limited to a few coastal routes, transportation by land proved considerably expensive and slow. After the French took Barcelona in February 1808, Napoleon instructed the navy to protect supply convoys destined for the Spanish port.[79] At the end of March 1809, he issued orders for a squadron of five ships and two frigates to escort a number of transports to Barcelona.[80] *Contre-amiral* Julien Marie Cosmao-Kerjulien sailed from Toulon on 24 April to protect seventeen transports loaded with 100,000 kg of gunpowder, one million musket balls, and 1,250 tons of wheat and flour. After unloading these supplies at the Gulf of Roses, 100 km northwest of Barcelona, Cosmao-Kerjulien slipped back into Toulon on 30 April, narrowly missing a British fleet of fourteen ships. Given the success of this sortie, Napoleon had another shipment of one million musket balls, 100,000 kg of gunpowder, 1,600 tons of wheat, flour, and biscuit loaded aboard another seventeen transports in September. Initially, *Vice-amiral* Ganteaume, now commander of the Toulon fleet, contemplated sailing with all fifteen of his ships, believing he outnumbered the British fleet of eleven ships under Admiral Cuthbert Collingwood. After Collingwood appeared to have abandoned his station off Toulon, Ganteaume suspected that the British fleet had returned to its port at Menorca. Taking advantage of this opportunity, Ganteaume opted to dispatch only a small squadron of three ships, two frigates, and two smaller craft, under the command of *Contre-amiral* François Baudin, to escort the convoy to Barcelona.[81]

---

77 CG, No. 20165, 9:126.
78 Around 385 cannon were dumped overboard during the attack to release some of the ships off sandbars and rocks. See Jules Sylvestre, *Les Brulots Anglais en rade de l'Île d'Aix (1809)* (Paris, 1912), 63; James, *Naval History*, 5:99–122; Troude, *Batailles navales*, 4:34–54; Chevalier, *Marine française consulat et l'empire*, 323–341.
79 CN, Nos 13635, 13638, 16:406, 409; Vincent Brun, *Guerres maritimes de la France: Port de Toulon, ses armements* (Paris, 1861), 2:491.
80 CN, No. 14970, 18:401–402.
81 Brun, *Guerres maritimes de la France*, 2:504–505, 507–509.

Baudin's departure on 21 October, however, did not go undetected, as Collingwood had left two frigates to monitor Toulon; they raced to Menorca to report the French movements. Although Ganteaume had correctly surmised that the British fleet's destination was that island, Collingwood had already returned to sea with fifteen ships and two frigates on 13 October after hearing rumors of the Toulon fleet's imminent departure. Easily deducing the French convoy's destination of Barcelona, Collingwood cruised to intercept it. After spotting the French convoy on the morning of 23 October, eight of the fastest British ships gave chase. While one of the French frigates raced back to the safety of Marseille, the rest of Baudin's squadron fled north toward the French coast. Upon reaching the port of Cette, only one of Baudin's ships and one frigate successfully navigated the shallow waters while the other two ships ran aground. Fearing that the British would capture them, the crews set fire to both ships.[82] The loss of two ships of the line proved too steep for Napoleon to take such risks again.[83] While planning another convoy in late 1810, the emperor warned Decrès that, "above all, I do not want to risk any of my ships of the line; I want to use only frigates."[84] While the overland trade routes into Spain may have been slow and expensive, attempts to provision his army in Spain by sea cost him two precious ships of the line and scores of smaller vessels.

As progress on the ships of the line in the Venetian dockyards continued, Napoleon relied on frigates and smaller vessels to vie for control of the Adriatic. With the onset of war with Austria in April 1809, he sought to concentrate his naval force at Venice in order to intercept shipping out of Trieste and reinforce the defense of Venice in case of an Austrian attack. In support of the three frigates and three brigs in the Adriatic, the emperor hoped to send additional corvettes, brigs, and sloops; he even contemplated sending two of his fastest ships of the line into the Adriatic to seize command the sea for two to three weeks, but this never materialized.[85] The British, however, continued to frustrate French efforts. To facilitate their operations in the Adriatic, the British had seized the island of Lissa, modern-day Vis, in the middle of the Dalmatian coast in 1807. In addition to several frigates, the British occasionally rotated a ship of the line into the Adriatic in anticipation of the launching of French

---

82 Private letter from aboard HMS *Sultan*, 1 November 1809, in *Naval Chronicle*, 22:457–460; Collingwood to Secretary of the Admiralty, 30 October 1809, ibid., 22:500–501; Martin to Collingwood, 27 October 1809, ibid., 22:501–502; Collingwood to Secretary of the Admiralty, 1 November 1809, ibid., 22:502–503; Hallowell to Collingwood, 1 November 1809, ibid., 22:503–505; Chevalier, *Marine française consulat et l'empire*, 362–363.
83 Napoleon was upset to learn that Baudin had been sent out with such a small squadron: CG, No. 22437, 9:1400.
84 CN, Nos 16935, 16955, 21:137–138, 147–148.
85 CG, Nos 20755, 20756, 20764, 9:453–454, 457–458.

ships from Venice. In March 1810, Napoleon wanted to reestablish a division of four frigates and other small ships at Ancona either to maintain "control of the gulf, or [to] force the enemy to keep ships of the line there."[86] Thus, Napoleon wanted to enjoy free use of the Adriatic Sea while he could, but would be content with making the British maintain large forces there. Not only would this divert British ships from his major ports, but it also would extend their logistics even further.

Adjusting his strategy slightly in 1810, Napoleon continued to prepare for expeditions to sail from all over his empire, but his primary intention was to utilize his fleet-in-being strategy to drain British resources rather than actually send these expeditionary forces to sea. Missiessy received instructions to conduct maneuvers from Vlissingen to force the British to maintain a blockading fleet, while the Dutch fleet of nine ships moved into the roadstead of Texel to present a threat to Britain. In the port of Cherbourg, the emperor gathered two ships, two frigates, two corvettes, and a number of transports capable of moving 10,000 soldiers. This expedition was to threaten the Channel Islands with invasion in the hope that this would force the British to maintain a squadron to blockade the port during the winter as well as garrison the island with more troops. Furthermore, a reduced flotilla at Boulogne capable of carrying 60,000 troops still threatened Britain with invasion. In the Atlantic, the ports of Brest, Lorient, and Rochefort were slowly building ships with the intention of assembling another large fleet at Brest. In the Mediterranean, the flotilla of transports at Toulon would continue to grow with the eventual goal of giving Napoleon the sealift capacity to carry 30,000 troops to Egypt, while a Neapolitan flotilla would threaten Sicily with an invasion force of 20,000 men. The French emperor continually instructed Murat to expand the Neapolitan navy as "it would force the English to keep an equal force against yours." In part, Napoleon believed that all of these mobilized forces would prohibit the British from deploying any ships to the Adriatic, thereby allowing the combined Franco-Italian fleet to command the sea. Meanwhile, he expanded ship orders as he looked to have 140 ships available for campaigns in 1812.[87] Napoleon finally learned to avoid costly expeditions until he could achieve naval parity with the British with the sole exception to this strategy being plans to rescue his remaining colonies in the Indian Ocean.

Although the campaign in the Indian Ocean had not started with any grand design, it evolved into Napoleon's primary center of effort against British commerce from 1807 to 1810. Between 1805 and 1810, Napoleon allocated eight

---

86   CN, No. 16315, 20:257.
87   CN, Nos 16418, 16433, 16462, 16490, 16515, 16686, 16851, 16916, 20:312, 323, 345, 365–366, 383, 511–512, 21:79, 121–122.

frigates to commerce raiding in the Indian Ocean. With one or two frigates dispatched each year, he continued to reinforce a *guerre de course* that showed promising results. While the British intercepted one of these frigates en route, the remaining seven frigates successfully made the long voyage from France and began plying the eastern waters. One example of early success was the frigate *Piedmontaise*. Having left France in December 1805, the *Piedmontaise* captured a number of rich prizes. In June 1806, it captured the East Indiaman *Warren Hastings*, valued at 3,000,000 francs, while a later cruise captured smaller prizes estimated to be worth some 2,000,000 francs.[88] However, another six-month cruise in early 1807 failed to garner any prizes. While the other frigates occasionally did better, they were not able to produce the same success as the earlier cruises.

While the early cruises in the Indian Ocean had caught the British unaware, the latter quickly took steps to remedy the problem. The Admiralty dispatched additional ships and frigates, thereby increasing their presence to six ships of the line, twenty frigates, and five smaller vessels by February 1807.[89] The British also captured the Dutch colony on the Cape of Good Hope, which eliminated a friendly port of call and threatened the line of communication back to France. Extensive use of the convoy system also limited the number of isolated ships that French commerce-raiders could easily snatch. Furthermore, extended operations in the Indian Ocean placed extensive pressure on the limited resources of Île de France (Mauritius). While stocks of naval stores ran low, port facilities and workers had to be rented from private owners. Without a proper supply of masts, frigates often had to cannibalize prizes to find replacements. Prices for copper and oil increased, and rope became a priceless commodity. All of this contributed to the expense of repairs. For example, the combined cost for repairs to the *Piedmontaise* and *Cannoniere* in 1806 exceeded 700,000 francs, more than the cost to build a frigate. In response, Napoleon sent a corvette loaded with naval stores in 1808, but British cruisers captured it en route. No longer preoccupied with threats elsewhere, the British commenced operations to capture the French colonies and end the threat to their commercial shipping. As it was difficult to maintain a blockade of the French islands from the Cape of Good Hope or India, which were both more than 4,000 km away, the British first seized the island of Rodrigues in August 1809. Control of this island, located just 600 km to the east of Île de France, allowed British cruisers to remain on station for a longer period of time, which made it

---

88 Ibid., 3:467–469; Harold C. Austen, *Sea Fights and Corsairs of the Indian Ocean, being the history of Mauritius from 1715 to 1810* (Port Louis, Mauritius, 1935), 93; Parkinson, *War in the Eastern Seas*, 293.

89 Parkinson, *War in the Eastern Seas*, 301–303.

more difficult for French frigates to operate. After assembling a sufficient number of troops, the British captured Île Bonaparte (Réunion) in July. While the French frigates succeeded in capturing three British frigates and sinking another at the Battle of Grand Port in August, this victory proved to be pyrrhic.[90] The British successfully invaded Île de France in December 1810, capturing all of the remaining French frigates in port and effectively ending Napoleon's campaign in the Indian Ocean.

After news of Île de France's capitulation reached France in February 1811, Napoleon turned his attention to the Dutch East Indies.[91] Napoleon urged Charles-François Lebrun, his administrator in the newly annexed Dutch territories, to prepare several Dutch expeditions for Java. In addition, he designated frigates and other small ships at Nantes and Saint-Malo to transport Dutch soldiers, munitions, and provisions to Batavia (Jakarta). In December 1810, the frigates *Méduse* and *Nymphe* from Nantes and the corvette *Sappho* from Bordeaux sailed with General Jan Willem Janssens, the new governor-general of the Dutch East Indies, several hundred troops, and munitions for Batavia. Reaching their destination safely in May, the *Sappho* left shortly with Janssens's predecessor while the *Méduse* and *Nymphe* sailed in late August just as the island was about to fall to the British. Despite British patrols, all ships eventually made their return to France. Napoleon debated sending expeditions from Nantes and Cherbourg to Batavia in February 1811, but he decided to cancel the expeditions from Saint-Malo and Cherbourg, sending the units back to their regiments. He continued to plan small expeditions to Java through the year, but none of them ever departed.[92] In the end, the feeble attempts to relieve Île de France and Batavia had little impact on the fates of these colonies, yet cost Napoleon two frigates and around 1,000 captured troops and sailors.

While Napoleon's efforts in the Far East caused the British great consternation and some economic loss, the accomplishments of the commerce-raiding campaign proved fleeting. Although the French had inflicted damage estimated to be worth tens of millions of francs, the campaign had eventually led to the loss of every vessel on a commerce-raiding mission. In addition to a seventy-four-gun ship, the French lost thirteen of the fourteen frigates

---

90   James, *Naval History*, 4:272–274, 5:277–296; Henri Prentout, *L'Île de France sous Decaen, 1803–1810* (Paris, 1901), 493–494, 522 ; Alnert Pitot, *L'Île de France: Esquisses Historiques (1715–1810)* (Port-Louis, Ile Maurice, 1899), 313–314.

91   Although he wanted to divert the three frigates preparing at Brest to Java, they had already set sail for Île de France. A British squadron captured two of the frigates upon their arrival in the Indian Ocean. See CN, No. 17390, 21:421–422.

92   CN, Nos 16872, 17092, 17107, 17161, 17164, 17390, 17420, 17595, 18306, 21:93, 246, 257, 289–290, 291, 421–422, 437, 22:54, 23:50–52; Jean-Paul Faivre, *L'expansion française dans le Pacifique de 1800 à 1842* (Paris, 1953), 202–206.

dispatched to the Indian Ocean. Yet, this campaign may have been worth Napoleon's effort as it did force the British to deploy four or five times as many ships and frigates in the Indian Ocean. Nevertheless, once the British decided to take the Mascarene Islands, Napoleon could do little to stop them.

Meanwhile, Napoleon's ambitious program faced continual delays in shipbuilding and shortages in manpower. As of March 1811, the emperor predicted that he would have 103 French ships and 76 frigates by 1813, plus an additional four ships and six frigates from the Kingdom of Italy, and two ships and four frigates from the Kingdom of Naples. As construction never proceeded as fast as he hoped, Napoleon was still expecting to achieve the same number of 103 French ships by September 1814. Assessing manpower requirements in 1810, he estimated that he needed 40,000 men for the navy and another 20,000 men for the flotillas. Short 20,000 men, the emperor turned to his marine regiments and conscripts from river regions. For a long-term solution, he looked to create training battalions for 40,000 young men. Within these battalions, the teenagers would learn basic infantry maneuvers, how to serve a gun battery, and how to conduct maneuvers on board a ship. Seeking to support his expanding navy with a formally educated naval officer corps, Napoleon also established special schools at Brest and Toulon in September 1810. With their total of 600 cadets studying for two or three years, he expected these schools to produce hundreds of new midshipmen a year.[93] Thus, Napoleon took important measures to ensure that his revitalized navy was properly manned.

As most of France's experienced sailors languished in British prisons, Napoleon looked to repatriate these men. In November 1809, he began sending conciliatory messages to Britain in an effort to establish a mass exchange of prisoners. While he wanted a comprehensive prisoner exchange involving the return of all prisoners from every belligerent, the British wanted to exchange their French prisoners only for British prisoners. This policy was unacceptable to Napoleon because most of the prisoners that Napoleon could exchange were Spanish, which meant that many French prisoners would remain in prison while all of the British returned home. The emperor even consented to pay for transportation costs of prisoners, but this did not work.[94] Negotiations collapsed, leaving most of France's experienced sailors in Britain.

With the loss of the colonies in the Caribbean and East Indies and his desire to conserve his ships of the line, Napoleon turned to his frigates and smaller vessels to conduct a *guerre de course*. While encouraging privateering in late 1811, Napoleon approved only one commerce-raiding operation in the Atlantic

---

93   CN, Nos 16663, 16802, 17452, 19488, 20:489–493, 21:46–69, 462–464, 24:427–430; Chevalier, *Marine française sous le consulat et l'empire*, 369.
94   CN, Nos 16014, 16431, 16839, 17035, 20:41, 319–322, 21:69–73, 211–222.

in 1812. From Nantes, *Capitaine de frigate* Jean-Baptiste-Henri Feretier led a small squadron of two frigates and one brig on an extended cruise in the Atlantic. Avoiding both a British frigate and a fifty-gun ship during his departure in January, this small squadron cruised for several months, destroying or capturing twenty-five merchant ships from various nations and netting 217 prisoners. Unable to enter the Mediterranean, Feretier eventually learned that Allemand had sailed with the Lorient squadron for Brest. Believing that the British squadron off Lorient would pursue Allemand, Feretier chose to make for this port. Spotted and chased by a British seventy-four-gun ship upon their approach to Lorient, all three French vessels ran aground. While local boats evacuated the crews and prisoners, the frigates caught fire, eventually exploding during the night after all personnel had been safely disembarked.[95]

In the Adriatic, three engagements in 1811 and 1812 crippled Napoleon's effort to contest the British for command of this sea. In 1810, the French emperor sent the enterprising *Capitaine de vaisseau* Bernard Dubourdieu to command his frigate squadron at Ancona. Having led a daring raid of the British base at Lissa with three frigates, two corvettes, and two brigs in October 1810, Dubourdieu took advantage of the departure of the only British ship of the line in the Adriatic to strike at the remaining British frigates and capture Lissa. With six frigates and six smaller ships, Dubourdieu sought to engage the British squadron of three frigates and one corvette off the coast of Lissa on 13 March 1811. During the resulting Battle of Lissa, a blast of triple shot swept the deck of Dubourdieu's flagship, killing him, and throwing the Franco-Italian squadron into confusion. While three of the frigates escaped, the British captured two of the Italian frigates, and Dubourdieu's frigate wrecked on the coast of Lissa. Of the three surviving frigates, one was shattered by a storm in November 1811, and another blew up in Trieste harbor in September 1812. Eight months after the Battle of Lissa, the British intercepted a French convoy of two frigates and one brig carrying artillery to Trieste, capturing one of frigates and the brig. To add to the imperial ire, the newly launched seventy-four-gun *Rivoli* was sent on its maiden voyage with only a light escort of three brigs in February 1812. Manned by an inexperienced crew, the *Rivoli* soon succumbed to the fire of the HMS *Victorious* after a four-hour firefight.[96] By early 1812, Napoleon's

---

95 Frigates – *Ariane* (40), *Andromaque* (40); brig – *Mameluck* (16). See CN, Nos 18106, 18369, 22:457, 23:108–109; Roger Lepelly, *Frégates dans la tourmente, 1812–1814* (Versailles, 1993), 42; Chevalier, *Marine française sous le consulat et l'empire*, 394–395; James, *Naval History*, 6:48–51; Troude, *Batailles navales*, 4:160–162.

96 CN, No. 17045, 21:219; Chevalier, *Marine française sous le consulat et l'empire*, 387–390; Troude, *Batailles navales*, 4:146–149, 155–158.

maritime aspirations in the Adriatic had suffered terribly due to the loss of his only ship of the line and six of his frigates.

Although upset by the loss of the *Rivoli* and his frigates, Napoleon remained optimistic about securing control of the Adriatic. After chastising Eugène for sending out the *Rivoli* poorly escorted, the emperor encouraged him "not to let this loss discourage you" as the French–Italian fleet in the Adriatic would soon have another three ships and one heavy frigate. This force would once again render them "masters of the Adriatic" or at least force the British to keep several ships in these waters.[97] Although he was poised to contest British sea power in the Adriatic in 1813, the collapse of the Grande Armée in Russia ended Napoleon's grand designs.

Overall, Napoleon's naval strategy remained constant in 1811. In March, he established his intentions for the 1811 season: "I do not want my squadrons leaving, but that they be provisioned as if they ought to leave." To facilitate this deception, Napoleon planned to fool his admirals into believing that they were destined to depart by frequently sending couriers with sealed orders to be opened at sea. Furthermore, he wanted 20,000 troops embarked on his fleets at Toulon and the Scheldt for a period of four to six weeks so that "the threat is real."[98] In particular, the emperor wanted the fleet at Antwerp, the Boulogne flotilla, and the squadron at Cherbourg to serve as three main points for menacing Britain and Ireland with invasion. As these forces steadily grew, Napoleon planned for these three expeditions to be completely ready by September 1813. At that time, he planned on the Scheldt expedition being capable of transporting 36,000 men and 3,000 horses, the Boulogne flotilla another 40,000 troops, and the Cherbourg expedition 18,000 men and 1,500 horses. As Napoleon and Decrès continued to discuss the organization of these expeditions, the former emphasized that "the threat could have an effect only if the operation is planned in a way that everyone believes it and that we can really attempt it." Napoleon did consider launching an invasion of Sicily or Sardinia from Corsica with forty small boats escorted by one frigate and one corvette in 1811, but this plan never materialized. If conditions improved, Napoleon envisioned launching these expeditions in 1812 or 1813. While the Toulon fleet would sail to either Sicily or Egypt, the Scheldt expedition would feign an invasion of Ireland, then head for the Caribbean to retake all of the French and Dutch colonies. Meanwhile, the Brest fleet would sail with 8,000 men to retake the Cape of

---

97 *CG*, No. 30171, 11:347–348.
98 For example, in October Napoleon ordered Missiessy to prepare for an expedition but provided him with no details as to its destination or potential date of departure: *CN*, Nos 17434, 18160, 21:446–448, 22:499.

Good Hope, thereby spreading "60,000 to 80,000 men across two worlds."[99] However, the contest in Spain remained a relative stalemate, and Russia started preparing for war.

Prior to launching his invasion of Russia, Napoleon and Decrès formulated plans for an expanded *guerre de course* in 1812. While the former wanted four frigate squadrons to sail immediately, the latter persuaded him to wait until the following winter. Not only were many of the frigates and corvettes unfinished or undergoing repairs, but the crews of many of these vessels were incomplete. Furthermore, the crews consisted mainly of new recruits led by inexperienced commanders. Decrès argued that postponing these cruises until the following season would allow the crews ample time to practice while the number of available frigates would increase to at least fourteen. Even as he marched into Russia, the emperor continued to think about his navy. After leaving Smolensk and having passed through hundreds of miles of pine forest, Napoleon urged Decrès to dispatch workers to fell trees for masts. In September, Napoleon issued Decrès his instructions for the naval campaign but only five of the fourteen frigates were ready.[100] With so few frigates available, the winter cruises of 1812/1813 proved ineffective. While each captain received the freedom to establish his own cruising grounds, Decrès reminded them to burn all prizes except for those laden with rich cargoes and able to reach a friendly port.[101] Although the French lost only one frigate, collectively they inflicted only minimal damage on British shipping.

Before commencing the 1813 campaign in Germany, Napoleon looked to his navy to support his attempt to save the empire and replace the men lost during the Russian campaign. After returning to Paris in December 1812, he ordered every soldier serving as a marine in the navy dispatched to the army. To help rebuild his artillery and engineering corps, Napoleon mobilized 1,200 naval workers. However, he did not wish to diminish his ship-building programs as this would hurt his navy's morale. Continuing the same production schedule as previous years, Napoleon deemphasized the need to complete ships, thereby spreading progress across all ships under construction so that he would have around twenty ships within one year. Even as Napoleon scrambled to recreate his army, he did not initially divert conscripts designated for the navy, as these recruits would be irreplaceable. Eventually, the emperor mobilized 12,000 men

---

99 CN, Nos 17434, 17946, 18010, 21:446–448, 22:343–346, 386–389.
100 CN, Nos 19082, 19150, 24:148–149, 184; Lepelley, *Frégates*, 58–62.
101 *Capitaine de frégate* Albin Roussin captured nine ships off the Azores. In total, Roussin's cruise captured or burnt thirteen ships valued at 2,600,000 francs and took 280 prisoners. See Lepelley, *Frégates*, 63–69, 80–84, 109–110, 129–35, 150–162; Félix Charyau, « Journal du chirurgien-major de la frégate l'Aréthuse," *Revue Maritime et Coloniale*, 200–227, 426–445; James, *Naval History*, 6:158–159 ; Troude, *Batailles navales*, 4:164–165, 171–173.

from the navy to rebuild the Grande Armée, warning Decrès that he might have to rely on the other 80,000 naval personnel to defend France if he suffered additional reversals. Meanwhile, the fleets in Antwerp, Brest, and Toulon were to prepare for expeditions to serve as "veritable diversions." Although formal relations between France and the United States remained tepid, the emperor wanted to keep the Antwerp fleet armed and ready to preoccupy the British navy as a form of indirect support for the Americans in their war with Britain.[102]

While keeping his fleets active in port, Napoleon relied on his frigates to strike directly at the British by raiding their commerce. In March 1813, he told Decrès to draft a plan for thirty frigates to "harm the enemy." In June 1813, the emperor ordered Decrès to send twenty frigates to sea by 15 September. The goal of this operation was threefold. Not only would this operation "harm" the British, it would also provide the novice sailors with experience. It also would satisfy the Americans, who had been clamoring for Napoleon to send frigates to "fatigue the enemy." On the eve of the Battle of Dresden on 7 August 1813, Napoleon approved Decrès's instructions. Fully aware of the risks, the latter forewarned the emperor that, "employing thirty frigates on cruise, you ought to calculate on there being ten captured before next June, therefore you need to replace them by pressing the construction of new frigates." Meanwhile, the increasingly precarious situation in Germany required Napoleon again to rely on sailors to replenish his losses. During the summer armistice, he diverted 10,000 conscripts originally designated for the navy to the army. After his decisive defeat at the Battle of Leipzig in October 1813, Napoleon contemplated pillaging his navy further to fulfill his growing demand for men to rebuild his army. However, he nonetheless wanted Decrès to "send out the frigates like nothing has happened." Still with an eye toward the future naval war, the emperor instructed Decrès not to disarm the frigates, stating: "frigates train sailors and harm the enemy; we must let them leave."[103]

The naval campaign of 1813/1814 pitted French frigate captains against the dominant British blockade in which the hunter could very quickly become the prey. Similar to the 1812/1813 winter campaign, each captain could select his own cruising waters. The only difference with Decrès's instructions was the requirement to burn all prizes. The subsequent campaign proved both futile and wasteful. Of the seventeen frigates that made it to sea, only eight returned to port. While this campaign provided the raw recruits with vital experience at sea, it came at a high price. Beyond losing nine frigates, the French navy

---

102   CN, Nos 19392, 19483, 19488, 19570, 19572, 19583, 24: 346–347, 425–430, 512–514, 523–524.
103   CN, Nos 19694, 20121, 20318, 20337, 20350, 20836, 25:58, 383–384, 518–519, 26:10–11, 26–27, 384.

suffered 175 sailors killed and another 2,800 captured. Furthermore, the eighty-plus merchant ships taken or burnt were only minimal commercial losses to Britain, whose own merchant fleet actually grew during this period. In the end, this campaign was all for naught as Napoleon abdicated in April 1814.[104]

When considering Napoleon's use of sea power, it is important to take into consideration the resources expended on coastal batteries, coastal flotillas, and port fortifications. In fact, the bulk of France's shipping relied on the coastal trade. Despite Britain's predominance at sea, the shallow draft of these coastal trading vessels allowed them to sail between nearby ports on a regular basis. Napoleon developed an elaborate system to protect this lifeblood of French commerce against attacks by smaller vessels such as brigs and sloops. By July 1810, he had established more than 900 coastal batteries across the empire. Armed with more than 3,600 cannons, these batteries required the employment of 13,000 gunners at a cost of 7,000,000 francs per year in the Ministry of War's budget. After the minister of war complained that this expenditure was useless, Napoleon retorted that the coastal batteries were necessary because small shipping was more active than ever. After hearing complaints by naval officers about the quality of these batteries, the emperor stated: "in the inferior state of our navy, you cannot have too many coastal batteries. The coastal shipping is strong and would grow more if the batteries were better serviced and composed of better materials."[105]

To supplement these coastal batteries, Napoleon ordered the development of small coastal flotillas to protect the ports and the major estuaries. Following attacks on coastal shipping in May 1808, he decreed the creation of a coast guard flotilla. As of July 1810, Napoleon wanted fourteen flotilla battalions of nearly 14,000 men to protect the entire Atlantic coastline. Serving aboard twenty-five brigs, 200 gunboats, luggers, and cutters, seventy barges, and more than 100 transports, these men were to ensure the safe arrival of coastal shipping. In the Mediterranean, Napoleon ordered the organization of four flotilla battalions at Toulon, Marseille, and Genoa. Thus, Napoleon could solve two problems at once. Not only could he protect his crucial coastal shipping, but he could also use these flotillas to train sailors to replenish losses in his navy.[106]

In addition to expanding the port facilities, the arsenals and fleets needed to be secured from attack. Following the British assault on Vlissingen and Antwerp in July 1809, Napoleon bolstered fortifications across his major ports. Even before the British had withdrawn from their failed attempt to capture Antwerp,

---

104   Lepelley, *Frégates*, 170–174, 193–198, 233–237, 259–261, 282, 302–306, 310–320, 370–393; James, *Naval History*, 6:279–281; Troude, *Batailles navales*, 4:193–194.
105   CN, No. 16633, 20 459–460.
106   CN, No. 13789, 16643, 17:45, 20:468–470; CG, No. 18125, 8:649.

the emperor ordered a massive expansion of the fortifications protecting the various approaches to his naval facilities. He spent millions of francs across Europe improving port batteries and fortifications.[107]

Overshadowed by his accomplishments on the battlefield and tainted by the infamous Battles of Aboukir Bay and Trafalgar, Napoleon's role in French naval affairs often has been overlooked or maligned. While more attention has been given to Napoleon's orders denying his officers permission to engage the British, he was not averse to his ships seeking to engage the British navy directly. For example, in 1807, the emperor issued orders for his fleets to attack the enemy under favorable conditions. After Napoleon received reports that the British had only a few ships off the ports of Vlissingen and Rochefort, he authorized attempts to capture them. Hearing of the capture of the HMS *Proserpine* in February 1809, he reaffirmed his desire to see similar actions. Of course, such maneuvers posed a potential risk as well. In November 1813, the Toulon fleet took advantage of the absence of a blockading fleet to conduct naval exercises. When the British fleet returned, a shifting wind nearly stranded five French ships, which had to fight their way back to the safety of Toulon.[108] Although the French escaped with minimal damage, this action demonstrated the inherent danger of even small sorties.

Fully understanding the importance of contesting Britain's control of the sea, Napoleon accepted the risks associated with such maneuvers. While ordering squadrons to engage in such operations in 1809, he tried to assuage concerns, stating that, "whatever the result of these expeditions, I will always approve the idea, even when I ought to lose some ships." Cognizant of the dangers, the French emperor did not want his commanders to take unnecessary risks, and cautioned them to await opportune moments. When Eugène de Beauharnais, his viceroy of Italy, sought to sail his fledgling flotilla against equal British forces in 1806, Napoleon declined, claiming that "their defeat is certain." When asked in 1807 if the Rochefort fleet should engage the British blockade, he exclaimed that "there is no doubt that [they] should not attack the enemy of equal force. All the more reason, if the enemy has superior forces." Although approving an admiral's request to make a sortie to chase after British cruisers in May 1810, Napoleon warned: "I wish that my squadron not be compromised in a naval battle, which does not enter into my projects; I would only approve an engagement with the English squadron as long as my squadron had at least one-fifth over the English." As Napoleon would later reiterate to Decrès in 1813, "my principle is to not risk my ships and to only send out frigates until

---

107   CG, Nos 22177, 22189, 9:1250–1254, 1261–1262; Maitland, *Surrender of Napoleon*, 122.
108   CN, Nos 12718, 13995, 14883, 15:308, 17:206, 18:333; Troude, *Batailles navales*, 4:170–171.

there is equilibrium between the two navies."[109] Thus, Napoleon's use of the fleet-in-being and commerce raiding were just interim strategies as he rebuilt the French navy.

Always interested in the fine details, Napoleon constantly sought ways to improve the navy. His frequent discussion of hydrodynamics with Decrès reflected his interest in developing ships with shallower drafts capable of entering shallower waters. Napoleon was also keen on adopting the best practices of other navies. In June 1807, he ordered Decrès to create rules for stowage based on the British system, while arming French ships with more carronades. He even asked Decrès to explore building smaller triple-decker ships of ninety-six guns like the British. On hearing reports of the prowess of the American super frigate USS *Constitution*, Napoleon sent officers to examine the frigate when it reached Cherbourg in 1811, as he was particularly curious about the number of its guns and the size of its crew. After learning that the British were developing super frigates on par with the Americans, the emperor ordered three frigates built along the American model.[110] Although not formally trained as a naval officer, Napoleon always remained curious about the details of the naval profession.

Since his rise to power in 1799, Napoleon had personally directed France's naval war against Britain. He regularly adapted his operational plans in reaction to the dynamic situation in Europe. In his naval strategy, he continually attempted to update his orders to reflect the ever-changing conditions, but the inherent difficulties in maritime communications generally rendered his efforts counterproductive. Moreover, construction delays and forces beyond his control negatively impacted his plans. For example, in early 1804, Napoleon had to delay the operation to invade Britain for another month because the invasion flotillas were not yet fully in place.[111] Then, Latouche-Tréville's death aboard his flagship on 19 August 1804 forced Napoleon to dramatically alter his plans, which had become increasingly complex and reliant on good fortune. Napoleon himself was not blameless. Likewise in 1804, after a potential security breach necessitated a complete revision of the plans to invade Britain, Napoleon did not issue new orders for nearly two months as he was

---

109   Napoleon did not completely rule out the idea, but insisted that it had to be "a feasible operation that would garner results." See *CN*, Nos 10112, 12115, 14883, 16393, 20121, 12:295, 14:496, 18:333, 20:297–298, 25:383–384.

110   *CG*, Nos 14080, 14354, 7:93, 208; *CN*, Nos 12806, 16760, 18133, 20334, 20337, 15:363–364, 21:16–18, 22:482, 26:7, 1C–11.

111   Correctly deducing that the British had anticipated his plan to rally with the ships in Spain, the First Consul adjusted the orders slightly on 2 July. Rather than heading to Cádiz and Ferrol, Latouche-Tréville would rally the five ships at Rochefort. *CG*, Nos. 8866, 8902, 8904, 8980, 9050, 4:701–3, 719–20, 756–57, 790; Desbrière, *1793–1805*, 3:425–29, 4:153–54; Monaque, *Latouche-Tréville*, 580.

predominantly preoccupied with the preparations for his coronation ceremony and other affairs. His attempts to adapt the naval campaign to the developing situation by issuing flurries of orders only hindered the campaign as his commanders received varying editions of his plans due to delays in maritime communications. This issue became paramount because of the numerous variables presented by the war at sea and the impact of those variables on planning. As a result, Napoleon could only hope that the Brest, Rochefort, and Toulon fleets could return to Europe in June 1805 with over forty ships to wrest command of the Channel from the British. Yet, even if the fleets failed to rally, he ordered Ganteaume's Brest fleet to head for the Channel if he had at least twenty-five ships and the winds were favorable.[112]

Although he began without any formal training, Napoleon eventually developed an astute understanding of naval affairs. As he did with almost every other aspect of the French state, Napoleon delved directly into any issue at hand with a remarkable knowledge of minute details. He was often able to micromanage every portfolio of the state, sometimes even when he was as far away as Poland. Yet, even genius has its limits, as there were times when he was completely preoccupied with other matters, particularly when conducting military campaigns across Europe. Already a man who had become more of a courtier than an admiral, Decrès was ill prepared to demonstrate initiative when Napoleon was away.[113] Despite his flaws and occasional mistakes, the emperor understood the importance of naval warfare. Not only did he spend vast sums on his fleets and ports, many of the annexations and conquests that mark his grand strategy were made to improve France's naval power. Although some of the most disastrous naval battles in history occurred during his reign, the tactical mistakes made by his naval commanders were as much to blame as Napoleon himself. Furthermore, Napoleon's tremendous efforts to rebuild the French and allied navies had them on track to rival the British navy. What Emperor Napoleon would have done with such a navy, however, remains open to speculation.

Bibliography

Albion, Robert G. *Forests and Sea Power: The Timber Problem of the Royal Navy 1652–1862*. Cambridge, MA, 1926.

Arthur, Brian. *How Britain Won the War of 1812: The Royal Navy's Blockades of the United States, 1812–1815*. Woodbridge, UK, 2011.

---

112   Cotton to Marsden, 19 March 1805, No. 459, Cotton to Marsden, 28 March 1805, No. 464, Gardner to Marsden, 3 April 1805, No. 468, in Leyland, *Blockade of Brest, 1803–1805*, 2:213–14, 216–17, 219–20. CG, No. 9732, 5:154.

113   Maurice Dupont, *L'amiral Decrès et Napoleon* (Paris, 1991), 87.

Baugh, Daniel A. *British Naval Administration in the Age of Walpole*. Princeton, NJ, 1965.

Baugh, Daniel A. "The Eighteenth-Century Navy as a National Institution, 1690–1815." In J.R. Hill, ed., *The Oxford Illustrated History of the Royal Navy*, 120–160. New York, 1995.

Black, Jeremy. *The War of 1812 in the Age of Napoleon*. Norman, OK, 2009.

Clowes, William Laird, Sir Clements Markham, A.T. Mahan, H.W. Wilson, Theodore Roosevelt, and L. Carr Laughton. *The Royal Navy: A History From the Earliest Times to Present*, 6 vols. London, 1897–1903.

Corbett, Julian S. *Some Principles of Maritime Strategy*. London, 1911; reprint, Annapolis, MD, 1988.

Davey, James. *The Transformation of British Naval Strategy: Seapower and Supply in Northern Europe, 1808–1812*. Woodbridge, UK, 2012.

Gates, David. *The Napoleonic Wars 1803–1815*. London, 1997.

Glete, Jan. *Navies and Nations: Warships, Navies and State Building in Europe and America, 1500–1860*, 2 vols. Stockholm, 1993.

Glete, Jan. "Navies and Power Struggle in Northern and Eastern Europe, 1721–1814." In Rolf Hobson and Tom Kristiansen, eds, *Navies in Northern Waters, 1721–2000*, 66–90. London, 2004.

Glover, Richard. "The French Fleet, 1807–1814: Britain's Problem; and Madison's Opportunity." *Journal of Modern History* 39 (September 1967), 233–252.

Hall, Christopher. *British Strategy in the Napoleonic War 1803–1815*. Manchester, 1992.

Hall, Christopher. *Wellington's Navy: Sea Power and the Peninsular War*. London, 2004.

Hamilton, Sir Richard Vesey, ed. *Letters and Papers of Admiral of the Fleet Sir Thomas Byam Martin*, 3 vols. London, 1898–1901.

Harding, Richard. "Sailors and Gentlemen of Parade: Some Professional and Technical Problems Concerning the Conduct of Combined Operations in the Eighteenth Century." *Historical Journal* 32 (1989), 35–55.

Herzog, Richard T. "The Royal Marine and Insurgent Operations in the Salamanca Campaign, 1812." In Gordon C. Bond, ed., *Proceedings, 1992: Consortium on Revolutionary Europe, 1750–1850*, 62–69. Tallahassee, FL, 1993.

Historical Manuscripts Commission. *Report on the Manuscripts of Colonel David Milne Home of Wedderburn Castle, NB*. London, 1902.

Horward, Donald D. "British Seapower and Its Influence upon the Peninsular War (1808–1814)." *Naval War College Review* 31 (Fall 1978), 54–71.

James, William. *Naval History of Great Britain from the Declaration of War by France to the Accession of George IV*, 6 vols. Reprint, New York, 1902.

Knight, Roger. *Britain Against Napoleon: The Organization of Victory 1793–1815*. London, 2013.

Knight, Roger. *The Pursuit of Victory: The Life and Achievement of Horatio Nelson*. New York, 2005.

Lambert, Andrew. *The Challenge: Britain Against America in the Naval War of 1812*. London, 2012.

Lavery, Brian. *Nelson's Navy: The Ships, Men, and Organization, 1793–1815*. London, 1989; reprint with revisions, Annapolis, MD, 1997.

LeFevre, Peter and Richard Harding, ed. *British Admirals of the Napoleonic Wars: The Contemporaries of Nelson*. London, 2005.

Lewis, Michael. *A Social History of the Navy: 1793–1815*. London, 1960.
Lieven, Dominic. *Russia Against Napoleon: The True Story of the Campaigns of War and Peace*. New York, 2009.
Londonderry, Charles Vane, Marquess of, ed. *Correspondence, Despatches, and Other Papers of Viscount Castlereagh, Second Marquess of Londonderry*, 12 vols. London, 1848–1853.
McCranie, Kevin D. *Admiral Lord Keith and the Naval War Against Napoleon*. Gainesville, FL, 2006.
McCranie, Kevin D. "The Recruitment of Seamen for the British Navy, 1793–1815: 'Why Don't You Raise More Men?'" In Donald Stoker, Frederick C. Schneid, and Harold Blanton, eds, *Conscription in the Napoleonic Era: A Revolution in Military Affairs?*, 84–101. London, 2009.
McCranie, Kevin D. *Utmost Gallantry: The US and Royal Navies at Sea in the War of 1812*. Annapolis, MD, 2011.
McCranie, Kevin D. "The War of 1812 in the Ongoing Napoleonic Wars: The Response of Britain's Royal Navy." *Journal of Military History* 76 (October 2012), 1067–1094.
Mackesy, Piers. *The War in the Mediterranean, 1803–1810*. Cambridge, MA, 1967.
Mitchell, B.R. and Phyllis Deane. *Abstract of British Historical Statistics*. Cambridge, 1971.
Musteen, Jason. *Nelson's Refuge: Gibraltar in the Age of Napoleon*. Annapolis, MD, 2011.
Parry, Clive, ed. *The Consolidated Treaties Series*, vol. 59 (1806–1808). Dobbs Ferry, NY, 1969.
Robson, Martin. *A History of the Royal Navy: The Napoleonic Wars*. London, 2014.
Rodger, N.A.M. *Command of the Ocean: A Naval History of Britain, 1649–1815*. London: W.W. Norton, 2004.
Rodger, N.A.M. *The Wooden World: An Anatomy of the Georgian Navy*. Reprint, London, 1996.
Ross, Steven T. *European Diplomatic History 1789–1815: France Against Europe*. Reprint, Malabar, FL, 1981.
Ryan, A.N. "The Defence of British Trade with the Baltic, 1808–1813." *The English Historical Review* 74 (1959): 443–466.
Ryan, A.N. "The Melancholy Fate of the Baltic Ships in 1811." *Mariner's Mirror* 50 (1964), 123–134.
Ryan, A.N., ed. *The Saumarez Papers: Selections from the Baltic Correspondence of Vice Admiral Sir James Saumarez, 1808–1812*. London, 1968.
Syrett, David. "The Role of the Royal Navy in the Napoleonic Wars After Trafalgar, 1805–1814." *Naval War College Review* (September–October 1979), 71–84.
Taylor, Stephen. *Storm and Conquest: The Clash of Empires in the Eastern Seas, 1809*. New York, 2007.
Wellington, Arthur Wellesley. *Supplementary Despatches, Correspondence and Memoranda of Field Marshall Arthur Duke of Wellington, KG*, edited by his Son, 15 vols. London, 1858–1872.
Whitehill, Walter Muir, ed. *New England Blockaded in 1814: The Journal of Henry Edward Napier, Lieutenant in HMS Nymphe*. Salem, 1939.

CHAPTER 14

Britain's Royal Navy and the Defeat of Napoleon

Kevin D. McCranie

Bodies, along with shards of wood, danced in the water as ships of the line belched smoke and fire. Deep within the bowels of one warship rested Britain's greatest admiral, dying in his moment of victory from a shattered spine. Trafalgar and the death of Horatio Nelson make for a thrilling story. Certainly, battle provided a dramatic, tangible manifestation of naval power and propelled Nelson to the apogee of fame. Although the Battle of Trafalgar, the last general fleet-on-fleet contest of the Napoleonic Wars, occurred on 21 October 1805, it did not contribute directly to Napoleon's overall defeat. Britain fought on for nearly a decade to force Napoleon from power in the spring of 1814. The Royal Navy's role in this decade of war necessitates a broader interpretation of how the British used naval power to obtain a comparative strategic advantage. Instead of being decisive in its own right, British naval power indirectly contributed to the defeat of Napoleonic France.

To better understand the Royal Navy's role in the Napoleonic Wars, fleet-on-fleet engagements like that of Trafalgar serve as an effective point of departure. That another general fleet-on-fleet engagement did not occur after Trafalgar frankly disappointed and surprised British contemporaries. John Wilson Croker, the secretary of the British Admiralty, wrote in 1811 that "it is now six years since we had a general sea fight and we are growing impatient."[1] Even an Admiralty official had become enchanted by the glory of battle. Moreover, British naval leaders viewed the French fleet "as the first object."[2]

The search for battle, however, could prove elusive. Wishing for a battle at sea and obtaining one were two different concepts. Julian Corbett has rightly argued that the greatest problem in naval warfare "was not how to defeat the enemy, but how to bring him to action."[3] In other words, the tactics of battle

---

[1] Croker to Pellew, 1 October 1811, William L. Clements Library, University of Michigan, Ann Arbor (hereafter cited as Clements Library), Croker Papers, Private Letter Book, 1/133–35. I would like to thank Brian DeToy for commenting on an earlier version of this paper at the 2013 meeting of the Consortium on the Revolutionary Era at Fort Worth, Texas, and for Frederick Black's comments on the entire chapter.

[2] Pellew to Melville, 25 December 1813, NLS, Melville Papers, MS 14839/108–15.

[3] Julian S. Corbett, *Some Principles of Maritime Strategy* (London, 1911; reprint, Annapolis, MD, 1988), 164.

posed less of an issue than the numerous points of fog and friction that occurred in naval operations that conspired to make battle itself less likely. Even ships propelled by wind had a high degree of mobility, often allowing weaker naval forces to escape. Since finding ships depended on lines of sight, the amount of light, and weather conditions, it often proved possible to avoid detection.

After 1805, the French reluctance to risk their capital ships in large fleet actions also made battle less likely. Concentrations of French warships generally stayed in or close to port, forcing the British to be ready to take advantage of chance such as a wind shift, which occurred in November 1813 and affected the French fleet while training outside the roadstead at Toulon. Admiral Sir Edward Pellew, the commander of the British Mediterranean Fleet, declared, "It was as near a godsend as could be." Rather than fight, the French harnessed a less than propitious wind to flee toward Toulon, though Pellew explained, "I can tell you we were very near dragging him out by the hair of his Head."[4] Even when French warships did come out, as in the case of Vice Admiral Honoré Joseph Antoine Ganteaume's Mediterranean Fleet in 1808, the French did not seek battle.[5]

The French shunned large-scale engagements, largely due to British proficiency in such encounters. This was the result of a long trend in which the British became increasingly effective at eliminating enemy warships at sea. Looking back to the 18th century, particularly during the American Revolution, fleet engagements generally did not result in the loss of a significant number of warships. This began to change in 1782 with the Battle of the Saints and early in the Wars of the French Revolution with the "Glorious" First of June in 1794. Nelson's actions at the Nile, Copenhagen, and Trafalgar along with Admiral Adam Duncan's maneuver at Camperdown allowed the British to hone their skill at capturing or destroying enemy warships. After Trafalgar, the concept was ingrained in British naval leadership that battles of annihilation were the desired objective. While commanding forces off the Scheldt in 1811, Admiral William Young asserted, "I should rather fight for the public good, than for my own fame; I should be better pleased to destroy the Enemy's Fleet with an equal force, than to defeat them partially with an inferior."[6]

Although the French remained less willing to risk their larger fleets after Trafalgar, single ships and small squadrons conducted an active war against

---

4 Pellew to Croker, 8 November 1813, Clements Library, Croker Papers, Box 4, Folder 18.
5 Piers Mackesy, *The War in the Mediterranean, 1803–1810* (Cambridge, MA, 1967), 231–258.
6 Young to Yorke, 4 June 1811, National Maritime Museum, Greenwich, UK (hereafter cited as NMM), Yorke Papers, YOR/20/8.

the British. The Royal Navy also applied the concept of annihilation in these encounters, which led to events such as the capture or destruction of five French ships of the line off San Domingo in February 1806 by seven British ships of the line and a successful frigate action off Lissa in 1811.[7] By 1813, Napoleon had come to recognize that a portion of these individual warships or small squadrons would be lost to the British.[8] Napoleon considered such losses to be an acceptable price to pay, as the loss of small squadrons did less to affect the overall balance of naval power. By carefully managing deployments, he could largely dictate the rate of loss. Furthermore, losing a smaller action did not have the same negative effects as Trafalgar, where twenty-seven British ships of the line met and defeated thirty-three Franco-Spanish opponents. Moreover, these smaller engagements did not always end in Britain's favor. One particularly brutal engagement occurred in the Indian Ocean during 1810 at Grand Port on the island of Mauritius or, as the French called it, Île de France. The battle left 2 British frigates captured and 2 others scuttled with more than 250 British seamen killed and wounded along with hundreds captured. In this case, the British attacked into a shallow port without sufficient hydrographic knowledge. Several frigates ran aground, making them easy targets. On an emotional level, this defeat stunned the Royal Navy. One contemporary explained, "No case, of which we are aware, more deeply affects the character of the British navy, than the defeat it sustained at Grand Port."[9] Strategically, however, Grand Port proved only a momentary setback, and the Royal Navy rapidly restored a favorable naval balance of power in the Indian Ocean.[10]

Though aggressive action incurred risks, a combination of audacious action, skill, and the navy's overall size gave the British significant advantages in pursuing dramatic results. Very different from the results Napoleon attained from his battles of annihilation on land, pursuing battles of annihilation on the seas had a tendency to affect the operational environment by removing or limiting the ability of the loser to conduct operations. Thus, battle proved only a means to an end rather than an event leading clearly or decisively to peace. A French naval victory, however large, would not have allowed the French to occupy England or cause the British to capitulate. The same also worked in reverse. A British naval victory would not lead to the occupation of Paris or compel

---

7   William James, *Naval History of Great Britain from the Declaration of War by France to the Accession of George IV*, 6 vols (Reprint, New York, 1902), 4:94–108, 5:232–245.
8   *CN*, No. 20337, 26:10–11.
9   James, *Naval History*, 5:168.
10 For a full-length treatment, see Stephen Taylor, *Storm and Conquest: The Clash of Empires in the Eastern Seas, 1809* (New York, 2007).

Napoleon to negotiate peace as the defeated party. Events on land, whether military, political, or economic, had to intercede to achieve war termination.

Although naval engagements would not directly lead to peace, battle did have the potential to provide the British with more freedom of action at sea. This proved particularly important when considering the limited size of the Royal Navy. It might seem counterintuitive to claim that the Royal Navy lacked in numbers considering that it dwarfed its rivals. After all, the British possessed approximately half the world's total warship tonnage by the late Napoleonic period.[11] Numbers certainly gave the British a degree of redundancy at sea that allowed them to rapidly restore situations, such as after the events at Grand Port in 1810; the losses in this engagement totaled but 4 out of a total worldwide naval strength of approximately 100 operational British frigates, and the French failed to add subsequent victories to create cumulative British losses. The real size issue for the Royal Navy was the wide range of British global commitments that left few warships in reserve, which forced London to carefully balance deployments. In the Mediterranean, Rear Admiral Pellew lamented, "I have an arduous task and force much Divided in all points."[12] His quandary was not an unusual one. First Lord of the Admiralty Robert Dundas, 2nd Viscount Melville, bemoaned "the difficulties we have to contend with in maintaining our Navy on its present scale."[13] A battle had the potential to eliminate a threat and allow for the redeployment of warships. By the French refusing battle and the likely losses that would result, Napoleon forced the British to conduct resource-intensive deployments.[14]

One major Royal Navy requirement involved blockade squadrons to mitigate the danger posed by post-Trafalgar French naval construction. French fleet concentrations developed in the Scheldt estuary and at Toulon on France's Mediterranean coast with smaller squadrons at numerous locations including the Dutch anchorage of the Texel and France's Atlantic ports such as Brest. The severity of the threat posed by French naval construction after Trafalgar remains contentious. In hindsight, it was extraordinarily flawed in terms of available French seamen, the logistical capability to sustain the buildup, and the quality of ship construction.[15] To British contemporaries, however,

---

11   Jan Glete, *Navies and Nations: Warships, Navies and State Building in Europe and America, 1500–1860*, 2 vols (Stockholm, 1993), 2:376.
12   Pellew to Keith, 12 September 1812, NMM, Keith Papers, KEI/37/9.
13   Melville to Pellew, 16 December 1812, Clements Library, Melville Papers, Box 28.
14   *CN*, No. 21059, 27:7.
15   Richard Glover has argued that the French fleet posed a dangerous strategic threat for Britain while N.A.M. Rodger has cast doubt on this argument by highlighting the various problems that made the French fleet less combat-effective. See Glover, "The French Fleet, 1807–1814: Britain's Problem; and Madison's Opportunity," *Journal of Modern History* 39

Napoleon's naval expansion appeared menacing. British leadership certainly gave serious consideration to French warship construction, as evidenced by the strength of Royal Navy blockade squadrons that accounted for more than half of Britain's ships of the line in the years 1811–1813.[16] The First Lord of the Admiralty from 1811 to 1812, Charles Philip Yorke, explained that a blockade "to watch the Enemy vigilantly appears to me to demand our principal attention at present."[17] This was particularly important given the strength and deployments of the Royal Navy. British ships of the line – the battleships of the era – were concentrated in blockade squadrons off French naval ports. This created a thin veneer of British naval strength. If a French fleet escaped, the British blockaders had to pursue the French before they could inflict damage on isolated naval units and vulnerable maritime commerce. As the number of French warships grew, the British had to commit increased naval strength to the blockade squadrons. Melville admitted this fact to Pellew regarding the situation in the Mediterranean: "If the Enemy Fleet shall be increased by additional ships ... you will probably feel it your duty under such change of circumstances to represent to us ... that your force has become inadequate."[18] Nevertheless, the British acknowledged the existence of a tipping point. One member of the Admiralty posited: "How it will even be possible to keep up the system of Blockade as he [Napoleon] increases his force is beyond my comprehension for it is totally impossible to increase our navy in that ratio."[19]

Although the Royal Navy was the largest in the world in the years following Trafalgar, it had a critical vulnerability in personnel. Manning issues have been described as the navy's "most intractable problem."[20] As the Napoleonic Wars continued, the issue became more acute. In 1813, Melville bemoaned that "the supply of seamen is so inadequate to the current demands of the service."[21] One contemporary observer was not far off when he explained:

(Sep. 1967), 233–252, and Rodger, *The Command of the Ocean: A Naval History of Britain, 1649–1815* (London, 2004), 562.

16   Ships in Sea Pay, The National Archives, Kew, United Kingdom (hereafter cited as TNA), Admiralty Papers (hereafter cited as ADM) 8/99–100.
17   Yorke to Young, 27 August 1811, NMM, YOR/20/22.
18   Melville to Pellew, 16 December 1812, Clements Library, Melville Papers, Box 28.
19   Hope to Keith, 17 June 1812, NMM, KEI/37/9.
20   Daniel Baugh, "The Eighteenth-Century Navy as a National Institution, 1690–1815," in J.R. Hill, ed., *The Oxford Illustrated History of the Royal Navy* (New York, 1995), 133. See also Kevin D. McCranie, "The Recruitment of Seamen for the British Navy, 1793–1815: 'Why Don't You Raise More Men?'" in Donald Stoker, Frederick C. Schneid, and Harold Blanton, eds, *Conscription in the Napoleonic Era: A Revolution in Military Affairs?* (London, 2009), 84–101; N.A.M. Rodger, *The Wooden World: An Anatomy of the Georgian Navy* (reprint, London, 1996), 145–204.
21   Melville to Keith, 3 September 1813, NMM, KEI/37/9.

Look at our ships, how they are manned at the breaking out of a war, and compare them with the generality of ships now commissioned, and the difference will be most striking: it cannot be otherwise, on account of the vast number of ships at this time in commission, which are now manned by a very small proportion of able seamen, and the remainder filled up with good, bad, and indifferent, *viz.* ordinary seamen, landsmen, *foreigners*, the sweepings of *Newgate*, from the *hulks*, and almost all the prisons in the country.[22]

Naval officers also supported this contention. In 1810, one captain opined that "we are delighted with the ship, but her crew is deplorably weak, the smallest people I ever saw."[23] Another described his crew as "not at all what I would wish them to be, or what they ought to be."[24]

The British seaman was a finite commodity, and the Royal Navy competed for his services against other, often better-paying and less onerous, employment opportunities.[25] The navy needed a constant flow of new seamen, but volunteers did not prove sufficient, and the navy's leadership resorted to forcible recruitment. Particularly, the British used impressment. The strategic imperative of keeping the Royal Navy operational provided naval leaders with a justification for this questionable practice, despite the fact that it was extraordinarily unpopular.[26]

The British navy had yet to create an effective means of managing maritime human resources, and this had strategic implications on the strength of the fleet. The lack of personnel contributed to a dwindling naval establishment from 595 deployed warships in July 1809 to 515 in July 1812. The reduction in the number of warships required approximately 12,000 fewer men at full manning levels.[27] Yet, full manning was in itself a misnomer. British warships when

---

22 To the Editor, signed Naval Patriot, May 1813, *Naval Chronicle*, 29:466–469.
23 Edward Hawks to Croker, 2 July 1810, Clements Library, Croker Papers, Box 2, Folder 5.
24 David Milne to George Home, 1 December 1811, in Historical Manuscripts Commission, *Report on the Manuscripts of Colonel David Milne Home of Wedderburn Castle, N.B.* (London, 1902), 150–151.
25 Rodger, *Command of the Ocean*, 497–501; Michael Lewis, *A Social History of the Navy: 1793–1815* (London, 1960), 95–101.
26 Rodger, *Command of the Ocean*, 497–501; Rodger, *Wooden World*, 164; McCranie, "'Why Don't You Raise More Men?'"; Lewis, *A Social History*, 92; Daniel A. Baugh, *British Naval Administration in the Age of Walpole* (Princeton, NJ, 1965), 147.
27 Ships in Sea Pay, July 1809 to July 1813, TNA, ADM, 8/98–100. The formula for determining these figures is as follows. The authorized complements of all deployed warships were totaled. Noncombat and stationary ships such as receiving and hospital ships were not included. Ships in ordinary and ships that had yet to be deployed or assigned to

compared to similar French and American warships sailed with smaller crews. A lieutenant aboard the 38-gun British frigate *Nymphe* learned that the complement of the American frigate *Congress* approached 400 men. He correctly asserted that "the *Congress* and *Nymphe* are nearly of a size, but the allowed establishment of the *Nymphe* is 315 souls, of which she has 300 (on paper only) … yet the Admiralty appears not to take the slightest trouble to man those frigates opposed to so superior a force."[28] Some considered manning levels less than optimal, causing one contemporary to posit: "The *matériel* and *personnel* were more than ever out of their due proportions."[29] The Admiralty certainly understood the issues but, with a limited manpower supply, more men aboard ships meant fewer ships on station, creating a difficult tradeoff that the Admiralty grudgingly answered with more ships over higher manning.

To husband strength, the high-ranking leadership sincerely desired to avoid exposing seamen to risky operations or what could be viewed as needless losses.[30] Service at sea was dangerous enough. Warships could be lost in foul weather as was the case when three ships of the line were lost in a Christmastime storm while exiting the Baltic Sea in 1811. This resulted in some 2,000 deaths, which amounted to more than four times the number of British killed at Trafalgar.[31] Daily operations also resulted in attrition. Tropical climates thinned crews. While participating in the capture of Java in 1811, the crew of the 74-gun *Illustrious* suffered 65 deaths from disease and sent 50 invalids ashore.[32] Daily operations in more moderate climates often proved similarly dangerous. While operating principally off the North American coast between March 1812 and January 1814, the 38-gun frigate *Junon* lost nearly 100 men out of an established complement of 315. Only five died in action and one was invalided for combat wounds, while sixty-two were discharged or died "principally arising from infirmity alone" and another twenty-nine deserted.[33]

The dangers of service along with recruitment difficulties meant that the Royal Navy had to carefully balance operational warships against threats. First Lord of the Admiralty Melville explained that "every additional man to the

---

commands were not counted because the manning of such ships was haphazard. Also, troopships were not counted given the incomplete statistics.

28　Walter Muir Whitehill, ed., *New England Blockaded in 1814: The Journal of Henry Edward Napier, Lieutenant in HMS Nymphe* (Salem, 1939), journal entry for 11 May 1814, 12–13.
29　James, *Naval History*, 5:426.
30　Drury to Minto, 20 July 1809, NLS, Letters to Minto, MS 11317/78–79.
31　James, *Naval History*, 5:231–232; A.N. Ryan, "The Melancholy Fate of the Baltic Ships in 1811," *Mariner's Mirror* 50 (1964), 123–134.
32　Broughton to Croker, 22 December 1811, TNA, ADM 1/184/37.
33　Upton to Griffith, 22 January 1814, NMM, Warren Papers, WAR/25/96.

Mediterranean must probably be taken from some other pressing service."[34] In other words, the navy in the years after Trafalgar did not have the luxury of expansion to meet threats; instead, forces in one location had to be reduced to meet expanding requirements in another.

Decisions about the distribution of naval forces were the province of the Admiralty. One British fleet commander sympathized with Melville's task: "I can readily believe that Your Lordship must find considerable difficulty in collecting Squadrons sufficient for the number of services that require them; we must all do the best we can with what can be afforded us; Your Lordship must attend to the whole."[35] In mid-1810, for example, the Admiralty withdrew ships of the line from distant stations so they could be deployed opposite the growing French naval concentrations in Holland and the ports around the Scheldt estuary including Antwerp and Flushing, while also increasing the number of large warships supporting the Anglo-Portuguese army at Lisbon and the Anglo-Spanish force at Cádiz.[36] Two years later, a member of the Admiralty lamented, "We have not at this moment a vessel of any description that we can call disposable."[37] Specifically, another member of the Admiralty explained, "We have been obliged by the demand upon us from America and the Baltic to strip the squadrons on the home stations of frigates and smaller vessels to the extent which we would willingly have avoided."[38] More than land armies, navies had greater mobility even in an age of movement dependent on the wind. In the decade after Trafalgar, British naval leadership constantly juggled warships by reinforcing stations facing threats and reducing naval forces in quieter locales. Even so, the British found it difficult to withdraw squadrons after they had established a naval presence. Cases in point involved the creation of two post-Trafalgar naval commands at Brazil and at the Cape of Good Hope. Rather than meet a temporary threat, both commands served to monitor regional maritime interests, the heart of which in both cases involved managing critical sea lines of communication. In the case of Brazil, the British expanded their operations first to encompass the eastern coast of South America and then deployed warships to the Pacific as Spanish colonial authority weakened. Moreover, the capture of the last French colonies in the Caribbean did not result in the withdrawal of the Jamaica and Leeward Islands stations. No longer did the British

---

34 Melville to Pellew, 16 December 1812, Clements Library, Melville Papers, Box 28.
35 Young to Melville, 10 August 1812, National Archives of Scotland, Edinburgh (hereafter cited as NAS), GD/51/2/1084/4.
36 Yorke to Saumarez, 10 August 1810, NMM, YOR/16A/9; Yorke to Warren, 20 July 1810, NMM, YOR/19.
37 Hope to Keith, 12 January 1813, NMM, KEI/37/9.
38 Melville to Young, 7 August 1812, NAS, GD/51/2/1084/3.

have to mount amphibious operations to capture French island colonies or combat squadrons of French warships. Instead, the British had to foster trade while minimizing the danger posed by commerce-raiders. Such a threat still required warships, albeit in smaller numbers and composed of different types.[39]

The need to maintain a naval presence, even after the elimination of regional threats, clearly highlighted the necessity for Britain to manage maritime communication. Naval theorist Julian Corbett argued that maritime communication, while rarely glamorous but always necessary, remains "the object of naval warfare."[40] Secure maritime communication allowed Britain to move soldiers, trade, and information in relative security across the ocean, facilitating both Britain's war effort and its economic might.

Controlling maritime communication involved layered deployments. Squadrons posted opposite French naval bases kept at bay enemies that could prey on commerce. Deployments around the British Isles established good order at sea and minimized the danger posed by privateers in home waters. Foreign stations were established either at maritime choke points such as the Cape of Good Hope or at the termini of sea lines of communication such as Brazil, Jamaica, and the East Indies. Along the oceanic highways, the British navy used patrolling warships and shepherded merchantmen in convoys.[41]

Convoys became more pervasive in the years following Trafalgar propelled by legislation that created legal requirements for merchants to sail in convoys. In September 1813, Melville explained that "the nature of naval service will nowhere admit of perfect and complete security. There must always be some risk, and our duty is to render it as little as possible." Specifically, he recounted about commerce: "We will not be responsible for ships sailing singly or without convoy … No amount of cruisers … could secure such ships from occasional capture."[42] The belief in the efficacy of convoys extended beyond the navy. A September 1814 report from Lloyds, the maritime insurer, added that "adequate security to our commerce can only be found in keeping it under convoy."[43] Convoys reduced maritime insurance rates by as much as 50 per cent when

---

39 Statement of the British Naval Force on the North American Stations, 1810–1813, in *Memoirs and Correspondence of Viscount Castlereagh*, ed. by Charles Vane, Marquess of Londonderry, 12 vols (London, 1848–1853), 8:286–287; Ships in Sea Pay, TNA, ADM 8/99–100.
40 Corbett, *Some Principles of Maritime Strategy*, 117.
41 Kevin D. McCranie, "The War of 1812 in the Ongoing Napoleonic Wars: The Response of Britain's Royal Navy," *Journal of Military History* (October 2012), 1071–1075.
42 Melville to Bathurst, 3 September 1813, in *Supplementary Despatches, Correspondence and Memoranda of Field Marshall Arthur Duke of Wellington, K.G.*, ed. by his Son, 15 vols (London, 1858–1872), 8:223–226.
43 Lloyds to Croker, 19 September 1814, TNA, ADM 1/3994.

compared to a similar unescorted voyage.[44] This facilitated commerce and protected insurers such as Lloyds from catastrophic loss, thus limiting economic risk and enhancing the stability of Britain's maritime communications as well as Britain's larger economic and financial systems.

As the use of convoys became more prevalent, Melville admitted that "it imposes on us the necessary duty of being liberal in regard to the number of convoys."[45] Convoys were defensive in nature, largely preventing the capture of merchant vessels. They did little to directly defeat France. Warships on escort duty had to protect their convoys rather than hunt commerce-raiders. Furthermore, convoys were unpopular with merchants. They only moved at the speed of the convoy's slowest ship. Moreover, the chairman of one British trading association asserted, "The loss, expense, and disappointment occasioned by this detention [of convoys] and in the arrival here of so great a number of vessels at once exceed calculation."[46]

Although the British navy proved less than decisive and faced serious limitations on its size, it remained the country's strongest and most flexible instrument of war. Not only did it dwarf other navies in a comparative numerical context, its advantage in infrastructure was even more pronounced. It was the only navy capable of sustaining far-flung deployments on a near global scale. This was no small accomplishment given contemporary ship-building materials and the mode of propulsion. Moreover, the mobility of warships allowed for rapid redeployments into deteriorating environments. Given these factors, British leadership sought to find a way to leverage the navy's advantages so as to obtain more decisive effects in its long war against Napoleonic France.

One way to use naval power offensively involved joint operations where the Royal Navy projected army forces to seize land objectives outside continental Europe. Such operations sought to secure British interests. Capturing colonies, however, was not merely designed as a means of territorial aggrandizement for an expanding British Empire; instead, London generally looked to the strategic advantage gained from the capture of a colony. In 1809, First Lord of the Admiralty Henry Phipps, 1st Earl of Mulgrave, wrote, "His Majesty's Government although not desirous of the capture of Guadaloupe [sic] as a colonial possession are yet of opinion that in a naval and political point of view, it is of sufficient importance to render its capture expedient."[47] The capture of the

---

44 Marryat to Melville, 10 May 1813, NAS, GD 51/2/882/3–4.
45 Melville to Croker, 30 April 1812, British Library, London, Add. RP 706.
46 Extract Chairman of the West India Association of Liverpool to Canning, 7 May 1814, Clements Library, Croker Papers, Canning Letters.
47 Mulgrave to Cochrane, 17 August 1809, NLS, Cochrane Papers, MS 2572 182.

Cape of Good Hope in 1806 provides an even stronger example of joint operations seeking a strategic advantage. By taking the Cape of Good Hope, the British removed a hostile base along their sea line of communication with India and China. Acquisition of the Cape further benefited Britain because at that time the British lacked a port between Saint Helena and India.

On the one hand, gaining possession of colonies removed bases for commerce-raiders and allowed for the development of British bases, and certain colonies became economically beneficial to the British state. On the other hand, some colonies proved difficult to occupy. The Île de France proved especially problematic given its isolated location in the Indian Ocean and the presence of a substantial number of French warships. Mauritius surrendered to the British in 1810 but only after they had incurred excessive costs including numerous naval operations, a stinging defeat at Grand Port, and a complex series of amphibious operations to secure outlying islands.[48] While removing the French presence at Mauritius improved British security in the Indian Ocean, other amphibious operations were based on more questionable objectives and resulted in the diversion of scarce warships and soldiers from other operations. In 1806 and 1807, the British attempted to seize key Spanish commercial centers in the Rio de la Plata region of South America. This was the brainchild of the naval commander at the Cape of Good Hope, who commanded the naval element of an unsanctioned invasion that led to the temporary occupation of Buenos Aires. In the end, a large British force surrendered and reinforcements did little to restore the situation.[49] One British official recounted, "It is, however, very intolerable still – bad in point of character, rendering doubly difficult all enterprises of a like nature." This same official explained a key British strategic imperative to avoid the "unprofitableness of the principle of simple conquest as applied by us to any great portion of the continental world."[50] In other words, the British army lacked the manpower for large-scale conquests, and the navy could not sustain operations against a continent-sized target. Only India proved the exception, but there the British relied on long-established bases and large, well-trained units of indigenous soldiers in the form of East India Company sepoys.

Even with missteps and facing difficulties, the British captured every French colony as well as many colonies belonging to states associated with France by 1811, from Guadeloupe in the West Indies to Batavia on the island of Java.

---

48   Taylor, *Storm and Conquest*.
49   Christopher Hall, *British Strategy in the Napoleonic War 1803–1815* (Manchester, 1992), 144–145.
50   Castlereagh to R. Dundas, 20 September [1807], in *Memoirs of Castlereagh*, 8:85–86.

Although such operations appeared offensive, they had a limited impact on the defeat of France since Napoleon's strength rested not in colonies but within the boundaries of continental Europe.[51] Britain's power largely hinged on the global economic system driven by trade and buttressed by colonies; however, the operative strength of Napoleon's French Empire was land-based, stretching from France through the German and Italian states, to the Russian border by 1807. To defeat France, Britain had to weaken this expansive domain. One method involved major amphibious operations directed at the European continent. Yet the failed attack on a continental target like Rio de la Plata in South America did not bode well for amphibious operations against the much more daunting opponent London faced in Napoleonic France. Even so, the British navy after Trafalgar put large forces ashore in Italy, Iberia, Denmark, and Holland. Although expeditionary land forces won battles like Maida in 1806 on the Italian peninsula, the navy had difficulty in sustaining forces ashore. A combination of limited amphibious lift and the intricacy of supplying land forces from the sea posed significant challenges. In particular, horses proved hard to transport, limiting British artillery, scouting forces, and logistics.

In some respects, the navy's greatest strength again proved to be defensive through its ability to evacuate the British army from the continent such as at both Coruña and Walcheren in 1809. Although the British navy successfully removed the armies, the inescapable fact was that these operations were at least partial failures. Fearing the long-term consequence of failure led one Briton to warn: "I wish these severe disappointments may not lead to the opposite extreme of desponding inactivity."[52] While British amphibious operations continued, their objectives often remained defensive with opposing naval forces as the object rather than offensive operations striking directly at the heart of Napoleon's continental land power. This was the case with the Danish fleet at Copenhagen in 1807. British amphibious operations also targeted Napoleon's naval forces in the Scheldt estuary in both 1809 and 1813–1814.

Not until late in the period after Trafalgar did London fully conceive the strategic effects attainable from land operations supported from the sea. This occurred in the Iberian peninsula, but the campaign's potential decisiveness became apparent only after several years of operations and much deliberation in London. Government leaders determined that the navy could play an essential role as explained by Britain's foreign secretary in 1810:

---

51 Statement of the British Naval Force on the North American Stations, 1810–1813, ibid., 8:286–287.
52 Memo by Melville, 1 January 1810, Clements Library, Melville Papers, Box 26.

> Great advantage has already been derived to the Spanish cause from operation of the British navy on the northern coast of Spain ... It would be very desirable to adopt a system of operations of a similar nature on a more extended scale embracing the whole coast of the Peninsula, and to connect these operations with those of Lord Wellington's army, and of the Garrison of Cadiz [sic].[53]

Iberia's peninsular geography allowed the British navy to nearly isolate the theater, while the region's poor road network and rough terrain made it difficult for the French to move supplies overland. In such favorable conditions, the British conducted a complex joint land and sea campaign. The Royal Navy made it possible to move supplies into Iberia by sea much more easily than the French could resupply their commands over land routes. Simultaneously, the navy provided a combination of mobility and a safety net for units operating along the coasts. The navy had the capability of providing the key support for the campaign, but First Lord of the Admiralty Yorke prudently asked in 1810, "The Question still is, what are our means for carrying it into execution?" He admitted, "As far as naval force is required it may be had on a sufficient scale but a disposable land force will still be necessary which ... is very difficult to be found or rather not to be had."[54] This led to a cautious strategy that maximized support from both Spanish and Portuguese allies while utilizing the existing base at Gibraltar and developing positions at Cádiz and Lisbon, the latter being of particular significance since it served as the British army's primary base of operations in Iberia. With the support of the Portuguese population and an increasingly capable Portuguese army, the British used its position on the far western side of Iberia to wear down the French in a long attritional struggle. Arthur Wellesley, the duke of Wellington, deftly refused to be drawn into battles not of his choosing while protracting the war and bleeding the French in combination with other operations. Highlighting Wellington's operations in western Iberia, however, does a disservice to the total extent of British operations. Large-scale land operations supported from the sea worked to assist Spanish land forces on Iberia's east coast. On the south coast, the navy played an integral role in the defense of Gibraltar and Cádiz. To the north, small British raiding forces proved particularly disruptive, especially in combination with Spanish irregular forces.[55]

---

53   Wellesely to Yorke, 18 September 1810, NMM, YOR/19.
54   Yorke to Wellesley, 19 September 1810, NMM, YOR/19.
55   Kevin D. McCranie, *Admiral Lord Keith and the Naval War Against Napoleon* (Gainesville, FL, 2006). See also Richard T. Herzog, "The Royal Marine and Insurgent Operations in the Salamanca Campaign, 1812," in Gordon C. Bond, *Proceedings, 1992: Consortium on*

Beyond Iberia, Europe's extensive coasts offered the Royal Navy significant opportunities to inflict damage on Napoleon's empire. To determine where, the British navy invested considerable resources to gather intelligence. Much of this effort focused on ascertaining the readiness of French warships. However, as the war continued, the Royal Navy closely monitored local sentiment toward France as well as the strength of French occupation forces. In mid-1812, the Admiralty reported that "all accounts from the Mediterranean are of the most favorable nature, as to the state of general discontent of all countries bordering it."[56] This worked hand in hand with London's desire to use "every principle of legitimate warfare."[57] Yet British leaders realized that they would have to wait for the right moment. In 1811, Yorke had argued that "nothing effective can be done till the Germans and Italians decide on imitating the Portuguese and Spaniards by making habitual war on the French determination to Conquer or Perish altogether."[58] In 1812, Yorke's successor as First Lord of the Admiralty, Melville, explained that "we should not push for the mere purpose of exciting or encouraging a rising, because we should probably be leading people to a resistance which would turn out to be unavailing and we would tend only to their own destruction."[59] The British did not want to deplete goodwill and lose carefully cultivated anti-French leadership in an effort that promised little chance of success. Circumstances began to change following Napoleon's 1812 Russian campaign. London responded by assisting those opposed to French rule, which often involved the navy landing arms to support anti-French insurgents in such places as the Vendée region of western France and Holland.

Nevertheless, the British realized they often would have to provide more than arms. The navy stood at the forefront supplying the initial assistance including ships and even the first men ashore. The crucial year, 1813, saw French fortunes in the Iberian peninsula ebb, particularly after their defeat at the Battle of Vitoria by Wellington's Anglo-Portuguese army. Napoleon's position

---

Revolutionary Europe (Tallahassee, FL, 1993), 62–69; Jason Musteen, *Nelson's Refuge: Gibraltar in the Age of Napoleon* (Annapolis, MD, 2011); James P. Herson, "The Siege of Cadiz, 1810–1812: A Study in Joint and Combined Operations During the Peninsular War" (PhD diss., Florida State University, 1998); Christopher Hall, *Wellington's Navy: Sea Power and the Peninsular War* (London, 2004); Paul Krajeski, "British Amphibious Campaigns and Operations of the Peninsular War, 1808–1814" (MA thesis, Florida State University, 1995).

56 George Hope to Alexander Hope, 7 July 1812, NAS, Papers of the Hope Family of Luffness, GD 364/1/1227/7.
57 Melville to Keith, 2 April 1814, NMM, KEI/37/9.
58 Yorke to Saumarez, 14 June 1811, NMM, YOR/16A/46.
59 Melville to Pellew, 12 August 1812, Clements Library, Melville Papers, Box 28.

in the German states deteriorated during the summer and autumn, climaxing with his dramatic military defeat at Leipzig. The British navy's role in such events proved peripheral. In general, the Royal Navy denied France the use of the sea. Particularly, warships supported Wellington's army, albeit at lower levels than expected. Several factors accounted for the lack of support including extensive deployments against the United States during the War of 1812 and the need to provide warships along the littorals of continental Europe. Such operations supported anti-French forces from the Baltic and the North German coast to Holland and around the Italian peninsula from Genoa to Venice and throughout the Adriatic.

Operations by the British navy proved nothing more than an irritant to France until Napoleon's weakened empire was on the verge of collapse. Even then, Secretary of State for War and the Colonies Henry Bathurst explained the quandary Britain faced while working within the coalition that opposed Napoleon. With regard to operations against Antwerp, Bathurst cautioned: "In this the Allies feel no common interest with us. Some, absurdly jealous of our maritime power, may even wish Antwerp to remain with France."[60] Added to this, naval operations during the twilight of Napoleon's empire remained limited in scope given the implications of the following question that Melville posed to Wellington: "Would *you* think that we were acting wisely, even in making those diversions, unless we could secure at the same time ... the fullest extent of our military superiority on the Peninsula?"[61] This question stemmed from the concern that Britain did not have unlimited means, and the lack of British soldiers forced London to prioritize between Wellington's operation and those in other regions of Europe, such as the Low Countries. Although the British did find troops for small-scale land operations outside Iberia, they placed an emphasis on British objectives vice those of the coalition fighting Napoleon.

Much of this came at the navy's behest as Bathurst aptly explained: "With respect to the Naval department, you say very justly that a service which offers no encouragement either of glory or profit, will not be well executed if it be not attentively watched."[62] British naval leadership was certainly preoccupied with the glory of gaining possession of French warships. If not through battle, the next best thing for the navy involved eliminating opposing naval assets in ports such as Antwerp, Venice, and Genoa. In addition, the prize money

---

60   Bathurst to Wellington, 31 December 1813, in *Supplementary Despatches of Wellington*, 8:450–452.
61   Melville to Wellington, 28 July 1813, ibid., 8:144–147.
62   Bathurst to Wellington, 31 December 1813, ibid., 8:450–452.

obtained from the capture of warships certainly motivated naval decisions. Regardless of these objectives, a deeper strategic logic that Bathurst did not recognize guided the navy. According to Melville, the capture or destruction of French warships would "liberate a large portion of our naval force and diminish greatly the public expenditure."[63] For the British, the primary goal was the development and sustainment of their maritime ascendency; anything that threatened to limit British economic and naval power – as well as the ability to sustain the latter which guaranteed the former – needed to be eliminated. For this reason, London prioritized its objectives when committing its small army for expeditionary operations outside Iberia. Thus, rather than focusing entirely on helping the Allies defeat Napoleon, the British attempted to diminish French naval power, which in turn would free their own naval assets, reduce the costs of the navy, and further their maritime economic supremacy.

The Royal Navy did not enjoy the unrestricted ability to influence events on land from the sea. Geographically isolated colonies of course proved most vulnerable, but these targets had but a small impact on Napoleonic France. Continental-sized targets were much more difficult to influence. A combination of geography and anti-French sentiment among the Portuguese and Spanish made operations in Iberia more effective, but even in this theater naval power experienced limitations. As noted, outside Iberia, the British had a tendency to prioritize naval targets over coalition development. This reflected both a strategic choice and the parochial interest of the navy, which had to support any operation, yet the Royal Navy was Britain's strongest and most flexible instrument of war as well as the tool that protected the moat shielding Britain's home islands.

Maximizing naval power led the British to grapple with more innovative ways of employing the Royal Navy against Napoleonic France. Naval power guaranteed London a comparative advantage in economic warfare. Britain benefited from the passive nature of naval operations through the protection of commerce, often through convoys, which fostered the economic vitality of the British state and buttressed tax revenues. As the Napoleonic Wars continued, Britain attempted to impose its will through a system of economic control. Most infamous were the Orders in Council, but these were just one manifestation of an effort to control the world's maritime economies. Particularly, in the years after Trafalgar, Great Britain developed a near-monopoly on trade in colonial produce including sugar, tobacco, and coffee.[64] Having monopolies on trade while also regulating other commerce created economic leverage.

---

63   Melville to Wellington, 28 July 1813, ibid., 8:144–147.
64   Hall, *British Strategy*, 16–17; Andrew Lambert, *The Challenge: Britain Against America in the Naval War of 1812* (London, 2012); 14–15; M.S. Anderson, "The Continental System and

British economic warfare involved multiple layers of regulation, protection, and coercion, all made possible by the Royal Navy, which served as the tool of enforcement. First, the navy deployed globally to protect trade and control maritime access to key trading nodes including existing and captured colonies as well as areas too large to directly occupy like Brazil, the United States, and China. The second element of global economic naval warfare comprised an ever more expansive convoy system that served the purpose of commerce protection while also supervising the flow of commerce. The final aspect involved managing the coastal regions of continental Europe. One means entailed blockades that became increasingly expansive in the years following Trafalgar, ringing the continent and eventually encompassing nearly every area associated with imperial France. Britain had to conduct multiple types of blockades. On the one hand, naval blockades focused on ports containing French warships and required a concentrated naval force, powerful enough to defeat the most powerful enemy force that could put to sea from that port. On the other hand, commercial blockades were designed to interdict trade. They generally required a dispersion of naval power opposite all ports and along trade routes with the number of warships more important than their size.[65] Beyond blockades, the British were careful to deal lightly with places such as Sweden and the Barbary States of North Africa because they had commodities that Britain needed. With Sweden, Britain valued neutrality at the choke point formed by the mouth of the Baltic. Moreover, Sweden served as a point of transshipment for moving colonial produce and British goods into Europe as well as naval stores such as hemp, timber, and tar to Britain. North Africa provided foodstuffs to support Britain's Mediterranean operations. Moreover, Britain sanctioned smuggling. Islands directly adjacent to the European coast such Heligoland in the North Sea proved a particularly relevant smuggling center. The British merely had to occupy the island to transform it into a massive point of transshipment for smaller smuggling craft that could more easily slip past Napoleon's customs officials. London explored similar opportunities in the Adriatic.

After Trafalgar, the French could not compete with the British in fleet engagements. At the same time, the Royal Navy became increasingly adept at controlling maritime trade. In response, Napoleon attempted to weaken British naval mastery through a series of actions known as the Continental System,

---

Russo-British Relations During the Napoleonic War," in K. Bourne and D.C. Watt, eds, *Studies in International History: Essays Presented to W. Norton Medlicott* (London, 1967), 76.

65 Jeremy Black, *The War of 1812 in the Age of Napoleon* (Norman, OK, 2009), 133–134.

which closed Europe's ports to British commerce.[66] As continental Europe served as Britain's largest export market, Napoleon's plan had the potential to economically devastate Britain and thus its ability to wage a protracted war.[67] However, the French became progressively less able to influence world markets throughout the Napoleonic period. British naval dominance and the loss of French colonies assured such an outcome. Although Napoleon understood the importance of continental Europe as a British market, he seemed less familiar with the global economic system. Moreover, he also lacked a true understanding of how market forces would work to undermine the strict economic control required for the Continental System to inflict maximum damage on Britain. The lack of such nuanced understandings allowed Britain to attack the strategy behind the system.

In the Baltic, Britain found a breach in Napoleon's wall. For the Continental System to prove effective, he needed other states to join. The 1807 Treaty of Tilsit brought Russia into the Continental System, thus closing Russian ports on the Baltic to British commerce.[68] Denmark readily joined the system after the British attack on Copenhagen. With the participation of Russia and Denmark, Napoleon hoped to compel Sweden to join, all but assuring that the Baltic would become a French lake. For Britain, this was especially dangerous given British dependence on the region's naval stores.[69] In response, the British pushed a fleet into the Baltic in 1808. One of its multiple missions concerned the regulation of regional trade with the key component involving Russia.[70] The Royal Navy was never far over the horizon. One British naval officer explained that "the object of our employment in the Gulf of Finland [the eastern Baltic] is the annoyance of the Russian trade and the destruction of her cruisers, combined with every possible protection and security of such vessels as may be sailing with licenses from the English Government."[71] Rather than stop trade in its entirety, Britain regulated it, licensing beneficial trading inter-

---

66 David Gates, *The Napoleonic Wars 1803–1815* (London, 1997), 154; Steven T. Ross, *European Diplomatic History 1789–1815: France Against Europe* (reprint, Malabar, FL, 1981), 272–275.
67 B.R. Mitchell and Phyllis Deane, *Abstract of British Historical Statistics* (Cambridge, 1971), 311.
68 Treaty of Tilsit, in Clive Parry, ed., *The Consolidated Treaties Series* (Dobbs Ferry, NY, 1969), vol. 59 (1806–1808), 248–249.
69 James Davey, *The Transformation of British Naval Strategy: Seapower and Supply in Northern Europe, 1808–1812* (Woodbridge, UK, 2012), 19–21.
70 Instructions to Saumarez, 16 Apr 1808, in A.N. Ryan, ed., *The Saumarez Papers: Selections from the Baltic Correspondence of Vice Admiral Sir James Saumarez, 1808–1812* (London, 1968), No. 10, 11–13.
71 Martin to Warren, 29 June 1808, in *Letters and Papers of Admiral of the Fleet Sir Thomas Byam Martin*, ed. Sir Richard Vesey Hamilton, 3 vols (London, 1898–1901), 2:119–120.

ests and restricting everything else. Such actions contributed to wild fluctuations in Russian trade, which in turn affected tax revenue and commercial enterprise. These issues created instability and contributed to Russia's paper currency losing a great deal of its value. In late 1811, the Russians prohibited French commerce while reopening ports to neutrals, but what constituted a neutral? British-flagged shipping was still considered belligerent trade, but much commerce in the region, though neutral in name, sailed under regulations set forth in a British licensing system. In effect, these were essentially British merchant ships in thinly veiled disguise, which only raised Napoleon's ire. Franco-Russian discussions on this matter along with other issues failed to resolve the situation, resulting in Napoleon's invasion of Russia in 1812.[72] By maintaining a presence in the region, the British had accelerated tensions between Russia and France and contributed to the escalation of the Napoleonic Wars in a manner that eventually crippled France and drew other states into Britain's coalition orbit.

This is not to say that the British steered a perfect course. Actions against Denmark at Copenhagen in 1807 and against the United States from 1807 to 1812 resulted in negative escalatory effects for Britain. These were much easier for Britain to mitigate, however, than the Iberian and Russian issues were for France. In 1807 after bombarding Copenhagen, the British forced the Danes to hand over their fleet. Such an egregious action led to intractable hostility directed against the British. After losing their battle fleet, the Danes had to rely on gunboats and privateers to wage war against Britain. Although these occasionally inflicted substantial losses on British Baltic convoys, the British made such occasions the exception rather than the norm and thus managed the threat. Moreover, Denmark's peninsular geography and numerous islands proved hard to defend, and its control of Norway, the Faroe Islands, and Iceland created maritime appendages that could be severed. Plus, the British could play on traditional hostility between Sweden and Demark.[73]

The United States proved more difficult to deal with but scarcely less vulnerable to British sea power. After the Americans declared war on Britain in 1812, the Royal Navy commander in North America received orders to use his British warships to "keep the American Navy in tolerably good order ... and hinder

---

72   Lieven, *Russia Against Napoleon*, 78; Anderson, "Continental System and Russo-British Relations"; Davey, *Transformation of British Naval Strategy*, 186–192.

73   Jan Glete, "Navies and Power Struggle in Northern and Eastern Europe, 1721–1814," in Rolf Hobson and Tom Kristiansen, eds, *Navies in Northern Waters, 1721–2000* (London, 2004), 66–90; A.N. Ryan, "The Defence of British Trade with the Baltic, 1808–1813," *English Historical Review* 74 (July 1959), 443–466.

them from making any formidable efforts by Sea."[74] Although this took more warships and lasted longer than expected, the British avoided catastrophic merchant ship losses from either American warships or privateers.[75] Again, the British navy had demonstrated its defensive strength. Offensively, Britain's greatest weapon against the United States involved a commercial blockade that stretched from New York to New Orleans by 1813 and that, eventually, by 1814, encompassed the entire eastern seaboard. The population density in the United States was low, and where people did concentrate it was generally near salt water or along navigable rivers, which made the Americans rely on maritime commerce as a substitute for a poorly developed internal road and canal network. The British navy rendered American maritime trade and population centers vulnerable to attack. Moreover, this denied the US government's largest revenue stream, which came from duties on maritime commerce.[76] The British naval leadership also looked to foment unrest among slaves and Native Americans as well as conduct major joint operations in the Chesapeake and against Maine, New Orleans, and Georgia. These, however, had mixed success and led one British army officer to write that operations against the United States "have sunk the country still deeper in disgrace – and have converted its navy and army into something little better than pirates."[77]

On the surface, the officer's opinion rings true. Deeper analysis showcases the inherent difficulty of understanding the efficacy of Britain's maritime power. Joint operations were difficult to manage, plus their scale was limited for numerous logistical and manpower factors. Unless aimed at islands like the French colonies in the West Indies or Mauritius, joint operations became little more than raids except when supported by large ground forces. The British obtained Allied support in Iberia, but elsewhere they failed to find enough friendly boots on the ground. Supporting irregular forces, revolts, or Allied armies proved even more difficult to manage. Local interests and objectives necessarily took precedence over British desires. Keeping such operations focused on British objectives required a sizable British land component, but logistics and the dispersed nature of the British army limited such opportunities, often making even important efforts appear to be nothing more than raids bent on plunder. The Royal Navy proved more adept at economic warfare. The outward manifestation of economic warfare involved the capture of

---

74 Melville to Pellew, 10 August 1812, Clements Library, Melville Papers, Box 28.
75 Marrayat to Melville, 1, 10 May 1813, NAS, GD 51/2/882/1, 3; McCranie, "War of 1812 in the Ongoing Napoleonic Wars."
76 Lambert, *The Challenge*, 15–17; Brian Arthur, *How Britain Won the War of 1812: The Royal Navy's Blockades of the United States, 1812–1815* (Woodbridge, UK, 2011), 57.
77 Brown to Alexander Hope, 4 April 1815, NAS, GD 364/1/1267/1.

commercial shipping; however, this appeared piratical to many onlookers, with captains and crews of Royal Navy warships bent on accumulating prize money from proceeds derived from their seizures. Capturing merchant vessels swept commerce from the sea, which British leaders viewed as an anathema to their economic system, but this was only the sharp end of Britain's strategy for controlling maritime economies. Trade regulations, blockades, and convoys quietly worked to provide slowly accruing cumulative effects. The economy of the United States proved particularly vulnerable to British sea power, but a continental empire like Napoleon's proved less so. In this case, the British had to compel Napoleon toward self-defeating actions through the interplay of naval, economic, and military factors buttressed by sound diplomacy. Not a quick solution, this strategy relied on the long-term interaction of numerous factors that often worked indirectly to undermine Napoleon's empire.[78] Overall, Britain positioned itself to take advantage of situations through allies and revolts facilitated by seemingly dispersed action made possible by a navy that to many onlookers appeared to function as predatory pirates instead of what one would normally consider a single decisive instrument of war.

Bibliography

Albion, Robert G. *Forests and Sea Power: The Timber Problem of the Royal Navy 1652–1862*. Cambridge, MA, 1926.

Arthur, Brian. *How Britain Won the War of 1812: The Royal Navy's Blockades of the United States, 1812–1815*. Woodbridge, UK, 2011.

Baugh, Daniel A. *British Naval Administration in the Age of Walpole*. Princeton, NJ, 1965.

Baugh, Daniel A. "The Eighteenth-Century Navy as a National Institution, 1690–1815." In J.R. Hill, ed., *The Oxford Illustrated History of the Royal Navy*, 120–160. New York, 1995.

Black, Jeremy. *The War of 1812 in the Age of Napoleon*. Norman, OK, 2009.

Clowes, William Laird, Sir Clements Markham, A.T. Mahan, H.W. Wilson, Theodore Roosevelt, and L. Carr Laughton. *The Royal Navy: A History From the Earliest Times to Present*, 6 vols. London, 1897–1903.

Corbett, Julian S. *Some Principles of Maritime Strategy*. London, 1911; reprint, Annapolis, MD, 1988.

Davey, James. *The Transformation of British Naval Strategy: Seapower and Supply in Northern Europe, 1808–1812*. Woodbridge, UK, 2012.

---

78 British footprints surround the events leading to Napoleon's 1812 invasion of Russia but the specific reasons for Napoleon's Russian campaign came down to the decisions made by Tsar Alexander and Napoleon.

Gates, David. *The Napoleonic Wars 1803–1815*. London, 1997.
Glete, Jan. *Navies and Nations: Warships, Navies and State Building in Europe and America, 1500–1860*, 2 vols. Stockholm, 1993.
Glete, Jan. "Navies and Power Struggle in Northern and Eastern Europe, 1721–1814." In Rolf Hobson and Tom Kristiansen, eds, *Navies in Northern Waters, 1721–2000*, 66–90. London, 2004.
Glover, Richard. "The French Fleet, 1807–1814: Britain's Problem; and Madison's Opportunity." *Journal of Modern History* 39 (September 1967), 233–252.
Hall, Christopher. *British Strategy in the Napoleonic War 1803–1815*. Manchester, 1992.
Hall, Christopher. *Wellington's Navy: Sea Power and the Peninsular War*. London, 2004.
Hamilton, Sir Richard Vesey, ed. *Letters and Papers of Admiral of the Fleet Sir Thomas Byam Martin*, 3 vols. London, 1898–1901.
Harding, Richard. "Sailors and Gentlemen of Parade: Some Professional and Technical Problems Concerning the Conduct of Combined Operations in the Eighteenth Century." *Historical Journal* 32 (1989), 35–55.
Herzog, Richard T. "The Royal Marine and Insurgent Operations in the Salamanca Campaign, 1812." In Gordon C. Bond, ed., *Proceedings, 1992: Consortium on Revolutionary Europe, 1750–1850*, 62–69. Tallahassee, FL, 1993.
Historical Manuscripts Commission. *Report on the Manuscripts of Colonel David Milne Home of Wedderburn Castle, NB*. London, 1902.
Horward, Donald D. "British Seapower and Its Influence upon the Peninsular War (1808–1814)." *Naval War College Review* 31 (Fall 1978), 54–71.
James, William. *Naval History of Great Britain from the Declaration of War by France to the Accession of George IV*, 6 vols. Reprint, New York, 1902.
Knight, Roger. *Britain Against Napoleon: The Organization of Victory 1793–1815*. London, 2013.
Knight, Roger. *The Pursuit of Victory: The Life and Achievement of Horatio Nelson*. New York, 2005.
Lambert, Andrew. *The Challenge: Britain Against America in the Naval War of 1812*. London, 2012.
Lavery, Brian. *Nelson's Navy: The Ships, Men, and Organization, 1793–1815*. London, 1989; reprint with revisions, Annapolis, MD, 1997.
LeFevre, Peter and Richard Harding, ed. *British Admirals of the Napoleonic Wars: The Contemporaries of Nelson*. London, 2005.
Lewis, Michael. *A Social History of the Navy: 1793–1815*. London, 1960.
Lieven, Dominic. *Russia Against Napoleon: The True Story of the Campaigns of War and Peace*. New York, 2009.
Londonderry, Charles Vane, Marquess of, ed. *Correspondence, Despatches, and Other Papers of Viscount Castlereagh, Second Marquess of Londonderry*, 12 vols. London, 1848–1853.

McCranie, Kevin D. *Admiral Lord Keith and the Naval War Against Napoleon*. Gainesville, FL, 2006.

McCranie, Kevin D. "The Recruitment of Seamen for the British Navy, 1793–1815: 'Why Don't You Raise More Men?'" In Donald Stoker, Frederick C. Schneid, and Harold Blanton, eds, *Conscription in the Napoleonic Era: A Revolution in Military Affairs?*, 84–101. London, 2009.

McCranie, Kevin D. *Utmost Gallantry: The US and Royal Navies at Sea in the War of 1812*. Annapolis, MD, 2011.

McCranie, Kevin D. "The War of 1812 in the Ongoing Napoleonic Wars: The Response of Britain's Royal Navy." *Journal of Military History* 76 (October 2012), 1067–1094.

Mackesy, Piers. *The War in the Mediterranean, 1803–1810*. Cambridge, MA, 1967.

Mitchell, B.R. and Phyllis Deane. *Abstract of British Historical Statistics*. Cambridge, 1971.

Musteen, Jason. *Nelson's Refuge: Gibraltar in the Age of Napoleon*. Annapolis, MD, 2011.

Parry, Clive, ed. *The Consolidated Treaties Series*, vol. 59 (1806–1808). Dobbs Ferry, NY, 1969.

Robson, Martin. *A History of the Royal Navy: The Napoleonic Wars*. London, 2014.

Rodger, N.A.M. *Command of the Ocean: A Naval History of Britain, 1649–1815*. London: W.W. Norton, 2004.

Rodger, N.A.M. *The Wooden World: An Anatomy of the Georgian Navy*. Reprint, London, 1996.

Ross, Steven T. *European Diplomatic History 1789–1815: France Against Europe*. Reprint, Malabar, FL, 1981.

Ryan, A.N. "The Defence of British Trade with the Baltic, 1808–1813." *The English Historical Review* 74 (1959): 443–466.

Ryan, A.N. "The Melancholy Fate of the Baltic Ships in 1811." *Mariner's Mirror* 50 (1964), 123–134.

Ryan, A.N., ed. *The Saumarez Papers: Selections from the Baltic Correspondence of Vice Admiral Sir James Saumarez, 1808–1812*. London, 1968.

Syrett, David. "The Role of the Royal Navy in the Napoleonic Wars After Trafalgar, 1805–1814." *Naval War College Review* (September–October 1979), 71–84.

Taylor, Stephen. *Storm and Conquest: The Clash of Empires in the Eastern Seas, 1809*. New York, 2007.

Wellington, Arthur Wellesley. *Supplementary Despatches, Correspondence and Memoranda of Field Marshall Arthur Duke of Wellington, KG*, edited by his Son, 15 vols. London, 1858–1872.

Whitehill, Walter Muir, ed. *New England Blockaded in 1814: The Journal of Henry Edward Napier, Lieutenant in HMS Nymphe*. Salem, 1939.

Afterword

Robert M. Citino

The German Way of War

Trying to evaluate outside or foreign influences on a neighboring country's "way of war" might seem contradictory, like trying to square a circle. After all, a national military culture is by definition home-grown. It arises out of domestic factors such as history, politics, and especially geography. It is a product of a sustained internal discourse, in other words, and foreigners usually need not apply.[1]

Certainly all these things were true with regard to Germany. Nature made it *die Macht in der Mitte*, "the power in the middle," crammed into a relatively tight spot in Central Europe, without much in the way of natural or defensible boundaries.[2] The Rhine River in the west is nicely broad and deep. Unfortunately, Germans live on both sides of it, and if a western enemy ever reached the Rhine, Germany had already lost a key strategic region in terms of population, resources, and industry. We might say the same for the Elbe River in the east. If an enemy managed to fight his way to the Elbe, the German people were in deep, deep trouble. International politics, as they so often do, reflected the geographical problem. Germany has historically sat ringed by enemies and potential enemies: France to the west, Austria to the south, Russia to the east, and, for much of German history, we might even add mighty Sweden to the north.

---

1 The term "ways of war," with its corollary of separate and unique national military cultures, appeared first in the seminal work of Russell F. Weigley, *The American Way of War: A History of United States Military Strategy and Policy* (New York, 1973), but has become much more prominent of late in military historical discourse. See, among others, Robert M. Citino, *The German Way of War: From the Thirty Years' War to the Third Reich* (Lawrence, KS, 2005); Isabel V. Hull, *Absolute Destruction: Military Culture and the Practices of War in Imperial Germany* (Ithaca, NY, 2005); Brian McAllister Linn, *The Echo of Battle: The Army's Way of War* (Cambridge, MA, 2007); and Peter A. Lorge, *The Asian Military Revolution: From Gunpowder to the Bomb* (Cambridge, 2008). For a useful introduction to the topic, see "Comparative Ways of War: A Roundtable," *Historically Speaking*, 11, 5 (November 2010), 20–26, including contributions by Citino, "The German Way of War Revisited"; Linn, "The American Way of War Debate: An Overview"; Lorge, "The Many Ways of Chinese Warfare"; and James Jay Carafano, "Wending Through the Way of War."

2 See Michael Stürmer, *The German Empire: A Short History* (New York, 2000), 12–13.

The combination of all these factors led to the rise of a distinctive "German way of war."[3] It was born in the Duchy of Brandenburg in the 17th century, flowered in the Kingdom of Prussia in the eighteenth, dominated military planning in the unified German *Reich* after 1870–1871, and would lead Germany into two world wars. Its bedrock conception was the vulnerability of the homeland. Incapable of defense, German armies had to attack. They could not fight and win a slow war of attrition, since their neighbors could always form a coalition to outnumber and outproduce them. Rather, the Germans had to fight a high-tempo war of maneuver, one designed to seek out and destroy as much of the enemy force as possible in the opening weeks of the fighting. They called it *Bewegungskrieg*, the "war of movement," and its principal purpose was to keep Germany's wars *kurtz und vives* (short and lively), in the memorable phrase of its most successful practitioner, Frederick the Great.[4]

The foundations of *Bewegungskrieg* were rigorous training, aggressive, risk-taking leadership at all echelons, and an independently minded officer corps expected to think for itself in battle. The last component was crucial. Standing alongside the supreme commanders was a feisty officer corps, men such as Georg von Derfflinger, Otto Christoph von Sparr, and Joachim Hennigs von Treffenfeld for Frederick William, the Great Elector of Brandenburg, and a whole host of them for Frederick the Great: Otto von Schwerin and Peter Du Moulin, Hans Joachim von Zieten, and Friedrich Wilhelm von Seydlitz. Allowing the initiative of subordinate commanders free rein on campaign, a trait that military historians call *Auftragstaktik*, although the Prussians were more likely to refer to it as the "independence of the subordinate commander" (*Selbständigkeit der Unterführer*), was a force multiplier for such a small and relatively impoverished state.[5]

The combination generated a parade of dramatic successes over the centuries: the Great Elector's signal victories at Warsaw in 1656, Fehrbellin in 1675,

---

3   For a more complete evocation of this argument, see Citino, *German Way of War*.
4   "Unsere Kriege kurtz und *vives* seyn müssen, massen es uns nicht konveniret die Sachen in die Länge zu ziehen, weil ein langwieriger Krieg ohnvermerkt Unsere admirable Disciplin fallen machen, und das Land depeupliren, Unsere Resources aber erschöpfen würde": Hugo von Freytag-Loringhoven, *Feldherrngrösse. Von Denken und Haldeln bevorragender Heerführer* (Berlin, 1922), 56.
5   See, among numerous examples from the German literature, Major Bigge, "Über Selbstthätigkeit der Unterführer im Kriege," *Beihefte zum Militär-Wochenblatt* 1894 (Berlin, 1894), 17–55, from the text of a lecture given to the Military Society in Berlin on 29 November 1893. See also General von Blume, "Selbstthätigkeit der Führer im Kriege," *Beihefte zum Militär-Wochenblatt* 1896 (Berlin, 1896), 479–534. For a twentieth-century example, see Erich Weniger, "Die Selbständigkeit der Unterführer und ihre Grenzen," *Militärwissenschaftliche Rundschau* 9, 2 (1944), 101–115.

and the Great Sleigh Drive during the East Prussian winter campaign of 1678–1679; Frederick the Great's triumphs at Mollwitz (after a slow start) and Hohenfriedeberg (the battle that won him the moniker "the Great"), as well as two of the greatest victories in all military history: Roßbach and Leuthen. The hallmark of all these victories was a lopsided casualty tally. It was something quite unusual for the age of linear tactics, in which both sides tended to form parallel fronts in a standing position, blasting away with their smoothbore muskets at ranges well under 100 yards, and trading losses.

The army that the Hohenzollerns and their Junker officer corps created was the finest in Europe – that was why contemporaries named Frederick "the Great," after all – and the reputation that it carried onto the battlefield acted as another kind of force multiplier. The great military historian Hans Delbrück spent a career pondering Frederick's battlefield exploits. While willing to admit the king's genius, Delbrück was a skeptic at heart, and certainly no friend of the Prussian officer caste. Frederick made his share of blunders during his career, Delbrück knew: in the approach, in battle, in the retreat. Alongside the great victories were a number of rash attacks that had ended in defeat, such as the attempt to surround and capture the entire Austrian army at Prague, or the assault on a force that had him outnumbered two to one and was sitting in solid defensive preparations at Kolin. But Delbrück also noted something else: how seldom Frederick's enemies had taken advantage of those blunders. Any fair analysis had to take that fact into account when assessing Prussian power:

> Victories like defeats of this kind had a spiritual significance that extended beyond the military result and was almost completely independent of that result. That was the tremendous respect which the king gained in the eyes of the opposing commanders. Why did they so seldom take advantage of the favorable opportunities that he offered them frequently enough? They did not dare. They believed him capable of everything.[6]

The fact that their enemies suffered from a "constant fear of being attacked," Delbrück noted, provided a certain moral advantage to Frederick and the Prussians.[7] It made them think twice, caused them to hesitate, and sometimes paralyzed them altogether.

---

6 Hans Delbrück, *History of the Art of War*, vol. 4, *The Dawn of Modern Warfare* (Lincoln, NE, 1990), 376.
7 Ibid., 4:353.

The Collapse

And then one day, a Great Captain rode out of the West. Apparently he wasn't all that impressed with the Prussian mystique, which he no doubt viewed as just another relic of a dead era, a quaint but obsolete idea like the "divine right of kings" or "hereditary privilege." His talents alone had carried him far since the outbreak of the French Revolution – indeed, they had allowed him to carve out his own throne as emperor of the French – and on a blustery fall day in October 1806 those same talents carried him to a battlefield outside the university town of Jena. Here (and simultaneously at a battlefield a dozen miles to the north at Auerstedt), his Grande Armée swatted the Prussian army – its mystique and its traditions, its history and its power – as if it were a fly.[8]

It was arguably Napoleon's finest hour. Certainly, he was at the personal peak of his powers. Consider the shape of this brief campaign: the rapid and secret French deployment south of the Thuringian Wood and its extension into Franconia; the tense uncertainty on both sides as the Grande Armée passed through the dark forests and headed north, aiming for Berlin; Napoleon's sudden realization that the Prussian army lay not north of him, as he expected, but west; the sudden French wheel to the left, catching the Prussians almost completely unaware. It was a breathtaking operational combination.[9] No army of the day could move or change direction like this one could, and no commander of the day had a more intuitive grasp of the overall operational situation, the ability to take it all in with a single "glance of the eye," a *coup d'oeil*, and make a snap decision.

Given their reputation in combat, it would be suitably dramatic to say that the Prussians went down fighting, but they did nothing of the sort. They simply went down. How could it be otherwise? Badly outmaneuvered from the start, the Prussians suddenly found themselves cut off from their capital. They now

---

8 Much of the work done on Jena is now quite old, although it is by no means obsolete. See the account by the German General Staff, *Studien zur Kriegsgeschichte und Taktik*, vol. 3, *Der Schlachterfolg. Mit welchen Mitteln wurde er erstrebt?* (Berlin, 1903), 28–38, as well as two early twentieth-century works by English authors, Colonel F.N. Maude, *1806: The Jena Campaign* (London , 1909), reprinted as *The Jena Campaign, 1806* (London , 1998), and Petre's *Napoleon's Conquest of Prussia*, reprinted by Hippocrene Books, New York, in 1972. Petre may occasionally puzzle American readers, as for example in his description of the village of Lobstädt on the Jena battlefield, "a village occupying much the same position in reference to Jena that Betchworth occupies in respect to Dorking" (121). The analytical treatment in Walter Görlitz, *History of the German General Staff, 1657–1945* (New York, 1953), 26–28, is still worthy. More modern accounts include Chandler, *Campaigns of Napoleon* , 479–488, 502–506; and Robert B. Asprey, *The Reign of Napoleon Bonaparte* (New York , 2001), 20–34.

9 For Napoleon's wheel, see German General Staff, *Der Schlachterfolg*, 34.

undertook a hurried retreat to the northeast, and Napoleon's great wheel thus found them prepared for neither a deliberate defense nor a vigorous attack. Strung out on the roads, they were incapable of concentrating for battle. Napoleon would actually fight an oversized rearguard at Jena (much to his dismay when he found out), while his greatest marshal, Davout, took care of business against what was left of the Prussian main body at Auerstedt.[10] Davout, in fact, would become the duke of Auerstedt for his inspired leadership that day. Nevertheless, Jena was as good as it got for Napoleon, and few other commanders have ever come close to a victory so complete.

The aftermath was nearly indescribable. As two twin streams of Prussian refugees, one from each of the defeats, crashed into one another on the high road to Weimar, command and control fell apart, and something that had rarely been seen in Prussian history made its appearance: panic. It was a veritable *sauve qui peut*, complete with acts of mutiny, looting, and curses and threats against officers who tried to reestablish order. Strewn along the path of retreat were hundreds and eventually thousands of Prussian infantry – reputedly the finest soldiers in Europe – who wanted nothing more than to find a Frenchman to take their surrender.

Into the midst of this chaos came the French pursuit, led by the cavalry of Marshal Murat. Never letting up the pressure, Murat made sure that the beaten rabble in front of him received no respite. Entire regiments surrendered without a fight to his dashing troopers, and so did fortress after fortress – fully equipped and manned positions opening their gates to French cavalry patrols who, I might add, posed no physical danger to the Prussian garrisons at all. Certainly there were a few diehards, but only a few. The French had to chase one division under Blücher all the way to Lübeck in Holstein.[11] Likewise, the Baltic fortress of Kolberg held out heroically under its grizzled old civilian militia commander, Joachim Nettelbeck, and a young officer destined for great things named August Neidhardt von Gneisenau.[12] For all intents and purposes, however, the kingdom and army of Frederick the Great had ceased to exist.

---

10   For Auerstedt, see Maude, *Jena Campaign*, 164–175; Petre, *Napoleon's Conquest of Prussia*, 149–164; and Chandler, *Campaigns of Napoleon*, 489–502.
11   For Blücher's retreat to Lübeck, see Petre, *Napoleon's Conquest of Prussia*, 254–287, complete with the surrender note, "I capitulate, since I have neither bread nor ammunition – Blücher" (286).
12   See the film *Kolberg* (1945, directed by Veit Harlan), with Heinrich George as Nettelbeck, Horst Caspar as Gneisenau, and a cast of thousands of Wehrmacht extras. It cost eight million Reichsmarks, making it one of the most expensive films ever produced by the Third Reich.

The entire debacle took only a few weeks, and even today it stands as one of the most abject collapses in all of military history. But as all students of the period know, the Prussians learned from their humiliation. The postcatastrophe period was the great era of Prussian reform: the introduction of combined-arms brigades, training the troops to fight in something approaching the French *ordre mixte*, stepping up the march rate from 75 paces per minute in the Frederician army to 108, experimenting with the creation of a people's army in the form of a *Landwehr* that would approximate the French *levée en masse*. In other words, the Prussians tried to create an army that could keep up with their wily French adversary.

And they showed that they could keep up, especially during the 1813 campaign. At Lützen (or Großgörschen) on 12 May, at Bautzen (20–21 May), and especially at the mammoth four-day Battle of Leipzig (16–19 October), the reformed Prussian army fought with verve and energy, even if it did not always win. Prussia was the fifth of the five great powers in size, resources, and manpower, and thus destined to be a bit player rather than a star. Nevertheless, it played an important material role in the struggle and, as Michael V. Leggiere has argued convincingly in his numerous works, the Prussian army was crucial in the spiritual realm as well, providing the anti-Napoleon coalition with a potent brew of passionate hatred and a burning desire for revenge.[13]

At Waterloo, Prussian materiel and morale were indispensable to victory. The arrival of the Prussians under the hard-driving Blücher was the decisive moment of the battle. Slamming into the French deep right flank at Plancenoit in late afternoon, Blücher's attack stretched the French beyond their breaking point. It forced Napoleon to commit his last reserves, the Middle Guard, against the Anglo-Allied center and the Young Guard and Old Guard against the Prussians. By evening he was locked in desperate fighting on all parts of the front. Anglophile historians who stress the Anglo-Allied repulse of the Middle Guard often fail to mention that the Prussians outfought the Old Guard in the south in some of the bloodiest fighting of the entire day. Kaiser William II once offended a British visitor by bragging that Blücher "had rescued the English army from destruction at Waterloo."[14] William did have a tendency to put his

---

13   See especially Michael V. Leggiere, *Napoleon and Berlin: The Franco-Prussian War in North Germany* (Norman, OK , 2002), and *Blücher: Scourge of Napoleon* (Norman, OK , 2014).

14   Andrew Roberts, *Napoleon and Wellington: The Battle of Waterloo and the Great Commanders Who Fought It* (New York , 2001), 84. His book embodies in its very title the problem of English-language scholarship on Waterloo. For a scholarly corrective, see the two-volume work by Peter Hofschröer that restores the Prussian contribution to its rightful place: *1815: The Waterloo Campaign*, vol. 1, *Wellington, His German Allies, and the Battles of Ligny and Quatre Bras* (London , 1998), and vol. 2, *The German Victory* (London, 1999).

foot in his mouth from time to time, but in this case he was only stating the truth.

Possible Legacies

Of course, a bare fifty years after Waterloo, the Prussians had broken out of role-playing status and become stars in their own right, the military giants of Europe. In a quick series of three wars in seven years, they smashed all their neighboring armies, booting the Habsburg Empire out of German affairs once and for all, humiliating the French and destroying the Second Empire, and making satellites of the small statelets of the German Confederation. Under the political leadership of Otto von Bismarck and the military genius of Field Marshal Helmuth Graf von Moltke, the Prussian army created a massive and powerful German Empire, or *Reich*, on the strength of its own bayonets. It was clear, and generally agreed upon by Prussian officers and military intellectuals alike, that something about the Napoleonic era had changed and strengthened Prussia, and Prussian war-making, profoundly.

But what? The foundations of Prussian success continue to arouse discussion and debate among historians. Technology played a role, but not a central one. Certainly the Prussians had a better rifle than the Austrians in the 1866 war. The famous Dreyse "needle gun" (*Zündnadelgewehr*) was the first production-model breechloader, and its high rate of fire inflicted massive casualties on Austrian storm columns. In 1870, however, the French had a rifle, the *Chassepot*, that outclassed it completely. The Prussians used their steel-tubed Krupp artillery to smash the French, it is true, but they had fought the Austrians with a serious disadvantage in artillery in the earlier war, and had still won. So technology, as important as it was, was not the only answer to the question.[15]

Likewise, the proverbial "military genius" of Moltke had played a role, but it was hard to say that it was decisive.[16] The long struggle against Napoleon had led the Prussians to do some hard thinking about genius, most notably in Carl

---

15   For a learned and nuanced discussion of the role of technology, see Dennis E. Showalter, *Railroads and Rifles: Soldiers, Technology, and the Unification of Germany* (Hamden, CT, 1976). It continues to serve as a model for the incorporation of operational history with broader trends in society, politics, and technology. See also Steven S. Ross, *From Flintlock to Rifle: Infantry Tactics, 1740–1866* (London , 1996).
16   The primary source on Moltke is Daniel J. Hughes, ed., *Moltke on the Art of War: Selected Writings* (Novato, CA , 1993), combining a selection of Moltke's most important works and incisive commentary.

von Clausewitz's *Vom Kriege* (Book 1, Chapter 3, "Der Kriegerische Genius").[17] Clausewitz had come to the conclusion that "genius" did not mean what it usually means in English. It was more than being smart or clever. Rather, it was a moral response to the demands that war places upon the individual. Since war was "the realm of danger," the commander had to have the attribute of courage.[18] Since it was "the realm of physical exertion and suffering," he had to have "strength of body and soul."[19] Since it was "the realm of chance," the commander would often find "that things are not as he expected."[20] In such cases, he had to be able to come to a rapid and accurate decision. He needed the *coup d'oeil*, in other words, the determination not to doubt himself, and the "presence of mind" to deal with the unexpected.[21] Above all, genius was a matter of will, which alone could overcome the tendency toward stasis. The default setting in a military headquarters is standing around, wondering what to do next, and "the inertia of the whole gradually comes to rest on the commander's will alone."[22] Clausewitz did warn that will must never degenerate into "obstinacy,"[23] however, where the commander rejects another point of view not from insight, but "because he objects instinctively,"[24] perhaps out of jealousy for his own authority. Will also needed to be tempered by intellect; it was instinctive, yes, but it required a great deal of hard work and study, since "a brave but brainless fighter" could never achieve anything outstanding.[25]

Did Moltke measure up? By most standards, yes. His moral strength and calm even when things seemed to be falling apart were legendary. But his three wars taught him some hard lessons, and he would reference them repeatedly for the rest of his life. "No plan survives contact with the enemy's main body," was his most famous aphorism,[26] along with "Strategy is a system of

---

17 See Carl von Clausewitz, *Vom Kriege. Ungekürzter Text* (Munich, 2000), 61–81.
18 "Der Krieg ist das Gebiet der Gefahr, es ist also Mut vor allen Dingen die erste Eigenschaft des Kriegers": ibid., 63.
19 "Der Krieg ist das Gebiet körperlicher Anstrengungen und Leiden; um dadurch nicht zugrunde gerichtet zu werden, bedarf es einer gewissen Kraft des Körpers und der Seele": ibid., 63–64.
20 "Der Krieg ist das Gebiet des Zufalls..", and thus "der Handelnde im Kriege die Dinge unaufhörlich anders findet, als er sie erwartet hatte": ibid., 64.
21 The German word is "Geistesgegenwart": ibid., 67.
22 "[L]astet nach and nach die ganze Inertie der Masse auf dem Willen des Feldherrn": ibid., 68.
23 The German word is "Eigensinn": ibid., 74.
24 "[A]us einem widerstrebenden Gefühl": ibid., 75
25 The phrase is "ein blosser Bravo ohne Verstand": ibid., 78.
26 A standard translation. Hughes, *Moltke: On the Art of War*, 92, has it, "Therefore no plan of operations extends with any certainty beyond the first contact with the main hostile force."

expedients."[27] You made plans and then hoped for the best, in other words, and you had better have a Plan B ready in your back pocket. Notions of a brilliant operational plan leading inexorably to victory were foreign to him. "Only the layman perceives the campaign in terms of a fixed original conception, carried out in all details and rigidly followed until the end," as he knew well.[28] Indeed, when all was said and done, if in 1866 the Army of Crown Prince Frederick William had arrived on the Königgrätz battlefield thirty minutes later than it did, military historians everywhere would be scoffing at Moltke today. Likewise, the climactic battle of the Franco-Prussian War, Saint-Privat, was an artless, wrenching brawl with massive casualties on both sides. On a grim ride back to his headquarters at Pont-à-Mousson after the battle, Moltke turned to an aide and muttered, "One thing we learned yesterday: you cannot be too strong at the point of decision."[29] He apparently was not feeling much like a genius that day. Individual genius was rocky soil on which to nurture a way of war, in other words, since a Napoleon comes around once per epoch, perhaps. Indeed, the whole point of creating and nurturing a Prussian (later German) General Staff was an attempt to replace Napoleon with a form of collective genius.

Likewise, while the Prussian army displayed a high level of aggression in its victories, aggression was not the sole cause of success. Even during the Jena campaign, there had been nothing passive about the Prussian army. Prussia may have lost in 1806, but it was not by being too operationally timid, but quite the reverse. Having decided on war, the Prussian commander, the duke of Brunswick, deployed his forces in a highly aggressive posture, one suited to a campaign of maneuver as he conceived of it. He opened the war by invading Saxony, impressed several Saxon divisions into Prussian service, and poised the army for the offensive. A defensive posture would have held the army behind the Elbe River, but in fact they opened the war well over the Elbe, massed to the west and south over the Saale, deep inside Thuringia, ready to meet a French thrust from the west. He had 125,000 men, well arranged to strike south or west against French lines of communication, or even to deal a powerful blow to the left flank of any French drive on Berlin.[30] He considered a number of options

---

27   "Die strategie ist ein System der Aushilfen." See "Generalfeldmarschall Graf von Schlieffen über den grossen Feldherrn der preussisch-deutschen Armee," *Militär-Wochenblatt* 125, 17 (25 October 1940), 805–807. For a general discussion of this point, see in that same wartime issue General Ludwig, "Moltke als Erzieher," 802–804.
28   Quoted in General Ernst Kabisch, "Systemlose Strategie," *Militär-Wochenblatt* 125, 26 (27 December 1940), 1235.
29   Quoted in Lieutenant General Marx, "Operative Zersplitterung in der Kriegsgeschichte," *Militär-Wochenblatt* 125, 3 (19 July 1940), 86.
30   For Prussian planning before Jena, see Citino, *German Way of War*, 109–112.

for the attack, but making a choice proved to be the problem. Disagreement and dithering arose within the Prussian high command, not helped by King Frederick William's uncertain attitude, and the Prussians were still arguing about which attack to launch when Napoleon's own plans overwhelmed them.[31] The point is, however, that the Prussians were not paralyzed with fear about falling into a "Jena," which has become our historical trope for a military disaster of infinite magnitude. They were, rather, fairly confident that they were about to refight the Battle of Roßbach.

Even the post-Jena "unreformed" Prussian army had more than enough aggression. In February 1807, the last remaining Prussian formation still in the field, styling itself a "corps" but in reality a great deal smaller than that, slashed its way though the ice and snow to fall in on the left of the badly battered Russian army at Eylau.[32] Its commander, General Anton Wilhelm von L'Estocq, had actually fought in the Battle of Zorndorf as a nineteen-year-old boy under Frederick the Great. He was now sixty-eight years old, one of those "superannuated" Prussian generals that have caused historians so much hand-wringing over the years. Maybe we all need to rethink the notion of "age."

L'Estocq did not bring a very large force, just eight battalions, twenty-eight squadrons, and two batteries of horse artillery. Even with the Russian stragglers he managed to sweep up in his approach, he certainly had fewer than the 9,000 men some sources credit. He probably had some 7,000, and with allowance for stragglers of his own, perhaps less than that. The exact employment of the force was, therefore, a crucial issue. Arriving at Althof, on the extreme northwest of the battle area, L'Estocq conferred with his "assistant" (*Gehilfe*), General Gerhard von Scharnhorst.[33] The Russians were *in extremis*, so perhaps the smart thing to do was to get in the battle as soon as possible, simply falling in on their right. The Russian commander, August Levin von Bennigsen, wanted them to split up the Prussian corps to provide relief at various points along the line.

Scharnhorst refused both options. The real danger lay on Russian left. And, so, the already-exhausted Prussian corps now set out on a swift ride clear across the rear of the Russian army. They came up into attack position at Kutschitten, quickly deployed into assault formation, and slammed into

---

31 Clausewitz, *Vom Kriege*, Book Six, Chapter 28 (p. 549), condemns the "viel-köpfigen Hauptquartier" ("hydra-headed staff") around the duke.

32 For the Eylau campaign, see Chandler, *Campaigns of Napoleon*, 535–555; Petre, *Napoleon's Campaign in Poland*, reprinted by Hippocrene Books (New York, 1975); Captain Meltzer, "Betrachtungen zum Feldzug und zum Schlacht von Pr. Eylau," *Militär-Wochenblatt* 121, 31 (12 February 1937), 1773–1776; and Citino, *German Way of War*, 119–128.

33 Meltzer, "Betrachtungen zum Feldzug und zum Schlacht von Pr. Eylau," 1773.

Davout's exhausted and freezing troops. The attack drove the French back in complete disorder.

Without insulting the thousands of brave Russian soldiers who died there, the arrival of L'Estocq's corps late in the day was the transforming event of the Battle of Eylau. It turned an almost certain Russian defeat into a draw, and fighting Napoleon to a draw in those days was as good as a win. For the previous seven years, most of the armies and commanders who had come up against the emperor wound up fleeing the battlefield in disorder. This time, it had been different, a fact that accounts in no small measure for the fascination that Eylau still compels.

Later German analysts and military operators would view Eylau as nothing less than the redemptive moment for the Prussian army. For a representative example of this argument, we need look no further than the 1906 work by Colmar Freiherr von der Goltz, the Prussian field marshal and military historian. In *Jena to Eylau: The Disgrace and Redemption of the Old Prussian Army*, he argued that history had been unfair to the "much-maligned army" of prereform Prussia. Despite its humiliation at Jena, it still possessed undeniable reserves of greatness, of what von der Goltz called "old-Prussian worth" and "old-Prussian valor." Jena had been shameful, yes, but there was still hope: "It was reserved for the weak, but brave and tenacious East Prussian corps to retrieve the honor of Prussian arms, and it was given to them to succeed. I have always held that it was at Eylau in 1807, and not in the War of Liberation in 1813, that the old army vindicated itself before the tribunal of history."[34]

To Goltz, success at Eylau had come not merely from Scharnhorst's intellect – the view modern analysts tend to prefer – but to old L'Estocq's toughness, his itch to get into a fight, his will. The general, "the last of Frederick the Great's school to hold a high command," still had "vigor, alertness, and daring enough to make the victory on 8 February possible." He not only recognized his assistant's "keener insight," but also "assumed full responsibility for its consequences."[35] As for the troops themselves, they had not changed at all since Mollwitz and Roßbach; they were "worthy of the famous days of old," and "in action their bearing was faultless."[36]

---

34 Colmar von der Goltz, *Jena to Eylau: The Disgrace and the Redemption of the Old-Prussian Army* (New York, 1913), vi.
35 Ibid., 325–326.
36 Ibid., 321.

The Legacy

To the Prussians, then, it was neither technology, nor genius, nor some peculiar national form of aggression that had given them a new edge since Waterloo. Rather, the strength of Prussian arms emerged from a matrix of changed operational conditions. With the rise of mass armies and people's wars, military forces had grown to an unheard-of size, so large that they could no longer function as unitary bodies. As German General Staff historian and analyst General Waldemar Erfurth put it in a seminal series of articles in 1939, the Napoleonic period had fundamentally changed the character of war. It had brought a new operational problem to the fore, the difficulty in managing what Erfurth called "the combined action of separate portions of the army" (*das Zusammenwirken getrennter Heeresteile*).[37] With independent bodies operating in open terrain, the commander could arrange operational combinations that had simply been impossible in Frederick's day – pinning the enemy frontally while separated armies came down on his flanks or rear. For the first time, a true battle of encirclement (*Kesselschlacht*) had become possible, gaining advantageous positions on the enemy's main body and then destroying him through concentric (*konzentrisch*) operations.

When Erfurth and his fellow General Staff officers looked back, they identified the precise moment when this became so: the 1813 campaign in Germany.[38] On the surface, the 1813 campaign seemed to be a parade of Allied strength. Three armies at first, and eventually a fourth, would advance on Napoleon and slowly wear him down. They included the Army of North Germany (Jean-Baptiste Bernadotte, once a Napoleonic marshal, now the crown prince of Sweden); the Army of Silesia (Blücher); the Army of Bohemia (Karl Philipp, the prince of Schwarzenberg); and the Army of Poland (Bennigsen). The Allies were as wary of Napoleon as always, however, and none of them wanted to meet him in person. Rather than risk battle with the greatest general of the age, perhaps of all time, they decided on the so-called Trachenberg–Reichenbach Plan. It was a strategy of fear: they would retreat whenever Napoleon attacked one of their armies in person, while the other Coalition partners would turn

---

37 Waldemar Erfurth, "Die Zusammenwirken getrennter Heeresteile," 4 Parts, *Militärwissenschaftliche Rundschau* 4, nos. 1–4, 1939, 14–41, 156–178, 290–314, and 472–499.

38 For Leipzig, see the three-part series "Der Herbstfeldzug 1813," parts 1–3, *Militär-Wochenblatt* 90, 5–7 (12, 14, and 17 January 1905), 100–105, 124–128, and 141–146. It is a synopsis and review of the first two volumes of Lieutenant Colonel Rudolf von Friederich, *Geschichte des Herbstfeldzuges 1813*, 3 vols (Berlin, 1903–1906); as always, these *Wochenblatt* articles were of enormous importance as a way of mediating detailed scholarly works to the German officer corps.

and attack French lines of communication. They would battle detached corps under his marshals, in other words, but not *der Mann* himself.

It seems a ridiculous strategy, and yet it worked. Napoleon won a decisive victory at Dresden in late August, for example. It was a grievous blow to the Allies, but that same week saw Blücher catch three French corps under Marshal Macdonald and smash them, while Schwarzenberg managed to do the same to a corps under General Dominique Vandamme. It may seem to us to be a simple principle, but the Allies had finally discovered that Napoleon could not be everywhere.

Still, there remained the problem of coming to direct grips with him. Dresden was the last major action for two complete months, as the Allies wrestled with a seemingly insoluble problem. The front had reached what a later German staff officer characterized as "a dead point." Even Napoleon seemed stumped, and as the French came to a standstill, so too did the Allies. That was the downside of the Trachenberg–Reichenbach Plan – it left all the initiative in Napoleon's hands. If he didn't move, then they wouldn't either. The Allied armies confronted Napoleon in a rough arc, with Bernadotte, Blücher, and Schwarzenberg arrayed from north to south, and the mighty Elbe River protecting both sides. Allied "operations" in this period consisted mainly of repeated calls from Schwarzenberg to Blücher for more troops. Since the Army of Silesia was already the smallest of the three armies, Blücher and Gneisenau stood fast against detaching any units to the south. Past experience being any guide, they would simply enlarge the Army of Bohemia without improving its fighting abilities, and diminishing either of the two smaller armies would place the entire Allied posture in jeopardy. For his part, Schwarzenberg rarely seemed to want to go beyond a posture of the "deliberate offensive" (*abgemessenen Offensive*), unlikely to achieve a decisive success against Napoleon.[39]

It was the Prussians who would force the action, finally breaking the stalemate along the Elbe. The idea was probably not Blücher's, more likely Gneisenau's. Deciding that the only way to get the front into motion again was to kickstart it, on 3 October the Army of Silesia concluded a flank march to the northwest along the Elbe, sliding toward its own right, slipping around Napoleon's left, and crossing the Elbe at Wartenburg against light opposition. Yorck's corps was in the van. He had been calling for more aggressive action for months, and thereafter he would be known as Yorck von Wartenburg.[40] The Prussian staff managed to talk Bernadotte into crossing as well. In coming

---

39 Erfurth, "Zusammenwirken getrennter Heeresteile," 33, 30.
40 For Yorck's crossing of the Elbe, see Major General Klingbeil, "Yorcks Elb-Übergang bei Wartenburg am 3. October 1813," *Militär-Wochenblatt* 123, 14 (30 September 1938), 857–861.

down from the north and west, the two armies would be exposing their communications to Napoleon, but he had already shown in this campaign that he was not the fast-moving dynamo of prior years.

When Napoleon did, indeed, turn on Blücher at Bad Düben on 9 October, the Army of Silesia retreated not back north over the Elbe, but west toward the Saale, that is to say that Blücher was retreating toward France, away from his own lines of communication. It was a "very unconventional move," to say the least, and once again both Blücher and Gneisenau had to work overtime to prevent a hasty retreat by Bernadotte and keep the Army of the North in the game.[41] Meanwhile, Napoleon's preoccupation with Blücher had allowed Schwarzenberg's main body to advance from the east and south, pushing back the other major wing of the French army, under Murat.

By now, Napoleon was more than *umstellt* (hemmed in or ringed round with enemies). He was physically encircled (*eingeschlossen*). His decision was to find a good position and fight it out, settling on the city of Leipzig. The maneuver on Wartenburg and the retreat to the Saale had trapped him. Old verities about the "superiority of the central position" and "interior lines" no longer applied. Analysts are wont to use such phrases until they take on the aura of revealed truth, but in fact they had become obsolete. What had worked for Frederick the Great, with his small and nimble armies of 30,000 or fewer – 22,000 at Roßbach, for example – was simply not possible with armies of 200,000 men. They couldn't turn easily, and they couldn't pounce rapidly, and reorganizing them after a battle was even harder. They took time to get into motion, and whichever way Napoleon was likely to turn, two other armies would have had a clear shot at him from behind.

The climax of the Fall Campaign was the great "Battle of Nations" (*Völkerschlacht*) at Leipzig. Here the combined forces of Austria, Russia, and Prussia formed a great arc around the city in a four-day battle the likes of which the world had never before seen. Even Bernadotte showed up, although he took his time, as always. The numbers involved were stupendous. Gneisenau wrote to his wife on the morning of the third day, "We have the French emperor completely surrounded. A half million men stand concentrated in a tight space, ready to destroy each other."[42]

The fighting at Leipzig was bloody, especially on the first and third days, with the heaviest fighting in the south, where Schwarzenberg and the Army of Bohemia launched repeated assaults against the French positions between the

---

41 Chandler, *Campaigns of Napoleon*, 918.
42 Gneisenau's phrase was *"ganz umstellt"*: quoted in Erfurth, "Zusammenwirken getrennter Heeresteile," 41.

villages of Wachau and Liebertwolkwitz. The emperor's plans for a great counteroffensive in this sector came to naught, however. The failure was at least partially because of Blücher's pressure from the north, pressing in on the French perimeter from the north through Möckern. Napoleon had to feed first one, and then a second corps earmarked for the blow against Schwarzenberg into the furnace at Möckern. The Prussian was in his element: in the heat of battle, driving forward, and killing Frenchmen. The inability to bring the northern front under control played a material role in Napoleon's decision to retreat on day four. The decision ended in disaster when a jittery grenadier exploded the demolition charges on the causeway over the Elster River to the west of the city while it was still crowded with retreating French troops.

Conclusion

The Battle of Leipzig, later German analysts believed, had been a turning point in military history. This campaign had been different from what had gone before, even counterintuitive. "If one considers the many unending difficulties that had to be overcome in order to conceive and execute this first great concentric operation with separate bodies of the army," Erfurth wrote, "then one can get a measure of how strange and unusual the operation must have appeared to the army commanders of 1813."[43] With the central position and interior lines no longer advantageous, and with mass armies too large to operate in a concentrated fashion, commanders had to unlearn a number of things, many of which Napoleon had driven home in the lessons of war he had taught. Armies now had to operate in widely separated sectors from widely separated bases, often hundreds of miles apart, completely out of contact with one another. They had to march on exterior lines, in fact, moving concentrically against the foe and linking up only on the day of battle itself. This new dispensation wasn't invented for its simplicity or elegance. Rather, logistical realities and the problem of feeding and supplying the new mass armies demanded it. In that sense, Leipzig occupied a special place of honor in the German way of war: it was nothing less than the first *Kesselschlacht.* It offered two equally important benefits to the Germans as a learning tool: it had arisen out of the art of war of someone whom they all recognized as a true genius, the master Napoleon himself. Equally important, it had arisen out of a Prussian victory, rather than a humiliation like Jena.

---

43 The phrase is "*die erste grosse konzentrische Operation*": ibid., 40.

The *Kesselschlacht* concept came to full fruition during the wars of German unification. The climactic battle of the war against Austria, at Königgrätz, was a representative example. Moltke had three armies in the field in Bohemia, each operating in isolation. He knew that one of them would encounter the Austrian main body somewhere, either on this or that side of the Elbe, and attack it. Either one or both of the other two armies would then have a clear shot at its flank or rear. It was a simple, flexible plan, more like a sketch, but Moltke did not think that the mass armies of the day were capable of anything more complicated. With the Austrians obliging by operating in a single mass formation under *Feldzeugmeister* Ludwig Benedek, the plan brought them to battle as envisioned. The 1st Army under the Red Prince, Frederick Carl, encountered the Austrians and attacked them even though he was vastly outnumbered.[44] He held them in place just long enough for the 2nd Army (the crown prince of Prussia, Frederick William) to arrive on their deep right flank and destroy them. Likewise, the Franco-Prussian war ended at the Battle of Sedan, with the last French army still in the field completely surrounded by the Prussians, under concentric attack, and eventually going into Prussian captivity. Among the haul of prisoners was the emperor of the French himself, Napoleon III.

The world wars of the 20th century would see the German army attempting to reproduce the *Kesselschlacht* with mixed results. The opening campaigns of the First World War featured a complete misfire on the western front, where the so-called Schlieffen Plan tried to manage no fewer than seven independent armies. The fact that they sometimes made wrong turns or tripped over one another still seems to surprise historians, but it was probably inevitable, given the primitive state of telegraphic communications in 1914. They nearly won anyway, coming perilously close to trapping the entire French 5th Army at Namur and being stopped only outside the gates of Paris at the Battle of the Marne.

The situation was very different in the east. Here, the vastness of the front, the relatively smaller force commitments, and the weakness of the opposition allowed the Germans to fight their preferred way of war. At Tannenberg in August 1914, the Germans managed to encircle and destroy the Russian 2nd Army, taking more than 80,000 prisoners. The commanders, General Paul von

---

44   For a brilliant exploration of the Red Prince's character, one that locates his genius precisely in his "boldness" (*Kühnheit*), see Hans Delbrück, "Prinz Friedrich Karl," in *Historische und Politische Aufsätze* (Berlin , 1907), 302–316.

Hindenburg and his chief of staff General Erich Ludendorff, would become national heroes, with fateful results.[45]

The Second World War was more "Tannenberg" than "Marne." This time, the combined action of separate portions of the army, made immeasurably more rapid and effective by mechanization, won one impressive operational-level victory after another. The opening of the war was a true onslaught, two triumphant years in which the German armed forces (Wehrmacht) reeled off one decisive victory after another.[46] With its tank (Panzer) formations operating as an apparently irresistible spearhead, and with a powerful air force (Luftwaffe) circling overhead, the Wehrmacht smashed every defensive position thrown in its path. The world called it *Blitzkrieg*, or "lightning war," but that was a term the Germans themselves never used in any formal sense.

By any name, it was impressive. The opening campaign in Poland (Case White), for example, saw German army groups operating concentrically and smashing the Polish army in eighteen days, although a bit more fighting was necessary to reduce the capital, Warsaw. Equally decisive was the simultaneous invasion of Denmark and Norway in April 1940 (code-name *Weserübung*). Both enemy capitals, Oslo and Copenhagen, fell on day one to a well-coordinated combination of ground forces, seaborne landings, and paratroopers. Allied formations tried to intervene, got a quick taste of the Luftwaffe, and soon evacuated under heavy fire.

A month later the Wehrmacht launched its great offensive in the west (Case Yellow). Once again, the Germans showed their mastery of concentric operations. One army group feinted through Belgium and the Netherlands, drawing Allied armies to the north to meet them. After the Allies had bitten, a second army group slashed its way through the Ardennes Forest, operating concentrically from the south. This second thrust contained most of the armor, out of Germany's ten Panzer divisions. The campaign smashed not merely the Poles or Norwegians, but the cream of the French and British armies, destroying the former and booting the latter off the continent in a frantic evacuation from the last port still in friendly hands, Dunkirk.

The pattern continued into 1941. A lightning drive into the Balkans in April overran Yugoslavia (Operation 25) and Greece (Operation Marita). When a

---

45 The authoritative source on the Battle of Tannenberg continues to be Dennis E. Showalter, *Tannenberg: Clash of Empires* (Washington, DC, 2004). See also Citino, *German Way of War*, 224–230.

46 For the Wehrmacht in the opening years of the Second World War, see Robert M. Citino, "The Prussian Tradition, the Myth of the *Blitzkrieg* and the Illusion of German Military Dominance, 1939–1941," in Frank McDonough, ed., *The Origins of the Second World War: An International Perspective* (London, 2011).

British force arrived to help defend the latter, the Wehrmacht kicked it from one position to another and eventually drove it off the mainland altogether, forcing the British into their third forced evacuation in less than a year. Their destination this time was Crete, and here they got hit by a real thunderbolt, Operation Mercury, the first all-airborne military operation in history. The British evacuated under fire yet again, this time to Egypt, where they made the acquaintance of General Erwin Rommel in the western desert.

There was a great deal of fighting yet to come, of course, and we all know the ending. Nevertheless, we should not minimize the achievement. Two years, after all, is a long time in modern war, and the Wehrmacht went through them undefeated. It had crushed one of its two great-power adversaries, and was keeping the other very much at bay. The Soviet Union was still an ally. The United States might as well have been on another planet, for all its impact on the immediate operational situation. German casualties had been minimal. Indeed, a few thousand losses among the paratroopers on Crete had led Hitler to cancel all future airborne landings. As he surveyed the strategic scene in May 1941, he believed they had become too expensive.

Certainly, the world was about to change. In Operation Barbarossa, the Germans would learn the paucity of their conception of modern warfare. The first six months of the fighting saw them achieve one massive encirclement after another, at Bialystok, Minsk, Smolensk, Kiev, Vyazma, and Bryansk. No matter how many encirclements or how concentric the maneuver scheme, however, overcoming a 5,000,000-man force like the Red Army required a number of other things: careful administration, sufficient transport, comprehensive logistics, a sensible strategy linked to politics. In all these areas, the Germans were deficient.

Nevertheless, they spent the rest of the war doing what they had always done, staying true to a way of war that they had created in the Frederician period, transformed during the fight against Napoleon, and perfected under Moltke. In all the later campaigns – the drive on Stalingrad and into the Caucasus, the abortive offensives at Kursk and the Bulge – the German army marched to the drum of its own history, certainly. The traditional military values still remained: aggression, high mobility, and independent battlefield command. Familiar names such as Derfflinger and Frederick and Seydlitz, Blücher and Moltke and Ludendorff, dominated the discourse of the German officer corps. A name rarely mentioned, however, was that of their greatest forebear, the commander of genius from whom they had derived so much inspiration, and one who had helped to define the modern "German way of war" as much as any of those past greats: Napoleon, *der Schlachtkaiser*.

Conclusion

John Severn

In academic life, scholars are judged on their performance in the triad of scholarship, teaching, and service. In light of this paradigm, how does one assess Donald D. Horward's legacy to the field of the French Revolution and Napoleon and the institution to which he devoted his entire career, Florida State University? To begin, there are the salient facts, those things that are beyond dispute. In Don Horward's case, a career spanning fifty years provides abundant evidence of a scholar, teacher, and mentor, and citizen of extraordinary quality. Professor Leggiere has outlined in superb fashion what can only be described as mind-boggling productivity. Allow me to add to Professor Leggiere's narrative to attempt to explain how Professor Horward was able to accomplish all that he did at Florida State University.

I arrived at Florida State in 1970 as a first-year graduate student, eager but naive. Professor Horward was on sabbatical and on his return in January 1971 I was introduced to something I had never experienced among the professoriate: a dynamo who hardly stopped to take a breath as he got to know you and attempted to explain what he expected. It was not just his conversation that exuded energy, his physical being was in constant motion. I walked out of his office both befuddled and mesmerized. When I returned later in the term for help with a research problem, the Professor (this is what I have always called him for even at age sixty-seven and having worked closely with him on innumerable projects, I cannot call him Don – it would seem disrespectful) – jumped out of his chair, grabbed his briefcase and said "let's go to the library". Then I learned what I could expect in the next four and one-half years. The Professor does not walk, he strides, and I was pressed to keep up with him as we made our way to the library next door. When accompanying the Professor to the library, the first thing one learned was that the eyes of the Strozier Library staff suddenly grew wider, almost saying "uh, oh, here he comes again." The library was truly his turf and whatever we, his students, wanted or needed, more often than not he got it for us. The Professor was an equal-opportunity task master. He demanded that we deliver but in turn he stood behind us when dealing with forces often beyond the control of students: such as libraries and administrators. How does one build a collection like that assembled by Don Horward? Easy, you do not give the library a choice. Several years ago we were at a conference at Cambridge University and on the last day the Professor and I went to see a bookseller on the outskirts of town. The collection was terrific and after a quick perusal, Don asked for boxes. Down came the books, dozens of them. And they were not inexpensive. His only comment was "I hope the library pays for these." But of course he knew it would. He had the staff well trained. But back to the original point: he introduced me to the key people I would be dealing with in my research, and showed me where I could locate the materials I would need. Then he left with the understanding that the rest was up to me. Most of my graduate student colleagues in the history department talked endlessly of the benign neglect they faced with their mentors. Mine pushed, encouraged, and, yes, cajoled. If you didn't know he cared so much he could be intimidating. At this distance in time, what stands out for me is the fact that very few of his students failed to complete their programs of study, even if there were few jobs awaiting them. Quitting was never an option with the Professor.

Working on a doctorate in history can be tedious and time-consuming. It is also an incredibly private task. One works alone in libraries and archives, and then in writing the dissertation. It is an all-absorbing endeavor and often it becomes self-absorbing. Graduate students that I have known almost always complained of their mentors sitting on their chapters and not offering much in the way of constructive criticism. Some such assessments were well founded, some not, but with the Professor complaints simply referred to all that he demanded. Chapters handed to him were back in short order, every page well marked either with questions of fact and interpretation, or style and grammar. I never really appreciated what he did for his students until I became an academic in my own right. At any one time throughout his career, the Professor had at least a dozen students at some stage of their programs. Add to this, upper-level courses filled with students, and one encounters a volume of work no normal human being could process. His grading and reading always occurred in his home office where he had his rocking chair and his classical music. There he rocked and read and graded with uncommon concentration and vigor. Essays were handed back in a week, and thesis and dissertation chapters were returned in an equally timely fashion. As I write I think, how extraordinary, how generous, how courteous! Some students required more care and guidance than others, but everyone got his undivided attention.

Now consider that on top of this he managed his own professional responsibilities with the same kind of energy. His students did not often see him at his research, so for us it just happened. What we did know is that he went to Europe every year (at least once) and that he worked at least twice as fast as mere mortals. He never talked much about what he was working on until it was done, when it appeared in the form of articles, papers, and books. The interesting thing is that his work accumulated in his own mind and he developed an encyclopedic knowledge of Napoleonic military history. Combine that with the fact that he walked every battlefield (including Russia, where he was the first modern scholar to trace Napoleon's retreat) and then brought it all to the classroom.

Behind this, the tangible parts of his career, there are several less obvious elements that characterize his work. First, he had to deal with the fact that there were always a significant number of students who wanted to work with him at a time when the job market in history was saturated in every field and especially military, political, and diplomatic history (more on this later). So there was something of an ethical question facing graduate education: should students be encouraged to pursue MAs and PhDs, spend a half-dozen years doing so, with few prospects for employment when they were done? The investment in time and resources was not inconsequential. The Professor was unique in giving this question considerable thought, and he dealt with it as he does with everything. Students were told forthrightly and honestly what to expect and, if they chose to proceed, he, at the very least, would do everything in his power to secure financial support in the form of assistantships and fellowships to minimize that part of the investment. And, when it came time to search for a job, there was nothing the Professor would not do to guide and support. Phone calls were made, letters of recommendation were written, by hand, again at his rocking chair – just another task I did not fully appreciate until it was my turn to do the writing. What cannot be quantified here is the worry. The Professor worried about his students and whether or not they could find suitable employment. This was the wonderful thing about the US Army's discovery of the Professor's program in the 1990s. These students had jobs; he was just providing them with additional tools. But, here again, the Professor seized the opportunity and then transformed it. The original intent was for these officers to return to school, complete an MA in Napoleonic History, rotate through West Point as an instructor, and then return to active duty. But the Professor captured their minds and imaginations, and many of them continued on and completed PhDs.

Next, it bears pointing out that Donald Horward began his academic life at a time when his discipline, history, was about to undergo redefinition. The traditional fields of study – political, diplomatic, military, intellectual, economic, national, and period history – were to give way to more narrowly defined fields to include gender, race, political theory, decline of imperialism, third world emergence, and more recently, world history as opposed to Western history (this list is by no means comprehensive). The debate over the future of historical studies was often uncivil and sometimes contentious, and occasionally split departments down the middle. It became not just an ideological struggle but one over resources, and it could often affect students directly, especially at the graduate level. Undergraduates were rarely asked their opinions on the matter; rather they were told, though they could vote when it came time to select courses. For Donald Horward, like many others trained in the traditional fields, this would prove a challenge. Was it simply the old giving way to the new? The inexorable progress of history? Or was it more complicated than that? His intellectual instincts told him it was the last and that it would be wrong, if not dangerous, to give up on tradition. He would remain true to that instinct into his retirement but he took care not simply to dismiss the other school of thought because, while he believed the new themes should not be compartmentalized, they could be incorporated into the traditional fields which would continue to serve as a framework for meaningful study. Thus the Professor accommodated and encouraged students interested in gender, race, colonialism, etc. He saw it as an enriching element in the compendium of scholarship he oversaw. Equally important, he made certain that his students were unaffected by departmental debates or discord, and he returned the favor when he sat on committees.

Much as we would like, none of us can escape historical bias, but the Professor did not obsess over the point. The bulk of his research concerned the Peninsular War, and most of the early dissertations (1960–1980) in one way or another focused on peninsular themes, either from the French or British side, or on the peninsular states of Spain and Portugal. And thus he began to rewrite Napoleonic military history. When he began his work, the history of the Peninsular War was dominated by the British school, based on Napier, Oman, and Fortescue. While these were monumental works, they were woefully out of date and the Professor knew it. When he arrived at Florida State he could not have imagined the opportunity that would unfold, but sometime in the early 1970s he began to see it. He looked carefully at prospective topics for his doctoral students, just as he assessed his students' strengths and weaknesses. Foremost among his concerns was language. Could the student work with skill in French, German, Italian, Portuguese, or Spanish? If so, where did the fertile ground lie? Thus he began a coordinated effort to rewrite the war's history. This did not happen accidentally, and what is extraordinary is the fact that the students were there to do it.

Taking the British side of the Peninsular War as an example, here is how the process worked. He began with Portugal, his field of expertise, assigning Mildred Fryman to Charles Stuart, Britain's ambassador in Lisbon, he gave Lord Liverpool to George Knight, and General Beresford to Samuel Vichness. Gordon Teffeteller examined the role of Sir Roland Hill while I got the Marquess Wellesley. Pacco de la Fuente studied the Portuguese and Forjas. The Professor did not assign these topics capriciously; they were carefully considered and taken together began the process of rebuilding the history of the Peninsular War. And what did we find? Mostly that the picture was far more complicated than British scholars had previously suggested. On military matters, he insisted that his students look at events from both sides as a check and balance, especially to Fortescue. In terms of diplomacy, Fryman discovered that the alliance with Portugal was not the smooth-sailing ship that we were led to believe. De la Fuente reinforced her work. These two historians provided the first close look at Anglo-Portuguese relations during the Peninsular War. Vichness added to the discussion with his work on Beresford. And Knight discovered just what a difficult character Wellington could be.

Consider this for a moment. Historians had long known of Wellington's strategy and the details of the construction of the Lines of Torres Vedras, but along comes Don Horward and he sets his students to work examining just how the Portuguese alliance worked. Where were the pressure points? Where were the obstacles? Who were the difficult personalities? The alliance was something to be managed, and scholars should have known that. Don Horward wanted to know, and through his students he began finding out.

As for the Spanish alliance, I discovered that there was a pronounced political dimension to the war, both in Spain and in Great Britain. Spain was problematic and in many ways challenged Britain's resolve, maybe even more than Napoleon. And so this too required a closer look. Other studies followed: James Herson studied the siege of Cádiz, Frederick Black looked at Anglo-Spanish relations in the first phases of the war, Jason Musteen examined the role of Gibraltar (these last students were army officers sent to Florida State).

As for Wellington himself, here too the Professor unpacked the microscope. Josh Moon wrote on Wellington's management of the politics of war, and Thomas Cornell looked at Wellington's contributions to tactics and strategy, while Steven Schwamenfeld went beyond battles and weapons to examine morale and patriotism in the duke's army. Specialized studies such as Mark Gerges's on Wellington's cavalry were supplemented by Paul Reese's work on John Hope, and Dan Gray's, on the King's German Legion. Richard Herzog put a bookend to all of this with his "Violence, Change and Politicians: The Campaign of 1813 and the Siege of San Sebastian."

Great Britain was, of course, first and foremost a naval power, and so it stands to reason that no history of the Peninsular War could exclude a discussion of the role of the navy. Again Professor Horward's students would be prolific, starting with Brian De Toy who wrote on Admiral Sir George Berkley. Paul Krajeski continued the tradition with a study of Charles Cotton, and Kevin

McCranie followed with one on Admiral George Keith Elphinstone, Viscount Keith.

Professor Horward's students also looked at Britain's role in the Napoleonic wars outside the peninsula. Gordon Bond, his first PhD, wrote the first detailed study of the expedition to the Scheldt in 1809. Little did the academic world realize what would follow. Philip Garland studied Anglo-Russian relations between 1807 and 1812, and David Raymond looked at the role of the Royal Navy in the same period and venue. Amy Johnston provided something very different with her dissertation on the United States and the Peninsular War. Erin Renn researched Britain's military and civil preparations for Napoleon's expected invasion in 1805. In this discussion alone, I have referenced twenty-four dissertations related directly to Britain in the Napoleonic Wars (that is half the total written under the Professor's guidance). Consider also that none of the Professor's students could be described as laconic or terse. If a study were done one would find the average length of a Horward dissertation to be somewhere between 450 and 550 pages. The Professor read every page, sometimes several times. In the process, his students' work became a part of him.

By the end of his career, the Professor's erudition on the subject of Napoleon was unparalleled. He was well versed in the major works and sources of the Napoleonic Wars long before he started directing students. His own work on Marshal Masséna led him through them. The extraordinary number of students who flourished under his direction, a trickle in the 1960s, a wave in the 1970s, and a tsunami in the 1990s, have been the primary beneficiaries of that erudition while at the same time contributing to it. All of us have made mistakes, but the tradition of inquiry and scholarship grew with each student who entered the Professor's clutches. We've mined the sources and complemented one another, all for the greater good of gaining a clearer understanding the Napoleonic era. There are of course many areas begging for inquiry but that is for another generation.

Another element in Professor Horward's construction of a program in Napoleon and the French Revolution relates to the creation of the Consortium on Revolutionary Europe. This organization took shape at a conference held at the University of Georgia in 1972. There he got together with colleagues from the University of Florida, the University of Georgia, Louisiana State University, and the University of South Carolina to discuss the feasibility of an annual conference hosted among these universities on the subject of Europe in the Age of Revolution, 1750–1850. Papers presented at the annual meetings would be published. Their thinking at the time was that because they were all southern universities they would hold the event in March thus providing their colleagues to the north not only an intellectual experience but also an escape

CONCLUSION 589

from the snow and cold. From this modest beginning grew a flourishing scholarly organization now with twenty sponsoring institutions, not all of them in the south.

The Consortium's first meetings were small but always headlined by noted scholars from North America and Europe. The first meeting to take place, in Tallahassee, featured Albert Soboul and R.R. Palmer. The Professor worked hard on this as Soboul, a card-carrying communist, needed special dispensation to enter the country. For his students, it meant managing logistics, setting up book displays, and accompanying participants to various venues. We referred to it as the corvée. The Professor treated participants not only to a scintillating program but to first-class entertainment as well. That meeting marked a turning point for the Consortium as it began to grow into a major event. As the size of the meeting grew year after year, graduate students found their way onto the program and it should come as no surprise that initially most of them came from Florida State University. This was not common practice at the time but it was a boon for students. In a competitive job market, presenting a paper and having it published was a leg up. The experience of standing before an audience of scholars and exposing one's research to critical minds was invaluable. It also showcased just what was going on in Tallahassee.

Eventually, as interest grew in the Consortium, the board changed the name from the Consortium on Revolutionary Europe to Consortium on the Revolutionary Era in order to broaden the scope to linking events in the rest of the world. One of the endearing features of the Consortium is that there tends to be something for everyone. The annual programs certainly reflect the interests of the host, but it always remains diverse. In any given year, one can still find the old standards dealing with the French Revolution, including church history, the slave trade and colonialism, ideology and war, as well as Napoleonic themes. But there will also be panels on literature of the period, art history, Latin American independence movements, India, Africa, the Ottoman Empire, and the rise of nationalism. Of course, this does not occur without an element of debate but the Consortium remains a most open-minded and supportive organization.

The growth of Professor Horward's program led to the creation of the Institute for Napoleon and the French Revolution in 1990. As part of the History Department and the College of Arts and Sciences at Florida State, it expanded studies in a multidisciplinary fashion to art history, English, geography, modern languages, the social sciences, music, theater, and the visual arts. The new scope expanded the appeal of the era to a wide variety of students and bears witness to Don Horward's own diverse historical interests in addition to his unbounded energy.

In the mid-1990s I was contacted by Florida State's Dean of Arts and Sciences to raise money the purpose of which was to create an endowed chair in Don Horward's name. I began by soliciting donations from former students and to my surprise by the end of the year I had received $20,000 in pledges. With that start and realizing that far more would be needed to create an endowed chair, Professor Horward was brought into the process and, after several meetings, the name of Ben Weider came up. Mr. Weider, who built a highly successful business in the health and bodybuilding industry, was a Napoleon aficionado. He had amassed an extraordinary collection of Napoleonic artifacts and had thrown his energies into proving the theory that Napoleon's death was due to assassination. Here, indeed, was a prospective donor who could make a real difference. In short order, the Professor cultivated a warm friendship with Ben Weider, one built on common interest and common personality. Weider made several visits to Tallahassee where the Professor introduced him to the academic life and the value of serious scholarship. In 1998 Ben Weider made a sizable contribution to the Institute. The value of the Weider bequest cannot be overstated. It assured the institute's future beyond Donald Horward's retirement by establishing two faculty chairs, one in Napoleonic history and the other in the revolutionary period. Equally important, it established fellowships for entering graduate students and dissertation fellowships for those finishing their programs of study. None of it would have occurred without Donald Horward. And, true to form, he grew the endowment with subsequent, substantial bequests.

And that brings us back to where I started: how does one measure Donald D. Horward's legacy? Does it rest on scholarship, teaching, or service? The answer reveals the unique accomplishment of this man: it is all three. The simple fact is that the Professor never thought of his career responsibilities as three separate entities. One simple passion informed his professional life and that was the process of learning and teaching, specifically learning and teaching about the French Revolution and Napoleon. To honor that passion, we have this *Festschrift*, carefully conceived, organized, and brought to fruition by Professor Leggiere. Appropriately, it focuses on Napoleonic military history and covers all the ground that Napoleon traversed, from Copenhagen to Cairo and from Lisbon to Moscow. Appropriately, the chapters are the product of the most recent scholarship, and they are penned not only by former students but also by students of students, and by colleagues who have rubbed shoulders with the Professor over the years. It bears witness to Professor Horward's abiding influence on a generation of scholars, and it speaks to the quality of the man whose integrity, honesty, and loyalty inspire us all.

Index

Aachen 65
Åbo (treaty) 375, 406
Abens River 348, 350
Abensberg (battle) 350–352, 364
Aboukir Bay (battle) 472, 543
Acqui 98, 106, 125–128, 130, 132, 213
Adda River 134–136, 138, 153, 172, 207
Adige River 73, 96, 120, 140–147, 160–161, 164, 167–187
Adriatic Sea 235, 518, 520, 528, 556, 558
Affi 181–182
Africa 509–510
  North Africa 558
Age of Mass War 257
Agincourt (battle) 8
Agogna River 132
Aisne River 364–365
Ala 140, 161
Albenga 129
Allemand, Zacharie Jacques Théodore 505, 509, 511, 520, 532
  "Invisible Squadron," 509, 511
Alessandria 90, 95, 114, 118, 124, 130, 132, 151, 209–214
Alessandria (convention) 216
Alexander I (Tsar of Russia) 222, 241–246, 276–277, 281–282, 294–295, 302, 372–374, 383–384, 387, 390–392, 394–396, 400–402, 406–410, 418, 421, 424–435, 442, 458, 465–472, 481
Alexandria 495, 518
Alpone River 173, 176
Alps Mountains 58, 89, 108, 110, 117, 119–120, 123–125, 160, 187, 196, 199–201, 203, 225, 344–345, 354
  Julian Alps 187
  Ligurian Alps 90, 117
  Maritime Alps 90, 117–119
Alsace 49, 54, 60–62, 452, 457–462, 464
Altare 102, 124
Althof 574
Alvinczi Borberek, József 72–73, 168–184, 190
Amberg 69, 347
Amberg (battle) 29
American Civil War 181, 182
Amiens (treaty) 145, 495, 499–500

Ampfing (battle) 78
Amsterdam 154, 455
Amstetten 239
Ancona 516, 518, 528, 532
Andalucía 310–311, 317, 327, 331, 339
Angiari 180
Ansbach 154, 156, 256
Antibes 520
Antigua 423
Antwerp 58, 463–464, 502, 519, 533, 535–536, 549, 556
Aosta 124–126, 130–131, 200–202, 206
Apolda 265, 267, 270
Apennines 117, 119, 124
  Ligurian Apennines 125
Apennine Passes 95, 97–98, 107–108
Aragón 309, 330
Aranjuez 308
Arcis-sur-Aube 467, 471
Arcole (battle) 73, 117, 163, 168–177, 190
Ardennes Forest 581
Argenteau, Eugène-Guillaume 101–102, 104, 106, 118, 120, 122–126
Argonne Forest 54
Arlon 62
Asolo 186
Aspern-Essling (battle) 342, 344, 354, 357–359, 362–363, 369
Asti 116
Astorga 317, 335
Asturias 311–312, 317
Atlantic Ocean 495, 499–501, 508, 416, 428, 431, 433–444, 457, 462, 470
  South Atlantic 318, 508, 511–512
Aube River 465, 468
Auerstedt 261, 265
Auerstedt (battle) 259, 269–70, 272, 427
Auffenberg, Franz Xaver von 156, 158
Auftragstaktik 566
Aufnahmstellung 466
Augereau, Charles Pierre François 70, 72–73, 97–98, 100, 101–102, 104, 107–108, 119, 122–129, 136, 142, 144–146, 149–177, 179–180, 186, 225, 257, 261, 266–267, 271, 277, 280, 283, 292, 380, 415
Augsburg 230, 232, 236, 347–348

Augustenborg, Christian Auguste de   267
Austerlitz   241, 245
Austerlitz (battle)   236, 241–247, 249–250, 253, 271, 276, 281, 365, 370, 403, 427, 431, 443, 481
Austria   52, 88–110, 116, 139, 189–190, 194–195, 223, 226–232, 250, 256, 275–276, 281, 294, 296, 303, 311, 315, 372–374, 377, 380, 387–388, 391–392, 418, 423–425, 507–508, 510, 518, 522, 527, 565
   army   128, 134, 151, 159, 184, 187, 223, 226, 234, 247, 259, 345–347, 351, 357–360, 363, 365–367, 369–370, 567, 571, 580
     Alvinczi Infantry Regiment   165
     Army of Italy   195, 345, 353, 360–361, 366
     Army of Bohemia, 450, 453, 459, 461–462, 463, 576–578
     Austro-Prussian War   571, 580
     Auxiliary Corps 1812   279
       Franco-Austrian War of 1809   342–370
     Friuli Corps   168
     General Staff   451
     Hauptarmee   346, 352–360, 363, 366–370
     Landwehr   346
     Tyrol corps   168
     Tyrolese volunteers   185
   Aulic Council   195, 224
   Bohemia   117, 237, 240, 246, 248–249, 261, 331–337, 580
   Franco-Austrian Treaty of Paris 1812   374
   Hofkriegsrat   224
   Landwehr   239
   Partitions of Poland   61, 265
   Schönbrunn Palace   359, 367
   Treaty of Paris 1812   267
   Vienna   50, 68, 76, 78, 87, 91, 95, 97, 137, 139, 160, 177, 185, 187, 190, 196, 199, 201, 208, 216, 223, 227–237, 239–244, 344–345, 352–363, 365–366, 369–370, 373, 387, 392, 422
     Tabor Bridge   239–240
   War of First Coalition   48–53, 56–58, 60–75, 91–92, 95–100, 102–116, 130, 391
   War of Fifth Coalition   235–264
   War of Second Coalition   78–79, 194–219
   War of Seventh Coalition   317, 366–367, 374

War of Sixth Coalition   317, 319, 423–425, 436, 439–441, 512–514
War of Third Coalition   223–247
1812 campaign   267, 273
Avenes   479
Avgustovo   380
Azores   508, 534

Badajoz   220–221, 224
Bad Düben   445, 513
Baden   146, 250, 456, 459
Baggovut, Karl, 388
Bagration, Pyotr Ivanovich   240–245, 385–386, 388–392, 395–398, 400–402, 404–405, 419, 421
Bailén (battle)   204, 207–208, 210, 217
Baird, David   220
Bajalić, Adam von Bajaházy   162–163, 178, 180–181, 188–189
Balâtre   371
Balkans   246, 360
Baltazar, Jacques-Henry   352
Baltic Sea   495, 516, 521, 548, 556–560, 569
Bamberg   69, 254, 256
Barbados   431
Barbary States   306, 558
Barbé-Marbois, François   405
Barbier, Antoine-Alexandre   377
Barcelona   317, 325, 454–455
Barclay de Tolly, Michael Andreas   385, 388–391, 393–397, 400–402, 404–406, 419, 421, 434, 465, 473
Barcon   169
Barrau, Pierre-Armand   304
Bar-sur-Aube   465, 469, 472
Bar-sur-Seine   467
Barthélemy, François-Marie   137
Basel   76–77, 451, 454, 456–465
Basel (treaty)   66, 88, 92
Bassano   72, 117, 158, 160–164, 167–170, 178, 180, 186–187
Bassano (first battle)   117, 163–164, 168
Bassano (second battle)   170
Bathurst, Henry   556
Baudin, François-André   526–527
Bautzen   433–434, 438
Bautzen (battle)   428, 433–436, 481, 467, 505
   Kreckwitz Heights   434–435

INDEX

Bavaria   52, 69, 79, 132, 137, 160, 197, 224, 227–280, 238, 246, 380, 344–346, 352–355, 359–361, 448
  army   227–228, 230, 241, 277, 347–348, 350, 362, 364, 448
  Munich   227, 230–231, 347
Bayonne   58, 308–309, 315, 328, 392, 519, 521
Beauharnais, Eugene de   256, 360–362, 364, 366, 377, 380, 424, 427, 520, 533, 537
  Viceroy of Italy   424
Beaulieu, Jean-Pierre de   71, 95–98, 100–104, 106–109
Beauregard, Joseph-Henri Costa de   108
Befreiungskrieg   425
Bedouins   393
Belfiore   173, 175
Belfort   75
Belgian-Bavarian exchange plan   52
Belgiojoso   132
Belgium   52, 423, 452, 454, 462–464, 465, 581
  Austrian Netherlands   48–61, 90, 92, 112
Belitsy   388
Belle-Alliance   475, 479
Belleville   480
Belluno   181, 187
Belvedere, Ramón Fernando Patiño y Osorio de   320, 325–218
Bembibre   332
Benavente   334
Benedek, Lajos (Ludwig)   580
Bennigsen, Levin August Gottlieb Theophil von   227, 277, 281–284, 286–287, 289–302, 390–391, 417, 437, 447, 574, 576
Berezina River   381–382, 388, 413, 415, 417–418, 420–421
Bergerac, Cyrano de   272
Bergeret, Jacques   525
Bernadotte, Jean-Baptiste   185, 188–189, 230, 234, 241, 257, 261, 267, 269–272, 281, 285, 287, 289, 290–291, 297, 364, 436–440, 453, 445, 447–450, 511–513
  Crown Prince of Sweden   374
Berry-au-Bac   470
Berthier, Louis-Alexandre   38, 76, 118, 135, 161, 170, 180, 189, 194, 199, 200–203, 209–211, 253–254, 261–262, 267, 290, 320, 328, 346, 348, 352, 359, 368–369, 385, 397–398, 400–401, 452, 460–462
Bessarabia   375
Bessières, Jean-Baptiste   309, 347
Bewegungskrieg   501
Bialystok   382, 390, 418, 582
Bicocca di San Giacomo   129
Bignon, Louis-Pierre-Édouard   277, 458
Bilbao   317, 323
Biron, Armand-Louis   51
Biscay (bay)   317, 319, 506
Bismarck, Otto von   571
Black Forest   69, 76–77, 197, 227, 230, 458–459
Black Sea   380–381
Blakeney, Robert   338
Blake y Joyes, Joaquín   317, 319–320, 325
Blücher, Gebhard Leberecht von   272, 290, 429, 436–440, 444–445, 451, 458, 460–461, 464–473, 475–480, 569–570, 576–578, 582
Bober (Bobr) River   381, 433, 439, 445
Bobruisk   382, 388
Bon, Louis-André   165–167, 173
Bonaparte, Jerome   380, 385–386, 397–398, 400–401, 420
Bonaparte, Joseph   128, 203, 308, 310–311, 313–314, 316, 321, 330, 469, 471, 513–514
Bonaparte, Louis   254, 514, 521
Bonaparte, Lucien   33
Bonnal, Henry   354, 397
Bordeaux   496, 519, 530
Borghetto   138, 158
Borgoforte   150
Borisov   382, 388, 401, 417
Borisov-Orsha line   401
Bormida River (Bormida di Spigno)   90, 100, 124–127, 212–215
Borodino (battle)   389, 406, 412–413, 416, 420–422
Boudet, Jean   201, 211–212, 215, 217
Boulogne   31, 221, 225–227, 237, 392, 501–522, 528, 533
Bourbon-Habsburg Alliance   50
Bourbons (French)   472, 493
Bourbons (Neapolitan)   92
Bourbons (Spanish)   92, 201, 237

Bourcet, Pierre-Joseph de   41, 55, 60, 74, 123, 195
  Principes de la guerre de montagne   21, 41
Bouvet de Maisonneuve, Pierre François Henry Étienne   465
Bouvet, François Joseph   498
Brabeck, Adolf   169
Bragança (dynasty)   307, 517
Braine-l'Alleud   478
Brandenburg   428, 437–438, 444, 566
Braunau am Inn   238, 247
Brazil   307, 513–514, 517, 549, 558
Breda   463
Brenner Pass   72–73, 189
Brenta River Valley   72, 140, 160–164, 167–172, 187
Brentino   143
Brentonico   180
Brescia   138, 140, 142–153, 155–157, 169, 172, 180
Breslau   377–378, 433
Breslau (treaty)   424
Brest   225–226, 391–392, 495, 497, 419, 502–503, 505–506, 508, 510–511, 513–514, 516, 519–520, 522–524, 528, 530–533, 535, 539, 545
Brest-Litovsk   381
Brienne   388
Brienne (battle)   465–466
Brissot, Jacques-Pierre   43, 45
Brittany   286
Brixen   189–190
Broglie, Victor-François de   29, 30, 40, 43
Broussier, Jean-Baptiste   456
Brunet, Gaspard Jean-Baptiste de   89
Brünn (Brno)   240–243, 365
Brunswick   224
Brunswick-Wolfenbüttel, Charles William Ferdinand of   53–61 *passim*, 264–265, 272, 573
Brussels   50, 56–57, 61, 64, 66, 454–455, 475, 477–478
Bryansk   582
Brye   476
Buat, Edmond   354–364
Bucharest (treaty)   375
Buenos Aires   552
Bug River   380–381, 386, 418

Bülow, Friedrich Wilhelm von   436
Bunzlau   438–439
Burgos   315, 317, 319–321, 323–324, 327, 329–330
Burgues de Missiessy, Édouard Thomas de   523, 528, 533
Burrard, Harry   313
Buxhöwden, Friedrich Wilhelm von   227, 238, 240, 277, 281–282, 286–287
Bužimski, Franjo Jelačić   232, 234, 239
Bykovo   307

Cacabellos   335
Cacault, François   100
Cadibona   99–100, 117, 124, 129
Cádiz   309, 312, 339, 495, 498, 502, 506–510, 513–515, 517, 520, 538, 549, 554
Cairo (Italy)   119, 122, 124–129
Calabria   303, 392, 513
Calder, Robert   505–507
Caldiero   171, 173–174, 177, 180
Caldiero (battle)   171
Calliano (battle)   170
Calmasino   144
Cambrai   62
Camon, Hubert   355
Camperdown (battle)   477
Campo Formio (treaty)   190, 392
Camporengo   143–144
Canale   178, 182
Canary Islands   509
Cannae (battle)   8
Cantabria   309, 319, 324, 336
Canto, Joseph d'Yrles   142, 150–151
Caporetto (Kobarid)   188
Capri   522
Caprino   141, 181–183
Carcare   90, 100–101, 110, 120–129
Caribbean Sea   495–498, 502–505, 508–509, 511–513, 515, 522–524, 531, 533, 549
Carmignano   170
Carnot, Lazare   32, 45, 58–66, 68–69, 77, 79, 87–91, 97, 107, 117, 132, 136–137, 207
Carpathian Mountains   381
Carrión de los Condes (battle)   328
Carrù   108
Cartagena   517
Carthage   304

INDEX 595

Cassano (battle)   195
Castaños y Aragones, Francisco Javier   311, 317, 319, 321, 324
Casteggio   134, 210–211
Castel d'Ario   165–166
Castelfranco   186
Castellino   107
Castello San Salvatore   187
Castelnuovo   138, 144–149, 176, 181
Castel San Giovanni   134
Castiglione   72, 117, 139–158, 190
Castlereagh, Robert Stewart   327
Catalonia   317, 325, 330
Cathcart, William Schaw   308
Catherine (Grand Duchess of Russia)   408
Catherine II (Tsarina of Russia)   373, 396
Cattaro (Kotor)   517
Caucasus Mountains   391
Caulincourt, Auguste-Jean-Gabriel de   310
Cavriana   158
Central America   308
Ceraino   182
Cerea   165–166
Cervoni, Jean-Baptiste   99, 102, 104, 119–120, 135
Cette   257
Ceva   70, 90–91, 100, 103–108, 110–111, 114, 117, 119–120, 122–124, 128–130
Chabran, Joseph   201–203
Châlons-sur-Champagne   467
Château-Thierry (battle)   467
Châtillon   202
Chambarlhac, Jean-Jacques-Antoine   201, 219–211
Champagne   54
Champaubert (battle)   467
Charlemagne   222
Charleroi   50, 63–64, 72, 473, 475
Charles (Archduke of Austria)   40, 68–79, 117, 160, 185–190, 223–225, 235–236, 241, 345–349, 361–370
Charles IV (King of Spain)   308–309, 314
Charles XII (King of Sweden)   377, 390
Charles XIII (King of Sweden)   374
Charles Frederick (Elector of Baden)   222
Chaumont (treaty)   472
Cherasco   95, 108–109
Cherasco (armistice)   71, 95, 109, 130, 136

Cherbourg   226, 519–520, 523, 528, 530, 533, 538
Chernishnya River   303
Chernyshev, Aleksandr Ivanovich   383, 387, 396
Chichagov, Pavel Vasiliyevich   406–407, 417–300, 311
Chiese River   138, 145, 152–153
China   131, 552, 558
Chivasso   207–208, 216
Chlapowski, Dezydery   320–321, 335
Chobrakit (battle)   395
Choiseul, Étienne-François de   15
Chuikevich, Pyotr   395
Cismon   162–163
Cittadella   163
Clausewitz, Carl von   40, 117, 119, 125, 127–128, 130, 137, 141, 145–146, 149, 151–152, 159, 167, 176, 183–184, 285, 394, 572
    friction   196
    Schwerpunkte [center of gravity]   120
    Vom Kriege   572
Clerfayt, François Sébastien de Croix de   65–67
Clinton, Henry   331, 337
Cobenzl, Johann Ludwig Joseph von   94, 97
Coburg   184
Codogno   134
Coignet, Jean-Roche   214, 324
Coimbra   325
Colbert de Chabanais, Auguste-François-Marie   335
Colborne, John   338
Col di Tenda   89, 117
Colin, Jean Lambert Alphonse   8–9
Colli, Michaelangelo Alessandro   91, 96, 98, 102–111, 118–130
Collingwood, Cuthbert   455
Colloredo-Mansfeld, Franz Gundacker von   97
Compiègne   479
Condé   59
Condé, Louis de Bourbon de   9
Conegliano   188
Coni   89–90, 114, 119
Constance   76–77

Constantinople, 372
Continental System   250, 307, 311, 372–374,
    512, 521, 559
  Berlin Decree   514
  Milan Decrees   514
Corbais   477
Corbett, Julian   542, 550
Córdoba   309
Corfu   391, 500, 520–521
Cornwallis, Samuel   505–506
corps and division system   9, 19, 31–32,
    40–42, 51, 59–60, 64, 66, 70, 75, 91, 96,
    103, 105, 110, 195–196, 225–227, 236,
    247, 257–259, 315, 370
Corsaglia River   107–108, 128–129
Corsica   13, 388, 390, 396, 533
Coruña   325, 331, 334–336, 338, 506, 553
  Monte Mero   336
  Piedralonga   338
Cosmao-Kerjulien, Julien Marie   526
Cosseria   102–105, 110, 124–128
Cotton, Charles   419
coup de main   144
coup d'oeil   22, 194, 216. 257, 312, 342, 568, 572
Courland   377, 391
Courtrai   52
Craonne (battle)   469–470
Creil   479
Cremona   135–136, 143, 146
Crespy   479
Crete   582
Croker, John Wilson   542
Cuenca   310
Cuneo   110
Curial, Philibert-Jean-Baptiste-François   455
Custine, Adam Philippe   55–56, 58–59
Czartorisky, Adam   387
Czenstochau   424
Czimochen   380

Dallemagne, Claude   132, 134–136, 146,
    152–154, 156, 167
Dalrymple, Hew Whiteford   313
Dammartin   479
Danton, Georges Jacques   54
Danube River   68, 76, 228–240, 342–344,
    347–348, 352–365, 369–370, 375,
    390–391, 406

Danzig   285, 293–294, 296, 302, 375–378,
    424–428, 443
Dardanelles   515
Daru, Pierre Antoine Noël Bruno   408
D'Aspré von Hoobreuk, Konstantin Ghi-
    lian   156, 158
Davidović, Pavle   140, 143–144, 147, 149,
    160–162, 168–177
Davout, Louis-Nicolas   234, 238, 243–244,
    257–273, 277, 279–280, 283–284, 289,
    292, 375–377, 380, 398, 400–402, 404,
    414, 418, 435, 438, 443, 447, 450, 479,
    481, 569, 575
  Duke of Auerstedt   270, 569
  Iron Marshal   479
Decaen, Charles Mathieu Isidore   499
Decrès, Denis   500–503, 506, 508, 510,
    515–518, 520–523, 527, 533–535,
    537–539
Dedem, Anton Gijsbert van   403
Dego   70, 90, 100–101, 103–106, 108, 110, 119,
    122, 124–129
Dego (1794 battle)   100, 126
Deime Channel   378
Dejean, Jean François Aimé   319
Delaborde, Henri-François   330
Delbrück, Hans   567
Delmas, Antoine Guillaume   185
Delmotte, Jean-Louis   497
Demont   90
Denmark   224, 312, 319, 373, 375, 553,
    559–561, 581
  Copenhagen   312, 516, 543, 553, 559, 581
  military convention with France   373
  navy   205, 560
  Schleswig and Holstein   373, 504
Dennewitz (battle)   445, 482
Derfflinger, Georg von   566, 582
Desaix, Charles Antoine   211–212, 214–215,
    217–218
Desenzano   143, 145–147, 152, 154, 156–157,
    180
Désirade   523
Desmoulins, Camille   43
Despinoy, Joseph   143, 146–147, 149, 152–158
Dessau   445
Dessolles, Jean-Joseph-Paul-Augustin   76,
    121

INDEX 597

Didelot, Charles-François-Luce 373
Dijon 194, 199
Dillon, Théobald 51
Dinaburg 393
Disna 388
Dnieper River 381–382, 388, 391, 393, 396, 402, 404–405, 416
Dokhturov, Dmitry Sergeyevich 243, 388–389, 412
Dokshitsy-Glubokoye line 401
Dolcè 140, 143
Dolgorukov, Mikhail Petrovich 166
Dommartin, Elzéar-Auguste Cousin de 106, 109, 127, 129
Donauwörth 228–232, 347–348, 351
Dornburg 190–195
Douro River 325
Drava River Valley 187, 189
Drissa 388, 393–395, 398, 401
Drogochin 381
Dubno 388
Dubois-Crancé, Edmond Louis Alexis 45
Dubourdieu, Bernard 532
Duckworth, John Thomas 511
Due Castelli 166
Duhesme-Philibert-Guillaume 201, 207, 212
Du Moulin, Peter 566
Dumouriez, Charles-François 48–51, 53–58, 61, 79, 390
Dupont, Pierre Antoine 202, 234, 237, 239, 309–313, 462
Dumas, Guillaume-Mattieu 222
Dun 50
Dunaburg 381–382, 388
Duncan, Adam 543
Dundas, Robert (Viscount Melville) 545–557
Dunkirk 50–51, 581
Duroc, Géraud-Christophe-Michel 76, 331
Dürrenstein 164–165
Düsseldorf 68
Dvina River 382–383, 385, 388, 393, 396

East India Company 552
  sepoys 552
  Warren Hastings 529
East Indies 306, 503, 530–531, 550
Éblé, Jean-Baptiste 404

Ebro River 311, 314, 317, 321, 330
Eisenach 264
Eggmühl (battle) 351–352, 364
Egypt 75, 211, 493, 495, 508, 515, 518, 522, 528, 533, 582
  Cairo 91, 103, 106, 108
Elba 317, 366, 397
Elbe River 375–376, 424, 427–428, 432, 438–447, 500, 509, 512–515
Elbing 377–378
Elchingen (battle) 158
Elphinstone, George Keith (1st Viscount Keith) 399
Elsnitz, Franz Anton von 209
Elster River 448–450, 579
Engen (battle) 77
Enghien, Louis Antoine de Bourbon de 222
English Channel 117, 225–228, 230, 238, 353, 473, 501–502, 504–507, 516, 519–520, 528, 539
Enns 239
Erfurt 252, 260–261, 264–266, 271
Erfurt (congress) 407
Erfurth, Waldemar 511, 514
Esla River 334
Espinosa (battle) 320
Essen, Ivan, 388
Essen, Magnus Gustav: 277, 287–288, 290
Estonia, 421
Eugene (of Savoy) 109
Extremadura 317
Eylau (battle) 275–276, 509–510

Fabius Cunctator, 396
Faipoult, Guillaume-Charles 101
Famars 58
Faroe Islands 560
Feltre 185, 187
Fère-Champenoise (battle) 471
Fehrbellin (battle) 566
Ferdinand (Crown Prince of Spain) 308
Ferdinand (Duke of Parma) 92, 116
Ferdinand IV (King of Naples) 519
Ferdinand Karl Joseph (Archduke of Austria) 225–226, 228, 231, 234
Feretier, Jean-Baptiste-Henri 532
Ferrara 181

Ferrol   502, 505–507, 517, 538
Fili   300
Finale   100
Finland   375, 379
Fiorella, Pascal Antoine   157–159
First World War   186, 580–581
  Schlieffen Plan   580
Fiszer, Stanislaw   383
Fleurus   473, 475
Fleurus (first battle)   63, 74
Fleurus (second battle)   63–65, 72, 78
Flanders   51, 54, 61–62
Flushing   549
Folard, Jean-Charles   12
Fombio   134
Fontainebleau   471
Fontaniva   168–170
Fort Bard   202–203, 206, 211, 216
Fort-de-France, 496
Fouché, Joseph   308, 552
Fournier, Jean-Louis   330
Foy, Maximilien-Sébastien   330
Franche Comté   452, 459–462
France   53, 87, 88, 91–96, 109–110, 194–195, 200, 221–226, 249–251, 259, 306, 308, 314, 344–346, 363, 372–376, 383–384, 387–388, 392, 410, 415, 418, 423, 425–426, 448, 450–452, 454, 458, 462, 464, 466, 471–472, 483, 493, 496, 518–519, 536, 538–539, 545, 553, 556, 565, 578
  ancien régime   8–48, 51, 55, 57–58, 62, 65, 74, 221, 225
  army   8–38, 40–51, 59, 67–69, 75–76, 221, 225, 249, 259, 472
    Army of Berlin   438–445, 481
    Army of Dalmatia   360, 362
    Army of England (Armée de l'Angleterre)   225, 392, 503
    Army of Germany   346–347, 351, 355, 361, 368–369
    Army of Hanover   221
    Army of Italy   30, 33, 58, 69, 72–73, 87–90, 92, 96–98, 103, 110, 112, 114–115, 117–119, 136, 145. 155, 167, 180, 185, 197, 204, 208, 227, 253–259, 390–392
      Instructions of 1794   90
      Instructions of 1795   90
      Instructions of 1796   88, 96, 117
    Army of Saint-Domingue   499
    Army of the Alps   88–89, 108, 367
    Army of the Ardennes   62
    Army of the Bober   440, 444, 482
    Army of the Center   49, 55
    Army of the Elbe   318, 321, 323
    Army of the Loire   472
    Army of the Main   424, 427, 429
    Army of the Midi   49, 56
    Army of the Moselle   60–62
    Army of the North (Armée du Nord)   27, 49–51, 53–54, 57, 60–62, 64, 463, 472, 475–476, 478–479
    Army of the Ocean Coasts (Armée des Côtes de l'Océan)   225–226
    Army of the Orient   493
    Army of the Pyrenees   367
    Army of the Reserve   194–214
    Army of the Rhine   49, 51, 55, 60, 75, 78, 196–197, 217
    Army of the Rhine and Moselle   68, 160
    Army of the Sambre and Meuse   63, 66–69, 160
    Army of Spain   315–316
    Army of the Upper Rhine   139
    Army of the Vendée   180
    Consular Guard   201, 214
    Corps of Observation of Italy   269
    Corps of Observation of the Ocean   269
    First Corps of Observation of the Elbe   269
    First Corps of Observation of the Gironde   307
    Honor Guard   461
    Grande Armée   9, 32–36, 221, 223, 226–241, 252–254, 257–268, 276–277, 279–283, 286–288, 293, 295–299, 315, 344, 346, 368, 375, 377, 380–381, 384–386, 394, 397–398, 403–404, 406–410, 412–416, 418–421, 423–424, 426–428, 431–433, 436, 438–440, 445, 447, 452, 462, 464, 480–481, 483, 508, 533, 535, 568
      Bulletins   270
    Grand Reserve   475, 482
    Imperial Guard   221, 237, 243–244, 254, 256, 261, 267, 277, 280, 292, 295,

INDEX 599

298–299, 300, 315, 320, 322–323, 330, 334, 346, 357–358, 362, 364, 380, 385, 401, 404, 415, 417, 423, 429, 431, 433, 438, 440, 443, 449, 454–455, 459–460, 462–464, 468, 472, 475, 478–479, 482, 505
Polish troops   322–323
Regular Reserve   475, 482
Reserve Cavalry   157, 239, 241, 243, 256, 277, 280–281, 283, 292, 295, 298–299, 346, 357–358, 364, 376, 405, 449
  I Cavalry Corps   380, 438, 440, 460–461, 465, 475–477
    1st Cuirassier Division   310
  II Cavalry Corps   380, 401, 433, 329, 438, 440, 454–455, 475–477
    2nd Cuirassier Division   310
  III Cavalry Corps   376, 380, 401, 438, 449, 454–455, 475
  IV Cavalry Corps   380, 438, 449, 475
  V Cavalry Corps   438, 454, 457, 459, 461, 464
I Corps   230, 234, 238–239, 243, 254, 266, 269, 272, 280, 287, 297, 300, 319, 330, 376, 380, 401, 414, 416, 438, 442, 475, 479
  2nd Division   330
II Corps   230, 236, 238, 241, 331, 335, 347–348, 358, 364, 376, 380, 433, 435, 438, 440, 449, 454, 457, 459, 461, 475, 479
III Corps   234, 239, 241, 243–244, 254, 256–257, 264, 267, 277–281, 284–285, 292, 295, 299, 319, 347–348, 350–351, 358, 364–365, 376, 380, 401, 414, 416, 429, 433–434, 438, 440, 475, 477, 479
  12th Division   310
IV Corps   234, 239, 244–245, 256–257, 266, 277, 280–281, 285, 289, 295, 297, 299, 319, 330, 347–348, 357–358, 364, 380, 404, 415, 429, 433–434, 438, 445, 449, 454, 460–461, 475, 477, 479
V Corps   232, 239, 243, 256, 260, 266, 277–281, 284–285, 290, 295, 325, 433–434, 438, 440, 454–455, 465, 477
VI Corps   232, 236, 239, 241, 256, 277–281, 285, 287, 292, 295–296, 298, 300, 319,

330, 380, 401, 433–434, 438, 440, 442, 454, 460–461, 470, 475, 478–479
  1st Division   234
  21st Division   477
VII Corps   238–239, 256–257, 277–281, 285, 292, 325, 347–340, 350, 380, 433, 435, 438
VIII Corps   239–241, 256, 295, 299–300, 348, 380, 404–405
IX Corps   273, 334, 362, 364, 380,
X Corps   380, 386, 400, 406, 449
XI Corps   380, 429, 431, 433–434, 438, 440, 454–455
XII Corps   433–434, 436, 438
XIII Corps   438, 443, 450
XIV Corps   438, 442, 447
Gribeauval artillery   20
Second Corps of Observation of the Elbe   375
5th Army   580
brigade system   52, 103–105, 107
Chassepot   571
citizen soldier   39–49
colonies   495–496, 499, 508, 513–514, 522–523, 528–531, 533, 550–553, 557, 559, 562
Committee of Public Safety   58–61, 63, 93
Conseil de la Guerre   14, 24–25, 34
Consulate   199
Coup of 18 *Brumaire*   194, 218, 395
Coup of 18 *Fructidor*   405
Directory   65–66, 68–69, 71, 75, 87–90, 92, 96–97, 111, 113–115, 125, 132, 142, 160–161, 164, 170, 184–185, 391–392, 400, 443
émigrés   49–50, 53, 167
Enlightenment   14, 42
Federalist Revolt   61, 90
fédérés   44
Franco-Prussian Treaty of Paris 1812   374
Franco-Austrian War of 1809   342–370
Gendarmerie Nationale   263
General Staff   59, 261–262, 481
Hundred Days   216
Jourdan Law   75
Legislative Assembly   52, 54
levée des 300,000   44
levée en masse   44, 58, 472, 479, 570
Military Convention of Paris   480

France (cont.)
  military state 251
  National Guard 43–44, 50, 457, 459, 462
  National Constituent Assembly 44
  National Convention 44, 46, 54, 56–57
  navy 226, 313, 493–539
    Andromaque 532
    Antwerp fleet 535, 533
    Ariane 532
    Banel 499
    Boulogne flotilla 522, 528, 533
    Brest fleet 495, 497, 502–503, 505–506, 508, 510–511, 516, 522–524, 528, 533, 535, 539
    Càdiz fleet 509, 515
    Cocarde 499
    Consolante 499
    Cybèle 510
    Desaix 499
    Diligent 510
    Jean Bart 525
    Lorient fleet 522
      port 497, 510, 513, 519–520, 523–524, 528, 532
      squadron 497, 520, 524, 532
    Mameluck 532
    Mediterranean fleet 518, 543
    Méduse 530
    Nymphe 530
    Ouessant (battle) 424
    Piedmontaise 529
    Poursuivante 498
    President 510
    Regulus 510
    Rivoli 532–533
    Rochefort fleet 502, 505–506, 515–516, 520, 525, 537, 539
      port, 497, 502, 505, 509, 513–514, 519, 523–525, 528, 537, 538
      squadron 497, 513–514, 520, 524
    Sappho 530
    Scheldt fleet 502, 533
    Surveillant 510
    Texel fleet 505
    Toulon fleet 498, 502–503, 515–516, 518, 522–524, 526–527, 533, 535, 537, 539
      port 495, 509, 513, 515, 518–528, 531, 536
      squadron 514, 520, 526

  Vlissingen fleet 519, 522–523
    port 498, 510, 519, 528, 536–537
  representatives on mission 46, 58, 64
  Royal and Catholic Army of the Vendée 61
  Paris 52–60, 107, 110, 185, 197–201, 218, 222, 226, 228, 250, 255, 345–346, 356, 369, 423, 426, 451–460, 463–469, 471–472, 479, 505, 513, 523, 534, 544, 580
    Opera 278
  Reign of Terror 58, 56
  Revolution 8, 24–25, 40, 43–46, 57–59, 74, 195, 199, 221, 462, 493, 503
  Revolutionary Wars 8, 9, 26–31, 33, 35, 39–75, 80, 88, 103, 223, 230, 257, 312, 451, 543
  Second Empire 571
  September Massacres 54
  Théâtre français 278
  Thermidorean Reaction 68, 90
  Topographical Bureau 61, 100, 117
  Treaty of Paris 1812 267
  Treaty of 1697 88, 95
  wing-command system 64–66
    5th Military District 454
    25th Military District 454
    26th Military District 454, 460
Francis II/I (Emperor of Austria) 94–95, 139, 150, 185, 223–227, 231, 235, 241, 244, 354, 373–374, 425, 448, 458, 481
  Holy Roman Emperor 137, 223
Franconia 264, 568
Franco-Prussian War 131, 573, 580
Frankfurt-am-Main 56, 58, 67–68, 256, 450, 456–458, 463
Frederick Augustus III/I (Elector/King of Saxony) 345, 376
Frederick Carl (Prince of Prussia) 580
Frederick (Duke of Albany and York) 59, 64
Frederick I (King of Württemberg) 376
Frederick II (King of Prussia) 10–11, 14, 47, 258, 393, 439, 566–567, 569, 574–575, 578, 582
  "kurtz und vives" 566
Frederick VI (King of Denmark) 373
Frederick William (Crown Prince of Prussia) 573, 580

INDEX 601

Frederick William (Elector of Brandenburg) 566
Frederick William II (King of Prussia) 55, 61
Frederick William III (King of Prussia) 250, 252, 264–265, 275–277, 295, 373, 424, 434, 458, 468, 471
Freiburg-im-Breisgau 458
Frere, John Hookham 327
Freytag-Loringhoven, Hugo 443
Friant, Louis 403
Friedland (battle) 197, 273–276, 300–302, 361, 420, 443, 481, 517
Frimont, Johann 472
Frische-Haff 290, 294, 377
Friuli 162, 164, 186–187
Fulda 260
Fulda Gap 254
Furnes 51

Galicia (Austria) 359, 363, 386
Galicia (Spain) 312, 317, 328, 331, 338, 517
Galluzo y Páez, José 317
Gamonal (battle) 320, 324
Ganteaume, Honoré Joseph Antoine 495, 498, 503, 505–507, 515, 520–521, 523–524, 526–527, 539, 543
Gardanne, Gaspard Amédée 211, 213, 217
Garessio 98, 101, 104
Gavardo 140, 143, 147, 152–156
Gazan de la Peyrière, Honoré Théodore Maxime 164
Gembloux 476–477
Gemona 187
Genappe 473
  King of Spain Inn, 481
Geneva 200–201
Genoa 70, 89, 90, 92, 98, 100–110, 199–201, 204–206, 208–210, 216, 518, 536, 556
Georgia 375
Gera 184–185, 189
Germany 52, 68–70, 73, 77, 89, 92, 94, 137, 139, 160, 188, 194–196, 222–231, 246, 253–254, 256–257, 302, 344–346, 353, 355–346, 360, 363, 367, 369, 375, 380, 387, 392, 395, 419, 444, 448–449, 450,
    459, 483, 508, 534–535, 553, 555–556, 565–566, 576
  Confederation of the Rhine (Rheinbund) 246, 250, 252, 271, 280, 345–346, 360, 425–426, 443, 450, 514
  German Confederation 506
  North Germany 360, 375, 380, 392, 395, 418, 427–428, 432, 444
  South Germany 52, 94, 188, 224–225, 228, 253–254, 257
Ghent 64
Gibraltar 306, 308, 503, 506, 554
Givet 50
Glogau 377–378, 423, 425, 433
Glorious First of June 477
Glubokoe 382, 401
Gneisenau, August Wilhelm Antonius Neidhardt von 476, 504, 577–578, 589
Godoy, Manuel de 308
Goito 146, 149–153, 155, 165
Goltz, Colmar von der 575
Golymin (battle) 283–285, 288
Golitsyn, Dmitry Vladimirovich 283
Gordon, Alexander 327–329, 332, 334, 336
Gorizia 188
Görlitz 438, 440
Gourdon, Antoine Louis de 418
Gouvion Saint-Cyr, Laurent de 325, 273, 299, 313, 377, 509
Gradisca 188
Graham, Thomas 138, 150
Granada 317
Grand Port (battle) 530, 544–545
Grasse, François-Joseph Paul de 406
Gratz 241
Graudenz 376
Gravina y Nápoli, Federico Carlos 497
Great Britain 221, 226, 250, 257, 276, 296, 302, 306–315, 353, 360, 372, 375, 392, 417, 423, 462, 471–472, 493, 495, 500–502, 506–509, 512–514, 516, 528, 531, 533, 535–536, 538, 542, 544, 553, 560
  Anglo-Danish relations 205
  Anglo-French War 1803–1805 222, 225–226, 372, 412–423
  Anglo-Portuguese army 483, 490

Great Britain (cont.)
  Anglo-Portuguese relations   307, 312–316, 339
  army   43, 313, 331, 334, 336–340, 552–553, 581–582
    British Isles   550, 557
    Channel Islands   528
    Continental System   307, 372–374, 512, 521, 558–559
    Industrial Revolution   379
    London   150, 246, 311–313, 439, 522, 545, 551, 553, 555–558
    Orders in Council   307, 557
    Parliament   221
    Peninsular War   306–340, 526
    Perfidious Albion   233, 516
    Royal Navy   200, 212, 272, 199–201, 205–206, 212, 286, 356, 493–539, 542–562
      Calcutta   509
      Channel fleet   506–507
      Illustrious   548
      Junon   548
      Mediterranean Fleet   119, 543
      Nymphe   548
      Proserpine   537
      Victorious   532
    Treaty of Orebro 1812   375
    War of American Independence   42, 477
    War of Fifth Coalition   246, 253
    War of First Coalition   48, 56, 71, 74, 89, 110, 114
    War of Fourth Coalition   251–253, 256
    War of Second Coalition   194
    War of Seventh Coalition   423, 472
    War of Sixth Coalition   423, 462, 471–472
    War of Third Coalition   224, 226, 236, 238
    War of 1812   556, 562
Great Saint Bernard Pass   90, 200, 213, 216
Greece   410
Grodno   381, 388–390
Großbeeren (battle)   440, 442–443, 445
Grouchy, Emmanuel de   218, 475–479, 481
Grünzburg   228
Guadalajara   322
Guadeloupe   495–498, 523–525, 551–552
Guernsey   502
Guibert, Charles-Benoît   13, 19

Guibert, Jacques-Antoine-Hippolyte de   8–39, 41–42, 55, 74, 79, 195
  cadenced step   11–13
  citizen soldier   42–45
  Colonnes de Guibert   16–17, 19, 25–26, 30
  column vs. line   10–18, 23, 26–30
  combined arms   20–21, 29, 30
  Défense du système de guerre modern   16, 42
  divisional system   19, 21, 24, 30–32, 41, 104–105
  General Staff   23
  Essai général de tactique   14, 16, 22, 41–44, 79
  grand tactics   18, 39
  L'instruction de 1769 pour les troupes legères   15, 17
  logistics   22, 33, 35, 40–41
  L'ordre mixte   18, 21, 25, 27–28, 505
  hommes de genie   15, 22–23, 33, 35, 78
  Provisional Regulations of 1789   24, 25
  war of movement   41
Guidizzolo   155, 157–158
Guieu, Jean Joseph   147, 149, 152–154, 156–157, 186–189
Guise   60
Gulf of Finland   559
Gulf of Genoa   125
Gulf of Juan   445
Gulf of Roses   526
Gumbinen (Gusev)   378
Günzberg   156, 158
Gustav IV (King of Sweden)   374
Gvozdanović, Petar Vid   140, 143, 147, 149–150, 152–157, 159–160, 162, 164, 168–169, 178, 181–183, 188
Gzhatsk   410, 412

Hadik Futaki, András   206, 209
Halle   264–266, 271
Hamburg   392, 424, 438, 443, 447, 450
Hanseatic Cities   272
Hanover   58, 221–222, 225, 230, 237, 250, 254, 392, 428, 514
Hardenburg, Karl August von   373
Haslach-Jungingen   232, 238
Haugwitz, Christian August Heinrich Kurt von   264

INDEX 603

Hausen-Teugn (battle)   350
Havana   511
Heilsberg (battle)   294–296, 298–300, 301
Heligoland   558
Hesse   54, 224
Hindenburg, Paul von   581
Hispaniola   497, 508
Hoche, Lazare   60, 75, 117
Hof   184, 188–189
Hohenfriedeberg (battle)   502
Hohenlinden (battle)   78, 140
Hohenlohe-Ingelfingen, Friedrich Ludwig zu   264–265, 272
Hohenzollern-Hechingen, Friedrich Franz Xaver von   169–171, 174, 185, 188
Holy Roman Empire   88, 151–152, 246, 250, 252
Hondschoote (battle)   59
Hospice of Saint Bernard   202
Hotham, Henry   387
Houchard, Jean Nicolas   59
Hougomont   478
Hourtoulle, François-Guy   194
Howell, Thomas   225
Hungary   160, 361–362
Huningue   454, 458–459

Iberia   306, 311–312, 393, 419, 439, 480, 553–557, 561
Iceland   560
Île Bonaparte (Réunion)   496, 530
Île de France (Mauritius)   496, 499, 529–530, 544, 552, 562
Iller River   228, 230, 232
Illyria   285–286
Imperia   129
Ingolstadt   347–348
India   306, 552, 589
Indian Ocean   478, 486, 496, 499, 508, 512–513, 522, 528–531
Inn River   256, 345, 342
Innsbruck   160, 162, 189–190
Insterburg (Chernyakhovsk)   378, 393
Ireland   503, 505, 509, 516, 522, 533
Isonzo River   185, 188–189
Isar River   350
Issy-les-Moulineaux (battle)   364

Italy   68, 71, 87–92, 94, 96–98, 103, 112–113, 116–120, 132, 137–142, 151, 153, 160, 168, 185, 190, 194–200, 216, 222–226, 228, 235–238, 246, 257, 345, 353, 355, 360–362, 364–366, 369, 426, 438, 451, 472, 497, 505, 516, 518, 520, 531, 537, 553, 555
   kingdom of   222, 225, 238, 255, 516, 518, 520, 531
Dalmatia   345, 359–360
Ivrea   200, 202–203, 207

Jamaica   549
Janssens, Jan Willem   530
Java   548, 552
Jemappes (battle)   44, 56
Jérémie   497
Jersey   502
John (Archduke of Austria)   78, 231, 237, 344, 355, 360–361, 366
Jomini, Antoine-Henri   40, 78, 141, 162, 168, 190–191, 384–385, 434, 481
Joseph II (Holy Roman Emperor)   50
Joubert, Barthélemy Catherine   73, 106, 126–127, 145, 169–171, 179–183, 186–190
Jourdan, Jean-Baptiste   30, 45, 60–72, 75, 78, 117, 160, 162
Junot, Jean-Andoche   154, 307, 313–314, 325, 405, 440
Jura Mountains   228, 450–451, 461
Jurien de la Gravière, Pierre Roch   524

Kaim, Johann Konrad Valentin von   206, 209
Kaiserslautern   445
Kaiserslautern (battle)   60
Kakuvyachino   402
Kalisch (treaty)   424, 426
Kaluga   409–410, 412
Kamensky, Mikhail Fedorovich   281–282, 286–287
Kankrin, Georg Ludwig von   396
Karlsruhe   458–459
Katzbach (battle)   440, 442–445, 482
Katzbach River   428, 439–440
Kaub   461
Kehl   455–458

Kellermann, François Christophe de   55, 89, 96, 102, 108, 117, 215
Kerpen, Wilhelm Lothar Maria von   189
Khorosh   381
Kienmayer, Michael von   228, 238
Kiev   388–391, 582
Kilmaine, Charles-Edouard   138, 143, 152, 157, 165, 167
Klagenfurt   189–190, 362
Kléber, Jean-Baptiste   64, 66
Klenau, Johann von   124, 147, 152, 166
Klinkhardt, Friedrich   308
Koblenz   66, 454–455, 457–458, 461
Köblös, Sámuel de Nagy-Varád, 178, 180–183, 188–189
Kolberg   376, 504
Kolin (battle)   567
Köln (Cologne)   457
Koltynyani   388
Königgrätz (battle)   573, 580
Königsberg   276, 281, 287–288, 292, 294, 299–302, 376–377
Kormend   236
Kovel   388
Kovno   380–382, 397
Kozietulski, Jan Leon Hipolit   302
Krajovai és Topolyai, Kray Pál   75–77, 195–200
Krasnyi   404–405, 415–416
Krems an der Donau   239–240
Kulm (battle)   162, 442, 444–445
Kurisches-Haff   378
Küstrin   376–378, 424, 426, 435, 443, 447
Kutschitten   574
Kutuzov, Mikhail Illaricnovich   222, 227, 230–232, 237–240, 242, 244–246, 281, 406–407, 409, 412–414, 416–417, 419–422, 426, 429

La Corona   143, 145, 170, 175, 177–178, 181, 183
La Croix au Bois (battle)   55
Lacrosse, Jean-Baptiste Raymond de   403–404, 409, 427
Lafayette, Gilbert du Motier de   49–54, 59
La Favorita   73, 166, 184
Lagny   479
Laharpe, Amédée Emmanuel François   70, 101–102, 104, 108, 119–129, 134, 136, 142

Lahn River   68–69
La Haye Sainte   477–478
Laibach (Ljubljana)   188–189
Lake Garda   72, 135, 138–143, 145–148, 154–155, 158–162, 169, 172, 178–179
Lake Geneva   200
Lake Idro   158
Lambro River   132
Landau   58, 454, 457–458, 460–461
Landrécies   62
Landsberg   447
Landshut   348, 350, 352
Langeron, Louis Alexandre Andrault de   243
Langres   450–451, 464, 468–469
Lannes, Jean   134–135, 144, 167, 173, 184, 201–203, 206–212, 214, 245, 257, 261, 265–267, 271–272, 277, 284, 295, 298–300, 321, 330, 347–348, 357–358
Laon   478–479
Laon (battle)   470
Lapoype, jean François Cornu de   212, 217
La Rochelle   496
La Rothière (battle)   465–466
La Spezia   125, 518
La Taulle   479
Latouche-Tréville, Louis-René Levassor de   495, 497, 499, 538
Latour-Maubourg, Marie Victor   380, 404
Lauer, Franz von   150, 160
Lauriston, Jacques   420
Lauter River   49
La Valette, Antoine   149–153
Lavis   161–162, 168–169
Lazise   144
League of Armed Neutrality   495
Le Bourget   374
Lebrun, Anne-Charles-François   377, 530
Le Cap Française   497
Le Cateau   62
Lech River   232, 347
Leclerc, Charles Victoire Emmanuel   183, 497–498
Lecourbe, Claude Jacques   197, 201, 217
Leeward Islands   484
Lefebvre, François Joseph   319, 322, 325, 347–348
Lefebvre-Desnouettes, Charles   334–335, 455

INDEX 605

Legnago 140, 142, 144, 160, 164–166, 178–180, 184
Legnano 73
Le Havre 496, 520
Leipzig 260–261, 265–266, 429, 447, 449, 578
Leipzig (battle) 423, 445, 447–449, 452, 535, 556, 570, 578–579
  Liebertwolkwitz 79
  Lindenau 447, 449
  Möckern 447–448, 579
  Battle of Nations (*Völkerschlacht*) 578
  Wachau 447, 579
Lejeune, Louis-François 216, 401
Le Noble, Pierre-Madeleine 336
Leoben (armistice) 190
León 320–321
Le Passage 519
Le Plessis 479
Lesser Antilles 513
L'Estocq, Anton Wilhelm von 289–290, 292, 294, 297, 574–575
Leuthen (battle) 8, 567
Levant 306, 493, 518
Leissègues, Corentin Urbain de 508, 511
Lhermitte, Jean-Marthe-Adrien 510, 525
Libava 388
Lieberich, Karl Mack von 224–225, 227–228, 230–232, 234–238
Liège 51, 63, 454, 473, 476
Lieven, Andreyevich Christophe 387
Ligny (battle) 475–476
Ligurian Riviera 119, 130
Ligurian Sea 119, 125
Lille 51
Linear warfare 9, 39–40
Linois, Charles-Alexandre Léon Durand 498–499
Linz 228
Lipthay, Anton de Kisfalud 132, 134, 149–153, 155, 169–170, 178, 180–183
Lissa (battle) 532
Lissa (Vis) 527, 532, 544
Lithuania 377, 384, 408
Little Saint Bernard Pass 90, 197, 201, 217
Livonia 377, 391
Lloyd, Henry E. H., 39
Lloyds of London 551

Loano 122
Loano (battle) 70, 90, 92–94, 97–98
Lobau Island 357–358, 361–364
Lodi, 135–136
Lodi (battle) 73, 135–137, 139
Logroño 317
Loire River 467, 472, 480
Loison, Louis-Henri 201
Lombardy 70–71, 88–96, 109, 114, 117–118, 131–137, 139–140, 150, 159, 197
Lonato 72–74, 138, 144–147, 149–157, 180
Lonato (battle) 147
Longwy 53–54
Lorge, Jean-Thomas-Guillaume 330
Lorient 497, 510, 513, 519–520, 523–524, 528, 532
Lorraine 452, 461, 464, 469
Loudon, Johann Ludwig von 168–169, 172, 185, 187
Louise (Queen of Prussia) 273
Louis Ferdinand (Prince of Prussia) 260
Louis XIV (King of France) 10, 88, 303, 482
  wars of 91, 95
Louis XV (King of France) 11, 15
Louis XVI (King of France) 25, 44, 49, 53, 56
Louis XVIII (King of France) 423, 471, 480
Louvain 57
Low Countries 61, 68, 204, 423, 451–452, 454, 456–457, 459, 462–463, 468
Lübeck 272, 279, 569
Lubino 405
Lublin 380
Luckau 433, 436, 445
Luckner, Nicolas 49–52
Ludendorff, Erich 581–582
Lukow 380
Lumini 180–182
Lusha River 306
Lusignan, Franz Joseph de 178, 180–183, 185, 187
Lützen (battle) 428–429, 431–432, 436, 570
  Großgörschen 429, 570
  Kaja 429
  Kleingörschen 429
  Rahna 429
Luxembourg 50, 454
Lyon 61, 89, 110, 472

Maastricht 57, 65–66, 477
Madagascar 496
Macdonald, Étienne Jacques Joseph Alexandre 380, 386, 406–407, 418, 420, 440, 444, 450, 452–455, 457, 462, 467–468, 470, 481–482, 577
Macquard, François 172–173
Madeira Island 508
Magdeburg 264–266, 272, 275, 277, 279, 375, 378, 424, 427, 429, 445
Maida (battle) 553
Mainoni, Joseph Antoine Marie Michel 201–202
Main River 67–68, 427
Mainz 29, 56, 58, 68, 230, 254, 271, 452, 454, 458, 460–461, 464
Maison, Nicholas-Joseph 463
Malet, Claude François 309
Mallare 101
Maloyaroslavets (battle) 412–413, 416, 420
Malta 221, 493, 495, 514
Mamluks 395
Mannheim 456–458, 461
Mantua 71–74, 96, 117, 120, 132, 135–153, 156–169, 172–185, 210, 213
Marbot, Jean Baptiste Antoine Marcellin de 320
Marcaria 146, 151, 157
Marceau, François-Séverin 64
Marengo (battle) 75, 194, 212, 214–218, 300, 361, 365, 404
Marescot, Armand Samuel de 127
Maria Ludovica 344
Marie-Galante 503
Marienburg 377–378
Marienpol 380
Marly-la-Ville 479
Marmont, Auguste Frédéric Louis Viesse de 201, 203, 213, 215, 360, 362, 366, 450, 452, 454–457, 459–461, 464, 467, 471, 481
Marne (battle) 580–581
Marne River 451–452, 461, 464, 466–469
Marseille 89, 100, 110, 119, 527, 536,
Martinique 496, 498, 502, 523–524
Mascarene Islands 496, 498–499, 531
Massenbach, Christian Karl August Ludwig von 264

Masséna, André 33, 70–74, 97–98, 101–102, 104–108, 119, 122–130, 135–136, 140, 143–147, 149, 152, 154, 158–159, 161–167, 169–171, 173–184, 187, 189, 195, 199–201, 204, 206, 208, 213, 235–237, 295, 347–348, 350–352, 357, 364–366
Maximilian IV/I Joseph (Elector/King of Bavaria) 151
Meaux 479
Mecklenburg-Strelitz 224
Medina de Rioseco (battle) 310
Mediterranean Sea 199, 223, 306, 311–313, 372, 392, 495, 507, 509, 513–515, 518–520, 523–524, 528, 532, 536, 545–546, 555, 558
Medyn 306
Meiningen 260
Melas, Michael Friedrich Benedikt von 194–217
Melito, André Miot de 321
Memel 302, 393
Memmingen 234
Menard, Jean-François-Xavier de 101, 104
Méneval, Claude François 377, 414
Menorca 526–527
Merseburg 190
Méry-sur-Seine 468–470
Mészáros, Johann von Szoboszló 140, 143–144, 150–151, 156, 158, 160–162, 164
Metternich, Klemens Wenzel Nepomuk Lothar von 374, 384–385, 425, 471
Metz 54, 451, 455
Meuse River 54, 57, 62, 450–451, 461, 469
Meynier, Jean-Baptiste 108, 119, 122–127
Michelsberg 235
Middle East 312
Milan 71, 113, 117, 120, 132, 136–138, 142–146, 149–150, 153, 155, 204, 206–209, 212–213, 224, 521
Milanese (Austrian Lombardy) 88, 114, 207
Millesimo 103–105, 110, 118–119, 124–125, 128
Miloradovich, Mikhail Andreyevich 389, 413–414
Mincio River 71, 120, 135, 138–139, 144–159, 165–168, 171–172, 180
Minsk 382, 384, 391, 400, 402, 405, 420, 582
Minto, Gilbert Elliot-Murray-Kynynmound of 306

Miollis, Sextius-Alexandre   184
Mittrowsky, Anton Ferdinand von Mittrowitz und Nemyšl   172–175
Möckern (battle)   429
Modlin   376–378, 385, 424, 426
Mogilev   382, 393, 402
Moldavia   375, 387
Mollwitz (battle)   567, 575
Moltke, Helmut von (Elder)   352, 571–573, 580, 582
Moncey, Bon-Adrien Jeannot de   201, 208, 212, 217, 319, 321
Mondego Bay   313
Mondovi   90, 103, 107–110, 119, 129
Mondovi (battle)   71, 108, 129, 131
Money, John   29
Monnier, Jean-Charles   211
Mons   49–52, 56
Montbrun, Louis-Pierre   323
Mont Cenis Pass   200, 202, 204–206, 345
Monte Albaredo   202
Monte Baldo   145, 181
Monte Baldo Ridge   140, 180
Montebello   143, 162–163, 169, 174, 176
Montebello (battle)   211, 213
Monte Castellazzo   122
Monte Legino   99–100, 103–104, 122–123
Monte Magnòne Ridge   178, 182–183
Monte Medalano   157
Monte Moscat   182
Montenotte   98, 101, 102, 104, 122–125
Montenotte (battle)   70, 102–105, 110, 122–123, 125, 136
Monte Pipolo   182
Montereau (battle)   362
Montezemolo   104–106, 110, 125, 128
Montesquiou-Fézensac, Anne-Pierre de   56
Montichiari   143–147, 149, 152–153, 155
Montmirail   467
Mont-Saint-Jean   473, 477
Moore, John   313–314, 317, 325–339
Moravia   154, 160, 164–166, 260–261
Moreau, Jean Victor Marie   68–70, 75–79, 117, 216–217
Morley, Stephen   332
Mormant (battle)   468
Mortefontaine (treaty)   403

Mortier, Adolphe Édouard Casimir Joseph   221–222, 239–240, 295, 325, 463
Moselle River   450–451, 461, 464
Möskirch (battle)   77
Mosty   388
Mousty   477
Mozhaisk   413
Mozyr   388
Muhlheim   459
Mulhouse   460
Mulassano (Murazzano)   109
Murat, Joachim   144, 167, 181, 201, 207–208, 212, 238–240, 257, 260–261, 265–266, 269–272, 279–280, 283, 292, 298–299, 308–309, 398, 401, 403–405, 410, 418, 444-445, 482, 504, 513, 517, 519

Naples/Two Sicilies (kingdom)   88, 92, 94, 132, 225–226, 236, 286, 513–516, 519, 531
  army   448
  Naples (city)   495, 509, 515, 519
  navy   443–444, 457, 461
  Sicily   435–436, 438, 447, 448, 452, 457, 464–465
Namur   50, 63, 459, 463, 476–477, 580
Nancy   461, 468
Nantes   405, 444, 447, 450, 460–462, 465, 468
Nanteuil   479
Napoleon I   8, 15, 32, 47–48, 64–65, 69–72, 74–76, 78, 87–110, 118–127, 194–218, 221–222, 246–247, 269–273, 275–294, 296–303, 306–307, 310–315, 334, 342–370, 423, 425–427, 480–483, 545, 569–571, 573, 575–579, 582
  as Guibert's *homme de genie*   9, 31, 33, 35, 81
  bataillon carré   31–32, 261, 267, 285, 288, 290, 298, 325
  Continental System   200, 317, 559
  coup de main   144
  Egyptian Campaign   493, 495, 508
  First Abdication   471
  First Consul   396
  First Italian Campaign   30, 71–76, 79, 87–191, 327, 337, 369–370, 391

Napoleon I (cont.)
  fleet-in-being strategy   388, 396, 434, 437, 439, 446, 472
  flying columns   202
  guerre de course   493, 508, 512, 529, 531, 534
  Josephine   245, 265, 270, 335
  logistics   34, 263–264, 285, 293, 346–347, 356
  manoeuvre sur les derrières   65, 76, 105, 108, 110, 116, 132, 136, 157, 160, 170, 172, 190, 194, 216, 240, 290, 299, 355, 427, 469, 471
  manoeuvre sur la position centrale   116, 119, 145, 159, 187, 190, 433
  Marie Louise   267, 319
  Napoleon III, 580
  navy   387–473, 476–480
  operational art   8, 9, 21, 31, 39, 41, 46–48, 52, 55, 57–59, 64–66, 69–71, 74–76, 78–79, 96, 110–111, 136, 172, 194–197, 204–206, 216–218, 237, 247, 249–273, 275, 279, 293, 309, 315–316, 319, 330, 339–340, 342, 350, 353, 357, 360–361, 367–370, 427–428, 431, 482, 569, 575–579
  Peninsular War   306–340, 312, 441, 451, 454, 465
  Proclamation (29 Sep. 1805)   156
  rumors of death   207, 309
  Schlachtkaiser   582
  Second Abdication   479
  Second Italian Campaign   31, 75, 194–218, 337
  stratégie de penetration   138
  strategy of central position   52, 70, 72, 74, 100, 110, 119, 122–123, 127, 145, 153, 171, 173, 175–177, 180, 184, 439, 442–443, 578–579
  War of Fourth Coalition   250–273, 275–305, 568–569, 573–574
  War of Fifth Coalition   342–370
  War of Second Coalition   194–218
  War of Seventh Coalition   472–480
  War of Sixth Coalition   423–471
    Fall Campaign   423, 428, 439–450, 575–579
    master plan of 1813   427–429, 435, 442, 445
    Spring Campaign   429–436
  1814 Campaign   450–471
    Six Days Campaign   467, 480
  War of Third Coalition   225–247
  1812 Campaign   372–387, 390–422, 555, 560
Narbonne-Lara, Louis   384
Naumburg   261, 264, 266–267
Navarre   330
Narew River   279–284, 286–287, 290, 380, 386
Natisone River   188
Naylies, Joseph de   324
Near East   312
Neckar River   457
Neerwinden (battle)   28, 57
Neiße River   433, 437, 444
Neptune Orientales   420
Neresheim   234
Netherlands   57, 65, 194, 376, 387, 451, 581
  Batavian Republic   407
  colonies   400, 402, 416, 436–437, 465
  Batavia   460–461, 552
  Cape of Good Hope   503, 514, 516, 529, 549, 553, 555–556
  Guianas   417
  Java   461
  Dutch East Indies   461
  Dutch Revolt   456, 462
  Holland   254, 360, 392, 452, 454–456, 462–463, 505, 514, 516, 521, 549, 553, 555–556
  navy   356, 398, 400, 409, 424, 437, 439, 457, 468
    Ajax   409
    Brutus   409
    Joan de Witt   498
    Neptunus   98
    sea camels   518
  War of First Coalition   57, 65
Nelson, Horatio   503, 506–507, 542
Nettelbeck, Joachim   569
Neuf-Brisach   458–459
Neumarkt   161, 190
Newfoundland   508

INDEX 609

Ney, Michel 28, 232–234, 238–239, 241, 257, 261, 267, 269–272, 280, 287–290, 292–293, 296–298, 301, 319, 321–322, 376, 380, 414, 416, 418, 432–436, 440, 444, 450, 468, 471, 475, 481–482
Nice 56, 93, 95, 97, 100, 110, 113, 117, 119, 124, 129–130, 200, 206, 209
Niemen River 302, 378, 380–381, 384, 388–389, 397, 400, 403, 418
Nile (battle) 387, 393–394, 543
Nile River 394–395
Nivelles 473, 476
Nogent-sur-Seine 467–468
Nollendorf 442
Nompère de Champagny, Jean-Baptiste de 266
North America 513
North Sea 224, 237, 353, 451–453, 558
Norway 374, 560, 581
  Oslo 581
Novara 207
Novgorod 388
Nove 170
Novi 212, 215
Novi (battle) 195, 215
Novyi Bykhov 402
Nuremberg 69, 160, 256, 347

Ocskay, Joseph von Ocskó 147, 152, 154–155, 178, 181–183, 188–189
Oder River 272, 277–278, 294, 391, 424–425, 427–428, 433, 435–438, 443–444
Offenburg 457
Oglio River 136, 138, 146, 149
Oise River 479
Old Castile 309–310, 325, 327
Oldenburg 236, 373
Olecko 380
Olmütz (Olomouc) 240–243, 246–247
Oneglia 89–90, 102
operational art of war 21, 39, 46–79, 130, 136, 172, 195, 221, 224, 247, 270
Oppenhein 458
Oppermann, Karl von 388
Ormea 98, 123–124, 129
Orsha 298, 309
Ospedaletto 187
Osteria 178, 182–183

Osteria Defile 178, 180, 182–183
Osterman-Tolstoy, Aleksandr Ivanovich 402
Ostrog 388
Ostrolenka 295, 380
Ostrovno 402
Ottoman Empire 372–375, 391–392, 406, 419, 515, 589
  Constantinople 372, 514–515
  navy 515
  Treaty of Bucharest 1812 375
Ott von Bátorkézi, Károly Péter 144, 147, 152, 154, 165–166, 208–211
Oudinot, Nicolas Charles 214, 348, 364–365, 376, 380, 401, 405, 420, 436, 438–440, 443–444, 463, 468, 481–482
Ourcq River 468
Ourthe River 66

Pacific Ocean 549
Padua 164, 178, 180, 186, 188
Paget, Henry Willim 328, 334
Pajol, Claude Pierre 476
Palafox y Melci, José Rebolledo de 317, 319, 321
Palatinate 49
Palermo 448
Palencia 316, 322, 330
Palmanova 188
Pamplona 317
Pancorbo (battle) 319
Papal States 439
Papelotte 478
Parma (duchy) 71, 116
Parthe River 447–448
Passau 228, 355–356
Paul I (Tsar of Russia) 442
Pavia 132–133, 136
Pélage, Magloire 409
Pellew, Edward 543, 545–546
Peri 177
Perpignan 58
Perret d'Hauteville, Joseph-François-Jerôme 94
Peschiera 71, 138, 144, 146–149, 156, 158, 168, 180
Peter I (Tsar of Russia) 388, 390
Pfuel, Karl Ludwig August Friedrich von 390, 393–395, 401

Philippeville 49, 478–479
Phipps, Henry (Earl of Mulgrave) 551
Piacenza 71, 73, 132–134, 136, 143, 208, 210, 212–213
Piave River 164, 168–170, 185, 187
Pichegru, Jean-Charles 61–62, 64, 75
Pijion, Jean Joseph 119–120, 154
Pillau 294, 376
Pillwiski 380
Pinsk 388
Pirna 440
Pitt, William 194, 246
Pittoni, Philipp von Dannenfeld 169
Pizzighettone 134–136, 138, 143, 146, 152
Plancenoit 478, 570
Pläswitz (armistice) 436, 438
Platov, Matvei Ivanovich 414
Pleiße River 447–448
Plock 377
Point-à-Pitre 409
Poland 52–53, 61, 66, 94, 273, 275–277, 280, 283–285, 295, 303, 315, 345, 354, 359, 372–373, 376–377, 380, 387–388, 391, 396, 406, 408–410, 428, 432–433, 436–437, 443, 515, 539, 581
  Grand Duchy of Warsaw 345, 359, 372–373, 376, 380, 383–385, 387, 391–392, 395, 397, 409, 424–427, 456
  Partitions 61, 66, 275, 372, 383
  War of the Fourth Coalition 345
  Warsaw 277–281, 294–295, 359, 376–378, 384–386, 396, 426, 458, 516
    Praga Suburbs 386
  Warsaw (battle) 566, 581
Polangen 381
Polesye Swamps 381, 390
Polotsk 401, 407
Pomerania 392, 395, 428
Pomerania (Sweden) 374
Pondicherry 410
Poniatowski, Józef 380, 387, 418, 450
Pont-à-Mousson 508
Pontebba 185
Ponte San Marco 145, 147–149, 152, 154
Pont Saint-Maxence 479
Po River 71, 87, 92, 117–118, 120, 125, 130, 132, 134–135, 143, 150–151, 200, 202, 204, 206–211, 213, 215

Port-au-Prince 497
Port-de-Bouc 518
Porto (Oporto) 312, 433
Portugal 307–308, 312–314, 325, 327–328, 331, 339, 508, 516–517, 521
  Lisbon 307, 312–313, 325, 327, 330, 339, 549, 554
  navy 517, 521
Prague 165, 428, 442–443
  siege 567
Predil Pass 187–189
Pregel (Pregolya) River 378
Prenny 380
Pressburg 366
  principles of war 74, 116, 130, 136, 160, 190, 204, 354
  economy of force 61, 74, 116, 126, 130, 171, 173, 177, 184, 190, 439, 473
  maneuver 70–71, 73–74, 79, 105, 108, 110–111, 116, 129–130, 132, 136, 145, 149, 157, 160, 167–168, 177, 184, 195, 204, 213, 216, 236, 246, 257, 279–281, 285, 299, 322, 355, 385, 397–400, 401, 404–405, 427, 435, 467, 480, 483
  mass 70, 74, 116, 122, 128, 130, 138, 145–146, 150, 159–160, 167, 177, 184, 190–191, 247, 278, 428
  objective 116, 119, 127, 129, 136, 158–160, 167, 177, 187, 190, 196, 206, 280, 293, 354, 356, 386, 428, 473, 481
  offensive 51, 55, 59–60, 66, 72, 97, 111, 113, 116, 122, 132, 136, 164, 167, 175, 177, 184, 190, 196, 209, 281, 294, 315, 361, 427–428, 437, 440, 442–443, 468, 475, 493
  security 116, 129–130, 134, 136, 190, 203, 216, 360, 522
  simplicity 116, 129, 134, 136, 145, 160, 177, 184, 190, 317
  surprise 66, 71, 74, 116, 130, 132, 136, 143, 160, 165, 167, 177, 190, 237
  unity of command 116, 190, 317
Pripyat River 381, 386
Provera, Giovanni, Marchese di 73, 91, 102, 104–106, 120, 124–126, 128, 168–184
Provins 470

INDEX 611

Prussia 94–95, 117, 249–252, 275–277, 279–281, 287, 289–290, 292–296, 298, 300–303, 372, 374, 376, 378, 380, 386, 388, 391–392, 395, 409, 423, 427, 481, 513–514, 566–567, 570, 573, 578
  army 10–11, 14, 259, 426, 432, 568–571, 575–576, 578
    Army of the Lower Rhine 472–473, 475, 477
    General Staff 131, 262, 445, 573–577
    Kesselschlacht 576, 579–580
    Krupp artillery 571
    Landwehr 426, 470, 570
    needle gun 571
    officer corps 567, 571
    Reform Era 570
    Royal Guard 275, 458, 465
    1st Army 580
    2nd Army 580
    I Corps 434, 447, 464, 466, 475, 477–480
      1st Brigade 478
    II Corps 429, 434, 442, 466
    III Corps 444, 476, 479
    IV Corps 444, 475, 477, 479
  Berlin 252, 254, 265, 273, 275, 277, 373, 376, 387, 424, 428–429, 432–433, 435–436, 440, 442–445, 481, 568, 573
  East Prussia 197, 378, 386, 392, 481
    winter campaign of 1678–1679 567
  Franco-Prussian Treaty of Paris 1812 374
  Partitions of Poland 61, 66, 383
  Russo-Prussian Alliance 1813 424–425
  Second Reich 566, 571
  Seven Years War 10, 14, 183
  Silesia 429–440 *passim*, 481
  Treaty of Basel 1795 66
  War of Fifth Coalition 246, 249–250–262
  War of First Coalition 48–66, 89
  War of Fourth Coalition 249–273, 275–305, 320, 503–510
  War of Liberation 575
  War of Seventh Coalition 472–480
  War of Sixth Coalition 423–471, 512–514, 570, 577–578
    Fall Campaign 423, 428, 439–450, 577–578
    Spring Campaign 429–436
    1814 Campaign 450–471

  War of Third Coalition 228–230, 237, 241, 250
  1812 campaign 372, 374, 376, 378, 380, 386, 388, 391–392, 395, 409
Pruth River 380
Pultusk (battle) 275, 279, 280–286, 289, 294
Pyrenees Mountains 58, 61, 66, 303, 315, 344, 423, 450, 472, 526

Quadrilateral Fortresses 71, 117, 120, 132, 135–153, 156–169, 172–185
Quadruple Alliance 471
Quasi War 403
Quatre-Bras 473, 476
Quatre-Bras (battle) 475–476
Queis River 433

Raab 361
Rampon, Antoine-Guillaume 122
Rastatt 68, 351–353
Rayevskii, Nikolai Nikolayevich 402
Red Sea 207
Regensburg 228, 344, 347–355, 358, 364, 369
Réglement 1754 11
  1791 8, 9, 25, 24, 35, 46
  1792 47
Reims 479
Reims (battle) 470
Reinosa 317
Réunion Island 496, 530
Reuß, Heinrich XV of 143, 147, 152, 154, 178, 182
Rey, Antoine Gabriel 180–183
Rey, Louis Emmanuel 73
Reynier, Jean Louis Ebénézer 380, 418
Rhineland 49, 55–56, 65
Rhine River 50–51, 53, 55, 63, 66–69, 75–77, 91, 94, 97, 110, 117, 139, 160, 162, 188, 190, 195–197, 223, 225, 227–228, 230–231, 235, 254, 423–424, 442, 448–464, 468–469, 471–473, 483, 565
Richepanse, Antoine 409
Riesch, Johann Sigismund von 158
Riga 377, 381–383, 388–389, 393, 406–407
Rigaud, André 403
Riva 155, 157
Rivalta 139, 170–171, 201
Rivaud, Jean-Baptiste 201

Riviera (Italian)   89, 92, 96, 98, 101, 110, 119, 127
Rivoli   124, 139–140, 158–159, 173, 175–185, 190
Rivoli (battle)   70, 177–185, 190
Robespierre, Maximilien   58
Rocchetta   127
Rochambeau, Jean-Baptiste Donatien de Vimeur de   49–51
Rodrigues (island)   496, 529
Roer (battle)   30
Roer River   66
Roguet, François   26, 455
Rocca, Albert Jean Michel de   324
Rochefort   497, 502, 505–507, 513–516, 519–520, 523–525, 528, 537–539
Romana, Pedro Caro y Sureda de la   319, 328, 332, 335
Romanov, Catherine Pavlovna   266
Rome, 410
Rommel, Erwin   582
Ronco   164–165, 173–175, 179
Rosasna   298
Roselmini, Gerhard von   169
Rosetta   393–394
Rosily-Mesros, François Étienne   510
Roßbach (battle)   14, 439, 567, 574–575, 578
Rousseau, Jean-Jacques   42
Roussin, Albin   534
Roverbella   138, 144, 146, 149–151
Rovereto   139, 161–162, 168, 177–178
Rovereto (battle)   161–162
Rudolstadt   264
Rüchel, Ernst von   264–265
Rügen   374
Rukavina, Matija Bojnogradski   122, 125, 151
Rumyantsev, Nikolai Petrovich   373, 396
Rusca, Jean-Baptiste Dominique   100–101, 104–106
Ruse (battle)   380
Russia   53, 222–223, 226, 275–303, 372–377, 379–385, 387–397, 399, 401, 403, 405–413, 415, 417, 419, 421–422, 439, 442, 465, 565, 578
  army   222, 247, 425, 481, 574–575, 578
    Army of the Danube   375, 390, 406
    Army of the Dnieper   393
    Army of the Dvina   393
    Drissa camp   388, 393–395, 398, 401

    Imperial Guard and Reserve   245, 295, 458, 465
    Scythian Plan   395–396
    2nd Army   580
    1st Western Army   385, 389–390, 394, 396–398, 401–402, 405
    2nd Western Army   385–386, 389, 397, 401–402, 405
    3rd Reserve Army of Observation   390
    IV Infantry Corps   402
    VI Infantry Corps   412
    VII Infantry Corps   402
  Belorussia   381–382
  Civil War   182
  Continental System   558–559
  Cossacks   409, 412–413, 417, 425–426, 445, 454, 458, 467
    Vlasov Regiment   467
  espionage   383–384
  Franco-Russian Alliance   302–303, 372–373, 408, 494
  Great Russia   395
  Moscow   381–382, 397, 404–410, 412, 415, 420, 481
  navy   313, 494
  Partitions of Poland   61
  Russo-Prussian Alliance 1813   424–425
  Saint Petersburg   223, 381–382, 386, 401, 407, 409, 414
  Soviet Union   413, 416, 582
    Red Army   582
    Stalingrad   582
  Treaty of Bucharest 1812   375
  Treaty of Orebro 1812   375
  Treaty of Saint Petersburg 1812   375
  Treaty of Velikiye Luki 1812   375
  War of Fourth Coalition   251–253, 260, 273, 275–303
    Eylau campaign   285–294, 574–575
    Friedland campaign   294–302
  War of Second Coalition   195
  War of Seventh Coalition   472–480
  War of Sixth Coalition   375, 423–471, 577–578
    Fall Campaign   423, 428, 439–450, 577–578
    Spring Campaign   429–436
    1814 Campaign   450–471

INDEX 613

War of Third Coalition 224–227, 230–247, 250, 320
1812 campaign 372–422
Ryazan 303

Saale River 261, 264–265, 429, 445, 448–449, 573, 578
Saalfeld 256, 260
Saar River 461
Sables d'Olonne 452
Sacile 188
Sahagún de Campos 328, 330–331, 338–339
Sahuguet, Jean Joseph 158–159, 165–167
Saint Denis 476
Saint-Dizier (battle) 471
Saint-Domingue (San Domingo) 495–499, 502, 544
 Santo-Domingo 497, 508, 511, 523
 Santo-Domingo (battle) 511, 522
Sainte-Menehould 55
Saint-Germain, Claude-Louis de 22–24
Saint Gothard Pass 197, 200, 206–208
Saint Helena 136, 177, 204, 208, 410, 424, 480, 522,
Saint-Hilaire, Louis-Vincent-Joseph de 156
Saint-Just 479
Saint-Lambert 477
Saint-Malo 530
Saint-Priest, Guillaume Emmanuel Guignard de 286, 384
Saint-Privat (battle) 573
Saint Polten 239
Saints (battle) 543
Salamanca 325, 328, 339
Saldanha 328–330
Salicetti, Antoine Christophe 97, 153
Salò 138, 140, 143–147, 149, 152–154, 156–157, 180
Salorno (battle) 189
Saltanovka (battle) 402
Salzburg 79
Samaná Bay 497
Sambre River 60–61, 549
San Benedetto 128–129
San Giacomo 124
San Giorgio 165–167, 184
San Giorgio (battle) 166–167
San Giuliano 212, 215

Sanguinetto 164–165
San Juan, Benito 322, 324
Sankt Veit 189–190
San Marco Chapel 178, 182–183
San Martino 171, 183
San Michele 107–108, 129
San Michele all'Adige 169
San Pietro in Gu 170
Saône River 51
Santander 309, 323
Sant'Antonio 166, 184
San Vito 185
Sarasa, Juan Manuel 320
Sardinia (island) 513, 515, 521, 533
Sardinia (Piedmont) 30, 57–58, 69–71, 87–115, 117, 119, 130, 195, 197, 203–204, 224
 War of First Coalition 69–71, 91, 116–131
Sassello, 120, 125, 127
Sauret, Pierre Franconin 142–143, 145–147, 149, 158
Savan, David 383–384
Savary, Anne-Jean 166
Savigliano (battle) 195
Savona 90, 96, 98, 100–102, 110, 119
Savoy (county) 56, 61, 93, 95, 110, 113, 117
Savoy (dynasty) 88, 224
Saxe, Maurice de 18, 42
Saxe-Coburg-Saalfeld, Frederick Josias of 57–58, 60, 62–65, 71
Saxony 224, 252–254, 271, 280, 294, 345, 362, 364, 376, 380, 418, 424–448, 573
 Dresden 264, 271, 384–385, 428–429, 438–440, 442, 444, 447, 449
 Dresden (battle) 440, 444, 447, 467, 577
Schaffhausen 76–77, 120
Scharnhorst, Johann David Waitz von 373, 390, 574
Schaumann, August 334
Scheldt Estuary 502, 543, 545, 549, 553
Scheldt fleet 502, 533
Scheldt River 462
Schérer, Barthélemy Louis Joseph 66, 87, 90, 91, 96–98, 100, 102,
Schleiz 184
Schönbrunn 221, 359, 367
Schöngraben 240
Schramm, Jean-Adam 457

Schübirz, Anton von Chobinin   134, 155, 169, 171
Schwarzenberg, Karl Philipp zu   380, 386, 405, 418, 436–451, 456–472, 576–579
Schwerin, Otto von   566
Scrivia River   210–211, 215
Sebottendorf van der Rose, Karl Philipp   101, 118, 131, 135, 144, 147, 160, 162, 164
Second World War   262, 357, 581–582
  Blitzkrieg   581
  Bulge (battle)   582
  Case White   581
  Case Yellow   581
  Hitler, Adolph   582
  Kursk   582
  Luftwaffe   581
  Operation Barbarossa   582
  Operation Marita   581
  Operation Mercury   582
  Operation   25, 581
  Panzer   581
  Wehrmacht   569, 581–582
  Weserübung   581
Sedan   54
Sedan (battle)   580
Sézanne   467
Segonzano   169
Segovia   322
Seine River   451, 466–468, 470
Selbständigkeit der Unterführer   566
Seltz   457
Senyavin, Dmitry Nikolayevich   313
Sepulveda   215–216
Sérurier, Jean-Mathieu-Philibert   70–73, 98, 100–102, 104–107, 119, 123–125, 128–129, 134, 136, 142–143, 146, 149, 151, 157–158, 180–181, 183–188
Servan, Joseph   43, 54
Sesia River   132
Seslavin, Aleksandr   417, 467–468
Seven Weeks War   571, 573, 580
Seven Years War   8, 13–15, 19, 30, 40, 42, 74, 119
Seville   309, 325, 330
Seydlitz, Friedrich Wilhelm von   566, 582
Sherman, William T., 257
Shavli   388
Sierra de Guadarrama   322

Guadarrama Pass   330, 332
Sierra Moreno Mountains   309
Simplon Pass   200, 206–207, 345
Slonim   382, 388–389
Slutsk   388
Smolensk   382, 384–385, 391, 396–397, 400, 402–406, 409–410, 412–416, 420, 465, 582
Soissons   469–470, 479
Solagna   162
Solferino   72, 155–157
Sombreffe   473, 476
Somosierra (battle)   322, 324
Sosnish   388
Soubise, Charles de Rohan de   14
Souham, Joseph   440
Soult, Jean-de-Dieu   28, 244, 257, 261, 267, 269, 271–272, 280–281, 289, 297–299, 325, 328–331, 336–337, 339, 441
South America   308, 312, 549, 552–553
  Rio de la Plata   552–553
Spain   87–89, 92, 94, 97, 306–340, 344–346, 366, 380, 390, 392, 406, 418, 423, 426, 468, 497, 502, 506, 516–517, 521–523, 527, 534, 538, 549, 552, 554
  alliance with France   502
  army   310, 325, 334, 340
    Army of Andalucía   311
    Army of the Center   315
    Army of Extremadura   320
    Army of the Left   315, 319
    Army of the Reserve   315
    Army of the Right   315
  Basque Provinces   330
  Catholic Church   339
  dos de mayo   309
  la guerrilla   309, 328–329, 332
  Madrid   93, 308–331, 338
    Retiro Heights   323
  navy   226, 339, 495, 497, 502, 506–507, 509–510, 516–517, 521
  Patriot Forces   315
  Peninsular War   200–233, 526
  Treaty of Velikiye Luki 1812   375
  War of First Coalition   56, 71, 74, 88–90, 92, 98
Spandau   376, 424

INDEX

Spanish America   513
Sparr, Otto Christoph von   566
Spilimbergo   185, 187
Sporck, Johann Rudolf von, 143, 147, 152–154, 156, 188
Spree River   433–434
Spremberg   433
Sprimont   65
Stadion, Johann Philipp   344
Stadtroda   264
Stains   479
Stalin, Joseph   306
Starhemberg, Louis   57
Starokonstantinov   388
Stengel, Henri Christian Michel de   109
Stettin   272, 277–278, 375, 377–378, 424, 426, 435, 443–444, 447
Steyr   163
Stockard von Bernkopf, Josef Otto   202–203
Stradella   208–209, 211
Stradella Pass   208
Strait of Otranto   520
Strasbourg   68, 160, 230, 454–455, 457–459, 461
Straubing   240
Stockach (battle)   77
Stura River   108
Suchet, Louis-Gabriel   209, 213
Suleika   307
Surazh   381
Suriname   514
Susa   90, 96, 204, 206
Susegana   187
Suvorov, Aleksandr Vasiliyevich   195, 222
Sventsyany   388
Swabia   137
Sweden   224, 296, 373–374, 390, 392, 419, 558–560, 565
  Riksdag   374
  Stockholm   374, 392
  Treaty of Saint Petersburg 1812   374
  War of Sixth Coalition   423, 436, 448, 450, 576
  War of Third Coalition   224, 226, 237
Swiss Guard   53
Switzerland   75, 195, 197–200, 216, 450–453, 457–460

Tagliamento River   185, 187–189
Tagus Estuary   308–309, 313
Tagus River   308
Talavera   325
Talleyrand, Charles Maurice de   307
Tanaro River   89, 96, 100, 104–109, 124–125, 128
Tannenberg (battle)   580–581
Tapiau (Gvardeisk)   378
Taranto   519
Tarvisio   185, 187–189
Tarutino   409–410, 416
Tasso Stream   178, 183
Tauentzien, Bogislav Friedrich Emanuel von   264
Tauroggen (convention)   418
Tavier (battle)   28
Terci   106
Terdoppio River   132
Texel River   505, 528, 545
Thaon de Revel, Charles-François   93–94, 109
The Hague   454
Thionville   454
Thorn   278–281, 287, 290, 293, 269–271, 278, 424, 426
Thugut, Johann Amadeus Franz de Paula   91, 94, 97
Thuringia   252, 573
Thuringian Forest   254, 258, 260, 568
Ticino River   207
Tiercelet   50
Tilsit   380, 382, 393
Tilsit (treaty)   273, 275, 302, 313, 345, 372–373, 407–408, 516, 520, 559
Toisinge, Jean-Gaspard Dichat de   129
Tolstoy, Leo   243
Torgau   424, 432, 435, 445, 449
Tori di Garafoli   213
Tormasov, Aleksandr Pretrovich   389–390, 405, 407
Torre River   188
Tortona   95, 114, 211
Toulon   61, 89, 110, 211, 495, 498, 509, 513, 515, 518–528, 531, 536, 543, 545
  fleet   502–503, 515–516, 518, 522, 526–527, 533, 535, 537, 539
  squadron   495, 514
Tourcoing (battle)   62

Tournai 49–51, 62
Tournai (battle) 62
Toussaint Louverture, François-Dominique 497
Trafalgar (battle) 308, 509–510, 512, 518, 537, 542–546, 548–550, 553, 557–558
Trambasore Heights 178, 182–183
Trannes 465
Trebbia River 195
Treffenfeld, Joachim Hennigs von 566
Trento 72, 140, 158, 161–162, 167–170, 178, 186–187, 189
Trier 49–50, 62, 459, 463
Trieste 527, 532
Troude, Amable Gilles 524–525
Troy 304
Troyes 466–470
Trubchevsk 388
Tsarevo Zaimische 406
Tsekhanovets 381
Tudela (battle) 321–322, 327
Tuileries Palace 53
Tunis 522
Tuscany 93
Turenne, Henri de La Tour d'Auvergne de 9, 482
Turreau, Louis Marie 202, 204, 206
Turin 87, 89–91, 94, 106, 108–114, 204–207, 209, 204, 206–207, 209
Tyrol 132, 137–140, 147, 158, 160, 162, 167–169, 172, 176, 185–187, 189, 225, 231–232, 234, 237–238, 241, 345, 353, 355, 360, 362

Ulla River 381–382
Ulm 69, 77, 160, 196–197, 200, 221, 227–242, 247, 385
United States of America 262, 311, 512, 535, 538, 549, 556, 558, 560–561, 582
  Chesapeake Bay 561
  Georgia 561
  Maine 561
  navy 548, 560–561
    Congress 548
    Constitution 538
  New Orleans 561
  New York 561
  War of 1812 556, 560–561

Unzmarkt 190
Ushant 504, 506
Utrecht 225, 462, 505
Uvarov, Fyodor 390

Valence (Valenza) 116, 130, 212
Valencia 310
Valenciennes 50–51, 58
Valladolid 322, 327
Valeggio 132, 134, 138–139, 146, 149–151, 158
Valmaçeda (battle) 319
Valmy (battle) 44, 54–55
Valsugana (Sugana Valley) 160, 170
Valvasone 188
Vandamme, Dominique René 162, 348, 380, 442, 512
Varennes 44
Var River 202, 208
Vaubois, Claude-Henri Belgrand de 73, 158–159, 161–162, 167–173, 175–176, 179
Vauchamps (battle) 362
Vaugirard 374
Velikiye Luki 388
Vendée 44, 61, 180, 194, 490
Venetia 71–74, 93, 137–185, 519, 527
  navy 518, 527–528
Venice 518, 520, 528, 556
Venezuela 313
Vercelli 207
Verdier 173
Verdun 53–55
Verdun, Jean-François 457
Verne 173
Verona 71, 73, 140–141, 143–145, 158–159, 162, 164, 167–181, 187, 190
Vicenza 140, 143, 162, 164, 169–171, 173, 177, 180–181
Victor Amadeus II (Duke of Savoy) 88
Victor Amadeus III (King of Sardinia) 88, 91–97, 106, 109, 117
Victor-Perrin, Claude 75, 201, 209–212, 214–215, 319–320, 324–325, 380, 418, 433, 435, 452, 454–461, 464, 468, 481
  Duke of Bellune 355
Vidor 187
Vieuville, Auguste-Joseph de la 459
Vigo 506–507
Vigo Bay 506

INDEX 617

Vilkomir 388
Villach 188–190
Villafranca 144, 149, 151, 176, 180
Villanuova 174, 176
Villaret-Joyeuse, Louis Thomas 497–498
Villars, Jean-Baptiste Dorothée 92
Villatte, Eugène-Casimir 319–320
Villimpenta 165
Villeneuve, Pierre-Charles 200, 503–507, 509–510
Vilna 375, 382–386, 388–391, 393, 397–398, 400, 405, 418, 420
Vilna (convention) 375
Vimeiro (battle) 313
Vincennes 374
Vinchant, Charles-Philippe de Gontroeul 189
Vins, Josef Nikolaus de 91, 94–95
Vistula River 276, 279–280, 282, 285, 287, 290, 293–294, 359–360, 377, 385–386, 424–425, 427–428, 432, 438, 443
Vital, Giuseppe Felice di 128
Vitebsk 381–382, 393, 401–403, 405, 409, 420
Vitoria (battle) 555
Vlissingen 498, 510, 519, 528, 536–537
  Fleet 522–523
Voghera 209–211
Volga River 385
Volhynia 386, 418
Voltri 96–98, 100–102, 119–120, 122, 125
Voralberg 225
Vosges Mountains 60, 345, 356
Donon Pass 356
Vukasović, Josip Filip 118, 125, 127–128, 132, 134–135, 151, 156, 178, 182, 207
Vyazma 413–414, 420, 582

Wagram (battle) 259, 342, 344, 354, 359–360, 364–368, 370, 427
  Russbach Heights 257–259
Walcheren Expedition 553
Walhain 477
Wallachia 375, 387
War and Peace 243
War of the Austrian Succession 92
War of the First Coalition 30, 48, 56, 71, 74, 58, 91–93, 116, 130, 223
  1792 campaign 48–53
  1793 campaign 56–60, 90
  1794 campaign 61–67, 90, 91, 102, 104
  1795 campaign 67–68, 91–92, 102
  1796 campaign 68–74, 87–177
  1797 campaign 74–75, 177–191
  Italian theater 87–191
  Sambre and Meuse theater 63–65
War of the Fifth Coalition 235–264
  Aspern-Essling campaign 353–359, 362–363, 375
  Marchfeld 235–237, 361, 363–364, 366
  Hungarian theater 361
  Raab (battle) 361
  Italian theater 345, 353, 355, 360–361
  Sacile (battle) 360
  Regensburg campaign 344–353, 369
  Schönbrunn (treaty) 344, 367
  Wagram campaign 359–366, 375
  Znaim campaign 365–368
  Znaim 366–367
War of the Fourth Coalition 173–197, 275–303, 480, 439, 568–569, 573–575, 579
  Jena-Auerstedt campaign 250–273, 275–277, 280, 350, 365, 370, 420, 427, 443, 568–569, 573–575, 579
  Eylau campaign 285–294, 574–575
  Friedland campaign 294–302
War of the Second Coalition 75–79, 194–219, 246
  German theater 76–78, 196–197
  Treaty of Lunéville 225
  1799 campaign 196
  1800 campaign 75–79, 194–219
War of the Seventh Coalition 472–480
War of the Sixth Coalition 423–471, 577–578
  Allied Headquarters 466, 468–470,
  Allied Monarchs 459, 463, 471
  Army of Bohemia 436–440, 442–445, 447, 450–452, 456, 463–465, 467–471, 511–514
    III Corps 465
    IV Corps 465, 468, 471
    V Corps 465, 471
    VI Corps 466–467, 471
  Army of North Germany 436–438, 443–445, 450–451, 454, 468–469, 576–578
  Army of Poland 436–437, 447, 576

War of the Sixth Coalition (cont.)
  Army of Silesia   436–438, 440, 444–445,
    447, 450–452, 457, 459, 461, 464,
    467–470, 576–578
  Fall Campaign   423, 428, 439–450, 511–514
  Frankfurt Proposals   450
  Reichenbach Plan   331–334, 339, 377,
    576–577
  Spring Campaign   429–436
  1814 Campaign   450–471
War of the Third Coalition   221–236,
    237–247, 375
  Austerlitz (Slavkov u Brna) (campaign)   221, 235, 241, 246–247,
    249–250, 253, 257, 271, 314, 427, 431,
    443, 481
    Goldbach Stream (Říčka)   243–244
    Prace   245
    Pratzen Heights   241–246
    Santon Hill   242–243
    Sokolnitz (Sokolnice)   242–245
    sun of Austerlitz   244, 296
    Tellnitz (Tellnice)   241–244
    Zuran Hill   166, 242, 244–245
  Ulm campaign   228–235, 260, 385, 427, 439
  Italian theater   224, 235–237
Wartenburg   445, 577–578
Wartensleben, Wilhelm von   69
Waterloo   473, 476–477
Waterloo (battle)   216, 218, 423, 473,
    476–477, 480, 570–571, 576
Watrin, François   201, 211
Wattignies (battle)   60–61
Wavre   476–479, 481
Weidenfeld, Franz   156
Weimar   265–267, 270, 569
Weißenberg   434
Weißenfels   266, 429
Wellesley, Arthur (Duke of Wellington)   313,
    339, 390, 396, 423, 439, 472–482,
    554–556
  Lines of Torres Vedras   393
  on Napoleon   8
Werneck, Franz von   234
Wertingen   232
Wesel   457, 463
West Indies   552, 561
Westphalia   380, 392, 400

Western Dvina River   381–383, 385, 388, 391,
    393–394, 396, 402
Weyrother, Franz von   168, 178, 242–244
Whittingham, Samuel   317
Wilkowiski   380
Willaumez, Jean-Baptiste   508, 511–512,
    523–526
William II (Emperor of Germany)   570
William Frederick (Crown Prince of Orange),
    64–65
Wilson, Robert   414
Wimpffen-Bournebourg, Louis-François
    de   25
Wintzingerode, Ferdinand von   471
Wissembourg   60
Wittenberg   272, 424, 432, 440, 443, 445, 449
Wittgenstein, Peter Ludwig Adolf von   388–
    389, 401, 405, 407, 417, 420, 429, 431,
    433–434
Wolzogen, Ludwig Adolf Friedrich von   390,
    393–394
Worms   56, 458
Wrede, Karl Philipp von   448
Wurmser, Dagobert Sigismund von   72–73,
    117, 139–169, 173, 176–177, 180, 184–185,
    190
Württemberg   174, 348, 350–351
Württemberg, Alexander of   391
Württemberg, Eugen of   417
Würzburg   69, 228–230, 253, 256
Wyszogrod   377

Yarmouth, Francis Seymour-Conway   435
Yermolov, Aleksey Petrovich   390, 400, 414
Yorck, Hans David Ludwig von   131, 418, 466,
    577
Yorck von Wartenburg, Hans Ludwig David
    Maximilian   130–131, 136, 139, 159,
    204, 212
Yorke, Charles Philip   546, 554–555
Young, William   543
Yugoslavia   581
Ypres   50, 64

Zach, Anton von   215
Zamosc   385, 424, 426
Zaragoza   310, 316–317, 322, 325
Zhitomir   388

Zieten, Hans Joachim von 566
Zittau 438
Zorndorf (battle) 574
Zündnadelgewehr 571
Zürich (battle) 195
Zwolle 454

Printed in the United States
By Bookmasters